K.C.C. v Shanghai, 1927 at K.C.C., Hong Kong

Courtesy : Maria Fincher

150 YEARS OF CRICKET IN HONG KONG

150 YEARS OF CRICKET IN HONG KONG

Peter Hall

The Book Guild Ltd
Sussex, England

The Book Guild Ltd
25 High Street,
Lewes, Sussex

First published 1999
© Peter Hall 1999

Set in Times

Typesetting by
Acorn Bookwork, Salisbury, Wiltshire

Printed in Great Britain by
Bookcraft (Bath) Ltd, Avon

A catalogue record for this book is
available from the British Library

ISBN 1 85776 313 0

This book is dedicated to the memory of all the Hong Kong cricketers who made the supreme sacrifice during the battle for Hong Kong in December 1941 and in internment thereafter.

CONTENTS

CONTENTS

MESSAGE FROM THE GOVERNOR

The history of cricket in Hong Kong brings together two of my greatest loves, the sport of life and a city of vitality.

Cricket has been a part of the History of Hong Kong since 1841, and this city boasts the unusual distinction of having the only cathedral in the world with a memorial window dedicated to a cricket team.

Sadly, *The Times*, that great recorder of the cricket scene, did not see fit to mention Hong Kong's part in the story of cricket until 1975, and then only to record the closure of the old Hong Kong Cricket ground. This splendid new history makes good all past omissions, and in its portrait of the vigorous condition of cricket in Hong Kong today, holds out great promise for the future. And if anyone doubts that promise, look back to the words of Chinese officials recorded in *The Times* by Richard Hughes in 1975, 'We well understand the rules and traditions of good sportsmanship, which have nothing to do with differing views on politics or ideology.'

Christopher Patten
Governor
1996

MESSAGE FROM THE PRESIDENT OF THE HKCA

Although on 30 June 1997 the United Kingdom relinquished sovereignty over Hong Kong to the Peoples' Republic of China it did not mark the dying of the quintessential English summer game of cricket that has been played in Hong Kong since the British people first arrived in 1841.

On the contrary the game continues to flourish in Hong Kong, and the strenuous efforts that have taken place in the 1990s to improve the quality of the cricket played and to widen its appeal to the local Chinese community are showing impressive results at this important moment in the development of Hong Kong, China.

Peter Hall's marvellous and timely book is a treasure trove of Hong Kong's cricket history and its various personalities. I'm sure it will delight not just old Hong Kong hands seeking to reminisce, but all cricket lovers, whilst at the same time illustrating the depth of tradition upon which the present game in Hong Kong is built.

The Hong Kong Cricket Association owes a debt of gratitude to Peter Hall for putting such time and effort into the research and writing of this excellent book, and on behalf of the cricket community of Hong Kong, I record our thanks to him for producing such a fine publication.

Terry Smith
President, HKCA
July 1997

FOREWORD

I am delighted to have been asked to write a foreword to Peter Hall's fascinating History of Hong Kong Cricket; all the more so because the British Forces, which I had the honour to command from 1973 to 1976, played cricket in Hong Kong from its very earliest days as a British Colony. They have contributed considerably to the well-being of the game, both providing players of quality to represent Hong Kong and also with sides to take part in the various leagues and club competitions which have been developed over the last 150 years. In return, cricket has helped the Armed Forces to integrate more with the people and the many races who go to make the citizens of Hong Kong and this has been greatly to their benefit.

Indeed, in many ways the cricket discussed and described in such well-researched detail by Peter Hall mirrors Hong Kong's remarkable history and development. Cricket started being played almost as soon as Hong Kong became British, on a ground already drained by the Army, and this ground, Chater Road - the home of the Hong Kong Cricket Club, became over the years one of the epicentres of Hong Kong's social life, sited as it was in the very heart of the shops, hotels and offices of Central and right next to the Hong Kong Club. It was just as if Londoners were playing cricket in Piccadilly Circus! How no one in the passing cars and trams ever got killed was a miracle; even Keith Miller, despite the generous reward from the Chairman of the Hongkong Bank, failed to break a window in the old Bank of China, and I personally saw Tony Greig pull a ball into the balcony of the Furama Hotel!

It was heady stuff and I remember so well playing in one of the last games on that famous ground before town planning pressures forced a move to the excellent new facilities and wickets of the Wong Nai Chung Gap. Here the great game which we all love continues to be played in a style and manner it deserves, as it is on so many other grounds throughout Hong Kong. For Hong Kong cricket, while it also and consistently appeals to the Saturday or Sunday cricketer, can also produce cricket of real quality, as typified by the profiles of the six Hong Kong cricketers who have done so much for the game there, by the one time Interport matches - Hong Kong's Test Cricket, and by the many visiting touring sides, which enabled Hong Kong to compete in the international arena.

Cricket is a very special game. It has a very special place in the life of Hong Kong, and I would be very surprised if after 1997 there was not still a considerable following for the game in Hong Kong and if visiting teams were still not falling over themselves to come to Hong Kong to play this great international game.

Peter Hall has done a great service to all who love the game of cricket, particularly those who over many years have had such fun and enjoyment playing it in that remarkable phenomenon call Hong Kong.

Field Marshal The Lord Bramall

SPONSORSHIP

The publication of *150 Years of Cricket in Hong Kong* has been made possible by the generous sponsorship of the following individuals, associations, clubs and companies, for which the author is most grateful:

Anderson, Peter
Anonymous   Jardines Cricketers: Past & Present
Peter Davies
Hatim Ebrahim
Dr Eddie Gosano
Peter Hall   In Memory of Mabel and George Hall
The Hongkong Land Co. Ltd   In Memory of Oscar Eager
John Hung
The Kowloon Cricket Club
Dr Douglas Laing
Geoffrey Lever
Peter Olsen
Lord Sandberg
Harry Wilken
Doris Zimmern   In Memory of Freddie Zimmern

The Hong Kong Cricket Association, through its Chairman Peter Slack, commissioned the author to write a history of Hong Kong cricket in 1992. This matter was minuted at an Executive Committee Meeting of the HKCA in November 1992 which the author attended. This daunting project was completed at the end of 1994, an appropriate date, as the 1993/94 cricket season saw the completion of 90 years of league cricket in Hong Kong. The complete text together with a folder of photographs was personally handed to the Chairman in Hong Kong in February 1995. In June 1997, the author was informed by the HKCA, that due to its commitment to the development of cricket in Hong Kong, it very much regretted it would not now be able to undertake the publication of this history.

CHRONOLOGY

1841	Cricket first mentioned in Hong Kong.
1851	The Hong Kong Cricket Club founded.
1866	First Interport v Shanghai.
1888	Diocesan Boys' School, first mentioned match.
1890	First Interport v The Straits and first match v Ceylon.
1894	Craigengower Cricket Club founded.
1897	The Hong Kong Parsee Cricket Club founded.
1903	The Civil Service Cricket Club and Police Recreation Club founded.
1903–04	First Division League Cricket commenced.
1904	The Kowloon Cricket Club founded.
1906	Club de Recreio founded.
1911	The Chinese Recreation Club founded.
1912	The University of Hong Kong Cricket Club founded.
1914–17	No competition – World War I.
1918	The Indian Recreation Club founded.
1921–22	Second Division League cricket commenced. Central British School (later KGV), first mentioned match.
1941–48	No competition – World War II and its after effects.
1948	Last Interport v Shanghai.
1951	100th Anniversary of The Hong Kong Cricket Club.
1952	Jack Chegwyn's Team – the first International side to visit Hong Kong.
1955	Interports v Malaya resumed.
1961	Craigengower Sixes commenced.
1962	St George's Cricket Club founded.
1964	Little Sai Wan Cricket Club founded.
1966	First MCC team to visit Hong Kong, and 100th Anniversary of first Interport.
1967–68	Gillette Cup Competition introduced.
1968	The Hong Kong Cricket Association (HKCA) replaced The Hong Kong Cricket League. Island School, first matches.
1969	HKCA became Associate Member of the International Cricket Council.
1970–71	Rothman's Cup Competition introduced.
1972–73	Ruttonjee 'Player of the Year' trophy introduced.
1973–74	Sunday/Saturday Leagues replaced First and Second Divisions.

1975	Last matches played at the HKCC Chater Road ground.
1975–76	Sunday/Saturday Leagues Cup and Plate Competition introduced. Saturday League – limited overs introduced.
1976–77	Ted Wilson Schools' Trophy introduced.
1982	Hong Kong's first participation in the ICC Trophy.
1982–83	Wimpey/Sime Darby sponsored the Sunday League. Artificial wickets introduced at KCC and Mission Road ground.
1983	Asian Cricket Council established.
1984	First South-East Asian Competition.
1984–85	HK Bank 'Player of the Year' Trophy replaced Ruttonjee.
1986	Annual Charity Cricket Festivals commenced. First 'Silk Cut' Single Wicket Competition in Hong Kong.
1986–87	Dunlop Slazenger sponsored the Sunday League.
1987	Last Interport v Singapore.
1990	The Volvo Cup inaugurated between Hong Kong and Thailand.
1991–92	Connaught Strategic Holdings sponsored Saturday and Sunday Leagues.
1991–92	Butani Cup and Plate replaced the Gillette.
1992	Malaysia joined the Volvo Cup – The Tuanku Ja'afar Cup inaugurated: Hong Kong, Malaysia, Singapore and Thailand – First Cathay Pacific/Wharf International Sixes at KCC.
1992–93	Connaught Strategic 'Player of the Year' replaced HKBank.
1993–94	90th Year of League Cricket.
1994	100th Anniversary of the Craigengower Cricket Club. 90th Anniversary of the Kowloon Cricket Club.
1994	First Beijing Sixes, China
1997	Inaugural Under-19 Youth Asia Cup

INTRODUCTION

Until the leasing of the New Territories from China in 1898, H J Lethbridge in his book, *Hong Kong*: *Stability and Change*, said: 'the geographical setting and minute area of Hong Kong meant that the territory could only support a small European population.' According to Endacott, 'the number of Europeans in Hong Kong in 1853, excluding service personnel, was 776.'

The Chinese as a race did not play cricket, thus the total 'pot' from which to draw cricketers was in those early days very small, mainly from five groups: officials (civil servants), merchants (the Hongs), the professional classes (lawyers, teachers, etc), the Police and the Services. The Garrison usually numbered less than 1,500 men, but the number fluctuated markedly at times, e.g. during the China Wars around 1840, 1860 and 1900. Also, Shanghai had developed faster than Hong Kong from the early 1860s, being viewed as more accommodating for the ambitious, as it grew into a wealthy international settlement.

John Luff, writing for the SCMP in March 1969, reminded his readers of an earlier report on a potential piece of ground for the establishment of cricket: 'A sloping dusty space in the winter and a muddy patch during the summer.' Was it to become a cricket ground for the few or a recreation area for the many? The arguments for and against were debated at public meetings and reported in detail by the press (see HKCC section). The military had formed part of the site by reclamation prior to 1851 and agreed to part with a slice, but always retaining their right to utilise the ground for ceremonial purposes. Thus the Hong Kong Cricket Club (HKCC) came into being in mid-1851. Cricket, although played in the Colony before that date, had now officially arrived.

In 1861, the profession of career civil servant was introduced into Hong Kong, allowing the Hong Kong Government to recruit highly educated young men from professional families in Great Britain. As only 22 cadets were appointed during the period from 1862–1900, their number hardly added to the 'pot' from which Interport cricketers were selected.

From the earliest days, Army unit sides, particularly the Sappers and Gunners, played cricket. This later led to triangular tournaments between the HKCC, Army and Navy, with the RAF forming a quadrangular tournament between the two world wars. The HKCC organised cricket in Hong Kong, their main influence being the Interports against Shanghai (from 1866) and The Straits/Malaya (from 1890).

xix

The Committee of the HKCC has accepted the invitation received from the Shanghai Cricket Club and has asked Mr T E Pearce (HKCC), Mr G R Sayer (CSCC) and Capt Davis (RGA) to select the Hong Kong team.

Hong Kong Daily Press, 6 April 1921

A strong HKCC influence remained right up to the period of the post-war years, when cricket was democratised during Ted Wilson's tenure as President of the HKCA.

During the late nineteenth century students from local schools were also playing cricket. They were to form the nucleus for the embryo local cricket clubs, such as Craigengower (CCC), the Hong Kong University (HKU), the Kowloon Cricket Club (KCC), the Indian Recreation Club (IRC) and Club de Recreio (Recreio). Government servants and members from the business fraternity supplied the HKCC, the Civil Service Cricket Club (CSCC) and the Police Recreation Club (PRC). These clubs, together with the Services, became the backbone of the league competition which commenced with the 1903–4 season.

Hong Kong's climate, with its high humidity, extremes of temperature and threat of typhoons, is very trying for half the year. Thus the official cricket season – clashing with other outdoor sports such as, hockey, rugby and soccer – runs annually from late September through to March.

The leagues have continued, with the addition of cup matches, to this day. The Shanghai Interport series ceased in 1948, while the Interports against the Straits/Malaya and Malaysia and Singapore continued up to 1987. The one-day game has, in the opinion of the author, unfortunately been allowed to become supreme, banishing the once renowned three-day Interport to the land of the dinosaurs.

Watching the Interport against Singapore in 1987, in the hot and humid atmosphere of the Padang, gratefully shaded by the colonial verandahs of the renowned Singapore Cricket Club, the author might have witnessed the demise of an historic occasion, the three-day Interport, a tradition since 1866.

Various causes can be attributable to the change: the faster pace of today's lifestyle; the boring number of drawn Interport matches from 1977 to 1983; Malaysia dropping out in 1983, and at that time, a generally lower standard of cricket on the Malayan peninsula. This, allied to a proliferation of one-day internationals worldwide, has focussed the attention of the local administrators to its short-term attraction.

Hong Kong became a member of the International Cricket Council (ICC) in 1969, and is affiliated to the Asian Cricket Council (ACC), which was established in 1983. As both organisations run one-day limited-over competitions, the die was cast. It was only a matter of time before the traditional three-day game, the builder of character, the extender of personality and the maker of lasting friendships, would sadly be thrust aside.

The Rt. Hon. R G Menzies, in his March 1956 Foreword to Arthur Mailey's book, *10 for 66 and All That*, said:

> For the truth is that cricket is a game not only of skill but of character. It is not something to be hustled through. It requires time, the setting and the delicacies of art to achieve its full expression.

The recent inauguration of the Volvo and Tuanku Ja'afar Cup competitions has added to the inevitability of the change. Entertainment value has over-ridden the purity of the great game.

Matthew Engel, the New Editor of *Wisden*, said in 1993 of one-day cricket: 'It distorts cricket's skills and produces a mutant game which, while it might on occasions be tense, is essentially shallow.'

Imran Khan, in a 1993 newspaper article, added: 'For me, with the exception of the World Cup, one-day cricket lacks drama, tension and the skills of Test cricket.'

Hong Kong's Test cricket was the three-day Interport, now struck off the cricket calendar. Surely, there should be room for both forms of cricket contests.

Apart from the Interports, international touring teams have been visiting Hong Kong since 1952, and continue to arrive to sample its hospitality as well as its cricket. Hong Kong teams have toured within the Far Eastern region and also ventured afar.

In 1994–95, the new HKCA President, my good friend John Terence Hung, son of Walter Alexander and Phoebe Hung (nee Kotewall), a fellow Eurasian and the first to be appointed to this prestigious post, was the right man for this difficult task of preserving Hong Kong cricket. The first Eurasian! As the HKCC ran the 'high profile' cricket in Hong Kong from its beginnings until the post-war years, and the club was very selective about its membership, it was unlikely that a non-Caucasian would have been appointed to this post at any time from the commencement of league cricket in 1903–04 till 1941. Post-war Presidents of the HKCA are listed in this book.

The HKCA has in recent years concentrated more on developing the local cricket scene by opening junior clinics in selective areas to encourage the indigenous population to play the game. There are encouraging signs that this policy is beginning to bear fruit.

A number of under 18 cricketers have recently attended two of the great schools of cricket – Lord's, and the Australian Cricket Academy of Adelaide, Australia.

The form and content of this book had been made more appetising by contributions from many persons I have cajoled, and others who have given freely of their knowledge and past records – some real bonuses have emerged. All the valued memories, photographs and assistance I very much appreciated and have acknowledged elsewhere. There are some stories in particular sections of the book whose authenticity I cannot vouch for, but as Michael Parkinson once said about a Rodney Marsh story: 'I just didn't want a marvellous yarn spoiled by the truth.' I have left such tales in the form presented to me. However, as some 'stories' were corrected by factual records, they had to be amended accordingly.

Hopefully, what I have written will provide, not only some background and a record of Hong Kong cricket, but also some nostalgia to savour and talk about with cricketing friends wherever.

[An asterisk * denotes 'not out' throughout the book unless otherwise explained]

Peter Hall
Heswall, England

THE PROFILES

[It is normal to use 'the author', but in this section I have decided to use the 'Royal' I]

Like *Wisden*'s Five Cricketers of the Year, whose Editor decides whom should be selected, I, as the author of this book have decided to whom a special tribute should be paid. Thus the selection of the following Hong Kong cricketers as my six Profiles. As *Wisden* is an annual production, I considered it reasonable to have six instead of only five Profiles, as this history covers a much longer period. I also felt it was very important to keep those selected as special.

I selected Dick Hancock, 'the father of Hong Kong cricket', Alec Pearce, Jalu Shroff, Carl Myatt, Peter Anderson and Dermot Reeve. Although the first two are no longer with us, I knew something about their cricket careers in Hong Kong, but not much else. Jalu, Carl and Peter were cricketing contemporaries of mine, whilst Dermot Reeve was the only Hong Kong-born cricketer to have played for England.

I started my research with the profile of the late Alec Pearce. Alec died in Kent in 1982 at his last known address in Hawkhurst. I wrote to Mrs Pearce at this address and added – PLEASE FORWARD. Two weeks later Mrs Nina Pearce telephoned me from her home, Quaves Cottage, near Guildford, Surrey. Luck had forwarded my letter. After briefly explaining my project over the phone, we then corresponded on the material I required for Alec's profile.

I was about to visit my brother in nearby Farnham, Surrey, so called on Mrs Pearce to look over some Hong Kong cricket material in her possession. On meeting Mrs Pearce again after an absence of many years, I discovered she had been a fellow internee in the Civilian POW Camp in Stanley, Hong Kong, during the Pacific war. When I later mentioned her maiden name to my elder brother, he immediately remarked: 'Nina Quin, she was one of the Camp beauties.'

In the meantime I had drafted profiles for Jalu and Carl, the first being resident in Hong Kong, while Carl was living in Honolulu. These were posted to them for their comments. I had also summarised Dermot Reeve's cricket career to date and wrote to him for some personal information, also asking for a photograph in either his England blazer or sweater. I thought there would be no problem with the photograph! Dermot admitted to me at the Lancashire/Warwickshire match in Liverpool in May 1993

1

that he's a hopeless correspondent. I found his personal material in the 1993 *Who's Who*, but had to wait until the Benson & Hedges final at Lord's in 1994 before I secured a photograph.

I realised my biggest hurdle would be Dick Hancock's profile. I contacted Laurie Kilbee, an ex-HKCC Optimist and good friend, who had played cricket in prewar Hong Kong. 'I'll think about it', he said. Then Nina Pearce called me after hearing from Laurie: 'I know where one of Dick Hancock's daughters lives, I think she can help you. But be careful with your approach, she's in her eighties!'

I jotted down the name, Marybud Chignell, who lived in Ditchling, Sussex. I then wrote to her, explaining the purpose of my letter and enclosed a rather blank profile for her to hopefully fill in the spaces for me. By return of post, I received a card which said: 'Just to let you know that it will take a little time to answer all the queries. But you will have the answers as soon as possible.'

I have since completed the most difficult of the Profiles, thanks to Marybud Chignell (nee Hancock). Very luckily for me, she was interested in cricket. In fact she's a member of the Association of Cricket Umpires in England. On completion of the H R B Hancock Profile, I sent her a copy to keep. Her comment to me was: 'I am thrilled with the profile which will be one of my greatest treasures, and an enormous interest to my two daughters.'

During a week in London in mid-October 1993 scouring the British Library (newspaper section) microfilm records for cricket scores from old Hong Kong newspapers, I took a day off to visit Mrs Chignell, who lives alone in Ditchling. She had left Hong Kong in 1930, but not before compiling a cricket scrapbook of immeasurable value to me and to Hong Kong cricket. She lent me her precious collection, the first time it had been out of her possession for 63 years. We chatted for two hours reminiscing about Hong Kong. Her father and mother had also been interned in Stanley POW Camp.

She had never heard of the Hancock Shield, played for since 1948 between HKCC and KCC, in fond memory of her father! I have since presented her with a photograph of the shield, and via the good services of Keith Garner, the then General Manager, a copy of the HKCC history published in 1989.

I left the work on the Anderson Profile to the last, mainly because Peter was resident in England, would have been too busy as chief executive of Somerset CCC to have answered me before the end of the 1993 season, and also because I had more information on him than the others!

The Profiles have been completed, including the last outstanding item – a photograph from Dermot, not the one I was initially looking for, but nevertheless one he is very proud of.

There are no doubt other Hong Kong cricketers, many of whom will have played their best cricket in the late 19th and early 20th century, such as Tam Pearce, father of Alec Pearce, who could also have been considered. To them all, I can only say, thank you for your contribution to Hong Kong cricket.

HERBERT RICHARD BUDD HANCOCK

H R B Hancock, Dick to his friends, was born in Hong Kong on 8 April 1877, the third son of Alfred Hancock and Hariot Elizabeth Rider (nee Budd). He was educated at Charterhouse School, England, where he played cricket for the 1st XI and for the school in the rackets pairs at Queen's, London. While still at school he played one match for Somerset CCC in 1895, scoring 80 not out.

Dick went out to Hong Kong immediately on leaving school, first working for Shewan Tomes in Canton, then for Stewart Bros., bullion brokers, in Hong Kong. When on overseas leave in England he played cricket for I Zingari and The Incogniti XIs. After his arrival in Hong Kong he joined the HKCC, where he distinguished himself at cricket and tennis for many years. He became Club President in 1922, a post he held until his retirement in 1947.

Dick was first selected to play for Hong Kong against both Shanghai and The Straits in a Triangular Tournament in 1901 in Hong Kong. He continued to play representative cricket for Hong Kong until 1929, having a highest score of 71 not out in 1914. At one time he was reported 'as being for 25 years the finest slip in the Far East.' He captained the Interport team for many years, being first appointed against Shanghai in 1904.

Dick and his brother Harry were for several years the Hong Kong Tennis doubles champions, and were also involved as administrators. In 1903, while in Shanghai with the Interport cricket team, he represented Hong Kong in an Interport tennis singles match beating E Buxton Forman 6–4, 6–0, 6–1 at the Country Club. The *Hong Kong Daily Press* reported at the time that: 'The play was so one-sided as to be uninteresting, Hancock admittedly outclassing his opponent.' Partaking in other sports at international level whilst on an Interport cricket tour was frowned upon by the Hong Kong cricket authorities, and stopped after this event. Dick's eldest daughter, Marybud, recalled a bet that her father won in Hong Kong: 'that he could not play a round of golf on all the Hong Kong Golf courses in a day.'

Dick married Mary Isabel Stobart on 12 March 1907 in St John's Cathedral, Hong Kong. Mary was brought out to Hong Kong by her brother 'Jamie', spare oar for Oxford, who was the best man at their

3

wedding. Dick and Molly had four daughters – Mary Budd, Honor Stobart, Rosamond Budd and Harmony Budd, all who married.

Dick and Molly were interned by the Japanese in the civilian POW Camp in Stanley, Hong Kong, for nearly four years. After the war he received wonderful kindness and help from the Australians during his six months hospitalisation in Australia.

Dick and Molly returned to England, where he died in 1948, a great loss to his family and to his many friends. Members of both the HKCC and the KCC, who held Dick in great esteem, immediately set up a memorial for him in the form of The Hancock Shield, played for each year by the two clubs since 1948. I am very glad to be able to say that this match is played to this day at the HKCC – truly a lasting memory to a Hong Kong cricketer, gentleman and friend.

THOMAS ALEXANDER PEARCE

Thomas Alexander Pearce, known as Alec to his friends and fellow cricketers, was born in Hong Kong on 15 December 1910, the elder son of Thomas Ernest Pearce and Eva (nee Leitch Rodger). He was educated at Charterhouse School, England, where he is remembered as a 'beautiful games player to whom hitting a ball came quite naturally. He was three years in the Charterhouse XI and two in the rackets pair.'

He played cricket for Kent from 1930, when A P F Chapman was the captain, till 1932, scoring 581 runs at an average of 24.13, and when on home leave from Hong Kong in 1937 and 1946. His highest County score of 106 was against Northants in 1946, a remarkable achievement, as he had only just been released from the Shamshuipo POW Camp in Hong Kong.

He was a tremendous scorer in club cricket in the UK and in Hong Kong. Unfortunately, his Hong Kong prewar club scores are not available. After the war he played for the HKCC Scorpions from 1948–49 to 1963–64, having a highest score of 105 not out in the 1952–53 season. He captained the Scorpions for eight seasons from 1948–49 to 1953–54 and from 1956–57 to 1958–59. He was the Club Captain for 11 consecutive years from 1948–49 to 1958–59 and President of the HKCC from 1961 to 1967.

Alec returned to Hong Kong in 1932 to join his father in business. In 1938 he became a bullion broker, and later as a 'Volunteer' fought in the battle for Hong Kong in December 1941. His father, Tam, was killed in action, and Alec became a prisoner of war until August 1945. After the war he rejoined Hutchison in London, then returned to Hutchison's Hong Kong office in 1946. He resigned in 1947 and worked as a stockbroker in his own firm, later joining Alec Potts as Potts, Pearce & Co. (Stockbrokers), until his retirement in 1970.

4

Alec played Interport cricket for Hong Kong from 1933 (against Shanghai) until 1955 (against Malaya). In 1933 and 1936, he captured 6–70 and 6–76 respectively in Shanghai's second innings. He had a highest score of 61 in Hong Kong's second innings in 1936. He and his father both played in the 1935 Interport against Shanghai in Hong Kong. After the war he captained Hong Kong in the first three Interports, against Shanghai in 1947 and 1948 and against Malaya in 1955. He also captained the Hong Kong team against Jack Chegwyn's Australian International side in 1952. In 1940, as a scratch golfer, Alec won the Colony Golf Championship, now called the Hong Kong Amateur Open Championship.

Alec married Nina Quin on 6th February 1948 in Hong Kong, and they had two daughters, Cynthia and Daphne. After Alec's retirement in 1970, he returned to his home in Hawkhurst, Kent, where he served on the Kent CCC cricket committee and was Club President in 1978. Alec died on 11 August 1982. A good friend remembers Alec: 'Alec relied on the typical racket player's lovely offside strokes, and first-class bowlers soon found ways of keeping him relatively quiet. His chief value to Kent was his glorious fielding anywhere. Above all, he was always fun.'

The author, as a schoolboy, played against Alec in the early 1950s: 'I was overawed by such names as Harry Owen Hughes, Donald Leach and Alec Pearce, all great personalities and Interport cricketers.'

JAL SORAB SHROFF

Jal Sorab Shroff, known to his cricketing friends as Jalu, a Parsee, was born in Shanghai, China, on 10 February 1937, the only son of Sorab Shroff and Khorshed (nee Bharucha). Jalu was educated at King George V School (KGV), Hong Kong, where he learnt his cricket and captained the 1st XI from 1953–54 to 1955–56. KGV played in the Second Division cricket league, and Jalu scored 892 runs in his last school season, a magnificent effort. He also captained the school 1st hockey and tennis teams. He furthered his education in England, where he represented London Universities. He scored 1,400 runs at an average 50.4 for London Polytechnic, helping them to win the London University cricket championship.

After his return to Hong Kong in 1959, he immediately stamped his mark on the local cricket scene and was selected to play for Hong Kong against Bangkok and Malaya. Jalu represented Hong Kong from 1959 to 1975, being Colony captain from 1967 to 1971. In the 1971 Interport against Malaysia in Hong Kong he scored 156, the then highest score in the Interport Series. He was also Chairman of Selectors from 1974–75 to 1975–76.

Jalu's 'best five years' of Hong Kong league cricket were from 1963–64 to 1967–1968, when he scored 3,065 runs. In 1970–71, he captained the First Division champions, the KCC Templars. A forceful batsman with a temperament for the big occasion and a superb slip fielder, Jalu was the backbone of Hong Kong representative cricket for many years. Carl Myatt reminisced:

> But it's the Ruby Hotel that I perhaps remember best, because of the copious amounts of *chow faan* consumed by Jalu, who whatever the circumstances of the match and its accompanying tensions, never lost his appetite. Fortunately his appetite for food has been matched through the years by his appetite for runs – a factor that Hong Kong can be thankful for.

The author recalled the vigorous training programme at KCC in 1965, prior to Hong Kong's tour of Malaysia and Singapore, when Jalu said his system was not built for the sprints and exercises we were put through, but 'he could bat all day' if the need arose. He was as good as his word on many occasions.

Jalu was KCC Club Cricket Captain from 1964–65 to 1973–74, and Club President from 1967 to 1971. He was made a KCC Life Member in 1981 and is an Hon. Member of the HKCC and the HKCA. He continued to play league cricket for a few years after his Interport days were over, then switched to lawn bowls, where his talents for the KCC First Division side continue to this day.

Jalu married Pervin Shroff on 25 September 1971 and they had three children, a son, Rasheed, and two daughters, Zarina and Sharmeen. A splendid 25th Wedding Aniversary buffet dinner for over 170 guests was held at the Hong Kong Jockey Club's Clubhouse in Shan Kwong Road to celebrate this occasion. Rasheed, in charge of the American operation in Dallas, Texas, rose to the occasion by asking his father whether it had been 'love at first sight'. Jalu responded by stating: 'Just look at the way we still look at each other!'

Jalu's a very successful businessman – Managing Director of S Framjee & Co. Ltd, a private family company he joined in 1959 after his return from the UK, and the Chief Executive officer of Fossil (East) Ltd, quoted on the American Nasdaq Stock Exchange.

PATRICK CARLISLE MYATT

Carl was born in India on 20 April 1936, the eldest son of John Myatt and Rica Ebert. While at St Thomas's College, Guruthalawa, Ceylon (now Sri Lanka), he captained the Under-16 cricket, hockey and soccer teams. Later in England, he played cricket for the Hove Grammar 1st XI. As well as cricket, Carl played club-level soccer in England and in Hong Kong.

Carl, together with his brother Tony, first played senior league cricket in Hong Kong for the Indian Recreation Club in the 1950s. He later joined Craigengower, where the wicket was most suited to his economical leg cutters. The ground was tiny by international standards and therefore tempting for batsmen to be aggressive, but Carl was 'impossible to hit' on that particular pitch. Later, when both CCC and Recreio, the home club of the Portuguese cricketers, found it difficult to field full sides in the senior league, they combined their remaining talents into a team called the Cavaliers, led by Carl. This very effective side, with players such as Buji Dhabher, Mike Barros and the Lalchandani brothers (Ram and Gopal), won the First Division championship in the 1968–69 season. On 7 January 1968, playing for CCC, Carl took all ten wickets, including the hat-trick against LSW. He performed the hat-trick five times in local cricket. In 1970–71, he joined KCC and continued to play for them right up to his farewell game in 1983, just prior to his departure to work at an Hawaiian university.

During Carl's first six seasons with KCC, when the club won the First Division championship four times, he took 285 wickets at 11.97 runs each. In 1974–75, he captained the winning Templars team, topping the league bowling averages at 8.33, and crowned a very successful season by being awarded the Ruttonjee Trophy as Player of the Year.

Carl was first selected for Hong Kong against Malaya in 1961, and played regularly for the Hong Kong team until 1977. He captained the side from 1971 to 1977, during which time Hong Kong beat Singapore in 1972 (Myatt 6 for 33 in the match) and Malaysia in 1974. In 1965 at Kuala Lumpur, Carl had Malaya, in all kinds of trouble, despite his lack of sleep, taking 5 for 17 as the Malayans struggled to 90 for 9 in their second innings. In 1969 in Hong Kong, he had his most successful Interport against Singapore, when he had a match analysis of 9 for 66.

In 1964 against E W Swanton's Commonwealth XI at KCC, which side included such players as Gary Sobers, Seymour Nurse, Nawab of Pataudi, Richie Benaud and Sonny Ramadhin, Carl bowled extremely well, taking 5 for 75. In fact, after Sobers had reached his century on a helpful bowlers wicket, he asked Tony Weller, the Hong Kong skipper, to put 'that chap over there' back on to bowl. Ram Lalchandani was the wicket-keeper. To Carl's first ball Sobers went down the wicket and 'missed' the ball. Ram was so surprised he failed to make the stumping, as the ball had not previously passed Sobers's bat. 'Watch the ball, sonny,' Sobers advised, and repeated the stroke to give Carl his well-deserved fifth wicket.

Carl has played representative cricket for Hong Kong in Australia, England, Malaysia, Singapore and Sri Lanka, where on numerous occa-

7

sions he has caused the opposing batsmen real problems with his particular type of bowling. It was his line, length and medium pace movement off the wicket, something many a first class bowler today cannot manage to maintain.

On Hong Kong's first official tour to the UK in 1976, Carl took four of the five MCC wickets to fall in Hong Kong's highlight match at Lord's. His victims included Eric Russell, Mike Smith, Ted Dexter and Bob Taylor, finishing with 4 for 73 in a drawn match. Carl considers this to be the pinnacle of his cricketing achievements.

The author recalls bowling to Carl, the batsman, where he had the very disconcerting habit of chewing his batting gloves as you ran in to bowl. Of course you stopped in your run-up, presuming he was not ready! It took awhile to get used to this idiosyncrasy of his.

Carl pioneered the coverage of Hong Kong cricket by the local press. His weekly column became compulsory reading for all cricketers and followers of the game. He was the *South China Morning Post* Sports Editor from 1964 to 1973, and Editor-in-Chief of the Sunday edition from 1973 to 1983. Apart from being the *SCMP*'s cricket and soccer correspondent for many years, his major sports assignments were: Olympic Games 1964 (Tokyo) and 1984 (Los Angeles); Asian Games 1966 and 1968, and the Ali-Frazier World Heavyweight Boxing Championship in Manila.

Since leaving Hong Kong in 1983, Carl has been coaching soccer successfully at all levels in Hawaii, where he lives with his wife Myra, and is currently Director Corporate Communications, Hawaiian Electric Company.

For his contribution to cricket in Hong Kong, Carl was elected an Honorary Life Member of KCC. He had been made an Honorary Member of the HKCC after the successful Interport against Malaya in Hong Kong in 1963.

Carl, as a player and a sportsman, was a valuable asset to any side, and his tremendous contribution to cricket in Hong Kong and South-east Asia will always be remembered.

PETER WINSTON ANDERSON

Peter Anderson, 'Plod' to his fellow cricketers in Hong Kong, was born on 19 May 1942 at Wokingham, Berkshire, England, the son of Charles William and Melanie (nee Tardival). He attended the Duke of York's Royal Military School in Dover, Kent, where he was awarded school colours for athletics, cricket, hockey, rugby, tennis and soccer. There is silence on his academic achievements!

Peter spent most of his working life in the UK West Country police force and played many seasons with the Torquay CC representing Devon in Minor Counties championship matches, and his last UK club was Tavistock CC, where he was the club captain. He married Sybil (nee Miller) in Beer, Devon, on 7 March 1963, and they had two daughters, Jayne and Emma.

Peter arrived in Hong Kong in 1975 to work for the ICAC (Independent Commission against Corruption). Between 1978 and 1986 it was unofficially known as the 'Institute for Cricket and Cricketers'. Goodness knows what he did in those years when he captained the Hong Kong cricket team! His lieutenant, Gordon Bacon, if he was allowed to, could probably tell us.

Peter first appeared on the Hong Kong cricket scene in the 1975–76 season, playing in the Saturday League for the Royal Navy, when he compiled 828 runs at an average of 51.75. He even managed to capture 36 wickets before the locals discovered his bowling was all talk!

From 1975–76 to 1986–87 (Saturday League and League Cup) he scored a total of 7772 runs, highest score 113 not out, at an average of 53.60, and topped the batting averages in four seasons. He played six times for the Royal Navy, five times for Island School, when he together with Geoff Lever assisted greatly in coaching and developing their cricket, and once for HKCC Gap Ramblers.

In the Sunday League and Rothman's Cup during the seasons 1977–78 to 1985–86, he scored 4356 runs, highest score 151 not out, at an average of 46.34. In the 1980–81 season, he was a member of the LSW team that completed the double by winning the Sunday League title and the Rothman's Cup. In the 1983–84 season, he topped the batting averages in both leagues, and was awarded the Ruttonjee 'Player of the Year' trophy, not only for his cricketing achievements but also for his tremendous contribution to Hong Kong cricket.

Peter first represented Hong Kong in the Interport against Singapore at KCC in November 1975, and continued to play for Hong Kong until the completion of the ICC Associate Members tournament in England in June 1986. He captained the Hong Kong team from 1978 till 1986, playing in Interports against Malaysia and Singapore; in ICC tournaments in 1982 and 1986, and in the first Asian Cricket Council competition in Bangladesh in 1984.

Once he became the Hong Kong captain, he led from the front, whether it was in Interports or in raising the necessary funds for them – 'watch it' it you didn't put your back into it! It wasn't the 'Plod' we thought we knew, but the Winston we didn't know, that provided the driving force. Motivation is so important, particularly in the Hong Kong context. The author managed to talk Peter into continuing as captain for the ICC tour in 1986. We needed his drive, determination and experience. He cursed the author more than once for putting him through yet another tough pre-tour training session – and at his age!

In 1986, Peter, together with Chakrapal Sinh, the very personable, cricketing Air India Manager in Hong Kong, were instrumental in arranging the first Hong Kong Overseas Schoolboys' cricket tour. Peter managed this successful tour to India in December 1986. Peter, like Carl Myatt, recalled the match for Hong Kong against the MCC at Lord's on 12 July 1976, as his most memorable cricketing moment, the more so as he had top scored with 39 runs.

In 1977, while on leave in the UK, he recalled playing in a six-a-side pro-am tournament and running Roger Tolchard (Leicestershire & England) out. Roger was recognised as 'pretty quick' between the wickets. This debacle led to a first-round elimination. A few months later, Roger arrived in Hong Kong with D H Robins' International side. Peter ran him out again: 'only this time it was by running around the midwicket boundary at KCC, picking up one-handed and throwing flat to the top of the stumps, whilst on the run. Roger was out by yards trying for two, and was still grumbling about me two days later!' 'Flat to the top of the stumps', sounds like one of those tall stories to me, but I'll allow just one from an old friend.

After leaving Hong Kong in 1988, Peter became Secretary, then Chief Executive of the Somerset CCC. Since that time, applying his 'Winston' personality, he has transformed the club – given it more purpose and improved its finances – and continues to strive for success on the field.

DERMOT ALEXANDER REEVE

Dermot was born in Hong Kong on 2 April 1963, the youngest of the four sons of Alec and Monica Reeve (nee Regan). He was educated at Kowloon Junior School, where his mother was a teacher, and later at King George V School, where his father was the Headmaster. He was coached by David Clinton, a sound batsman who had played cricket for Hong Kong and had fashioned many KGV schoolboys into good cricketers. Dermot captained the 1st XI in his last year. Three schools currently play cricket in the Hong Kong Saturday League, so schoolboys are, as Dermot put it, 'literally thrown in at the deep end at an early age,' to give them valuable experience, and any sign of talent would be quickly developed. Dermot was not known as a bowler at school.

A few days before his 17th birthday, playing for the independent side 'Vagabonds' in the final of the Rothman's Cup, he literally won the match for them, carrying his bat for 117 runs and taking 2 for 13. In May the same year, he was selected to tour Malaysia and Singapore and played in

10

the three-day Interport against Singapore, becoming the youngest player postwar to play Interport cricket for Hong Kong. In 1980–81, he topped the Sunday League batting, scoring 917 runs, average 70.54 (five centuries, highest 119). He was second in the Saturday League with 1029 runs, average 64.31 (two centuries, highest 145), and was awarded the Ruttonjee 'Player of the Year' trophy.

In 1982, he was selected to play for Hong Kong in the ICC Associate Members tournament in England. When selection was being made for the same tournament in 1986, the author, who was Chairman of Selectors, contacted Dermot, now a Sussex County player, to enquire whether he would be available for Hong Kong. Whilst appreciating the invitation, Dermot said: 'I'd rather not be selected, as I hope to play for England one day.'

Dermot then joined the Lord's Ground Staff in late 1981, played cricket in Perth, Western Australia during the English winters, had trials with Warwickshire and Nottinghamshire, and finally signed a two-year contract with Sussex on 7 June 1983.

The 'boy from Hong Kong' had arrived, and as luck would have it, with first team members 'falling like flies at the wayside', for one reason or another (Monica, a fervent follower of her son's cricketing fortunes, probably 'pointed the bone'), Dermot grasped his chance with both hands, something he would continue to do whenever opportunities arose. He played for Sussex from 1983 till 1987.

> The 1983 season began with the sore news that Imran and Tony Pigott both had stress fractures. Garth Le Roux had a serious groin strain and was not one hundred per cent fit. The arrival of Dermot Reeve, nicknamed 'Enid' because of his extraordinary story telling powers, helped to revive fortunes.
>
> Christopher Lee *From the Sea End*, the Official History of Sussex
> CCC

Dermot was later called 'Huck' (after the young scamp in Mark Twain), a much more suited name for this 'tall, fair, rather tousled-haired, athletic and friendly extrovert'.

In 1986, he was awarded his cap as well as the 'Man of the Match' against Lancashire in the NatWest Final. He had dismissed the dangerous Clive Lloyd for a duck.

In 1986, he married Julie Chester, whom he had met while playing cricket in Perth. They had a daughter. Dermot and Julie have since parted amicably. In 1988, he joined Warwickshire, being awarded his cap in 1989 during which year he won his second 'Man of the Match' award in the NatWest Final against Middlesex. On 30 March 1990, Dermot was made an Hon. Member of the Kowloon Cricket Club.

11

In 1991, he made his debut for England, playing in the one-day International against the West Indies at Lord's on 23 May, the only Hong Kong-born cricketer to achieve this distinction. He was then selected, as a member of the England team, to tour New Zealand and to take part in the Benson & Hedges World Cup. He played in all three Tests and the three one-day Internationals against New Zealand, scoring 59 runs in his first Test and being named 'Man of the Match' in the first of the one-day Internationals. In the World Cup, he played in nine matches, including the semi-final and the final against Pakistan, only missing England's disastrous game against Zimbabwe.

In August 1992, he played against Pakistan in the last two of the five one-day Internationals. He was then selected to tour India and Sri Lanka in early 1993 and played in all the one-day Internationals – India (six) and Sri Lanka (two).

Dermot was appointed Warwickshire captain in 1993 and led them to an exhilarating win at Lord's in the NatWest Final against Sussex in September, after Sussex had scored 321 in their 60 overs.

> ... without him, without his weird strokes and imaginative placings, Warwickshire could never have won.
>
> Robin Marlar, *The Times*, September 1993

In early October 1993, he was once again 'Man of the Match', when England won the second Hong Kong International Sixes under the captaincy of Graham Gooch. Dermot visits Hong Kong regularly and was appointed the Hong Kong squad coach for the ICC tournament in Kenya in February/March 1994.

Dermot has always had a certain belief in himself. Some call it cockiness. The author has known him from his early schoolboy days – even then he was an extrovert. He never gives up, but takes his chances believing he'll win. In order to succeed in this very competitive age you have to be different – that's what he is, but as Jack Bannister said: 'He does get up people's noses!'

Prior to the Benson & Hedges final at Lord's on 9 July 1994, Derek Pringle, writing for the *Independent on Sunday*, said in a Profile on Dermot Reeve:

> Reeve's talent, as such, is that of the conjuror or the escape artist, most effective when cornered, with few options and large stakes to play for. Nobody is quite sure how he does it, but give the man a demanding and pressurised situation and he usually pulls something out of the bag.

After Warwickshire had won the trophy, Colin Bateman of the *Daily*

Express reported: 'While Lara provided inspiration, Reeve provided the belief.' Paul Smith, a team member, added: 'He's been a great captain, his confidence and personality rub off. These are the most exciting times I've known at Edgbaston.'

Statistics – County Cricket Record to Season 1995

Batting	Inn	NO	HS	Runs	Ave	Bowling	Runs	Wkts	Ave	Best
Sussex	101	31	119	1761	25.16		6728	239	28.15	7–37
Warwicks	201	42	202*	6133	38.57		4982	200	24.91	6–73
	302	73	202*	7894	34.47		11710	439	26.67	7–37

Dermot continued as captain of Warwickshire in 1994 and 1995. In 1994, with Brian Lara as their overseas player, they won three of the four County titles – the County Championship, the Benson & Hedges Cup and the Sunday League, the first time any County had achieved this distinction. In 1995, with Allan Donald as their overseas player, they repeated winning the County Championship and also won the NatWest Trophy. Dermot was honoured with the OBE in the 1996 Queen's New Year Honours List. He was selected as a replacement for the injured Craig White in the 1996 World Cup in India and Pakistan. *Wisden* has also honoured Dermot by naming him as one of their Five Cricketers of the Year for 1995.

Very sadly, 'Warwickshire's inspirational leader, the most successful county captain of modern times, retires with hip complaint,' reported Mike Beddow, *Daily Telegraph*, 20 July 1996 – a torn cartilage in the hip joint would no longer stand up to 'the rigours of batting, bowling and chivvying'.

Even more sadly in the author's opinion, speaking your mind is sometimes all right in the right context, but when you decide to go into print, as in *Winning Ways*, you should also very carefully consider your words before you finally commit yourself. In Robin Marlar's excellent review of Reeve's book in *The Cricketer International*, January 1997, he has summed up the present Reeve character when he said: '... Reeve's self-confidence has long since crossed the frontier of bumptiousness to a less attractive conceit, the superiority complex.'

LEAGUE CRICKET

In no other game do events of import hang so bodefully on a single act. In no other game does one little mistake lead to mischief so irreparable.

Neville Cardus, *Cricket,* 1929

Cricket was established wherever the Royal Navy, British Army, British Traders or settlers went: in the Americas, Australia, New Zealand, India and in the Far East. Before the birth of Hong Kong in 1841, Macau, the pied-à-terre where European merchants had established trade with China, could boast its own 'racetrack and cricket ground' – adjacent to the Portas de Cerco. Wherever he went, the overseas Englishman always took horse racing and cricket with him.

G R Sayer, in his book, *Hong Kong 1841–1862*, stated: 'In January 1846 the formation of a cricket ground and racecourse at Wiang La Chung was mooted in the *Friend of China*.'

We know 'Wiang La Chung' as Wong Nai Chung in Happy Valley, Hong Kong. The draining of the swamps in Happy Valley in 1846 to create a suitable environment for sporting activities, including cricket, coincided with one of the most notable events in the history of cricket, the formation of the first All England XI on 31 August 1846, 'a side of itinerant professionals.' William Clarke, a lob bowler, took over 2,300 wickets in six seasons from 1849. Presumably some of Hong Kong's early bowlers were also lob bowlers?

From that time the various sporting facilities formed at Happy Valley were mainly utilised by the Services. However, as Hong Kong began to develop into a thriving port, more civilians arrived to swell the business community, resulting in a call for additional recreational facilities.

The military parade ground on the north side of Queen's Road at the end of Des Voeux Road became a target for a cricket ground. This distinct possibility became a fact in 1851, when the Hong Kong Cricket Club (HKCC) was formed.

The new HKCC organised cricket matches between its own members, against Service teams and, from 1866 and 1890, against Shanghai and Malaya respectively. In addition to these Interport matches, the HKCC had sent teams to Swatow, Amoy and Foochow in China, but these trips were looked upon more as pleasure tours rather than cricket contests, ana-

15

logous to the tours to Bangkok and Manila now made by the KCC, Centaurs and HKCC respectively.

Inter-unit cricket matches amongst the Services – the Royal Engineers, Royal Artillery, Royal Garrison Artillery, RAMC, Ordnance Corps, the 49th, 55th and 98th Regiments and others were mostly played at Happy Valley on Hong Kong Island.

THE EMERGING YEARS 1903–41

In the latter part of the 19th and early part of the 20th century, civilian teams, such as Craigengower Cricket Club (CCC), the Hong Kong Parsee Cricket Club (HKPCC), the Civil Service Cricket Club (CSCC), the Kowloon Cricket Club (KCC), and the Police Recreation Club (PRC), were being formed to become the basis for the beginnings of a league cricket system in Hong Kong. At an initial suggestion of Mr A E Asger, Hon. Secretary of CCC, a league competition commenced on 24 October 1903.

The *South China Morning Post* (SCMP) generously provided a handsome shield for this new competition. However, not everyone was in favour of an organised league, several critics describing the set-up as 'second class'.

The eight teams participating in the inaugural league for the SCMP shield were: HKCC 'A', CCC, HKPCC, Royal Engineers, RAMC, Army Ordnance Corps, CSCC and HMS Tamar. The Army Ordnance Corps had the distinction of being the inaugural winners of the First Division League competition in the first league season of 1903–04.

The criticism levied against the HKCC for its 'lack of commitment' to the league competition in 1903–04 was answered by a member of the HKCC.

In the second season, the KCC and the PRC (both founded in 1904), together with the RGA and Army Staff, joined the league, whilst HMS Tamar and the Parsees withdrew. The Hon. T Sercombe Smith, Police Magistrate, who played Interport cricket for Hong Kong against Malaya and Shanghai, became the first President of the league, a position he held until he left Hong Kong in 1906.

In 'Plum' Warner's book, *My Cricketing Life*, after winning the rubber against Australia on 3 March 1904, during his first tour as captain of England, congratulatory messages were received from all over the world, including a postcard from Hong Kong with just three words: 'Veni, Vidi, Vici'. Making an educated guess, the author considered the message would most likely have been sent by the Hon. T Sercombe Smith, as President of the Hong Kong Cricket League, a typical lawyer's learned comment.

16

The following clubs were then founded: Club de Recreio (Recreio) in 1905, the Chinese Recreation Club (CRC) in 1911, the Hong Kong University Cricket Club (HKUCC) in 1912 and the Indian Recreation Club (IRC) in 1918.

During WWI only friendly cricket matches were played. In 1917–18, just prior to the re-commencement of the league, the top Colony batting (runs/averages) and bowling (wickets/averages) were:

T E Pearce (HKCC) 833 69.41   P H Cobb   (KCC)   72   6.73
H E Muriel (HKCC) 564 42.85   F W Hamilton (HKCC) 48   8.26
J Stalker   (KCC)   508 33.86

At the Hong Kong Cricket League annual general meeting held on 9 October 1918, it was decided to revert to league cricket with one division only.

After the Treaty of Versailles in 1919, when the ravaged Western world was beginning to return to normality, there were enough keen cricketers in Hong Kong to form another division in the league. Thus the league Second Division came into being for the 1921–22 season, with KCC becoming the first champions. Although the divisions of the league were termed 'First' and 'Second', they were in effect two separate competitions, with a higher standard of cricket in the First Division.

In those earlier days, the Army, HKCC, KCC, IRC, the Civil Service, Craigengower, the Police and the University were the mainstays of the league. Now in the 1990s, all these clubs, some in different guises, are still in existence, although not all are playing on their original grounds. The Army/British Forces, a very important element in the local cricket scene since the Hong Kong flag was first raised in 1841, left Hong Kong at the end of June 1997 with the loss of some of their very valuable grounds.

In the 1926–27 season, Bill Brace of KCC, who played for Hong Kong from 1927 to 1929, scored a record 1025 runs with a highest score of 126.

At the end of the 1928–29 league season, two important matches were played:

Apr 6 The Rest: 126 (E C Fincher 68, W Brace 7–12)
       Hong Kong XI: 171 (T E Pearce 65, W Brace 33, Capt
                                 A G Dobbie 4–32)

Played at the HKCC, the Hong Kong XI won by six wickets.

Apr 13 HKCC: 121 (H R B Hancock 31, W Brace 6–26)
        The Rest: 97 (W C Hung 30, H V Parker 5–16)

Another perfect day awaited the last important match of the season, and the wicket though not good, might have been considerably worse. There is no getting away from the fact that the batting in the Colony is in a pretty low ebb, even when one discounts liberally for a bad wicket. I would be only too glad to explain it by saying the bowling is of a very high standard, but I fear that would hardly be true.

R ABBIT, *Hong Kong Daily Press*

R ABBIT also had some scathing remarks to make about the game's administrators.

The Rest were told the game was for twelve-thirty, while the HKCC were under the impression the match started at two p.m. and turned up accordingly. But, of course, you can confidently count that anything the League management has a hand in will be mucked up; and I suggest that next year officials are put in who (a) have some intelligence, (b) some intention of devoting more than an hour a season to their job, and (c) are on the telephone. In the meantime let us be thankful that the League doesn't run the Interport or we should probably find ourselves two short with no tiffin.

During these 'Emerging Years' the HKCC and KCC dominated the First Division, while IRC were dominant in the second. Most of the highlights of these league matches are recorded under the various club histories.

A particular feature of those earlier matches was the continuation of the game after the winning side had passed their opponents' score. No doubt due to the many low scores and relatively few games, cricketers wished to make the most of their Saturday afternoons, so often continued playing until stumps were drawn. Presumably the various sides had their own scorers, but how did they work out the averages at the end of each season?

The annual fixtures schedule also seemed to be fairly flexible. Sometimes only one league match would be played on a Saturday, the remainder of the grounds being used for friendly matches, or a match would have been arranged to commence and finish at times different to that laid down by the League Committee.

R ABBIT wasn't the only person to criticise the administration. Three years later, more flak came from a different direction. *Cricket Notes* by 'Leg-break', *SCMP,* 2 March 1932:

The Cricket League seems to confine its activities to holding an annual meeting when a balance sheet is passed, and perhaps some contribution being made to schools. For a body which is supposed to control local cricket, I think this is a sad state of affairs.

During this period many friendly matches were played, not only by the league sides, but also by schools and associations, such associations as the China Light & Power and the Hong Kong Electric Recreation Clubs. Apart from the Chater Road ground, the others were located at King's Park in Kowloon, where the 'grounds were surrounded by few trees and bare hills', and at Happy Valley and Sookunpoo on Hong Kong Island.

1933   Cent. Brit. Assn: 67 (F E Filmer 27, A B Clemo 5–43,
                                    R A J Simpson 4–24)
Nov 12 China Light RC: 36 (N Whitley 3–0 'hat-trick')

1934   University: 181–5 dec (E L Gosano 72, K P Gan 44,
                                    L T Ride 35*)
Oct 20 HKCC: 146–4   (H Owen Hughes 51)

E. L. Gosano, the University captain, played one of the finest innings I have seen him figure in. He was never afraid to hit the ball hard, his score of 72 included 13 boundary hits.

R ABBIT

1935   League XI: 204–9 dec (A M Rodrigues 48, A H Madar 44*,
                                    G Ricketts 4–64)
Mar 16 HKCC: 156–9   (A W Hayward 31, H Owen Hughes
                                    23, A R Minu 3–55)

By 1939, league cricket in Hong Kong was severely affected by the worsening political scene in Europe, as club members and service personnel returned to the United Kingdom. A direct result of this situation was a proposal by Harry Owen Hughes (HKCC) at the Cricket League annual meeting held on 12 September 1938, that league matches should commence in January and end in March. This proposal was adopted and applied to league matches in 1939–40 and 1940–41. In the first of these seasons, the HKCC dropped out, to be followed by the Army in the next season. In the last prewar season, 1940–41, there were only six teams left in the First Division: CSCC, CCC, HKU, IRC, KCC, and Recreio.

KCC won both the senior and junior titles in the last prewar season, the senior team retaining the SCMP shield by defeating the CSCC on 5 April 1941 by six wickets. The fight for the junior division title was a close encounter between KCC and CCC, who were level on points prior to their final clash. In that match, KCC bowled CCC out for 95 and then scraped home by two wickets, the winning run being an overthrow!

The cricketers who remained in Hong Kong were nearly all members of the Hong Kong Volunteer Defence Corps and/or the Hong Kong Volunteer Naval Reserve, who were later embroiled in the battle for Hong Kong against the Japanese Imperial Forces in December 1941. Many made the supreme sacrifice, including:

H A Alves	D J N Anderson	A Baker
F E dos Remedios	E F Fincher	L E Lammert
M Mendonca	T E Pearce	S A Reed
	E Zimmern	

Alfred Prata, an ex-DBS pupil and younger brother of A M 'Toto' Prata, who played for Hong Kong against Shanghai in 1948, played for Recreio prewar and for the Centaurs in their formative years in the 1950s, recalled the immediate prewar cricket scene in Hong Kong:

> I really cannot recall any matches I played in which were un-interesting (even in defeat!) or un-enjoyable. Those were fantastic days ... we were all 'youngsters' playing against really 'seniors' in every respect – some were Interporters: the likes of Teddy and Ernie Fincher, Harry Owen Hughes, Alec Pearce, the Rumjahns and Madars. We all looked forward to these matches weeks ahead in keen anticipation and, what was more, we were never disappointed! The 'greats' were GREAT.
>
> 'There were also the Gosanos (at one time five brothers were playing for Recreio – Lino, Bertie, Luigi, Zinho and Gerry). A truly remarkable cricketing family! The Reeds – Willie and Reggie (four of the brothers died in the battle of Hong Kong); the Zimmerns – Ernie, Freddie, Francis and Archie, who with Robbie and 'Tinker' Lee, were all 'greats' of Craigengower; A R Minu, Karsa Nazarin and F D Pereira of IRC; H A Barros, H A 'Dickie' Alves, Ferdie Cavalho, Dr H L Ozorio, Dr Albert Rodrigues, E M L 'Ginger' Soares, P M N da Silva, the two Guterres, Dr and George, all of Recreio AND the THREE who brought cricket to us at DBS – J L Youngsaye, C B R Sargent and G A Goodban ... the TWO at CBS – Mulcahy and McLellan and, Asome at St Joseph's/La Salle.

Bertram Lay, a schoolboy contemporary of Alfred's and fellow cricket enthusiast who played prewar for KCC, recalled his early impressions of cricket in Hong Kong:

> What impressed me when I started to play cricket here were the grounds and wickets the game was played on. I must say that the grounds in Hong Kong in the 30s were, on the whole, very functional and not at all as pictureque as one would have hoped and imagined cricket grounds to be. Hong Kong grounds suffered mainly from a lack of trees and character, and were usually on the small side.

20

I am reminded of the Navy ground in King's Park, the Army ground in Sookunpoo, the grounds in Happy Valley (Craigengower, Civil Service & Police), which one must admit, could not be said to have been very appealing. The KCC was a nice ground, but I cannot say I was inspired by the HKCC ground, where it used to be. However, in those days, I was under the spell of the game and all cricket grounds were wonderful.

THE POSTWAR YEARS 1948–73

During the fighting for Hong Kong and the immediate aftermath, looting by local gangs was widespread – in *Kowloon Cricket Club – A History, 1980*, it was recorded:

> ... the Club (KCC) was soon stripped of not only its stocks of food, drinks and furniture, but in time its doors, window frames and eventually its wooden flooring for use as firewood. The Club-house and main ground were used by the Japanese for stabling horses and mules during the war years.

All the private recreational clubs in Hong Kong suffered similar fates to that of KCC, some to a greater and others to a lesser degree, with the result that the prewar league shields and wooden 'Honour' boards, listing Presidents and Captains of Cricket from each club's inception, were destroyed, causing irreparable loss of cricket archival records.

The KCC main ground was in such bad shape through lack of drainage and improper usage during nearly four years of total neglect, that it was not possible to play any form of sport until 1947, when through the sheer hard work and guiding hand of Bill Hitchen, friendly cricket matches were resumed. Other grounds also started to come back to life – the Army played the Navy at Sookunpoo (Oct 1947); the Dockyard RC played against the Chief & Petty Officers' CC at King's Park (Nov 1947), and the HKCC played the Army at Chater Road (Dec 1947).

In late 1996, after sending the 'Governor's Message' for my book, Chris Patten showed his further interest in my project by having his office send me a news cutting dated 10 September 1945, recording the 'first postwar cricket match' in Hong Kong. It briefly outlined 'an informal cricket match' between two naval teams on the HKCC ground, 'after the Club's groundsman put in a couple of patient hours preparing a pitch in the middle of the ground....'

On 1 January 1948, the annual Hong Kong Electric Co. Recreation Club fixture 'which had been played for 25 years', took place at Sookunpoo.

21

Local Staff: 149–8 dec   (S H Khan 45 retd)
European Staff: 144   (A G Gardner 50, I Haroon 4–38)

The two league divisions recommenced in the 1948–49 season. The First Division had ten teams playing on a home and away basis, with four points for a win and one each for a draw.

In the 1950s and 1960s, a cricketer could go to the nets at HKCC and KCC to practise on any afternoon without calling on any fellow cricketers, as the two premier clubs had very capable Chinese ground staff bowlers, who would bowl to you as long as you wished to bat. One of these Chinese bowlers later played for the Scorpions and eventually for Hong Kong – his name was Benny Kwong. He was a specialist leg spinner with a superb googly – ask Alan Smith, the 1994 TCCB chief executive, who had faced Benny at the HKCC, but not for long! Benny was also a capable batsman and superb fielder.

The Services, strengthened with 'recruits' from the Korean War regiments and United Kingdom National Service personnel, dominated league cricket during this period, such Hong Kong representatives as H S Bedson, M Birley, Pat Howard-Dobson, J Lipscombe and Bill Withall spearheading the strong Army presence.

Led by Alec Pearce, with two experienced stalwarts in Harry Owen Hughes and Len Stokes, the HKCC sides put together seven championship wins – the Scorpions had two early wins, in 1949–50 and 1952–53, before the Army started inscribing their name on the A H Madar Shield. Harry's association with the HKCC dated back to the 1920s, and he continued as a diehard Scorpion almost to his 60th birthday, while Len was a prewar Shanghai Interporter. But the real destructive weapon was one Frank Howarth, an 'old Lancashire Pro' whose 'flight and subtle variations of pace' won many a match. In the 1949–50 season he captured 103 wickets at 6.78, a postwar record to this day, which included five wickets plus 13 times!

The first 'tampering' with the points system came in 1960–61 when bonus points were introduced – two points being awarded for a 'winning' draw. The CCC Sixes were introduced in 1961. Little Sai Wan CC joined the First Division in the 1964–65 season.

Ted Wilson, known locally as 'Uncle Ted' or 'Smoothy Wilson', depending upon the occasion, led the Scorpions to their next victory in 1966–67, after a lapse of 13 seasons. Ted had commented on the Scorpions lack of success and after 'proving his point', handed the mantle over to John 'Foxy' Fawcett, one of Hong Kong's leading postwar all-rounders: an accomplished left-hand batsman, right-arm medium-fast bowler and an excellent close to the wicket fielder. John thanked Ted and went on to retain the title.

1966   Scorpions defeat the RAF – 'Fawcett, single-handedly took the
Nov 12 RAF apart, scoring 91* and capturing 6–31.'

1967   Scorpions: 223–2 dec   (J Fawcett 82*, A Weller 61*)
Nov 17 Saracens: 68   (E Wilson 5–20, J Murphy 4–21)

Dec 9 Scorpions: 167–2 dec
        LSW: 73   (J Murphy 6–17)

'Saiwan shattered by the pace bowling of Julian Murphy.'

1968   Scorpions: 155–9 dec
Mar 9 LSW: 53   (J Fawcett 7–24)

'Fawcett grabbed seven wickets, including four caught and bowled.'

The other HKCC side, the Optimists, spread their three championship
wins equally over the period from 1959–60 to 1971–72. In the first of these
successes under 'Guy' Pritchard, the Optimists required a draw in their last
match against KCC. The KCC Captain, David Coffey, needing a win for
the championship, won the toss and put the opposition in to bat ... to bat
... to bat, which they did, declaring with 168 runs on the board, leaving
KCC 'the impossible task of scoring 169 runs in 42 minutes.' This caused
'aggro' between the two clubs for some time. If you had been the Optimists captain, would you have acted differently?

The Optimists winning sides in 1963–64 and 1971–72 were captained by
John Baker and Peter Davies respectively, with the youthful Mike Duggan
playing in both these winning sides. The author well remembers John
Baker's farewell dinner held at the old HKCC. Cricketers and friends had
been drinking in the mens' upstairs bar and when the time came to eat,
hadn't noticed that the fresh oysters were 'off'. Forty-eight hours later,
three were in hospital with hepatitis while many others had suffered
varying degrees of 'Eastern Trot'.

John Baker had Peter 'Dad' Langston in his side. 'Dad' Langston, rolling
in on his long run up to the wicket, shirt hanging out, would duck his head
on delivery and promptly put batsmen back in the pavilion, with his decep-
tively late inswingers. The author recalled Jim Swanton's look of incredulity
when he watched 'Dad' opening the bowling against his Commonwealth XI
in 1964 at KCC. His whole delivery action was unbelievable, but on his day,
'Dad' was very effective. Ask many former Army and Recreio cricketers!

1968   Cavaliers: 26   (G McLeod 12, P Langston 7–16, P Greene 3–10)
Oct 12 Optimists: 27–3

'Langston enjoying a swinging time on his favourite ground.' (at Recreio)

Peter Davies, who captained the last of these winning sides, had already started his prolific run scoring in the league for the Optimists. From the seasons 1966–67 till 1987–88 . . . 'don't be a spoil-sport' Hall, let's have it from the horse's mouth.'

> Surprising though some will find it, I did not keep a precise record of all my scores over the years, but I do have all the Handbooks for the relevant period and as clear as I can get it, my statistics for HKCC Optimists are –
>
> Inns   318   NO   29   Runs   11464   Av   39.67
>
> That runs from November 1966 to March 1988.
>
> Peter Davies, December 1993

1970   Optimists: 193–7 dec (D Roberts 99*)
Nov 22 Police RC: 92   (M Duggan 5–23)

> Peter Davies declared 'for some inconceivable reason'. Mike Prew sportingly offered an additional over, but Davies's decision prevailed.

Army defeated Scorpions to win the inaugural Rothman's Cup in the 1970–71 season. Denys Roberts, President of the HKCA, in thanking Ian Gow of Rothman's said: 'I hope that this tournament will become a regular fixture in the cricket calendar.' Thanks to the generosity of Rothman's and the foresight of Ian Gow, the Rothman's Cup remains a much-coveted annual trophy to win.

KCC Templars grabbed the honours at the end of this period with wins in 1970–71 and 1972–73, captained by Interporters Jalu Shroff and Buddy Carnell respectively. The 1972–73 side included the father/son Vachha's, Jangu and Yarman.

1970   RAF: 143 (B Dhabher 6–30)
Dec 6 Templars: 95 (B Dhabher 32)

> 'Templars crash to their second defeat of the season.'

1971   RAF: 45   (C O'Brien 14, P Hall 7–21)
Nov 28 Templars: 48–0 (J T Hung 35*)

> 'Sweet revenge, even without a contribution from Buji Dhabher!'

Apart from the teams already mentioned, Recreio, coupled with the name Cavaliers, a combination of CCC/Recreio cricketers, were the only other 'club' to win the senior division title during the postwar years. Recreio winning in 1948–49, with five Gosano brothers all playing a part, and again in 1961–62, while the Cavaliers, led by Carl Myatt, took the honours in 1968–69. Friendly matches were played on Sundays and whenever there was a gap in the league programme.

1955   Secretariat: 194–7 dec (R J C Howes 101, D C C Trench 43*)
Nov 12 Legal Dept: 205   (J Pakenham-Walsh 71, W Tingle 3–42)
        at HKCC.

Nov 20 Govt. Exec. Officers: 83   (J Harris 3–8)
        Police RC: 84–7 (J Harris 26, D C Readman 3–23)
        at Happy Valley.

Alongside the senior league, an International Series was launched in the 1959–60 season, and continued until 1962–63. The winners were:

    1959–60   England
    1960–61   England
    1961–62   England & Indian Sub-Continent / Malaya (jointly)
    1962–63   Indian Sub-Continent / Malaya

This was followed for one season by a Knock-out Shield in 1963–64, won by the PRC.

A Single Wicket Competition, played at KCC, then followed for two seasons, for the 'Torrie' Wilson Trophy, the winners being:

    1964–65   J K Fawcett (HKCC Scorpions)
    1965–66   R G Daniel (Army)

The 'Torrie' Wilson Trophy was donated by Arnold Graham in memory of T W R Wilson, the Shanghai Interporter. The 1947 *Interport Brochure* reported a brief sketch of 'Torrie': 'Can bowl wicket-leg-break and effect spectacular slips in the field. As a batsman if he gets going he can spin his shot into the Supreme Court or the Naval Yard.'

In order to try and improve the standard of cricket, an innovative idea for the 1967–68 season was to create a 'Super' league on Sundays. This league consisted of four teams – HKCC, the Combined Services, Kowloon (KCC & Recreio) and the Valley (CCC, IRC, LSW & PRC). The experiment only lasted two seasons, as many cricketers did not wish to sacrifice their Sundays for cricket. HKCC was the inaugural winner and the Valley the last.

25

When this idea fell through, the HKCA then decided for the 1969–70 season, to switch the First Division from Saturday afternoons to Sundays, in the belief that the longer game would better prepare top players for Interports and overseas tours. The Second Division continued on Saturdays. Col Metcalf (LSW), became the first winner of the Ruttonjee 'Player of the Year' Trophy in the 1972–73 season.

The relative success of switching the First Division from Saturdays to Sundays prompted the HKCA Committee to capitalise on this and provide for separate Saturday and Sunday leagues. These came into being in 1973–74, the beginning of the 'Modern Years'. The First Division became the Sunday League and the Second Division became the Saturday League. The Saturday programme was then extended with the introduction of Cup and Plate competitions. These competitions, which are commercially sponsored, are played on a knock-out basis at the end of the official league season.

Craigengower CC v Little Sai Wan CC

Venue: Sai Wan, Hong Kong Island – 7 January 1968

Sai Wan CC

K Pitchforth, b Myatt	15	*Bowling*
P Everett, st Lalchandani b Myatt	27	
D Raderecht, c Dhabher b Myatt	9	
L O'Meara, b Myatt	4	
P Davison, c G Lalchandani b Myatt	6	
E Birch, b Myatt	0	
B Millar, b Myatt	4	
A Morgan, not out	13	
T Millar, b Myatt	2	
G Williams, c & b Myatt	0	
I Arkley, st Lalchandani b Myatt	4	
Extras	12	
Total	96	

	O	M	R	W
G Lalchandani	8	1	28	0
G Williams	4	0	12	0
C Myatt	9	1	23	10
J Ashworth	5	1	21	0

Fall of wickets: 1–39, 2–46, 3–59, 4–60, 5–60, 6–73, 7–74, 8–93, 9–93

Craigengower CC

R Lalchandani, not out	48	*Bowling*
J McLeod, b Morgan	48	
J Ashworth, not out	3	
B Dhabher		
G Ebert		

	O	M	R	W
P Davison	8	0	20	0
T Millar	2	0	17	0

A Ma			P Everett	2	0	19	0
T Ramesh			I Arkley	2	0	13	0
C Myatt	} Did not bat	A Morgan	4	0	14	1
G Lalchandani		L O'Meara	2	0	11	0
G Williams		G Williams	0.5	0	5	0
D Peter						

Extras   0

1 wicket for   99

Fall of wickets: 1–86

Craigengower won by nine wickets as Carl Myatt 'bagged the lot', but not being satisfied, also put a 'hat-trick' in the bag. The *SCMP*, 8 January 1968 reported:

> ... with the last two deliveries of his sixth over, he bowled O'Meara and Birch. Then, with the first ball of his seventh, he had Davison taken at short mid-wicket by Gopal Lalchandani to complete his 'hat-trick'.

St George's CC v IRC

Venue: Mission Road, Kowloon – 8 February 1969

St George's CC: 195–3 dec (A Gough 60 *, M Lonsdale 51)

IRC

T Chiney, b Allbutt	0	*Bowling*	
S Songerwalla, c Gough b Allbutt	0		

		O	M	R	W
O Rathoir, b Allbutt	5				
S Ebrahim, c Self b Allbutt	10	G Allbutt	10.4	1	23	10
K Gohel, c Kotch b Allbutt	22	J Kotch	2	0	10	0
S Mansukhani, b Allbutt	0	J Williams	8	2	14	0
K Lalchandani, b Allbutt	0					
R Melwani, b Allbutt	0					
K Gabuji, c Lonsdale b Allbutt	6					
P Choksi, b Allbutt	4					
J Ward, not out	0					

Extras   0

Total   47

Fall of wickets: 1–0, 2–1, 3–7, 4–20, 5–20, 6–22, 7–22, 8–38, 9–43

St George's CC won by 148 runs.

Geoff Allbutt, St George's lanky fast bowler, getting plenty of lift off the matting wicket, mowed down IRC for 47 in a Second Division match at Mission Road. He was twice on a 'hat-trick', but failed to achieve this double.

SCMP, 9 February 1969

IRC won the first postwar Second Division title, the Ezra Abraham Shield, then disappeared from any further interest in the roll of championship winners.

The Services, like their seniors, dominated the Second Division from 1950–51 to 1962–63, winning nine championships during this period. KCC broke up this monopoly from time to time in the 1950s with five championship wins, mainly through their bowling strength:

1949–50 – 'Tinker' Lee 54 wickets at 7.87 and D G White 50 wickets at 8.16

1951–52 – under the astute leadership of the experienced Teddy Fincher

1955–56 – A J Catley 78 wickets at 8.60 and G Webster 54 wickets at 9.20

1957–58 – R Williams 67 wickets at 8.33 and G Webster 70 wickets at 9.39

1959–60 – F Apps two 'hat-tricks' and a century from M Guilford against Centaurs.

St George's CC, founded in 1962 by Graham Wills, a young schoolmaster, joined the Second Division the following season. Graham took 49 wickets before Christmas, then none for the next three weeks. Graham wryly remarked at the time: 'Getting married had an imperceptible effect on my game.'

The Centaurs and HKCC Nomads took over the winning mantle from 1963–64, each winning twice, with the 1967–68 title shared jointly. Island School joined the Second Division in the same last mentioned league season.

1967	Army:	144–9	
	St George:	52	(D Paul 8–15)
Oct 7	Centaurs:	42	(N Oei 17, L Roberts 6–14)
	Nomads:	45–7	(R Beevor 23, Andrews 5–19)

THE MODERN YEARS 1973–97

The last 20 years have seen many changes to the cricket scene in Hong Kong. This started with the re-structuring of the First and Second Divisions, just mentioned. The KCC Templars, led by Buddy Carnell, and HKCC Nomads, led by Peter Green, became the first holders of the new league titles.

With Services cricket gradually losing its impact on the local scene and ground problems becoming a reality, the two Happy Valley grounds (CCC and PRC), IRC and Recreio, all ceased as cricket grounds – the two larger clubs HKCC and KCC, each with numerous teams, dominated cricket during the modern years by winning over 70 per cent of each of the divisional championships.

The standard of cricket in Hong Kong will initially be the poorer without the Service players. Indeed, it is thanks to the generous way in which the Service chiefs have made their players and facilities available for cricket on a regular basis that added an extra dimension to the league system.

The closure of the historic Chater Road ground then followed in 1975. The HKCC moved to its new home 'up the Hill' at 137 Wong Nai Chung Gap Road, Hong Kong Island.

It was appropriate and fitting that the Army, whom the site originally belonged to, should feature at its demise, when General Edwin Bramall, Commander British Forces, scored 112 not out on 15 March 1975, the last league century at the Chater Road ground.

During the 1975–76 season, limited overs cricket with bonus points for runs scored and wickets taken was introduced by the author for Saturday cricket, to allow for a fairer allocation of playing time. Previously, some of the weaker teams had occupied the crease for three of the four available hours.

'Tug' Willson, an effective and aggressive right-hand batsman and deceptive slow left-arm bowler, who had captained the United Kingdom Combined Services, led LSW and Kai Tak to their first league titles in the Sunday and Saturday leagues respectively.

In 1976–77, Ted Wilson, President of the HKCA, donated the Ted Wilson Schools' Trophy for an annual competition among four secondary schools: DBS, Island School, KGV and South Island School. Brian Wigley led the PRC to their first senior league title, and the author's KCC Saracens captured the inaugural Jangu Vachha Memorial Shield, designed by the author in memory of a fellow cricketer and true friend.

In 1977–78, the Vagabonds Cricket Club (Vags) joined the senior league and the HKCC Wanderers won their first championship title under the 'dictatorial' Bob Toes. Tartars became the third KCC club side to join the

Saturday league. The following season KCC added another side, when the Infidels, led by the exuberant Aussie, Eric Hurst, joined their team mates, the Templars, in the senior league. Three Saturday batsmen were dismissed on 99 runs.

During that same season, Arthur Barnett, 'Silver Fox', an HKCC stalwart, recalled an incident involving another character, one Martin 'Bullers' Bulfield:

> He arrived for a match late and rather under the weather. He was helped into his gear and directed out to the middle to keep wicket. The first ball flew down the leg side for four byes. The next ball went past him for four byes down the off side. Off the third ball there was a little nick and Bulfield took the catch. 'There you are,' he said triumphantly, 'you all thought I was pissed, but I caught him first ball!'

The first signs of a 'higher plane' cricketing future for 16 year old Dermot Reeve emerged at the end of the 1979–80 season, when he scored 117 not out, to play a dominant role in Vagabonds Rothman's Cup win over the Police at KCC.

| 1980 | Vagabonds: | 220–3 | (D Reeve 117*, F McLeod 33, D Clinton 30) |
| Mar 30 | Police: | 116 | (M Hammett 25, B Gohel 2–12, D Reeve 2–13) |

At the end of the same season, Brian Wigley, a fierce competitor and Police stalwart, finished 0.12 behind Gopal Lalchandani in the Saturday league bowling averages. The match at Sookunpoo between Police Sentinels and the Royal Navy would haunt Brian for the rest of his cricketing days. Shortly after Elias Ismail reached his fifty, Wigley said to Martin Walker (Royal Navy): 'Isn't that the worst 50 you've ever seen?' About an hour later, Walker said to Wigley: 'Aren't they the two worst 100's you've ever seen?' The Navy pair had put on 203 in a total of 281–1 in 35 overs. Wigley's figures were 1–114!

Gordon Bacon, playing for the Navy in the same match, recalled another incident:

> When Walker deposited one delivery high over the sightscreen into the middle of the adjoining hockey pitch, Wigley said: 'My God that was a good shot, I almost lost control of myself and applauded.'

The affable Harry Lucas (Kai Tak) scored a monumental 1622 runs, including five centuries and a 99, in the Saturday league, a record which still stands.

The next season was to become unofficially known as the year of the 'Tony Turner Triumphs', when, led by Tony, LSW won seven of their last nine matches to take the senior league title – then, inspired by Gordon Bacon's unbeaten half-century, they also wrapped up the Rothman's Cup. Down amongst the smaller print, five bowlers achieved 'hat-tricks' in the Saturday league.

1980	LSW:	160	(P Anderson 61, R Lalchandani 38, Y Vachha 6–64)
Dec 31	Templars:	152	(J Bygate 41, D Evans 36, Y Vachha 30, A Turner 6–48)

Turner topples Templars in tense tussle.

1981	LSW:	207–8 dec	(R Lalchandani 61, B Kwong 4–69)
Jan 4	Scorpions:	26	(A Turner 6–15, G Lalchandani 4–11)

One of the greatest hidings ever handed out to the HKCC Scorpions.

Mar 9	Vagabonds:	191	(D Reeve 83, C Metcalf 3–26)
	LSW:	192–9	(P Anderson 55, S Myles 4–41)

Last man Geoff Lever joined Col Metcalf at 183–9. Metcalf, the non-striker watched while Lever calmly hit a six for the winning runs in this nail-biting finish. Col Metcalf must have been quite 'shocked' to see the normally calm, slightly hunched, pipe-smoking Geoff, in such a belligerent mood.

1981	Taverners:	139	(M Sabine 40, A Turner 3–21, G Bacon 3–42)
Apr 6	LSW:	141–7	(G Bacon 55*, J Hughes 3–23)

The Rothman's final played at HKCC was rather tentative and nervous until Bacon decided to adopt an aggressive approach. Nobody had hit a six – Bacon hit four, for Saiwan to complete a unique league and cup double, the first time it had been achieved. In 1981–82, the HKCC Scorpions, led by Nigel Beaton, ended a long drought going back to the 1967–68 season, to capture the senior league title. Four Sunday league batsmen exceeded 150.

1981	Vagabonds:	239–3 dec	(D Greenwood 102*, D Race 101)
Sep 27	Wanderers:	222–5	(M Sabine 106, P Anderson 33*)

Oct 11   Scorpions: 80   (D Parsons 23*, C Collins 6–38)
          Infidels: 81–9 (R Gill 17*, B Kwong 5–26)

Then the Scorpions reversed the process and 'stung' the Infidels into submission at HKCC.

Dec 6   Scorpions: 327–5 (B Kwong 153*, J Hollioake 133)
         Infidels: 85–9 (P Williamson 24, D Way 4–20, D Clarke 3–23)

The Infidels batted for 68 overs and not one of the first five batsmen reached double figures.

On 21 March 1982 at KCC, the KCC Infidels (15 points) received a 'walk-over' from British Forces, who could not raise a full team.

In 1982–83, Wimpey/Sime Darby sponsored the Sunday league and artificial wickets were introduced at KCC and Mission Road, in what was to become the wettest cricket season in living memory, luckily garnished with many close and exciting finishes.

1982   LSW: 114   (J Hawkesley 29, D Swift 8–49) at Sai wan.
Dec 5   Optimists: 115–6 (J Hughes 25)

Dec 19 Vagabonds: 197   (S Myles 74, B Hansen 56, T Smith 7–61) at
                          Mission Rd.
        Wanderers: 200–9 (M Walsh 51, M Darke 32, S Myles 4–47)

        Infidels: 173 (E Hurst 80, I Lindsay 4–26) at Sookunpoo.
        Brit. Forces: 179 (G Jones 36, J Peters 35, R Starling 5–74,
                           C Collins 4–58)

1983   Templars: 184   (D Evans 38, F Jowharsha 37, G Davies 31,
                          G Lalchandani 6–61)
Jan 2   LSW: 180   (E Ismail 71, K Johnston 30, J Jenkins 4–29)

        Infidels: 117   (J Hansen 28, D Way 4–30) at HKCC.
        Scorpions: 114   (P Varty 44, C Collins 8–39)

Prior to the last round of the Sunday league, any one of the five top teams in the challenge for the league title had a chance to win. The table read:

Team	Points
KCC Templars	124
HKCC Wanderers	122

LSW	120
HKCC Scorpions	116
KCC Infidels	116

With 15 points for an outright win, you could perm any one from the five teams:

- Templars would win the league if they beat Vagabonds, so when Vagabonds had been bowled out for 181 runs at Mission Road, it appeared to be all over.
- At Sookunpoo, British Forces had declared at 250 for 4 against Wanderers, not a promising outlook for the second placed team.
- Scorpions had scored a respectable 210 for 8 at home, before declaring against LSW.
- IRC, without a win all season, had compiled their highest score to reach 244 for 9 declared against the Infidels.
- Templars made a complete hash of their excellent opportunity, and struggled to 117 for 9, gaining three points = 127 points.
- Wanderers, after a good start, also slipped down the ladder, disappointingly ending on 154 for 8 also gaining three points = 125 points.

Now three out of five could still win! If both Infidels and Scorpions won, they would tie on 131 points each. If both failed to win and LSW won, the title would go to LSW.

- At KCC, the last batsman was run out trying to achieve the impossible. Infidels all out three runs short for 242, gaining no points = total 116.
- At HKCC, with two balls left, LSW were 208 for 8, still requiring three runs to win. From the penultimate ball LSW scored two, the teams were level on runs and wickets lost. The batsmen scrambled a single off the last ball for LSW to clinch the senior championship title. What an amazing finale to the 1982–1983 season.

Except for the HKCC, all the other available cricket grounds in Hong Kong have laid down artificial wickets. The HKCC and KCC are the only clubs to also play on turf wickets. The change in playing surface has made it much easier for the average batsman with an iota of ability to score runs, with the more accomplished notching up 200 runs plus per innings. At the other end of the scale, artificial wickets have destroyed the spirit of the average bowler, and all but removed the spinner from the game.

When Mike Womersley (PRC) turned up for a Saturday league match at KCC against the Tartars in the 1983–84 season, and saw the artificial

33

wicket for the first time, he asked the author and Buji Dhabher why he hadn't been informed earlier of this 'batsman's paradise'. He went away happy after scoring exactly 100 runs that day.

In 1983–84, the Scorpions, led by Paul Varty, stormed through the second half of the season without loss, to capture their second senior title in three years. The Saturday league produced a haul of 31 centuries, and no bowler aggregated 50 wickets.

1984   LSW: 132   (R Muirhead 32, J Jenkins 4–41, L Prabhu
Jan 2   Templars: 133–8   (J Lamsam 39, G Bacon 5–47)

This match at Sai wan saw both sides bat for a little over 51 overs each.

Vagabonds: 262–4 dec   (N French 56*, D Greenwood 52,
                               D Sharwood 47, A Rutt 33*)
Infidels: 264–6   (C Collins 78, P Williamson 53, P Taylor
                               38, E Hurst 34*, D Jones 33)

'A good batting display brought Infidels their first victory.'

Jan 15   Infidels: 261   (E Hurst 62, P Williamson 50, A Lethbridge
                               46, M Darke 4–67)
        Wanderers: 255–5   (M Sabine 80*, M Swift 62, D Griffiths 37)

Mar 18 Templars: 107–2   (J Bygate 60) in 28 overs.
        LSW:
Match abandoned at Sai wan due to fog!

   25   Wanderers: 265–6 dec (P Anderson 130, M Darke 83, J Jenkins
                               3–53)
        Templars: 269–7   (R Brewster 74, Y Vachha 64*, J Lamsam
                               42, T Smith 3–89)

A Rothman's Cup semi-final at Sookunpoo saw LSW narrowly defeat Kai Tak by one wicket with two balls remaining.

Mar 11 Kai Tak: 187–7   (T Willson 80*, N Sawrey-Cookson 27)
        LSW: 189–9   (N Perera 64, M Grubb 48, T Willson 3–33)

In a Saturday league match at the Army's Blackdown Barracks ground near Kai Tak airport, KCC Tartars snuffed out the Army's challenge with one run to spare.

34

1983   Tartars: 191–4 (N Broadhurst 71)
Nov 19 Army: 190   (P Wood 72)

In 1984–85, the Ruttonjee 'Player of the Year' trophy was replaced by one donated by the Hongkong Bank. British Forces, led by 'Player of the Year' Peter Wood, captured their final senior league title. The HKCC Nomads made it three Saturday league titles in a row.

1984   Optimists: 204–8 dec (W Orchard 59, D Kilgour 55, M Sant 36,
                             Y Vachha 5–52)
Oct 7   Templars: 205–2   (B Catton 85*, R Brewster 85)

        Scorpions: 130   (S Caley 49, S Weatherley 9–53) at HKCC
        Vagabonds: 60   (S Polaris 27, R Fotheringham 7–20)

After Steve Weatherley's magnificent nine wickets, his team mates succumb to 'Fothers' for a meagre 60 runs.

Dec 30 Infidels: 270–3 dec (K Kumar 133, D Evans 57, S Myles 33)
        Optimists: 272–6   (J Barrington 127, A Morgan 44,
                             W Orchard 39, S Myles 3–61)

A great win for the Optimists at HKCC.

        Wanderers: 202–5 dec (P Anderson 83*, M Walsh 58*, N Gulzar
                             3–71)
        IRC: 203–7   (A Ebrahim 82, M Ahmed 37*, N Gulzar
                             30, T Smith 3–75)

This deserved win by lowly IRC shocked the HKCC Wanderers.

1984   Brit. Forces: 157 (P Wood 41, I Wright 35, D Way 5–65,
                           B Kwong 4–20)
Dec 30 Scorpions: 108   (R Fotheringham 29, P Wood 6–48,
                           K Hardman 4–52)

Skipper Peter Wood led from the front; he and Kevin Hardman bowled throughout for this hard-fought victory.

KCC Infidels, skippered by Norman Broadhurst, won their first senior championship pipping KCC Templars. Young Simon Myles, playing for Infidels in the Rothman's Cup, hit two centuries. Glyn Davies's side, with 17 wins from 17 matches, emphatically inscribed KCC Saracens name on the Vachha Memorial Shield.

Mightier with the pen than with the bat, Barry Ellis, a 'part-time' cricketer, paints a picture of cricket in Hong Kong, in a lead article for the 1986 Hong Kong ICC *Trophy* magazine:

For me, probably the most enjoyable aspect of cricket in Hong Kong is the cosmopolitan nature of the sides, most of which boast a mixture of British, Australian, New Zealand, Indian, Sri Lankan and Pakistani players. Unfortunately, only a handful of Chinese are currently playing as the local schools do not have the facilities for the game. As one would expect, with the large number of Antipodeans in Hong Kong cricket here is played hard and with a degree of importance rarely to be found anywhere outside the West Indies. Where else in the world would the Chief Justice be appointed merely on the strength of a full umpire's qualification!! The Government long recognised that a strong cricket league contributes greatly to the prosperity and orderliness of Hong Kong, keeping, as it does, so many expatriates off the streets and out of trouble, particularly when the Police are playing. This seriousness does not, however, mean that our players display the behavioural excesses shown by their professional counterparts in other regions of the globe. Microphones buried beneath the stumps would report nothing to cause distress to any matronly aunt. Gentle banter and encouragement to opponents, colleagues and umpires alike are the order of the day.

The kindness of Hong Kong cricketers is legendary. The way Doug Beckett never failed to remind absent-minded batsmen where the pavilion was on getting out. Or indeed, what the great John Bygate did for the Guild of Bat Manufacturers. Only batting with a new bat each week, John would ceremoniously destroy the instrument on being given out, but not before reaching the sanctuary of the dressing room, so as not to upset the sensibilities of any watching tree environmentalists. A great tradition now carried on by the young Simon Myles.

No, dear readers, Hong Kong still strives to retain the best of what is after all the best of games. Perhaps this is truly epitomised on the top balcony of HKCC, where the 'all-time greats', now in the twilight of their careers, such as 'Dipper' Duggan, Arthur 'Silver Fox' Barnett and Peter Berry more than willingly pass on their vast experience through good-natured badinage to the youngsters, like Peter Anderson and Peter Davies, attempting to perform below.

Dunlop Slazenger took over sponsorship of the Sunday league in 1986–87. KCC just about cleared the board of trophies, as John Thirkell's Infidels – 'their strength in depth with bat and ball' – took the Sunday league title;

the Templars thrashed the Police by 152 runs to capture the Rothman's Cup, and Jim Middleton's Tartars grabbed the Saturday league title and Gillette Cup. Nigel Stearns (PRC) headed the senior league batting averages with 106.71.

1987 Templars: 235–7 (N Perera 88, B Catton 81, G Davies 2–21)
Apl 12 Police: 83 (N Stearns 37, B Gohel 4–16, N Perera 2–20)

'KCC Templars retain the Cup with emphatic win over Police in a disappointing final.'

The summarised scores of matches from the 1980–81 season to the 1984–85 season would not have been possible without the dedicated and time-consuming efforts of Malcolm Grubb, who voluntarily entered the details of all Sunday league matches in the annual HKCA Handbooks, for the interest of future generations of cricketers and cricket enthusiasts. But for his efforts, the contents of this book would have been the poorer.

HKCA Chairman John Bygate and his committee re-introduced the 'Super' league in 1987–88, but like its predecessor in the 1960s, it failed to capture the imagination of the players and slid back into the archives after one season. Bryan Hemshall's HKCC Wanderers achieved the double, winning the senior league title and the Rothman's Cup.

1988–89 saw the KCC Infidels capture their third senior league title in four years. Pat Fordham (Templars), from the competitive Yorkshire Bradford League, chalked up a Hong Kong career best score of 178 not out. HKCC Nomads made the Saturday league title look like a personal possession, winning it for the sixth time. Ian Collier (Army) did a demolition job on the once proud Centaurs, taking 10 wickets for 13 runs. B K Sipahimalani, 'Sippy' to local cricketers, retired as HKCA Hon. Secretary after 10 most valuable years of service.

Rod Eddington landed the treble, not at the racetrack, but on the local cricket scene in 1989–90. His Kai Tak team captured both the Saturday league and the Gillette Cup. He then led Taikoo to victory over the Scorpions, his senior league teammates, in the Rothman's Cup. John Bygate stepped down after seven years as Chairman of the HKCA.

Tragedy removed two talented and well liked Hong Kong cricketers from the local scene. In the words of the new Chairman of the HKCA, Brian Catton:

On a sadder note we record with deep regret the sudden and tragic passing of Chris Collins and David Paull and his wife Jay. Both cricketers were giants in their own way and contributed immeasurably to the game, both on and off the field.

David's six wickets for Hong Kong at KCC against the full Australian side on 18 October 1988 will long be remembered, while Chris's full blooded Aussie presence on and off the field always added colour to the scene. RIP.

KCC captured three of the four major titles in the 1990–91 season, when Mark Eames took Infidels to yet another championship ahead of the Templars. Templars defeated old rivals Optimists for the Rothman's pot, while Tartars, 'led' by Nanda Perera, deprived Nomads of their seventh title. An Australian, Stewart Brew, masquerading under DBS colours in the Saturday league, amassed 1505 runs (eight centuries) at an average of 215.00. His wife, Karen Lay Brew, became the first and only postwar woman league cricketer, playing for LSW in the Saturday league – was she the only woman ever to play league cricket in Hong Kong? Her first victim, Shiroy Vachha, was stumped by Geoff Lever. Probably Shiroy's only claim to cricket fame in Hong Kong!

Mar 17 Optimists: 218–7 (J Barrington 71, A Morgan [Tony] 48,
T Fitzsimmons 37, J Middleton 4–48)
KCC Templars: 219–6 (K Kumar 70, C Goonesena 48*, S Atkinson
47, G Howells 3–45)

At 142 for 4, Templars needed seven runs an over for victory. A sparkling 48 not out in 39 balls from Charlie Goonesena brought Templars victory with an over to spare.

The HKCC Scorpions, spearheaded by South African all-rounder Warren Symcox, broke the KCC monopoly to take the senior league title in 1991–92, winning eight of their first nine matches to put the title out of anyone else's reach.

The season introduced the first individual 200 plus run-makers, when Adnan Butt (LSW), personally extracted 201 not out from the Scorpions. Not to be outdone, Aussie Stewart Brew put Police Strollers on the rack to the tune of 204 not out in the Saturday league, where 31 centuries were scored and no bowler took 40 wickets. HKCC Nomads made it seven Saturday league titles, and Hong Kong University captured the inaugural Butani Cup which replaced the Gillette. Taikoo CC defeated HKCC Wanderers by nine runs to win the Rothman's Cup, giving them their third Cup win in eight years to match that of the Templars. Connaught Strategic Holdings became the new sponsors of both leagues, the Saturday league being sponsored for the first time.

1992–93 saw Hong Kong captain, Pat Fordham, lead from the front to become the Connaught 'Player of the Year'. He scored 807 runs at the top

38

average of 100.88, and helped Templars to their first senior league title since their 'golden' era in the 1970s. Yarman Vachha, one of the victorious eleven, was also a juvenile member of the winning 1974–75 side. The Templars added the prestigious Rothman's Cup to their spoils for the season, beating the Pakistan Association in the final.

Mar 21 Templars: 374–3 (R Farcy 124*, S Atkinson 110*, P Fordham 79, J Penrose 30)
KCC Pak. Assn: 251 (S Malik 67, I Wasim 66, M Hafeez 38, Y Vachha 3–46)

Chris Parsons put another 200 plus on the board, whilst Jason Penrose went 20 runs better with 221 in the Rothman's Cup in partnership with Nanda Perera, in a record first wicket stand of 358 against HKCC Casuals. Ross Greer, a professional footballer with a talent for the smaller ball, appeared for St George's, and claimed the highest score in league cricket, 233 not out against CCC. How the late Lee brothers, Robbie and 'Tinker', and George Souza would have cringed at the onslaught against their old club.

More records went in 1993–94, the 90th Anniversary Year of league cricket in Hong Kong, as the strong KCC Templars convincingly retained their title. Their chances of the 'Double' were thwarted by Hong Kong's participation in the ICC Competition in Kenya in February/March 1994, as Pat Fordham, Steve Atkinson, Paul Cresswell, Bharat Gohel, Ravi Sujanani and Yarman Vachha were all called up as members of the Hong Kong team.

In the following seasons, the KCC teams take a backseat as HKCC's Optimists once more move into first gear to take the Sunday league title in 1994–95 and 1996–97, nudged by the Pakistan Association who won in 1995–96. The Merchants, with a sprinkling of Pakistan Association players captured the Saturday league in 1995–96 and 1996–97.

BATTING AND BOWLING HIGHLIGHTS – 1903 TO 1939

The following highlights have been recorded from information obtained by the author at the British Library, North London, from press cuttings lent by Bertram Lay, Marybud Chignell (Hancock) and Dr Eddie Gosano, and from *Cricket* (see Services). It is by no means comprehensive of the period, but on the basis that some information is better than none, these statistics have been included under league cricket.

(F) Friendly matches

Batting

Year	Names/Teams		Centuries
1909	L/Sgt Power (RE) v KCC		111*
	T E Pearce (HKCC'B') v Telegraphs		111
	R Hancock (HK) v Navy	(F)	103*
	A Osman (CCC) v Police		103*
1910	Comdr Lewis (Navy) v Army	(F)	149)
	Staff/Sgt Power (Army) v Navy	(F)	144*) Same match
	Capt Baird (Army) v Navy	(F)	125)
1914	Cpl Morrish (RE) v Police		110
1919	R Hancock (HKCC) v Navy	(F)	156
	A A Claxton (HKCC) v Army	(F)	125
	Capt P Havelock-Davies (Army) v Navy)	(F)	105*) Same
	Col Coles (Army) v Navy	(F)	100) match
1920	T E Pearce (HK) v Shanghai/Malaya	(F)	111*
	Capt Olliver (RGA) v HKU		100
	K R Macaskill (KCC)		100*)
	E J R Mitchell (HKCC)		102*) League Table
	A H Rumjahn (IRC)		106*) Ave.
	Bowen (Staffs)		100*)
1924	G E Livock (Malaya) v KCC	(F)	133*
1926	Capt E I M Barrett (S'Hai) v U.Services	(F)	133
	H V Parker (Vols) v CRC	(F)	100*
	Lt Hankey (KOSB) v CRC	(F)	104*
	Capt Morris (Army) v Vols	(F)	121
1928	A W Hayward (HKCC) v KCC	(F)	143
1931	A M Rodrigues (HKU) v RAMC	(F)	128*
	D J N Anderson (HKU) v CSCC	(F)	110*
	W Brace (KCC)		100*) League Table
	Lt Musson (RA)		102)Ave. (1st Div.)
	Skinner (KCC)		100*) League Table
	Remedios (Recreio)		101) Ave. (2nd Div.)
1932	R H Dowler (B & S) v HKBank	(F)	102
1933	D J N Anderson (HKU) v CSCC		100
1934	A M Rodrigues (HKU) v RN		103*
	Lt J P Williams (E Lancs) v Lincolns	(F)	120
1935	E L Gosano (HKU) v CCC		102*
	E L Gosano (Meds) v Eng. (HKU)	(F)	104
	H Owen Hughes (HKCC) v KCC		104*
1936	Capt Walsh (RASC) v RAMC		132 2nd Div.
	J E Richardson (HKCC) v CSCC		104*

40

| 1938 | R T Broadbridge (KCC) v USRC | (F) | 103 |
| 1939 | B D Lay (KCC) v Army 'B' | | 111* 2nd Div. |

Bowling

1903	E R Herton (CCC) v RAMC		8–30
	E Crabtree (Tamar) v CSCC		7–26
1906	J D Noria (Parsees) v Civil Service 'A'		7–33
	H Mackay (HKCC) v League XV	(F)	10–59
1909	Capt Baird (HKCC'A') v HKCC'B'		7–19
	R E O Bird (HK) v Swatow	(F)	7–59
1913	H H Taylor (CCC) v KCC		8–55) Same
	K R Macaskill (KCC) v CCC		7–44) match
1914	Cpl Morrish (RE) v Police		7–34
1918	T E Pearce (HKCC) v 25th Middx	(F)	7–38) Same
	Pte Taylor (25th Middx) v HKCC	(F)	7–50) match
1919	Sig Hack (Navy) v KCC		7–42
1920	Capt P Havelock-Davies (Army) v Navy	(F)	10–38
	F A Redmond (HKU) v RGA		7–71
1924	T W R Wilson (S'Hai) v Kowloon	(F)	7–34
	W Edmonds (CSCC) v RN		7–22
	F N Young (KCC) v HKCC		8–12 2nd Div.
1926	A B Clemo (China L.) v CCC	(F)	8–45
	Capt A Dobbie (KOSB) v CRC	(F)	7–31
	A C I Bowker (HKCC) v KCC		8–20
1928	G R Vallack (Hancock's) v Hayward's	(F)	7–38
	C D Wales (HKCC) v KCC	(F)	7–49 & 7–29
1929	F C Baker (RN) v HKCC		7–86
	W H Edmonds (CSCC) v HKCC		7–39
	W Brace (HK XI) v The Rest	(F)	7–12
1931	Gnr Bryant (RA) v HKU	(F)	8–31
	G C Burnett (KCC) v HKU		4–33 'hat-trick'
	G C Burnett (KCC) v Vols	(F)	8–25
1932	Bdr Bryant (RA) v IRC		8–39
	A C Beck (HKCC) v KCC		7–36
	E L Gosano (HKU) v Comb.Schools	(F)	7– 5
1933	R Divett (HKCC) v HKU		8–29
	U M Omar (CCC) v HKU		8–43
	N Whitley (CBAssn) v China L.	(F)	3– 0 'hat-trick'
1934	F D Pereira (IRC) v CSCC		7–12
	CSM Elwin (Army) v HKU	(F)	7–44

Bowling (cont'd)

Year	Names/Teams		Analyses
	Capt D B Mitchell (Army) v HKU	(F)	7–16
1935	E L Gosano (HKU) v RN		8–23) Same
	Lt Crunden (RN) v HKU		7–18) match
	E L Gosano (HKU) v KCC		7–67
	P B Tata (HKU) v CCC		6–13 'hat-trick' 2nd Div.
	A E Perry (CSCC) v HKU		8–63
	E L Gosano (Youngsaye's) v Phoenix	(F)	7–30
1936	E L Gosano (HKU) v IRC		8–20
1938	A J Hulse (Sargent's) v HKU	(F)	7–11
	C N Matthews (DBS) v Queen's		4–18 'hat-trick'
	C B R Sargent (KCC) v Army		7–14 2nd Div.
	Capt Parsons (USRC) v KCC	(F)	7–78
	H Overy (Abraham's) v Robinson's	(F)	7–50
1939	D J N Anderson (KCC) v Army		7–28

THE HONG KONG CRICKET ASSOCIATION – CHAMPIONSHIP WINNERS

	Emerging Years 1903–41		Postwar Years 1948–73		Modern Years 1973–97	
	1st	2nd	1st	2nd	1st	2nd
Army/Units & British Forces	4	3	12*	9	1	
Cavaliers (Recreio/CCC)			1			
Club de Recreio	1		2			
Civil Service CC / Centaurs	2	1		4*		2
Craigengower CC	4*	1				
Hong Kong CC	10*	2	7	3*	10	8
Hong Kong University CC	3	1				
Indian Recreation Club	4#	6		1		
Kai Tak CC						3
Kowloon CC	8	4	4*	5	8	6
Little Sai Wan CC					3	2
Merchants CC						2
Pakistan Association					1	
Police Recreation Club		1		1	1	1
RAF				2		

THE HONG KONG CRICKET ASSOCIATION – CHAMPIONSHIP WINNERS (cont'd)

	Emerging Years 1903–41		Postwar Years 1948–73		Modern Years 1973–97	
	1st	2nd	1st	2nd	1st	2nd
Royal Navy	1	1				
St George's CC			1			
	37	20	26	26	24	24

* Jointly (once) and # Jointly (twice)

1903–41 1st Dominated by HKCC/KCC (48.6%) – 2nd by IRC (30%)
1948–73 1st Dominated by Army (46%)/HKCC (27%) – 2nd by Army (35%)
1973–97 1st Dominated by HKCC (42%)/KCC (33%) – 2nd by HKCC (33%)/KCC (25%)

HKCA – First Division Winners

Season	Champion	Season	Champion
1903–04	Army Ordnance Corps	1926–27	Kowloon Cricket Club
1904–05	Craigengower CC	1927–28	Hong Kong University
1905–06	Kowloon Cricket Club	1928–29	Hong Kong Cricket Club
1906–07	Kowloon Cricket Club	1929–30	Kowloon Cricket Club
1907–08	Craigengower CC	1930–31	Indian Recreation Club
1908–09	Hong Kong Cricket Club 'B'	1931–32	Indian Recreation Club
1909–10	Hong Kong Cricket Club 'A'	1932–33	Hong Kong University
1910–11	RE & Departments	1933–34	Hong Kong Cricket Club
1911–12	Craigengower CC	1934–35	Hong Kong Cricket Club
1912–13	Hong Kong Cricket Club 'B'	1935–36	Kowloon Cricket Club
1913–14	Hong Kong Cricket Club	1936–37	HKCC & IRC (jointly)
1914–17	No Competition	1937–38	CCC & IRC (jointly)
1917–18	Hong Kong Cricket Club	1938–39	Club de Recreio
1918–19	Royal Garrison Artillery	1939–40	Kowloon Cricket Club
1919–20	Royal Garrison Artillery	1940–41	Kowloon Cricket Club
1920–21	Civil Service CC	1941–48	No Competition
1921–22	Kowloon Cricket Club	1948–49	Club de Recreio
1922–23	Hong Kong University	1949–50	HKCC Scorpions
1923–24	Hong Kong Cricket Club	1950–51	Army
1924–25	Civil Service CC	1951–52	Army 'A'
1925–26	Royal Navy	1952–53	HKCC Scorpions

HKCA – First Division Winners (cont'd)

Season	Champion	Season	Champion
1953–54	Army 'A'	1963–64	HKCC Optimists
1954–55	Kowloon Cricket Club	1964–65	Army
1955–56	Army 'South'	1965–66	Army
1956–57	Army 'South' & KCC (jointly)	1966–67	HKCC Scorpions
1957–58	Army 'North'	1967–68	HKCC Scorpions
1958–59	Army 'South'	1968–69	Cavaliers
1959–60	HKCC Optimists	1969–70	Army
1960–61	Brigade	1970–71	KCC Templars
1961–62	Club de Recreio	1971–72	HKCC Optimists
1962–63	Army	1972–73	KCC Templars

Sunday League Winners

Season	Champion	Season	Champion
1973–74	KCC Templars	1985–86	KCC Infidels
1974–75	KCC Templars	1986–87	KCC Infidels
1975–76	Little Sai Wan	1987–88	HKCC Wanderers
1976–77	Police Recreation Club	1988–89	KCC Infidels
1977–78	HKCC Wanderers	1989–90	HKCC Optimists
1978–79	HKCC Optimists	1990–91	KCC Infidels
1979–80	HKCC Optimists	1991–92	HKCC Scorpions
1980–81	Little Sai Wan	1992–93	KCC Templars
1981–82	HKCC Scorpions	1993–94	KCC Templars
1982–83	Little Sai Wan	1994–95	HKCC Optimists
1983–84	HKCC Scorpions	1995–96	Pakistan Association
1984–85	British Forces	1996–97	San Miguel Optimists

HKCA – Second Division Winners

Season	Champion	Season	Champion
1921–22	Kowloon Cricket Club	1930–31	Indian Recreation Club
1922–23	Indian Recreation Club	1931–32	Indian Recreation Club
1923–24	Royal Engineers	1932–33	Craigengower CC
1924–25	Civil Service CC	1933–34	Indian Recreation Club
1925–26	Royal Engineers	1934–35	Royal Army Service Corps
1926–27	Indian Recreation Club	1935–36	Indian Recreation Club
1927–28	Hong Kong University	1936–37	Kowloon Cricket Club
1928–29	Hong Kong Cricket Club	1937–38	Royal Navy
1929–30	Hong Kong Cricket Club	1938–39	Kowloon Cricket Club

HKCA – Second Division Winners (cont'd)

Season	Champion	Season	Champion
1939–40	Police Recreation Club	1959–60	Kowloon Cricket Club
1940–41	Kowloon Cricket Club	1960–61	Garrison
1941–48	No Competition	1961–62	Garrison
1948–49	Indian Recreation Club	1962–63	Army
1949–50	Kowloon Cricket Club	1963–64	Centaurs
1950–51	Army	1964–65	HKCC Nomads
1951–52	Kowloon Cricket Club	1965–66	St George's School
1952–53	RAF	1966–67	Police Recreation Club
1953–54	Army 'B'	1967–68	HKCC Nomads & Centaurs
1954–55	RAF	1968–69	HKCC Nomads
1955–56	Kowloon Cricket Club	1969–70	Army
1956–57	Army 'North'	1970–71	Army
1957–58	KCC Hornets	1971–72	Centaurs
1958–59	Army 'North'	1972–73	Centaurs

Saturday League Winners

Season	Champion	Season	Champion
1973–74	HKCC Nomads	1985–86	KCC Saracens
1974–75	Centaurs	1986–87	KCC Tartars
1975–76	Kai Tak CC	1987–88	Kai Tak CC
1976–77	KCC Saracens	1988–89	HKCC Nomads
1977–78	HKCC Nomads	1989–90	Kai Tak CC
1978–79	KCC Crusaders	1990–91	KCC Tartars
1979–80	Centaurs	1991–92	HKCC Nomads
1980–81	Police Sentinels	1992–93	Little Sai Wan
1981–82	KCC Crusaders	1993–94	HKCC Nomads
1982–83	HKCC Nomads	1994–95	Little Sai Wan
1983–84	HKCC Nomads	1995–96	Merchants CC
1984–85	HKCC Nomads	1996–97	Merchants CC

Rothman's Cup

Season	Winner	Season	Winner
1970–71	Army	1975–76	KCC Hornets
1971–72	KCC Templars	1976–77	HKCC Optimists
1972–73	Police Recreation Club	1977–78	Little Sai Wan
1973–74	HKCC Wanderers	1978–79	Police Recreation Club
1974–75	Police Recreation Club	1979–80	Vagabonds CC

Rothman's Cup (cont'd)

Season	*Winner*	*Season*	*Winner*
1980–81	Little Sai Wan	1987–88	HKCC Wanderers
1981–82	Little Sai Wan	1988–89	Police Recreation Club
1982–83	HKCC Wanderers	1989–90	Taikoo CC
1983–84	Little Sai Wan	1990–91	KCC Templars
1984–85	Taikoo CC	1991–92	Taikoo CC
1985–86	KCC Templars	1992–93	KCC Templars
1986–87	KCC Templars	1993–94	Vagabonds CC

Saturday League Cup

1975–76	Army	1977–78	KCC Saracens & LSW
1976–77	Centaurs	1978–79	HKCC Nomads

Gillette Cup

1979–80	HKCC Nomads	1985–86	Army
1980–81	HKCC Nomads	1986–87	KCC Tartars
1981–82	Kai Tak CC	1987–88	KCC Tartars
1982–83	KCC Crusaders	1988–89	KCC Saracens
1983–84	HKCC Nomads	1989–90	Kai Tak CC
1984–85	HKCC Witherers	1990–91	Hong Kong University

Butani Cup

1991–92	Hong Kong University
1992–93	HKCC Nomads

Dragonair Cup

1993–94	Kai Tak CC

Hong Kong – Player of the Year

Sponsored by: H J Ruttonjee 1972–73 to 1983–84
Hongkong Bank 1984–85 to 1991–92, and
Connaught Strategic from 1992–93 to 1994–95
Clerical Medical International 1995–96

Season

1972–73	Colin Metcalf	Little Sai Wan
1973–74	Peter Davies	HKCC Optimists
1974–75	Carl Myatt	KCC Templars
1975–76	David Clinton	Little Sai Wan & KGV School
1976–77	Brian Wigley	Police Recreation Club
1977–78	Tony Turner	Little Sai Wan

1978–79	Gopal Lalchandani	IRC & KCC Saracens
1979–80	Des Greenwood	Vagabonds & CCC
1980–81	Dermot Reeve	Vagabonds & KGV School
1981–82	Gordon Bacon &	Little Sai Wan/Royal Navy &
	Rod Eddington	HKCC Scorpions/Kai Tak CC
1982–83	No Award	
1983–84	Peter Anderson	HKCC Wanderers & HKCC Gap Ramblers
1984–85	Peter Wood	British Forces & Army
1985–86	Nigel Stearns	Police Recreation Club & KCC Crusaders
1986–87	Martin Sabine	HKCC Wanderers & Hong Kong University
1987–88	Craig Dean	Vagabonds/Independents & KGV School
1988–89	Ian Collier	British Forces & Army
1989–90	Stewart Brew	HKCC Optimists & Centaurs
1990–91	Salauddin Tariq	Little Sai Wan
1991–92	Warren Symcox	HKCC Scorpions & CCC
1992–93	Pat Fordham	KCC Templars & KCC Saracens
1993–94	Stewart Brew	HKCC Optimists
1994–95	Mark Eames	KCC Infidels & KCC Crusaders
1995–96	Rahul Sharma	KCC Templars & KCC Saracens
1996–97	Pat Fordham	KCC Templars & KCC Saracens

First Division/Sunday League

Second Division/Saturday League

Team Codes (see top Batting, Bowling & Wicket-keeping averages)

(A)	Army	(A)	Army
(B)	British Forces	(C)	Craigengower
(C)	Craigengower	(Ce)	Centaurs
(Ca)	Cavaliers	(Cr)	KCC Crusaders
(In)	KCC Infidels	(D)	DBS
(Ir)	IRC	(GR)	HKCC Gap Ramblers
(L)	LSW	(H)	HKU
(O)	HKCC Optimists	(KG)	KGV School
(P)	Police	(Kt)	Kai Tak
(R)	Recreio	(L)	LSW
(S)	HKCC Scorpions	(M)	Merchants
(T)	KCC Templars	(N)	HKCC Nomads
(V)	Vagabonds	(Ra)	RAF
(W)	HKCC Wanderers	(RN)	Royal Navy
		(S)	KCC Saracens
		(SG)	St George's
		(St)	Police Sentinels
		(T)	KCC Tartars
		(W)	HKCC Witherers

BEST BATTING PERFORMANCES

(1) indicates position in league table

First Division/Sunday League 1965–66 to 1993–94

Season	Player	Team	Aggregate 900 plus
1993–94	Rahul Sharma	Templars	1072 at 89.33 (3) incl. 5 centuries
	Stewart Brew	Optimists	1005 at 111.67 (2)
1973–74	Peter Davies	Optimists	968 at 46.10 (1)
1989–90	Stewart Brew	Optimists	939 at 93.90 (1)
1990–91	Stewart Brew	Optimists	929 at 66.35 (4)
1980–81	Dermot Reeve	Vagabonds	917 at 70.54 (1)

Second Division/Saturday League 1965–66 to 1993–94

1979–80	Harry Lucas	Kai Tak	1622 at 73.73 (1) incl. 5 centuries
1990–91	Stewart Brew	DBS	1505 at 215.00 (1) incl. 8 centuries
1976–77	Peter Anderson	Royal Navy	1225 at 72.06 (1)
1983–84	'Tug' Willson	Kai Tak	1076 at 56.63 (6) incl. 6 centuries
1978–79	John Bygate	Crusaders	1067 at 53.35 (4)
1977–78	John Bygate	Crusaders	1065 at 53.25 (4)
1979–80	Peter Olsen	Centaurs	1062 at 55.89 (3)
1983–84	Damian Sharwood	Islanders	1054 at 52.70 (8)
1988–89	David Jones	KGV	1032 at 79.38 (2)
1980–81	Dermot Reeve	KGV	1029 at 64.31 (2)
1987–88	David Evans	Tartars	999 at 62.44 (7)
1983–84	Des Greenwood	CCC	986 at 82.16 (2)
1989–90	Stewart Brew	Centaurs	982 at 89.27 (1)
1979–80	Paul Varty	Nomads	981 at 57.70 (2)
1992–93	Steve Foster	Nomads	971 at 88.27 (2)
1976–77	John Bygate	Crusaders	965 at 50.79 (4)
1979–80	John Bygate	Crusaders	957 at 53.17 (6)
1975–76	Graham Turner	Nomads	948 at 49.89 (5)
1979–80	Martin Walker	Royal Navy	948 at 47.40 (8)
1987–88	Mark Eames	Tartars	948 at 79.00 (4)
1971–72	Jim Rhodes	St George's	947 at 45.10 (3)
1977–78	Graham Richardson	Tartars	939 at 52.17 (5)
1975–76	'Tug' Willson	Kai Tak	934 at 66.71 (2)
1981–82	David Jones	KGV	930 at 51.67 (5)
1972–73	David Clinton	St George's	925 at 66.07 (1)
1979–80	Andy Lorimer	Nomads	925 at 48.68 (7)
1985–86	Krish Kumar	Saracens	907 at 64.78 (5)

Second Division/Saturday League 1965–66 to 1993–94 (cont'd)

1979–80	'Tug' Willson	Kai Tak	901 at	45.05	(11)
1989–90	Steve Atkinson	St George's	900 at	75.00	(2)
1992–93	Ross Greer	St George's	900 at	90.00	(1)

Sunday League/Rothman's Cup

Season	Player	Team	Highest Score 150 plus
1991–92	Adnan Butt	LSW	201* v HKCC Scorpions
1992–92	Chris Parsons	LSW	201* v British Forces
1992–93	Steve Foster	Wanderers	192 v LSW (Rothman's Cup)
1988–89	Pat Fordham	Templars	178* v IRC
1974–75	Guy Richardson	Police	174 v Army
1988–89	Doug Beckett	Infidels	171 v Vagabonds
1975–76	Ian Nicholson	Police	167 v Army
1989–90	Stewart Brew	Optimists	166* v KCC Templars
1984–85	Tarun Sawney	Police	165* v IRC
1981–82	Dave Race	Vagabonds	161 v British Forces
1993–94	Jonathan Orders	Scorpions	158* v IRC
1985–86	Krish Kumar	Infidels	158 v British Forces
1973–74	Ian Stevens	Optimists	157* v HKCC Scorpions
1981–82	Dermot Reeve	Vagabonds	156* v British Forces
1993–94	Rahul Sharma	Templars	156 v HKCC Scorpions
1990–91	Martin Sabine	Wanderers	155* v British Forces
1981–82	Paul Dean	British Forces	155 v Vagabonds
1990–91	James Barrington	Optimists	155 v IRC
1993–94	Steve Foster	Wanderers	155 v HKCC Optimists
1981–82	Benny Kwong	Scorpions	153 v KCC Infidels
1992–93	Andrew Dartnell	LSW	153 v IRC
1987–88	Dermot Reeve	Templars	152* v LSW
1977–78	John Bygate	Templars	151* v HKCC Scorpions
1981–82	Peter Anderson	Wanderers	151* v IRC
1971–72	Martin Alexander	Army	151 v KCC Templars

Saturday League

1992–93	Ross Greer	St George's	233* v CCC
	Steve Foster	Nomads	222* v CCC
1991–92	Stewart Brew	DBS	204* v Police Strollers
	Pat Fordham	Saracens	195 v CCC
1975–76	Rupert Litherland	Army	178* v DBS
	Guy Richardson	Police	173 v Army

49

Saturday League (cont'd)

1980–81	John Hollioake	Nomads	170	v HKU
1991–92	Ian Hardy	Kai Tak	169*	v LSW
1992–93	Seamus O'Brien	Gap Ramblers	165	v Police Strollers
1974–75	Jim Rhodes	St George's	161	v HKCC Witherers
1975–76	'Tug' Willson	Kai Tak	160	v Royal Navy
1981–82	John Murphy	Centaurs	160	v Army
1973–74	Mark Tress	Nomads	159*	v KCC Crusaders
1990–91	Craig Dean	KGV	158*	v Police Strollers
1985–86	Steve Elliott	Gap Ramblers	158	v HKU
1979–80	Martin Walker	Royal Navy	155*	v Police Strollers
1992–93	Jason Penrose	DBS	155	v Kai Tak
1979–80	Harry Lucas	Kai Tak	152*	v LSW
1991–92	Ian Hardy	Kai Tak	152	v KGV
1992–93	Jonathan Orders	Kai Tak	151*	v Islanders

BEST BOWLING PERFORMANCES

First Division/Sunday League 1965–66 to 1993–94

Season	Player	Team	Analyses
1967–68	Carl Myatt	CCC	10–23 v LSW incl. 'hat-trick'
1950–51	Frank Howarth	Scorpions	9–11 v Recreio
1971–72	Benny Kwong	Scorpions	9–14 v LSW
1993–94	Rahul Sharma	Templars	9–16 v Vagabonds
1949–50	Frank Howarth	Scorpions	9–26 v CCC
1967–68	Peter Hall	Templars	9–27 v Police
1969–70	Mike Duggan	Optimists	9–29 v IRC
1960–61	Bob Bell	KCC 'A'	9–32 v RAF
1966–67	Ian Lacy-Smith	Police	9–32 v IRC
1984–85	Neil Smith	Scorpions	9–32 v Police
1965–66	Mike Barros	Recreio	9–33 v Army
1981–82	Don Swift	Optimists	9–33 v IRC
1990–91	Rohan Chandran	IRC	9–36 v HKCC Wanderers
1967–68	Peter Langston	Optimists	9–49 v Army
1960–61	Vic Fairhall	KCC 'A'	9–52 v Recreio
1984–85	Steve Weatherley	Vagabonds	9–53 v HKCC Scorpions
1957–58	Guy Pritchard	Optimists	9–56 v Police
1991–92	Warren Symcox	Scorpions	9–82 v KCC Templars
	incl. 'hat-trick'		

First Division/Sunday League 1965–66 to 1993–94 (cont'd)

Season	Player	Team	Analyses
1985–86	Neil Smith	Scorpions	9–83 v British Forces
	Jim Sutherland	British Forces	9–85 v Vagabonds

NB: HKCC players included from 1948–49
KCC players included from 1960–61

Second Division/Saturday League 1965–66 to 1993–94

Season	Player	Team	Analyses
1969–70	Bernie Nichol	LSW	10–6 v IRC incl. 4 in 4 balls
1988–89	Ian Collier	Army	10–13 v Centaurs incl. 'hat-trick'
1968–69	Geoff Allbutt	St George's	10–23 v IRC
1976–77	Ron Grisenthwaite	Royal Navy	9–11 v DBS
1977–78	Levin Prabhu	Crusaders	9–20 v LSW
1982–83	Graham Fletcher	Centaurs	9–22 v DBS
1977–78	Tom Richardson	St George's	9–28 v Royal Navy
1966–67	Keith Giles	Crusaders	9–30 v Police
1973–74	Gopal Lalchandani	IRC	9–35 v KCC Crusaders

TOP AVERAGES

First Division/Sunday League

Top Batting Averages 1965–66 to 1993–94

Season	Player		Ave	Player		Ave	Player		Ave
1965–66	Daniel, R G	(A)	55.27	Hall, P A	(T)	48.38	Shroff, J S	(T)	48.33
1966–67	Fawcett, J K	(S)	54.10	Davies, P H	(O)	42.09	Shroff, J S	(T)	38.10
1967–68 a	Wilson, E H	(S)	44.44	Abbas, G	(T)	39.55	Mills-Owen R	(O)	35.90
1968–69 a	Davies, P H	(O)	39.53	Abbas, G	(T)	38.22	Clinch, M R V	(O)	36.33
1969–70 e	Daniel, R G	(A)	91.40	Jarman, G P	(S)	66.83	Abbas, G	(T)	60.73
1970–71 d	Daniel, R G	(A)	53.60	Lalchandani, R	(Ir)	47.11	Davies, P H	(O)	37.92
1971–72	Alexander, M	(A)	55.07	Brown, R	(T)	48.55	Hall, P A	(T)	40.20
1972–73 c	Marshall, I	(S)	43.36	Davies, P H	(O)	37.29	Nolan, G	(S)	36.57
1973–74	Davies, P H	(O)	46.10	Bygate, J	(T)	43.15	Cumings, C G	(P)	40.18
1974–75	Richardson, G	(P)	42.53	Cumings, C G	(T)	40.33	Davies, P H	(O)	37.92
1975–76	Willson, B J	(L)	73.44	Clinton, D	(L)	72.75	Davies, P H	(O)	56.25
1976–77	Bygate, J	(T)	38.44	Smith, R G	(A)	35.86	Litherland, R	(A)	33.53
1977–78	Sabine, M	(W)	61.44	Clinton, D	(V)	52.45	Shroff, J S	(T)	48.13
1978–79	Greenwood, D	(V)	78.00	Anderson, P W	(L)	50.70	Clinton, D	(V)	46.90
1979–80	Greenwood, D	(V)	54.45	Eddington, R I	(S)	44.50	Davies, P H	(O)	44.20
1980–81	Reeve, D A	(V)	70.54	Bygate, J	(T)	52.39	Davies, P H	(O)	50.50
1981–82	Greenwood, D	(V)	72.50	Sabine, M	(W)	72.00	Hollioake, J	(S)	58.73
1982–83	Bygate, J	(T)	45.22	Myles, S D	(V)	39.90	Hollioake, J	(S)	39.00

First Division/Sunday League (cont'd)

Top Batting Averages 1965–66 to 1993–94

Season	Player		Ave	Player		Ave	Player		Ave
1983–84	Anderson, P W	(W)	61.45	Brewster, R	(T)	46.36	Varty, P	(S)	42.89
1984–85	Collins, C	(In)	66.29	Anderson, P W	(W)	64.40	Kumar, K	(In)	54.64
1985–86	Stearns, N	(P)	63.45	Kumar, K	(In)	55.67	Bygate, J	(T)	53.42
1986–87	Stearns, N	(P)	106.71	Sabine, M	(W)	72.55	Davies, P H	(O)	60.78
1987–88 b	Perera, N	(T)	64.00	Greenwood, D	(V)	59.50	Eames, M	(In)	54.56
1988–89	Sabine, M	(W)	99.29	Speak, M	(O)	84.00	Beckett, D	(In)	79.83
1989–90	Brew, S	(O)	93.90	Atkinson, S R	(T)	77.80	Evans, D	(In)	51.56
1990–91	Speak, M	(O)	77.56	Fordham, P	(T)	73.55	Foster, S	(W)	67.60
1991–92	Brew, S	(O)	65.89	Fordham, P	(T)	54.18	Speak, M	(O)	54.13
1992–93	Fordham, P	(T)	100.88	Penrose, J	(T)	85.75	Atkinson, S R	(T)	82.43
1993–94	Fordham, P	(T)	159.00	Brew, S	(O)	111.67	Sharma, R	(T)	89.33

Qualification: 10 Innings/300 runs

a Excludes 'Super' League as separate averages were incomplete.
b Includes 'Super' League as Handbook had aggregated totals.
c Excludes IRC as details were not submitted.
d R G Daniel also topped the bowling averages in 1970–71.
e The author has included Daniel's original 1969–70 batting average per the 1970–71 Handbook. His Army captain Tony Vivian, Ian Vaughan-Arbuckle and Peter Davies, all recalled he was 'not out' many times, as he batted in the middle order.

First Division/Sunday League

Top Bowling Averages 1965–66 to 1993–94

Season	Player		Ave	Player		Ave	Player		Ave
1965–66	Myatt, C	(C)	8.29	Barros, R M	(R)	8.43	Bennett, J	(A)	8.51
1966–67	Metcalf, C	(L)	7.80	Murphy, J C G	(S)	9.96	Fawcett, J K	(S)	10.25
1967–68 a	Myatt, C	(C)	8.63	Lacy-Smith, I	(P)	8.78	Hall, P A	(T)	9.51
1968–69	Lalchandani, G	(Ca)	6.29	Barros, R M	(Ca)	7.73	Pike J I D	(A)	9.13
1969–70	Mitchell, P A	(A)	8.54	Myatt, C	(Ca)	8.79	Duggan, M	(O)	10.25
1970–71 b	Daniel, R G	(A)	12.89	Duggan, M	(O)	13.47	Myatt, C	(T)	13.58
1971–72	Ashworth, J	(O)	12.48	Myatt, C	(T)	12.87	Metcalf, C	(L)	14.38
1972–73	Carnell, B C N	(T)	8.40	Metcalf, C	(L)	10.96	Myatt, C	(T)	11.74
1973–74	Wellard, D	(W)	10.43	Myatt, C	(T)	12.12	Metcalf, C	(L)	12.76
1974–75	Myatt, C	(T)	8.33	Butler, G	(W)	11.37	Robinson, O L	(L)	13.39
1975–76	Lewis, M	(O)	10.77	Ashworth, J	(O)	12.70	Myatt, C	(T)	13.02
1976–77	Wigley, B T	(P)	9.58	Smith, P	(L)	11.94	Stenner, L	(L)	12.38
1977–78	Willis, S	(O)	11.41	Smith, P	(L)	12.57	Forse, C	(V)	13.27
1978–79	Poynton, R	(W)	11.36	Duggan, M	(W)	13.44	Forse, C	(V)	14.15
1979–80	Hislop, M	(S)	12.70	White, I	(B)	13.41	Hughes, J	(O)	13.70
1980–81	Lalchandani, G	(L)	12.00	Way, D	(S)	13.87	Turner, A	(L)	14.81
1981–82	Bacon, G	(L)	12.10	Clarke, D	(S)	12.11	Myatt, C	(T)	13.74

First Division/Sunday League (cont'd)

Top Bowling Averages 1965–66 to 1993–94

Season	Player		Ave	Player		Ave	Player		Ave
1982–83	Lalchandani, G	(L)	12.14	Kwong B	(S)	12.41	Jenkins, J	(T)	14.04
1983–84	Jenkins, J	(T)	12.94	McLeish, A	(O)	13.00	Smith, N	(S)	13.50
1984–85	Jones, Brad	(W)	14.47	Fotheringham R	(S)	16.27	Kwong B	(S)	17.04
1985–86	Gohel, B	(T)	14.28	Telford, A	(W)	15.03	Beckett, D	(In)	15.40
1986–87	Collins, C	(In)	13.10	Gohel, B	(T)	14.75	Barnett, A	(W)	15.03
1987–88 c	Jones, Brad	(W)	13.65	Gohel, B	(T)	20.94	Uttamchandani D	(V)	23.63
1988–89	Collier, I	(B)	17.03	Davies, G	(In)	18.41			
1989–90	Davies, G	(In)	14.42	Fotheringham R	(S)	18.37	Paull, D	(O)	19.52
1990–91	Symcox, W	(S)	16.66	Brettell, D	(In)	17.26	Tariq, S	(L)	18.84
1991–92	Symcox, W	(S)	13.02	Davies, G	(In)	16.55	Fotheringham R	(S)	17.27
1992–93	Ashman, A	(O)	15.60	Johnson, M	(S)	16.19	Cresswell, P	(T)	16.70
1993–94	Foley, A	(In)	15.39	Strachan, J	(O)	16.58	Gohel, B	(T)	17.79

Qualification: 30 wickets

a   Excludes 'Super' League as separate averages are incomplete.
b   R G Daniel also topped the batting averages in 1970–71.
c   Includes 'Super' League as Handbook has aggregated totals.

Second Division/Saturday League

Top Batting Averages 1965–66 to 1993–94

Season	Player		Ave	Player		Ave	Player		Ave
1965–66	Fishwick, R	(Ra)	40.18	Iranee, B	(C)	35.73	Snoxall. DJ	(Ce)	31.82
1966–67	Bedlington, L	(Cr)	34.40	Tyrrell, B	(A)	26.00	Barnes, WSD	(N)	24.62
1967–68	Self, B	(SG)	38.10	Booth, G	(C)	37.64	Barnes, WSD	(N)	25.24
1968–69	Cooper, AG	(P)	50.50	Snoxall, DJ	(Ce)	37.56	Bailey, A	(A)	31.82
1969–70	Booth, D	(C)	51.20	Moores, S	(Cr)	45.31	Rhodes, J	(SG)	40.17
1970–71	Danks, J	(N)	45.13	Jackson, G	(C)	37.79	Rhodes, J	(SG)	37.41
1971–72 a	Garner, K	(C)	55.00	Joynt, CR	(W)	53.78	Rhodes, J	(SG)	45.10
1972–73	Clinton, D	(SG)	66.07	Rhodes, J	(SG)	55.71	Green, P	(N)	50.31
1973–74	Stopford, R	(A)	90.50	Tress, M	(N)	74.50	Green, P	(N)	65.18
1974–75	Clinton, D	(KG)	62.31	Rhodes, J	(SG)	61.50	Tipper, R	(W)	49.09
1975–76	Clinton, D	(KG)	78.38	Willson, BJ	(Kt)	66.71	Shroff, JS	(Cr)	55.33
1976–77	Anderson, PW	(RN)	72.06	Vergelius, R	(L)	61.33	Clinton, D	(KG)	55.81
1977–78	Anderson, PW	(RN)	92.44	Hurrell, G	(S)	61.69	Greenwood, D	(C)	59.00
1978–79	Clinton, D	(KG)	123.33	Race, D	(H)	65.11	Garner, K	(C)	63.33
1979–80	Lucas, H	(Kt)	73.33	Varty, P	(N)	57.70	Olsen, P	(Ce)	55.89
1980–81	Anderson, PW	(RN)	83.50	Reeve, DA	(KG)	64.31	Oliver, G	(N)	54.50
1981–82	Reeve, DA	(T)	91.60	Stearns, N	(St)	88.78	Eddington, RI	(Kt)	87.10
1982–83	Olsen, P	(Ce)	83.71	Lorimer, A	(N)	77.86	Greenwood, D	(C)	71.92
1983–84	Anderson, PW	(GR)	92.57	Greenwood, D	(C)	82.16	Davies, G	(S)	74.50
1984–85	Willson, BJ	(Kt)	95.75	Veivers, P	(N)	89.43	Barrington, J	(Kt)	75.75

Second Division/Saturday League (cont'd)

Top Batting Averages 1965–66 to 1993–94

Season	Player		Ave	Player		Ave	Player		Ave
1985–86	Stearns, N	(Cr)	98.17	Sabine, M	(H)	81.13	Greenwood, D	(C)	70.40
1986–87	Dean, C	(KG)	60.40	Telford, A	(W)	55.00	Davies, G	(S)	53.82
1987–88	Dean, C	(KG)	121.83	Marsden, R	(KG)	98.50	Sabine, M	(H)	87.57
1988–89	Fordham, P	(S)	80.86	Jones, DA	(KG)	79.38	Rothman, J	(W)	73.29
1989–90	Brew, S	(Ce)	89.27	Eames, M	(T)	75.89	Atkinson, SR	(SG)	75.00
1990–91	Brew, S	(D)	215.00	Farouq, R	(N)	106.20	Foster, S	(N)	90.71
1991–92	Speak, M	(H)	91.00	Noble, M	(L)	66.57	Fisher, D	(L)	64.00
1992–93	Greer, R	(SG)	90.00	Foster, S	(N)	88.27	Glenwright, P	(H)	76.00
1993–94	Garden, J	(N)	71.67	Samuel, A	(W)	63.70	Husain, S	(M)	55.20

Qualification: 10 Innings/300 runs

a K Garner also topped the bowling averages in 1971–72.

Second Division/Saturday League

Top Bowling Averages 1965–66 to 1993–94

Season	Player		Ave	Player		Ave	Player		Ave
1965–66	Davies P	(SG)	7.74	Gohel K	(KG)	7.97	Varty G	(KG)	8.24
1966–67	Barnett A	(N)	7.98	Paul G	(A)	8.34	Kotch J	(SG)	9.18
1967–68	Varty G	(KG)	6.10	Finch J	(P)	6.78	Hemshall BG	(Ce)	7.02
1968–69	Dennis NJ	(N)	8.94	Langstaff D	(A)	10.08	Allbutt G	(SG)	10.22
1969–70	Tilley A	(C)	8.50	Bridger A	(A)	8.70	Berry PJ	(N)	9.31
1970–71	Gubbins B	(A)	8.97	Green M	(A)	9.60	Miles MJ	(W)	10.70
1971–72 a	Garner K	(C)	10.32	Hemshall BG	(Ce)	12.55	Rhodes J	(SG)	13.02
1972–73	Hammond A	(Ce)	9.07	Buckland G	(C)	10.10	Swift A	(SG)	10.15
1973–74	Robinson OL	(L)	7.94	Lalchandani G	(Ir)	8.39	Garner K	(C)	8.45
1974–75	Robinson OL	(Ra)	8.82	Swift A	(SG)	9.68	Bird K	(Ra)	11.09
1975–76	Stenner L	(L)	9.12	Willson BJ	(Kt)	9.65	Starling R	(Cr)	10.35
1976–77	Lalchandani G	(S)	9.68	Toes R	(Ce)	10.30	Nissim R	(S)	10.47
1977–78	Richardson T	(SG)	6.65	Gipson R	(SG)	9.69	Grisenthwaite R	(RN)	11.45
1978–79	Lalchandani G	(S)	13.27	Ismail E	(RN)	13.47	Prabhu L	(Cr)	13.87
1979–80	Lalchandani G	(S)	12.41	Wigley BT	(Se)	12.53	Gregson T	(A)	13.32
1980–81	Filus E	(Kt)	9.67	Archer S	(A)	11.06	Reeve DA	(KG)	11.59
1981–82	Lacy-Smith I	(Se)	10.33	Harris A	(Cr)	11.45	Wigley BT	(Se)	12.09
1982–83	McLeish A	(Ce)	14.47	Fletcher G	(Ce)	14.53	Greenwood D	(C)	15.22
1983–84	Scott A	(L)	12.73	Prabhu L	(Cr)	13.21	Bacon G	(L)	13.91
1984–85	Hardman K	(A)	13.40	Poynton R	(D)	14.10	Robinson S	(Cr)	14.75
1985–86	Vachha Y	(S)	12.41	Middleton J	(T)	13.45	Prabhu L	(Cr)	13.57
1986–87	Prebble A	(GR)	12.81	Gohel B	(SG)	13.15	Swift D	(H)	13.40
1987–88	Prabhu L	(Cr)	13.45	Duggan M	(W)	13.90	Shugrue R	(Se)	15.20
1988–89	Collier I	(A)	9.60	Davies G	(Se)	11.84	Gohel B	(SG)	13.43

Second Division/Saturday League (cont'd)

Top Bowling Averages 1965–66 to 1993–94

Season	Player		Ave	Player		Ave	Player		Ave
1989–90	Beaman L	(Kt)	10.41	Pierce D	(SG)	13.37	Gohel B	(SG)	13.85
1990–91	Swift D	(N)	13.90	Tse E	(D)	15.00	O'Hara D	(T)	16.67
1991–92	Todd S	(Se)	15.48	Fotheringham R	(N)	16.21	Lethbridge A	(Cr)	18.11
1992–93				No bowler achieved 30 wickets					
1993–94	Eddington RI	(Kt)	7.84	Johnson M	(W)	15.18	Tse E	(D)	15.33

Qualification: 30 wickets

a   K Garner also topped the batting averages in 1971–72.

First Division/Sunday League

Top Wicket-keepers/Fielders 1965–66 to 1993–94

Season	Player			Player			Most Catches		
1966–67	Johnston V	(LSW)	35	Holman J	(A)	26			
1967–68	Patten PJM	(S)	25				Wilson EH	(S)	15
1968–69							Fawcett JK	(S)	17
1969–70	Lalchandani R	(Cav)	32				Hammett M	(P)	18
							Whittaker I	(A)	15
1971–72	Gilkes D	(S)	29	Bartlett P	(A)	25	Ashworth J	(O)	16
1972–73	Foster GA	(O)	27	Grandfield N	(T)	26			
1973–74	Grandfield N	(T)	33	Bulfield M	(W)	30	Booth R	(P)	17
							Wigley BT	(P)	16
1976–77	Foster GA	(O)	28	Vergelius R	(LSW)	26			
1977–78	Bulfield M	(W)	31	Foster GA	(O)	28			
1979–80	Walker M	(BF)	33						
1980–81	Gill R	(Inf)	32	Grandfield N	(T)	30			
1981–82	Olsen P	(O)	26				Bacon G	(LSW)	15
1983–84	Gill R	(V)	25						
1984–85	Gill R	(V)	28	Olsen P	(O)	27	Catton B	(T)	17
1985–86	Higgs J	(P)	30	Broadhurst N	(Inf)	29			
1986–87	Evans D	(Inf)	26				Lerwill T	(BF)	27
							Beckett D	(Inf)	15
1989–90	Evans D	(Inf)	26						
1992–93	Brewster R	(Inf)	25						

Qualification: 25 dismissals   15 Catches

Second Division/Saturday League

Top Wicket-keepers/Fielders 1965–66 to 1993–94

Season	Player			Player			Most Catches		
1966–67							Barnes WSD	(N)	18
1969–70							Garner K	(C)	18
							Maloney	(P)	16
1970–71	Jones A	(SG)	33				Huang L	(D)	17
							Bailey A	(Ce)	15
1971–72	Jones A	(SG)	46	Coppin J	(Ce)	25	Williams J	(SG)	15
1972–73	Bradley P	(SG)	49	Kent G	(S)	33			
1973–74	Tipper R	(W)	42	Grandfield N	(SG)	38	Lee Warner M	(N)	17
							Swift A	(SG)	15
1974–75							Garner K	(C)	15
1975–76	Pearson J	(Kt)	30	Thadani R	(Ir)	28	Lunn J	(W)	19
							Woolfe B	(L)	17
1976–77	Robinson K	(RN)	40	Tipper R	(W)	28	Clinton D	(KG)	22
							Mountstevens E	(1L)	19
1977–78							Richardson G	(T)	17
							Smith M	(C)	17
1978–79	Jowharsha F	(S)	28	Olsen P	(Ce)	27			
1979–80	Walker M	(RN)	49	Hurren D	(A)	32	Sibree D	(N)	15
1980–81	Evans D	(KG)	36	Tipper R	(W)	35	Evans J	(KG)	15
1981–82	Grandfield N	(SG)	25						
1983–84	Gill R	(S)	26	Jones D	(N)	26	Wood P	(A)	16
1984–85	Brewster R	(Cr)	30	Gill R	(S)	26	Anderson PW	(Isl)	16
1985–86	Howden A	(C)	28	Broadhurst N	(T)	25	Clinton D	(KG)	16
1986–87	Howden A	(C)	29						
1988–89							Foster N	(GR)	15
1989–90	Grandfield N	(SG)	34						
1992–93	Brewster R	(Cr)	32						

Qualification: 25 dismissals   15 Catches

OFFICIALS

Hong Kong Cricket League

Seasons	Chairman	Hon. Secretary	Colony Captains	Chairman of Selectors
1948–49	H Owen Hughes		T A Pearce	H Owen Hughes
1949–50	H Owen Hughes			
1950–51	T A Pearce	G Hong Choy		
1951–52	T A Pearce	G Hong Choy		
1952–53	T A Pearce	G Hong Choy	T A Pearce	T A Pearce
1953–54	T A Pearce	G Hong Choy		
1954–55	T A Pearce	G Hong Choy		
1955–56	T A Pearce	G Hong Choy	T A Pearce	T A Pearce
1956–57	T A Pearce	G Hong Choy		

Hong Kong Cricket League (cont'd)

Seasons	Chairman	Hon. Secretary	Colony Captains	Chairman of Selectors
1957–58	T A Pearce	G Hong Choy	F Findlay	
1958–59	T A Pearce	G Hong Choy		
1959–60	T A Pearce	G Hong Choy	G H P Pritchard	T A Pearce
1960–61	T A Pearce	G Hong Choy		
1961–62	T A Pearce	G Hong Choy	F Findlay	
1962–63	J B H Leckie	G Hong Choy	D G Coffey	J B H Leckie
1963–64	J B H Leckie	G Hong Choy	F A Weller	D W Leach
1964–65	J B H Leckie		D G Coffey	
1965–66	J B H Leckie	M J Jones	D G Coffey	
1966–67	D T E Roberts	M J Jones	D G Coffey	G T Rowe

| | *President* | | | |
| 1967–68 | D T E Roberts | M J Jones | J S Shroff | G T Rowe |

Hong Kong Cricket Association

1968–69	D T E Roberts OBE	P H Davies	J S Shroff	E H Wilson
1969–70	D T E Roberts OBE	P H Davies	J S Shroff	E H Wilson
1970–71	D T E Roberts OBE	P H Davies	J S Shroff	E H Wilson
1971–72	D T E Roberts OBE	P H Davies	Shroff/Myatt	B C N Carnell
1972–73	E H Wilson	P H Davies	C Myatt	E H Wilson
1973–74	E H Wilson	B G Hemshall	C Myatt	B C N Carnell
1974–75	E H Wilson	B G Hemshall	C Myatt	J S Shroff
1975–76	E H Wilson	B G Hemshall	C Myatt	J S Shroff
1976–77	E H Wilson	B G Hemshall	C Myatt	P A Hall
1977–78	E H Wilson	B G Hemshall	C Myatt	P A Hall
1978–79	E H Wilson	B G Hemshall	Myatt/Anderson	P A Hall
1979–80	E H Wilson MBE	#B K Sipahimalani	P W Anderson	P A Hall

	Chairman			
1980–81	E H Wilson MBE	*B G Hemshall	P W Anderson	P A Hall
1981–82	E H Wilson MBE	B G Hemshall	P W Anderson	P A Hall
1982–83	Sir Denys Roberts	B G Hemshall	P W Anderson	P A Hall
1983–84	Sir Denys Roberts	J A Bygate	P W Anderson	P A Hall
1984–85	Sir Denys Roberts	J A Bygate	P W Anderson	P A Hall
1985–86	Sir Denys Roberts	J A Bygate	P W Anderson	P A Hall
1986–87	Sir Denys Roberts	J A Bygate	Anderson/Vachha Y	P A Hall
1987–88	Sir Denys Roberts	J A Bygate	Vachha/Fordham	P A Hall
1988–89	Sir Denys Roberts	J A Bygate	P Fordham	P A Hall
1989–90	H Ebrahim	J A Bygate	Fordham/Davies G	Hall/Eddington
1990–91	H Ebrahim	B Catton	P Fordham	R I Eddington
1991–92	H Ebrahim	B Catton	P Fordham	R I Eddington
1992–93	H Ebrahim	E P Slack	P Fordham	R I Eddington
1993–94	H Ebrahim	E P Slack	P Fordham	R I Eddington
1994–95	J T Hung	E P Slack	P Fordham	R Starling

Hong Kong Cricket Association (cont'd)

1995–96	J T Hung	E P Slack	P Fordham	M Walsh
1996–97	T Smith	E P Slack	P Fordham	M Walsh

Notes: #   B K Sipahimalani 'Sippy' continued as Hon. Secretary until he retired in 1988–89. M Speak was Hon. Secretary from 1989–90 till 1990–91. J Cribbin has been Hon. Secretary since 1991–92.

φ   E H Wilson 'Ted' was elected an Hon. Life Member of the MCC.

*   B G Hemshall 'Bryan' was appointed to the new post of Chairman in 1980–81. The Chairman is the Chief Executive, the role of President became that of a figurehead.

The following persons have been elected Hon. Vice Presidents of the HKCA for services to Hong Kong cricket:

1980	General Sir Edwin Bramall KCB, OBE, MC	
	(now Field Marshal The Lord Bramall)	
	T A Pearce Esq	deceased 1982
	Hon. Sir Denys Roberts KBE, QC, JP	
	G T Rowe Esq	deceased 1992
	Hon. M G R Sandberg OBE, JP	
	(now Lord Sandberg)	
	K H Sillett Esq	
	Hon. P G Williams OBE, JP	deceased 1983
1982	B C N Carnell Esq	
	E H Wilson MBE	
1994	Papu Butani, Esq	
	Hatim Ebrahim, Esq	
	Rod I Eddington, Esq	
1995	George Hong Choy, Esq	deceased 1997
1996	John T Hung, Esq	

PRE PACIFIC WAR – HONG KONG CAPTAINS

Hong Kong v Shanghai		**Hong Kong v Straits / Malaya**	
1866			
1867			
1889		1890	E J Coxon
1891		1891	E M Blair
1892	Capt J Dunn		
1897		1897	
1898	Dr J A Lowson		
1901		1901	
1903			
1904		1904	
1906			

PRE PACIFIC WAR – HONG KONG CAPTAINS (cont'd)

Hong Kong v Shanghai		Hong Kong v Straits / Malaya	
1907			
1908			
1909		1909	
1912			
1914			
1920	H R B Hancock	1920	
1921			
1922	H R B Hancock		
1923	T E Pearce		
1924	H R B Hancock	1924	H R B Hancock
1925	Rev E K Quick		
1926	T E Pearce	1926	H R B Hancock
1927	T E Pearce	1927	T E Pearce
1928	H R B Hancock		
1929	H R B Hancock	1929	T E Pearce (Hancock unwell)
1930	T E Pearce		
1931	T E Pearce		
1932	E J R Mitchell		
1933	H Owen Hughes	1933	H Owen Hughes
1934	H Owen Hughes		
1935	T E Pearce		
1936	T A Pearce		

HONGKONG CRICKET LEAGUE & HKCA – SPECIAL AWARDS

From the late 1960s, various companies, mainly those concerned with drinking and smoking, introduced incentive packages to excite the local cricketer. It worked well in many cases!

1. State Express (1969–70)
   A player who in any league or representative match during the season, scores 50 runs, takes 5 wickets or 3 catches in an innings, is entitled to receive 200 State Express cigarettes. Superseded by Benson & Hedges from 1970–71 to 1973–74.

2. Benson & Hedges – Monthly and Annual (1974–75 to 1986–87)
   Monthly: One batting award and one bowling award each month for each league competition (tour). Highest runs scored by a batsman and highest number of wickets taken by a bowler in a match. Double award for a tie. Each award will be 400 cigarettes.

Annual: Six annual awards will be given. Best batting, bowling and wicket-keeping in the league competitions, minimum qualification ten matches. Each award will be in the form of a gift voucher, cigarettes (ceased 1978–79) and a suitable memento – to be presented at the annual presentation dinner.

British American Tobacco Co. (HK) Ltd

3. HKCA Awards (1987–88 to 1990–91)
Three awards for each of the leagues in the form of tankards. Best batting and bowling averages and best wicket-keeping (victims per match).

4. Long John (1969–70 to 1982–83)
A bowler who in any league (1975–76: league cup/plate) or representative match during the season takes 5 or more wickets in an innings, will be entitled to receive one bottle of Long John 'Special Reserve' Scotch whisky.

H. Ruttonjee & Son Ltd

5. Ballantines Award (1983–84 to 1985–86)
One bottle of Ballantines Scotch whisky replaced Ruttonjee's Long John 'Special Reserve' Scotch whisky.

Gibb Livingston & Co. Ltd

6. Haig and Napoleon (1969–70 to 1972–73)
A player in any league or interport match during the season, who scores 70 runs* or more will be entitled to receive a bottle of Haig Gold Label whisky. A player who in any league or interport match takes a hat-trick, will be entitled to receive one bottle of Bisquit Napoleon Cognac.

* Replaced VAT 69 for scoring 69 runs or more

Gande Price & Co. Ltd

7. Johnnie Walker 'Red Label' (1973–74 to 1987–88)
One bottle of Johnnie Walker 'Red Label' whisky replaced Haig's Gold Label whisky. [1975–76 Handbook stated 100 runs or more!]

Caldbeck Macgregor & Co. Ltd

8. Long John 'Imperial Quart' (1976–77 to 1982–83)
   This Ruttonjee award replaced the Gande Price Bisquit Napoleon Cognac.

9. Ballantines 'Vintage' Award (1983–84 to 1985–86)
   This Gibb Livingston award replaced Ruttonjee's Long John 'Imperial Quart'.

10. Hiram Walker Wine Awards (1986–87)
    These awards replaced both Ballantines awards. Any bowler taking 5 wickets or more in an innings or performing the hat-trick will receive a regular size bottle of Curlier Bordeaux Wine.

    Hiram Walker & Co.

11. Bell's Whisky Award (1972–73)
    In alternate weeks of league cricket, the player with the highest score (two or more will each receive a bottle) and the player taking the most wickets (if two or more, the best average will receive a bottle) of Bell's whisky.

    East Asiatic Co. Ltd

12. Ballantines Vintage Award (1986–87)
    The first batsman to score 500 runs and the first bowler to take 30 wickets in each of the Sunday and Saturday leagues will receive a bottle of Ballantines 15-year-old whisky.

13. Ballantines Special Awards (1987–88 to 1990–91)
    Awards as Ballantines Vintage (above), no mention of actual awards.

14. Ruttonjee 'Player of the Year' (1972–73 to 1984–85)
    This award will be made to a player selected by a sub-committee appointed by the Executive Committee of the Association (the selection sub-committee chaired by the Chairman of Selectors) as the 'Player of the Year'. It will consist of a permanent trophy with the player's name inscribed thereon each year.

    Presented by H. Ruttonjee & Son Ltd

15. Hongkong Bank 'Player of the Year' (1985–86 to 1990–91)
    This trophy replaced the Ruttonjee Trophy.

    Presented by The Hongkong and Shanghai Banking Corporation

16. Connaught 'Player of the Year' (1991–92 to 1994–95)
    This trophy replaced the Hongkong Bank Trophy.

    Presented by Connaught Strategic Holdings Ltd

17. Jangu Vachha 'Umpire of the Year' (1973–74 to 1996–97 ongoing)
    This award will be made to the umpire who receives the most votes
    from the captains of the First Division/Sunday league, as the 'Umpire
    of the Year'. It will consist of a permanent trophy with the umpire's
    name inscribed thereon.

    Presented by Jangu Vachha

THE NETWORK

CRICKET ADMINISTRATION

Two days before league cricket commenced in Hong Kong in 1903, a meeting of persons from all the interested clubs took place in the Craigengower CC pavilion with Mr W D Braidwood, President of CCC, presiding.

The following Rules and Conditions were drawn up:

The name of the League to be 'The Hongkong Cricket League'.

Each club to play two matches with every other club. Two points to be reckoned for a win and one point for a draw. The club scoring the highest number of points to be declared Champion Club and be entitled to hold the trophy for one season.

Every player must be a bona-fide member of the club he represents. No player may represent more than one club in the same season.

The cost of a trophy to be subscribed for by the competing clubs; contributions to be unlimited. The entrance fee to be $10 per season for each club. Souvenirs and general disbursements to be paid for out of this fund.

The next meeting, to elect office-bearers, etc., will be held on the 2nd November, and entries for the competition close on 31st October. Eight clubs have, at present, entered for the League. All communications should be addressed to Mr A E Asger, care of The Hongkong Land Investment Co., who has undertaken to act as Hon. Secretary and Treasurer, pro.tem.

The first major change in cricket administration came in 1968, when the Hong Kong Cricket Association (HKCA) was formed to replace the original Hongkong Cricket League (League), after legal and financial complications required the former League to be incorporated under the Hong Kong Companies Ordinance. The lead roles in this modernisation were played by Sir Denys Roberts, the Attorney-General and President of the HKCA, and Peter Davies, a leading solicitor and the HKCA Hon. Secretary.

The HKCA is now fully responsible for the development of the game in Hong Kong: the domestic arena, in which 17 Saturday and 9 Sunday sides take part in separate leagues and limited over competitions; all arrangements for representative tours to and from Hong Kong; and the organisation of the prestigious Cathay Pacific/Wharf International Sixes. The HKCA became an Associate Member of the International Cricket Council (ICC) in June 1969, and is affiliated to the Asian Cricket Council.

The HKCA works closely with the Hong Kong Association of Cricket Umpires and Scorers (HKACUS), and an annual handbook is produced listing the fixtures and rules for the impending season, extensive coverage of the immediate past season, and details of previous results and records. This invaluable source of information ceased after the 1992–93 season, when only the rules and fixtures were produced for 1993–94. Somebody wanted $20,000 to do the handbook!

Over the last 45 years, Hong Kong has become a very popular venue for visiting cricket teams, as distinct from Interport sides, which are mentioned separately. These visiting teams range from international cricketers to local sides from Australia, England and other countries. It goes without saying that it is the excellence of the local cricket which attracts the numerous overseas teams, not the vibrancy of Hong Kong, with its temptations of shopping, its easy access to China, and other dubious delights tantalisingly available in the exotic Orient!

The visits are, however, not all one way. The HKCA has also organised tours to Sri Lanka, East and West Australia, and to England, these tours being separate from those when Hong Kong participated in the Associate Members' World Cup matches in 1982 and 1986 (England), 1990 (Holland), 1994 (Kenya) and 1997 (Kuala Lumpur), and the South East Asian competitions in 1984 (Bangladesh) and 1992 (Singapore). More recently, additional international tournaments have taken place in South East Asia for the Volvo and Tuanku Ja'afar Cups. In the past, to play in the Interports, the Far Eastern 'Test Matches', which began against Shanghai in 1866 and ended against Singapore in 1987, was every local cricketer's dream.

All tours, whether to or from Hong Kong, required a great deal of planning. This, apart from the problem of arranging nine Saturday fixtures on only six available grounds, or concocting polite replies to numerous touring team organisers, all of whom wished to visit Hong Kong during the same week, having given a week's notice of their intentions!

New Articles of Association were adopted in 1980 and further amended by the 1991 Annual General Meeting (AGM). The main purpose of the new Articles was to provide for a Chairman of the HKCA, in addition to the President, which position had become more or less honorary, and to provide for the establishment of the Executive Committee with a definition of its membership and powers. These changes were necessary to handle the recent increased workload and to provide for a more efficient administration.

Individual cricket membership is now over 300, and from 1991–92, the membership fee was increased to $150 per season. The previous season saw the first increase in 'living memory' from $10 to $75. A Life Membership was also introduced at $1,500. Reciprocal rights to nine English County Cricket Clubs was added as a sweetener to help swallow the new fee.

The present fees are: Life $3,000, Full $300 and Junior $150.

In late 1990, after discussions with the Hong Kong Government Sports Development Board, who provided generous support for cricket, a Four Year Rolling Development Plan 1991–95, was drawn up. The main objectives of the Four Year Plan are:

1. To administer, co-ordinate and develop the sport;
2. To support the ICC, the International governing body of cricket and the Asian Cricket Council (ACC);
3. To encourage participation at all levels of the sport; competitive, social and school, and encourage the sport amongst the indigenous population;
4. To promote Hong Kong's participation and performance in international competitions, particularly the 4-yearly ICC Trophy and the South-East Asia Competition;
5. To improve the quality and quantity of coaches and umpires, and
6. To invite international teams to visit and compete in Hong Kong and promote international events.

Following on from this Plan, David Wilson, a former Scottish coach was appointed as a Development Officer. This post reverted to a member of the Executive Committee, and a qualified coach, Lal Jayasinghe, was brought over from Sri Lanka. Lal and Rahuman Farcy are the present Executive Development officials.

The main objectives of the original four year Plan continue to be pursued. A more recent important aim of the HKCA has been to provide opportunities for youngsters at domestic and international level. This has been made possible through the support of sponsoring companies and individuals who became founder members of the Development Trust Fund instituted in 1995, together with financial backing from the Hong Kong Sports Development Board.

The HKCA also formed its own charitable trust to – 'raise funds for charity and organise the annual charity cricket festival.'

In 1994–95, members of the Executive Committee were: the four

Officers, one representative of each club participating in the league competitions (16), an umpires representative and sub-committee chairmen (currently 10 active).

President: Mr John Hung
Chairman: Mr Peter Slack
Hon. Secretary: Mr John Cribbin
Hon. Treasurer: Mr John Holgate
Hon. Statistician: Mr Jim Middleton

The principal sub-committees and chairmen were:

Development: Mike Speak*
Finance: John Holgate*
Fixtures: Bob Fotheringham
Membership: Tony Slack*
Rules Revision: Graham Fletcher*
Selectors: Rod Starling
Sixes: Hatim Ebrahim
Visiting Teams: Suzie Ledger*
Charity: Shyam Chakrabarti
Social Cricket: John Larvin

* also a member of the Executive Committee in another capacity

The Executive Committee has discussed structural changes from time to time, but has not been willing to adopt a more streamlined structure. Clearly, it is important that clubs be represented in the organisation of the game, but with the growth of HKCA activities beyond the domestic league and cup competitions embracing development, international affairs, the national team, charity, the Sixes and, in future, a permanent office and staff, there is an urgent need for a more efficient executive and management structure than is presently the case.

John Cribbin, Hon. Secretary, HKCA, April 1993

Hong Kong cricket has been very fortunate in the past, having had keen, dedicated and experienced voluntary administrators, a far cry from the ones as described by 'leg-break' in the SCMP in 1932 (see League Cricket – the 'Emerging Years'). As the HKCA moves into a more sophisticated era, a permanent office, within the Hong Kong Stadium complex, has been set up. The appointment of paid staff is an improvement and will take some of the pressure off the 'dedicated' volunteers who continue their good work.

In 1996–97, the HKCA Executive consisted of:

President:	Terry Smith
Chairman:	Peter Slack
Hon. Secretary:	John Cribbin
Hon. Treasurer:	Martin Sabine
Exec. Director:	Russell Mawhinney
Development officers:	Lal Jayasinghe
	Rahuman Farcy
Administration:	Chris Speak
Sport Administrator:	Simone Kwan

In September 1997, the HKCA went into Cyberspace. Their web-site is hosted by a UK based non-profit organisation called 'Cric Info' at *http://www.cricket.org* The HKCA's web-site address is: *http://www.hkca.cricket.org* 'We hope to expand the site to include Chinese language pages and more on junior cricket,' said an HKCA spokesman.

Finance

The changing HKCA financial scene must not be ignored. The apparent total dependence on shared funds received from the World Cup Tournament every four years seemed to be leading the Executive Committee, like lemmings, to a financial catastrophe. They should put a greater emphasis on better usage selection and also take a much firmer grip on expenditure.

In the Treasurer's Report of 1979–80, after the inclusion of $27,000 from the Prudential World Cup, the accounts showed a surplus of $25,756. The Treasurer, Nigel Beaton said:

> Our overall position is sound, we do not aim to make profits, and we can look forward to next year with confidence as our regular income is sufficient with husbandry to maintain our present standards.

At that time the cost of providing for visiting teams to Hong Kong was mainly covered by local sponsors, whilst overseas tours by Hong Kong teams were mainly self-financing, with funds raised predominantly by the players and by sponsorships from local companies.

How times have changed. The HKCA, as an Associate Member of the International Cricket Council, now receives substantial sums from the proceeds of World Cup matches and remains responsible for the structure of cricket in Hong Kong, which is now akin to a business enterprise – even the annual accounts for the year ended 31.12.93 extended to 14 typed pages!

Fifteen years ago, we were talking about 'peanuts'. In 1993 total income amounted to $711,575, an increase of 123% over 1992, while expenditure reached an alarming $1,085,506 with three individual items alone exceeding $100,000!

Administration fee (paid staff)	$162,600
National Coach expenses	213,776
Visiting teams deficit	195,928
	$572,304

The deficit for the year of $373,931 was only cushioned by the exceptional income of $351,150 received during the year from the shared proceeds of the World Cup Tournament.

In 1996, total income had increased to $1,711,920, an increase of 140% since 1993, mainly from the ICC $534,375, the Sports Development Board subvention $445,147 and the surplus from the International Sixes $319,168. Total expenditure at $1,678,378 included $686,956 (deficit on the development programme and schools coaching), $254,895 (administration), and $106,800 (deficit on Scoreboard). Ground improvements at $47,770 was $102,725 less than in the previous year. While a small accumulated surplus was carried forward, the bank overdraft increased slightly to $82,978.

The HKCA had to introduce a development programme and the junior clinics in an endeavour to improve the standard at junior levels and to interest the indigenous population in the game, and by making the game available to a wider sector. This would also strengthen its claim to the retention of its diminishing cricket grounds.

I have been back to Hong Kong five times since my retirement in early 1990, and have noticed a decline in the general standard of league cricket. In my opinion, I think the HKCA is spreading its wings too wide, bearing in mind the diminishing availability of talent due to the exodus of the services and expatriates, who have been the backbone of the leagues. As the qualification rules for international cricket are now much stricter, a concentration on the Under 19 squad, who also play league cricket, should be the main objective.

Hong Kong Association of Cricket Umpires and Scorers

Until the formation of the Hong Kong Panel of Umpires (the Panel) in 1963–64, affiliated to the Association of Cricket Umpires (ACU), London, this most important aspect of the great game of cricket was mainly carried out by 'volunteers', players and ex-players, each team providing its own umpire. In fact, even after the Panel was formed there were not enough qualified umpires to supervise every First Division/Sunday league match. The Second Division/Saturday league sides have continued to provide their own umpires to this day.

During the prewar triangular Interports in Hong Kong, players and appointed officials from Hong Kong, Malaya and Shanghai would act as umpires. Arthur Bliss and J P Robinson were two well known prewar KCC umpires. They umpired league matches, friendlies, club matches against Malaya and Shanghai and Interports. The author's father, George Hall, travelled to Shanghai with the Hong Kong team in 1930 as the official Hong Kong scorer.

Among some of the active umpires in the mid-1960s were Bert Mellowes, Bert Varty, John Hackling, Maurice Roberts, Bernard Moore, Bob Henderson, John Morgan, Frank Apps, Wally Hampton, George Lemay (the original designer of the now famous HK scorebook) and Dave Smith. Several of these gentlemen can be seen, in their long white coats, on pictures around the walls of the two major clubs in Hong Kong.

At the time the Panel was formed, a gentleman called Michael Shu, who umpired with the DBS first team, became the first Chinese umpire, one of the Colony's 12 qualified umpires.

Dickie Bird, highly strung, given to mannerism and conscientious in the extreme, now world renowned, became a first class umpire in England in May 1970. He said:

You can't coach umpires, umpires are born not made. You can learn the laws backwards and forwards and every way there is, but that isn't the secret of successful umpiring. Knowing the laws is only a small part. The real job is standing up to the pressure and commanding the respect of the players.

Fortunately for Hong Kong, where all the players, umpires and scorers are unpaid, the pressures on umpires are not as great as in countries where the game is played on a professional basis, controlled to a large extent by the marketing men, where money now dictates much of the play, pushing good sportsmanship onto the sideline.

By the early 1970s, Bert Mellowes had assumed the role of instructor and, quite deservedly, by 1976 had been honoured with Life Membership of the Panel. Those aspiring umpires who attended his courses were impressed by the wisdom, enthusiasm, enjoyment and wit he showed in putting over the then 46 laws of the game. His list of how an umpire

69

should conduct himself on the field of play remains as relevant today as it did then.

The Panel was strengthened by several qualified British and Australian Forces personnel from the 1970s onwards, with Dean Khan, John Stainton, Bill Hallett, Tony Millett and Tom Green all serving as officers of the Panel.

There have been many 'incidents' between players and umpires over the years, but nothing that could not be resolved amicably. One such incident took place at KCC between the Police and the Saracens, when the umpire walked off the field after he had been given 'a torrent of foul, abusive language which was most deporable and unacceptable.'

The author was batting at the time this so-called incident took place. He didn't hear what the bowler said, but it certainly upset the Forces umpire, who walked off the field, muttering that such behaviour was unacceptable.

One of the earliest postwar lady scorers (KCC-1953) and (Hong Kong/ Malaya-1955) was Mickie Chamberlain, who introduced the coloured pencil system. She first scored in a Western Command match at Chester in 1942, where her husband was a senior W/O. Other names that followed included Gerry Stokes (Police), Eddie Cunningham (Centaurs), Bill Conway (LSW, later to become Manager of the HKCC), Shelagh Dewar and Margaret Miles (HKCC), Janet Bygate, Mary Cooper and Peter Horton (KCC) and Monica Reeve (KGV), who became an official scorer for England in India in 1993. D Khan, Chairman H K Panel 1976–77, said:

> We in Hong Kong suffer from the calls of Crown and commerce which cause so much movement in the cricket population. So all too frequently we find ourselves searching around for anyone willing and able to stand, and let us bear in mind too, that Hong Kong has quite a full and lengthy cricket season. Training has been given to anyone aspiring to become an umpire. Most players recognise that an umpire is an important adjunct to the game; we have no axe to grind except our love for the game.
>
> D Khan, Chairman, HK Panel, 1976–77

With the retirement of Bert Mellowes to Australia in 1978, instruction for prospective umpires (and refresher courses for established ones) relied upon British Forces instructors coming out to Hong Kong. Courses and subsequent examinations were under the tutelage of retired RAF officer Bill Fawley, with the final oral examination conducted under the keen scrutiny of the then Chief Justice, Sir Denys Roberts.

The post of Training Officer was established in the early 1980s with

Alan Swift as the incumbent. Alan must like the job, because in 1998, he was still conducting courses as Bert Mellowes had done before him, always striving to improve the standard of umpiring in Hong Kong. Sir Denys continued to administer the oral examinations until he retired from Hong Kong in 1988, helped out by Syd Gale, a UK umpire and examiner, who visited Hong Kong from time to time during his wintering 'annuals' in Bangkok.

The Panel in 1982 included stalwarts such as Tony Gough, Geoff Lever, Nigel Grandfield, Tom Handley, Jim Middleton, Roger Nissim and Alan Swift. Other active members were Dave Stevenson and Peter Anderson (now Chief Executive of Somerset CCC).

At the AGM in 1982, it was proposed that the committee should revise the Constitution. In March 1986, the Umpires Panel was registered under the Hong Kong Societies Ordinance, as the Association of Cricket Umpires – Hong Kong (ACU-HK). This was later changed to the Hong Kong Association of Cricket Umpires (HKACU), and in June 1994 was further amended to the Hong Kong Association of Cricket Umpires and Scorers (HKACUS), to bring it into line with the ACUS, the parent body in England. The later amendments to the Constitution and re-registration as a Society were mainly carried out by the author – President from 1988 to 1990 and now an honoured Life Member of the HKACUS.

In the late 1980s a Scorers' Representative was first elected onto the committee and a good deal of valuable work was carried out by Jean Lever, Linda Goodwin and Kathy Walker. Kathy took on the role of Scorers' Instructor and her courses proved both popular and successful, resulting in the addition to the scorers' list of Kay Barnett and Alice Jones – Alice achieved a remarkable 100% in her examination.

Other Sunday league scorers have included Meera Chandran (IRC), Gopa Chakrabarti, Noel Morris (KCC Infidels and the composer of their team song which has echoed round the KCC bar on many a Sunday evening), Gayle Gill, Linda Goodwin, Corinne Varty, Suzi Ledger, Arati Nimkar and Jenny Lethbridge, who is the present Scorers' Representative. Jean and Kathy have been instrumental in updating George Lemay's marvelous scorebook to make it more applicable for the game today.

A recent umpires' course and examination has added a number of new faces to the list: Rod Starling, now umpiring regularly since his playing seasons with the Police and KCC have ceased; Mike Walsh, HKCC Captain of Cricket; Bob Fotheringham, an HKCC and Hong Kong Representative stalwart for many years; Bob Painter and Martin Darke (HKCC) and Paul Guest and Chris Pyke (Police). Kevin Eaton, a newcomer from Australia, has been ever-present on the field in

71

1993–94, and Mike Tetlow has maintained the presence of excellent Services umpires.

Over the years the Hong Kong umpires and scorers have handled First Division/Sunday league and Rothman's Cup matches – Interports – visiting tours – Silk Cut Single Wicket (Lever and Swift) – International Sixes (Lever, Starling and Swift were privileged to share the duties in the first Sixes with the West Indies' Steve Bucknor, India's Papan Punjabi and Australia's Tony Crafter, in deciding the fate of some of the world's greatest cricketers from all the Test nations) – ICC matches (Lever was asked to umpire the 1994 final in Kenya between the United Arab Emirates and Kenya but was unable to change his flight schedule, much to his and Hong Kong cricket's great disappointment) – South-East Asian Competition – Volvo and Tuanku Ja'afar Cup tournaments.

The HKACUS Committee in 1997–98:

President	Nigel Grandfield
Chairman	Herb Whitlock
Secretary	Alan Swift
Treasurer	R R Sengupta
Training Officer	Alan Swift
Scorers' Representative	Jenny Lethbridge
Fixture Secretary	Bob Fotheringham
HKCA Representative (League/Cup committee)	Nigel Grandfield
HKCA Executive Member	Alan Swift

With such dedicated personnel in charge, the HKACUS remains a thriving body, determined to maintain the high standards of umpiring and scoring that has become a byword on the Hong Kong cricket scene.

Umpires and Scorers officially selected for Overseas Tours

	Umpires	*Country*
1979	Tony Gough	S-E Australia
1980	Bernard Moore	Malaysia & Singapore
1984	Geoff Lever	Bangladesh (S-E Asian Competition)
1990	Alan Swift	Holland (ICC)
1992	Rod Starling	Singapore (S-E Asian Competition)
1993	Mike Tetlow	Bangkok (Tuanku Ja'Afar Cup)
1994	Geoff Lever	Kenya (ICC)
1997	Herb Whitlock	Malaysia (ICC)

Scorers	Country
1982 Noel Morris	England (ICC)
1987 Jean Lever	Singapore (Interport)
1992 Suzi Ledger	Singapore (S-E Asian Competition)
1993 Kathy Walker	Bangkok (Tuanku Ja'Afar Cup)
1994 Linda Goodwin	Kenya (ICC)
1997 Arati Nimkar	Malaysia (ICC)

Jangu Vachha – Umpire of the Year Award

Winners		Winners	
1973–74	Bert Mellowes	1986–87	Alan Swift
1974–75	Dean Khan	1987–88	Alan Swift
1975–76	John Stainton	1988–89	Alan Swift
1976–77	Tony Gough	1989–90	Tony Gough &
1977–78	Tom Green		Nigel Grandfield
1978–79	John Morgan	1990–91	Simon Friend
1979–80	Don Cruikshank	1991–92	Tony Gough
1980–81	Tony Gough	1992–93	Mike Tetlow
1981–82	Alan Swift	1993–94	Alan Swift
1982–83	Trevor Cutts	1994–95	Tony Gough
1983–84	Geoff Lever	1995–96	Bob Fotheringham
1984–85	Roy Green	1996–97	Herb Whitlock
1985–86	Alan Swift		

Hong Kong Association of Cricket Umpires & Scorers

Honorary Life Members:	H F Mellowes	Jean Lever
	P A Hall	Linda Goodwin
	A R Gough	T Handley
	G H Lever	

Umpires Panel	Chairman	Representative
1955–56	F/S. C Robinson (RAF)	
1956–66		
1966 67		J Hackling
1967–68		
1968–69		

73

Hong Kong Panel of Cricket Umpires

	Chairman	Secretary
1969–70		Dr M Leahy
1970–71		Dr M Leahy
1971–72		M S Roberts
1972–73	W J Hampton	Lt Col R F Pierce
1973–74*	H F Mellowes	M S Roberts
1974–75	H F Mellowes	Sgt T Groves
1975–76	H F Mellowes	D Khan
1976–77	D Khan	J Stainton
1977–78	M B C Teale	M B C Teale
1978–79	A R Gough	Capt J Morgan
1979–80		A R Gough
1980–81		B More
1981–82	A R Gough	J Middleton
1982–83		WO2(SQMS) A Millett
1983–84		

Association of Cricket Umpires – Hong Kong

	President	Chairman
1984–85	Sir Denys Roberts	A R Gough
1985–86	Sir Denys Roberts	A R Gough
1986–87	Sir Denys Roberts	A R Gough
1987–88	Sir Denys Roberts	A R Gough

Hong Kong Assocation of Cricket Umpires

1988–89	P A Hall	G H Lever
1989–90	P A Hall	G H Lever
1990–91	A R Gough	G H Lever
1991–92	A R Gough	G H Lever
1992–93	A R Gough	G H Lever
1993–94	A R Gough	G H Lever

Hong Kong Association of Cricket Umpires & Scorers

1994–95	A R Gough	G H Lever
1995–96	G H Lever	T Handley
1996–97	A Swift	H Whitlock
1997–98	N Grandfield	H Whitlock

* affiliated to the Association of Cricket Umpires & Scorers, London, England.

THE CLUBS AND ASSOCIATIONS

Chinese Recreation Club

In 1910, through the efforts of Sir Kai Ho Kai and Sir Po-san Wei Yuk, Chinese members of the Legislative Council, and other influential Chinese gentlemen, a playing field for the Chinese community was allotted by the Government at Causeway Bay. In 1911, the Chinese Recreation Club (CRC) was founded to promote games and other athletic pastimes and to encourage social activities between members. All Chinese gentlemen were eligible to join. Soon after, with donations from enthusiastic supporters, the ground was levelled and turfed.

In 1912, mainly through the issue of debentures to members, a modest two-storey clubhouse, designed by Mr A R F Raven (who in 1932 designed the KCC clubhouse), was built by Mr Lam Woo at cost, on the club site in Tung Lo Wan Road. Mr Raven was made an honorary life member of the club, but there was no mention of any recognition for Mr Lam Woo!

The present CRC is a far cry from its original concept, when there were only 120 members. The present two-storey clubhouse provides a restaurant, bars, health centre, badminton court, billiards and snooker room, while row upon row of floodlit all-weather tennis courts, swimming pools and a car park have replaced the original playing fields.

Cricket began soon after the ground was turfed, for in 1914, a CRC team with the legendary tennis star Ng Sze Kwong, played against the KCC. The CRC's cricket eleven comprised Chinese and Eurasian players, mainly former students of Queen's and St Joseph's Colleges.

The following are First Division league matches unless otherwise stated:

1918   CRC: 74 (Ng Sze Kwong 22, C Severn 4–25, W E Dixon 3–5,
                R E O Bird 3–13)
Mar 2 CSCC: 87 (C Severn 29, Un Hew Fan 6–37)

CRC were all out in 21 overs whilst CSCC batted for 32 overs.

1919   CRC: 89 (G Lee 32, Ng Sze Kwong 21, RQMS Allan
                5–33)
Mar 8 Manchesters: 53 (Pte Walker 30, Yew Man Tsun 6–26)

This friendly match on matting was played '... on the military ground at Happy Valley.'

Hong Kong Daily Press

The First Division league batting averages at the end of March 1919 showed Ng Sze Kwong as second, having scored 380 runs (ave. 42.22).

1920 CRC: 162–2 dec (Ho Wing-kin 95, Lo Man-pan 48*)
Feb 27 CSCC: 181–6 (H Bevan 77*)

CSCC batted 39 overs to CRC's 32 in this second team friendly match.

1926 HKCC: 60 (Ng Sze Kwong 5–25)
Nov 20 CRC: 99 (J L Youngsaye 26)

1928 HKCC: 167–7 dec (Capt A G Dobbie 49*, H Owen Hughes 32,
W C Hung 3–26)
Dec 22 CRC: 52 (Tsui Wai-pui 26, Capt Dobbie 4–22)

Tsui Wai-pui 'only player to reach double figures'.

Tsui Wai-pui, with his brother, dominated tennis doubles in Hong Kong for many years. They were the sons of that famous standby of the HKCC, Tsui Ting Wa, whom hundreds of past cricketers had referred to familiarly as 'Tadpole'.

Others who played for CRC included: W H Sling, H Hung, Tsui Hung-pui, H C Hung, H S Lee, K L Chau and Yew Man Hon, captain of the second XI in the early 1920s (also see scoresheet of match against HKU). Cricket continued to be played until the late 1920s, when, probably due to diminishing interest, coupled with a growing demand from tennis members, the ground was made over to tennis for which it was now well known.

CRC came through the Pacific war better than most recreation clubs, due to its use by the Japanese occupation forces as a sports club. With a current membership of over 2,000, CRC remains the premier Chinese club for tennis in Hong Kong. Many of Hong Kong's top tennis players, past and present, are members, with Dr Stanley Ho as its President.

Chinese Recreation Club v Hong Kong University

20 November 1920

CRC

		Bowling				
Lo Man-pan, b Yeoh	17					
George Lee, c Samy b Yeoh	22		*O*	*M*	*R*	*W*
Wei Yee-san, c Mogra b Hunt	1					
Un Hew-fan, c Samy b Yeoh	39	D K Samy	10.4	3	24	1
*Sin Man-ping, b Hunt	4	C H Yeoh	17	4	51	4
Henry Ching, lbw Hunt	6	H C Hunt	10	1	37	4
Charlie Choa, b Hunt	0	I T Pun	4	–	15	1

James Wong, c Barney b Yeoh	5
Lai Kuen, b Pun	12
Hung Man-to, not out	15
Wu Pak-fook, b Samy	7
Extras	18
Total	146

Hong Kong University

		Bowling				
H C Hunt, b Ching	2					
I T Pun, lbw Ching	6		*O*	*M*	*R*	*W*
T L Cheah, b Ching	3					
D K Samy, not out	67	George Lee	11	1	28	–
T E Yeoh, not out	28	Henry Ching	10	1	38	3
R W Barney		Un Hew-fan	3	–	21	–
K S Cheah		Sin Man-ping	4	–	19	–
K E Mogra	Did not bat					
F Baker						
M K Yue						
C H Yeoh						
Extras	9					
3 wickets	115					

Match drawn.

*alias G A V Hall, father of the author, who later joined KCC.

Civil Service Cricket Club – Centaurs

In the first match ever to be played in the Hongkong Cricket League on 24 October 1903, one of the new sides, the Civil Service Cricket Club (CSCC) played Craigengower (CCC) at Happy Valley, CCC scoring 71 for 4 wickets in reply to CSCC's 100 runs.

Stalwarts of that early period were R C Witchell, G A Woodcock (who later became a Magistrate), P T Lamble, H T Jackman and Dr Atkinson (the Principal Medical Officer and Member of the Executive and Legislative Councils, the governing bodies in the Colony).

1904	CSCC:	60–7 (R A Witchell 24, Raven 4–18, Weaser 3–16)
Mar 5	RE:	35 (P T Lamble 6–22, R A Witchell 3–0)

Other CSCC players: Hon. Dr Atkinson, G A Woodcock,
H T Jackman, J Lander, H J Gidley, W H Woolley, L E Brett,
F T Robins and W Pitt.

Although the foremost cricket ground in Hong Kong was Chater Road, the home of the HKCC from 1851 until 1975, most of the early cricket in Hong Kong was played at Happy Valley, which after being drained in 1846, provided the largest flat area of land. The CSCC's home ground at Happy Valley was on the site recently vacated by The Royal Hong Kong Regiment (The Volunteers). On 10 April 1909, the *Hong Kong Daily Press* reported:

> Now they have a permanent habitation. A handsome pavilion of bricks and tiles has been erected on the site of the old quarters and with a nice garden in front it will look perhaps the most picturesque in the valley.

The clubhouse with bar, dressing and bathrooms cost around $3,500. Its inauguration was expected on Thursday, 14 April, when it was hoped the Governor, Sir Frederick Lugard, would perform the opening ceremony.

1909	CSCC:	194	(R O Hutchison 67, H R Phelips 63, T E Pearce 6–45)
Mar 27	HKCC'B':	195–9	(H Hancock 68, A O Lang 37, Comdr Lewis 36, S Moore 29*, L E Brett 5–76)

1920	CSCC:	149	(R C Witchell 46, Capt Davis 4–38, Gnr Baines 4–54)
Feb 27	RGA:	205–4	(Capt Oliver 93, Capt Davis 84)

The RGA only batted for 27 overs, whilst CSCC took 49 at Happy Valley – '... the first league match for several weeks.'

1924	Royal Navy:	52	(W Edmonds 7–22)
Mar 2	CSCC:	48	(Pay Com Osborne 4–12, PO Tisley 3–11)

'... narrow win for the Navy at Happy Valley.' A Second Division match.

1926	CSCC:	170–4	(G R Sayer 69, E Fincher 56*)
Nov 27	IRC:	112–6	(S Ismail 47*)

1928	HKCC:	163–4 dec	(Capt A G Dobbie 66*, H Owen Hughes 33*, A Hayward 30)
Dec 1	CSCC:	92	(G R Sayer 27, C D Wales 4–40)

HKCC batted for 36 overs, while CSCC were all out in 28 overs.

1929   CSCC: 76   (Rev E K Quick 6–39) A friendly match.
Jan 26 HKCC: 173–9 (L W Hayward 31, Quick 31, extras 34,
                         W H Edmunds 7–39

CSCC won the First Division championship in the 1920–21 season, with the redoubtable Witchell still leading the batting, along with schoolmaster J de Rome (Queen's College) and G H Piercy, F J Ling and Geoffrey Sayer. In 1924–25, CSCC achieved a fine double, winning both the First and Second Division championships. Sayer was still batting well in the first team. In the 1940–41 season, the last before the Pacific war, CSCC lost a closely contested match by two wickets to the KCC, the eventual double league champions.

Geoffrey Sayer, Interport cricketer and later Director of Education, was largely responsible for promoting the game of cricket, both in the Civil Service and in the schools, in the years preceding the Pacific war.

1931   University: 194–2 dec (D J N Anderson 110*, A M Rodrigues 59)
Dec 12 CSCC: 131–9   (J E Richardson 36, R Wood 30,
                           E L Gosano 3–10, D J N Anderson 3–12)

This was a first team friendly played at Pokfulam.

1932   CSCC: 140–9 dec (J E Richardson 46, B D Evans 43,
                            E L Gosano 4–24, D J N Anderson 4–22)
Feb 13 University: 140   (D McLellan 4–13)

'... the last University man running himself out with the scores level at 140! McLellan was the most successful trundler for the Civil Service.'

Dec 24 CSCC: 134–8 dec (G R Sayer 67, D Anderson 5–39,
                            A T Nomanhboy 2–8)
        University: 129–7 (D Anderson 71, A Rodrigues 24,
                            B D Evans 4–24)

This was a first team friendly played at Happy Valley.

1934   CSCC: 91   (A W Grimmett 28, D Roy 4–16, P B Tata 4–49)
Mar 10 University: 100   (F S Fernando 30, H F Westlake 5–28)

     18 CSCC: 18   (A A Rumjahn 5–14, A R Suffiad 4–3)
        IRC: 30–1

This was a second team friendly!

79

1936   HKCC: 175–7 dec (N P Fox 41*, I S Forbes 34, A E Perry
                     3–36)
Mar 23 CSCC: 204–4   (J E Richardson 104*, A E Perry 29,
                     I McInnes 3–62)

Such players as Bill Colledge (later to join KCC), Ken Attwell, Arthur
Perry (who joined the HKCC Optimists on their formation in 1948), and
Michael Wright (later Director of Public Works), all played leading roles.

Civil Service cricket ceased after the Japanese invasion of Hong Kong in
December 1941. Subsequent looting wrecked the clubhouse and although
efforts were made after the war by a few individuals to rekindle interest,
this failed, due mainly to the absence of many older former members and
the tendency of new civil service recruits joining such clubs as the HKCC
and KCC. Interport players such as George Rowe, Ivor Stanton and Tony
Weller (HKCC) and Pat Dodge (KCC). In October 1949, the Financial
Secretary, declared the CSCC defunct.

On Saturday, 5 October 1957, a group of Government officers led by
Alan Bailey, Jimmy McGregor and Norman Whitley, a prewar cricketer,
formed the Centaurs who joined the league Second Division. Their first
league match at the KGV School ground was against Docklands CC. The
Centaurs were all out for 121 runs, many lbw, and lost by six wickets.
Alan Bailey and Norman Oei scored 40 and 39 respectively.

Why Centaurs? Sir Denys Roberts, who would have qualified as a senior
Centaur, said in his foreword to the booklet *75 Not Out: Seventy-five
Years of Civil Service Cricket in Hong Kong*:

> The first Centaur was the offspring of an adulterous relationship
> between a concupiscent Thessalian King and a cloud shaped like
> Zeus's mistress.

The Centaurs, instead of 'The Hong Kong Government Officers' Team',
are regarded as the Government team composed of civil servants of one
variety or another, although there have been a number of exceptions, especially of late.

Louis Hall recalled in the early 1960s the difficulty in getting certain of
the more senior civil servants to matches in Kowloon:

> One of my abiding impressions of how keen the Centaurs were in the
> 1960s concerns J D 'Jimmy' McGregor and L W R 'Laurie' Mills.
> These two worthies were the rising stars in the Commerce and Indus-
> try Dept – very busy and therefore needing to be collected from the
> old Fire Brigade Building at 12:30 p.m. with a view to crossing on the
> vehicular ferry to the KGV ground in Kowloon. They were rarely

ready so their transport, often myself or Peter Lewington, would proceed to take our place in the queue of cars for the ferry. We then bit our nails until we sighted the two of them encumbered with their cricket gear dashing through the parked cars to collapse on the rear seat.

Although playing well for many seasons, the Centaurs did not win the league title until 1963–64, ably led by Alan Bailey. John Gowler took 110 wickets, which remains the Second Division league record to this day. The title was won again in the 1967–68 season, being shared with the HKCC Nomads. The new star was Bryan Hemshall, who took 47 wickets at an average of only 7.02 runs per wicket. The Centaurs' most successful period was from 1971–72 through to 1974–75, when, under the astute and determined captaincy of Bryan Hemshall, they won the league title three times. Possibly the change of home ground from KGV School to Sookunpoo also played a part. Prominant players during this fruitful period were Jim Danks (Royal Navy CPO), Keith Broadbridge, Tony Hammond, Bryan Hemshall, Jim Hughes, Peter Olsen (also a fire services footballer and team joker), Mark Weedon (ex-Cambridge University), Terry Wood, Nigel French and Martin Lewis.

1975   DBS: 27   (T Wood 7–15, A Hammond 3–12)
Nov 22 Centaurs: 31–0

The league title was won once more in the 1979–80 season. More recent sides, with a greater mix of honorary members, have had disappointing results. However, as Tony Clark, a Centaurs stalwart himself said in *75 Not Out:* '... hope springs eternal'. Another writer said: 'the Centaurs are a team of characters ... striving hard to play cricket fairly and firmly with determination – a flamboyant team who played it hard.' The author can certainly vouch for 'playing it hard', especially under the captaincy of Bryan Hemshall in the 1970s.

Tony Clark, in his history of the CSCC/Centaurs, singled out two outstanding postwar Centaurs players who have given much time to and provided valuable service for cricket in Hong Kong. Bryan Hemshall – apart from leading the Centaurs so successfully during their 'golden period', has also been a very able and thorough Secretary and Chairman of the HKCA, deeply involved with the administration of the game in Hong Kong. Alan Bailey – one of the founder members of the Centaurs and a performer in every department of the game – also served on the HKCA Executive Committee, and was responsible for producing the cricket square at the HKCC's new ground at Wong Nai Chung Gap, which was successfully transplanted from the Chater Road ground.

81

The author would add the names of Tony Clark and Graham Fletcher, for their own contributions to Hong Kong cricket, apart from their cricketing enthusiasm – Tony with the 'pen' and Graham with the 'camera'. Also the late Eddie Cunningham, for his many years of dedicated service as the loyal Centaurs scorer. Many persons, too numerous to name, have also played their part in making the Centaurs a successful side, not only in results, but in the way the game was played.

Geoff Fawcett, one of the earlier members of the Centaurs, remembers:

All the team were genuine civil servants. Our attitude was very Gower-like (if not our skills). Once BGH came on the scene, we were more Gooch-led, but with better results! But it was more fun before, and I think we set a better example of sportsmanship when we played the lads at DBS, KGV and later Island School.

1989   Centaurs: 216–4   (S Brew 107*, A Ruxton 41)
Dec 30   Witherers: 133   (A Ruxton 5–37)

This brief history would be short-changed without a reference to a Centaurs overseas social cricket excursion.

The Centaurs have made periodic tours to Thailand, with matches culminating at the RBSC in Bangkok, for the Bailey-Morris Trophy (after Alan Bailey, co-founder and one-time President of Centaurs, and Eric Morris, doyen of RBSC cricket). Prior to the 'big game', the Centaurs usually sampled Chiangmai hospitality in northern Thailand:

... where their hosts' overwhelming hospitality saw to it that no-one got to bed before 3:00 a.m. in an insidious attempt to ensure that the first overseas team to visit Chiangmai would forget the true purpose of their visit. The sight of the ground the next morning was enough to make the bleary eye and sore head forget their excesses. The grass track is reminiscent of an English ground, ringed by huge trees, and with seating and refreshments under a marquee.

The author had, during his cricket playing days in Hong Kong, always found the Centaurs to be a tough nut to crack, but a team who enjoyed their game of cricket.

Centaurs – Batting Performances 1965–66 to 1993–94

Season	Player	500 runs plus	Centuries
1965–66	D Snoxall	541 at 31.82 (3) (only batsman 500 plus)	
1969–70	J March		117* v PRC & 100* v DBS
1971–72	J March	640 at 33.68 (10)	
	K Broadbridge	645 at 29.32	
	J Danks	544 at 25.90	
1972–73	K Broadbridge	501 at 25.05	
	P Olsen		105 v PRC
	J Hughes		102* v KCC Saracens
1973–74	N French		102* v HKU
1975–76	P Olsen	604 at 46.46(7)	125* v KCC Crusaders
1976–77	N French	621 at 32.68	124 v HKCC Witherers & 102 v DBS
	P Olsen	573 at 31.83	
	B G Hemshall	727 at 31.61	
1977–78	P Olsen	510 at 39.23	
	B G Hemshall	513 at 30.18	
1978–79	J Hughes	643 at 40.19(7)	102 v KGV
	P Olsen	731 at 38.47(9)	
	N French	673 at 37.39	115 v HKCC Witherers
	B G Hemshall		135* v HKU
1979–80	P Olsen	1062 at 55.89 (3) (70 runs plus 7 times)	111* v CCC & 107 v KGV
	B G Hemshall	804 at 36.55	100* v DBS
	B G Hemshall & L Hall 213* (1st) v DBS (3)		
1980–81	P Olsen	698 at 43.63 (10)	
	B G Hemshall	641 at 35.61	
1981–82	P Olsen	598 at 42.71	
	J Murphy	692 at 38.44	160 v Army
1982–83	P Olsen	586 at 83.71(1)	131* v KCC Saracens
	J Murphy		103* v DBS
1983–84	P Olsen	597 at 45.92	102* v DBS
1984–85	B G Hemshall	577 at 32.06	107* v HKU
1988–89	M Burrell	524 at 32.75	118* v HKU & 101* v Police Strollers
	D Atkinson	540 at 30.00	107* v Kai Tak
1989–90	S Brew	982 at 89.27(1)	116* v Islanders, 112* v St. G 107* v HKCC Witherers & 104* v KCC Tartars
	A Ebrahim	541 at 31.82	105 v KGV
	M Peck	525 at 30.88	
1990–91	M Burrell		103 v HKCC Gap Ramblers
1991–92	A Ruxton		102* v CCC
1993–94	G Baker		121 v KGV

(1)   Position in averages
(1st) Partnership position in table

Centaurs – Bowling Performances 1965–66 to 1993–94

Season	Player	50 wickets plus	7 plus (for 50 runs or less)
1965–66	P Lewington		7–41 v CCC
1966–67	V H Andrews	55 at 9.22 (4)	7–37 v Army
1968–69	B G Hemshall	50 at 13.08 (10)	
1969–70	B G Hemshall	65 at 10.95 (9)	
	J C A Hammond	56 at 11.42	8–29 v PRC
1970–71	B G Hemshall	52 at 11.09 (6)	
1971–72	B G Hemshall	74 at 12.55 (2)	7–33 v IRC
	J C A Hammond	67 at 15.72	
1972–73	J C A Hammond	57 at 9.07 (1)	8–30 v DBS
	B G Hemshall		7–49 v HKCC Nomads
1973–74	J C A Hammond	67 at 14.67	7–42 v CCC
	B G Hemshall	64 at 16.94	
1974–75	T Wood	50 at 12.38 (7)	6– 5 v KCC Crusaders (Excep.)
	J C A Hammond		7–14 v HKCC Nomads
1975–76	T Wood	73 at 12.33 (5)	7–15 v DBS & 7–67 v HKU
	J C A Hammond		'hat-trick' v St George's
1976–77	R Toes	54 at 10.30 (2)	
	C C Roberts		'hat-trick' v DBS
1977–78	M Hislop	67 at 12.85 (6)	8–49 v St George's
1978–79	M Hislop	55 at 14.62 (4)	
1982–83	G Fletcher		9–22 v DBS
	A McLeish		'hat-trick' v Islanders
1983–84	R Dalgleish		7–10 v Police Strollers
	J Hughes		'hat-trick' v KCC Crusaders
1986–87	R Dalgleish		7–32 v KCC Crusaders

(1) Position in averages

Club de Recreio

The Club de Recreio started as a Co-operative Savings Society in 1905 with 19 members. The Society prospered, and within 15 months, the subscribed capital was refunded and the profits were applied towards the formation of a club with the chosen name 'Club de Recreio', which in English means 'Recreation Club', with a registered membership of 35. The club occupied very humble premises in Barrow Terrace, Granville Road, Kowloon. Recreio was officially incorporated on 13 November 1911 'to promote the game of tennis and other athletic sports and pastimes, and in particular social intercourse among members of the Portuguese community in the Colony of Hong Kong.'

The seven signatories to the Memorandum and Articles of Association were:

C A da Roza,	Lowe, Bingham & Matthews
A M Roza,	Pereira, Broker
B Basto,	Noronha & Co.
V Gonsalves,	David Sassoon & Co.
J J Remedios,	International Banking Corporation
F V Vandenbert,	Reiss & Co.
J M F Basto,	Cruz, Basto & Co.

A vacant piece of land situated on the corner of Nathan and Kimberley Roads was leased and a clubhouse was built, together with two tennis courts.

As more Portuguese families began to live on the Kowloon Peninsula, larger recreational facilities were required. The Government, in recognising the importance of the Portuguese community as permanent residents of the Colony, offered Recreio the choice of a site at King's Park, in the Town Planning Scheme of 1922.

The present club premises were officially opened on 4 February 1928. In his reply to the President's address of welcome, His Excellency the Governor, Sir Cecil Clementi, said: 'The growth of Kowloon is well illustrated by the growth of the Club de Recreio, which began in 1905 with 19 members and it now has 220 members.'

After the leasing of the spacious grounds at King's Park, cricket was learnt, with special encouragement and assistance from the HKCC. The following were all First Division matches:

1927　　Recreio: 174–4 dec　(R C Reed 42, H A Alves 40*, E de Sousa
　　　　　　　　　　　　　　35*, H M Xavier 33)
Nov 19　PRC:　　111　　　(W E Meadows 21, W Dyer 21, R Reed 3–19)
　　　　　　　　　　　　　　at Recreio.

Other Recreio players were: D P Xavier, J E Noronha, L J Guterres, M Pinna, D Lopes, F H Cavalho, and C M Sousa

1934　　Recreio:　　82　　(A P Pereira 24*, S A Reed 4–29, E L Gosano
　　　　　　　　　　　　　　3–18, H Ozorio 3–27)
Feb 2　　University: 91–3　(E L Gosano 30*, B K Ng 27, L T Ride 26)
　　　　　　　　　　　　　　at Recreio.

1939　　Recreio: 68 (A E Perry 3 wickets)
Jan 28　CSCC:　 59 (A T Lay 22, E L Gosano 5–18, H Ozorio 5–37)
　　　　　　　　　　　　at the CSCC ground.

Recreio won the First Division championship in the 1938–39 season with such players as Dr Albert Rodrigues (Capt) and Dr E L (Eddie) Gosano, who had played for Hong Kong against Shanghai in the last prewar Interport in 1936 in Shanghai.

When league cricket was resumed in 1948–49, Recreio won the First Division championship, with five Gosano brothers all having a hand in the pie. G N (Gerry) Gosano, 'one of Hong Kong's finest post-war sportsmen', also played for Hong Kong against Shanghai in 1947 and 1948, the last in the series of these Hong Kong/Shanghai Interports.

1948   Recreio: 196–3 dec (A P Pereira 54, G N Gosano 51,
Jan   L G Gosano 50 ret'd)
        CCC: 54   (L G Gosano 5–13)

1961   IRC: 57   (Mahmood 21*, A P Pereira 6–17, M Barros 4–40)
Jan 28 Recreio: 58–8 (A E Noronha 17, O Adem 5–18)

'The man responsible for wrecking the Recreio innings was Osman Odem, IRC's pint-sized off-spinner, who, in one glorious over, captured four wickets including the 'hat-trick' without conceding a run.'

Recreio won their last senior championship title in 1961–62. The decline in Recreio's cricketing fortunes thereafter coincided with the migration of many Portuguese families from Hong Kong to Australia, Canada and the USA in the 1950s and 1960s.

1967   Recreio: 97
Sep 20 Saracens: 49 (R M Barros 6–10)

'KCC Saracens found Mike Barros impossible to handle at King's Park only Reg Cooper reached double figures.'

Oct 28 Recreio: 152–7
        Army: 74   (R M Barros 8–31)

'Barros bowling with his old fire and zip smashed through the Army batting at Sookunpoo.'

This migration had a dramatic effect on the ability of Recreio to raise a cricket eleven. When Portuguese cricketers were again involved in winning the First Division, it was as the Cavaliers in 1968–69, a team mix of players mainly from Recreio and CCC.

1970   Cavaliers: 207–6 dec (G Lalchandani 88, R Lalchandani 48)
        Army: 134–5   (R Daniel 70*, I Vaughan-Arbuckle 50)

Mar   Cavaliers: 213
           LSW: 48 (C Myatt 7–21)

The Portuguese were amongst Hong Kong's keenest and most versatile sportsmen, excelling in cricket, hockey, lawn bowls, tennis, baseball and softball. Unfortunately, cricket ceased to be played on the Recreio ground after the 1969–70 season. Non-Portuguese Associate Members were then introduced by the club committee to offset the decreasing Portuguese membership.

The original one-storey clubhouse with the verandah now closed in is still at King's Park, with hockey, lawn bowls and tennis being played, tennis predominating on grass and on artificial surfaces. Lisbello D'Alla-cantara Sarrazola Xavier was the club's first Presidente, whilst Arnaldo de Oliveira Sales 'Sonny' remains its present long-standing Presidente.

Soldiers blow up

Mike Barros and Chappie Remedios, Recreio's all-swing attack, ignited a fuse under Army, and the league leaders blew up in the most sensational cricket match of the season 1967–68 on 4 February 1967 at King's Park. Barros, a chunky left-hander, and Remedios, a right-hander with the ability to 'wobble' the ball in the air, shattered the complacency of the soldiers completely after Recreio had been dismissed for a paltry 73 runs.

Recreio		*Army*	
J Basto, c Holman b Paul	9	A Vivian, c Gosano b Remedios	9
H Barros, b Broomes	3	K Hamblin, c L Remedios b Remedios	0
J Gosano, c Holman b Paul	0	I Vaughan-Arbuckle, b Barros	0
D Gosano, run out	25	J Holman, b Barros	0
G Souza, c Holman b Paul	2	P Allamby, lbw Barros	0
D E Remedios, b Davison	7	L Guy, b Remedios	0
D Castro, st Holman b Paul	12	W Kinkaid, lbw Barros	0
M Barros, c Holman b Paul	0	G Broomes, b Barros	0
W McGrann, b Davison	3	M Davison, b Remedios	5
C Yvanovich, not out	5	J Arnold, b Barros	0
L E Remedios, b Davison	4	G Paul, not out	1
Extras	3	Extras	1
Total	73	Total	16

Fall of wickets: 1–13,2–13,3–13,4–16   1–6,2–10,3–10,4–10,5–10,6–10,7–10,
5–37,6–56,7–56,8–63,9–67   8–15,9–15

Bowling

	O	M	R	W		O	M	R	W
G Broomes	6	1	20	1	M Barros	8	3	7	6
G Paul	10	1	41	5	D Remedios	7.5	4	8	4
M Davison	4.5	1	9	3					

Recreio won by 57 runs.

The author was playing at KCC that Saturday afternoon and went into the club bar after the match. He noticed a West Indian, 'Granny' Broomes, sitting in the corner of the bar looking completely dumbfounded and shaking his head! 'Man, how can it have happened, we were all out for 16 and the captain scored 9!!' With Barros and Remedios at Recreio, anything could happen and often did. Very few sides could score 100 runs on that wicket facing those bowlers. Mind you, other teams could cause as much havoc there, so you never knew who was going to come out on top in a King's Park encounter.

Any history of Club de Recreio, no matter how brief, which does not speak highly of the sporting Gosano family, is not in the opinion of the author a deserving one. The Gosano family was a part of Portuguese sporting history in Hong Kong, and as such, deserves a special place in this history.

'Cricket is a game not normally taken up by the Portuguese.'
Dr E L Gosano, January 1994

Eddie Gosano's grandfather, Leonardo Jose Gosano, was born in Tojal, Portugal. The Gosanos were farmers. Grandfather Gosano came out east and was an ensign attached to the Police Guard of Macau, retiring with the rank of Major on 12 November 1891. Eddie's father, Julio Jesus dos Passos Gosano, was born in Macau on 24 August 1882. He married Adeliza Atomasia Maria Marques at the Roman Catholic Cathedral in Hong Kong on 15 September 1906. They had seven sons and two daughters. Eddie's father died in Hong Kong in 1923. Also very sadly, Carlos, the third son and first to play cricket for Recreio, died when only 25. In 1969, there was another family tragedy, when Gerry, the dominant sporting member of the family, who played 'virtually every sport with in-born ability, excelling at cricket and softball', died aged 45.

The two eldest brothers, Lino and Bertie, were brilliant soccer players, Lino being considered – 'the finest Portuguese footballer the Colony ever produced.' All seven brothers played baseball and softball, with 3 to 6 being members of prewar champion baseball and softball teams. Eddie, Luigi and Zinho (five, seven and nine in the family) were members of the

88

Recreio cricket championship side of 1938–39. When Recreio captured the title again in 1948–49, amazingly, five of the brothers were involved: Bertie, Eddie, Luigi, Gerry, Zinho and Lino as 12th man. Eddie played cricket for Hong Kong against Shanghai in 1936, while Gerry played for Hong Kong against Shanghai in 1947 and 1948. Eddie, Gerry and Bertie also played hockey for Hong Kong.

They were endowed with 'natural ability', so it was their fielding in cricket that was outstanding – they would catch anything, anywhere, were quick onto the ball and could throw accurately – all part of the baseball/ softball upbringing which developed quick reflexes and co-ordination. As batsmen and bowlers, they were less predictable, relying more as batsmen on their keen eye and willingness to give the ball a 'good belting.' But it was their natural ability which made them formidable sportsmen.Unfortunately for certain Gosanos, the cricketing hierarchy at the time of their prominence, still tended to incline toward the 'Pukka Sahib' fraternity.

The author knew many of these brothers and played cricket against their sons. The Gosano name in Hong Kong sporting circles was revered and much talked about. This is just a small tribute to their sporting memory.

Bowling Performances 1965–66 to 1969–70

Season	Player	50 wickets plus	7 plus (for less than 50 runs)
1965–66	R M Barros	47 at 8.43 (2)	9–33 v Army, 7–19 v Police & 7–19 v Saracens
1966–67	R M Barros	52 at 10.35 (4)	
	D E D'Almada Remedios		'hat-trick' v Templars
1967–68	R M Barros	70 at 9.60 (4)	8–31 v Army, 7–14 v IRC
	D E D'Almada Remedios	54 at 11.05 (8)	

(1) Position in averages
KCC – Saracens & Templars (First Division)

Micky D'Almada Remedios – The Portugese Connection

My first introduction to cricket was in the early 1930s, when my uncle gave me his old bat – a Canon by Gunn – which I cut down and planed to what I thought was a 'Harrow' size bat.

We played cricket in Homantin, the Garden City, where many of us Portuguese built our homes in 1918 along Liberty Avenue and Peace Avenue. My father and other office workers travelled to Hong Kong by railway and junk ferry (total fare 15c). Later on, Soares, Julia and Emma Avenues were developed. [Julia, Emma and Soares Avenues were named after the Portuguese Vice-Consul, F X Soares's daughter, wife and family names. He was the prime mover in the development of Homantin. The streets are still there, but none of the original homes exist.]

Our cricket was played in the Homantin Oval bounded by Peace and Liberty Avenues. We would pick-up 'Test teams' with Gerry and Zinho Gosano, Philip and Bill Yvanovich, the Silva brothers, Jock Collaco, Sonny Monteiro and three or four D'Almada Remedios' and a few others. Our 'Test matches' lasted many hours each day. We had lots of fun.

I also vividly recall our first and only cricket instruction by 'Toto' Prata (he married Nancy Banker who lived in Liberty Avenue). During a visit he saw us and was kind enough to take the time to teach us the fundamentals of the game. He encouraged us to want to be cricketers. It turned out that some of us would play for him when he was the captain of Club de Recreio. He led the Club with great enthusiasm for many years.

At La Salle, a few of us from Homantin formed the nucleus of the school team – Gerry and Zinho Gosano, Sonny Cavalho (son of Ferdie Cavalho, who was a cricket enthusiast and probably the force in starting cricket at Recreio), John Arculli (later IRC), Frank Cotton (whose father was a captain in the RAMC, with whom we always had a fixture), Dickie Silva, myself and a few others. Other fixtures would be against DBS – Denham Carey, Matthews, Francis Lay, John Fenton, Head-master Sargent and Housemaster J L Youngsaye; Ellis Kadoorie School, with more Arcullis', Abbas's etc.; CBS (Central British School) – Hose-good, Pride, Terry Lockhart and his brother, Mitchell and Tony Weller.

On to bigger things. In 1938, while still at school, I started playing for Recreio second XI, captained by Ferdie Cavalho, with Zinho Gosano, Elysio and Dick Alves, F E (Effy) dos Remedios, Polly Xavier, Jackie Noronha, Henry Barros (father of Mike and Quito), Ronnie Soares, A V and Bertie Gosano (the senior Gosanos, who were well known soccer players who represented Hong Kong in many Interport matches).

Recreio cricket has always been played with shortages, with probably only 60 per cent to 70 per cent regulars and the balance made up of 'fill-ins', generally friends cajoled from other sports. Recreio offered so much in those days – soccer (1920s to 1941), hockey, baseball, softball, tennis, bowls and cricket. You will no doubt observe that all the sports can be played over a couple of hours, except cricket, which took up all afternoon.

90

Most of the young athletes preferred the shorter games, which allowed them time for girlfriends and other activities. Most of the Recreio cricket team played softball, hockey and tennis on Sundays.

The 1938–39 season was the year that Recreio won the First Division league with 'Toto' Prata, Dr Rodrigues, Dr Gosano, Luigi Gosano, Zinho Gosano, Dr H L Ozorio, Spotty Pereira, Nick Beltrao, Eddie Soares, Phyrio Nolasco da Silva and Willie Reed. I think I have got them all, but it is difficult to go back so many years, particularly so far away in Seattle, to bring up these faces of 50 years ago.

Some of the above first played cricket with Professor (then Colonel, then Brigadier General) L T Ride of Hong Kong University. Yes, Doc Gosano, Doc Ozorio and Doc Rodrigues played for the University, as did Spotty Pereira and Luigi Gosano, and I think 'Toto' Prata, who worked there (no doubt specially selected for the job by Ride).

Recreio in those days had a strong attacking team, with Doc Gosano and Spotty Pereira spear-heading with their fast bowling, followed by Doc Ozorio with his googlies and Eddie Soares's left-arm spinners. Of course Luigi (left-arm) and Gerry Gosano were still inexperienced, but very positive change bowlers. With a good fielding side Recreio always managed to play close games.

We had some very hard hitters in that lot, particularly Eddie Gosano and Eddie Soares. I can remember these two regularly hitting sixes to the Philippino Club bowling green (Eddie Soares, a left-hander, did most of these) and to the Kowloon Indian Tennis Club court (Eddie Gosano specials), and both of them with lofted straight drives up to the China Light & Power clubhouse to the north and the squash courts of the Army Recreation Club (USRC) across Gascoigne Road to the south. I think it appropriate to say here that few men have driven the cricket ball so hard, so high, and so often in so many different directions, than these two in their prime for Recreio.

We also had a couple of very good 'ticklers' all around the wicket. To mind comes Doc Rodrigues and Willie Reed, never hitting very hard, but gently deflecting the ball and playing it where they directed.

Luigi Gosano was a stylish left-hander, who stalwartly opened the batting for Recreio for 20-odd years. A good all-rounder who enjoyed his game. Gerry Gosano was second to none. A good bowler, a good forceful bat and a superb fielder. He made it look so easy and appeared to have so much time to play his strokes and to make outstanding catches in the slips.

Phyrio Nolasco da Silva was a very enthusiastic cricketer and played secretary to the team. He organised parties and was good for the team. He also played many good innings (he collapsed on the golf course in Vancouver, BC, and died many years ago).

By the end of the 1950s, many of the older players had retired after good and happy innings, while others were lost through immigration to the States and Australia, so once again the struggle to find 22 players for the two divisions became a weekly problem.

The backbone of Recreio comprised of a few older cricketers – Luigi Gosano and Eddie Noronha (our opening bats), myself and my brother Chappie (a good all-rounder), Leonardo D'Almada Remedios (our 'chucker' who represented Hong Kong against Malaya), and a few budding cricketers ex-Australian schools – Alvaro Alonco (a good bat and excellent fielder); the Guterres brothers (Manuel the wicket-keeper and Antonio, a good all-rounder); the Barros brothers (Quito the determined batter and Mike the opening bowler); Gerry Noronha (wicket-keeper and useful bat) and Jojo Basto (an enthusiastic all-rounder). These and the second XI regulars at the time – Frankie Correa (bowler), Dennis McGrann (fast fielder), Danny Gosano (a hard-hitting batsman/wicket-keeper who played well for both the first and second elevens), Edo Noronha (useful bat), Maciano Baptista (promising bat, now Rev M Baptista, Society of Jesus, Jesuits Order) and Robert Guterres (promising bat), plus a bundle of 'fill-ins', gave us the required 22 each week.

For the 1961–62 season, the usual problem to raise enough players became too much, so it was decided (in my absence on UK leave) to field one team in the Second Division. On my return and in time to change, I insisted on one team in the First Division.

Fortunately for us, the Remedios brothers (Frisco and Edo) had finished schooling in England and joined the team. Well, historical data will show that Recreio won the First Division title that year. Chappie, Mike Barros and Edo's bowling, and the team's excellent fielding, gave us the required edge that put us in contention which led to eventual success.

Chappie and Mike supplemented each other well, and the difference between them caused discomfort to our opponents, and very often a quick demise. These two were consistently successful for many years. Records will show that many a side were dismissed below 50 runs, and I recall that a good and contending Army team was dismissed for 16.

It was so easy to captain the side when they were on form. I captained Recreio for some 15 years and always enjoyed playing with them – we had lots of fun together.

Edo Remedios, with his medium off-spinners and his solid and aggressive batting and outstanding fielding, was a real plus to the team. His three years with Recreio cricket made a difference, and his cheerful demeanor left an indelible mark.

Another promising young cricketer returned from schooling in England in 1964–65 – young Joe Gosano (Danny's brother). He was a polished bat with tremendous inherited athletic ability. However, he could not find the enthusiasm for cricket and did not continue the greatness that was within his capability.

Recreio cricket was always fun with lots of challenges. Somehow a few would come through each game, if not with bat or ball, then some spectacular fielding often turned the tide.

I left Hong Kong on 17 December 1967, but continued to play a straight bat in the office passages of Boeing with imaginary bat and ball for many years. Recreio cricket has given me many years of active pleasure and many more years of happy reminiscing.

Peter, you also asked me about cricket in the POW camp. Early on there were efforts made to play a few games (I played in two), but it soon became obvious that we could not afford the luxury of expending our energy on cricket. Not on a minimal diet of rice and vegetables and little at that.

There were lots of cricketers in camp – the Pearce brothers, Gosano brothers, Dr Tony Coombes, Bosanquet, the Lee brothers ('Tinker' and Robbie), Teddy Fincher, Terry Lockhart, Tony Weller and many others.

Towards the end when things were looking better – good news of the Allied advance up towards Japan and two Red Cross parcels, and a good feeling that we would survive – Alec Pearce held a cricket clinic for Eddie Noronha, Gerry Gosano, Alfred Prata and myself. We had a few good hours together and our morale rose to a higher level each time, although our weight did not rise (I was 117 lbs at the end).

[The author had played against Micky's Recreio side in the mid-1950s and later from 1963 until Micky left Hong Kong in 1967. Many thanks Micky for the memories.]

Club de Recreio – Cricketers

Prewar	*Postwar*
Dick Alves (killed in action 1941)	A Alonco
* E A R Alves	H Barros Jnr
* J A Alves	R M Barros
H A Barros	M Baptista
C P Basto	J J Basto
* N Beltrao	D Castro
F Cavalho	F Correa
* M D'Almada Remedios	C A D'Almada Remedios
F E dos Remedios (killed in action 1941)	D E D'Almada 'Chappie' Remedios
A V Gosano	L J D'Almada Remedios
Bertie Gosano	R A D'Almada Remedios
* Dr E L Gosano	Edo dos Remedios

* Luigi Gosano   F dos Remedios
* Gerry Gosano   D Gosano
* Zinho Gosano   J Gosano
    Dr A P Guterres   A P Guterres
    G A Guterres   C A Guterres
* H 'Spikey' Guterres   E Guterres
    M Mendonca (killed in action 1941)   J Guterres
    J A Noronha   L G Guterres
* Dr H L Ozorio   R Guterres
* A P 'Spotty' Pereira   D McGrann
* A M 'Toto' Prata   E J Noronha
* W Reed   G Noronha
    Sir Albert Rodrigues   A R Osmund
* P N da Silva   Alfred Prata
    E M L Soares   Eric Remedios
    R Soares   D Rodrigues
    P Xavier   P Yvanovich
         E (Manuel) Xavier

*Also played postwar.

Most of the postwar cricketers had learnt their cricket at schools in either Australia or the United Kingdom.

[Quito Barros, February 1995]

Craigengower Cricket Club

The Craigengower Cricket Club (CCC) was founded in 1894, one of the earliest cricket clubs in Hong Kong, when Mr W D Braidwood, the Principal of the Victoria English School, converted a turfed piece of ground into a cricket field by Bonham Road, near Breezy Point on Hong Kong island.

Cricket was enthusiastically received, both by the students and their parents. Mr Braidwood required a name for this new activity, and legend has it, settled upon the name Craigengower, which was the name of the building housing the school. However, according to Nick Barnett, former CCC player and Hong Kong High Court Justice, CCC was named after Braidwood's home in Scotland.

There was one drawback to this particular cricket ground, for whilst hitting the ball over the boundary was an easy matter, recovering it was less straightforward. The land beyond the boundary was the site of an old cemetery, and the students had to find the ball from amongst skulls and damaged urns scattered there. Not unnaturally, many balls were not recovered from this macabre site, so Braidwood looked for a more suitable piece of land upon which cricket might be played.

At this point of time, Happy Valley was a large area of open ground which was being utilised for a wide variety of sporting activities, including that of the Hong Kong Jockey Club. Braidwood selected an area in the north-eastern corner of Happy Valley for his new cricket club. Parents of the cricketing students provided funds to construct a matshed. This pavilion was subsequently destroyed by a typhoon and replaced by a more permanent wooden structure. The Club's early benefactors included such well known personalities as R E Belilios, L E Lammert, J H N Mody, R Pestonji and J H Ruttonjee.

Even this corner site was not without its problems, as it was the start for the Jockey Club races. Consequently, Saturday afternoon cricket matches were interrupted at regular intervals, while horses and their riders were lined up for an enthusiastic, if not altogether professional gallop around the perimeter of Happy Valley. The Jockey Club activities did not deter Braidwood and his cricketers. Indeed, it was not long before a formal and permanent racetrack was constructed, which no longer encroached upon the cricket field or vice versa!

CCC was a very go-ahead club. Early on, it introduced the award of a shield to the player who headed the batting averages. Unfortunately, the shield was allowed to be won outright by a certain R Basa in 1903, possibly because club funds could not extend to a new shield, or maybe because it was a good idea, the club secretary, A E Asger, suggested an open cricket competition on league principles.

On 22 October 1903, Mr Braidwood, the CCC President, convened a meeting in the CCC Pavilion of parties interested in forming a cricket competition. Rules were established during the meeting, and two days later CCC played the Civil Service Cricket Club (CSCC) at Happy Valley in the first match of the Hongkong Cricket League. The match was drawn. Winning the toss was of vital importance even in 1903. CSCC's 100 runs was scored in 43 overs, leaving CCC only 13 overs in which they scored a creditable 71 for 4. A local newspaper, the *South China Morning Post,* donated a shield for this new competition which consisted of eight teams. This distinctive shield (see League Cricket), last won by KCC in the 1940–41 season, was lost during the Pacific war.

| 1909 | CCC: | 186–2 | (A Osman 103*, J D Noria 45) |
| Mar 27 | Police: | 93 | (Edwards 59, Hancock 3–11) |

| Apl 3 | CCC: | 205–9 | (A O Brawn 86, R Pestonji 53) |
| | Kowloon: | 101 | (Capt Balderstone 48*, Battliwara 3–5, A Osman 3–10) |

Dec 4   Telegraphs: 180–4 (Oliver RN 55, Young 46, Hose 32, Manning 28)
         CCC: 104   (G A Hancock 24, Shields 5 & Young
                            3 wickets)

   Other CCC players: R A Cavalho, W H Viveash, R Pestonji, J D Noria,
L A Rose, R Basa, L E Lammert, P Currie, S E Green and S Battliwara.

1913   CCC: 114 (E L Braga 44, K R Macaskill 7–44)
Mar 8   Kowloon: 87 (A R F Raven 18, H H Taylor 8–55)

1920   CCC: 61 (S Jex 21, F A Redmond 5–35, T E Yeoh 4–19)
Feb 27   HKU: 69 (Y Abbas 4–9, L E Lammert 4–42)

   '... the first league match for several weeks' – closely contested.

1926   CCC: 123   (Leonard 55, A B Clemo 8–45)
Nov 27   China Light RC: 93–8 (Tinson 42)

The next three First Division matches were played at HKCC, Pokfulam
and Happy Valley.

1929   CCC: 168   (F Oliver 36*, D Rumjahn 36, B W Bradbury 35,
                       H V Parker 5–34)
Jan 12   HKCC: 141–6 (T E Pearce 35, Capt A N Evers 26, S Abbas
                       5–34)

1932   University: 120 (F R Zimmern 32, A M Rodrigues 26, R E Lee
                          6–27)
Mar 12   CCC: 95 (W Paterson 33, D J N Anderson 6–25)

1939   CCC: 148   (G Souza 45, H P Lim 24, E Zimmern 24*)
Jan 28   IRC: 87–9 (P J Billimoria 3–29)

Until the Pacific war, CCC continued to be a leading force on the Hong
Kong cricket scene. It won the First Division championship on four occasions, in 1904–05, 1907–08, 1911–12 and jointly in 1937–38, and the
Second Division in 1932–33. Cricket in Hong Kong came to an abrupt
halt in 1941. The CCC clubhouse was badly damaged when the Japanese
attacked Hong Kong that December.
   The Club's ground was taken over by the Japanese as a work site, the
area being used for the shaping of large granite blocks, possibly for the
building of the grandiose Japanese War Memorial, which was partially
erected on one of the peaks overlooking Hong Kong harbour.

The clubhouse was rebuilt after the war due mainly to the dedication of a handful of old members, such as B W Bradbury, L C R Souza and A E Coates. On 21 January 1951, an extension was officially opened by Sir Arthur Morse. This same structure can be seen today at 188 Wong Nai Chung Road, Happy Valley. Also in 1951, CCC was officially incorporated as a company, its subscribers being Richard Basa, Bertram Walter Bradbury, Alfred Edward Coates, Navel Pestonji Karanjia, Chi Wei Lam, Sorab Rustom Solina and Li Sui Wing. After cricket recommenced in the 1948–49 season, although CCC always performed creditably, there were few successes in the various competitions.

Several postwar cricketers as CCC members played representative cricket for Hong Kong, such as Buji Dhabher, George Souza Snr, Carl Myatt, Roy Gresley, John Ashworth, Des Greenwood and Steve Waller. Until recently, CCC held the Saturday league record of 315 runs scored in the 1974–75 season. Available records show that Keith Garner remained the only postwar Second Division player to have topped both the batting and bowling averages in the same season (1971–72).

| 1961 | CCC: | 201–8 dec | (C Myatt 87*) |
| Dec | IRC: | 110 | (C Myatt 5–12, B Dhabher 5–31) |

'CCC's skipper Myatt coming in at No. 9 stopped the rot.'

A particular CCC highlight was its victory against KCC in the first Six-a-Side tournament in Hong Kong held at the Chater Road ground on 24 December 1961. Peter Kuruneru donated six tankards to the winners.

| 1967 | Recreio: 127 | (G Lalchandani 7–34) at King's Park. |
| Nov 4 | CCC: | 59–9 |

'Gopal Lalchandani bowled with great fire throughout the afternoon.'

| 1968 | LSW: | 96 | (P Everett 27, C Myatt 10–23) |
| Jan 7 | CCC: | 99–1 | (R Lalchandani 48*, G McLeod 48) |

From the records perused by the author, this is the only postwar First Division match when ten wickets have been captured by a bowler. Carl also achieved the 'hat-trick' in this remarkable spell.

Unfortunately as space in Hong Kong was at a premium, the under-utilised grass of the club's ground was eyed, not only by property developers, but also by the club's tennis players and lawn bowlers. Sadly, one

Saturday afternoon in early 1976, the cricket team arrived at the club to find that half the ground had been dug up to a depth of two feet. The last cricket match at CCC was played with half the fielding side dodging around heaps of earth and tripping over lumps of concrete. After that unhappy occurrence, it was no longer possible to play cricket, and the long association with the Happy Valley ground ended. The same ground where Carl Myatt, on a helpful wicket, was almost unplayable, and Jack Johnson smashed you out of the ground, whether your name was Buddy Carnell or not!

1976   CCC: 223–4 (K Garner 102*, N McCann 47)
Mar 20 Army: 190–8 (R Smith 50, P Richards 37)

Shortly before the ground was lost to cricket, CCC inaugurated their annual six-a-side competition in Hong Kong, some 15 years after the initial event at HKCC. It was won by the Centaurs who beat KCC in a very 'dark' final, when KCC failed to find the ball as the Centaurs batsmen kept running. The author was one of the KCC fielders lying flat on the ground trying to pick out the outline of the ball against the lighted clubhouse. The competition, now played annually on the KCC ground, is an established and very popular cricket fixture expertly run by CCC players, past and present.

The CCC cricket team is now nomadic, receiving assistance from the HKCA, its own club committee and other league clubs, and playing on any available ground on a Saturday afternoon. CCC are not the only team to have lost its playing area in recent years, as changes in club membership quite often determined the utilisation of the ground, usually to the detriment of cricket. This has created some difficulty for the HKCA, which is responsible for cricket in Hong Kong. As the number of cricket grounds continues to dwindle, it is possible that CCC will cease to have an eleven. However, Nick Barnett commenting in *Scoreboard* in 1981 said:

Taking its cue from the name Happy Valley from where it originates, CCC are a happy side. Generally, but let it be admitted not always, CCC try and put enjoyment and pleasure before points on a Saturday afternoon. In spite of the lack of a home ground, there is a good team spirit which bodes well for the future.

Nick's words are still valid today. Although the flesh might be weaker, the good spirit still prevails in the matches played by CCC. CCC players, past and present, have made regular tours to the West Country in England, another example of the camaraderie that has been built up and sustained over the years.

It is perhaps significant for cricket at CCC, and in Hong Kong, that some 98 years after the club was formed to teach schoolboys the game, the HKCA in December 1992 held a series of coaching sessions for the sons of club members at CCC.

For the 90th Anniversary of the first league match in Hong Kong, the CCC committee arranged for their 1993–94 league fixture against the Centaurs (the postwar 'civil service' side) to be played on 23 October 1993 at Sookunpoo.

> Centaurs: 229–8 (W Tootall 68, M Peck 67, J Hughes 32,
> S Weatherley 2–55)
> CCC: 162–8 (M Darke 50, K Styles 35, M Lewis 3–57,
> G Fletcher 2–27)

Centaurs players, averaging 55 years, beat CCC averaging about 42 years, by 67 runs. 'I'm sure I could have seen him off', said a despondent Des Greenwood after succumbing to Graham Fletcher's long hops!

A cocktail party in the clubhouse on the preceding evening saw John Pau, a member since 1931, and Harry Esmail, a member since around 1928, who had played in the 1937–38 First Division championship side, in attendance.

As part of CCC's 100th Anniversary celebrations in 1994, club skipper, Kevin Styles, gathered together a plethora of cricketers for a cricket tour of Shanghai, the first since the last Interport in 1948. Kevin said:

> Whatever changes the future may have in store – to be in Shanghai for cricket at this time is a wonderful expression of co-operation and sporting goodwill. A winning draw to CCC in the first, and also a win on Sunday – but winning wasn't the point of the weekend.

CCC now boasts nine all weather floodlit tennis courts, two very fine bowling greens, a spacious badminton hall, a gymnasium, a swimming pool and two squash courts.

The author would like to use a little of this space to give his heartfelt thanks to Kevin Styles for his enthusiastic assistance in helping to put together this brief cricket history of CCC. CCC continues to play its own important part in the cricket scene in Hong Kong, albeit at the lower scale of the ladder, thus the spiritual signs are – cricket is far from dead in the Valley.

Civil Service C C v Craigengower C C

Venue: Happy Valley, Hong Kong – Saturday, 24 October 1903

Civil Service CC

P T Lamble, c & b Pestonji	9	**Bowling**				
R Witchell, b Pestonji	3		*O*	*M*	*R*	*W*
J Lander, b Pestonji	6					
L E Brett, c Cross b Pestonji	12	A O Brawn	10	2	23	–
W Brand, c Pestonji b Herton	2	R Pestonji	16	3	30	6
W Pitt, c Taylor b Herton	5	E R Herton	9	3	20	3
W Andrews, b Pestonji	3	L E Lammert	2	–	10	–
J Deveney, lbw Herton	31					
W H Woolley, c Stuart b Pestonji	6					
W Parkinson, run out	3					
H Gidley, not out	3					
Extras	17					
Total	100					

Craigengower CC

J L Stuart, c Pitt b Witchell	0	**Bowling**				
J D Kinnaird, not out	11		*O*	*M*	*R*	*W*
A O Brawn, c Woolley b Lamble	5					
E R Herton, c Parkinson b Brett	48	R Witchell	5	–	25	1
L A Rose, b Brett	5	P T Lamble	3	–	16	1
L E Lammert		J Lander	3	–	18	–
R Basa		L E Brett	2	–	10	2
T L Cross						
R Pestonji	Did not bat					
J H Ruttonjee						
H H Taylor						
Extras	2					
Total (for 4 wickets)	71					

Result: Match drawn

Craigengower C C v Little Sai Wan C C

Venue: Sai Wan, Hong Kong Island – 7 January 1968

LSWCC

		Bowling				
K Pitchforth, b Myatt	15					
P Everett, st Lalchandani b Myatt	27		*O*	*M*	*R*	*W*
D Raderecht, c Dhabher b Myatt	9					
L O'Meara, b Myatt	4	G Lalchandani	8	1	28	–
P Davison, c G Lalchandani b Myatt	6	G Williams	4	–	12	–
E Birch, b Myatt	0	C Myatt	9	1	23	10
B Millar, b Myatt	4	J Ashworth	5	1	21	–
A Morgan, not out	13					
T Millar, b Myatt	2					
G Williams, c & b Myatt	0					
I Arkley, st Lalchandani b Myatt	4					
Extras	12					
Total	96					

Fall of wickets: 1–39, 2–46, 3–59, 4–60, 5–60, 6–73, 7–74, 8–93, 9–93

Craigengower CC

		Bowling				
R Lalchandani, not out	48					
G McLeod, b Morgan	48		*O*	*M*	*R*	*W*
J Ashworth, not out	3					
B Dhabher		P Davison	8	–	30	–
G Ebert		T Millar	2	–	17	–
A Ma		P Everett	2	–	9	–
T Ramesh	Did not bat	I Arkley	2	–	13	–
C Myatt		A Morgan	4	–	14	1
G Lalchandani		L O'Meara	2	–	11	–
G Williams		G Williams	.5	–	5	–
D Peter						
Extras	0					
1 wicket for	99					

Fall of wickets: 1–86

Craigengower won by 9 wickets.

... with the last two deliveries of his sixth over, he bowled O'Meara and Birch. Then, with the first ball of his seventh he had Davison taken at short mid-wicket by Lalchandani to complete his 'hat-trick'.

First Division – Batting Performances 1965–66 to 1969–70
Cavaliers

Season	Player	500 runs plus	Centuries
1969–70	R Lalchandani	660 at 41.25 (8)	
	B P Dhabher		113* v KCC Templars

(1) Position in averages

First Division – Bowling Performances 1965–66 to 1969–70
Craigengower CC

Season	Player	50 wickets plus	7 plus (for 50 runs or less)
1965–66	C Myatt	59 at 8.29 (1)	7–40 v KCC Saracens
1966–67	C Myatt	53 at 10.50 (5)	
1967–68	C Myatt	70 at 10.27	10–23 v LSW incl. 'hat-trick'
	G Lalchandani		7–34 & 7–46 v Recreio

Cavaliers

1968–69	G Lalchandani	62 at 6.29 (1)	
	R M Barros	64 at 7.73 (2)	8–37 v KCC Saracens, 7– 5 v LSW, 7–10 v Army & 7–13 v RAF
1969–70	C Myatt	64 at 8.79 (2)	7–21 v LSW and 'hat-trick' v RAF
	G Lalchandani	54 at 14.64 (6)	8–41 v RAF

(1) Position in averages

Second Division/Saturday League – Batting Performances 1965–66 to 1993–94

Season	Player	Centuries

Craigengower CC

1965–66	B Iranee	124* v IRC

Recreio/Craigengower CC

Season	Player	500 runs plus	Centuries
1967–68	D Booth	527 at 37.64 (2) (only batsman 500 plus)	100 v DBS
1968–69	D Booth	467 at 51.20 (1)	

Craigengower CC

1970–71	G Jackson	529 at 37.79 (2)	119* v Saracens
1971–72	G May	605 at 27.50	
1972–73	D Booth	811 at 42.68 (4)	125 v DBS
	G May	740 at 41.11 (5)	106 v Nomads
1974–75	J Sharman		129 v St George's
	D Beecroft		118* v Islanders & 100* v LSW
	J Johnson		110* v St George's
1975–76	K Garner	782 at 48.88 (6)	102* v Army
1976–77	D Greenwood	859 at 42.95 (6)	111* v Islanders & 100 v DBS
	K Garner	687 at 36.16	121* v Islanders

K Garner & D Greenwood 221* (1st) v Islanders (1)

1977–78	D Greenwood	885 at 59.00 (3)	115* v HKU & 106* v Islanders
1980–81	S Waller	574 at 33.76	
1981–82	D Greenwood	702 at 46.80 (8)	103* v Army
1982–83	D Greenwood	863 at 71.92 (3)	116* v DBS & 103* v Sentinels
1983–84	D Greenwood	986 at 82.16 (2)	127* v Nomads, 119 v Kai Tak 116 v Tartars & 111 v Centaurs
	M Walsh		111* v Witherers
1984–85	D Greenwood	533 at 48.50 (10)	104* v Centaurs
1985–86	D Greenwood	845 at 70.40 (3)	100* v Gap Ramblers
	M Darke	846 at 60.40 (6)	116* v DBS
1987–88	M Darke	739 at 73.90 (5)	137* & 107* v Witherers
1988–89	D Greenwood		138* v Nomads
1991–92	W Symcox		108* v Gap Ramblers
	J de Angelis		100* v Strollers.
1992–93	P Fitzgerald		100* v Tartars §

§ Butani Cup
(1) Position in averages
    HKCC – Gap Ramblers, Nomads & Witherers
    KCC – Saracens & Tartars
    Police – Sentinels & Strollers

Second Division/Saturday League – Bowling Performances 1965–66 to 1993–94

Season	Player	50 wickets plus	7 plus (for 50 runs or less)

Recreio/Craigengower CC

| 1968–69 | J Matthew | | 8–14 v KCC Crusaders |

Craigengower CC

1969–70	A Tilley	68 at 8.50 (1)	
	J Johnson		'hat-trick' v St Georges
1970–71	A Tilley	62 at 11.08 (5)	
	K Garner	60 at 11.55 (8)	6–12 v DBS (excep.)
1971–72	K Garner	52 at 10.32 (1)	
	J Johnson		7–22 v HKU
	A Tilley		7–27 v HKCC Nomads
1972–73	G Buckland	52 at 10.10 (2)	3–0 v IRC (excep.)
1973–74	R Cooper	64 at 10.91 (4)	7–33 v Royal Navy
	G Buckland		5–2 v DBS (excep.)
1974–75	R Cooper	49 at 14.26	7–14 v RAF
	G Buckland		7–35 v KCC Crusaders and 'hat-trick' v KGV
1975–76	R Cooper	52 at 20.33	
1976–77	D Greenwood	58 at 15.19	
	M Smith		7–21 v Islanders and 7–44 v HKCC Nomads
1977–78	M Smith	53 at 17.21	7–43 v KGV
1985–86	K Garner		'hat-trick' v Police Strollers

(1) Position in averages

Craigengower Cricket Club

List of Presidents

Year	Name
1894–c.1914	W D Braidwood
1920s	R Basa
1930s)	C Rosselet and
1940s)	B W Bradbury

1947–51	Dr C W Lam
1951–52	Dr N P Karanjia
1952–63	H A de Barros Botelho
1963–64	J A Fox
1964–91	H A de Barros Botelho
1991–96	Dr Louis Hsu
1996–	Paul Tam

Dragons

The Dragons, the first ever Chinese cricket team, formed under the auspices of the HKCA as part of their recent four-year development programme to promote cricket amongst the Chinese community in the region, successfully completed their first tour, a visit to Taiwan.

| 1993 | Dragons: | 135–6 | (P Wong 23, F Fung 20) |
| Sep | Taipei CA: | 135 | (Sandip 43, M Ling 4–19, E Tse 2–20, D Ling 2–23) |

The last Taipei wicket fell to Maurice Ling with two balls remaining.

| | Dragons: | 105–7 | (P Wong 26) |
| | Taipei CA: | 106–8 | (R Lamsam 3–22) |

Eddie Tse, who has played league cricket in Hong Kong since 1976, captained the side. Bharat Gohel, Hong Kong-born and a Hong Kong representative cricketer, managed the squad, whilst Lal Jayasingh, the HKCA coach, trained the team.

The batsmen performed reasonably well in that they could protect their wickets, but they need to be able to score the singles and perhaps play more attacking shots.

Bharat Gohel, *Scoreboard*, December 1993

A visiting school team, Ewell Castle School, from Surrey, were the Dragons next opponents in a 40-over match at the HKCC.

| 1994 | Ewell: | 148–8 | (R Tapping 48, McMillen 27, Sutton 25, Wien-fung 4–24, M Wong 2–18) |
| Jan 3 | Dragons: | 150–9 | (E Tse 56*, P Fung 23, Sutton 3–31, Evens 2–21) |

A match-winning innings from the captain Eddie Tse steered the Dragons to a one-wicket victory.

In November 1994, the Hong Kong selectors included Tony Correa, Maurice Ling and Eddie Tse in the squad participating in the Tuanku Ja'afar tournament in Hong Kong. The nominated three all played in one match against Malaysia capturing two, one and two wickets each in an easy Hong Kong victory.

After the Dragons first arrived on the local cricket scene, the HKCA, in their endeavours to enlighten the Chinese in the concept of cricket, appeared to be 'pampering' the squad too much by favouring them with regional tours, first to Taipei in 1993, as previously recorded, and then in September 1994 to Beijing for the inaugural sixes in the Olympic Stadium. They then returned to Beijing in September 1995, and later in the same year visited Shanghai.

1994   Beijing CC: 116   (Extras! 34, W Fung 4–30, R Lamsam 4–35)
        Dragons: 117–1   (T Correa 59*, P Wong 37*)

The very sporty track (uneven bounce) was reflected by extras!

In the inaugural sixes, the Dragons provided three teams, while Beijing CC's teams were from the contingents of Australia, Bangladesh, England, India, Pakistan and Sri Lanka. In a low-scoring final, Dragons I, 38 runs (E Tse, B Gohel, T Correa, R Lamsam, K Lowcock and B Lin) defeated Australia, 29 runs.

In the return match against Beijing CC, '... the exhaustion from 2 days of cricket began to show.'

        Dragons: 176   (E Tse 43, K Lowcock 27)
        Beijing CC: 177–8 (P Wong 3–46, K Lowcock 2–25)

Manager-player Gohel said: 'There has been much improvement in attitude, commitment and technique, but the finer points of cricket-thinking need to be improved. Many people were surprised that the Chinese could not only play cricket, but at a reasonably competitive level.'

Tony Fisher and his charming wife Jasmine, formerly of the KCC, were delightful hosts and ensured no inconvenience was caused to the squad.

In September 1995, on their return to Beijing for the sixes, the Dragons defeated Sri Lanka, the Commonwealth and Japan to reach the final against England (the British Embassy), losing on the second last ball of the day in near total darkness! This event has gained a high degree of publicity in the media (including the BBC Worldwide Service) and an acknowledgement from the ICC.

In October of the same year, the Dragons played the Shanghai CC in two 40-over matches at the Meiling Cricket Ground. In the first match, the

Dragons scored 242, with runs flowing freely from the bats of Roland To and Roy Lamsam, and captured 17 of Shanghai's wickets for 139, memories of All-England v 20 of Sheffield in 1846. In the return match, Bharat Gohel scored 72 of the Dragons 142, with Shanghai being bowled out for 128.

Hong Kong Cricket Club

During the HKCC Centenary Celebrations, from Saturday, 29 September until Saturday, 13 October 1951, four cricket matches took place on the Chater Road ground, the scene of many a flannelled contest. These were Old Shanghailanders v Old Hong Kong Stagers (6 October); HKCC v The Rest (7/8 October); Hong Kong v Singapore Services (9/10 October), and Hong Kong v Combined Singapore & Hong Kong Services (12–14 October).

HKCC beat The Rest by 7 wickets, no one scored a fifty. Harry Owen Hughes said: 'bowling honours were fairly evenly distributed, with Teh of the University looking the most impressive, and the fielding throughout was very creditable.' Rest of the Colony: 146 and 125 – HKCC: 216 for 9 and 57 for 3.

In the next match, HKCC beat the Singapore Services by 5 wickets. Guy Pritchard added: 'the Services won the toss, and HKCC took the field in conditions of considerable heat and great humidity which characterised the weather during the week.' Only Capt. R Marriott of the Services, with a fine 69 runs in their second innings, exceeded 50. The most successful bowlers were C B Connett (HKCC) and F/O P Martin (Services), with match analyses of 9 for 72 and 9 for 135 respectively. Singapore Services: 171 and 161 – HKCC: 234 and 100 for 5.

In the last match Hong Kong beat the Combined Services by 6 wickets. Noel Arthy with 81 not out and 46 not out was easily the best of the Hong Kong batsmen, while R Craig with 7 for 62 (first innings) and Gerry Gosano with 6 for 58 (second innings) were Hong Kong's most successful bowlers. Alec Pearce reported: 'whilst Weller bowled remarkably steadily finishing with the excellent analysis of 3 wickets for 11 runs in 14 overs, 9 of which were maidens.' Combined Services: 144 and 146 – Hong Kong: 188 and 103 for 4.

The most amusing report comes from that 'old leg-puller' Arnold Graham, in describing the first match between the Old Hong Kong Stagers and the Old Shanghailanders. The following participated: Old Hong Kong: Dicky Richardson, 'Punchy' Stapleton, Teddy Fincher, Eric Mitchell, Lindsay Ride, Arthur Perry, 'Fatty' Minu, R H Hughes, N P Fox, David Robb and W Stoker.

107

Old Shanghai: 'Peanut' Marshall, Solly Shroff, Harold Bidwell, M J Divecha, George Mills, J C Pullen, Charlie Smith, Lolly Goldman, Arnold Graham, Fali Kermani and Torrie Wilson.

'The rain had cooled the atmosphere and left the pitch easy and slow for dimmed eyes and reluctant reflexes. Teddy Fincher and 'Punchy' Stapleton saw the ball well from the start but did little with it. Doc Ride survived just long enough to demonstrate the classical half-cock shot – Fali Kermani's bowling shoulder immediately joined his achilles tendon in semi-retirement. Torrie shuffled up to the wicket and bowled an impeccable length with much of the same easy action that I first saw twenty odd years ago – an amazing youngster of sixty China Coast summers. Glimpses there had been of former greatness with ball and bat and in the field. Above all, the bonhomie and the friendly cheerful atmosphere of the game will be long remembered by those who took part in it. Only a comparative few years ago one witnessed and enjoyed similar scenes in Shanghai, Tientsin and Hankow – a pleasant memory.'

Hong Kong: 149–7 – Shanghai: 135–8. The result was not important.

The time capsule now reverts back to the 1850s to the beginnings of serious cricket in the young Colony of Hong Kong. Around 1850 in England:

wicket-keeping gauntlets were on the scene; leg-guards were becoming popular as the round-arm bowlers built up their speed, and in 1853–54 cane-handled bats were invented.

Tony Lewis, *Double Century*

This description of the beginnings of protective equipment for cricketers, coupled with the likely local ground conditions – the southern portion of the Army parade ground recently extended by reclamation, with an 'unprepared' cricket square – gives a vague picture of the circumstances which faced the early pioneers of cricket in Hong Kong.

In describing the location of that early piece of ground to the more recent visionary, John Luff wrote in the *SCMP* in March 1969:

measure with your mind's eye a stretch of ground beginning just below St John's Cathedral and running north to the limit of the Hong Kong Cricket Club Ground, taking in such buildings as the Hilton Hotel and part of Beaconsfield House, and the Bank of China, then south east to the cricket ground.

[The former HKCC ground is now Chater Gardens and the Hilton Hotel demolished – 1996]

On Saturday, 7 June 1851, at a public meeting chaired by Joseph Frost Edgar, who with William Jardine, were elected the first unofficial members of the Legislative Council in Hong Kong, the secretary, A Shortrede, read out the object for a meeting of members of the community:

> That the sanction of His Excellency (Sir Samuel George Bonham) be obtained to the adaptation of the Parade Ground carried into effect on the opening of the new road by the waterside by levelling and turfing all the space from the upper part of the Parade Ground to the new road.

Apart from the chairman, others on this ad hoc committee were: Mr William Bridges and Mr R C Antrobus – representing the Civil Profession. Captains Lodder and Chadwick – representing the Army. Mr James Smith and Mr T A Lane – representing the Trades People.

The chairman said the Government would not give the land for private use, so it was decided that it be developed for 'public recreational purposes.' Despite the *China Mail*, on 12 June 1851, questioning whether the proceedings represented the wishes of the bulk of the community in the matter of 'a place for public recreation and not simply a cricket ground,' that historic meeting of some 30 persons, including the Governor, launched *The Hong Kong Cricket Club* (HKCC), one of the first cricket clubs outside England, a club and ground which was to become world famous. Only three of the eighteen English County cricket clubs were formed before the HKCC – Sussex (1839), Nottinghamshire (1841) and Surrey (1845). Although a majority of the public were not aware of the 'recreational' aspect of the Chater Road ground, they could freely enter whenever a game of cricket was being played.

At a meeting later in the year, various objections were raised:

1. Cricket players in Hong Kong are a very small section of the community and it appears that they already possess the means of indulging in the pastime, both on this and on the opposite shore.
2. The space available, say 250 or 300 yards, by a mean width of half that length is insufficient for a good cricket player, whose ball, well struck, might be sent from the lower part of the ground through the stained glass windows in the transepts of St John's Cathedral.
3. Whilst a game of cricket is going on, Pedestrians, Equestrians, and those in Carriages, will be continually liable to a black eye, or other disagreement, as they are passing the playground.

4. And the suggestion is one of the unprotected Females – A very pretty thing indeed, Sir, that as I am taking my evening stroll I am to be shocked with the sight of several lusty young men stripped to their doublets whizzing their bats about and shouting 'Hurrah, for the next innings'.

One questioner, whose suggestion came true 125 years later, said:

'The construction of a capacious shrubbery – garden plots here and there – pretty little fountains with granite images of Chinese cupids – grotesque arbours a la Chino'se – a small lake in the centre with a few swans in it – shady paths with seats at little distances ...'

The Friend of China & Hong Kong Gazette, 1851

In May 1883, it was reported in the *Hong Kong Telegraph* that 'Sir Arthur Kennedy had no right to take away from the public what was undoubtedly their exclusive privilege.' In October 1883, the same paper returned to the attack and championed the formation of a rival cricket club, The Victoria Cricket Club, and that this club should be allowed to share the ground. Nothing more was ever heard.

The matter of whether the Chater Road ground should be a cricket ground or a place for public recreation, was raised again by Mr Y K Kan (later Sir Y K) in the Legislative Council on 18 March 1963.

These discussions dragged on until 1968, when Mr Hilton Cheong-leen, Chairman of the Urban Council, said that the 1968 Report of the Advisory Committee on Private Recreational Leases, recommended that the HKCC should be granted a fresh lease in 1971 for a term of ten years. However, with a 'scorpion' sting, he added: 'The City Hall and Statue Square have become the cultural heart of Hong Kong. We need to expand this cultural heart, and we can best do this by turning the Cricket Club into public open space.'

Seconding the motion, Mr D J R Blaker said conditions had changed entirely from the time when the HKCC originally took up its position on the edge of what was then a relatively small village. He added: 'It is now in the midst of a thriving, bustling city. I hardly think that is a symbol that the majority of our community would choose to have as its City Square.'

Another Urban Councillor in March 1968 said: 'It has been a political issue for some time. It is disappointing that we have had to have racial discrimination in the centre of town. The Cricket Club is symbolic of discrimination.'

After much correspondence on this matter, George Rowe, President of the HKCC, commented in the *SCMP* on 11 March 1969: 'It has been referred to as – "a symbol of racial discrimination". There is no racial discrimination at The Hong Kong Cricket Club, and many members would resign if there was. I certainly would. Membership is not restricted by race, colour, creed or nationalities; indeed, we probably have more nationalities than any other club in Hong Kong.' Well spoken, George, and I'm sure you believed it to be true. However, I'm afraid in reality the picture was different.

Prewar and in the immediate postwar period, His Excellency the Governor as a special guest, was always present for Interport matches played at the HKCC. Unfortunately, due to Hong Kong's lifestyle, this is no longer possible. I doubt the 'do-gooders' would have suggested a change in the location, if the Governor had continued to attend these local 'Test' matches.

Throughout the 124 years since cricket was first played at Chater Road, those who have played on it will remember the nostalgia which affects many cricket lovers, the bright winter days, the cacophony echoing around the ground, the comradeship, the excitement of winning, the gloom of losing and the uplifting of the spirit, all inwardly experienced on this central piece of turf.

On 27 April 1975, to mark the closing of this historic ground, Cathay Pacific via the driving force of Keith Sillett, brought to Hong Kong a superb collection of great Australian players mainly from the 1950s, names such as Alan Davidson, Neil Harvey, Ian Johnson, Ray Lindwall, Bobby Simpson, plus Clarrie Grimmett, Harold Larwood and Bert Oldfield.

Unfortunately for the keen followers of the game, the 'Great' Don Bradman (later Sir Donald) was unable to join the team. However, he sent a personal message:

I regret that I cannot be with Cathay Pacific's cricket Superstars for their historic games marking the end of the Crown Colony's famous cricket ground. The Australian team is comprised of men of great distinction in cricket. I wish the celebration, with all its heavy nostalgia, great success and an exciting and pleasurable end to another chapter in the greatest game of all.

Carl Myatt, ex-Hong Kong captain and acknowledged SCMP scribe, takes us through the highlights of the main game – HKCC v The Superstars, played exactly to the day, 134 years on since the first cricket match was recorded as having been played in Hong Kong:

An opening partnership of 107 by HKCC skipper Peter Davies (68) and Noel Hooper was a warning to the visitors that this was going to be serious stuff. This was followed by an innings of pure brilliance by Peter Green. His magnificent innings of 95 contained two huge sixes and 16 fours. He was applauded all the way back to the pavilion by the Australians – a tribute indeed. The Superstars were left to score 236 at almost a run a minute. A century partnership between Bob Simpson and Jim Burke set the foundations for a fine finish. Simpson cut loose immediately, scoring 85 (18 fours) in only 38 minutes! After a slight middle order crisis, the experience of Rod Marsh and Alan Davidson saw the Superstars through to a comfortable win. No joss sticks or incense were burnt in traditional Chinese style to appease the ghosts of the past. Perhaps the vintage of the cricket did that.

On the day before, in a match between W A Brown's XI and I Johnson's XI, Bobby Simpson, opening for Brown's XI scored the last century (103) on this historic ground.

Bert Oldfield, after donating a pair of his wicket-keeping gloves to the HKCC, said:

Unaccustomed as I am to public speaking, let me say on behalf of all cricketers throughout the world and the Superstars in particular – may you take the 125 years of cricket history with you from Chater Road to Wong Nai Chung Gap, and may your club go from strength to strength, always maintaining the real spirit of cricket.

The last matches to be played on this historic ground were: Club Past (pre-1966) and Club Present (post-1966) and Weller's XIV and Steven's XIII on 3/4 May 1975. In the Past v Present match, each side batted 13; 24 wickets fell; 24 bowlers were tried and the match ended in a tie, each with 220 runs. You couldn't have contrived a better finish!

The last match saw 'Youth', 10 for 253 runs, defeat 'Experience', 13 declared for 250 runs. Few of the crowd of spectators, players, umpires and club staff who witnessed the sad 'Beating the Retreat' by the band of the Royal Hampshire Regiment could control the lump in their throats, as the club flag was lowered, leaving an eerie feeling of uncertainty, as nearly 125 years of cricket memories passed by in the evening light.

Back in 1972, the decision had been taken to move to the new site 'up the Hill' on Wong Nai Chung Gap, which site had been filled in and set aside by the Government for this purpose. The first pavilion at Chater Road was a matshed in the north-east corner of the ground. This was soon replaced by a more solid structure which was used until 1893. This was itself replaced by a larger single-storey building immediately across the road from the present old Bank of China building. In 1923, the last club-house was built in the north-west corner near the Hong Kong Club building. This two-storey structure was finally demolished after the move up the hill, and the ground handed over to the majority of the community for the creation of 'Chater Gardens'.

According to *The Friend of China & Hong Kong Gazette* on Friday/ Saturday, 21/22 November 1851, Dr Lewis of the Medical Staff and ten men of the 59th Regiment played against six officers of the Garrison and five civilians. This was the first recorded match played on the HKCC Chater Road ground.

The author considers, from the available records, this match to be the first played on the new HKCC ground at Chater Road. From the make-up of the teams, with only five civilians participating, the cricket at this early stage appeared to be under Services control. The playing area had been part of the Army Parade ground, which could revert at any time to its former usage.

Dr Lewis of the Medical Staff and ten men of the 59th
Verses
Six Officers of the Garrison and five civilians

at HKCC – Friday & Saturday 21/22 November 1851

Dr Lewis & 59th Men

Dr Lewis, stumped out Smith	0	not out	32
Penton, b Lane	32	b Lane	12
Harding, c Smith b Pollard	4	stumped out Smith	2
Mitchell, b Lane	1	b Bowring	3
Drady, c Lane b Pollard	31	b Bowring	7
Woods, b Lane	8	b Bowring	1
Bergen, c Lane b Bowring	0	c Gray b Bowring	4
Timbrill, b Bowring	4	run out	0
Scott, not out	11	b Bowring	2
Moore, c Bowring b Pollard	12	run out	6
Wright, b Bowring	14	run out	1
byes	32	byes 16, wide 1	17
Total	141	Total	87

Fall of wickets ⎫
⎬ not recorded.
Bowling ⎭

Officers & Civilians

Lieutenant Chadwick, b Harding	0	b Drady	12
Lieutenant Lloyd, c Timbrill b Drady	0	b Penton	4

113

Lieutenant Wilson, hit into wicket	2	run out	4
Lieutenant Lugg, run out	3	b Harding	0
Lieutenant Gray, stumped out	0	c Drady b Penton	2
Lieutenant Dobyns, b Harding	1	not out	0
Lane, c Bergen b Harding	0	b Penton	4
Napier, c Wright b Harding	14	c Scott b Penton	0
Smith, not out	18	run out	22
Pollard, c Woods b Penton	12	b Harding	1
Bowring, run out	0	b Penton	3
byes 7, no-balls 2	9	byes 6, wides 2, no-balls 1	9
Total	55	Total	60

NB: Total scores add up to 59 and 61 respectively.

Fall of Wickets }
Bowling } not recorded

The light lads of the 59th, putting not their trust in shoe leather, showed that, however stiff they may appear on military parade as soldiers, on cricket parade they were as active as weasels.

The Friend of China & Hong Kong Gazette, 1851

During the first league season in 1903–04, there had been some acrimonious correspondence in the local press about the HKCC's lack of commitment to the new cricket league, as their team languished second from the bottom of the table at the end of December 1903.

League Table 3 Dec 1903	Played	Won	Lost	Drawn	Points
Army Ordnance	8	7	1	–	21
Civil Service CC	6	5	–	1	16
Craigengower CC	7	3	2	2	11
Royal Engineers	5	2	3	–	6
HMS Tamar	5	2	3	–	6
RAMC	5	1	3	1	4
HKCC 'A'	4	–	4	–	0
HK Parsee CC	4	–	4	–	0

Win (3 points) and draw (1 point)

A member of the HKCC, who signed himself – A Cricketer, answered the criticism:

The HKCC Committee had voluntarily debarred 17 or more of the best civilian players in the club, to say nothing of all naval and military members. There can be little doubt to anyone who knows anything about Hong Kong cricket that the Senior Club could put a team into the field which would be far too strong for the first eleven of any other club in the Colony.

The HKCC had by far the largest membership of any club in Hong Kong, having been in existence since 1851. Most other clubs were formed or were being formed around the turn of the 20th century or later. The HKCC also had many Service members.

1903	HKCC:	160	(T Sercombe Smith 46, R Hancock
Dec 25			33, Sub/Lt Barron 5–29)
& 26	United Services:	171–6 dec	(H Hancock 45, A G Ward 30,
			M C Williams 3–54)
		149	(F L Horsey RN 59, Sub/Lt Cornabe
			RN 38*, T Sercombe Smith 4–4,
			R Hancock 2–31)
		168–4	(Lt Heath 110th Mahratta L.I. 97)

Match drawn. The SCMP reported: 'Arthur, Pearce and Cooper were noticeably absent. The match was watched with much interest by quite a large number of spectators, including several ladies.'

A Cricketer's point was duly proved at the end of the season, when a United League XV played an HKCC XI on the Chater Road ground, the senior club winning by 31 runs, while some of its best players watched the match!

1904	HKCC XI:	162	(R Hancock 33*, H Hancock 20,
Mar			A G Ward 20)
	United League XV:	131	(Sgt/Maj Webb AOC 38, R Hancock
			4–12, T Sercombe Smith 3–23)

On 11 March 1905, Lord Hawke, Captain of Yorkshire and subsequently President of the MCC, played for the HKCC against a team representing the Ladies Recreation Club. The LRC players were all gentlemen. Lord Hawke was bowled by Dick Hancock for two runs.

1906	League XV:	156	(Br Kerrick 27, A O Brawn 22, H Mackay
Mar 24			10–59 W Dixon 3–50)
	HKCC XI:	124	(W C D Turner 34, W J Daniel 31*, Br Kerrick
			4–29)

1909   HKCC 'B': 258–4 (T E Pearce 111, A Claxton 56*, H Hancock
Mar 13   56)
         Telegraphs: 117   (Young 58, Shields 26, H D Sharpin 6–43)

Apl 10   HKCC 'A':   39 (Capt Baird 7–19, H D Sharpin 3–19)
         HKCC 'B': 221 (Capt Baird 78, T E Pearce 53, H Hancock 37,
                          W Waterhouse 5–63)

Not only did the so-called 'B' team smash the 'A' team, but they won 15
of the 16 league matches to comfortably capture the senior league title.
The points system: Win 1, draw 0 and lose –1, which produced an interesting table at the end of the season.

League Table	Played	Won	Lost	Drawn	Points
HKCC 'B'	16	15	1	0	14
Civil Service CC	16	11	3	2	8
Telegraphs	16	9	5	2	4
HKCC 'A'	16	7	5	4	2
CCC	16	5	6	5	–1
RGA	12	4	7	1	–3
Police RC	15	2	10	3	–8
Kowloon CC	14	2	10	2	–8
RE	13	1	9	3	–8

Apr 11 Hong Kong: 142 (R E O Bird 45, J Hall 37, J Harrison 4–11)
        Swatow: 126 (F C Butcher 43, S J Weekes 20, R E O Bird
                         7–59)

1912   HKCC 'A':   142   (T E Pearce 42, W W Waterhouse 4–7)
Mar 5   Tels. & Dodwells: 119–7 (W Manning 40, R E H Oliver 28,
                                  H Makin 3–40)

Mar 12 Kowloon: 82 (J H Mead 45, S S Moore 3–33)
        HKCC 'A': 194 (T E Pearce 42, A Claxton 30, R Hancock 31,
                        F J de Rome 5–76)

1918   25th Middx: 68 (L/Cpl Tebbutt 28, T E Pearce 7–38)
Mar 2   HKCC: 176 (H E Muriel 76, M M Maas 33, Pte Taylor
                         7–50)

After the Triangular Interport had been completed in 1920, Hong Kong
played the visitors (Malaya & Shanghai). The Wiltshire band was in attendance.

| 1920 | Hong Kong: | 296–6 | (T E Pearce 111*, R Hancock 69) |
| Nov | Visitors: | 244 | (D W Leach 94, A Holmes-Brown 64, P Havelock-Davies 5–82) |

| Mar 13 | HKU: | 182–9 dec | (D K Samy 63, I T Pun 33, E W Day 5–71) |
| | HKCC: | 196–0 | (E J R Mitchell 82*, C Blaker 80*) |

| 1924 | KCC: | 53 | (F N Young 8–12) |
| Mar 15 | HKCC: | 248 | (L D McNicholl 70, D E Nicholson 48, J A Fraser 4–54, H Overy 4–65) |

| 1926 | HKCC: | 221–6 | (H V Parker 46*, R Hancock 39*, T E Pearce 34, J C Lyall 3–73) |
| Feb 27 | KCC: | 44 | (S Jex 19*, A C I Bowker 8–20) |

In 1923, at the time the last clubhouse on Chater Road was opened by the President, Dick Hancock, membership was around 500, with 248 resident playing members. In 1975, when the last game was played, the membership stood at around 750. By 1 January 1994 the membership had become much more complicated, with ordinary, subscriber, junior sporting members and corporate nominees, totalling 1,426. There were also 39 honorary members.

Dudley Coppin, a member of the HKCC in the 1920s, whose father had been a member before him, remarked that for many years membership of the HKCC was based on 'rank' rather than on cricket prowess, and even recalled instances of outstanding players, who were not considered of necessary rank, being forced to play elsewhere. Most of the Eurasian players of ability were members of the CCC, CRC and later the KCC. Traditionally, a member of the HKCC, on reaching the age of 30, would be invited to join the prestigious Hong Kong Club.

The HKCC was very much a male stronghold. There were two bars, one on the first floor, and a men-only bar on the second floor. Adjacent to the men-only bar was the restaurant, and to the right of the main part of the clubhouse, at ground floor level, were the mens' changing rooms. Light refreshments and drinks were served to bench seated members and their friends in the area below and in front of the clock. This very central location, a great place to be during lunchtimes when overseas teams visiting Hong Kong were playing, was exchanged for a remoter but much better establishment up in the hills of Wong Nai Chung Gap.

Sir Denys Roberts said in his foreword to *A History of The Hong Kong Cricket Club, 1851–1989*:

I have thus watched the Club change in the past 20 years, from being a happy place with air-conditioned beer, an unreliable lunch, a young bachelor membership and a central location. It has become a family centre, with greatly improved facilities of all kinds. The old clubhouse enjoyed a membership which varied from six to eight hundred and was prepared to elect almost anyone who applied, except those who were literate and thus looked upon with grave suspicion. The present one has twelve hundred members and a substantial waiting list. And so, far from admitting anyone who asks, it only elects those who are likely to preserve the atmosphere of courteous incompetence which has been so carefully encouraged since the move.

The move 'was an extremely harrowing experience', recalled Alan Bailey, who took on the huge responsibility of keeping the grass alive after its transportation from Chater Road in 14 lorry loads. After negotiations with the Government, the HKCC was offered:

1. A levelled area of 146,000 sq.ft. with basic drainage;
2. A private recreational lease of 21 years from 1971;
3. A direct grant of HK$75,000 and
4. A loan of HK$75,000 repayable over 10 years at 6% p.a.

The total cost of the new development, designed by Spence Robinson, was estimated at HK$3.8 million. The clubhouse was opened by Sir Denys Roberts, KBE, QC, on 26 September 1975.

A number of structural changes, modifications and additions have been made since the official opening: a staff quarters building, poolside cafeteria, extended dining room, ground floor bar, enclosed cricket scorers' room, air-conditioning the squash courts, floodlighting the cricket nets and tennis courts, and additional multi-storey car parking, all enhancing the original new clubhouse, one of the best in the territory.

Bill Conway, a member, was the first General Manager in the hot-seat at the transition time. A pleasant and popular person, Bill retired in 1987, in the same year as Sir Denys, the long-serving President, difficult batsman to dislodge (ask Buddy Carnell), slow left-arm bowler of dubious ability (ask Ted Wilson), and after-dinner speaker extraordinaire.

Terry Smith, a chartered surveyor by profession, ex-Captain of Cricket and cricketer of variable talents, was appointed the new President, while Keith Garner, a school teacher, and a very personable ex-CCC player, was appointed General Manager. Keith, who has been tremendously helpful to the author, retired to live in France in late 1994, the position of General Manager being filled by that 'elegant stylish batsman', Nigel Stearns.

Major A E W Salt from Hereford referred to a match in which he played for the University against the HKCC in the spring of 1914. Admiral Sturdee, who was watching the game said he thought it was the first time, to his knowledge, that Chinese had ever played on the Club ground. Salt said they may have been Chinese undergraduates playing for the University, but the bulk of the team was made up of good cricketing professors.

HKCC Centenary Booklet, 1851–1951

Since 1903, when First Division league cricket came into being, and in 1921, when the Second Division was added, the HKCC has won the senior division 26 times (once jointly) and the junior division 12 times (once jointly).

Pre the Pacific war, the most successful periods for the first team were 1908–09 to 1913–14 and 1933–34 to 1936–37, together with the double league titles in 1928–29. In those earlier league seasons, the HKCC entered 'A' and 'B' teams, until they decided to amalgamate the sides for the successful 1913–14 season. Players of special note in the prewar days, excluding services members, were R E O Bird, Dick Hancock, Acky Bowker, Harry Owen Hughes, and Tam and Alec Pearce.

The results of many of the league matches played at this time between the HKCC and other clubs, also appear in the League cricket section.

1924	Ladies XII:	190	(Mrs Reed 101 retd., Mrs Bower 28,
Dec 5			Comdr. Osborne 2–14, R E O Bird 2–32)
	Gentlemen XI:	131–6	(Lt Comdr. Lockhart, Comdr. Osborne,
			E W Hamilton, L D McNicoll, all retd on
			20, Mrs Lucey 5–56)

The acting Governor, Sir Claud Severn, was 8 not out batting No. 12.

The Rules were: Gentlemen catch with one hand, two hands forfeits 6 runs. Retire at 20. Boundaries 2 runs, boundary byes 1 run. Ladies: Boundaries 6 runs, boundary byes 4 runs. Umpire will call 'no-ball' if he considers Gentlemen bowl too fast.

1928	Single:	163–9 dec	(Owen Hughes 34, Lt Col Wyatt 5–56,
Oct 20			Lt Col Christian 4–65)
	Married:	126–6	(A W Hayward 51)

An early season annual fixture.

| 1928 | R Hancock's XI: | 142 | (A C I Bowker 41*, J Bonnar 6–35) |
| Oct 6 | | 104 | (G R Vallack 7–38) |

8   A W Hayward's XI: 113 (O Moor 43, C D Wales 7–22)
                       149 (W K Tait 45, A Reid 5–29, V M L
                            Stanion 4–42)

Hayward's XI won this opening match of the season by four wickets but batted on until they were all out.

Oct 27 IRC: 188–8 dec (A R Minu 41, J S A Curreem 35*)
         HKCC: 150–6   (H R B Hancock 32, O Moor 30)

IRC batted for 51 overs at HKCC, leaving the home side 100 minutes/30 overs to score the required runs for victory.

Nov 17 HKCC: 153–6 dec (Capt A N Evers 35; Rev E K Quick 31)
         RN: 101–9   (H V Parker 5–38)

This Saturday friendly match was played on the Navy ground at King's Park on the 'second level'. The Queen Elizabeth Hospital now occupies the site.

Dec 15 Under 30: 153   (V Stanion 45, H J Armstrong 30*, H V Parker
                       30)
        Over   30: 117–8 (T E Pearce 38, A W Hayward 31)

The only newspaper comment on this match: 'The bowling was weak.'

1929   HKCC: 267 (Rev Quick 65, G R Sayer 39, Owen Hughes 36,
Jan 1   T E Pearce 36, Comdr F C Baker 7–86)
      RN: 67 (C D Wales 4–31)

In this annual 'friendly' match, C D Wales had 3–3 off 10 overs until Pay Lt C F Waters, coming in at No. 10, 'knocked him about' for 20 runs. 'Baker was the most prominent bowler for the Senior Service maintaining a good length in his 25 overs. He is medium pace and comes across from the leg.'

Jan 5   HKCC: 165 (Capt A N Evers 46, O Moor 44, M R Abbas
                  4–24, A H Madar 3–36)
      IRC: 92 (A H Madar 25, A K Minu 25, Owen Hughes
                  3–14, Bowker 3–22)

HKCC batted for 33.1 overs on the IRC Sookunpoo wicket. IRC were all out in 26.3 overs, only the two mentioned IRC batsmen reaching double figures.

Jan 12   CCC: 168   (F Oliver 36*, D Rumjahn 36, B W Bradbury 35,
                             H V Parker 5–34)
          HKCC: 141–6 (T E Pearce 35, S Abbas 5–34)

On the HKCC ground, CCC had lost six wickets for less than 50
runs, then Bradbury, Rumjahn and Oliver, the 'tail-end' took the
score to 168 after 52.1 overs. Batting for only 27 overs, HKCC fell
short by 28 runs.

Feb 2   University: 130   (C W Lam 30, A Reid 4–45)
         HKCC: 131–4   (H Owen Hughes 61*)

It must have been close on 4.45 p.m. when they went in to get 131 in
an abominable light … with the unfortunate scorers peering from
their lofty box through the crepuscular gloom trying to make sure if
the game was over or not still being played.

                                                           R ABBIT

Feb 24   RN: 68   (C D Wales 5–23, Capt A G Dobbie 5–41)
         HKCC: 203–6 (H V Parker 51, Capt A G Dobbie 50*, Rev E K
                           Quick 39, H Owen Hughes 34)

Wales and Dobbie bowled unchanged throughout the 31.5 overs the
Navy were at the crease. 'After the match had been won, Parker and
Dobbie hit out merrily.'

The previous four recorded matches were all First Division played on
Saturdays.

Mar 2   HKCC 1st: 200–7 dec (A W Hayward 79, H Owen Hughes 34*)
         HKCC 2nd: 57   (C D Wales 5–31)

This was a 'so-called' friendly club match!

Mar 9   Mr A W Hayward's XI: 251–6 dec   (A W Hayward 81,
                                             H Owen Hughes 67*)

         Mr H R B Hancock's XI: 192–9   (Lt Maxwell 50,
                                             V Stanion 32, R Hancock
                                             26*, J L Bonnar 5–51)

The bowlers on either side were expensive on a wicket which favoured
high scoring.

                                                           R ABBIT

Marybud Chignell (nee Hancock), the eldest daughter of Dick Hancock, provided much of the information covering the 1929–30 season in Hong Kong, mainly concerning matches in which the HKCC played.

1929   HKCC: 183–6 dec   (E R Duckett 71, K H Batger 37, H J
Nov   Armstrong 31)
      RN: 110   (G E R Divett 3–11)

Two Interports trials were held at Chater Road after the end of the 1931–32 season.

Apr 23   E J R Mitchell's XI: 160   (E J R Mitchell 36 ret'd., A H Madar
                                  28, E F Fincher 27, E Zimmern 21,
                                  A C Hamilton 4–28)
        A Reid's XI: 108–8 (G C Burnett 2–17, F D Pereira 2–20)

The batsmen are good enough to keep the bowlers out of their wickets so long as they do not try to score anything but a stray single once every two overs. The bowlers can keep them stuck up like this but can't get 'em out!

R ABBIT

May 7   A Reid's XI: 136   (D Anderson 37*, A Beck 2–10, A Hamilton
                             2–14, A Madar 2–14
       Interport XI: 126   (A Minu 26, A H Madar 21, D Anderson
                             4–39, A Reid 3–3)

A colourless game on the club ground. The fielding was fair, but might have been better. However, under the gruelling sun they put up a good show on a pitch which was kicking rather badly.

R ABBIT, *The Daily Press*

1933   HKCC: 182–0 dec (E J R Mitchell 81*, H Owen Hughes
Feb 25   79*)
      University: 143   (L T Ride 69, A M Rodrigues 34,
                             R Divett 8–29)

This First Division match was played on the University ground at Pokfulam.

1934   RE: 62   (H J D Lowe 6–19)
Mar 10 HKCC: 118–9   (J E Potter 43 ret'd., H J Armstrong 43, Sgt
                         Stripp 4–31)

1935   HKCC: 179–6 dec   (C K Hill Wood 66, I McInnes 41*,
Feb 16   E T Wood 4–38)
        University: 80   (K P Gan 20, G R M Ricketts 6–10)

'University trounced by champions, Ricketts has 6 for 10.'

David Parsons, ex-Central British School, now KGV, recalled nets at the HKCC:

> I can remember walking from Jardines offices in Pedder Street to the HKCC most evenings (before the war) and spending an hour or two at the nets. We used to put 10 cents on the middle stump and the ground staff (Chinese) used to bowl to us. Some of them were very good too, as they had been at it for a number of years.

After the Pacific war, when league cricket commenced again in the 1948–49 season, the First Division squad was split into two teams, one called the 'Optimists' and the other the 'Scorpions', captained respectively by Laurie Kilbee and Alec Pearce. The team names were conjured up by Laurie and Alec. Laurie informed the author that while at Dover College, England, he played hockey for a side called the 'Folkestone Optimists', and felt the name 'Optimists' would be an appropriate name for a Hong Kong team he was about to captain, having survived internment in Hong Kong during the Japanese occupation. When the author asked Alec Pearce's widow, Nina, in early 1993 about the name 'Scorpions', without hesitation she said: 'Alec named the side Scorpions – sting in the tail.'

Postwar, the Optimists and Scorpions have won the senior championship seven and eight times respectively. The HKCC's third senior side, the Wanderers, joined the fray when the Sunday league came into being in the 1973–74 season, and later added a further two senior championship wins to the HKCC stock.

According to Stuart Barnes the name 'Wanderers' came about from an 'Occasionals' team that had played social cricket in the 1950s. After Stuart's arrival in Hong Kong in the early 1960s, the team under his helm, then known as the Wanderers, became a regular Sunday social side. When Sunday league cricket became a reality in the 1973–74 season, the Wanderers had the choice of joining the league or drifting back to their former occasional role. The rest is history.

There are also three Saturday league teams, the longest standing and most successful being the 'Nomads', which in the late 1950s was technically a CCC side which had an unofficial arrangement with the HKCC, whereby some HKCC members played in this team captained by a member of CCC, a sort of 'nomadic' existence. Eventually, the proportion of players swung in favour of the HKCC, and it became an official HKCC team in

123

the 1960s. From 1964–65 up to and including the 1993–94 season, the Nomads have won the Second Division/Saturday league title ten times (once jointly). They have also won the Saturday league/Gillette/Butani Cup five times. It was something special if you could beat the Nomads!

Again according to Stuart Barnes, who led the original 'Witherers', the name was proposed by George Rowe, after a past HKCC team of that name. The Witherers joined the Second Division league in 1970–71, and have been runners-up in the Saturday league four times since 1973–74. They won the Gillette Cup in 1984–85.

The most recent addition to the league, the 'Gap Ramblers' was formed as a Saturday league side, because, according to *The Pinkun* in October 1982: 'Early in 1983, many cricketing members of the club had been complaining that they were unable to get a game on Saturday.'

The name referred to the club's location at the time, and the likelihood that the team would be required to play most of their fixtures away from home. As the club already had a nomadic side, the name 'Ramblers' was adopted. The Gap Ramblers joined the Saturday league in 1983–84 and immediately picked up a trophy, the Gillette Cup.

There is still another side, the Hong Kong Stragglers. This side is akin to the original Stragglers of Asia, formed in India after World War I, by Army officers who had returned to the United Kingdom. Until recently, to qualify for the Stragglers of Asia, you had to have played cricket 'so many thousand miles east of Suez'. The 'Hong Kong Stragglers', formed by Stuart Barnes in 1969, are still playing regular friendly matches as part of the annual HKCC cricket calendar.

In the first postwar season, 1948–49, two Scorpions, one in the form of Len Stokes (85), a prewar Shanghai opening batsman, and the other Alec Pearce (82), a prewar Hong Kong player, put together a record first wicket partnership of 172 against the Optimists, a record not surpassed during George Lemay's 20 years as the HKCC statistician. The following season saw the 'old Lancashire Pro' Frank Howarth at his best: 'the bowling was dominated by Howarth, by now in his 40s. He delivered 311 overs and captured a staggering 103 wickets – a record which is never likely to be surpassed.'

Frank, with his medium-pace off-cutters, topped the HKCC bowling for three consecutive seasons, from 1948–49 till 1950–51. Peter Langston, who first appeared on the Hong Kong cricket scene in 1962–63, was the only other HKCC bowler to match this three-card trick during the seasons from 1962–63 till 1964–65.

Laurie Kilbee, another Hong Kong prewar player, celebrated his final season in charge of the Optimists in 1950–51 with a first victory against the Scorpions. At that time West Australian, Noel Arthy (Scorpions), topped the club batting averages for the three seasons 1949–50 to 1951–52. Like his contemporary Peter Langston in the bowling department, Peter

Davies was the only other club batsman to top the batting for three consecutive seasons, 1973–74 to 1975–76. The 'Great Man' had first played in the 1966–67 season. How did Peter Davies acquire this status?

The 'Great Man' reported the *SCMP*'s Sports Editor, Carl Myatt, after HKCC's Peter H Davies had hit KCC's Peter Hall's first four balls for four on 25 January 1969 at KCC. If only one of those deliveries had swung, as they usually did, the whole course of history might have been changed! The author did feature again as the 'Great Man' was reaching his century – bowled Hall for 97.

In the middle 1950s, Guy Pritchard, an astute skipper, who first appeared in 1949–50, like Alec Pearce and Laurie Kilbee, another 'Man of Kent', led the Optimists for 11 successive seasons, especially satisfying being their 10-wicket 'thrashing' of the Scorpions in 1954.

27 Nov Scorpions: 142   (T P Mahon 6–50)
        Optimists: 143–0 (C J B Leader 89*, G H P Pritchard 54*)

Ray Hughes, Optimists, was the only HKCC wicket-keeper to record 30 dismissals during the 20 seasons from 1948–49 to 1967–68. In the 1958–59 season, he stumped six Recreio batsmen off Pritchard's 'special teasers'. Guy then led Optimists to their first championship title in 1959–60, 'Providing the backbone in both batting and bowling.' Guy was well supported by John Leader, veteran George Rowe, and bowlers such as the economical Ken Spink, slow left-armer Gordon Williams, and young off-spinner Mike Duggan, who collected 25 wickets apiece.

The Optimists owed much to Peter Langston for their second postwar title in 1963–64. His total of 61 wickets at 8.11 included seven hauls of five wickets or more, with a best of 7 for 5 against Recreio at King's Park.

Dean Barrett (Scorpions), who toured Malaya in 1961 with the Hong Kong team, exceeded 500 runs over three consecutive seasons, 1959–60 to 1961–62. The Scorpions were beginning to stir again, aided by a flow of talented players arriving in Hong Kong in the early mid-1960s: John Fawcett, an accomplished all-rounder, and Hamish Muirhead in 1963–64; Noel Hooper in 1964–65; Ted Wilson, an experienced campaigner who had captained East Africa, and Julian Murphy in 1965–66. Wilson soon 'talked' his way into the captaincy of the Scorpions and led them, in convincing style, to the title in 1966–67.

1967   Scorpions: 223–3 dec (J Murphy 100, J Fawcett 69*)
Jan 28 Recreio: 81   (E Cannon 5–5, all bowled)

Wilson became Captain of Cricket, so Fawcett took over the captaincy the following season and retained the title.

1967   Scorpions: 245–4 (E Wilson 94*, J Murphy 43*, I Graham 43,
Oct 7   J Fawcett 39)
          Police: 170

Wilson scratched around for 40 minutes and made 20 runs. He went on to reach 94 not out, being dropped at 16, 17 and 55.

SCMP

Oct 11   Hong Kong CC: 118 (E Wilson 41, R Pellew 4–20)
         Singapore Services: 118 (K Riley 40, J Fawcett 8–57)

Fawcett getting the ball to lift and turn on this lively Chater Road pitch ... weathered some heavy punishment at the hands of West Indian left-hander Riley, then struck several decisive blows as the HKCC fought out a dramatic tie. This is believed to be the first tie in a representative fixture involving local and visiting teams.

SCMP

History was made in this same season, when a former club ground staff bowler, Kwong Wah, was selected to play for the Scorpions. Kwong Wah, better known as Benny Kwong, achieved

the unique distinction of being the first Chinese to play for the HKCC. Several generations of his family had served on the ground staff. Attacking middle order batsman, leg-spinner, seamer and excellent fielder.

Benny went on to play representative cricket for Hong Kong from 1969 till 1984.

1970   Scorpions: 219–1 dec (G Jarman 102*, N Hooper 100*)
Jan   IRC: 110   (Basri 28, B Kwong 5–33, P Harper 3–18)

Stuart Barnes's Witherers joined the Nomads in the Second Division league in 1970–71.

1971   Optimists: 232–3 dec (C Rowe 112, R Mills-Owen 69)
Jan   Scorpions: 200–6   (E Wilson 63, K Sillett 43, T Booth 30,
                               M Duggan 4–63)

Apr 10   HKCC: 284–5 dec (D T E Roberts 123, G Jarman 70,
                               M Smith 44)
         Sabah CA: 183–8   (A Dews 68)

126

'Give him a 1, give him a 2, give him a 3 ...' – Denys Roberts puts it together.

The Optimists collected their third title in 1971–72. Peter Davies scored the bulk of the runs, whilst John Ashworth was 'the pick of the bowlers'.

In the 1973–74 season, when the First and Second Divisions became separate Saturday and Sunday leagues, with cricketers playing in both leagues if they so wished, the HKCC entered their third Sunday side, the Wanderers. They immediately marked their presence by defeating the league champions, KCC Templars, to capture the Rothman's Cup.

| 1975 | Wanderers: | 260–8 dec | (M Bulfield 133, R Remnant 44, R Litherland 4–47) |
| Dec 7 | Army: | 236–7 | (D Budge 90, R Litherland 67) |

[Note: Bulfield's century was not recorded in the *HKCA Handbook* 1976–77. The information coming from Marlene Willson's newspaper cuttings.]

| 1976 | Nomads: | 235–2 | (M Tress 133, G Turner 58, H Patterson 42*) |
| Feb 28 | CCC: | 195–8 | (D Beecroft 78, P Berry 3–72) |

Over the next eight seasons from 1977–78 till 1984–85, HKCC teams captured 15 major titles. The Wanderers picked up their first senior league championship in 1977–78, when 'the elegant left-hander Martin Sabine was the linchpin of the batting.' The Optimists then won in 1978–79 and 1979–80 'under the shrewd guidance of John Ashworth', who completed his tenth season, seven as captain. He had a key strike bowler in 'big-hearted medium pacer Steve Willis.'

1980–81 saw the Nomads complete 'an unprecedented 'hat-trick' of Saturday League Cup victories', the last two under Gillette sponsorship.

| 1981 | Optimists: | 272–5 dec | (P Davies 132*, I Laidlaw 70) |
| Feb 1 | IRC: | 64 | (A Kirpalani 24, N Tonkinson 6–21) |

'Optimists tear the IRC bowling apart for Tonkinson to cut through their batting.'

| 1982 | IRC: | 87 | (D Swift 9–33) |
| Jan 3 | Optimists: | 89–1 | (P Davies 49*, D Kilgour 38*) |

Don Swift, the fitness fanatic, carved through the brittle IRC batting.

The Scorpions came back into business after a long lean period. The presence of three talented Aussies – Dave Clarke, Rod Eddington and John Hollioake, well backed by Dennis Way and the resurgence of Benny Kwong, had something to do with them taking the title in 1981–82.

1982   HKCC: 117–9 (B Kwong 26, B Wigley 3–16, G Bacon 3–21)
          HKCA: 114   (P Anderson 33, D Way 4–14, C Swann 3–36)

Only 'smoothie' Wilson could have conjured up such a win in his farewell match at the HKCC.

The 1983–84 season saw the third HKCC side Gap Ramblers join the Saturday league.

1983   Gap Ramblers: 227–2 (P Anderson 101*, S Caley 80)
Dec 10 Saracens: 207–8 (J Shroff 61, R Gill 49*, Y Vachha 41,
                                P Anderson 4–41)

The 'three-pronged' attack of Bob Fotheringham, Neil Smith and Benny Kwong guided the Scorpions to another title in the same season. These three captured 120 of the team's 135 wickets. For the first time in the Sunday league, the three HKCC sides took 1st, 2nd and 3rd positions.

1983   Scorpions: 205 (S Caley 45, D Cutting 41, S Myles 4–58)
Nov 6 Vagabonds: 60 (S Myles 35, N Smith 7–16)

Nomads, led by David Sibree, retained the Saturday league title in grand style, losing only once in the 17-match programme, their strengths being solid batting with Paul Veivers the star, reliable medium pace bowling, backed up by excellent fielding. A full-course recipe for success.

    After the previous season's top one-two-three positions in the Sunday league, all three teams slid down the table suffering from changes of personnel and a failure of expectations. However, the club's flag was kept flying by the two Saturday sides, Nomads and Witherers, who took the top two places – for David Sibree, a fitting farewell to Hong Kong cricket. Witherers also captured the Gillette Cup by defeating KCC Hornets by 33 runs.

Mar 23 Witherers: 224–8 (B Kwong 41, G Foster 39, R Stiller 39,
                           M Darke 35)
        Hornets: 191   (N Stearns 61, N Broadhurst 47, R Brewster
                           26, J Chandler 4–16)

The 1987–88 season saw Bryan Hemshall's Wanderers brush aside the bickering of the revised competition schedules to score a memorable league and cup double, only the second time this feat had been accomplished. Hemshall's 'who dares wins' attitude, memories of his leadership days with the Centaurs, was a refreshing change, and with players as diverse as the 'exuberant' Brad Jones and the 'evergreen' Arthur Barnett victimising the opposition, Bryan's approach produced the desired results. Martin Darke's version is not recorded!

From 1988–89 through to 1993–94, only the Optimists in 1989–90 under Tony Morgan, who had 'Player of the Year' Stewart Brew in his side, and the Scorpions in 1991–92 led by John Garden's consistent batting line-up and Warren Symcox's 55 wickets, kept KCC's Infidels and Templars from claiming the Sunday league title as their own right over this period.

However, the club could be thankful for the presence of the ever-marauding Nomads, who took the Saturday league title three times, plus the Butani Cup in 1992–93. Simon Brennan, in a match against the KCC Tartars at Mission Road in 1988–89, hit Hong Kong's Sri Lankan fast bowler Nanda Perera for six sixes in an over to end the game. In 1991–92, under Mike Walsh, they equalled the KCC Saracens 1985–86 record by winning all 17 matches played. In 1993–94, John Garden scored 860 runs, over 200 more than anyone else, as Nomads clinched the third of their three titles.

1993–94 also saw Stewart Brew, Optimists, become the first HKCC player to score over the magic 1000 runs in senior league cricket, a stupendous feat matched only by KCC Templars' Rahul Sharma, whilst Jonathan Orders and T Smart, Scorpions, amassed a huge 300-run partnership against IRC. Brew also became the first Hong Kong cricketer to be awarded the 'Player of the Year' trophy twice.

Stewart Brew continued his excellent form at the ICC tournament in Kenya in February 1994, in a much higher class of cricket. He was Hong Kong's most successful cricketer, scoring a total of 255 runs including 124 against West Africa and capturing 18 wickets.

The slow wickets in Malaysia during the ICC tournament in 1997 didn't suit Stewart's style of cricket and he was less successful. But he did emerge with another honour, that of Hong Kong captain, after Pat Fordham decided to call it a day after a long innings.

When ex-Interporter Nigel Stearns became the club's new General Manager, after the retirement of Keith Garner, the author remarked that it would be interesting to see whether the HKCC cricket section regained its pre-eminence. Nigel's presence and influence seems to have provided an impetus, as the Optimists won the Sunday league in 1995–95 and 1996–97. Unfortunately, the Wanderers dropped out of the Sunday league after 20 years, due to 'a shortage of numbers and talent.'

Hancock Shield

The Hancock Shield, in memory of Dick Hancock, was a gift from the 1948 HKCC President and members and Dick's many KCC friends. The donors stipulated that two two-day matches were to be played, one at the beginning and one at the end of each season, at KCC and HKCC. If a game was drawn, the team leading on the first innings would be declared the winner. The first match was played at the KCC on Saturday/Sunday, 9/10 October 1948.

HKCC: 253–8 dec (L D Kilbee 102 retd., N Oliver 57, A Panton 44,
              G E Taylor 4–75)
       85–6 dec (C P Smith 3–26, R E Lee 3–43)
KCC: 226   (W H Colledge 56, E C Fincher 40, G E Taylor 28,
              C P Smith 25*, D McLellan 6–39)
       81–5   (G E Taylor 29*, McLellan 3 wickets)

The HKCC had actually won the match, but Mr Vic Labrum, KCC Vice President, said:

> The Shield would remain with the KCC for three months and then it would be handed over to the HKCC for a similar period until the next match in April. In conclusion, he remarked that the Shield served to cement the friendship between the two clubs.

Just after leaving Sydney Grammar School and returning to his home in Hong Kong, the author played in the Hancock Shield at KCC and HKCC in the 1953–54 season.

1953   KCC: 150 (P V Dodge 39, P A Hall 31, I L Stanton 6–41,
Oct 11   F van Oorde 4–25)
& 12   89   (D G Coffey 29, I L Stanton 5–48)
       HKCC: 125 (L D Kilbee 48, R Franklin 31, R E Lee 5–47,
                   P A Hall 3–37)
       115–9 (R Franklin 36, D G Coffey 5–25, P A Hall 3–52)

HKCC won by one wicket in a closely fought early season match at KCC.

1954   HKCC: 205–8 (A Harvey 54, G T Rowe 50, H Owen Hughes
Mar 27   35, W Withall 5–25)
& 28   122–9 (C J B Leader 39, B C N Carnell 4–21, W N J
                   Withall 3–26)
       KCC: 282–9 (R E Lee 75, P Wood 44, P A Hall 32)

130

KCC won on the first innings to recapture the shield at HKCC.

In the early to mid-1960s, KCC dominated these annual matches between the two premier clubs.

1966   HKCC: 274–6 (M Bulfield 100*, J K Fawcett 100, C Shaw 34)
             112   (G T Rowe 35*, H Dickson 5–32, P A Hall 3–25)
        KCC: 255   (G Abbas 88, R B Jones 54, G Jones 49*,
                      G Williams 5–90)
             124   (J Shroff 62, J Fawcett 6–44, M Miles 3–55)

HKCC won by seven runs in a 'thrill-packed match at Cox's Road', the first time KCC had lost for six years.

The author asked Keith Garner for his assistance to find some of the Hancock Shield match results played at Chater Road in the 1960s. Keith said he was 'sorry to have to report that he could only find two Hancock Shield match details from the 1960s – the earlier scorebook does not seem to have been transferred to Wong Nai Chung Gap.'

1967   HKCC: 95   (J Fawcett 33, I Vaughan-Arbuckle 27*,
Apr 8   J Vachha 5–28, Carnell 4–29)
& 9   213–6 dec (I Vaughan-Arbuckle 49*, P Davies 36,
                      G Rowe 31, I Stevens 30*)
        KCC: 98–9 dec (J Shroff 26, G Williams 7–28)
             181–6   (J Shroff 71, A Tebbutt 36*, B Roach 34)

Match drawn, KCC won on first innings.

1969   KCC: 246   (P Hall 91, D Dalrymple 60, J Fawcett 4–65,
Apr 12   E Wilson 3–5)
        HKCC: 80–0

Match abandoned because of rain at HKCC.

Peter Davies was HKCC captain at Chater Road in the 1970s, when it was agreed between the two club captains that the side winning the match would keep the shield in perpetuity, as there was only one remaining 'small shield' for inscription. KCC led on the first innings in a drawn game, so became the proud permanent holders of the Hancock Shield.

A little time after this event, the author thought it would be appropriate to similarly honour a KCC cricketer. The name E C 'Teddy' Fincher immediately sprang to mind. Teddy had first played for Hong Kong in 1926 against Malaya, was still playing league cricket after WWII, and was KCC President in 1968–69. A Teddy Fincher shield was designed, constructed and donated by KCC and HKCC in memory of Teddy to replace the Hancock Shield.

Further thought was given to this 'replacement' idea, and mainly at the instigation of Geoff Foster, HKCC Captain of Cricket at the time, it was decided by both clubs that the annual memorial shield matches should be for the Hancock and Fincher Shields, the Hancock Shield when played at the HKCC, and the Fincher Shield when played at the KCC. That format continues, but due to heavy pressure on the cricket calendar, only one annual match is played, the matches rotating between the two grounds.

1983   HKCC: 181–7   (P Anderson 70, L Prabhu 5–80)
               204–5   (D Kilgour 68, P Anderson 52*, P Davies 30)
        KCC: 182–6   (J Bygate 62, G Davies 42, R Toes 4–38)
               207–6   (G Davies 90*, J Bygate 36, B Kwong 3–58)

KCC won by four wickets. 'Man of the Match' – Glyn Davies.

The respective cricket captains then decided these HKCC/KCC shield matches should be played for on a 50-overs basis. Like so many others, these memorial matches have also 'succumbed' to the limited overs format.

1990   KCC: 224–7   (N Stearns 42*, J Marsden 31)
        HKCC: 176   (S Brew 70, B Gohel 5 wickets)

KCC won by 48 runs.

1991   HKCC: 293–5   (S Brew 63, L Beaman 50*, J Barrington 41,
Dec 1   S Foster 33, J Garden 32)
        KCC: 220–9   (P Fordham 68, R Brewster 48, G Davies 36,
               S Foster 4–31)

HKCC won by 73 runs. Due to an injury, KCC only batted ten players.

1995   KCC: 231–6   (M Eames 110, N Waters 46, A Ashman 3–34)
Nov. 26 HKCC: 232–6   (S Brew 93, S Foster 34, R Bannister 32,
                 O'Reilly 4–50)

HKCC – Honorary membership for interport cricketers

At an HKCC General Committee meeting on 10 September 1963, it was minuted:

> J H B Leckie advised that the names of 17 former Interport Crick-
> eters had been submitted by the various clubs and the Committee
> agreed that letters inviting the persons should be signed by the Chair-
> man. It was unanimously agreed that the name of Mr George Hong
> Choy, Hon. Secretary of the Hong Kong Cricket League, be added to
> this list.

The author asked the General Manager Keith Garner about this list in November 1994. Keith said: 'A search of the minutes, both backwards and forwards, does not shed any light on identities!'

After Hong Kong beat Malaya at Chater Road in November 1963, the first win against Malaya since 1929, the 1963 recommendation of the HKCC General Committee, with later amendments, was implemented by George Rowe (President 1968–73), and the practice of honoring Interport cricketers in recognition of their contribution to Hong Kong cricket continued for a few years thereafter.

Initial Honorary Members	Honorary Members post 1963
Bell, R W (dec'd)	Cumings, C G
Carnell, B C N	Daniel, R G
Coffey, D G	Ebrahim, H D
Dhabher, B P	Hung J T
Hall, P A	Kwong, B
Kermani, F (dec'd)	Lacy-Smith, I F
Lalchandani, R	Lalchandani, G
Myatt, P C	Wigley, B T
Remedios, E J	
Shroff, J S	
Sillett, K H	
Souza, G Snr (dec'd)	
Stapleton, C I (dec'd)	
Zimmern, A (dec'd)	
Zimmern, F R	
Hong Choy, G * (dec'd)	

* Not an Interport cricketer – see Minute quoted above.

The author has compiled this list from available records, but its complete accuracy cannot be confirmed, even after checking with some of the original Honorary Members.

There was a hiccup in the mid-1970s over the granting of these Honorary Memberships to 'persons who had not contributed to the Club'. The matter was resolved at an HKCC Annual General Meeting at Chater Road attended by Buji Dhabher and the author, when Denys Roberts was the incumbent President.

Club centuries

The *Hong Kong Daily Press* and the *South China Morning Post* were the main daily newspapers in the Colony when the cricket league commenced in the 1903–04 season.

This schedule of centuries scored by HKCC members from 1866 to 1904 was a spectacular find, for not only does it provide a unique record, but it also gives us a window into the variety of cricket teams partaking in the game during those early years.

South China Morning Post Club Centuries

The Record of the H.K.C.C.

The following centuries have been scored by members of the H.K.C.C. in club matches since 1866:

Match	Date	Player	Score
East v. West	1866	Captain Perry	129
H.K. v. United Services	1871	F. S. Head	109
West v. East	1874	A. R. Handley	125
H.K. v. Fire Brigade	1877	A. K. Travers	126
H.K. v. Garrison	1878	W. Hynes	122 not out
Garrison v. R.N.	1878	Lieut. Saunders	112
Over 30 v. Under 30	1879	S. M. Munro	105
H.K. v. Army and Navy	1879	S. M. Munro	157 not out
H.K. v. Fire Brigade	1879	Lieut. Friend	157
Bankers and Brokers v. The Merchants	1880	S. M Munro	126
H.K. v. Army and Navy	1880	W. Dunman	118 not out
Dockyard v. Garrison	1881	Lieut. Purdon	103
Over 30 v. Under 30	1881	W. Hynes	114
Old Residents v. New Comers	1881	W. Dunman	152

Match	Date	Player	Score
Fire Brigade v. H.K.C.C.	1881	W. Dunman	105
H.K. v. Amoy	1883	H. G. Rice	120
H.K. v. Garrison	1884	C. A. Stuart	100
Ireland v. The World	1885	E. Druitt	147
'A. to LL.' v. 'M. to Z.'	1887	M. D. Graham	113
H.K. v. Garrison	1887	W. B. Robertson	113
Lieut. Graham's XI v. Sercombe-Smith's XI	1887	E. J. Coxon	100
H.K. v. Garrison	1887	T. E. Davies	121
H.K. v. R.N.	1889	E. M. Blair	155 not out
H.K. v. Navy	1889	A. J. Campbell	103
H.K. v. Southern Division R.N.	1890	Capt. Dunn	120
H.K. v. H.K. Football Club	1890	Capt. Dunn	208 not out
H.K. v. R.M.S. *Empress of India*	1890	Capt. Dunn	187
H.K. v. Bankers, Lawyers and Brokers	1891	Dr. J. A. Lowson	120 not out
H.K. v. Shanghai	1892	Capt. Dunn	107
H.K. v. Garrison	1892	Dr. Lowson	102
H.K. v. Garrison	1892	F. Maitland	144 not out
H.K. v. United Services	1893	F. Maitland	103
Over 30 v. Under 30	1893	F. Maitland	103 not out
H.K. v. Shanghai Past & Present	1893	E. J. Coxon	104
H.K. v. Jockey Club	1893	Dr. Lowson	108
H.K. v. Wigwam L.T.C.	1894	Dr. Lowson	109
H.K. v. Civil Service	1894	B. E. M. Waters	112
H.K. v. Wigwam L.T.C.	1894	Ross Thompson	100
H.K. v. Football Club	1894	Dr. Lowson	130
The World v. Scotland	1897	A. G. Ward	105
H.K. v. West Yorks Regt	1897	Lieut. Campbell	100 not out
H.K. v. West Yorks Regt	1897	F. Maitland	100
H.K. v. H.K.F.C.	1898	Capt. Dyson	109
H.K. v. H.K.F.C.	1898	Capt. Langhorne	121
H.K. v. Garrison	1898	Dr. Lowson	163
H.K. v. R.N.	1898	T. Sercombe Smith	122
H.K Shanghai XI v. Stay at Homes	1898	A. S. Anton	112 not out
H.K. under 28 v. H.K. over 28	1898	Lieut. G. D. Campbell	104 not out
„ v. „	1898	H. R. B. Hancock	119
„ v. „	1898	Lieut. Powlett, R.N.	111
„ v. „	1898	Capt. Langhorne	110 not out

Match	Date	Player	Score
H.K. v. United Services	1900	Dr. Tuck	102
H.K. v. Garrison	1900	F. Maitland	156
United Services v. Civilians	1901	A. G. Ward	132
H.K. v. Army	1902	T. Sercombe Smith	156 not out
H.K. v. Army	1902	Lieut. Hayhurst	111
H.K. v. Cruisers	1902	Capt. Kriekenbeek, B.I.	100 not out
H.K. v. Public-Schools	1902	Capt. Kriekenbeek	108
H.K. v. Navy	1902	Lieut. Hayhurst	117
H.K. v. The Navy	1903	G. A. Cooke, R.N.	102 not out
H.K. v. The United Services	1903	J. T. Dixon	118
Over 29 v. Under 29	1903	A Punnett, R.N.	104
Public Schools and Varsities v. The Rest	1903	G. Moore, R.N.	113
H.K. v. Shanghai	1903	Lieut. W. F. Lumsden	136
H.K. v. The Peak	1903	T. Sercombe Smith	101
H.K. v. A United Service team	1904	W. C. D. Turner	104
H.K. v. The Garrison	1904	W. C. D. Turner	115 not out
H.K. v. The United Services	1904	W. C. D. Turner	198
H.K. v. The United Services	1904	R. Hancock	130

First Division/Sunday League – Batting Performances 1948–49 to 1993–94

Season	Player		500 runs plus	Centuries
1948–49	L F Stokes	(S)	613 at 55.73	
1949–50	N E Arthy	(O)	676 at 42.25	
	L F Stokes			118 v 3rd Cdo. Brigade
	L D Kilbee	(O)		101* v Army
1951–52	N E Arthy		596 at 42.57	
1952–53	I L Stanton	(S)	696 at 40.94	120* v IRC & 111 v CCC
	T A Pearce	(S)		105* v HKU
1954–55	G H P Pritchard	(O)	568 at 33.35	102 v CCC
	C J B Leader	(O)		101 v KCC
1955–56	F A Weller	(S)	574 at 41.00	123* v PRC & 106 v Recreio
1956–57	C J B Leader		503 at 33.53	
1957–58	H Owen Hughes	(S)	586 at 36.62	
	R M Macpherson	(O)		124 v PRC
1958–59	G T Rowe	(O)	500 at 38.46	
1959–60	D Barrett	(S)	660 at 55.00	
	I L Stanton		509 at 33.93	
	C J B Leader			100 v Brigade

136

First Division/Sunday League – Batting Performances (cont'd)

Season	Player		500 runs plus	Centuries
1960–61	G T Rowe		525 at 35.00	
	D Barrett		519 at 32.43	
	G H P Pritchard			110 v KCC 'B'
1961–62	G H P Pritchard		580 at 38.66	
	D Barrett		598 at 37.37	
	K H Sillett	(S)	530 at 29.44	
	I L Stanton			103* v Seawings
1962–63	R Newman	(S)	542 at 54.20	104* v CCC
	F A Weller			104* v RAF
1963–64	F A Weller		564 at 35.25	
	D T E Roberts	(S)		125* v Saracens
1964–65	J K Fawcett	(S)		110* v Army
	R J McAulay	(O)		102* v Saracens
1965–66	J K Fawcett			106 v IRC & 101* v Optimists
	D Barrett			100* v PRC
1966–67	J K Fawcett		541 at 54.10	
	J C G Murphy	(S)		100 v Recreio
1967–68	P H Davies	(O)	732# at 33.27	
	E H Wilson	(S)	593# at 49.42 (1)	
	J K Fawcett		511# at 28.39	
	J R Kilbee	(O)		126* v RAF
	I L J Stevens	(O)		105 v VALLEY #
	R Mills-Owen	(O)		103* v LSW
1968–69	P H Davies		780# at 41.05	103 v RAF
	J K Fawcett			115* v SERVICES #
1969–70	G P Jarman	(S)	802 at 66.83 (1)	115* v Saracens & 102* v IRC
	N B Hooper	(S)	814 at 50.86 (3)	104* v LSW & 100* v IRC
	J M Smith	(O)	734 at 48.93 (4)	100 v Army
	P H Davies		876 at 48.67 (5)	116 v Templars
	M R V Clinch	(O)		133 v Wanderers
	K H Sillett	(W)		122* v LSW
1970–71	C Rowe	(O)		112 v Scorpions
1971–72	G Nolan	(S)	522 at 40.15 (4)	106* v RAF
	P H Davies		674 at 39.65 (5)	103 v Army
	R Mills-Owen		516 at 34.40 (8)	112 v RAF
	N B Hooper			143 v Templars
	M de Vries	(O)		117 v Army
1972–73	I Marshall	(S)	607 at 43.36 (1)	
	P H Davies		522 at 37.29 (2)	103* v Wanderers
	G Nolan		512 at 36.57 (3)	110 v Police
	G Turner	(W)		140* v Scorpions
	I L J Stevens			140* v Scorpions
1973–74	P H Davies		968 at 46.10 (1)	110 v Police & 110 v Scorpions
	I L J Stevens		659 at 38.76 (4)	157* v Scorpions
	C Shaw	(S)	584 at 30.74 (10)	
	R Wright	(W)	530 at 27.89	116 v Police

137

First Division/Sunday League – Batting Performances (cont'd)

Season	Player		500 runs plus	Centuries
	P Murray	(W)	544 at 27.20	
	B Kwong	(S)		111 v Army
1974–75	S Kirkness	(S)		120* v IRC
	R Mulready	(S)		115* v IRC

S Kirkness & R Mulready 216* (3rd) v IRC (1)

1975–76	P H Davies		675 at 56.25 (3)	134* v Wanderers & 102* v Scorpions
1976–77	J Lunn	(W)		138* v IRC
	M Lewis	(O)		118 v Scorpions
1977–78	M Sabine	(W)	553 at 61.44 (1)	133* v IRC
	B Kwong			119 v Army
	C Townsend	(S)		105* v IRC
	P H Davies			103* v Scorpions
1978–79	R Poynton	(W)	533 at 44.14 (5)	
	P H Davies		511 at 39.31 (6)	117* v Scorpions
	A Lorimer	(O)	573 at 38.20 (8)	111* v LSW
	I L J Stevens			124* v Wanderers
	C Swann	(W)		106* v Police
1979–80	P H Davies		663 at 44.20 (3)	113* v Templars
	N Beaton	(S)	640 at 40.00 (7)	108* v Infidels & 107 v IRC
	P Varty	(S)	597 at 39.80	108* v LSW, 108 v Police & 103* v IRC
	R Eddington	(S)		100* v IRC
1980–81	P H Davies		505 at 50.50 (3)	132* v IRC & 125* v Templars
		(T)		126* v Brit.Forces§
	J Hollioake	(T)		100 v Police§
	A Lorimer			104 v Brit.Forces
	M Sabine	(T)		112* v Brit.Forces§
1981–82	M Sabine		576 at 72.00 (2)	106 v Vagabonds & 103*v LSW
	J Hollioake	(S)	646 at 58.73 (3)	138 v Brit.Forces, 133 v Infidels & 112 v Templars
	A Lorimer		567 at 56.70 (4)	128* v Infidels
	P W Anderson	(W)	500 at 50.00 (5)	151* v IRC
	P H Davies		615 at 43.93 (8)	102 v Brit.Forces
	M Walsh	(W)		127* v Infidels
	D Kilgour	(O)		118 v Infidels
	B Kwong			153* v Infidels
	D Kilgour	(O)		118 v Infidels
	B Kwong			153* v Infidels

J Hollioake & B Kwong 230 (2nd) v Infidels (2)

1982–83	D Kilgour			116* v Wanderers
	P W Anderson			115* v Templars
	P Henley	(S)		105* v IRC
	J Hollioake			104* v IRC
	P Olsen	(O)		102* v IRC

P Henley & J Hollioake 228* (1st) v IRC (1)

George Souza Snr. (Craigengower) allowing one to pass on the off. A. Zimmern (Kowloon) keeping wicket. Picture taken during the First Division match at Happy Valley. The others in the picture are N.A.E. Mackay (fielder) and J.P. Robinson (umpire).   Courtesy: Irene Souza

Hong Kong Bund   Courtesy: Mike Hammersley (copied postcards)

1992-93 Stewart Brew (HKCC) Batsman, Mark Eames (KCC) Fielder. Courtesy: Peter Ford

HKCA - Handbooks

Craigengower C.C. - Champions First Division 1937-38

Courtesy: C.C.C.

Club de Recreio - Champions First Division 1938-39

Courtesy: Dr. E.L. Gosano

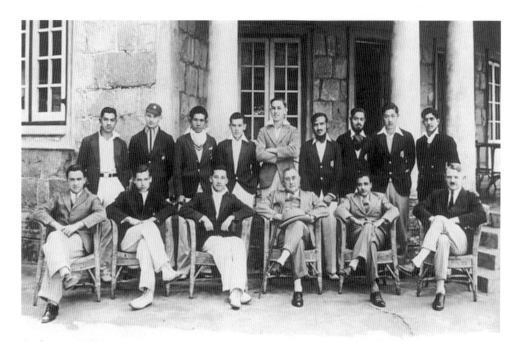

Hong Kong University - Champions First Division 1932-33   Courtesy: Dr. E.L. Gosano

HKCC First pavilion   Courtesy: The Hongkong Cricket Club

Neil Harvey on his way to a stylish 65 for the Australian Superstars v HKCC President's XI at Chater Road, Hong Kong, 20th April 1975. Wicket-Keeper: Ram Lalchandani

Courtesy: HKCA

The Three 'Musketeers' - flown to Hong Kong by Cathay Pacific - on the occasion of the closing, old Clubhouse, 1975. L to R: Denys Roberts (President HKCC), Bert Oldfield, Harold Larwood, Clarrie Grimmett, Ted Wilson (President HKCA)

Courtesy: Ted Wilson

Indian Recreation Club Champions First Division 1930-31

Kowloon Cricket Club - The Matshed and cricket First XI -1904

The shipwreck of the Bokhara: The Hong Kong and Shanghai Cricket Teams - 1892

Courtesy: Jean Lever

Templars Champions First Division 1972-73

Courtesy: Peter Hall

Saracens Champions Saturday League 1976-77   Courtesy: Peter Hall

LSWCC - Champions Sunday League and Rothman's Cup 1980-81   Courtesy:Geoff Lever

First Division/Sunday League – Batting Performances (cont'd)

Season	Player		500 runs plus	Centuries
1983–84	P W Anderson		676 at 61.45 (1)	130 v Templars
	R Davies	(S)		101* v Templars
	P W Anderson & M Darke 203 (3rd) v Templars (1)			
1984–85	P W Anderson		580 at 64.40 (2)	134* v Brit.Forces & 127 v Optimists
	W Orchard	(O)	681 at 48.64 (6)	131* v Vagabonds
	M Walsh		603 at 46.38 (9)	102 v Police
	R Stiller	(S)	528 at 40.62	108* v Vagabonds
	M Sabine		510 at 39.23	100* v Vagabonds
	S Caley	(S)	572 at 38.13	
	B Kwong		509 at 31.81	
	J Barrington	(O)	(580 at 82.85 nine innings)	139* v IRC, 133* v Police, 127 v Infidels & 100 v Vagabonds
1985–86	M Walsh		614 at 47.23(5)	112 v Scorpions & 108 v Police
	P H Davies		555 at 46.25(7)	100 v LSW
	R Eddington		508 at 46.20(8)	
	N Sawrey-Cookson			134* v IRC
	M Sabine			111* v Brit.Forces
	A Morgan	(O)		108* v Vagabonds
	W Orchard			103 v Vagabonds
1986–87	M Sabine		798 at 72.55(2)	127* v Brit. Forces
	P H Davies		547 at 60.78(3)	124* v Brit.Forces & 113* v IRC
	R Davies			103 v Brit.Forces
1987–88	I Chakrabarti	(W)		128* v IRC
	M Darke			105* v Brit.Forces
	M Sabine			100* v LSW
	I Chakrabarti & D Chandiok 201 (4th) v IRC (1)			
1988–89	M Sabine		695 at 99.29 (1)	135* v Brit.Forces
	M Speak	(O)	840 at 84.00 (2)	145* v Infidels & 111 v Templars
	D Thomas	(S)		118 v IRC
	A Morgan			111* v Vagabonds
1989–90	S Brew	(O)	939 at 93.90(1)	166* v Templars, 124 v Infidels & 103* v LSW
	M Swift	(W)		141* v IRC
	W Symcox	(S)		135 v Brit.Forces
	J Barrington			122 v Infidels
	J Garden	(S)		117 v Templars
	R Nuttall	(O)		107* v Templars
	S Brew & R Nuttall (O) 273* (1st) v Templars (1)			
	S Brew & J Barrington (O) 248(1st) v Infidels (2)			
1990 91	M Speak		698 at 77.56 (1)	151* v IRC, 111* v Vagabonds
	S Foster	(W)	676 at 67.60 (3)	135 v Brit.Forces, 101*v Vagabonds
	S Brew		929 at 66.35 (4)	105 v Vagabonds, 104 v Infidels

139

First Division/Sunday League – Batting Performances (cont'd)

Season	Player		500 runs plus	Centuries
				104 v Wanderers & 100* v IRC
	J Barrington		652 at 59.27 (6)	155 v IRC & 100* v LSW
	P Barker	(S)	611 at 55.55 (7)	112* v Infidels
	M Sabine		550 at 50.00 (9)	155* v Brit.Forces & 112 v Scorpions
	J Garden			137* v Templars
	N Helm	(S)		106* v Brit.Forces
	M Speak & S Brew	(O)	261* (1st) v IRC (1)	
	J Barrington & M Speak	(O)	211(5th) v IRC (2)	
1991–92	S Brew		593 at 65.89 (1)	115 v Templars
	M Peck	(W)	622 at 47.85 (7)	111 v Templars & 101 v IRC
	D Thomas		507 at 46.10	
	M Sabine		507 at 42.25	105 v Vagabonds
	J Penrose	(O)		123 v Infidels & 112* v LSW
	S Foster			122* v Optimists, 105* v Vagabonds &138* v Taverners§
	J Barrington			109 v Wanderers
1992–93	M Sabine		669 at 60.82 (6)	130* v IRC & 102 v Vagabonds
	S O'Brien	(O)	632 at 57.45 (7)	129 v Brit.Forces
	S Foster		509 at 36.36	193 v LSW§ & 132 v Scorpions
	J Dally	(O)		123 v Brit.Forces
	L Beaman	(O)		115* v Vagabonds
	D Thomas			105* v Templars
	J Hawkesley	(O)		103 v IRC
	J Orders	(S)		101* v Brit.Forces
	S O'Brien & J Dally	(O)	246 (4th) v Brit.Forces (2)	
	S Foster & M Sabine	(W)	240 (2nd)v LSW (2)§	
	D Thomas & J Orders	(S)	206* (3rd) v Brit.Forces (4)	
1993–94	S Brew		1005 at 111.67 (2)	138* v Vagabonds, 124* v Infidels
				120* v Pak.Assn. 110 v Vagabonds
	J Orders		573 at 63.67 (7)	158* v IRC & 126 v Brit.Forces
	S Foster			155 v Optimists & 109 v Optimists§
	T Smart	(S)		147 v IRC & 102 v Brit.Forces
	M Watson	(O)		118* v Infidels
	P Lacamp	(S)		110* v Brit.Forces
	R Nuttall			124 v Wanderers§
	J Orders & T Smart	(S)	303 (3rd) v IRC (1)	

(1) Position in averages Wicket partnership (1st)
\#   Includes 'Super' League
§   Rothman's Cup

HKCC – (C) Centredemics (O) Optimists (S) Scorpions (T) Taverners (W) Wanderers
KCC – Infidels/Saracens/Templars

First Division/Sunday League – Bowling Performances 1948–49 to 1993–94

Season	Player		50 wickets plus	7 plus (for 50 runs or less)
1948–49	F Howarth	(S)	53 at 10.91	'hat-trick' v IRC
	T P Mahon	(O)	49 at 12.10	
	T A Pearce	(S)		8–31 v KCC
1949–50	F Howarth		103 at 6.78	9–26 v CCC, 8–45 v Cdo.Brig.
			(5 plus 13 times)	7–26 v CCC & 'hat-trick' v Recreio
	T P Mahon			7–19 v Royal Navy
	A L Snaith	(O)		7–26 v IRC
1950–51	F Howarth			9–11 v Recreio & 7–45 v IRC
	F A Weller	(S)		7–23 v HKU
	G H P Pritchard	(O)		7–43 v IRC
1951–52	C B Connet	(S)		8–18 v CCC
	R G Craig	(O)		8–45 v RAF
1952–53	C B Connet			'hat-trick' v Royal Navy
	H Owen Hughes	(S)		7–25 v CCC
1953–54	K G E Spink	(O)	58 at 8.38	
	D W Leach	(S)		7–42 v Royal Navy
	T P Mahon			7– 8 v Recreio
1955–56	G H P Pritchard		50 at 14.34	7–48 v CCC
1956–57	T P Mahon		49 at 11.75	
1957–58	L White	(S)	51 at 13.88	
	F Howarth		58 at 14.09	
	G H P Pritchard			9–56 v Police
1958–59	R H Campion	(S)	53 at 12.07	7–49 v Army 'North' & 'hat-trick' v Police
	T P Mahon			7–29 v PRC
1959–60	G H P Pritchard			7–42 v IRC
1960–61	M Duggan			7–23 v Scorpions
	L Sheldon	(O)		7–30 v IRC
	K G E Spink			7–42 v CCC
	W E G Williams	(O)	61 at 10.86	7–47 v KCC 'B'
1962–63	J Robson	(S)	54 at 11.40	7–31 v IRC
1963–64	P A Langston	(O)	61 at 8.11	7– 5 v Recreio & 7–15 v Army II
			(5 plus 7 times)	
1964–65	F A Weller			8–31 v LSW
	J K Fawcett	(S)		'hat-trick' v CCC
1966–67	J C G Murphy	(S)	50 at 9.96	
	J K Fawcett		64 at 10.25	
			(5 plus 5 times)	
	P A Langston			8–14 v Recreio
	I L J Stevens	(O)		'hat-trick' v Army
1967–68	J K Fawcett		66 at 11.03 #	7–24 v LSW
	M Duggan		61 at 13.38 #	
	J C G Murphy		56 at 12.36 #	
	P A Langston			9–49 v Army
	W E G Williams			'hat-trick' v Saracens

141

First Division/Sunday League – Bowling Performances (cont'd)

Season	Player		50 wickets plus	7 plus (for 50 runs or less)
1968–69	F A Weller			8–18 v Cavaliers
	M Duggan			8–40 v IRC
	P A Langston			7–16 v Cavaliers
1968–69	J Macdonald	(O)		7–16 v Saracens
	P G H Green	(O)		7–24 v Army
1969–70	M Duggan		75 at 10.25 (3)	9–29 v IRC
	N Dennis	(W)		7–28 v Templars
	P A Langston			7–39 v RAF
	R Dewar	(S)		7–40 v RAF
1971–72	J Ashworth	(O)	52 at 12.48 (1)	
	B Kwong	(S)	60 at 17.25 (6)	9–14 & 8–88 v LSW
1972–73	J Ashworth		52 at 14.25	
	R Bullen	(W)		7–24 v IRC
1973–74	D Wellard	(W)	69 at 10.43	7–17 v Optimists & 7–34 v LSW
	L Williams	(S)		8–41 v Army
	M Duggan		54 at 14.44 (7)	
1974–75	G Butler	(W)		7–22 v Police & 7–30 v IRC incl. 'hat-trick'
	P Francis	(S)		7–24 v Police
	J Hughes	(O)		'hat-trick' v Police
1975–76	J Ashworth			8–56 v Wanderers
1976–77	B Kwong			7–16 v Army
	D Way	(O)		7–35 v Wanderers
1978–79	M Hislop	(S)		7–32 v Police
1979–80	M Hislop		61 at 12.70 (1)	
	T Smith	(W)		7–35 v Vagabonds
	R Toes	(W)		7–36 v IRC
1981–82	D Swift	(O)		9–33 v IRC
	D Way	(S)		7–37 v Vagabonds
1982–83	D Swift			8–49 v LSW
1983–84	A McLeish	(O)	61 at 13.00 (2)	7–41 v Brit.Forces
	N Smith	(S)		7–16 v Vagabonds
1984–85	N Smith			9–32 v Police
	B Jones	(W)		8–36 v Wanderers & 7–32 v IRC
	R Fotheringham	(S)		7–20 v Vagabonds
	B Kwong			7–20 v IRC
	A Telford	(W)		7–49 v Brit.Forces
1985–86	R Fotheringham		54 at 16.81 (1)	(only bowler 50 plus wickets)
	N Smith			9–83 v Brit.Forces
	D Swift			7–39 v Templars
	A Morgan	(C)		7–44 v Taikoo§
	R Toes			7–47 v Police
1986–87	R Fotheringham		53 at 18.32 (6)	8–49 v Infidels (only bowler 50 plus wickets)
1987–88	B Jones			8–61 v Brit.Forces & 7–32 v Templars

First Division/Sunday League – Bowling Performances (cont'd)

Season	Player		50 wickets plus	7 plus (for 50 runs or less)
1988–89	A Scattergood	(W)		7–31 v IRC
1989–90	R Fotheringham			8–39 v Brit.Forces
	D Neutze	(S)		7–46 v Optimists
1990–91	W Symcox	(S)	41 at 16.66 (1)	'hat-trick' v Infidels
1991–92	W Symcox		55 at 13.02 (2)	9–82 incl. 'hat-trick' v Templars
				& (only bowler 50 plus)
				'hat-trick' v Wanderers
1992–93	A Ashman	(O)	40 at 15.60 (1)	
	M Johnson	(S)		7–47 v IRC & 'hat-trick'
				v LSW
1993–94	J Strachan	(O)		7–20 v Brit.Forces

Second Division/Saturday League – Batting Performances 1965–66 to 1993–94

Season	Player		500 runs plus	Centuries
1969–70	P J Berry	(N)	540 at 31.76 (7)	100 v HKU
1970–71	D B Minns	(N)	514 at 36.71 (4)	
	J Danks	(N)		133* v IRC
	C Strachan	(N)		114* v CCC
	B E Hurges	(W)		100 v Nomads
1971–72	B Temple	(W)	618 at 41.20 (4)	
	D B Minns		513 at 39.46 (7)	116* v Crusaders
	G Turner	(N)	508 at 39.08 (8)	
	W Templeman	(W)	579 at 30.47	
	M Watts	(W)		103* v Police II
	I Marshall	(W)		102 v Police II
1972–73	P Green	(N)	654 at 50.31 (3)	101* v St George's
1973–74	M Tress	(N)	894 at 74.50 (2)	159* v Crusaders, 103* v IRC
				& 102* v Army
	P Green		717 at 65.18 (3)	
	M Bulfield	(W)	599 at 46.08 (5)	
	R Tipper	(W)	706 at 39.22 (7)	102* v IRC
	R Joynt	(W)	549 at 32.29	
	R McGregor	(W)		113* v DBS
	K H Sillett	(N)		113 v DBS
1974–75	R Tipper		540 at 49.09 (3)	
	M Bulfield		577 at 41.21 (6)	
1975–76	G Turner		948 at 49.89 (5)	
	M Tress		548 at 34.35	133 v CCC
	R Tipper		515 at 34.33	104* v DBS
	J Lunn	(W)		105 v KGV
	R Mulready	(W)		100 v LSW
1976–77	R Tipper		615 at 34.17	
1977–78	G Turner		667 at 44.47 (6)	
1978–79	A Lorimer	(N)	777 at 43.10 (6)	
	P Varty	(N)		102* v Crusaders

Second Division/Saturday League – Batting Performances (cont'd)

Season	Player		500 runs plus	Centuries
1979–80	P Varty		981 at 57.70 (2)	122* & 102* v St George's
	A Lorimer		925 at 48.68 (7)	136* v Kai Tak, 104 v CCC &
				114* v Witherers
	N B Hooper	(N)		118 v St George's
1980–81	A Lorimer		841 at 44.26 (7)	100 v Witherers
	J Hollioake	(N)		170 v HKU
	M Walsh	(N)		110 v Royal Navy
1981–82	A Lorimer		690 at 49.29 (6)	
	K McConnell	(N)	534 at 38.14	
	M Walsh			115* v Crusaders
	P Staveley	(N)		104* v Islanders
1982–83	A Lorimer		545 at 77.86 (2)	116* v Kai Tak
1983–84	P W Anderson	(GR)	648 at 92.57 (1)	106 v CCC, 101* v Saracens &
				100* v Centaurs
	K McConnell		596 at 66.22 (5)	104 v St George's
	M Darke	(W)	794 at 46.70	100 v Islanders
	W Kitson	(W)	523 at 37.25	
	P Varty		501 at 31.31	
	D Sibree	(N)	523 at 30.76	
	S Caley	(GR)		119* v Tartars
	P Veivers	(N)		104 v Saracens
1984–85	P Veivers		626 at 89.43 (2)	124* v Crusaders & 117* v
				LSW
	B Kwong	(W)	598 at 35.18	114* v KGV
	M Darke		631 at 31.55	
1985–86	M Walsh		588 at 34.59	
	S Elliott	(GR)		158 v HKU
	B Jones	(W)		116 v Army & 102 v Centaurs
	M Hammersley	(N)		108* v Kai Tak
1986–87	P Durack	(N)	562 at 51.09 (5)	122* v Strollers & 105 v
				Centaurs
	I Laidlaw	(GR)	513 at 32.06	102 v HKU
	B Jones			143 v Nomads & 143 v HKU
	A Telford	(W)		130 v LSW & 104 v Centaurs
	M Cornett	(N)		112 v Saracens
1987–88	P H Davies	(W)		111 v Islanders
1988–89	J Rothman	(W)	513 at 73.29 (3)	112* v Strollers, 105* v Army &
				107 v Centaurs
	R Muirhead	(N)	518 at 43.17	
	M Walsh		549 at 32.29	
	P Varty			106* v Witherers
	R Farouq	(N)		105* v DBS
	D Cutting	(GR)		100* v Strollers
1989–90	J Rothman		591 at 53.73	
	N Foster	(GR)	549 at 39.21	104* v Islanders
	S Ellis	(W)		112* v KGV
1990–91	R Farouq		531 at 106.20 (2)	

144

Second Division/Saturday League– Batting Performances (cont'd)

Season	Player		500 runs plus	Centuries
	S Foster	(N)	635 at 90.71 (3)	105 v Crusaders
	D Sharwood	(W)		133* v KGV
	J Cole	(W)		107 v CCC & 106 v KGV
	R McNeil	(GR)		101* v Crusaders
1991–92	S Foster		542 at 38.71	101 v Crusaders
	T Addison	(GR)		106* v KGV
	D Cutting			102* v HKU
1992–93	S Foster		971 at 88.27 (2)	222* v CCC, 147* v St George's
				120* v Islanders & 120* v MCC
	S O'Brien	(GR)	857 at 61.21 (7)	165 v Strollers & 139 v Islanders
	B Catton	(W)	559 at 55.90	125* v MCC
	M Swift	(N)		124 v CCC
	R Fotheringham	(N)		123 v KGV
	D Kilgour	(W)		120* v Centaurs & 107* v Saracens
	R Stiller	(N)		108* v Crusaders§
	S Foster & M Swift	(N)	255 (2nd) v CCC (2)	
	B Catton & D Kilgour	(W)	221 (1st) v Centaurs (4)	
1993–94	J Garden	(N)	860 at 71.67 (1)	132 v G Ramblers, 124 v Strollers,
				122* v Saracens, 118 v Centaurs & 102 v Crusaders
	A Samuel	(W)	637 at 63.70 (2)	137* v Saracens, 104 v Islanders & 102 v Kai Tak
	S O'Brien		595 at 49.58 (8)	139 v Strollers
	M Winstanley	(GR)	618 at 47.53 (9)	
	B Catton		532 at 44.33 (10)	117 v Islanders
1993–94	M Swift			147 v G Ramblers
	S Foster			113* v LSW, 106 v Tartars & 137 v St George's§
	M Johnson	(W)		111* v G Ramblers
	A Melloy	(W)		101* v Centaurs
	M Swift & J Garden	(N)	256 (2nd) v G Ramblers (1)	
	A Samuel & B Catton	(W)	203 (2nd) v Islanders (4)	
	P Varty & S Foster	(N)	206 (1st) v St George's (1)§	

§ Butani Cup
(1) Position in averages
(1st) Wicket partnership
HKCC – (GR) Gap Ramblers (N) Nomads (W) Witherers
KCC – Crusaders/Saracens & Tartars
Police – Strollers

Second Division/Saturday League - Bowling Performances 1965-66 to 1993-94

Season	Player		50 wickets plus	7 plus (for 50 runs or less)
1966–67	A Barnett	(N)	53 at 7.98 (1)	8–29 v Crusaders
	J D Abbis			'hat-trick' v IRC
1967–68	A Barnett		62 at 9.32 (6)	
1968–69	T Norris	(N)		8–16 v LSW
1969–70	R Wilson	(N)		7–16 v DBS
1970–71	M J Miles	(W)	54 at 10.70 (3)	
	N Dennis	(N)	55 at 12.34	
1971–72	A Barnett		52 at 21.56	
1972–73	D Wellard	(N)		8–32 v HKU
1973–74	M Pulford	(W)	60 at 11.81 (5)	8–62 v Police & 7–27 v LSW
	M Duggan	(N)	58 at 13.29 (9)	
	T Henderson	(N)		7– 5 v DBS
1974–75	R Rankin	(W)		7– 7 v DBS
1977–78	C Swann	(N)		7–20 v HKU
1980–81	P J Berry	(N)		7–22 v LSW
	M Sant	(N)		'hat-trick' v Kai Tak
1982–83	P Dunnett	(N)		'hat-trick' v DBS (wide ball within 'hat-trick')
1985–86	T Seddon	(W)		7–24 v CCC (4 in 4 balls)
	T Addison			'hat-trick' v Centaurs
1986-87	B Kwong	(W)		7–16 v Army
	A Telford	(W)		7–24 incl. 'hat-trick' v St George's
	R Fotheringham	(N)		7–31 v Strollers
1989–90	T E Smith	(GR)		6– 3 v Strollers (excep.)
1990–91	D Swift	(N)	40 at 13.90 (1) (only bowler 40 plus)	

(1) Position in averages
   HKCC – (GR) Gap Ramblers (N) Nomads (W) Witherers
   KCC – Crusaders
   Police – Strollers

Officials

Presidents		Captains of Cricket	
Season	President	Season	Captain
1851–66			
1866–67	Hon W H Alexander		
1867–72			
1872–75	J Greig		
1876–77	H B Gibb		

Presidents		Captains of Cricket	
Season	*President*	*Season*	*Captain*
1878			
1879–81	H B Gibb		
1882–86	A Coxon		
1887–88	W H F Darby		
1889–90			
1891	W M Deane		
1892–95	A J Leach		
1896–97	A Coxon		
1898–1900	Justice Wise		
1901–04	E W Mitchell		
1905			
1906	E W Mitchell		
1907–22	F Maitland		
1923–47	H R B Hancock		
1948–61	H Owen-Hughes	1948–59	T A Pearce
1961–67	T A Pearce	1959–62	G H P Pritchard
1968–73	G T Rowe	1962–65	F A Weller
1973–87	Sir D T E Roberts	1965–67	G T Rowe
1987–	T E Smith	1967–71	E H Wilson
		1971–77	P H Davies
		1977–83	G A Foster
		1983–87	T E Smith
		1987–89	R Eddington
		1989–92	B G Hemshall
		1992–	M Walsh

Hong Kong Parsee Cricket Club

An English schoolmaster named Boswell introduced cricket to Parsee boys in a Bombay school, thus cricket to Parsees is a blend of Iranian genes and English culture. In 1848, the Parsees founded their first cricket club, the Oriental Cricket Club, in Bombay, India.

A pioneering cricket tour to England in 1886, led by Dr Dhunjishan Patel, P D Kanga, Dr Mehelashah Pavri and K M Mistry, had one thing in common with more recent cricketers, such as Polly Umrigar, Rusi Modi, Nari Contractor, Rusi Surti, and Farokh Engineer – they delighted spectators with their 'stroke-play, bravery, fair-play and sense of fun.'

The Hong Kong Parsee Cricket Club (HKPCC) was started by Ardeshir

Bamji, a relative of the Tatas, who was working for Tata & Co. in Hong Kong in 1897. There is a Minute Book written in the beautiful handwriting of Bejonji Tata, the secretary of the club. Bejonji was the father of Phiroze 'Fish' Tata, an old friend of the author's.

Jalu Shroff, ex-Hong Kong Interport cricket captain, produced a copy of the *Rules and Regulations of The Hong Kong Parsee Cricket Club*, which for the season 1900–1901 listed F D Setna as President & Acting Hon. Secretary & Treasurer, and J M Master as the cricket captain. There were other English names, R B & H N Cooper, among the members for that same season, which intrigued me. When I asked my 'contemporary' Tata why there appeared to be English members of the HKPCC, he said: 'They were not English, but Parsees working for English firms, so took the name of the firm as their own name.'

Other members at that time with familiar sounding names were: S B Bhabha (Dhabher!), H K Eranee, H Ruttonjee, F P Shroff and B D Vatcha.

One of the Rules and Regulations stated: 'Non-resident members (Canton members excluded) shall pay an annual subscription of 50 cents ...'

In 1903–04, the first season of league cricket in Hong Kong, R N Cooper was the captain of the HKPCC. They won one game and lost 13. In the second season the Parsees withdrew from the league, due to their inability to raise an eleven for all their matches. This inability was most likely caused by their disastrous first season in the league, with the result that their best players joined Craigengower, whose ground was also at Happy Valley. Parsees continued to play for CCC for many years.

Although the HKPCC's league cricket experience was short-lived, my 'contemporary' Tata remembered friendly matches being played for a few years in the early 1930s, on Sundays against CCC and IRC. These matches were organised by Behman Iranee, the father of Khorshed, Carl Myatt's first wife, a lovely lady.

The HKCC which, up until the late 1960s as a matter of policy, only admitted Caucasians as members, had two distinguished Parsee members prior to the Pacific war. One was the father of Dhun Ruttonjee, and the other was R Pestonji. Both were polished cricketers who played for CCC.

When the Cricket Club of India, led by Polly Umrigar, captain of India in the middle to late 1950s, took to the field at KCC in 1967 against the Hong Kong team led by Jalu Shroff, it was the first and only occasion in the history of Hong Kong cricket that two Parsee captains had opposed each other at this level.

During the match, Polly was deeply puzzled for awhile as to how his instructions in Gujerati were being 'read' by the opposition. Hong Kong's two renowned cricketing Parsees, Buji Dhabher and Jalu Shroff, were listening intently to the chatter and thoroughly enjoying the opposition's dilemma. In spite of this local knowledge, Hong Kong failed to take advantage of the situation to win the match.

Although there are Parsees still playing cricket in Hong Kong, the Hong Kong Parsee Cricket Club, as such, remains only as a distant memory of past cricket in Hong Kong.

Hong Kong Parsee C C v Civil Service C C

19 December 1903 at Happy Valley

HK Parsee CC

K D Mistry, c & b Witchell	0	*Bowling*					
R Pestonji, b Jackman	0		O	M	R	W
J M Mehta, c Robbins b Witchell	5					
D R Captain, c Lamble b Jackman	1	W T Jackman	9.2	3	20	6
R B Cooper, b Jackman	8	P T Lamble	6	1	9	2
J D Noria, c & b Lamble	9	R Witchell	3	–	8	2
J A Chinoy, c & b Jackman	2					
R J Ruttonjee, b Lamble	4					
J M Master, not out	8					
C B Nowrawalla, b Jackman	0					
M D Vania, c Lamble b Jackman	0					
Extras	4					
Total	41					

Civil Service CC

Dr Atkinson, c Cooper b Noria	25	*Bowling*					
R Witchell, b Noria	13		O	M	R	W
W T Jackman, c Noria b Cooper	12					
P T Lamble, c Ruttonjee b Noria	0	J D Noria	11	1	27	5
W H Woolley, c Cooper b Noria	0	K D Mistry	3	–	19	–
J Deveney, b Cooper	0	R B Cooper	8	–	37	5
F T Robbins, b Noria	10					
L E Brett, b Cooper	14					
H Gidley, not out	6					
W Pitt, c Vania b Cooper	3					
J Parkinson, b Cooper	0					
Extras	6					
Total	89					

149

NB: Matches continued after an opponent's score had been exceeded, presumably, because total scores tended to be low and not many matches were played.

Hong Kong Parsee C C v Civil Service 'A'

3 March 1906 at Happy Valley (friendly)

HK Parsee CC

		Bowling				
Vasunia, not out	45					
Cooper, b Willis	8		*O*	*M*	*R*	*W*
Chinoy, b Babcock	6					
Noria, c Dawson b Babcock	5	Willis	12	6	16	1
Captain, b Babcock	0	Hurlow	4	–	21	–
Kanga, b Gast	12	Babcock	9	1	14	4
Bejonji, c Coombs b Gast	8	Hoggarth	3	–	11	–
Tarapore, c Hurlow b Gast	0	Cooper	5	–	15	–
Tavadia, b Gast	3	Gast	4	1	10	4
Mowdivala, b Babcock	0					
Extras	4					
Total	91					

Civil Service 'A'

		Bowling				
Cooper, b Captain	6					
Dawson, c Tarapore b Noria	13		*O*	*M*	*R*	*W*
Adams, c Vasunia b Noria	12					
Kelly, c Tavadia b Noria	12	Noria	12	1	33	7
Willis, b Noria	0	Captain	4	–	11	1
Babcock, b Noria	7	Tavadia	7	–	17	2
Coombs, b Noria	3					
Gourley, b Tavadia	1					
Hoggarth, b Tavadia	0					
Gast, c Tavadia b Noria	8					
Hurlow, not out	1					
Extras	4					
Total	67					

HK Parsees won by 24 runs, although they had only ten cricketers playing.

150

Hong Kong University Cricket Club

Various student clubs were incorporated with the HKU Athletic Association. The HKUCC was founded on 2 November 1912. Earlier in the year, on 11 March, the University was officially opened by the Governor, His Excellency Sir Frederick Lugard.

The original University Athletic ground at Pokfulam, known as the Pavilion, was presented to the University by the Government of Hong Kong in March 1915. It was mainly due to the efforts of Sir Kai Ho Kai, Dr Francis Clark and Mr S W T'so that it was levelled and turfed. In 1923, it was extended and returfed. However, it was not big enough, had an awkward shape, also catered for soccer, and finally when cricket moved to Sandy Bay, became part of the foundation site for the Flora Ho Hall, donated by Dr Stanley Ho in memory of his mother.

The Editor of the University Union Magazine (*The Union*) writing in 1923 said:

> Go to the playing fields and learn to be a sport. Go and expand your lungs with life and feel the vigours of thought, the gasp of intellect flowing through your veins. Go and chase after the fleeting ball and learn the miracle of fresh air. Most of you think that scholarship is all that matters.

1924   HKU: 154 (A A Rumjahn 58, W Ponsonby-Fane 23*, F J Ling
Mar 2   5–13)
        CSCC: 82 (A E Wood 38*, H N Balhatchet 3–14)

In spite of having a fine columned Pavilion and the encouragement of Sir William Hornell (Vice Chancellor 1924–37), the eccentric cricket lover, Richard Ponsonby-Fane, and later by those enthusiasts, Sir Lindsay Ride (Vice Chancellor 1949–64) and Professor Edmund Blunden (author of *Cricket Country*), cricket remained the love of only a handful of devoted students, mostly from the DBS, Malaya, Singapore and a few teachers from the United Kingdom.

The HKUCC won the First Division championship three times: in 1922–23 and 1927–28, when Arthur Rumjahn was captain, and in 1932–33, when Albert Rodrigues was captain.

The highlights of the 1927–28 season were the winning of both the First and Second Division titles, and Arthur Rumjahn's 'hat-trick' against the Royal Navy. Commenting on the 1927–28 season, *The Union* said:

> Mention was made of the able captaincy of Mr Rumjahn in skippering last season's team to victory in the Senior League of the Colony with

an unbeaten record. Mr Rumjahn, the captain, was again the mainstay of the side: in batting he secured the largest aggregate and the biggest individual score, and in match after match he batted finely.

In spite of winning both the titles in 1927–28, *The Union* had little to say on the results of actual league matches:

The match against Kowloon was a sensational one, and for once the 'far corner' of Pokfulam was generally patronised by cricket lovers. The fielding and batting of both sides was exceptional, in fact it was miraculous, and though we lost, we went down fighting.

(see attached Appendix for first & second XI statistics 1927–28)

In HKCC's first senior division league match of the season played on the Pokfulam ground, the *Hong Kong Daily Press* commented:

The ball on some occasions broke completely off the wicket owing to the bad turfing; this also was dangerous to the batsmen, Anderson having to retire for one run after being badly hurt.

1929   University: 152–7 (L T Ride 50*, S V Gittins 28, A C Beck 3–35)
Oct   HKCC: 160–6 (J R Hinton 37)

Donald Anderson, 17 years old on 31 October 1929, selected against Shanghai in November 1929, was the then youngest player pre WWII to represent Hong Kong.

The University first team made mincemeat of the Royal Artillery, the RAMC and the Royal Navy in three friendly matches, the first two at Pokfulam and the third at King's Park.

1931   University: 136 (A T Lee 37, A M Rodrigues 37, Gnr Bryant
Nov 18   8–31)
        RA: 85 (Lt Wolfe Barry 23, E L Gosano 5–19,
                         H Nomanbhoy 3–19)
  28   University: 221–2 dec (A M Rodrigues 128*, A T Lee 89, Cpl
                              Davies 2–55)
        RAMC: 76 (Sgt Patterson 19, E L Gosano 4–14,
                         H Nomanbhoy 3–18)

1932   University: 209–2 dec (D Anderson 62, A M Rodrigues 50, E L
Jan 30   Gosano 45*, L T Ride 33*)
        Royal Navy: 65–9 (A Baker 4–12, D Anderson 4–14)

The University first team came home with a flourish at the end of the 1931–32 season.

1932 University: 120 (F R Zimmern 32, A M Rodrigues 26,
Mar 12   R E Lee 6–27)
   CCC: 95 (W Paterson 33, D Anderson 6–25)

 19 HKCC: 57 (A C Beck 26*, E L Gosano 4–9,
         A Baker 3–15)
   University: 67–1 (A M Rodrigues 38*)

Apr 16 University: 130 (A M Rodrigues 38, D Anderson 28, Lt Villiers
        3–18)
   Royal Navy: 40 (D Anderson 3–14, E L Gosano 3–15)

After coming third in the league in 1931–32, *The Union* said:

> F R Zimmern must have thought that he was a wicket-keeper in the Oldfield class and consequently did not need practice. Anderson was not half as good as he was the season before, though he did take quite a number of wickets and scored two hundreds.

In the April of that same season, the Phoenix XI defeated L T Ride's XI in a friendly.

Apr 3 Phoenix XI: 127 (A T Lee 38, F D Pereira 5–34, G C Burnett
       4–28)
  L T Ride's XI: 111 (A Baker 21, D Anderson 5–19)

The successful 1932–33 team included: D J N Anderson, E L Gosano, H Nomanbhoy, A T Lee, Dr Lindsay Ride, A M Rodrigues and F R Zimmern. *The Union* commented:

> Gosano was the live wire of the side. He was a quick and prehensile field, a dashing batsman with a very good eye, and an attacking bowler, especially with the new ball. He made them swing late while the shine was on, and when it was off, he would break them back nastily from the off. Gosano did very good all-round work for the 1st XI. He is probably the best all-round sportsman in the University at the present time. Teamwork may be said to be responsible for the success of the team.

The 1932–33 season proved to be the last time the University was to win the First Division championship. How they stormed through, losing only against the HKCC.

1933   CSCC: 168–8 dec   (J E Richardson 50, H G Wallington 44,
                                        E L Gosano 5–41)
Jan 1   University: 183–2   (D Anderson 100, A M Rodrigues 64)

'Brilliant batting by Donald Anderson, the season's first premier league century.'

Feb 11 University: 80 (E L Gosano 24, A R Minu 4–20, F D Pereira
                                3–31)
        IRC: 70 (D Anderson 5–18, A T Lee 5–29)

'Bowling with a deceptive off-break, Anderson walked through the side.'

Mar 11 University: 164 (H Nomanbhoy 49, F R Zimmern 32, G Burnett
                                4–54)
        KCC: 96 (E C Fincher 30, E L Gosano 5–23, A T Lee 5–51)

'University dash Kowloon's hopes of winning the championship. It was a great win and the University fully deserved it. Both Gosano and Lee were irresistible, and clean bowled eight batsmen.'

Mar 12 CCC: 133 (E Zimmern 61, C W Lam 26, A T Lee 6–28)
        University: 136–8 (L T Ride 60, E L Gosano 22, U M Omar
                                8–43)

The undergraduates had lost 7 wickets for 103 runs when Ride proceeded to use the long handle with great success, and with A T Nomanbhoy took the score to 132 before Ride was given out for obstruction.

By Athole

The following were all First Division league matches.

1934   HKU: 178–7 dec (A M Rodrigues 103 *, A B Lewis 4–41)
Mar 10 RN: 153–9   (Lt Webster 42, Lt Larkin 39, D K Samy 5–23)

1935   CCC: 130–9 dec (G A Souza 22, A T Lee 20, E L Gosano
Feb 16   4–22, H Ozorio 3–37)
        University: 144–8   (E L Gosano 102*, L Hubbard 2–16)

154

'Gosano hit 22 boundaries in a hurricane innings at Happy Valley.'

On the same day in a Second Division match at Pokfulam the University dismissed Craigengower for 21 runs (P B Tata 6–13 including the 'hat-trick'). The author asked Phiroze 'Fish' Tata, a friend for many years, about this feat. Although he vaguely remembered the 'hat-trick', memories of receiving his 'Phoenix', second team colours, was very clear. Eddie Gosano had remarked: 'He can't bat, bowl or field!', to which Lindsay Ride had replied: 'but he's the keenest cricketer we have, always willing to fill any vacancy.'

1936　　HKU: 150　(E L Gosano 51) – scored in 18 minutes!)
Mar 21　IRC: 　 46　(E L Gosano 8–20)

　　The University – in the person of Gosano – won by 104 runs!

In 1936, the University hockey and football clubs also used the ground. In 1941, Professor Lindsay Ride presented the club with a shield named after Sir William Hornell, 'who perhaps more than anybody else fostered the game here.' Ride said: 'The shield was presented with the purpose of encouraging good cricket in inter-faculty competitions and not to see the Medicals lick the others.'

　　During the Japanese occupation, the pavilion and ground were used as stables, vegetable gardens and finally as a cemetery, the pavilion being partially destroyed. The field was completely bare of grass in 1946, and despite the encouragement given by the keen cricketing Vice Chancellor, Sir Lindsay Ride, the general response to sporting activities was poor.

　　Cricket was played again towards the end of 1946 under very adverse conditions. Despite the shortage of players, equipment and the lack of a ground, the foundation for cricket was re-established by the committee, the HKCC lending its ground for net practice.

　　Most of the sports clubs within the University held annual Intra-Varsity tournaments. The cricket club held an inter-hostel league and such annual fixtures as a Past v Present XI's on 1 January, and the Vice Chancellor's XI v the President of the Students' Union XI. Apart from the league matches, prewar friendly matches had been played against Lingham University of Canton, with matches against the University of Malaya initiated in 1949.

　　In 1949 and 1950, mention is made of J C Koh being 'ranked as one of the Colony's best bowlers'. Thereafter *The Union* made little mention of cricket right up to 1960. Obviously, a non-cricketing editor was in charge, for on 14 November 1959, on the KGV ground, there was no comment on one of the most amazing league bowling performances.

HKU: 164–5 dec (A R Kitchell 60*, J T Hung 43)
KGV: 9   (S M Teh 5.4 overs, 8 for 0) Six of the runs
                were extras!

In the 1960s, guided by Jimmie Duthie, a team known as the 'Phoenix Ashes' made up of students, with a sprinkling of occasional Alumni members, struggled to remain in the Second Division – a far cry from the successful seasons in the late 1920s and early 1930s. This had largely been brought about by a radical change in the students' structure at the University, with mainly Chinese students in attendance with not the slightest interest in cricket, the cricketing students from Malaysia and Singapore having ceased to enrol.

At the end of the 1960s, Dafydd Evans and Stewart Richards, with much enthusiasm and dedication, revived the interest in cricket, and apart from a 'no show' in 1969–70, this keenness has been maintained to the present day.

Prior to a cricket match on the Pokfulam ground, until it closed in 1981, the pitch area was watered, then rolled for a matting wicket to be laid on the 'smoothed' surface. The author played many a game on this 'sporting' ground, where a driven ball could 'take off' at any time on its course either towards a fielder or the boundary.

1976   HKU: 251–3 dec (B Lovegrove 101, A Cooper 65)
Jan 17 Police: 135–9   (K Wellburn 47, B Peacock 4–26, A Cooper
                         3–42)

After an absence of 46 years, a HKU side won a league trophy, the Saturday League Cup in the season 1978–79. Led by their captain Sippy, who used to 'sneak' the ball to you with his low round-arm action, they saw off KGV, the previous year's champions.

KGV: 142   (A Cooper 4–17)
HKU: 143–9 (D Race 25)

'The University were finally steered to victory by Sippy 12 not out, and their last man Stewart Richards 10 not out.'

B. Sipahimalani, better known as 'Sippy', after this achievement, and his best ever league 6–36 earlier in the season, stepped into the busy chair of Hon. Secretary of the HKCA in 1979–80, a position he made his own until he retired after the 1988–89 season.

During Sippy's HKCA tenure of office, a HKU milestone was reached when, on 7 September 1985, the first ball was bowled in earnest on ground

156

number four at the Stanley Ho Sports Ground at Sandy Bay, on the western side of Hong Kong Island. Though not easily found, it is well worth a visit on a nice sunny day, for it is surely the most scenic ground in the territory.

Malcolm Merry described the HKU approach to the game of cricket, before the advent of the 'S' men – Sabine and Speak, who played for the HKCC in the Sunday league.

HKU certainly likes to think of itself as a friendly side. The University's bowling indeed, is notoriously friendly, the ally of many a sagging batting average. The University's fielders are absurdly generous, regularly giving opposition batsmen another chance; HKU bowlers soon learn to treat a chance that is taken as an unexpected bonus. Our batting has of occasion manifested a tough veneer, but the soft middle has often provided a pleasant surprise for unsuspecting opposition bowlers. Our umpiring is surely the fairest in the league, our umpires giving on average three times as many lbws as are given in our favour.

Players such as Martin Aske, Krish Chandran, Tony Cooper, Brian Jones, Barry Lovegrove, Brian Peacock, Dave Race, Harry Ricketts, Don Swift and others, backed by the stalwarts Sippy, Stewart Richards and Richard Wood, have all kept the flag flying.

1984   Army: 184
Mar 31 HKU: 182 (K Chandran 120)

Despite Krish Chandran's valiant 'solo' effort, HKU failed by two runs in this Gillette Cup Pool 'A' match.

1989   Kai Tak: 168–6 (B Willson 77, N Sawrey-Cookson 43)
Jan 7   HKU: 173–4 (M Speak 85, P Glenwright 53*)

'Skipper Mike Speak led the run chase with a hard-hitting 85 which included eight sixes and six fours...'

With the participation of the 'S' men – Sabine and Speak, and now largely dependent on staff and others with more thinly veiled links, the Saturday league and cup teams have recently performed well in the league, also winning the Gillette Cup in 1990–91 and the Butani Cup in 1991–92.

The HKU has recently upgraded its cricket facilities at its Sandy Bay sports ground with a permanent pitch and high quality floodlit twin practice nets. Its renowned friendly fixtures list continues to the present

157

day, and their relaxed approach to this great game provides a welcome contrast to the hectic environment of bustling, commercial Hong Kong.

Championship Winners – First & Second Division 1927–28

1st and 2nd Team Statistics

1st XI (in batting average order)
J Barrow (31.00), A A Rumjahn, E A Lee, S V Gittins,
A P Guterres, F I Zimmern, W H Sling, D Laing, C W Lam and
D K Samy.
also batted:
F H Trayes, B K Ng, A T Lee, W M Gittins and S R Kermani.

Best Bowling:
S V Gittins   9 wickets for 40 runs (4.44 ave.)
A P Guterres 26 wickets for 150 runs (5.77 ave.)
A A Rumjahn   12 wickets for 159 runs (13.25 ave.)

2nd XI (in batting average order)
S R Kermani (39.12), W M Gittins, F Hiptoola, A Chan Fook,
S F Chen, B N Sudan, H T Barma, A Baker, M B Osman,
A B Sulieman and K T Loke.
also batted:
N P Karanjia and A M Rodrigues.

Best Bowling:
F Hiptoola 37 wickets for 343 runs (9.27 ave.)
B N Sudan   23 wickets for 253 runs (11.00 ave.)
W M Gittins 10 wickets for 119 runs (11.90 ave.)

Sir Albert Rodrigues, CBE, ED – Reminiscences

After joining the Medical Faculty at the University of Hong Kong, Albert was encouraged to play cricket again when asked to join the XYZ eleven. He played cricket on Sundays, usually against a team of schoolboys led by G R Sayer, a senior member of the Education Department, whose keenness helped build up some good cricketers. Guy Sayer, son of G R, was later to become the Chief Manager of the Hongkong Bank.

From this beginning, Albert moved up to become captain of the HKU 1st XI. He was at the University from 1928 till 1934. In the 1927–28 season, the HKU won both the First and Second Division league titles ... Arthur Rumjahn and F Hiptoola being the respective captains.

Sir Albert recalled the highlight of his cricketing career whilst at the HKU:

> I was later to captain the side that won the First Division in 1932–33 ... with a strong side comprising – Donald Anderson (we were the opening bats), the Zimmerns (Fred, Francis and Ernie), Tinker Lee, Lindsay Ride, Eddie Gosano, Ozo, Spotty Pereira (who worked in the University Registry), Bill Hong Sling and myself.

Sir Albert also recalled a painful incident while playing for the University first team:

> While fielding near the boundary I let pass many fours as I found it painful to bend down. After the game many budding doctors looked me over, and the diagnosis was – gas pains or possible appendicitis. That night I was rushed to hospital (St Paul's, where I am now the Superintendent), and they operated on me for a ruptured appendix. All were surprised I survived, for at that time penicillin had not been discovered. But I guess I was very fit, or the good Lord was not ready for me.

After graduating from Hong Kong University, together with Pereira, Gosano, and Ozo, he played cricket for Recreio, which only had a team in the Second Division. Recreio soon entered a team in the First Division, and the senior league title was won in 1938–39.

Sir Albert Rodrigues, now 88 years old, enjoys his cacti plants, walking and a little swimming in his Kadoorie Avenue pool, retired as Pro-chancellor of HKU and Superintendent at St Paul's Hospital, in 1996 after suffering a stroke in 1995.

As Sir Albert didn't play any postwar league cricket, the author did not have the opportunity of playing with or against him. However, the author has known Sir Albert for many years and takes this opportunity to thank him for his assistance and his comments in 1994 on prewar cricket in Hong Kong.

Second Division/Saturday League – Batting Performances 1965–66 to 1993–94

Season	Player	500 runs plus	Centuries
1970–71	A Suffiad	665 at 30.23 (8)	124* v HKCC Witherers
	D Rivers	508 at 26.74 (9)	114* v Centaurs
1973–74	A Cooper	766 at 38.30 (9)	127* v PRC & 102 v DBS
	I Watson	615 at 29.29	

A Cooper & I Watson 218 runs (2nd) v PRC (1)

Season	Player	500 runs plus	Centuries
1975–76	B Lovegrove	572 at 30.11	101 v PRC
	A Cooper	525 at 25.00	
1976–77	B Lovegrove	516 at 22.43	
1978–79	D Race	586 at 65.11 (2)	
	B Lovegrove	657 at 32.85	
1979–80	A Cooper	588 at 30.95	
1980–81	B Lovegrove	522 at 24.86	
1981–82	B Hansen	593 at 32.94	103* v Saracens (Gillette Plate)
	D Race		101* v Army
1982–83	D Swift	481 at 60.25 (4)	
1983–84	K Chandran	572 at 38.13	120 v Army
	A Cooper	613 at 36.06	
1984–85	M Sabine		111 v Tartars
	A Cooper		100* v Sentinels
1985–86	M Sabine	649 at 81.13 (2)	127 v Crusaders & 102 v Tartars
	A Cooper	610 at 40.67	
1987–88	M Sabine	613 at 87.57 (3)	102* v Strollers
	M Speak	650 at 34.21	
1988–89	M Speak	1044 at 65.25 (5)	157 & 114* v KGV
	P Glenwright	574 at 52.18 (10)	
	M Sabine	702 at 50.14	114* v Centaurs
	A Asundi	531 at 31.24	
1989–90	M Sabine	615 at 68.33 (4)	
	M Speak	682 at 68.20 (5)	144* v Army & 102 v Centaurs
1990–91	M Sabine		101 v Kai Tak
	M Speak	728 at 91.00 (1)	108 v LSW
	J Logan		127 v St George's & 104 v HKCC Witherers§
	J Penrose		145* v St George's§ & 120 v LSW§
	P Glenwright		103* v CCC

160

Second Division/Saturday League – Batting Performances (cont'd)

Season	Player	500 runs plus	Centuries
1992–93	P Glenwright	760 at 76.00 (3)	112 v Strollers
	M Speak	619 at 68.78 (5)	153 v Centaurs & 125* v Tartars
	M Sabine	490 at 61.25 (6)	142 v Saracens
1993–94	P Glenwright	534 at 38.14	
	M Sabine		100* v KGV

§   Butani Cup
(1)   Position in averages
(1st)   Wicket partnership
KCC – Crusaders/Saracens/Tartars
Police – Sentinels/Strollers

Second Division/Saturday League – Bowling Performances 1965–66 to 1993–94

Season	Player	50 wickets plus	7 wkts plus (for 50 runs or less)
1965–66	T Millar		7–30 v LSW
1969–70	I Watson		'hat-trick' v LSW
1970–71	P Twentyman		4– 0 v KGV (excep.)
1971–72	D Evans	51 at 16.02	7–36 v CCC
1973–74	A Cooper	60 at 17.47	9–43 v LSW
	T Allsop		8–18 v Royal Navy
1974–75	A Cooper		7–38 v PRC
	D Ricketts		6– 9 v DBS (excep.)
1975–76	D Ricketts		7–18 v Islanders
	A Cooper	49 at 17.96	7–25 v LSW
	B Peacock		'hat-trick' v DBS
1976–77	D Ricketts		8–43 v DBS
1977–78	A Mahtaney	50 at 18.92	
	B Peacock		8–58 v St George's
1980–81	M Aske		'hat-trick' v KGV
1985–86	M Aske		(5 wickets plus 4 times)

The Indian Recreation Club

The Pacific war in the Far East had many things to answer for; one lesser factor was the destruction of many of the records of the private recreational clubs, most of which had been formed in the early part of the 20th century.

Through the good services of Arthur Abdul Aziz Rumjahn, an IRC cricketing stalwart, who played Interport cricket for Hong Kong against Shanghai in 1921 and 1923, I am indebted for the following historical background to the IRC, one of these early clubs:

> Our forefathers were ultra-conservative, super-conventional and uneducated. The Government Central School (later Queen's College) did not admit non-Chinese students until 1867.

The ultra-conservatism and conventionalism relaxed a little around 1900 when

> Our youngsters did not need to hide the fact that they would play games in the open.

The pioneers who encouraged the youngsters to play games also realised they lacked a proper ground where their natural talents could be developed. These pioneers – Osman el Arculli, 'Cheese' S E Ismail, D Rumjahn, M B Suffiad, 'Shortie' Ismail, S. Juman, 'OB' Kitchell, A Pillai Madar, N M Bux, S Harteem and others, formed in 1910 the Muslim Recreation Club, the predecessor of the IRC. They met in 1917 to make an application to the Government for a sports ground for the Indian community 'to meet the flaming passion of a conglomeration of young Muslim boys ever seeking to climb up to greater heights in the field of sports.'

The application was rejected. Fortunately for the MRC, the CSCC, based in Happy Valley at this time, offered the use of their clubhouse and ground on Sundays.

Arthur's elder brother, A H (Abdul) was playing for the HKUCC where the Governor's private secretary, Richard Arthur Ponsonby-Fane, was a team-mate. Arthur was a student at Queen's College, where Ponsonby-Fane had been engaged as a replacement teacher. In a school cricket encounter, Arthur told Ponsonby-Fane that he would like to play for CCC after he left school, as the MRC's application for a sports field had been refused by Government. This chance remark set various 'cogs' in motion, and once Ponsonby-Fane had reviewed all the facts of the case and was satisfied that the MRC could raise two cricket XI's, he informed Arthur's brother and father, Usuf Rumjahn, that the Government would look favourably at a new application. A meeting was called and held at the residence of J D Noria, a fine Parsee sportsman. It was resolved to form a new club called The Indian Recreation Club, and the following were elected office bearers:

162

President: J H N Mody
Vice Presidents: Messrs U Rumjahn and H M H Nemazee
Hon. Secretary
& Treasurer: D Rumjahn

A suitable site acceptable to the authorities had yet to be found. After a Maulood at the Rumjahn's house, Arthur jokingly mentioned the 'Coffee Garden' where he caught crickets. An appointment was immediately set up with Ponsonby-Fane to meet at the corner of the Victoria English School, where the Po Leung Kuk is now situated. The party met and walked along a narrow path in a southerly direction to the area where Chinese funerals for coffee garden burials usually started their noisy rites from this thickly shrubbed area. This site, Plot C, Sookunpoo Valley, was later allotted to the club and has remained the home of the IRC ever since.

In 1918, less than a year after the application was approved, the site had been cleared, filled and levelled, and in 1919 the club ground was opened. A matshed clubhouse was erected and a cricket team under the captaincy of A H Rumjahn was entered in the cricket league.

1920 IRC: 106 (A A Rumjahn 38, Pte Durton 5–28)
Mar 6 Staffs & Dept: 103 (Sgt Connor 32, A A Rumjahn 4–3)

Typhoons played havoc with the matshed, but because the ground was still settling, it wasn't until 1931 that a multi-columned Indian style building could be contructed. Mr Gonella of Messrs Hazeland & Gonella was the architect, and the main subscribers to the building fund were: A T M Barma, Khan Sahib Nawab Khan, Khan Sahib Mohinder Singh, J H N Mody, Abbas el Arculli and U Rumjahn. Their names were inscribed on a tablet which was lost when the present clubhouse was built after the Pacific war. The previous one had been damaged beyond repair during the battle for Hong Kong and the Japanese occupation. The present two-storeyed flat roofed structure accommodates a badminton hall, bar and changing rooms, and is now the home for a cosmopolitan club with 20 or more different nationalities.

Certain local schools at the time of the IRC's founding, such as Queen's College, the Diocesan Boys' School and St Joseph's College, had many an Indian student showing a definite keenness for cricket, and it was this aptitude that convinced the founder members, one such as Abbas el Arculli OBE, a former President and Cricket Captain, that cricket should be a prominent activity of the Club.

1929 HKCC: 184-8 (Capt F Sillitoe 65, T E Pearce 32*)
     IRC: 78–2 (A el Arculli 38*)

'... darkness interfered', after IRC had batted for 28 overs at HKCC.

IRC has won both the First and Second Division championships on many occasions, the most successful period being in the 1930s, particular mention being made of the seasons 1930–31 and 1931–32, when IRC won both divisions. Players of special note during this golden period were Arthur Rumjahn, 'Fatty' Minu and Frank Pereira. Arthur remembers Frank:

> surely one of the finest, fastest bowlers ever to wear a Hong Kong cap. There was a certain poetry in the long loping approach and silken delivery of the man. Glorious was the sight of this slim six-footer running about twelve effortless paces, then releasing the ball with a synchronism of movement that almost took one's breath away.
>
> His crowning achievement in local senior cricket was against the HKU side – a team that had won the senior league championship a season or two earlier – and this remarkable feat was achieved on a perfect batsman's wicket.
>
> His analysis: 4.5 overs, 3 maidens, 5 runs and 10 wickets!
> [see scoresheet on page 168]

The following details are summarised results of First Division matches, unless otherwise indicated, played between 1932 and 1983.

1932   IRC: 153 (S R Kermani 40, A T Lee 4–27)
Jan 9   HKU: 37   (F D Pereira 4–11, A R Minu 4–21)

1932   IRC: 130 (F D Pereira 54, Bdr Bryant 8–39)
Mar 5   RA: 48   (A R Minu 5–28, F D Pereira 4–19)

Minu and Pereira then repeated the same dose against the Artillerymen.

On 12 March the final match of the season between IRC and KCC was postponed till 2 April, due to the death of Mrs W F Fincher, mother of Interporters Teddy and Ernie.

Apr 2   IRC: 197   (A H Madar 93, A H Rumjahn 27*, G C Burnett 4–63)
        KCC: 120–2 (E F Fincher 39*, P Madar 24, E C Fincher 24, A R Minu 2–52)

KCC: 98 (F M el Arculli 3–17)
IRC: 99 (A M Rumjahn 28*, F M el Arculli 27, J Chadwick
3–25) Second Division at KCC.

'IRC win league, were nine for 70 runs at one stage.'

Apr 9 IRC: 198–5 (A H Madar 82*, A H Rumjahn 48, S R
Kermani 21)
The Rest: 107 (J Richardson 26, A Minu 4–33, A H Madar
3–5, F Pereira 3–30)

'The Indians bundled out The Rest ten minutes before time.'

IRC: 135 (F M el Arculli 40, A R Abbas 31, Cpl
Meehan 3–13)
The Rest: 149–2 (F S W Smith 86*, F E Lawrence 39)

The Indian second team couldn't match their elder brothers' performance.

1933 University: 80 (E L Gosano 24, A R Minu 4–20, F Pereira 3–31)
Feb 11 IRC: 70 (D J N Anderson 5–18, A T Lee 5–29)

'The Indian's first defeat for three seasons as Anderson, bowling with
a deceptive off-break, walked through the side.' [This is not correct,
as IRC lost to CCC at Happy Valley after winning the Shield in 1931]

1933 IRC: 166 (A H Rumjahn 58, R E Lee 4–38)
Nov 25 CCC: 28 (F D Pereira 6–9)

CCC: 93 (T Yeoh 37, A A Rumjahn 5–28, A A Aziz 3–2
incl. 'hat-trick')
IRC: 119–5 (A R Abbas 58*) Second Division match.

1934 IRC: 153–9 dec (F Pereira 29, A H Madar 28, H G
Wallington 3–14)
Mar 3 CSCC: 87 (J E Richardson 25, G R Sayer 22, F Pereira
7–12)

1935 Recreio: 24 (F D Pereira 5–8, A R Minu 2–11)
Mar IRC: 33–3

'Pereira bowling very fast ...'

165

1937   IRC: 156   (F M el Arculli 57, K Nazarin 26, R E Lee 4–27)
Mar 13 KCC: 145–4 (D J N Anderson 72, E F Fincher 41*, A R Minu
                        3–73)

'Time saved the IRC.' KCC only had 36 against IRC's 46.5 overs.

1956   Police: 68   (P English 28, A Myatt 5–7, C Myatt 3–44)
Mar 17 IRC: 73–4 (L G Ebert 38)

It was a great shame for Hong Kong cricket that Tony Myatt didn't continue with the game. It would be hard to imagine trying to score runs against both the Myatts, Carl and Tony.

1959   KGV: 18   (O Adem 10–10)
Nov 7   IRC: 22–1

'Young IRC off-spinner Osman Adem set an all-time Colony record by capturing 10 KGV wickets for 10 runs in 6.5 overs.'

SCMP

[Not an all-time Colony record, see Frank Pereira's 10 wickets for five runs – 19 Jan 1935]

In January 1961, Osman Adem followed this performance with a 'hat-trick' against Recreio in the First Division.

1971   RAF: 90   (C Hull 25, H Ebrahim 8–33)
Jan 24 IRC: 91–6 (G Lalchandani 40*, R Graham 4–40)

'Hatim Ebrahim's teasing drifters had the RAF in a spin.'

Feb 14 IRC: 102 (L Stenner 6–27)
        LSW: 43 (G Lalchandani 6–21)

With left-arm seamer Stenner swinging the ball in and right-arm seamer Lalchandani moving it away, what chance did the batsmen have!

1975   LSW: 133 (G Lalchandani 5–40, Zahid 5–48)
        IRC: 130 (R Lalchandani 50)

1976   CCC: 177–8 (Zahid 7–78)
Jan 17 IRC :   65   (G Lalchandani 31, J Mason 6–7, R Cooper 4–54)

1981   Brit. Forces: 206   (N Newell 58, M Cooper 51, R Litherland
Oct 11   42, A Ebrahim 5–65)
          IRC: 207–9   (V Sharma 63, R Thadani 36, A Kirpalani
                               30)

A nail-biting victory for IRC, so often the underdog in recent years.

Coming into the last match of the 1982–83 season, IRC had played 14, lost 11 and had not looked like winning a game. The KCC Infidels needed to win the match to have a chance of capturing the Sunday league title. There didn't seem to be much doubt in the KCC camp that they would win this match, all the portents were there.

1983   IRC: 244–9 dec (H Ebrahim 64, B Gohel 51, N Deva 47)
Apr 17 Infidels: 242   (N Broadhurst 55, I Nicholson 44, N Stearns
                               38, B Gohel 6–68)

At KCC the last man was run out going for an impossible run and IRC had gained their first win of the season and denied Infidels a chance of the title.

HKCA Handbook, 1983–84

Bharat Gohel proved once again that when he's 'on song', there's a good chance his team can win the match.

In prewar years, the club's sporting activities branched out to include tennis and later to lawn bowls. Unfortunately, the IRC ground ceased to be used for cricket after the 1979–80 season; like CCC and Recreio, tennis and lawn bowls had taken precedence. The IRC team is now another of the nomadic sides that play cricket in Hong Kong.

Postwar players such as: J C Koh; the Myatt brothers: Carl and Tony; the Lalchandani brothers: Ram and Gopal; Hatim Ebrahim (a past President of the HKCA), together with many other anonymous cricketers, have all provided sterling service to IRC cricket over the years, and some of the above named, also to Hong Kong cricket like the Madars, Minu, Nazarin, Rumjahn and Pereira before them. Though no longer a cricket team with its own ground, a few enthusiastic members of the club have managed to collect together enough players to keep the flag flying. IRC might not now be such an influence on cricket as in the 1930s, but the club adds flavour to the cricket scene in Hong Kong, and continues to play its part in the Sunday league.

University v IRC

Pokfulam – 19 January 1935

University

D Hunt, b Pereira	0				
K P Gan, b Pereira	0	*Bowling*			
A B Tata, b Pereira	0		*O*	*M*	*R*	*W*
E L Gosano, b Pereira	1				
L T Ride, lbw Pereira	4	F D Pereira	4.5	3	5	10
B K Ng, c Y el Arculli b Pereira	0	A R Minu	4	4	0	0
D S Blake, c Y el Arculli b Pereira	0				
S A Reed, c Y el Arculli b Pereira	0				
P Power, c Y el Arculli b Pereira	0				
H L Ozorio, b Pereira	0				
D Roy, not out	0				
Extras (B5, WB2)	7				
Total	12				

Fall of wickets: 1–1, 2–1, 3–6, 4–10, 5–10, 6–11, 7–11, 8–11, 9–11

IRC

A H Rumjahn, b Ozorio	7	*Bowling*			
S A Ismail, b Gosano	0		*O*	*M*	*R*	*W*
A S Suffiad, b Blake	9				
A Rahmin, not out	6	E L Gosano	5	1	8	1
A M Omar, c Power b Roy	22	H L Ozorio	4	2	5	1
F D Pereira		D S Blake	3	1	10	1
M P Madar		S A Reed	2	0	10	0
A R Abbas	Did not bat	L T Ride	1	0	11	0
M K el Arculli		D Roy	1.3	0	0	1
Y el Arculli					
A R Minu					
Extras (LB4)	4				
Total (for 4 wickets)	48				

Fall of wickets: 1–1, 2–15, 3–26, 4–48

F D Pereira was a terrifyingly fast bowler with a low action. The ball
came very fast off the pitch and kept low with occasional bumps. He
was murderous on our matting wicket – this match was a nightmare
for us.

Dr E L Gosano, February 1994

First Division/Sunday League – Batting Performances 1965–66 to 1993–94

Season	Player	500 runs plus	Centuries
1970–71	R Lalchandani	424 at 47.11 (2)	104 v Army
1979–80	K Chandran		110 v HKCC Wanderers
	H Ebrahim		103 v LSW
1984–85	M Ahmed		111* v HKCC Optimists
	A Ebrahim		101* v Police
1985–86	Chatrapal Sinh	511 at 31.90	
1986–87	S Tariq		115 v LSW & 105 v Brit. Forces
1987–88	V Ramani		118* v KCC Infidels
1991–92	A Hasan		101 v HKCC Scorpions
1992–93	T Nimkar	542 at 36.13	139 v LSW
	S Malik		125* v Vagabonds
1993–94	T Nimkar	631 at 42.07	102 v Vagabonds

(1) Position in averages

First Division/Sunday League – Bowling Performances 1965–66 to 1993–94

Season	Player	50 wickets plus	7 wkts plus (for 50 runs or less)
1970–71	H Ebrahim		8–33 v RAF
1973–74	G Lalchandani	54 at 15.52 (7)	8–32 v HKCC Scorpions & 7–40 v Army.
1978–79	G Lalchandani		8–67 v Police
1987–88	K Krishnan		8–43 v Brit.Forces
1990–91	R Chandran		9–36 v HKCC Wanderers & 8–37 v Vagabonds
1992–93	V Naresh		'hat-trick' v HKCC Scorpions

Second Division/Saturday League – Batting Performances 1965–66 to 1976–77

Season	Player	500 runs plus	Centuries
1970–71	K Sharma		100* v HKCC Witherers
1973–74	F Jowharsha	695 at 28.96	
	S Chulani		100* v Police
1975–76	G Lalchandani	750 at 35.71	
	R Thadani	514 at 25.70	

Second Division/Saturday League – Bowling Performances 1965–66 to 1976–77

Season	Player	50 wickets plus	7 plus (for 50 runs or less)
1970–71	S Punjabi		6– 7 v KCC Saracens (excep)
1973–74	G Lalchandani	33 at 8.39 (2)	9–35 v KCC Crusaders &
			8–29 v LSW
	R Bhavnani		7–44 v Royal Navy
1975–76	G Lalchandani	94 at 12.02 (4)	7–47 v Centaurs

(2) Position in averages.

Kowloon Cricket Club

The Kowloon Cricket Club (KCC) was founded in 1904 by a group of enthusiastic and dedicated cricketers who, according to the late J P Robinson, discussed such a formation and implementation in the back-room of the Kowloon Dispensary of Messrs A S Watson & Co. Ltd. Kowloon was undergoing its own changes, one of which was the construction of a road from Kowloon Inland Lot 652, Hunghom, to Sixth Street, Yaumati, a road planned to 'afford the much needed communication between the villages of Hunghom and Yaumati.'

The KCC, bounded by Jordan Road, Cox's Road, the Kowloon Bowling Green Club/Austin Road, and the Gun Club Hill Barracks to the east, is situated in the bustling centre of the Kowloon peninsula. Once a low lying marshy field, it is now the recreational home for over 1,300 multi-racial members and their families. Just over half the membership is Chinese, the remainder being a mix of most of the world's differing races. The criteria for membership has always been: is he or she a decent and English-speaking person?

A matshed was the first clubhouse, with membership around 75. This was followed by a wooden structure on the west side of the ground, the foundation stone being laid by the President, Mr H N Mody, on 18 January 1908, and officially opened on 11 July 1908 by the Governor, His Excellency Sir Frederick Lugard. The present clubhouse was officially opened on 17 September 1932 by Mrs W T Southern, wife of His Excellency the Officer Administering the Government. Membership in the early 1930s was about 300.

The clubhouse has been structurally altered so many times that only the front facing Cox's Road is still recognisable from 1932. The main building contains the restaurant, coffee shop (over a four-lane ten-pin bowling alley), kitchen, mixed bar and lounge, snooker rooms, Fincher Room,

170

ladies' changing room, library and manager's flat. Adjacent to the main building are two structures – one a multi-storey car park with attached air-conditioned squash courts, office and staff quarters, roofed by two floodlit all weather tennis courts. The other, completed in 1993, houses the mens' changing room over a multi-purpose exercise area.

It is one of the few private recreational clubs with bowling greens separate from the main playing field. Beyond the playing field, a swimming pool complex provides the members with a very popular facility, where the annual children's swimming galas are held.

KCC now caters for five league cricket teams, as well as hockey, lawn bowls, squash and tennis as competitive league sports. Cricket has always been the major sport, although this has been challenged from time to time, when either the hockey or lawn bowls sections have been seasonally more successful.

Early matches were played on grounds loaned to KCC by the Hong Kong Parsee CC and others at Happy Valley, Hong Kong island. KCC played its first league match on 15 October 1904 on the Parsee CC ground:

> The day was exceedingly warm for cricket and the ground hard. As is the usual custom, players who know for a fact that they are to play in a match generally make it a habit of turning up late, causing great inconvenience.
>
> *SCMP*

AOCCC		Kowloon CC	
Webb, b Swan	10	Capt Lightfoot, c Merritt b Edwards	2
Edwards, b Swan	9	Harrop, c McGibbon b Edwards	7
Lieut Doran, c & b Swan	6	E R Lapsley, run out	1
Thurlow, c Swan b Cranston	1	J Robinson, b Bradford	0
Skinner, c Swan b Cranston	2	Dr Swan, b Bradford	1
McGibbon, b Cranston	7	J Scott Cranston, c Bromley b Bradford	0
Bradford, run out	7	Blackledge, b Edwards	1
Olive, run out	3	Clelland, c Bilton b Bradford	0
Bromley, c Robinson b Cranston	3	P Mass, not out	3
Merritt, c Harrop b Swan	1	C Filtock, c Skinner b Edwards	0
Bilton, not out	1	C W Brett, B Edwards	7
Extras	3	Extras	3
Total	53	Total	25

171

The Kowloon Club, although they lost the match, played a very promising game. One word that can be said of the team is that their bowling was good, and as regards their batting, more hard practice will find them a good team.

SCMP

1906   Kowloon: 128   (W Dixon 82, H Beer 27, Shepherd 4–42)
        Police: 29   (Davis 10*, W Martin 6–8, W Dixon 4–21)

W. Dixon was one of the first recorded century-makers for the Club, scoring 120 not out in the successful 1906–07 season.

In January 1914, KCC defeated a cricket team from the Chinese Recreation Club, scoring 196 (Capt Liddell 91) to their opponents' 113 (L J Blackburn 5–24). How many Hong Kong cricket followers were aware that the Chinese Recreation Club had played league cricket?

An historic advertisement in the *SCMP* for cricket equipment placed by Lane, Crawford, appeared regularly in 1918–

CRICKET BATS Surridge's 'Patent Rapid Driver'
$13.50 and $15.00 each. Wisden's cricket balls
$3.75 and $4.75 each. Special terms to Clubs,
Colleges and Service Teams

KCC was known as Kowloon in the league and in friendly matches right up to the mid-1920s, until presumably Recreio, another Kowloon side, began playing league cricket.

Various matches from 1909 till 1939 are recorded here. Someone might recognise the name of a grandfather, father or uncle who played cricket in prewar Hong Kong.

1909   Kowloon: 112   (J P Robinson 28, J H Mead 23, Cpl
                            Macgregor 4–20, Cpl Osman 4–32)
Dec 4   RE: 197–3   (L/Sgt Power 111*, Cpl Macgregor 58,
                            W Brewer 2–73)

Other Kowloon Players: W L Weaser, Lt Bunbury, J P Douglas, W F Brewer, Lt G G Richardson, W J Mackenzie, E H Pond, W T Elson and T Chee.

1924   Kowloon: 136   (Lt Col E D Matthews 26, T W R Wilson 7–34)
Nov 19   Shanghai: 185   (D W Leach 40, J A Quayle 25, Dr W E O'Hara
                            24, D C Burn 21, B D Evans 4–28, F Goodwin
                            3–40)

172

Other Kowloon Players: G Lee, S Jex, E C Fincher, Capt Parkes, Sgt Gifford, T D E Pendered, F N Young, J C Lyall and D H F McMaster.

	Kowloon:	221–9	(A E Wood 73, Lt Col Matthews 54, E C Fincher 42, A E Holmes-Brown 4–53)
	Malaya:	235–2	(G E Livock 133*)

1926	KCC:	176–3	(A W Ramsay 64*)
Dec 11	CCC:	91	(N H Ross 5–17)

1927	KCC:	196–8	(Capt Erskine 84*, F/O Mellor 44, Rawsthorne 4–41)
	Shanghai:	185–7	(D W Leach 66*, J A Quayle 57, Erskine 4–55)
	Malaya:	323–7	(Capt C H Condon 72, N H P Whitley 63, F Goodwin 4–90)
	KCC:	140–9	(A W Ramsay 42)

1928	HKCC:	399–4	(A W Hayward 143, Rev E K Quick 97, H
Nov 10		30–6	Owen Hughes 81*, G P Lammert 42)
& 12	KCC:	141	(F Goodwin 45, W Brace 40, C D Wales 7–49)
		116	(E F Fincher 46, C D Wales 7–29)

'Coming in first, Hayward early on mastered the bowling and made full use of his powerful drives and cuts in a flawless innings (22 4s). The wicket yesterday (Monday) was none too easy. The follow on was not averted.

HOW THE MIGHTY HAVE FALLEN

Last March (1928) at KCC, KCC scored a record 470, then dismissed HKCC twice for just over 300 runs in all. The KCC bowling has been sadly weakened by the loss of Lyall and Reynolds and the injury to Brace's bowling arm.'

Dec 8	HKCC:	172–7	(Capt Dobbie 87)
	KCC:	108–6	(E C Fincher 33, G A V Hall 32*)

Feb 16	KCC:	150	(W Brace 62, E F Fincher 28, E C Fincher 26, C D Wales 6–49)
	HKCC:	185–3	(T E Pearce 68, E J R Mitchell 51)

'HKCC passed their opponents total for the loss of only one wicket. The winners went on to score 185–3 when stumps were drawn.'

This was a feature of prewar cricket, when the side batting second would continue until stumps were drawn. They certainly made full use of Saturday afternoon cricket. No wonder the season's averages were not published!

Mar 16 HKCC: 238–8   (H Owen Hughes 61, E J R Mitchell 61, Capt
                            Dobbie 38, J L Bonnar 37*, E F Fincher
                            3–34)
         KCC: 136–3   (W Brace 79*)

1932   University: 175   (D J N Anderson 53, E L Gosano 52, G C
Jan 16   Burnett 4–33 including a 'hat-trick', J Lyall
                             4–64)
         KCC: 154–8   (E C Fincher 37, N A E Mackay 34, A Baker
                             6–47)

The following recorded highlights of matches till 1935 were all friendlies:

1932   CLPRC: 134–9   (A C Tinson 34, O B Raven 24*)
Mar 20   KCC: 64   (A A Dand 21, A B Clemo 5–22)

'... Clemo ran through the KCC.'

Mar 27   KCC: 174   (E F Fincher 44, G C Burnett 27, N A E
& 28   Mackay 26, J C Lyall 24, A C Beck 7–36)
                     222   (E F Fincher 56, P Madar 56, Mackay 24,
                             A C Hamilton 6–65)
         HKCC: 277   (G R Sayer 89, E J R Mitchell 52*, J E
                             Richardson 36, Lyall 4–86)
                     98   (L T Ride 42*, Mitchell 21, Burnett 6–44,
                             F Goodwin 4–23)

'Club needing 119 for victory found Burnett in deadly form.' KCC won an enthralling match by 21 runs at KCC.

Apr 9   KCC: 91   (D S Green 21*)
         HKFC: 85   (J E Potter 45*)

'The match was distinctly an enjoyable affair.'

174

1933 KCC: 176–9 (G C Burnett 42, C I Stapleton 40, L Alvis
Nov 11   4–35)
      Malaya: 176–9 (L Alvis 51, W C Hung 4–64, G C Burnett
                          4–65)

What a finish! Must have been a match to watch.

  19 Shanghai: 250–8 (D W Leach 60, J N F Mayhew 50*)
      KCC: 193–9 (E C Fincher 44, D W Leach 4–31)

1934 KCC: 92   (G Lee 32, Pte Forsythe 5–22, L/Cpl
Mar 10   Vaughan 4–24)
      RASC: 93–8   (L/Cpl Vaughan 24, F A Dunnett 4–28)

1935 KCC: 182–7 (E F Fincher 48, F I Zimmern 46, W C
                          Hung 36, E L Gosano 7–67)
      University: 96–9   (E L Gosano 41, R E Lee 5–31)

1936 Royal Navy: 130   (S V Gittins 6–34)
Mar 21 KCC: 135–4 (N A E Mackay 50)

On the same day, the University had thrashed IRC who were heading for
the senior title. The following week in a crucial match, KCC defeated University by 87 runs.

Mar 28 KCC: 173–4 (N A E Mackay 74, E C Fincher 36, E F
                          Fincher 31)
      University: 86   (R E Lee 5–30, F Goodwin 3–22)

KCC clinched the title from IRC by one point. The final table read:

	Played	Won	Lost	Drawn	Points
KCC	7	5	–	2	17
IRC	7	5	1	1	16

1938 DBS: 129   (F J Lay 48, A J Prata 34, G A V Hall
                          4–14, D Anderson 4–20)
      KCC 2nd: 137–8 (K M Baxter 62, C B R Sargent 4–46)

Mar 5 KCC 2nd: 154–9 (R Baldwin 33, C Sargent 26, R Broadbridge
                          26, Pte Coombs 5–26)
      Army: 40–9   (C B R Sargent 7–14)

Army were all out as one player was absent in this match at KCC. Bishop Sargent was a former Headmaster of DBS.

12   KCC: 230 (R T Broadbridge 103*, F Goodwin 39, Capt Parsons 7–78)
USRC: 202 (Lt Weedon 79, Lt Beadnell 39, G F O'Bryen 5–45)

26   Abraham's XI: 54   (S Jex 27, W Nash 6–18)
                       121–3 (S Jex 66 ret'd., G E Clarke 32)
Robinson's XI: 143–9 (J P Robinson No.11 – 33*, A A Dand 27, H Overy 7–50)

'KCC old-timers have a day in the field. Over 1,000 years were represented by the players, their ages aggregating 557 and 549 ranging from 65 (J P Robinson) to 41 (George Hall).'

1939   KCC: 165–7 (D J N Anderson 41, G C Burnett 32)
Jan 28 Army: 131   (Drv Logan 51, D J N Anderson 7–28)

'... with two wickets to fall in the last over, R E Lee had Major Swyres lbw with his first ball, and then clean bowled Pte Hatfield with his next.'

In a Second Division match on the same day at Sookunpoo: 'B D Lay of Kowloon, claimed the honour of having scored the first league century ...'

Army: 191–4 (Spr Ratcliffe 75*, Cpl Webb 51)
KCC 2nd: 213–5 (B D Lay 111*)

1921–22 saw the formation of a Second Division. KCC became double league champions that season. This achievement was repeated in 1940–41, the last cricket season before the Pacific war interrupted league cricket until the 1948–49 season. Although the war ended in August 1945, a devastated Hong Kong took a long time to recover from the havoc the war had caused.

The KCC clubhouse was looted of its furniture, doors, window frames and floorboards, and its cricket field was used by the Japanese for stabling horses and mules during the war years. This was just one example of a ransacked recreational club. As a consequence, the cricket league did not recommence until the 1948–49 season, with KCC having one team in each division.

1948   KCC: 181   (N Hart-Baker 59, Sterns 6–40)
Jan 1   RN: 125–8 (R E Lee 6–40)

Must have been a traditional New Year's day match at King's Park, the KCC ground being reserved for children's sports day.

1956   KCC: 71 (R C Jenner 23, Yates 4–11)
Mar 17 Army South: 25 (B C N Carnell 6–11, R W Bell 3–9)

'Leaders wilt before fiery onslaught of Bell and Carnell.'

Despite this embarrassment inflicted by Archie Zimmern's team, Army South went on to clinch the title in 1955–56.

Despite criticism, KCC played only one team in the First Division up till 1959–60. In 1960–61, the Club entered an 'A' (captain Bob Bell) and 'B' (captain Robbie Lee) team in the First Division and a team in the Second Division. Prior to the departure on leave of Buddy Carnell and Mike Jones in November, the 'A' team had 28 points out of a maximum 32. 'The failure to obtain any points from "lesser" sides such as Police, Recreio and KCC "B" in the early second half of the season allowed Brigade to pip the "A" team at the post.' J Shroff with 529 runs at 31.11 was the only batsman with 500 runs, including a 'flawless unbeaten century against CCC.' Carnell topped the bowling with 23 wickets at 12.95, whilst Vic Fairhall and Bob Bell collected 49 and 35 wickets apiece.

By this time the number of active playing members had increased, and many were unhappy about the lack of any identity for the club sides, so a competition was held to 'Name the Teams'. According to veteran Interporter Bob Bell, he came up with the winning combination: Templars, Saracens and Crusaders. In the 1961–62 season, the Templars and Saracens played in the First Division, with the Crusaders in the Second. From 1962–63 till 1969–70, the Saracens struggled in a league really beyond their ability. In fact, in the two seasons mentioned, they failed to win a single match. In 1962–63, they were even challenged by the Crusaders! However, the Saracens did have their moments:

1966   Saracens: 163–4 dec (P A Hall 38*, D G Coffey 35*)
Dec 10 Police: 101   (R Kay 33, M Hammett 31, P A Hall 5–26)

1967   Saracens: 185–6 dec
Oct 7   IRC: 83   (P Brockman 6–18)

'IRC had little answer to the left-arm spin of Brockman.'

1968   Kowloon: 146   (B Roach 52, P Hall 29, H Ebrahim 3–11,
                            C Myatt 3–17)
Feb 11 Valley: 109   (K Cumings 59, P Hall 6–30)

Hall's big dippers ruin Valley Clubs. – *Super League*

Mar 9 'Barry Jones, the Saracens captain, adjusted his sights, zeroed in on the Police bowlers (Lacy-Smith, Cumings, Wigley, Wilson and Kwong Tim) and blazed away'. Barry scored 86 (17 4s).

SCMP

The name Buddy Carnell was prominent during the 1965–66 season for the Templars.

> Templars: 208–3 dec (J S Shroff 129, G Abbas 37*, K Lo 31)
> Army: 167 (G Daniel 62, J Bennett 35, G Abbas 5–58, P Hall 3–29)

Jalu Shroff's century puts the task of winning out of Army's reach at Sookunpo.

> Templars: 173–5 dec (P Hall 46, D Coffey 34)
> IRC: 73 (R Lalchandani 27, B C N Carnell 7–28)

Buddy Carnell scatters the IRC batsmen at Sookunpoo.

> Templars: 160–3 dec (P Hall 88*, D Coffey 40*)
> LSW: 53 (B Carnell 7–20, P Hall 3–14)

While Peter Hall had a fruitful day, Buddy Carnell demolished LSW at KCC.

> Templars: 212–5 dec (J Shroff 87, D Coffey 44, P Hall 35, G Lalchandani 4–72)
> IRC: 112 (R Lalchandani 40, G Lalchandani 26, G Abbas 7–35, B Carnell 3–24)

Only the Lalchandani brothers prevented a massacre by Templars at KCC.

Serious damage inflicted by Templars on their opponents in 1967–68, reported by the *SCMP*:

1967
Oct 14 Templars 165–4 declared, beat LSW by 127 runs at Sai Wan.

'Saiwan were completely mesmerised by the pace of big Buddy Carnell ... as seven batsmen fail to score.' Only Dick Zarnke (20) reached double figures.

Oct 28   Templars 136–4 declared, defeat Police by 64 runs at KCC.

'HALL JUST MISSES A FULL BAG
'Peter Hall, swinging the ball tremendously, finished with the remarkable analysis of nine for 27, eight batsmen being bowled.'

Dec 9   Templars 136–5 declared, beat RAF by 79 runs at Kai Tak.

'Carnell captures 6–23, only the RAF No. 10 reaches double figures.'

1968
Jan 13   Templars 140–4, defeat CCC by 76 runs at Happy Valley.

'Templars inflict first defeat on league leaders. Splendid batting by
skipper Jalu Shroff (44) and great bowling by Peter Hall (5–16) and
Buddy Carnell (4–30).' Only Andy Ma (29) reached double figures.

Jan 20   Templars 160–5 (J Shroff 78), defeat LSW by 79 runs.

'Lively bowling by Peter Hall (6–32) quickly shatters Saiwan.'

During the 1968–69 season in a match at Kai Tak, the RAF lost to Templars by 10 wickets. The author recalled Mussie Fincher, daughter of
Teddy Fincher, arriving at the ground just as the Templars batsmen were
walking off the field. She thought it was a bit early for the tea break!

RAF: 19   (P A Hall 6–11, R B Jones 4–7)
Templars: 21–0

'The Templars polished off the Royal Air Force in an hour and a half
at Kai Tak. It was probably the quickest result achieved in the league
since the war. The airmen, at one time were six for 11, and they
managed to scramble to 19.'

In 1970–71, the Saracens joined the Crusaders in the Second Division, and
the Templars, after 15 lean years, won the First Division after defeating
IRC by five wickets in the last league match of the season (C Myatt 6–67).
The *SCMP* reported: 'The Templars never looked like a championship
side. In fact their fielding was simply appalling.'
Since the inauguration of each of the league championships and the cup
competitions, KCC has won the First Division/Sunday league 19 times
(once jointly), the Second Division/Saturday league 15 times (once jointly),
and the Rothman's Cup six times. Since its double league titles prewar,

179

KCC, fielding more than one team in each league, has completed the double a further three times, in 1985–86, 1986–87 and 1990–91.

The most successful league period for the club was during the seasons 1970–71 to 1974–75, when the senior division championship was won four times, the missing season being 1971–72, when a crucial match was 'carelessly' lost to the HKCC Optimists.

Optimists: 109 (N Sturgeon 38, M Bulfield 29, P Hall 4–23,
             B Carnell 4–42)
Templars: 90 (G Williams 3–10, M Miles 3 wickets)

Only 110 to win at KCC, with Shroff and Abbas opening the batting. Abbas took two fours off Peter Langston's first over – then it all went wrong. A win on that day would have given KCC Templars a record of five consecutive championship titles. But that's cricket!

The Hong Kong representatives who played for KCC during these eventful years were: Ghulam Abbas, John Bygate, Buddy Carnell, Kit Cumings, Buji Dhabher, Nigel Grandfield, Peter Hall, John Hung, Carl Myatt, Jalu Shroff, and Jangu and Yarman Vachha.

KCC had provided many Interporters pre-WWII for the matches against Shanghai and The Straits/Malaya. The youngest to represent Hong Kong during that period was the very talented Donald Anderson, who had learnt his cricket at DBS under the enthusiastic tutorship of J L Youngsaye. The most successful were probably the all-rounder Bill Brace with 1,025 runs in 1926–27, after the 1927 Interport against Shanghai in Hong Kong, an 'Observer' remarked: 'It was disappointing for Hong Kong that we did not have Brace in the Colony for more than a few years, as he was undoubtedly one of the best all-round cricketers we have seen.' and the batsmen brothers, Teddy and Ernie Fincher, Teddy, usually as steady as a rock, and Ernie, who scored 127 not out in the 1936 Interport against Shanghai. R ABBIT, who wrote for the *Hong Kong Daily Press*, said of the KCC team after the 1930–31 season:

The KCC are a bit of a tragedy. Without Brace, they are Hamlet without the Prince of Denmark. I suggested before the season that their bowling would be weak, but I did not realise what tripe it was going to become. Really, the trouble was that they depended on Frank Goodwin, and Frank got a date with a typhoid germ and bowled like the inverse ratio of Vitamin D.

After WWII, KCC provided many Captains of the Hong Kong team, from Frank Findlay (1957–61) continuously – except for the Interport against Malaya in 1959 when Guy Pritchard was captain, and for the game against

180

E W Swanton's Commonwealth side when Tony Weller was captain – to David Coffey (1962–66), Jalu Shroff (1967–71) and Carl Myatt (1971–77). More recently, after Peter Anderson retired in 1986, the captaincy had again reverted to KCC, with first Yarman Vachha, then Glyn Davies and more latterly Pat Fordham (1990–97), carrying on the great honour of this post.

The position of Chairman of Selectors was also cornered by KCC in the early 1970s, from Buddy Carnell (1971–73) to Jalu Shroff (1974–75) and then Peter Hall (1976–90). Rod Starling took over briefly in 1993–94 after the retirement of HKCC's Rod Eddington.

The Chairman of the Hongkong Cricket League and later the HKCA had always been a member from the HKCC until the 1980s, when KCC managed to get a 'foot in the door' with first John Bygate (1983–89), followed later by Brian Catton (1990–91) and then Peter Slack (1992–98).

In 1994–95, John Terence Hung became the first postwar KCC member to be elected to the prestigious post of President of the HKCA.

In 1973–74, the Templars, ably led by Buddy Carnell, became the first winners of the Sunday league (formerly First Division). Meanwhile in the Second Division, Jangu Vachha, working his magic for the Saracens, completed the double, scoring 567 runs and taking 54 wickets. Lance Bedlington in 1966–67, playing for Crusaders, also achieved this distinction, scoring 516 runs, the only batsman to exceed 400 runs, and capturing 50 wickets.

| 1975 | Crusaders : | 174–1 dec | (J Bygate 115*, D Clegg 42*) |
| Dec 20 | St George's: | 143–9 | (A Lonsdale 36, N Jones 4–37) |

| 1976 | Optimists: | 107 | (P Davies 30, J Chandler 8–32) |
| Jan 11 | Templars: | 108–0 | (J Bygate 60*, J Lamsam 46*) |

| Mar 28 | LSW: | 167 | (B Willson 62, C Myatt 7–44) |
| | Templars: | 171–6 | (K Cumings 56*, D Clegg 45) |

'… Templars spearheaded by brilliant bowling by skipper Carl Myatt …' [Note: This Sunday league cup match analysis was not recorded in the handbook 1976–77]

In September 1976, Jangu Vachha died suddenly in his 50th year; a tribute from Carl Myatt is memorialised here:

Few men in cricket will be missed more than Jangu Vachha, sportsman, administrator and gentleman. Jangu probably did more for the game in the short period of time he lived here than most men have done in a lifetime of residence in Hong Kong. He arrived in Hong Kong from India in the mid 1960s and joined the KCC where he made a legion of friends. He was always kind and full of good advice – a man who laughed a lot and genuinely loved life and the game of cricket. In Hong Kong, he could bowl intelligently and economically over long spells and on any wicket that gave him assistance, really spun the ball. He devoted much of his spare time to coaching the youngsters who congregated at the KCC on Sunday mornings. We mourn the passing of a fine and gentle man.

That season, a new Saturday league shield, designed by the author, then captain of the Saracens, was designated The Jangu Vachha Memorial Shield by the HKCA.

This Saracens side, led by Peter Hall, with Jangu guiding from above, won the coveted new shield, spearheaded by Gopal Lalchandani's 'top of the chart' 76 wickets at an average of 9.68.

1976   Saracens: 152–8 (D Williams 36, G Lalchandani 35, E Hurst 28,
Oct 9   G Hamson 4–40)
        LSW: 85   (D Compton 33, G Lalchandani 7–23, B Carnell
                            3–19)

'Carried by a superb all-round performance from Gopal Lalchandani Saracens humiliated LSW in a 67 run victory.'

Dec 11   Saracens: 187–7 (F Jowharsha 59, E Hurst 51*, P Hall 25,
                            P Berry 4–64)
         Nomads: 74   (D Wellard 28, G Lalchandani 5–22, P Hall
                            3–12)

'Leaders Saracens cut down Nomads with an emphatic 113 run victory at HKCC.'

In 1977–78, the club entered a third team, the Tartars, in the Saturday league and cup, while John Bygate (Templars & Crusaders) scored a total of 1648 runs.

In 1978–79, the Infidels, under the captaincy of the effervescent Aussie Eric Hurst, joined the Sunday league. John Bygate added another 1616 runs to his aggregate.

1980   Templars: 239–2 dec (J Bygate 136*, R Makhija 47)
Sep 21 IRC: 43   (L Prabhu 7–13)

'A thunderous win for Templars by 196 runs.'

From Bygate's first season in Hong Kong 1973–74, up to and including 1985–86, he scored a total of 16,929 runs in league/cup competitions which included 26 centuries.

1981	Infidels:	229–8 dec	(D Jones 100*, P Williamson 42)
Jan 11	Scorpions:	180	(J Hollioake 74, D Parsons 39*, R Starling 6–76)
Dec 20	Infidels:	253–0 dec	(I Nicholson 124*, J Hansen 102*)
	IRC:	81	(A Mahtaney 20, D Jones 5–26, C Collins 4–46)
1983	Saracens:	237–3	(G Davies 111*, R Gill 45)
Nov 26	KGV:	98–8	(S Myles 26, G Davies 4–26) – Saturday league
1984	Vagabonds:	91–9	(D Clinton 30, N Perera 7–17)
Dec 9	KCC Wasps:	92–2	(C Collins 37*, K Kumar 33*)

KCC Wasps won this Rothman's first round match by eight wickets.

1985	Templars:	211–9	(F Jowharsha 39, Y Vachha 39, R Brewster 34,
Mar 17			B Anderson 33, S Robinson 5–36)
	Infidels:	215–3	(C Collins 53*, N Broadhurst 52*, K Kumar 51, D Evans 45)

'A closely contested "Home Derby" saw the Infidels triumph once again over team-mates Templars'.

KCC 'almost grabbed all the trophies' in 1985–86. The Infidels, well led by Norman Broadhurst, won their first senior league title, followed into second place by club mates Templars. Krish Kumar with 835 runs, including three centuries, was the backbone of the batting, whilst Doug Beckett and Chris Collins spearheaded the bowling attack. The Templars defeated Police in a disappointing Rothman's Cup final by five wickets.

Police:	185	(G Davies 82, T Sawney 29, N Perera 3–23, D Cotton 3–43)
Templars:	187–5	(R Brewster 39, J Bygate 39, M Price 37*, B Catton 34)

In earlier rounds, Infidels Simon Myles had hit two centuries, 110 against British Forces and 112 against the Police.

The Saracens, with an unprecedented 17 wins out of 17 matches captured the Saturday league title, with skipper Glyn Davies leading the way with 754 runs and 33 wickets, ably supported by Krish Kumar's 907 runs and Yarman Vachha's 51 wickets.

In 1986–87, Infidels skippered by John Thirkell retained the Sunday league title, 42 points ahead of second placed Scorpions, whilst Templars retained the Rothman's with another crushing win over Police by 154 runs.

Templars: 237–7 (N Perera 88, B Catton 81)
Police: 83   (N Stearns 37, B Gohel 4–16)

Jim Middleton led the Tartars to the Saturday double of the league title and the Gillette Cup, his side's formidable all-round strength proving too much for the other teams. Thus, KCC wrapped up all the major titles and honours in a remarkable season.

In 1988–89, the Infidels under Mark Eames's captaincy captured their third Sunday league title in four years. The name Fordham with a total of 1192 runs, appeared for the Templars. A re-arranged Gillette Cup final in miserable weather saw Saracens deservedly upset Nomads to take the honours.

February 1990 saw the departure of Peter Hall, KCC stalwart, ex-Interporter, Chairman of Selectors, and supporter of Hong Kong cricket for many years, on retirement to England.

In 1990–91, KCC dominated Sunday cricket, with Infidels captained by Mark Eames, just heading off the Templars for the league title. The Templars then defeated the HKCC Optimists by six wickets to win the Rothman's Cup.

Optimists: 218–7 (J Barrington 71)
Templars: 219–4 (K Kumar 70, C Goonesena 48*)

Tartars, 'led by' Nanda Perera, pipped HKCC Nomads for the Saturday league title.

After an absence of 18 years, Steve Atkinson's Templars finally mounted the rostrum and took the Sunday league title for 1992–93. They then marched on to capture the Rothman's Cup by defeating the Pakistan Association, only the third team to hold both titles in the same season.

Mar 21 Templars: 374–3 (R Farcy 124*, S Atkinson 110*, P Fordham 79, J Penrose 30)
Pak. Assn: 251 (S Malik 67, I Wasim 66, M Hafeez 38, Y Vachha 3–46)

To round off a very successful season for KCC, Pat Fordham, the current Hong Kong captain, was named the Connaught 'Player of the Year', only the second 'full-blooded' KCC cricketer to win this coveted trophy since its inception in 1972–73, the other being Carl Myatt (1974–75). Gopal Lalchandani (1978–79: IRC & KCC Saracens) and Nigel Stearns (1985–86: Police & KCC Crusaders) have also won this coveted trophy.

The author's selection of the best KCC players to have represented Hong Kong in Interport cricket, during his years of involvement with cricket in Hong Kong, are:

Bowlers – Buddy Carnell and Carl Myatt.
Batsmen – Jalu Shroff, John Bygate and Nigel Stearns.

Many others, too numerous to mention by name, have played their part, whether as player or official, representating the KCC and Hong Kong sides over the years. However, a few special league performances should be mentioned. From records researched, there have been only six KCC bowlers who have taken nine wickets in an innings in postwar league/cup matches:

In 1960–61, for KCC 'A', Bob Bell with 9–32 v RAF and Vic Fairhall 9–52 v Recreio; in 1966–67, Keith Giles (Crusaders) 9–30 v Police; in 1967–68, Peter Hall (Templars) 9–27 v Police; in 1977–78, Levin Prabhu (Crusaders) 9–20 v LSW, and in 1993–94 Rahul Sharma (Templars) 9–16 v Vagabonds.

90 years after the commencement of league cricket in Hong Kong, KCC Templars, in the year of the Club's 90th Anniversary, retained the coveted Sunday league title.

From the season 1985–86 till 1993–94, the Infidels and Templars have won the Sunday league title six times, with Templars being runners-up four times (three times to the Infidels). The Templars have also won the Rothman's Cup four times, being runners-up once. Meanwhile, not to be outdone by their seniors, the Saracens and Tartars have won the Saturday league title and Gillette Cup three times. A very successful period for KCC cricket, probably something to do with the magnificent facilities which have tempted prospective sporting members to join KCC.

KCC had for some time been planning for its 90th Anniversary in 1994. The celebrations kicked off in mid April with a Sixes tournament. Three famous Aussie Test cricketers, Bruce 'Roo' Yardley, Geoff 'Swampy' Marsh and Tom Moody helped to lift the 'colourful' occasion to great heights. The Governor, Chris Patten, gave permission for a team to be named the Governor's VI, and even left his desk to grace the festival, the first Hong Kong Governor to visit the KCC as its Patron since the early 1960s. Despite the added 'quedos' and the mighty Moody, the Governor's VI lost to the HKCC's Victorians, led by the craft of Rod Eddington.

Tony Gough, writing for *Scoreboard*, gave the occasion a nostalgic nod by referring to KCC's first Captain of Cricket, Dr J H Swan, as 'looking down from the railings of the Great Pavilion in the Sky':

'Look at those queer boys in all those multi-colours; that's not cricket; they've only got six players a side and look at the sight-screens! Some blighters had the effrontery to paint 'em light blue!'

'and anyway the clubhouse is in the wrong position', he would have added.

The Club's 90th Anniversary celebrations ended with a Grand Ball in December 1994.

Although KCC teams have failed to win the Sunday league title in the last three seasons from 1994–95 to 1996–97, they have secured the individual honours in the 'Player of the Year.' First with Mark Eames, an elegant left-hand bat from the English Midlands; secondly, Rahul Sharma, a top-order batsman and medium pace bowler, ex Ranji Trophy player; and finally, now a 'two-timer' as 'Player of the Year,' Pat Fordham, former Hong Kong captain, forceful batsman and superb wicket-keeper from the county that provides a certain breed of person, Yorkshire.

The KCC, firmly backed by its dedicated officials and its multi-national membership, has already carried its great traditions across the Chinese transformation, and now looks forward to its Centenary in the 21st century.

Annual friendly matches

Annual local friendly matches prewar were played against the HKCC, various schools and Service teams. Postwar, friendly matches were played against CCC (the Robbie Lee Shield and the HKCC (the Hancock/Fincher Shields). The Robbie Lee Shield was inaugurated in 1964 in memory of the late KCC President, who had been a member of CCC before he joined KCC. The Hancock Shield, in memory of H R B 'Dick' Hancock (see Profile), is now played at the HKCC, whilst the Fincher Shield, in memory of E C 'Teddy' Fincher, Interporter and late President of KCC, is played at KCC.

The Fincher Shield initially 'replaced' the Hancock Shield, until a later decision brought both 'Shield' matches into the annual competition between the HKCC and the KCC (see the comments in the HKCC section). The first Fincher Shield match in 1980 was played at the HKCC, as the resurrection of the Hancock Shield took place at a later date.

1980	HKCC:	224–8	(J Hollioake 56, A Lorimer 62)
Dec 27		217	(B Kwong 68)
& 28	KCC:	218	(B Catton 77, R Toes 7–71)
		227–9	(F Jowharsha 40, O Hegarty 27*)

'When the last over commenced the score was 220–8. R Starling facing Toes with Hegarty 21 not out watching. Starling swung at the first four deliveries and missed, being bowled by the fourth. The last batsman Jim Middleton blocked the fifth ball to John Ashworth at short mid-on and ran, Ashworth fumbled, the batsmen crossed safely. There was a long pause while "all the HKCC players" told Toes where to bowl the last ball (the vociferous members on the verandahs were doing the same). Toes finally bowled the last ball which Hegarty heaved over the long-on fence onto the Urban Council tennis courts below. KCC had won by one wicket.'

What a memorable game, made possible by the spirit in which it was played, the example being set by the two captains, Eric Hurst (KCC) and Geoff Foster (HKCC). A fitting memory to those two renowned prewar Interporters, Teddy Fincher and Dick Hancock.

1981	KCC:	171	(D Reeve 68, C Collins 32, R Eddington 5–35)
Dec 26		224–6	(D Evans 44, D Reeve 39, C Collins 38,
& 27			P Williamson 30, D Way 4–48)
	HKCC:	177	(P Davies 45, M Walsh 35, B Kwong 32,
			Y Vachha 3–20,G Lalchandani 3–35)
		177–7	(P Varty 37, P Davies 27, G Lalchandani 3–27,
			R Starling 3–39)

HKCC won on the first innings. *Scoreboard*'s comment: 'Uninspiring cricket from the foremost cricket clubs.'

In 1990–91, after an absence of three years, the Hancock Shield returned to the cricket calendar, the format being changed for both Fincher and Hancock Shields to one-day 50-over matches. KCC won the new format match by 48 runs.

KCC:	224–7	(N Stearns 42*, J Marsden 31)
HKCC:	176	(S Brew 70, R Farouq 29, B Gohel 5 wickets)

187

At the end of the 1992–93 season, two of the strongest sides to represent the KCC and HKCC for many years faced each other on an overcast chilly day on a perfect batting wicket at Cox's Road.

```
1993     KCC:    276–7  (R Farcy 73, J Penrose 47, N Stearns 33,
Apr 5                    G Davies 32* M Eames 31, W Symcox 3–90)
         HKCC: 140       (J Orders 33*, S Foster 32, B Gohel 5–58,
                         R Farcy 3–31)
```

Riaz Farcy was joined by Nigel Stearns at the crease and they really began to increase the tempo putting on an excellent 95 run partnership. KCC got off to the best possible start with skipper Glyn Davies having Stewart Brew caught in the slips in the very first over. Excellent ground fielding, superb catching and tight bowling had the HKCC facing an uphill battle, eventually folding for a meagre 140 all out.

Roger Nissim, Scoreboard, 1993

KCC won by 136 runs. 'Man of the Match' deservedly went to Bharat Gohel. Mussie Fincher, daughter of Teddy Fincher, presented the Fincher Shield to KCC captain Glyn Davies.

The 1994 derby match reverted to the HKCC for the Hancock Shield, the match being sponsored by Connaught for the first time, where Captain of Cricket Mike Walsh and General Manager Keith Garner, had carried out all the necessary preparations.

```
Mar 20 KCC:    196–8  (P Fordham 54, M Eames 38, R Sujanani 38,
                       S Foster 4–37)
       HKCC: 158       (S Foster 63, S Brew 43, N Stearns 4–26)
```

It was an excellent game that waxed and waned for both sides. The match was played in a competitive but friendly spirit appropriate for both the fixture and the game.

Roger Nissim, Scoreboard 1994

```
1995     HKCC: 174   (R McGregor 62, M. Swift 32, R. Sujanani 3–32)
Apr. 30 KCC:    175–8  (D Hunt 69, G Davies 51)
```

'Glyn Davies ... played a prominent role in helping KCC retain their dominance over arch-rivals HKCC in this annual clash.'

Regular matches have been played against the Royal Bangkok Sports Club (RBSC) since 1959, on a home and away basis, while KCC sides have also toured Malaysia, Singapore, Taiwan and Thailand.

The KCC and RBSC matches are something special. From the first match in 1959 in Hong Kong, engineered by two old prewar friends, Robbie Lee and Tommy Madar, when David Coffey hit a 'sparkling unbeaten century' playing for R E Lee's XI – to a game in 1980, when two RBSC players scored centuries, and John Bygate failed for once to score a century in a match against the RBSC, he was out for 99 in the KCC second innings – the games have been played hard but with plenty of spirit!

In 1964, the RBSC's Labhamal Sachdev donated two trophies named after him for 'Interport Cricket and Hockey.' This generous gesture was immediately matched by Ralph Capell, the President of KCC.

1966　　KCC: 242–3　(P A Hall 74*, B P Dhabher 72*, K Lo 35)
Easter　　　191–4　(G Wills 63*, G Abbas 44, R B Jones 31*)
　　　　RBSC: 188　　(M Nana 53, J Clarke 44, T Baiden 33, B C N
　　　　　　　　　　Carnell 4–25, P Hall 3–38)
　　　　　155　　(A Pereira 65, J S Shroff 5–32, P Hall 3–30)

KCC won by 90 runs.

1968　　KCC: 128
Easter　　　231–3 dec　(P Hall 90, B Dhabher 70*, G Abbas 51)
　　　　RBSC: 183　　　(D Thompson 49, N Coulson 39, J N Vachha
　　　　　　　　　　4–56)
　　　　178–5　　(D Thompson 52*, N Coulson 34)

RBSC won by five wickets.

Certain stories cannot be printed, but some are worth recording – Jalu Shroff's five wickets in an innings in 1966, a sixth wicket was refused by a fielder (the author), who considered five was enough; the honour bestowed on the perennial 'Interporter' Buji Dhabher (pre-married days), who was presented with an RBSC blazer in 1979 in Bangkok, for services to cricket! After Buji retired, Jimmy Keir and Jim Middleton have continued the cementation of the bond between the two clubs.

Buji's *Confessions of a Veteran*, written in 1983, are hereby added:

That amazing scoreboard in Bangkok which read KCC 180–7, last man 143. The 'batsman' being none other than Buddy Carnell, with 13 gigantic sixes. Tim Mills taking a marvelous catch and then turning to acknowledge the thousands of voices in appreciation, only

189

to realise that the roar was for the start of the sixth race. The Welsh-man George Jones, who went for his 'bath' one evening, ended up in the countryside, and was not seen until lunchtime the next day. The effervescent Anton who, when he batted was more often than not closer to the bowling wickets when he struck the ball, and whose flowing pen the next day gave everybody their due, be it good or bad, in a style and manner that could only be Perera. Charles Stewart with the ever present cigarette holder in his mouth, singing and dancing Thai and holding his own against the Thai dancers. Miles de Vries, whose affinity for the Thai lifestyle caused him 'a bit of bother.'

There's also the Tony Lewis story, while on tour with the MCC in 1970, which every cricketer visiting Bangkok can relate to:

I shall never forget my first night in Bangkok. Don Wilson and I were escorted around the town by one Charles Stewart, a charming and most generous host. A fascinating procession through bars and restaurants – an incredible city by night. In the early hours we retreated home. Charles with a chuckle wished us strength for the coming day's play. With a chuckle we revealed that we were two of the three not playing. He was shattered. He was certain he had seen off the 'skipper' and Don Wilson.

Like most decades, circumstances change and, what started purely as a cricket encounter, with hockey as a sideline, very soon became cricket and hockey, and then mixed tennis and whatever. However, the initiative and 'spirit' provided by the early pioneers, the many friendships made and strengthened over the years, together with the hospitality from both sides, lives on. That's all important.

Many inter-club friendly cricket matches have also taken place. One that has survived since the 1950s with a few blips, having been resurrected by the author when he discovered its purpose whilst researching the club's history in the late 1970s, was the J P Robinson Shield.

J P Robinson was a member of the 1st XI in 1904–05. After he retired from playing for the club, he continued for many years as an umpire. The club's Annual Report for 1950–51 reported the death of J P 'Robbie' Robinson, founder and Life Member:

He was Captain, Hon. Secretary, 'Fa Wong', Umpire, Scorer, Special Secretary, Children's Sports and Christmas Draw Organiser, and additionally had participated in every phase of the Club's sporting and social activities.

190

The J P Robinson Shield, introduced in his memory, was to be played for by the President's XI (over 40s) and the Captain's XI (under 40s). For many years his daughter, Bonnie Penny, still going strong in her 92nd year (1997), presented a tankard via the author for the 'Man of the Match'.

The other 'Shield Match' which should also be remembered was the Robbie Lee Shield, in memory of the KCC President who died suddenly in 1962 on the edge of the KCC ground during a match. Robbie played for Craigengower before joining the KCC. This Shield was for matches between these two clubs. Happily, after an absence of too many years, matches were resurrected in 1996 by the then KCC Captain of Cricket, Tony Lethbridge.

The KCC ground, apart from its use for local league and friendly cricket, has been the venue for Interports against Malaysia and Singapore; the South East Asian tournament; touring sides from a host of countries, including Australia, the Indian sub-continent, Sri Lanka, Thailand and the United Kingdom; the 'Silk Cut' single wicket competition; local sixes and charity matches, and more recently the prestigious Cathay Pacific/Wharf Holdings International Sixes.

Apart from cricket

The Children's Sports, inaugurated on New Year's Day 1906, with a few unavoidable exceptions, has been an annual event ever since.

Just prior to June 1908, the Hong Kong Amateur Athletic Association laid down a cinder track for athletic events, but after one meeting in November that year, the track was grassed over.

In June 1908, a hockey team was formed, but after some poor and discouraging results and understandably less enthusiasm, hockey did not survive as part of the club's activities. However, organised hockey restarted at KCC in 1958–59 and has never looked back, with the men's and ladies' teams winning many championships and drinking much champagne! The section is very much alive and thriving.

In 1909, a golf section was formed and was very popular with members until the course was taken over by the Government in 1923 to make provision for other recreational facilities in King's Park.

The lawn bowls section formed in 1918 continues to have a large keen following, with the men's and ladies' teams and individuals winning many local championships and league titles. KCC lawn bowlers have also represented Hong Kong in the Commonwealth Games and the World Championships.

Tennis has been part of the club's fabric since its inception. Mark Bailey its brightest star, has represented Hong Kong in the Davis Cup. Squash commenced in 1962–63.

KCC has also produced rugby and soccer sides. The Blarney Stones Sevens tournament in 1958 was threatened by a KCC team up to the semi-finals! Mike Kennedy's soccer side were undefeated in the 1977 Sunday summer league. Soccer has been resurrected in recent years.

The first dramatic change in the club's membership came in 1963 after the completion of the new swimming pool complex. As this resulted in a large influx of new members, you no longer knew everyone anymore.

General Managers up to the late 1970s really acted as 'caretakers'. Ian Powell, a former WOI in the RAOC, saw many dramatic changes during his long tenure of office from 1981 to 1994, with the holding of the International Cricket Sixes probably being the most taxing. After his retirement, Mike Williams, a former RAF Squadron Leader, a specialist in physical education took over the responsibility of managing this prestigious club in the heart of Kowloon. The present General Manager, Marian Conbeer, is the first lady to occupy this post. She was previously general manager with the United Services Recreation Club.

The Governor in Office has always been the Patron of the club. The last Governor, the Right Honourable Christopher Patten has, it seems, also been the last Patron of KCC. In late 1998, Mr Tung Chi Wah, the Hong Kong Chief Executive, has graciously agreed to be Patron.

Officials

Presidents

1904–05	J Macgowan
1905–06	Dr J H Swan (acting)
1906–07	C F Fochen (died)
	T Skinner (acting)
1907–10	H N Mody
1910–23	Dr Chas Forsyth
1923–41	Justice R E Lindsell
1941–45	
1946–54	E Abraham
1954–62	R E Lee
1962–63	R E Lee (died Nov 62)
	R S Capell
1963–67	R S Capell
1967–68	A C McDonald
1968–69	E C Fincher

Club Captains

1904–06	Dr J H Swan
1906–07	S Lightfoot
1907–08	J H Mead
1908–09	S Lightfoot
1909–10	J P Robinson
1910–11	Major Chitty
1911–12	C J Jeffrey
1912–13	W L Weaser
1913–20	J P Robinson
1920–21	J Stalker
1921–24	J P Robinson
1924–25	J C Fletcher
1925–27	J C Lyall
1927–29	F Goodwin
1929–30	W Brace

Officials (cont'd)

Presidents		*Club Captains*	
1969–70	E C Fincher (died Oct 69)	1930–31	J C Lyall
	C A Adam	1931–40	F Goodwin
1970–74	C A Adam	1940–41	E C Fincher
1974–77	B C N Carnell	1941–47	
1977–80	J S Shroff	1947–51	R E Lee
1980–83	P G O'Dea	1951–53	S V Gittins
1983–87	J S Armitage	1953–54	P V Dodge
1987–90	P T Horton	1954–56	A Zimmern
1990–93	T J McKinlay	1956–58	D G Coffey
1993–96	M D McMillan	1958–59	F Findlay
1996–97	T J McKinlay	1959–61	R W Bell
1997–	C O'Brian	1961–63	F Findlay
		1963–64	D G Coffey
		1964–74	J S Shroff
		1974–76	H J Dickson
		1976–82	P A Hall
		1982–84	J Hansen
		1984–85	E Hurst
		1985–87	B Catton
		1987–88	B P Dhabher
		1988–90	N Stearns
		1990–92	G A Swift
		1992–94	R Nissim
		1994–95	D Hunt
		1995–97	A Lethbridge
		1997–	B Gohel

First Division/Sunday League – Batting Performances 1965–66 to 1993–94

Season	Player		500 runs plus	Centuries
1965–66	J S Shroff	(T)	580 at 48.33	129 v Army
1966–67	J S Shroff		572 at 38.10	
1967–68	J S Shroff		802 at 33.42 #	120 v Services#
1969–70	G Abbas	(T)	668 at 60.73 (2)	107* & 106* v Scorpions & 102* v Saracens.
	R Brown	(S)	641 at 45.79 (6)	102* v Templars
	D Dalrymple	(T)		114* v RAF
	S Hill	(T)		100* v Army

193

First Division/Sunday League – Batting Performances (cont'd)

Season	*Player*		*500 runs plus*	*Centuries*
1971–72	R Brown		534 at 48.55 (2)	
	R Booth	(T)		102 v Scorpions
1973–74	J Bygate	(T)	561 at 43.15 (2)	102* v Optimists
	J S Shroff			101* v Army
1974–75	C G Cumings	(T)		114 v Police
1975–76	J Bygate		757 at 54.07 (4)	113 v IRC
1976–77	J Bygate		615 at 38.44 (1)	108 v Scorpions
	F Jowharsha	(T)		106 v Army
1977–78	J Bygate		583 at 41.64 (7)	151 v Scorpions &
				128 v Vagabonds
	C G Cumings			121* v IRC
1978–79	J Bygate		549 at 34.31	138 v Infidels
	J King	(T)		102* v LSW & 101* v Infidels
1979–80	M Palmer	(I)	620 at 41.33	102 v Wanderers
	A Timms	(I)	531 at 40.85	
	B Catton	(T)	530 at 35.33	
1980–81	J Bygate		681 at 52.39 (2)	136* & 128* v IRC
	R Makhija	(T)		147 v Vagabonds
	F Jowharsha			132 v Scorpions
	D A Jones	(I)		100* v Scorpions
1981–82	I Nicholson	(I)	537 at 48.82 (6)	124* v IRC
	J Hansen	(I)		103* v IRC

J Hansen & I Nicholson 253* (1st) v IRC (1)

1982–83	J Bygate			147 v Infidels
	P Williamson	(I)		106* v Wanderers
	G Davies	(T)		104 v Optimists
1983–84	R Brewster	(T)	510 at 46.36 (2)	
1984–85	C Collins	(I)	464 at 66.29 (1)	
	K Kumar	(I)	765 at 54.64 (3)	133 v Optimists &
				124* v Scorpions
	B Catton		749 at 53.50 (4)	114* v Wanderers, 104 v IRC
				& 105 v Optimists
	R Brewster		616 at 47.38 (7)	
	D Evans	(I)	502 at 33.47	
	N Broadhurst	(I)		123* v Vagabonds & 100 v
				Brit.Forces
	N Perera	(T)		110* v IRC

First Division/Sunday League – Batting Performances (cont'd)

Season	Player		500 runs plus	Centuries
1985–86	K Kumar		835 at 55.67 (2)	158 v Brit.Forces, 115 v Police & 106v Wanderers
	J Bygate		641 at 53.42 (3)	121 v Wanderers
	N Perera			107* v Vagabonds
	S Myles	(I)		107 & 110 v B.F§ & 112 v Police§
	R Brewster			103 v Police
1986–87	K Kumar		546 at 54.60 (5)	
	D Evans		584 at 48.67	
	D A Jones			118* v Brit.Forces
	D Beckett	(I)		116 v IRC
	N Perera			114* v Wanderers
	P Fordham	(T)		102 v Vagabonds
1987–88	D A Reeve	(T)		152* v LSW
	D Evans			135 v Comb.Serv.# & 104* v Brit.Forces
	P Fordham			117* v IRC & 108* v Independents#
	N Perera		384 at 64.00 (1)	
1988–89	P Fordham		626 at 78.25 (3)	178* v IRC & 102*v Wanderers
	M Eames	(I)	553 at 50.27 (8)	132 v Brit.Forces
	D Beckett		479 at 79.83 (six innings)	171 v Vagabonds & 114 v Templars
	K Kumar			120* v LSW
	R Brewster			107 v Scorpions

P Fordham & K Kumar   236* (1st) v IRC   (1)
M Eames & N Stearns   234 (2nd) v Brit.Forces   (2)

Season	Player		500 runs plus	Centuries
1989–90	S Atkinson	(T)	778 at 77.80 (2)	129* v Vagabonds, 127 v Infidels & 100 v Scorpions
	D Evans			127* v Scorpions
1990–91	P Fordham		809 at 73.55 (2)	125 v Optimists, 122* v Scorpions & 112* v Vagabonds
	K Kumar		602 at 60.20 (5)	
	D Brettell	(I)	591 at 45.16 (10)	111 v IRC
	M Eames			118 v Scorpions
	A Dartnell	(I)		115* v Vagabonds

First Division/Sunday League – Batting Performances (cont'd)

Season	Player		500 runs plus	Centuries
1991–92	P Fordham		596 at 54.18 (2)	133 v Optimists, 119* & 102 v Scorpions & 194 v Pak. Assn.§
	M Eames		512 at 51.20 (4)	124* v Brit.Forces & 102* v IRC
	C Goonesena	(T)		131* v IRC
1992–93	P Fordham		807 at 100.88 (1)	136 & 129 v Wanderers
	J Penrose	(T)	686 at 85.75 (2)	138* v LSW, 113 v Scorpions, 105 v Wanderers, 221 v HKCC Casuals§ & 112 v PRC§
	S Atkinson		577 at 82.43 (3)	116* v Optimists & 110* v Pak. Assn.§
	R Brewster		522 at 43.50	123* v Scorpions & 117* v IRC
	D Thompson	(I)		123 v Vagabonds
	M Eames			116* v Brit.Forces
	N Perera	(T)		156* v HKCC Casuals§
	R Farcy	(T)		124* v Pak. Assn.§
	H Davis	(T)		116* v Vagabonds§

J Penrose & N Perera (T) 358 (1st) v HKCC Casuals (1)§
P Fordham & J Penrose (T) 224 (1st) v Wanderers (3)
P Fordham & J Penrose (T) 200 (2nd) v Scorpions (5)

Season	Player		500 runs plus	Centuries
1993–94	P Fordham		636 at 159.00 (1)	121* & 110* v Vagabonds
	R Sharma	(T)	1072 at 89.33 (3)	156 v Scorpions, 145 v LSW, 142* v IRC, 121 v Pak.Assn & 111* v Vagabonds
	M Eames		515 at 85.83 (4)	106* v Pak. Assn. & 104 v Optimists
	S Atkinson			127* v Optimists
	R Brewster			119 v Optimists

P Fordham & R Sharma 244* (1st) v Vagabonds (2)
R Brewster & M Eames 222 (1st) v Optimists (3)

#	Includes 'Super' league
§	Rothman's Cup
(1)	Position in averages
(1st)	Wicket partnership over 200 runs
	(I) Infidels (T) Templars
	HKCC – Optimists/ Scorpions/ Wanderers

First Division/Sunday League – Bowling Performances 1965–66 to 1993–94

Season	Player		50 wickets plus	7 plus (for 50 runs or less)
1965–66	B C N Carnell	(T)	58 at 8.78 (4)	7–20 v LSW & 7–28 v IRC
	P A Hall	(T)	53 at 10.47 (7)	
	G Abbas	(T)		7–35 v IRC & 5– 1 v RAF
1966–67	R B Jones	(T)		7–13 incl. 'hat-trick' v Police
	H J Dickson	(S)		4–0 (4 overs) v Optimists
1967–68	P A Hall		66 at 11.05 (3) #	9–27 v Police
	R B Jones			7–24 v RAF
	B C N Carnell			7–32 v Saracens
1968–69	R B Jones		53 at 15.21 (8) #	
1969–70	R B Jones		62 at 15.24	8–32 v HKCC Wanderers &
				8–39 v KCC Saracens
1970–71	P A Hall			7–21 v RAF
1972–73	C Myatt		54 at 11.74 (3)	
	R B Jones			7–43 v Police
1973–74	C Myatt		59 at 12.12 (2)	8–60 v HKCC Scorpions
1974–75	C Myatt		42 at 8.33 (1)	
			(only 2 bowlers	
			40 plus)	
1975–76	J Chandler	(T)	51 at 13.50 (4)	8–32 v Optimists & 'hat-trick'
				v IRC & Scorpions
1978–79	I Talbot	(I)	52 at 16.85 (9)	
			(only bowler	
			50 plus)	
1979–80	J Chandler	(I)		7–46 v IRC
1980–81	L Prabhu	(T)		7–13 v IRC
1982–83	C Collins	(I)		8–39 v HKCC Scorpions
	G Davies	(T)		7–30 v LSW
	M Giles	(I)		7–47 v Vagabonds
1983–84	J Jenkins	(T)	47 at 12.94 (1)	
			(second highest	
			total)	
1984–85	N Perera	(W)		7–17 v Vagabonds§
1985–86	B Gohel	(T)		7–45 v Vagabonds
1986–87	C Collins			8–36 v HKCC Optimists
1989–90	G Davies		48 at 14.42 (1)	7–34 v HKCC Optimists
			(highest total)	
	C Milnes	(T)		8–41 v IRC
	P Fordham	(T)		7–28 v Brit.Forces
	N Perera	(I)		7–38 v LSW

First Division/Sunday League – Bowling Performances (cont'd)

Season	Player		50 wickets plus	7 plus (for 50 runs or less)
1990–91	D Brettell	(I)		7–33 v HKCC Optimists
1991–92	G Davies		49 at 16.55 (3) (second highest total)	
	P Cresswell	(T)		8–35 v IRC
1992–93	R Greer	(T)		8–53 v IRC
1993–94	A Foley	(I)	33 at 15.39 (1)	8–32 v Brit.Forces
	R Sharma	(T)		9–16 v Vagabonds

Includes 'Super' League
§   Rothman's Cup
(1)   Position in averages
     (I) Infidels (S) Saracens
     (T) Templars (W) Wasps

Second Division/Saturday League – Batting Performances 1965–66 to 1993–94

Season	Player		500 runs plus	Centuries
1966–67	L Bedlington	(C)	516 at 34.40 (only batsman 500 plus)	
1969–70	S Moores	(C)	589 at 45.31 (2)	102* v Army
1971–72	P Varty	(S)	630 at 35.10 (9)	102* v Crusaders
	R Cooper	(S)	527 at 27.74	
1973–74	J Bygate	(C)	870 at 45.79 (6)	117 v Police
	K Lo	(C)	690 at 30.00	
	J Vachha	(S)	567 at 28.35	
	R Booth	(S)		101 v Centaurs
1974–75	J Bygate		702 at 46.80 (5)	
	G Richardson	(C)		124* v Islanders

J Bygate & G Richardson (C) 215* (2nd) v Islanders (1)

1975–76	J Bygate		788 at 46.35 (8)	128* v Kai Tak & 115* v St George's
	E Hurst	(S)	613 at 29.19	107 v Crusaders
	F Jowharsha	(S)	506 at 23.00	
	G Richardson			118* v Nomads
1976–77	J Bygate		965 at 50.79 (4)	135* & 124 v CCC
	M Palmer	(C)	525 at 37.50 (10)	

198

Second Division/Saturday League – Batting Performances (cont'd)

Season	Player		500 runs plus	Centuries
	G Lalchandani	(S)	643 at 35.72	
	F Jowharsha		611 at 25.46	
	D Clegg	(C)		100* v Nomads
1977–78	G Hurrell	(S)	802 at 61.69 (2)	102* v KGV
	J Bygate		1065 at 53.25 (4)	144* v HKU, 106 v Tartars & 102 v CCC
	G Richardson	(T)	939 at 52.17 (5)	131* v HKU
	M Palmer		621 at 36.53	
	I Nicholson	(T)	725 at 32.95	107 v Crusaders
	F Jowharsha		631 at 27.43	
1978–79	J Bygate		1067 at 53.35 (4)	121* v St George's, 110 v Saracens, 101 v Tartars.
	G Richardson		674 at 44.93 (5)	105* v CCC
	T Mills	(T)	559 at 34.94	
	G Sims	(T)	537 at 31.59	
	G Lalchandani		545 at 27.25	102 v DBS
	F Jowharsha		520 at 21.67	
1979–80	R Makhija	(C)	766 at 54.71 (4)	114* v Nomads, 109* & 100 v Strollers & 104* v KGV.
	J Bygate		957 at 53.17 (6)	142* v St George's
	B Catton	(C)	667 at 33.35	
	O Hegarty	(C)		102 v DBS
	G Lalchandani		540 at 54.00 (5)	
	P Nunn	(T)	583 at 30.68	
	C Dirckze	(T)	509 at 29.94	
	D Williams	(S)	520 at 27.37	

J Bygate & B Catton (C) 225 (1st) v St George's (2)

Season	Player		500 runs plus	Centuries
1980–81	B Catton		740 at 52.86 (4)	
	J S Shroff	(S)	622 at 44.42 (6)	
	P Williamson	(S)	661 at 44.07 (8)	103 v Royal Navy
	F Jowharsha		778 at 38.90	109 v KGV & 105* v Army
	J Bygate		733 at 36.65	
	C Dirckze		662 at 33.10	104 v Royal Navy & 101* v Islanders
	N Shroff	(C)	527 at 32.94	
1981–82	D A Reeve	(T)	458 at 91.60 (1)	
	J Bygate		845 at 52.81 (4)	111* v Witherers
	B Catton		532 at 33.25	
	F Jowharsha		564 at 29.68	

Season	Player		500 runs plus	Centuries
	P A Hall	(S)		109* v Royal Navy
	E Hurst			103* v Royal Navy
1983–84	G Davies	(S)	894 at 74.50 (3)	111* v KGV & 100* v Islanders
	R Brewster	(C)	645 at 40.31	
	N Broadhurst	(T)	759 at 37.95	103* v Saracens
	J Hansen	(T)	567 at 31.50	
	J Bygate		536 at 29.77	
1984–85	N Stearns	(C)	681 at 68.10 (4)	
	J Bygate		690 at 53.08 (6)	109* v Gap Ramblers
	K Kumar	(S)	782 at 52.13 (7)	
	N Broadhurst		631 at 45.07	
	R Brewster		668 at 33.40	102 v Tartars
	R Marsh	(T)		101* v Saracens

N Stearns & J Bygate 215 (1st) v Gap Ramblers (2)

Season	Player		500 runs plus	Centuries
1985–86	N Stearns		589 at 98.17 (1)	132* v HKU & 105* v Army
	G Davies		754 at 68.55 (4)	
	K Kumar		907 at 64.78 (5)	104* v LSW
	B Catton		690 at 43.12	
	J Bygate			103* v Tartars
	J Thirkell	(T)		100* v St George's
	C Dirckze			100 v Gap Ramblers
1986–87	G Davies		592 at 53.82 (3)	104 v CCC
	D A Jones	(T)	601 at 37.56	114 v LSW, 108 v CCC &
				103 v KGV
	D Evans			119 v Saracens
1987–88	M Eames	(T)	948 at 79.00 (4)	
	D Evans		999 at 62.44 (7)	139* v St George's &
				111* v Saracens
	J Bygate		548 at 49.82	113* v St George's
	N Stearns		519 at 47.18	118* v Centaurs
	R Brewster		505 at 36.07	
	P Fordham			113 v Crusaders & 104* v HKU
1988–89	P Fordham		566 at 80.86 (1)	113 v Sentinels
	R Brewster		855 at 71.25 (4)	
	C Jones	(S)	585 at 53.18 (8)	
	D Evans		742 at 53.00 (9)	
	K Kumar			113 v Sentinels
	H Tyrwhitt-Drake	(C)		103 v Centaurs

Second Division/Saturday League – Batting Performances (cont'd)

Season	Player		500 runs plus	Centuries
	M Eames			103* v Army
1989–90	M Eames		683 at 75.89 (2)	
	R Brewster		508 at 42.33	
	D Evans		581 at 38.73	109* v DBS
	A Braund	(T)		127* v KGV
	N Perera	(T)		116 v Centaurs
1990–91	M Eames		600 at 85.71 (4)	122* v HKU & 103 v KGV
	D Hunt	(C)	630 at 52.50 (5)	
	A Braund		568 at 43.69 (8)	
	D Evans		511 at 36.50	
1991–92	M Eames		695 at 53.46 (8)	106* v MCC
	P Fordham			195 v CCC & 138* v Centaurs
	A Beard	(T)		109 v Sentinels
	N Perera			109 v KGV §

P Fordham & C Jones (S) 206* (1st) v Centaurs (1)

Season	Player		500 runs plus	Centuries
1992–93	R Brewster		522 at 43.50	117* v Islanders & 100* v Kai Tak
	H Davis	(T)	537 at 41.31	125 v Saracens
	D Thompson	(T)		149 v St George's
	P Fordham			133* v Tartars, 109 v HKU & 107 v MCC.
	K Krishnan	(S)		103* v Gap Ramblers
	R Farcy	(T)		102 v Nomads §
1993–94	M Eames		501 at 38.54	124 v DBS
	R Farcy			132* v LSW & 105* v MCC
	P Fordham			126 v Kai Tak
	S Atkinson	(S)		120 v Nomads
	N Stearns			104 v Gap Ramblers §

§ Butani/ Dragonair Cups
(1) Position in averages
(1st) Wicket partnerships over 200 runs
(C) Crusaders (S) Saracens (T) Tartars
HKCC – Gap Ramblers/ Nomads/ Witherers
Police – Sentinels/Strollers

Second Division/Saturday League – Bowling Performances 1965–66 to 1993–94

Season	Player		50 wickets plus	7 plus (for 50 runs or less)
1966–67	L Bedlington	(C)	50 at 11.74 (9)	
	K Giles	(C)		9–30 v Police
1968–69	B Johnson	(C)		7–29 v Nomads
1969–70	S Paton	(S)		7–26 v LSW & 7–30 v DBS
1971–72	B Johnson			7– 7 v IRC
	K Giles			7–12 v HKU
1972–73	Y Vachha	(S)	55 at 11.38 (5)	6– 6 v Police
	L Prabhu			7–35 v Witherers
1973–74	J N Vachha	(S)	54 at 13.04 (7)	
	L Prabhu	(C)	54 at 18.33	
1974–75	L Prabhu			8–14 v Royal Navy
	R B Jones	(S)		8–54 v Centaurs
1975–76	R Starling	(C)	51 at 10.35 (3)	7–20 v HKU
	J N Vachha		60 at 12.52 (6)	8–36 v Kai Tak & 'hat-trick' v LSW & Kai Tak
	L Prabhu		57 at 14.40 (9)	
1976–77	G Lalchandani	(S)	76 at 9.68 (1) (7 wkts 4 times)	7–21 v Islanders, 7–23 v LSW & 7–37 v St George's
	J Middleton	(C)	56 at 16.29	
	R Nissim	(S)		'hat-trick' v Police
1977–78	L Prabhu		50 at 14.94	9–20 v LSW
	J Middleton	(T)	50 at 19.36	8–31 v Islanders & 7–30 v HKU
	P A Hall	(S)		7–13 v Witherers
	G Hunt	(S)		'hat-trick' v Royal Navy
1978–79	G Lalchandani		44 at 13.27 (1)	
	L Prabhu			7–29 v RGJ (Army)
	P Nunn	(T)		7–20 v LSW
1979–80	G Lalchandani		53 at 12.41 (1)	
	J Middleton		50 at 20.58	
1981–82	S Punjabi	(T)		8–13 v Army
	A Harris	(C)		'hat-trick' v LSW
	M Giles	(C)		'hat-trick' v Royal Navy
1983–84	G Davies	(S)		7–19 v St George's
1985–86	Y Vachha		51 at 12.41 (1)	7– 8 v DBS
	J Middleton		55 at 13.45 (2)	
	L Prabhu		51 at 13.57 (3)	
	J Hansen	(T)		'hat-trick' v Saracens
1986–87	J Tedd	(C)		'hat-trick' v DBS

202

Second Division/Saturday League – Bowling Performances (cont'd)

Season	Player		50 wickets plus	7 plus (for 50 runs or less)
1987–88	L Prabhu		49 at 13.45 (3) (only bowler 40 plus)	
1990–91	P Cresswell	(S)		'hat-trick' v HKU
1991–92	P Cresswell			7–22 v Islanders
	D O'Hara	(T)		'hat-trick' v HKU
1992–93	A Lethbridge	(C)		'hat-trick' v MCC

      (1)   Position in averages
             (C) Crusaders (S) Saracens (T) Tartars
             HKCC – Nomads/ Witherers

Lamma Island Cricket Club

The club's history can be traced back to the early 1980s, when Lamma played an annual game against the Hong Kong University Social XI at Sandy Bay, a tradition that survives to this day.

Around 1992, Lamma's growing community began to include keen cricketers and this led to the formation of a more organised social club. The club was inaugurated at a meeting held at the Waterfront Restaurant on Lamma, and the first practice session was on a helicopter pad. This remains one of the few areas of 'flat' land on the island, not that flat though, as the first the batsman saw of the bowler was his head appearing over the horiazon from his up-hill run-up! At that time the club possessed one bat, one ball and some tatty pads by way of equipment. They had, however, some keen players and their first sponsor was the Island Bar, so they became the Lamma Island Bar Cricket Club. The club has since secured generous sponsorship from Hong Kong Electric and Foster's Lager.

Early games did not meet with much (any) success but the club persevered, encouraged by a love of the game and the undeniable fact that they could do no worse. As players improved and new ones appeared, matches were won, with the most successful social season being 1994/95, when they won every social game played and also reached the third round of the Saturday league cup, beating the Champagne XI and KGV, before losing by one (very dubious) run to the eventual winners, HKCC Witherers.

As grounds became increasingly difficult to find, Lamma began to tour in Thailand, Manila, Sri Lanka and Angeles City, where they won a sixes tournament. Lamma eventually achieved admission to the Saturday league in the 1996/97 season, taking the place of LSWCC, during which time the club remained firmly at the foot of the table, but were learning fast, and won the Craigengower CC Sixes tournament at KCC. During the 1997/98 season, the club showed a marked improvement achieving 10th place (17 teams), and progressed to the quarter-finals of the Saturday league cup, going out closely once again to the HKCC Witherers.

It remains to be seen whether Hong Kong's immigration laws, revised since June 1997, will impact on the continuation of the club in the local league, as British citizens entering Hong Kong are now restricted to a maximum stay of six months and are not allowed to look for employment.

Little Sai Wan Cricket Club

The Little Sai Wan Cricket Club (LSWCC) was established in 1964. The initial playing talent came from the British Ministry of Defence, who operated a 'China Listening Post' at a former RAF base, called 'Little Sai Wan', situated on the eastern seashore of Hong Kong island. These players were supplemented by a few servicemen from the Royal Australian Air Force, who were seconded to the base, and by school teachers working at British Military Schools. A club insignia of a 'Lion and Kangaroo standing each side of a set of stumps' was chosen as an appropriate design for this new club. The cricket facilities were housed in a colonial style two storey verandahed building, raised on a grass embankment, known as 'The Hill', which overlooked the playing field, and had extensive views out to the sea lanes which approached the Lei Ye Mun channel separating Hong Kong island from Kowloon. A fine sunny January day would bring the whole family out to enjoy the expansive grounds which touched the shore, cupped by the surrounding hills. On a cold, windy day ...

From the outset LSWCC was known as one of the most hospitable clubs in the league. Long bar sessions were mandatory for visiting teams. How you got home was another matter. It was also a 'do it yourself' club, with the outfield and pitch being prepared by team members. A grass wicket was played on during the first seven or eight years; however, due to the unpredictability of 'high tides,' a matting wicket was used from the early 1970s.

1966   Saracens: 151–5 dec (D G Coffey 63, P A Hall 59*, B Binder 4–43)
        LSW: 118–7   (D Zarnke 41, R W Bell 3–16)

LSW gained bonus points in a drawn match at KCC.

LSWCC performed with limited success in its formative years, despite the talents of such players as John Ackroyd, Ted Birch, Peter Everett, Vic Johnson, Col Metcalf, Jim Rhodes, Alan Swift and Geoff Wells.

```
1971      IRC:    102  (L Stenner 6–27)
Feb 14    LSW:     43  (G Lalchandani 6–21)
```

Gopal Lalchandani had a soft spot for LSW, whom he later joined.

LSWCC's fortunes changed in the early 1970s with the introduction of a 'guest' player policy. Members' acceptance of this policy was far from universal, but success on the playing field overcame early objections. The persons instrumental in both ensuring that this policy was tactfully implemented (Conway) and that the ground was in a fit condition for play (Mellowes), were Bill Conway and Bert Mellowes. Their names are synonymous with the name LSWCC: 'Bert was controversial, not always the most placid of individuals on or off the field, and he succeeded in incurring the wrath of players, officials, and the media alike on various occasions.'

His involvement with LSWCC, especially in its early years, will not be forgotten by others who were there, whilst his pioneering work with umpiring in Hong Kong has been expanded in the section under league cricket. Bill Conway served as club mentor and President in the early 1970s, as well as general factotum and scorer.

Bill's charm and diplomacy held the club together during difficult times. On his retirement from the Defence Ministry, he became the Manager of The Hong Kong Cricket Club, a job he conducted with distinction for several years, until his final departure from Hong Kong.

LSWCC's first major success came in the 1975–76 season, when after 10 years of endeavour, the club won the Sunday league title. This was achieved under the astute captaincy of 'Tug' Willson. In his late 30s when he joined LSWCC, he proved to be one of the club's and Hong Kong's most outstanding cricketers in the 1970s. He and David Clinton, a school teacher and talented cricketer, were the mainstays of the batting, ensuring high scores were achieved with several prolific opening partnerships. They were ably supported by Les Stenner and Peter Smith, who provided an outstanding swing and pace attack.

```
1975      LSW:         200–8 dec  (B Willson 82, M Duggan 4–36)
Jan 12    Wanderers:    94         (O Robinson 4–34, P Smith 3–35)

Feb 23    Wanderers:   153         (G Butler 31, A Turner 4–36)
          LSW:         154–6       (B Willson 105*)
```

'The LSW batting was dominated by 'Tug' Willson who scored a magnificent 105 not out in the Rothman's Cup semi-final at Sai Wan.'

Oct 19   Army: 109   (D Budge 55, B Willson 6–19, A Swift 3–48)
             LSW: 111–1 (D Clinton 54*, B Willson 51)

Nov 2   Police: 99   (I Nicholson 48*, P Smith 6–40, L Stenner 3–3)
             LSW: 102–4 (B Willson 71*)

'Police collapsed against LSW's left arm pair of Smith and Stenner.'

1976   Army: 103   (R Litherland 37, A Swift 4–33, B Willson 3–7)
Jan 11   LSW: 104–0 (B Willson 73*)

Feb 29 Optimists after declaring at 205 for 6 (P Davies 95) lost to LSW, with 'Tug' Willson once again getting involved to the tune of 126 runs.

Mar 7   LSW: 248–4 (D Clinton 79, B Willson 78, M Wilkinson 44)
           Police: 115   (P Smith 4–49, A Swift 3–52)

'LSW are Sunday League Champs.'

21   Optimists: 243–5 dec (I Stevens 98, R Mills-Owen 40)
      LSW: 244–8   (D Clinton 80, R Vergelius 57, B Willson 40)

'LSW out-hit the Optimists to win by two wickets.'

In 1977–78, the Saturday League Cup trophy was shared with KCC Saracens when the final was abandoned at KCC due to adverse weather conditions.

A 'golden era' had started for LSWCC, who went on to win the Sunday league in 1980–81 and 1982–83 and the Rothman's Cup in 1977–78, 1980–81, 1981–82 and 1983–84. The highlight of the club's history was in 1980–81, when under the 'inspired' captaincy of Tony Turner, they became the first team to achieve the double, winning the Sunday league title by defeating KCC Infidels in the rain at Mission Road and then the HKCC Taverners in the Rothman's Cup final.

1979   LSW: 174 (B Willson 80, R Poynton 4–21, M Darke 3–44)
Feb 4   Wanderers: 153 (D Griffiths 30, G Bacon 6–47)

'Skipper Toes, was run out when running with his runner off the last ball!

1981   LSW: 207–8 dec (R Lalchandani 61, B Kwong 4–69)
Jan 4   Scorpions: 26   (A Turner 6–15, G Lalchandani 4–11)

'Saiwan thrash Scorpions at Sai Wan.' This must be one of the heaviest defeats suffered by the HKCC Scorpions in league cricket.

1982   Infidels: 168   (P Williamson 55, J Hansen 30, M Grubb 3–26)
Feb 14 LSW: 171–6 (B Willson 67, M Giles 3–33)

A Rothman's Cup match at Sookunpoo.

Mar 7   LSW, declaring at 206 for 8 (A Turner 53, R Lalchandani 36, C Metcalf 24), defeated the Optimists 185 in 'wet and miserable conditions ... ' at KCC.

Apr 5   Vagabonds: 150–9 (D Greenwood 48, D Reeve 33, A Turner 2–15)
        LSW: 151–7 (A Turner 57, G Bacon 40*, C Wrigglesworth 32, B Gohel 3–42, D Reeve 2–11)

'Saiwan became the first team to successfully defend the Rothman's Cup with another nerve–racking triumph in a closely fought final at KCC.'

During this 'golden era', LSWCC was ably served by Peter Anderson, Gordon Bacon, David Clinton, Elias Ismail, Gopal and Ram Lalchandani, Alan Scott, Peter Smith, Tony Turner, Roger Vergelius and 'Tug' Willson, all of whom had represented Hong Kong, coupled with the names of Richard Flood, Malcolm Grubb, Keith Johnston, Geoff Lever, Robert Muirhead and Chris Wrigglesworth, to name a few.

1983   LSW: 150 (M Grubb 38, C Wrigglesworth 32, G Davies 3–26)
Oct 9   Police: 48 (A Scott 7–19, G Bacon 3–13)

Dec 10 CCC: 63   (D Greenwood 41, A Scott 6–23)
        LSW: 69–5 (N Maloney 25*, D Greenwood 3–14)

A low-scoring Saturday league match.

1984   LSW: 240   (G Lalchandani 68, R Muirhead 67, P Veivers 52,
Feb 19   C Collins 7–97)
        Infidels: 232–5 (C Collins 96, P Williamson 53*, K Kumar 45)

'Collins day nearly turns up trumps for Infidels at KCC.'

Dec 16   Wanderers: 215–9 dec (P W Anderson 39, M Walsh 36, S Grant
                                5–75)
         LSW: 216–8   (R Muirhead 84, P Veivers 78, B Jones
                                4–44)

Another excellent win for LSW, despite Anderson's 'defection' to HKCC Wanderers, spearheaded by loose-limbed West Indian medium pace bowler Sid Grant.

After the relocation of the Ministry of Defence facilities to Chung Hom Kok, on the southern side of Hong Kong Island, in the early 1980s, the Sai Wan ground was earmarked by Government to be developed for residential and light industrial use.

LSWCC continued to operate out of an abandoned yacht club on the Sai Wan seashore for two seasons, until finally forced into a nomadic existence in 1985. The survival of the club after 1985 owed much to the drive and determination of a few devoted members, who continued to ensure the right spirit was maintained despite the lack of any clubhouse facilities. One such rallying point has been the end of season, lively/presentation evenings held at the Deep Water Bay Golf Club, when 'special' guests were invited to sample LSWCC's hospitality. Other occasions not to be missed were the 'home' matches at DBS with the very tasty and spicy lunchtime 'Indian takeaways', organised when Gopal Lalchandani was captain.

The team continued to be competitive, with notable contributions in recent years from Rizwan Farouq, Andy Medhurst, Mike Mehaffey and Saluddin Tariq, but major titles had become elusive, except for the Gillette Plate Final in 1984–85. Finally in the 1992–93 season, came LSW's first-ever success in the 20-year-old Saturday league competition. The ever-popular independent club, led by Rizwan Farouq, edged out defending champions HKCC Nomads by two points to win the Saturday league title. Skipper Farouq said:

Winning the title for the first time obviously has a special meaning and calls for a special celebration. It's been a great team effort throughout the season.

HKCA handbook, 1992–93

In 1993–94, the senior side came second to the powerful KCC Templars in the Sunday league. Riaz Farcy with over 700 runs including three centuries, being the main strength of the side. In the following season, under

208

the captaincy of Monty Noble, Saiwan recaptured the Saturday league title. Unfortunately, they played their last Saturday league season in 1995–96. However, in the 1997–98 season under Mohanna Marzook, Saiwan were runners-up in the Sunday league.

Tony Turner is still the President, 'although not very active,' he said. I feel sure that, despite their nomadic existence, as long as the guiding hand of the President, and such enthusiastic captains as Mohanna remain, LSWCC will continue to be a force in local cricket.

It seemed appropriate that a brief history of the Adastrals CC, the fore-runner to the LSWCC, should be included here. John Skelton reported.

Following the departure of the RAF from the station (at Sai Wan) during the death throes of UK National Service, in the natural order of things, a group of Air Ministry civilians established the first independent cricket club at Little Sai Wan, although the RAAF had been operating an eleven, based at Kai Tak, for several seasons.

There were no inherited funds, little by way of gear and equipment, a lot of enthusiasm and a sports field which had been ravaged by sea water, flooding and neglect. As a result of a crash fund-raising effort, a club was formed in the early part of 1960 and was named the Adastrals. Slim financial resources and the lack of a qualified groundsman contributed to the inability to exploit the obvious potential of the site as a major cricketing centre, and it was to the RAF that the club had to turn for assistance; thus Kai Tak for our first venture became the home ground. We were accepted into the Second Division of the Hongkong Cricket League, and set about the task of demoralising Centaurs, Nomads, Crusaders and the rest. We could dream...

That first term was an arduous one, and under the captaincy of Brian Ashton, we painfully proceeded to explore every inch of Kai Tak's broad and dusty acres. Successes were rare, and the so-called selection committee, beset by the calls of shift work on its playing members, went almost beserk. Hope springs eternal, and with the move to Sookunpoo by the following season, a step nearer home, the light seemed better and winning became less of an hysterical occasion. Indeed the slow build-up of the club continued and we heard no more talk of burning the score books.

Bottles of VAT 69 and Long John offered to players in those days for a score of 69 or the taking of five wickets, seemed to bolster the alcoholic tendencies of our opponents rather than ourselves. League honours were to become pipe dreams, although an occasional performance made the head-lines – the dismissal of arch-rivals 'Nomads' for the miserly sum of 12 runs at CCC being one to savour.

The avowed intention of establishing Little Sai Wan as an acceptable cricketing centre was eventually brought to fruition in 1964, when after three seasons at Sookunpoo, the amalgamation took place of the Civilian and Service (RAAF) interests (heresy, some said) and a composite LSWCC commanded the strength to enable teams to be entered in both divisions of the league. The annual blood matches were allowed to be perpetrated, so all was not lost by way of national fervour. Thus the Adastrals were edged into the archives and the new club Little Sai Wan Cricket Club – was inaugurated.

Officials

Honorary President

Bill Conway

Chairmen / Presidents		*Captains of Cricket*	
1964–67		1964–67	Col Metcalf
1968–69	Geoff Hardy	1968–69	Geoff Hardy
1969–75	Bill Conway	1969–70	Col Metcalf
		1970–74	Jim Rhodes
		1974–76	B J 'Tug' Willson
1976–79	Tony Turner	1976–77	David Clinton
1979–81	John Morgan	1977–81	Tony Turner
1981–86	Maurice Morgan	1981–84	Gordon Bacon
		1984–85	Geoff Lever
		1985–86	Gopal Lalchandani
1986–	Tony Turner	1986–87	Chris Wrigglesworth
		1987–88	Rizwan Farouq
		1988–90	Gopal Lalchandani
		1990–93	Tarun Sawney
		1993–94	Rizwan Farouq
		1994–95	Riaz Farcy
		1995–96	Lal Jayasinghe
		1996–97	Mohanna Marzook

First Division/Sunday League – Batting Performances 1965–66 to 1993–94

Season	Player	500 runs plus	Centuries
1972–73	C Metcalf	563 at 31.28 (7)	112 v Optimists
1973–74	C Metcalf	626 at 36.82 (5)	
1975–76	B J Willson	661 at 73.44 (1)	126 v Optimists
	D Clinton	873 at 72.75 (2)	123* v IRC & 109 v Templars

First Division/Sunday League – Batting Performance (cont'd)

Season	Player	500 runs plus	Centuries
1977–78	P W Anderson		130 v Templars
1978–79	P W Anderson	507 at 50.70 (2)	
1979–80	P W Anderson	502 at 33.47	101 v IRC
1980–81	P W Anderson	527 at 43.92	106* v Templars & 101* v Templars§
	R Flood		102* v Brit.Forces
1984–85	R Lalchandani		118* v IRC
	C Wrigglesworth		104* v IRC
	R Lalchandani & C Wrigglesworth 240* (1st) v IRC (1)		
1985–86	R Farouq	530 at 35.33	108 v Infidels & 100* v Optimists
	G Lalchandani		103* v IRC
	A Turner		101* v Vagabonds
1986–87	R Farouq		138 v Optimists
	G Lalchandani		121 v Vagabonds
	M Haines		103* v Scorpions & 102* v Police
1987–88	M Mahaffey		108* v IRC
	M Haines		102* v Wanderers
	N Gulzar (Independents)		104* v KCC #
1988–89	A Medhurst	500 at 50.00 (9)	111* v IRC, 109* & 106* v Vagabonds
	M Abid		119* v IRC
	M Abid & A Medhurst 218* (2nd) v IRC (3)		
1989–90	A Medhurst	512 at 42.67 (6)	
1990–91	A Medhurst		121 v IRC
	S Tariq		118* v Brit.Forces & 101 v IRC
	T Sawney		112* v IRC
	R Farouq		106* v Scorpions
1991–92	A Butt	500 at 50.00 (5)	201* v Scorpions
	D Fisher		120* v Wanderers & 118 v Optimists
1992–93	C Parsons		201* v Brit.Forces
	A Dartnell		153 v IRC & 104 v Scorpions
	A Dartnell & C Parsons 258 (2nd) v IRC (1)		
1993–94	R Farcy	709 at 70.90 (6)	144 v Infidels, 103* v Wanderers, 100 v Pak.Assn & 122 v Vags.§
	P Howe		103* v IRC
	N Waters		102 v IRC

#	'Super' league
§	Rothman's Cup
(1)	Position in averages

(1st)   Wicket partnership over 200 runs
        HKCC – Optimists/ Scorpions/ Wanderers
        KCC – Infidels/ Templars

First Division/Sunday League – Bowling Performances 1965–66 to 1993–94

Season	Player	50 wickets plus	7 plus (for 50 runs or less)
1965–66	C Metcalf		8–21 v CCC & 7–13 v Optimists
1966–67	C Metcalf	51 at 7.80 (1)	
1967–68	P Davison	60 at 13.20#	8–50 v Recreio
	D Raderecht		'hat-trick' v Police
1972–73	C Metcalf	55 at 10.96 (2)	
1973–74	C Metcalf	59 at 12.76 (3)	
	A Swift		7–38 v HKCC Scorpions
1976–77	P Smith	50 at 11.94 (2)	7–17 v IRC
	L Stenner		7–42 v HKCC Wanderers
1978–79	G Bacon		7–23 v KCC Infidels
1979–80	G Bacon		7–46 v Vagabonds
	E Ismail		7–50 v KCC Templars
1980–81	G Lalchandani	38 at 12.00 (1)	
1981–82	G Bacon	52 at 12.10 (2)	7–27 v Brit.Forces
		(only bowler 50 plus)	
	G Lalchandani		7–35 v Brit.Forces
1983–84	A Scott		7–19 v Police
	G Lalchandani		7–50 v HKCC Optimists
1985–86	E Ismail		7–46 v Vagabonds
1989–90	N Varley		8–90 v HKCC Optimists
1990–91	S Tariq	50 at 18.84 (3)	8–63 v Vagabonds
	A Medhurst		'hat-trick' v IRC
1993–94	M Ling		4– 0 v IRC incl. 'hat-trick'

NB: Although less than 50 wickets top of the averages has been included.

     #   Includes Super League
     (1) Position in averages

Second Division/Saturday League – Batting Performances 1965–66 to 1993–94

Season	Player	500 runs plus	Centuries
1971–72	A Morgan		124 v IRC
1975–76	R Vergelius	512 at 42.67 (10)	

212

Second Division/Saturday League – Batting Performances (cont'd)

Season	Player	500 runs plus	Centuries
1976–77	R Vergelius	736 at 61.33(2)	113* v Centaurs
1977–78	A Turner	694 at 40.82(8)	118* v DBS
1978–79	E Elsworthy		102* v HKCC Nomads
1983–84	R Muirhead	620 at 32.63	
1985–86	M Roberts	621 at 34.50	100 v Islanders
1986–87	M Roberts	573 at 40.93	105 v Centaurs
	M Haines		110* v Army
1987–88	R Muirhead		123* v Islanders
1988–89	A Medhurst	571 at 47.58	110* v KCC Tartars
1989–90	J Thompson	604 at 67.11(6)	112* v DBS
	N Gulzar		111 v ?
	M Mahaffey		100* v DBS
1990–91	K Hemshall		100* v St George's
1991–92	D Fisher		129* v St George's &
			116 v Centaurs
	M Noble		123* v HKCC Gap Ramblers &
			101 v DBS
1992–93	D Fisher	519 at 57.67(9)	128* v HKCC Witherers &
			120 v KCC Tartars
	R Farouq	681 at 52.38	115* v Kai Tak &
			106 v KCC Saracens
1993–94	D Happell		110* v HKCC Witherers

(1)   Position in averages

Second Division/Saturday League – Bowling Performances 1965–66 to 1993–94

Season	Player	50 wickets plus	7 plus (for 50 runs or less)
1966–67	D Wake		7–45 v CCC
1969–70	B Nichol		10–6 v IRC (incl 4 in 4 balls)
1971–72	I Arkley		7–27 v HKCC Witherers
1972–73	A Thorpe		7–26 v KCC Crusaders
1973–74	O L Robinson	31 at 7.94 (1)	
	J Brereton	52 at 14.44	
1975–76	L Stenner	82 at 9.12 (1)	8–35 v HKCC Nomads &
			7–14 v DBS
1977–78	A Turner	62 at 13.77 (9)	
	L Stenner		7– 7 v Kai Tak
	D Foley	53 at 16.09	7–49 v Centaurs & 'hat-trick'
			v RGI (Army)

Second Division/Saturday League – Bowling Performances (cont'd)

Season	Player	7 plus (for 50 runs or less)
Season	*Player*	*7 plus* (for 50 runs or less)
1979–80	A Turner*	7–44 v Centaurs

* Recorded as B Turner in the 1980–81 Handbook
(1) Position in averages

Merchants Cricket Club

The Merchants Cricket Club (MCC) was started by a KCC member, Papu Butani, an Indian businessman in Hong Kong, who is a cricket fanatic. He sponsored the Saturday League Butani Cup and Plate for the seasons 1991–92 and 1992–93; the diamond-studded gold cricket bat for the Cathay Pacific/Wharf Holdings International Sixes, and for many years prizes at annual cricket functions.

Butani formed a Diamond XI in the 1989–90 season to play social cricket. As interest and support increased, he applied to the HKCA to enter a team in the Saturday league for the 1991–92 season, and this was accepted by the league committee. He then changed the name of the side to the Merchants Cricket Club, its initials having obvious connotations. The MCC have come 10th and 11th out of 18 league teams in their first two seasons, a creditable performance for a new side.

The Merchants CC were clear winners of the Saturday league title in 1995–96, and repeated their success in the following season. Interestingly, the new association started by an Indian now has an infiltration of players from the Pakistan Association, including their star player and captain, Sada Hussain. Hong Kong has always been a place where various nationalities have mixed amicably.

Saturday League – Batting Performances 1991–92 to 1993–94

Season	Player	500 runs plus	Centuries
Season	*Player*	*500 runs plus*	*Centuries*
1991–92	M Chohan	524 at 34.93	
	M Hafeez		111* v DBS
1992–93	T Nimkar		117 v Police Sentinels
1993–94	S Hussain	552 at 55.20 (3)	140 v HKU
	G Mudbhatkal		113 v Centaurs
	T Nimkar		104* v Police Sentinels

J Iqbal & S Hussain 232 (1st) v HKU (3)

Saturday League – Bowling Performances 1991–92 to 1993–94

Season   Player   *7 plus* (for 50 runs or less)

1993–94 J Iqbal   7–30   v LSW
         M Sagir   7–40   v Islanders

Pakistan Association of Hong Kong Ltd

In the year 1955 a society was formed under the name of 'Pakistan Muslim Society' which functioned as a body for the enhancement of religious, social and cultural affairs of the Pakistanis in Hong Kong.

On 15 May 1960, the 'Pakistan Muslim Society' was dissolved and all its records, funds etc., were handed over to the 'Pakistan Association of Hong Kong' which was formally incorporated on 4 May 1960. Since its inception the Association has been active in the promotion of various social, economic, educational, religious, cultural, recreational and welfare activities for the Pakistani community in Hong Kong.

On land provided by the Hong Kong Government near the junction of Chatham and Gascoigne Roads, Kowloon, the Association built a clubhouse with assembly hall, squash courts, tennis court and children's playground. It has its own in-house catering service. The Association is prominent in local hockey, with Farooq Saeed being nominated 'Player of the Year' in 1993–94, and squash, where Fahim Khan was the Territories No. 1 player.

A cricket team was entered in the Rothman's Cup competition in the 1991–92 season. A senior team entered the Connaught Sunday league in the 1993–94 season, where they came eighth out of the ten participating teams. Members such as Messrs Saeeduddin, M T Amdani, Mohammad Amin, Matin Farooqi and ex-member Asad have been the 'pivotal personalities' in this section, well supported by Amin Saba (President).

The Pakistan Association of Hong Kong Ltd., Independence Day 1994
brochure

No doubt, once all the members and prospective members are fully aware of this senior cricket facility, its popularity will increase with a resultant improvement in team playing standards. A budding Wasim Akram, Salim Malik, Mushtaq Ahmed or Waqar Younis might be just around the corner, and in no time at all they will be winning the senior championship! The author is sure the HKCA welcomed the Pakistan Association into the Sunday league, and hopefully the Pakistani community in Hong Kong will long continue to be involved in many local affairs.

The Pakistan Association romped home with the Sunday league title in 1995–96, and created the highest league team total of 469 runs in 49 overs. The formation of junior teams has resulted from the success of the senior team which has led to great enthusiasm in the local Pakistan community. Each match has a following of 100 to 200 supporters.

Ably led by Sada Hussain, other useful players being Muneer Hussain, Waseem Imtiaz, Javed Iqbal, Salim Malik and Mohammad Zubair, to name a few.

Sada has a great eye and hits the ball like a bullet. One of the best fielders in Hong Kong.

Scoreboard, April 1996

It has been the combined efforts of everyone which has won the laurels for us. We are also thankful to our supporters. Curry rice is always available when we are on home ground.

M T Amdani, Chairman Cricket Committee

Sunday League – Batting Performances 1991–92 to 1993–94

Season	Player	500 runs plus	Centuries
1991–92	A Hasan		156 v KCC Templars§
1993–94	S Hussain	660 at 44.00	101 v HKCC Wanderers
	W Imtiaz		121 v KCC Templars &
			100 v Vagabonds
	§ Rothman's Cup		

Police Recreation Club

The Police Cricket Club was founded in 1903, and a Police cricket team joined the new official Hongkong Cricket League for the inaugural 1904–05 season. They, like most cricket teams at that time, played at Happy Valley, where in 1907 the Police Recreation Club (PRC) was formed. The rough matshed was replaced by a more permanent one-storey clubhouse by Leighton Road, opened by His Excellency the Officer Administering the Government on 2 May 1919.

1927   Recreio: 174–4 dec   (R Reed 42, H Alves 40*, E de Sousa 35*, H
Nov 19   Xavier 33)
        PRC: 111   (W E Meadows 21, W Dyer 21, R C Reed
                             3–19)

This First Division match was played at the Recreio ground, King's
Park.

Other PRC players were: C F Alexander, Dr J R Craig, W le B
Sparrow, T H King, B J Baker, A Reynolds, S Randall, B J
Thorpe, L J Wayland.

The PRC cricket ground must have been one of the smallest anywhere in
the world to be used for league cricket. A main feature was the nullah
running along the northern boundary over which the clubhouse was built.
Prewar, players had to cross a small bridge from the clubhouse over the
nullah. In the winter, the cricket season, the nullah became a dry 'mud'
bed and stank to high heaven. 'Fah Wongs' were permanently on duty,
ready to recover balls covered in slime by means of a small wire basket on
the end of a pole.

Postwar, due to the small size of the ground, it was decided no sixes
could be scored. This naturally led to the development of local knowledge
and the perfection of the PRC cut.

The PRC cut was played to either a half volley bowled outside the off
stump on the front foot, or a ball on a similar line pitched short of a
length on the back foot. The ball came off the inside edge, missed the
leg stump by a whisker and sped to the fine leg boundary, a mere 25
yards away.

A fielder had no chance to react before the ball had reached the boundary.

The PRC's only prewar championship win was the Second Division in
1939–40. After which time, most of the triumphant team spent the war
years interned in the POW Camp at Stanley. Postwar they won their only
First Division title in 1976–77 and the Second Division in 1966–67. Its successor, the Saturday league, was won by the Police Sentinels in 1980–81.

Police cricket during the decade covering the period 1950–60 was run by
'The Big Five,' Tim Williamson, Peter English, Geoff Woodhouse, Robin
Day and Maurice Hulbert. The regular batsmen were Harry Brearley, John
Rumbelow and Mike Womersley, while the bowling chores were borne
by Danny Renton, Tony Whitehead, Andy Anderson and Alan Wilson
together with Denis Salter, the prewar stalwart, who retired in 1955. Prominence is given to the above cricketing enthusiasts, because they were

217

instrumental in getting the cricket section going again after the deprivations of war-torn Hong Kong.

Two important annual fixtures were arranged in the early 1950s. One was an annual Sunday match played at Sookunpoo against the Commander British Forces XI, which was initiated by Major Pat Howard-Dobson, who represented Hong Kong v Malaya in 1955. The other was the first annual fixture between the Auxiliaries and the Regular Police, which began in 1953.

The Auxiliaries were very strong, having such Interport players as George Souza Snr, Ivor Stanton and Tony Weller representing them in these all-day matches. The first match at the PRC was a grand affair with the Auxiliary Police Band in attendance. One of the 'Big Five' remembered an amusing episode:

> Robin Day ran in to open the bowling to the last few bars of 'Alexander's Ragtime Band'. Robin, being a jazz enthusiast, completely lost the rhythm of his run-up and fell in a heap at the bowling crease, much to the amusement of the crowd.

Knowing Robin, the crowd probably thought it was all part of the day's entertainment!

This smallest ground in the league, made even smaller in 1951 when the Hong Kong Football Club built their stand, shared the same overall field with CCC, who had a greater portion of the whole area. When two matches were being played simultaneously, confusion reigned over the boundaries, and it was extremely dangerous when big hitters like Buji Dhabher (CCC) and Peter English (PRC) were in full cry. You required eyes in the back of your head!

On 5 October 1965, when the Police Second Division team took to the field against the HKU side at Happy Valley, another snippet of cricket history was about to be created. Included in the Police eleven was PC 7761, Kwong Tim, the first Chinese Police constable to play league cricket in Hong Kong. He was the son of the head groundsman at the HKCC, and elder brother of Benny Kwong.

> He can bowl right-arm medium pace seamers or cutters, he is a fielder with an extremely safe pair of hands, and as a batsman, is blessed with a fine eye and quick reflexes.

1968   CCC: 84   (I Lacy-Smith 6–41)
Jan 20 PRC: 89–9

> 'CCC's batsmen had no answer to the two Police pacemen, Lacy-Smith and Cumings, and the brittle pitch.'

218

1969   Police: 257–9 (I Nicholson 87)
Dec 21 Optimists: 133   (B Wigley 7–17)

'The first three Police batsmen scored 217 runs, the next five one run!'

1970   Police: 181   (M Hammett 123*, J Armour 4–39, A Prins 3–47)
Jan 18 LSW: 143–8 (G Hardy 55*, D Summerbell 5–52)

The 1975–76 season witnessed the last matches played on this unique piece of ground, where many a player smashed the ball against the concrete walls of the HKFC, across the CCC turf and/or out of the ground, endangering the local population with the constant bombardment of cricket balls. Many thought the reason for the move to the Police Training School at Wong Chuk Hang, Aberdeen, was due to the planned construction of flyovers in that area of Happy Valley. Not so, according to a Police spokesman. The 'real reason' was for environmental purposes!

Before the imminent final departure, a memorable farewell game for Geoff Woodhouse was played, where on the fall of each wicket, a tray of drinks was 'solemnly' conveyed out to the players on the field. Luckily, there were no drink/drive laws in Hong Kong at the time. The author still vaguely remembers the privilege of playing in this memorable match.

1976   Police: 279–6 (G Richardson 118)
Apr 3   Nomads/   161   (R Tipper 73, I Lacy-Smith 4–16, B Wigley
        Witherers   4–19)

Rothman's Cup match at Happy Valley, the last official match on the smallest of grounds.

The first season played on the recently laid 'cricket' ground at Aberdeen, produced the first and only Sunday league championship win in 1976–77 for the PCC, led by Brian Wigley. The PRC had reverted back to its original 1903 name of the Police Cricket Club.

Many league teams objected to the state of the ground and the wicket in particular. The Police players, as previously stated, were very adept at making full use of any home advantage, and knew where the various 'rocky' sections were to be found under the matting and over the outfield.

In May 1981, the Police cricketers took a break from their normal duties to participate in a six-match cricket tour to Singapore and Malaysia. Half the matches were rain affected, and the last by human nature, when the RHKP were dismissed for 34 runs! 'Caught on a very sticky wicket after a surfeit of cricket, late nights and super hospitality.'

Nigel Stearns hit the highest score of 81 runs against the Ipoh Club President's XI, whilst Ian Lacy-Smith was the most successful bowler. However, winning was not all-important, it was the experience of taking part. The matches were played in unaccustomed 'hot, steamy conditions'. Jim Finch's meticulous organisation made it a memorable experience, well matched by the generous hospitality and careful planning of their police hosts.

| 1982 | Police: | 257–5 | (G Davies 112, N Stearns 83) |
| Feb 14 | HKCC Taverners: | 90 | (M Walsh 21, B Wigley 3–7) |

'Police made it a rout ...' second round Rothman's Cup match at PTS.

1984	Optimists:	260–9 dec	(K McConnell 91, J Barrington 79, G
Feb 19			Davies 6–81)
	Police:	215–9	(N Stearns 106, M Sant 5–71)
Nov 18	Optimists:	260–1 dec	(J Barrington 133*, K McConnell 54*,
			W Orchard 52)
	Police:	263–7	(N Stearns 144*, T Sawney 57, D Swift 3–77)

After opposing teams had baulked at the lack of facilities and on the 'nature' of the ground, a new bar and changing facilities were incorporated into the expansion of the Training School Complex in 1984. It was even rumoured that sightscreens, a proper scoreboard and cricket nets might be erected! However, the PCC considered there was nothing wrong with the mobile blue/cream and red/cream screens provided by the bus companies, CMB and KMB, at the nullah end of the ground. Nobody kept the scoreboard up to date anyway, and the Police players felt it was unsporting to practise in the nets before or during the season.

During the 1970s and 1980s, the Police teams were acknowledged as the renowned exponents of the limited overs game, winning the Rothman's Cup four times: in 1972–73, 1974–75, 1978–79 and in 1988–89. They were also runners–up on four occasions. The author rated Brian Wigley's side of 1972–73 as 'one of the best'.

Led by Brian, other members of the side were: P Barclay, Roger Booth, Kit Cumings, Ian Lacy-Smith, Jim Middleton, Ian Nicholson, Mike Prew, Danny Renton, Geoff Woodhouse, Mike Womersley with Gerry Stokes (scorer). Other players of that era included Jim Finch, Mike Hammett, John Hawkesley, John Pettengell, Guy Richardson and Rod Starling –

what a collection of Inspectors! Some have even been elevated to the higher echelons of the Force!

The club nearly always had difficulty raising full sides, from 1988–89, so it confined itself to running two Saturday league teams, the 'Sentinels' and the 'Strollers', whose matches against each other were usually 'needle' affairs, mixed with sardonic humour, quite uncomprehensible to anyone outside the Force. However, when it came to the Rothman's, they would rustle around and gather together a formidable side for this particular competition, as though this 'Cup' rightly belonged to them.

Many Police cricketers have been selected to represent Hong Kong: Kit Cumings, Glyn Davies, Mike Hammett, Ian Lacy-Smith, Jim Middleton, Tarun Sawney, Rod Starling, Nigel Stearns and Brian Wigley. One of the most successful batsman in the 1980s was undoubtedly the 'stylish' Nigel Stearns, who holds the record for the highest Interport score, 169 runs against Singapore in 1984.

The most durable senior players have been Ian Lacy-Smith, Brian Wigley and Mike Womersley, who all started their Hong Kong cricket careers in the 1960s. Ian and Brian have both assisted the HKCA in different ways overs the years, Brian being the Manager of the Hong Kong Interport teams to Malaysia and Singapore in 1977, 1980 and 1983, Manager of the 1979 Hong Kong tour to Eastern Australia, and Manager of the Hong Kong team on their first ICC Trophy competition in 1982. He deserved a medal for handling this mixed bunch of individualistic *homo sapiens*. Ian retired from the Police force in 1994, while Brian and Mike retired in early 1995.

One member of the Police 'team' who also deserved a special place in this short history is their scorer for many years, Gerry Stokes. Gerry began scoring for the Police in the 1965–66 season and continued until the 1987–88 season, when the Police team left the Sunday league. He continued to score the Rothman's Cup matches until 1990.

After the retirement from Hong Kong of such cricket stalwarts as Brian Wigley and Mike Womersley, what would the expatriate Police roll be after 1997? The future of the PCC as a cricket venue would depend on the answer to this question. For since Kwong Tim in 1965, there has not been another Chinese constable playing cricket in Hong Kong.

At the end of the 1994–95 season, the Police Strollers and Sentinels were right at the bottom of the pile, lying 18th and 19th (19 teams in the league). The committee decided on only one team for the following season, and by end February 1996, was favourably placed 6th (18 teams). But with the inevitable drift of expatriates away from Hong Kong, by end February 1998, the team had descended the ladder to 14th (17 teams.)

First Division/Sunday League Batting Performances 1965–66 to 1987–88

Season	Player	500 runs plus	Centuries
1967–68	C G Cumings	585 at 29.25 #	
1969–70	M Hammett	551 at 34.44	123* v LSW
	C G Cumings		102* v KCC Saracens
1973–74	R Booth	579 at 36.19 (6)	
	G Richardson	582 at 32.33 (8)	109 v IRC
	C G Cumings		114 v IRC
1974–75	G Richardson	553 at 42.53 (3)	174 v Army & 101* v LSW
1975–76	G Richardson	724 at 48.27 (5)	173 v Army, 139 v Scorpions & 121* v Wanderers
	I Nicholson		167* v Army
	J Hawkesley & G Richardson 225 (3rd) v Scorpions (1)		
1977–78	N Stearns	524 at 47.64 (4)	
	R Starling		124* v Army
	M Hammett		114 v Army
1978–79	N Stearns		100* v Optimists
1979–80	I Nicholson	529 at 33.06	102* v ? **a**
1980–81	P Ramsay-Horler		102* v Brit. Forces II **b**
1981–82	G Davies		112 v HKCC Taverners
1983–84	G Davies	577 at 41.21	
	N Stearns		106 v Optimists
1984–85	T Sawney	619 at 51.50 (5)	165* v IRC
	N Stearns	562 at 46.80 (8)	144* v Optimists & 103 v Wanderers
1985–86	N Stearns	698 at 63.45 (1)	149* & 108 v Brit.Forces & 121* v IRC
	G Davies	597 at 42.64 (10)	
	T Sawney	512 at 32.00	
1986–87	N Stearns	747 at 106.71 (1)	
	G Davies	571 at 47.58 (9)	118* & 116 v Scorpions, 109 v Wanderers & 108 v Brit. Forces

NB. 1987–88 was the last season in the First Division.

a Ian Nicholson's 102* appeared in the averages but not in the statistics for 70 runs or more, thus opponents not known.

b I P Ramsay-Horler playing for Police 'Bluebottles' in the Rothman's Cup.

\# Includes 'Super' League

(1) Position in averages

HKCC – Optimists/Scorpions/Wanderers

First Division/Sunday League Bowling Performances 1965–66 to 1987–88

Season	Player	50 wickets plus	7 wkts plus (for 50 runs or less)
1966–67	I Lacy-Smith		9–32 v IRC
1967–68	C G Cumings	60 at 16.35 #	8–41 v IRC & 8–49 v LSW
1968–69	B T Wigley	70 at 10.90 #	
	I Lacy-Smith	57 at 13.42 #	
	E Evans		'hat-trick' v KCC Saracens
1969–70	B T Wigley		7–17 v HKCC Optimists
1972–73	C G Cumings		7–39 v IRC
1973–74	J Middleton		7–40 v LSW
1976–77	B T Wigley	48 at 9.58 (1)	8–51 v Army
	R Starling	56 at 13.68 (4)	
	J Middleton		8–50 v HKCC Optimists

Includes 'Super' League.
(1) Position in averages

Wicketkeeping Performances 30 plus dismissals

1985–86 J Higgs   30 (1)

Second Division/Saturday League Batting Performances 1965–66 to 1993–94

Season	Player		500 runs plus	Centuries
1968–69	A G Cooper		404 at 50.50 (1)	
	R L Macdonald			116 v LSW
1970–71	R L Macdonald			105 v KCC Saracens
1976–77	J G Hawkesley		565 at 40.36 (9)	
1978–79	M Womersley	('A')	655 at 32.75	100* v Kai Tak
	J G Hawkesley	('B')	590 at 31.05	101 v HKU
	B T Wigley	('A')	582 at 30.63	
	M P de E Collin	('B')	631 at 30.05	
1979–80	N Stearns	(Se)	613 at 47.15 (9)	
	M Womersley	(Se)	636 at 35.33	
	J Hawkesley	(Se)	607 at 33.72	144 v Royal Navy & 100 v CCC
	N Trape	(St)	503 at 22.86	
1980–81	I Nicholson	(Se)	789 at 34.22	119* v Islanders
	B T Wigley	(Se)	659 at 31.38	103* v LSW
	M Hammett	(Se)	596 at 31.37	
	J Hawkesley	(Se)	546 at 27.30	106 v Islanders

Second Division/Saturday League – Batting Performances (cont'd)

Season	Player		500 runs plus	Centuries
1981–82	N Stearns	(St)	799 at 88.78 (2)	104* v Sentinels
	G Davies	(Se)	691 at 38.39	
1982–83	N Stearns	(St)	540 at 60.00 (5)	
	B T Wigley	(Se)		106* v CCC
1983–84	B T Wigley	(Se)	788 at 49.25 (9)	
	M Womersley	(Se)		100 v KCC Tartars
1984–85	J Hawkesley	(Se)	560 at 35.00	
	B T Wigley	(Se)	617 at 32.47	
1985–86	B T Wigley	(Se)	761 at 38.05	
	I Nicholson	(Se)	696 at 36.63	
	J Hawkesley	(Se)		102* v KCC Tartars
1986–87	B T Wigley	(Se)	627 at 41.80	
1988–89	R Hawes	(Se)	511 at 36.50	126* v HKU & 104* v HKCC Gap Ramblers
	G Davies	(Se)		104 v Army
1989–90	R Hawes	(Se)		105* v DBS
1991–92	R Hawes	(Se)	629 at 52.42 (9)	
	J Hawkesley	(St)		112 v KCC Saracens
1992–93	G Jones	(Se)		128 v Kai Tak
	N Macdonald	(St)	577 at 38.47	104 v KCC Tartars
	C Ball	(St)		100* v KCC Saracens
1993–94	T Sawney	(Se)	543 at 54.30 (4)	
	J Hawkesley	(St)		102 v Kai Tak

(1)   Position in averages
(Se)   Sentinels   (St) Strollers

Second Division/Saturday League – Bowling Performances 1965–66 to 1993–94

Season	Player		50 wickets plus	7 plus (for 50 runs or less)
1969–70	J Pettengell			8–17 v HKU
	Kwong Tim			8–102 v IRC
1974–75	I Lacy-Smith		58 at 14.41	
1975–76	B T Wigley			7–23 v Islanders
1976–77	J Pettengell		62 at 16.29	
1979–80	B T Wigley	(Se)	62 at 12.53 (2)	7–17 v HKU
1981–82	I Lacy-Smith	(Se)	42 at 10.33 (1)	7–35 v St George's
	R Starling	(Se)		7–15 v Kai Tak

Second Division/Saturday League – Bowling Performances (cont'd)

Season	*Player*		*7 plus* (for 50 runs or less)
1987–88	R Shugrue	(Se)	7–15 v Police Strollers
1988–89	G Davies	(Se)	7–20 v HKCC Nomads
1990–91	S Todd	(Se)	7–26 v HKCC Witherers

NB. Although less than 50 wickets top of the averages has been included.

(1)   Position in averages
(Se) Sentinels   (St) Strollers

RAF – Kai Tak/Taikoo

The RAF, after winning the Second Division championship twice in the early 1950s (1952–53 and 1954–55), thereafter entered the league intermittently, finally dropping out of Hong Kong cricket after the 1974–75 season. The RAF had also participated in the senior league from the immediate postwar season 1948–49 till 1971–72, their Kai Tak ground being right next to the eastern apron of Kai Tak Airport.

1961	Recreio:	60	(A P Pereira 20, J S Harris 5–19, D Cornfield
Feb 4			5–37)
	RAF:	63–4	

On the same day Recreio beat the RAF in a Second Division match by 58 runs.

Recreio: 130 (M J Baptista 79, T Crabtree 7–49)
RAF: 72 (V Stjornqvist 23, Barros 4–24, F Correa 4–39)

The next three matches were all First Division.

1968	RAF:	74
Mar 2	LSW:	78–8 (G Sefton 6–41)

Police: 126 (D Brownlow 7–50)
RAF: 72 (I Lacy Smith 5–28, K Wallis 4–10)

'Brownlow revelling under the damp conditions at Happy Valley.'

1971   Optimists: 203–6 dec (P H Davies 77, R Mills-Owen 66,
Jan 3   R Graham 6–42)
          RAF: 169–9   (C Hull 112*)

RAF's place in the 1975–76 Saturday league was taken over by Kai Tak, the team taking its name from its then venue. The Kai Tak ground closed after the 1976–77 season; thereafter home matches were at Mission Road. The Kai Tak team, comprised of RAF personnel and Cathay Pacific employees skippered by recently arrived B J 'Tug' Willson, former captain of UK Combined Services, who immediately stamped his mark on the local cricket scene by capturing the league title. After his last season in the UK in 1974, Air Chief Marshal Sir Derek Hodgkinson said:

> I am writing to congratulate and thank you for the splendid way you have captained the side during the season ... with the splendid victories over the Navy and the Army fresh in mind. Well done.

[... his best score ever was 218 runs for the RAF v D H Robin's XI in the late 1960s, which side included Jim Laker, Clive Lloyd, Rohan Kanhai, John Shepherd and Brian Langford.]

1975   Nomads: 126–9 (M Tress 37, B Willson 7–46)
Dec 6   Kai Tak: 127–4 (B Willson 57, G Sperring 42)

Sep 27   Army: 130   (G Chance 61, B Willson 4–31)
          Kai Tak: 132–0 (B Willson 76*, B Phillips 52*)

          Kai Tak: 101–7 (B Phillips 27)
          Royal Navy 13   (B Phillips 6–5)

One of the lowest scores ever recorded for a Saturday match.

1975   Kai Tak: 53 (E Evans 5–25, J Pettengell 3–15)
Oct 18   Police: 44 (B Phillips 7–26, D Rose 3–9)

'An incredibly low scoring game at Kai Tak.'

1976   St George's: 135–6 (Hardy 47, Pennell 43, G Sperring 3–48)
Jan 17   Kai Tak: 139–2 (B Willson 81*)

This win clinched the Saturday league title for Kai Tak. The match that followed was a league cup match.

Feb 28   Kai Tak: 229–5 (B Willson 160*)
         Royal Navy: 140–1 (P Anderson 95*)

An awesome score in a 35-over match at Sookunpoo.

1979   Kai Tak: 215–5 (H Lucas 103, B Willson 74)
Oct 27   HKU: 118   (J Bell 4–23, I Gervais 3–28)

Nov 10   Kai Tak: 230–1 (H Lucas 129*, B Willson 55)
         CCC: 195   (N Pearson 52, P Fox 51, J Johnson 45,
                            H Lucas 5–36)

1980   Kai Tak: 173–5 (B Willson 72, T Dennett 40*, P Thompson
Jan 5   3–49)·
         Tartars: 174–6 (P Nunn 81, J Keir 30)

'Kai Tak were surprised by Tartars, with Phil Nunn out-gunning
'Tug' Willson.'

Feb 23   Saracens: 190–7 (E Hurst 81*, C Penman 31, G Sperring 3–60)
         Kai Tak: 169   (F Gillett 40, J Bell 40, P Murphy 4–38, P Hall
                            3–23)

Mar 1   Kai Tak: 286–1 (H Lucas 152*, B Willson 126)
         LSW: 138–4 (R Pearce 47*, A Turner 35)

Lucas and Willson put on 280 runs for the first wicket in this Gillette
Cup match.

    15   Witherers: 196–6 (D Holland 65*, D Parsons 47*, J Lunn 34, H
                            Lucas 5–49)
         Kai Tak: 198–2 (H Lucas 99, B Willson 69)

    22   Kai Tak: 221–8 (H Lucas 96, F Gillett 37, T Hart 5–39) tied
                            with
         Army: 221   (T Gregson 62, J Aldridge 53, H Lucas 3–50)

'... only nine runs from the last two overs, three run-outs proved
fatal for the Army.'

Apr 19   Kai Tak: 229–5 (H Lucas 128, B Willson 42)
         Royal Navy: 173   (M Walker 59, G Bacon 31, I Gervais 3–45)

27 Nomads: 135 (M Walsh 47, D Sibree 37, J Bell 4–17)
    Kai Tak: 134 (B Willson 40, N Walker 3–22, R Jewkes 3–32)

On a very damp wicket at KCC, '... it seemed that Kai Tak must take their first league cup [Gillette] title when they got within six runs of the target with three wickets standing ... J. Bell run out from the second last ball of the day going for a suicidal single.'

Mark Giles *SCMP*

1981   Army: 142–7 (J Dean 42, R Eddington 4–59)
Nov 28 Kai Tak: 144–2 (R Eddington 55*, B Willson 35)

1982   Kai Tak: 128 (R Eddington 41, D Morgan 5–27, M Saunders
Jan 9   3–9)
        LSW: 127 (A Gear 56, B Willson 5–17, R Eddington 3–48)

'Saiwan required four from the final over but Sperring bowled out the last man ...'

1982   Centaurs: 187–8 (J Murphy 55, J Hughes 41, R Eddington 3–30)
Apr 17 Kai Tak: 191–1 (R Eddington 80*, B Willson 72)

'High flying Rod steers airmen home.'
'Rod's batting policy is to avoid being dismissed. [21 innings 11 times not out]
'He has a magnificent defence, and this ability teamed up with two of the fastest scoring opening partners in the local scene [Willson – Kai Tak] and [John Hollioake – Scorpions, father of Adam and Ben], produced two champion teams. [Scorpions won the Sunday league]'

Malcolm Grubb, *SCMP*

1983   Kai Tak: 180–3 (B Willson 108)
Oct 8   Gap Ramblers: 138–8 (P Anderson 41, C Bennett 33, W Garvey
                               6–40)

Dec 17 Kai Tak: 186–6 (B Willson 131, N Jepson 3–27)
        HKU: 187–5 (D Swift 67, A Cooper 38*)

'Willson scorched his way to a superb century – and finished on the losing side.'

1984   Kai Tak: 187–7 (B Willson 80*)
Apr 1   LSW: 189–9 (N Perera 65, M Grubb 48, B Willson 3–33)

'Keith Johnston cracked two sixes in the final over ...' to win an enthralling Rothman's Cup semi-final.

Dec 29 Kai Tak: 210–7 (J Barrington 97, B Willson 77, R Nissim 4–73)
        Centaurs: 119   (B Hemshall 31, J Barrington 3–4, P Hay 3–9)

1985   'Tug' Willson completed his 100th century in Kai Tak's win over
Jan 19 St George's.

Willson's statistician – his wife Marlene – has been carefully counting his tons, and revealed that after last season's efforts, when he hit six Saturday league tons, he was within striking distance of the magical figure of a century of centuries. After putting on 219 for the first wicket with Nigel Sawry-Cookson (102), he was informed by his new partner that he needed two from the final delivery of the innings. He played a straight drive, set off for a comfortable single and came for a suicidal second. Sure enough, he was run out, and thought it was for 99. Then came the good news – he had actually made exactly 100.

SCMP

Jan 26 Kai Tak: 163–7 (B Willson 83, N Smith 3–19) tied with
        LSW: 163–8 (G Lalchandani 57)

Feb 9   Kai Tak: 179–4 (B Willson 95*)
        Nomads: 173–5 (B Jones 48, M Walsh 38, K McConnell 30)

Mar 2   Kai Tak: 195–9 (B Willson 37, N Sawrey-Cookson 36,
                          L Prabhu 4–40)
        'Hornets': 196–8 (N Broadhurst 94*)

'... 30 runs from the opening 11 overs ... Broadhurst came to the wicket at 46 for three and proceeded to blast the attack to all parts of the ground.' A Gillette Cup quarter-final match at Mission Road.

Kai Tak's alter ego 'Taikoo', a team that only participated in the Rothman's Cup, captured this prestigious trophy at their first attempt in 1985, with 'out-station' men, James Barrington, Willie Boulter and Rod Eddington being flown in by Cathay Pacific for the crucial matches.

Dec 9   Taikoo: 365–6 (J Barrington 134, B Willson 100, T
                          Fitzsimmons 41)
        Taverners: 133   (R Fawcett 26)

229

'Taikoo had an incredible 247 without loss at lunch, with both Barrington and 'Tug' Willson having completed their centuries.'

1985   Optimists: 175–8 (P Olsen 48*, A Morgan 47, K McConnell 32)
Mar 24 Taikoo: 179–4 (B Willson 77*, W Orchard 45)

'Willson leads Taikoo home. 'Tug' Willson, one of the best men you could have for a big occasion – led Taikoo to a marvelous Rothman's Cup triumph.'

In late 1997, as 'Tug' was suffering from cancer, I faxed him the Kai Tak/ Taikoo section of my book for his early perusal. 'If I can make one truly heartfelt request it would be for some mention of my 100 average in league cricket at the age of 50.'

'Tug' Willson, Feb 1998

1984–85	Inns	NO	HS	Runs	Ave
Saturday league	13	5	118*	766	95.75
Rothman's Cup	4	2	100	290	145.00
	17	7	118*	1056	105.60

[He said his proudest moment was his averaging over 100 in his 50th year. 'Tug' died on 14 February 1998.]

Kai Tak captured the Saturday league title again in 1987–88, with such players as James Barrington, Rod Eddington and 'Tug' Willson, all Hong Kong Interporters, as their nucleus. They proved that they didn't have to have the facilities and administrative advantages of the HKCC and KCC to be successful in the field.

1988   Kai Tak: 193–2 (A Burge 99, B Willson 41*)
Jan 16 Sentinels: 160– (T Sawney 68*)

30   HKU: 209–   (M Sabine 84*, M Speak 61)
      Kai Tak: 210–   (J Barrington 70, B Willson 37*)

'Rod Eddington's men managed to reach a daunting 210 with just three balls left.'

Feb 6   Tartars: 198–6 (M Eames 95, D Evans 47, J Hansen 32)
        Kai Tak: 199–4 (A Burge 63*, N Sawrey-Cookson 43, B Willson 30)

'Kai Tak picked up their first Saturday league title for 12 years when they beat defending champions Tartars ...' [Mark Eames scored 95 off only 61 balls]

We were always very relieved to see the back of 'Tug'. I think Levin Prabhu [Crusaders] with his accurate gentle outswingers probably 'worried' 'Tug' more than any other Saturday league bowler. 'Tug' was a very good cricketer, but off-field he could be difficult at times.

The season 1989–90 was magical as Rod Eddington's Kai Tak/Taikoo sides, with their outstanding teamwork, accomplished the unique feat of winning all they entered for – the Saturday league and Gillette Cup (Kai Tak) and the Rothman's Cup (Taikoo).

| 1990 | Taikoo: | 241–7 | (B Willson 97, L Beaman 70, D Jones 3–58) |
| Jan 14 | Infidels: | 229 | (C Collins 46*, D Jones 39, M Clarkson 4–55) |

| Mar 3 | Kai Tak: | 184–6 | (L Beaman 60, N Sawrey–Cookson 34, J Barrington 32) |
| | Army: | 117 | (D Wells 47, D Crowe 4–12, L Beaman 4–31) |

| 11 | Taikoo: | 187 | (L Beaman 45, A Burge 32, S Brew 3–44, M Wiggett 3–49) |
| | Optimists: | 139 | (C Johnstone 33, L Beaman 4–35) |

| 1990 | Kai Tak: | 220–7 | (A Burge 101, J Barrington 66) |
| Mar 24 | Witherers: | 162 | (J Rothman 45, M Wiggett 35, D Crowe 4–24, L Beaman 3–36) |

'Cathay Pacific pilot Alan Burge successfully landed the first leg of a possible title treble ... the opening batsman struck a well–paced century ...'

| 25 | Taikoo: | 218–8 | (L Beaman 87, R Nuttall 45, W Symcox 2–19) |
| | Scorpions: | 178–9 | (N Helm 45, J Garden 36, L Beaman 4–45, D Crowe 3–18) |

'Taikoo produced a tremendous team effort ... some accurate bowling, backed up by keen fielding and impeccable catching, ... '

Jeremy Walker, *SCMP*

| 1990 | Sentinels: | 128–5 | (R Hawes 31) |
| Apr 21 | Kai Tak: | 129–6 | (L Beaman 31) |

231

Kai Tak had to draw on all their character and team spirit to round off a memorable season with a hard fought victory to clinch the Saturday league championship.

'Sentinels made us fight all the way so it was a great way to end a terrific season,' said Eddington. Eddington added: 'This is the first time any team has won three of the four titles in Saturday and Sunday cricket, largely because most people play for different teams on the two days.'

Jeremy Walker, SCMP

Rival teams hoped that Cathay would allow some of their 'grounded cricketers' to return to flying duties in 1990–91. Rod attributed his teams' successes to a combination of tight bowling, good fielding and excellent catching. The author would add another vital ingredient for these triumphs, the astute and experienced captaincy of the skipper.

1991–92 saw the powerful Taikoo side beat HKCC Wanderers by nine runs in the Rothman's final. They had previously defeated holders KCC Templars in a high scoring semi–final.

    Taikoo: 360–3 (J Barrington 154*, A Burge 120)
    Templars: 312–7 (D Albrecht 81)

Appropriately in 1993–94, Kai Tak (Swire's team with their family connection Dragonair), won the inaugural Dragonair Cup which replaced the Butani Cup. This trophy originally started life as the Saturday League Cup in 1975–76, being replaced by the Gillette Cup, when Gillette first stepped in as sponsors in 1979–80.

Rod Eddington took over the 'hot seat' as Chairman of Selectors from the author in early 1990, a job he directed for five years. Despite his all-consuming position as Chief Executive of Cathay Pacific, Rod found time to continue playing local cricket. Such breaks are very important for winding down in a 'helter skelter' place like Hong Kong.

As Kai Tak/Taikoo's home ground at Mission Road, a long-leased Army ground lying close to the Kai Tak Airport flight path, has recently been returned to the Hong Kong Government, the future of the ground for cricket appears decidedly bleak. Its levelled area would provide a firm base for a large residential development once the new airport at Chep Lap Kok, Northern Lantau Island, becomes operational in 1998 in place of the present one. This would be another sad loss for the game in Hong Kong. At present the future of this ground is 'on hold'.

Royal Air Force

First Division – Batting and Bowling Performances

Season	Player		Centuries
1970–71	C Hull		112* v HKCC Optimists

7 plus (for 50 runs or less)

Season	Player		Centuries
1967–68	G Sefton		'hat-trick' v Kowloon #
	D Brownlow		7–50 v PRC
1969–70	J Gordon		7–36 v IRC
	C Hull		'hat-trick' v KCC Templars

Second Division – Batting and Bowling Performances

Season	Player		Centuries
1974–75	B J Willson		123 v Nomads & 108* v HKU

50 wickets plus

Season	Player	
1965–66	G Browne	61 at 11.95
1974–75	O L Robinson	56 at 8.82 (1)

(1) Position in averages
\# Super League

Kai Tak Cricket Club

Saturday League (incl. Cup & Plate) – Batting Performances

Season	Player	*500 runs plus*	Centuries
1975–76	B J Willson	934 at 66.71 (2)	160* v Royal Navy &
			105 v Crusaders
1979–80	H Lucas	1622 at 73.73 (1)	152* v LSW, 129* v CCC,
			128 v Royal Navy, 103 &
			101* v HKU
	D J Willson	901 at 45.05	132 v Saracens & 126 v LSW
	F Gillett	521 at 30.65	
	H Lucas & B J Willson	280 (1st) v LSW (1)	

233

Saturday League (incl. Cup & Plate) – Batting Performances (cont'd)

Season	Player	500 runs plus	Centuries

Season   *Player*   *500 runs plus*   *Centuries*

1980–81 B J Willson   121   v CCC

1981–82 R Eddington   871 at 87.10 (3)

         B J Willson   646 at 43.07

1983–84 B J Willson   1076 at 56.63 (6)   145   v CCC, 131 v HKU, 109

                                            v Army

                                         108   v G Ramblers, 106 v

                                             Sentinels &

                                         104   v DBS

         J Barrington   113   v Sentinels

1984–85 B J Willson   766 at 95.75 (1)   118* v Strollers, 100 v St

                                             George's &

                                         100   v HKCC Taverners φ

         J Barrington   606 at 75.75 (3)   124* v G Ramblers & 134 v

                                             Taverners φ

         N Sawrey-Cookson   102   v St George's

         N Sawrey-Cookson & B J Willson 219 (1st) v St George's (1)

1987–88 B J Willson   655 at 50.38 (10)

         N Sawrey-Cookson   102   v CCC

1988–89 R Nuttall   586 at 58.60 (7)   115* v Tartars

         B J Willson   526 at 35.07

1989–90 A Burge   521 at 43.42   130* v Centaurs

         R Nuttall   128   v Centaurs

         N Sawrey-Cookson   100   v DBS

         A Burge & R Nuttall   240 (1st) v Centaurs (1)

1990–91 J Barrington   530 at 48.18 (7)   103   v Saracens & 103 v St

                                             George's

         I Hardy   102   v Sentinels

1991–92 J Barrington   655 at 59.55 (5)   146* v Saracens & 154* v

                                             Templars φ

         I Hardy   755 at 58.08 (7)   169* v LSW, 152 v KGV &

                                             109   v Sentinels

         A Burge   107* v St George's, 100 v

                                             Centaurs &

                                             120   v Templars

1992–93 J Orders   151* v Islanders & 111 v

                                             Nomads §

         I Hardy   137* v Nomads, 118* v MCC

                                             & 108 v Saracens

Saturday League (incl. Cup & Plate) – Batting Performances (cont'd)

Season	Player	Centuries
	J Barrington	132 v Sentinels, 125 v HKU, 103* v KGV & 100 v Saracens

J Barrington & R Eddington 229* (1st) v Sentinels (3)
J Barrington & I Hardy 205 (1st) v Nomads (7)

Season	Player	Centuries
1993–94	J Barrington	148 v Centaurs
	I Hardy	108 v Centaurs

J Barrington & I Hardy 246 (1st) v Centaurs (2)

Saturday League – Bowling Performances

Season	Player	50 wickets plus	7 wkts plus (for 50 runs or less)
1975–76	D Rose	49 at 15.78	
	B Phillips		7–26 v Police
	B J Willson		7–46 v Nomads
1976–77	D Rose		'hat-trick' v CCC
	I Gervais		'hat-trick' v IRC
1979–80	I Gervais	51 at 16.51	
1980–81	E Filus	30 at 9.67 (1)	'hat-trick' v CCC
1981–82	R Eddington	50 at 12.98 (only bowler 50)	'hat-trick' v HKU
	G Sperring		7–29 v Witherers
1983–84	D Sturmey		'4 in 4' v KGV
1984–85	E Filus		6–12 v LSW (excep.)
1989–90	D Crowe		'hat-trick' v Army
1993–94	R Eddington	31 at 7.84 (1)	
	I Hardy		7–20 v G Ramblers

NB: Although less than 50 wickets top of the averages have been included.

φ	Rothman's Cup
§	Butani Cup
(1)	Position in averages
(1st)	Wicket partnership over 200 runs
	HKCC – Nomads/Witherers
	KCC – Crusaders/Saracens/Tartars
	Police – Sentinels/Strollers

St Georges Cricket Club

The St George's Cricket Club (St George's) was founded in 1962 by a young maths master, Graham Wills, originally as St George's School Cricket Club, a team selected from around a dozen keen and able schoolboys, whose ages varied between 14 and 18 years, and several schoolmasters of indeterminate age, ability and keenness.

In the first year, friendly matches were played against Army Units associated with the school, the RAF, Adastrals and the occasional KCC side. Graham remembered:

> Playing RAF in a large field, with a marquee for the pavilion, and vast acres sprawling out to Kai Tak Airport – any hit escaping a boundary fielder and going onto the concrete apron, seeming to escape into the far blue yonder.

A decision was made in the following year to enter St George's in the Second Division of the Hongkong Cricket League for the season 1963–64. The team structure was nine students, plus Graham and Alun Stevens. The next season brought an influx of staff wanting to play – Graham had certainly started something beyond his wildest dreams – so the team mix swung very much in favour of the staff, with Tony Gough taking over the captaincy halfway through the season from sixth-former John Tanner.

St George's won the Second Division title in 1965–66, winning 16 of the 21 games played, and only losing two. Stalwarts being P Davies, M Braithwaite, Malcolm Lonsdale and Trevor Uff, all in the top ten batting averages, with John Kotch taking 46 wickets. St George's thereafter challenged for the top honours many times, but have only managed that one championship title.

1967   KGV: 115 (K Gohel 84*)
Nov 25 St. George's: 89 (G Varty 8–18, seven being bowled)

'Gohel and Varty 'man-handle' St George's at Mission Road'.

Many fine cricketers have played for the club, players such as David Clinton, Barry Ellis, Bharat Gohel, Tony Gough, Nigel Grandfield, Harold Harris, Gordon Jones, Chris Langford, Malcolm Lonsdale, Jim Middleton, Tom Richardson, Pete Smith, Alan Swift and Trevor Uff, to name quite a few. An important ingredient were the scorers such as Bob Brown and Linda Goodwin. Two 'giants' of St George's cricket – in the words of Tony Gough were:

236

Geoff Allbutt, all six foot eight, and Jim Rhodes. Geoff took 63 wickets in 1969–70 and 48 in the following season, the fastest bowler in Hong Kong at that time. Jim arrived in 1969 and promptly made a name, as one of, if not the hardest straight hitting batsmen in Hong Kong.

1969   St. George's: 195–3 (A Gough 60*, M Lonsdale 51, E Roberts 38)
Feb 8   IRC: 47   (K Gohel 22, G Allbutt 10–23)

Geoff Allbutt, St George's lanky fast bowler, getting plenty of lift off the matting wicket mowed down IRC for 47 at Mission Road. He was twice on a 'hat-trick' but failed to achieve this double.

When Jim Rhodes was batting you didn't field too close, and if batting with him, you watched for the ball coming back down the wicket off some hapless bowler as 'Rhodes middled another one'.

The 25th Anniversary St George's booklet produced many memories of noble past deeds, a selection:

Tony Gough: A day in the 1967–68 season when league leaders HKCC Nomads were bowled out for 74. A schoolboy who batted at No. 10 then proceeded, with his innocuous looking leg-spinners, to bowl out St George's for 55! That same schoolboy went on to play County cricket for Kent – Charles Rowe. One dreadful afternoon when Jim Rhodes resorted to under-arm bowling against a HKU side that batted on till 4:25 p.m., leaving St George's 19 overs to score 170! At the old Chater Road ground in a friendly game against George Rowe's HKCC Wanderers – 'bowling a head high full toss to Sir Denys Roberts on 99, and then catching the dolly return one-handed and claiming it all as a subtle plan.'

Nigel Grandfield: In the 1972–73 season, when Jim Rhodes made a brutal attack on the KCC Crusaders, scoring 105 not out, out of a total 156. 'His powerful fore-arms exerted such a force through wood to ball that chances were often dropped because of the sheer pace of the ball.' Harold Harris's bowling 18 overs against LSW and taking 8 for 30. 'Harold was unplayable on the spongy matting wicket.'

Alan Swift: His first game in the 1971–72 season, when the Police were bowled out for 30! Jim Rhodes compiled a patient, out of character 15, the only double figures in the match against Kit Cumings and Roger Booth to lead St George's to a narrow victory. In the 1972–73 season, when St George's 'had the temerity to enter the Rothman's Cup,' and in the first round to proceed to beat the HKCC Optimists by six wickets. A certain John Barclay, later to captain Sussex, did not trouble

237

the scorers that day. In 1975, witnessing Harold Harris's 'hat-trick', when he clean-bowled the Army numbers 2, 3 and 4 (number 2 being Sir Edwin, now Lord Bramall). Those slightly longer in the tooth might well remember the Pete Smith B/W Newsreel Specials. Well, a certain policeman called Paul Foster remembers, while trying his damndest to forget, Pete Smith's cricket 'Specials'. From 1975, on five consecutive occasions, Paul was bowled first ball by Pete! More recently, St George's has looked like a team of KCC reserves. In one game against Mark Giles's Crusaders, St George's had 10 KCC members in their team against the home side's eight. The KCC balcony were so confused they cheered the away team!

More latterly the number of teachers playing cricket has sadly diminished, but due to the club's strong tradition of friendly and enjoyable competition, it has managed to attract many able and sociable cricketers from other clubs.

Overseas tours have been successfully made to Beijing, South West England and Manila. In 1983, St George's in Beijing, a memorable highlight and probably the first by a Hong Kong side. That tour has even been recorded for posterity in *Tales from Far Pavilions* by Allen Synge and Leo Cooper under the apt heading 'Peking Duck,' with apologies to Dave Whitfield of St George's. This was the first cricket tour of China since 1948, when the Hong Kong Interport team visited Shanghai before the Communist takeover in 1949.

The second and most important of the three matches for the Middleton Trophy against the Beijing Cricket Club, formed in the previous year, was won by St George's after Malcolm Grubb hit a fine 117 out of a total of 237 for 6. The Beijing CC, comprised of members from the Embassies of Great Britain, Australia, India, New Zealand and Pakistan, managed 145 runs, having to bat on a rain-affected wicket. That evening, St George's were treated to a Chinese banquet at the Fragrant Hill Hotel, north-west of Beijing, the occasion being graced by the presence of the Australian Embassador and his wife, both cricket enthusiasts. Nine members of the team took the slow train back to Hong Kong via Shanghai, covering over 2,000 miles in four days.

In January 1993, Hong Kong representative all-rounder Ross Greer became the highest scorer in a recorded league match played in Hong Kong: 'Greer demolishes Saturday league mark.' Greer peppered the Sek Kong boundary, cracking fifteen 6s and twenty-two 4s off only 108 balls for his 233 not out. St George's declared at 322–3 off 31.2 overs, beating CCC by 188 runs.

Later in the year in a more normal game – Greer must have been elsewhere – St George's continued their winning ways.

1983   Islanders: 122–9 (A Rutt 50, B Gohel 5–48, D Scott 3–13)
Dec 10 St. George's: 126–4 (N Perera 76*, N Smith 2–31)

1990   St. George's: 237–4 (S Atkinson 126*, D Brettell 63, A White
                              32*, M Peart 3–50)
Mar 3   HKU: 191–6 (M Speak 62, M Sabine 41, M Peart 30*,
                              G Jones 3–37)

Since 1983–84, St George's most successful seasons have been in 1988–89 (5th), 1989–90 (3rd) and in 1992–93 (6th) in the Saturday league. As the last of the British Army regiments left Hong Kong in June 1997, and St George's School has since closed, British Forces personnel would no longer form the basis of St George's CC. However, as players are drawn from a wide circle, especially from KCC, the club continues to fly the St George's flag. At the end of February 1998, the team was handily placed 4th in the Saturday league.

Second Division/Saturday League – Batting Performances 1965–66 to 1993–94

Season	Player	500 runs plus	Centuries
1969–70	J Rhodes	723 at 40.17 (2)	116* v KCC Crusaders
	M Lonsdale	513 at 32.06 (5)	106 v HKU
1970–71	J Rhodes	823 at 37.41 (3)	100 v HKCC Witherers
1971–72	J Rhodes	947 at 45.10 (3)	100* v KCC Crusaders
1972–73	D Clinton	925 at 66.07 (1)	100* v KCC Crusaders
	J Rhodes	780 at 55.71 (2)	105* v KCC Crusaders
1973–74	D Clinton	884 at 49.11 (4)	104* v Royal Navy
	J Rhodes	881 at 38.30 (9)	116 v HKCC Nomads &
			113 v HKCC Witherers
1974–75	J Rhodes	738 at 61.50 (2)	161 v HKCC Witherers

J Rhodes & A Swift 208 (2nd) v HKCC Witherers (2)

Season	Player	500 runs plus	Centuries
1975–76	N Grandfield	501 at 23.86	
1976–77	A Swift	617 at 41.13	
1977–78	G Potton	563 at 31.28	133 v Police
1978–79	R Gipson	575 at 38.33	
	C Langford	752 at 37.60	115 v Kai Tak
1979–80	A Swift	625 at 34.72	
	C Langford		104 v DBS
1980–81	B Ellis	547 at 32.18	

Second Division/Saturday League – Batting Performances (cont'd)

Season	*Player*	*500 runs plus*	*Centuries*
1983–84	N Perera	721 at 55.46 (7)	
	B Gohel	561 at 37.40	
1984–85	A Morgan	548 at 34.25	
1985–86	D Westwood	502 at 38.62	148 v Sentinels & 102 v Centaurs
1986–87	G Jones		107* v HKCC Witherers
1987–88	B Gohel		104 v KCC Tartars
1989–90	S Atkinson	900 at 75.00 (3)	133 v KCC Tartars & 126* v HKU
	D Brettell	506 at 46.00	101* v Strollers
1991–92	G Jones	521 at 37.21	
	S Atkinson		129* v Centaurs
	T White		105* v Strollers
	R Greer		117 v HKU§ & 102* v Kai Tak§
1992–93	R Greer	900 at 90.00 (1)	233* v CCC, 117 v KCC Saracens,
			106* v Stroller & 132 v Islanders§
	S Atkinson		142 v KCC Tartars
	R Greer & G Jones 257 (3rd) v CCC (1)		
1993–94	R Greer		134 v Islanders§
	R Archer		112 v Legal Eagles§

§   Butani/Dragonair Cups
(1)   Position in averages
(1st)   Wicket partnerships over 200 runs
       Police – Sentinels/Strollers

Second Division/Saturday League – Bowling Performances 1965–66 to 1993–94

Season	*Player*	*40 wickets plus*	*6 plus (for 50 runs or less)*
1965–66	J Kotch	46 at 10.30 (6)	6–20 v RAF
	A Gough		7–32 v KGV
1966–67	M Lonsdale		6– 6 v DBS
1968–69	G Allbutt	57 at 10.22	10–23 v IRC
1969–70	G Allbutt	63 at 9.50 (5)	8–48 v CCC/Recreio &
			7–48 v LSW
	J Williams		'hat-trick' v KGV
1971–72	A Swift	56 at 14.11 (6)	
	J Rhodes		7–17 v LSW

Second Division/Saturday League – Bowling Performances (cont'd)

Season	Player	40 wickets plus	6 plus (for 50 runs or less)
1972–73	A Swift	81 at 10.15 (3)	8–31 v IRC & 8–33 v Army
1973–74	H Harris	53 at 13.43	7–24 v HKCC Witherers
1974–75	A Swift	40 at 9.68 (2)	
	J Ackroyd	49 at 14.65	7– 4 v DBS
1975–76	H Harris	46 at 17.04	'hat-trick' v Army
1977–78	T Richardson	43 at 6.65 (1)	9–28 v Royal Navy
1979–80	P Etherington		7–10 v LSW
1988–89	B Gohel		7–15 v CCC
	N Whyborn		7–31 v Police Sentinels
	D Brettell		6–18 v LSW
1989–90	D Pierce		7–15 v Police Strollers
	D Cross		'4 in 4' v KCC Saracens
1992–93	R Greer		7–36 v Pak. Assn.§

[According to Nigel Grandfield (see Text), Harold Harris captured 8–30 against LSW in 1972–73. However, these figures do not appear in the HKCA handbook.]

§   Butani Cup
(1)   Position in averages

Vagabonds Cricket Club

As is usual with the formation of independent cricket clubs, their beginnings are sparked by some enthusiasts who feel frustrated by the normal run of things. In the case of the Vagabonds (persons with no fixed home), the cricket fanatic was one Robert Smith, who couldn't get a regular Sunday game with either the HKCC or the KCC, so in August 1977, with a group of fellow enthusiasts, formed the Vagabonds Cricket Club (the Vags). The Vags managed to secure the use of Mission Road (the leased Army ground) for their home Sunday fixtures, and so organised, joined the Sunday league for the 1977–78 season.

The team, captained by Des Greenwood, a Hong Kong representative player, had a healthy mix of youth and experience, the players coming from several Saturday league sides, notably CCC, HKU and KGV School. The Vags soon proved to be an ideal nursery for aspiring schoolboy cricketers, when KGV School teacher, David Clinton, who had also represented Hong Kong, brought his most talented schoolboys into the Sunday league via this channel.

241

The blend of youth and experience soon paid dividends, when in 1980, the Vags, captained by David Clinton, came within a 'hair's breadth' of completing the senior cricket double of league championship and Rothman's Cup. At KCC on 30 March, they won the Rothman's Cup by defeating the 'Cup' experts, the PRC, by 104 runs – propelled by a match-winning performance from KGV's 16-year-old Dermot Reeve. Dermot, who opened the batting, hit nine 4s and four 6s in his 117 not out, scored out of a total 220 for 3. Unfortunately, the Vags lost the crucial last game of the league season against the 'Optimists' by a handful of runs, and ended as runners-up in only their third season in the premier league.

1980	Brit. Forces:	247–7 dec	(T Gregson 74, J Bell 47, I White 47,
Oct 26			J Desmond 38*)
	Vagabonds:	169–9	(D Reeve 108, J Aldridge 6–64)

1981	Vagabonds:	239–3 dec	(D Greenwood 102*, D Race 101)
Sep 27	Wanderers:	222–5	(M Sabine 106, P Anderson 33*)

Nov 1	Brit. Forces:	281	(J Dean 155, R Litherland 47, D Muir 38,
			K Gohel 7–61)
	Vagabonds:	282–2	(D Race 161, D Greenwood 90*)

1984	Optimists:	132	(J Snoxall 49, D Reeve 8–67)
Dec 23	Vagabonds:	133–1	(D Reeve 105*)

Sussex's Dermot Reeve, home on his Christmas holidays, single-handedly took the HKCC Optimists apart at Mission Road.

The ultimate Hong Kong individual cricket trophy, the 'Player of the Year', has been won by three Vagabonds players: Des Greenwood in 1979–80, and schoolboys Dermot Reeve in 1980–81 and Craig Dean in 1987–88.

Juniors who have graduated to better class overseas cricket included: Simon Myles, Damon Sharwood, Ravi Sujanani, Jonathan Ellis and Andy Rutt.

Stalwarts include such players as: Barry Lovegrove, David Race, Steve Weatherley, Rob Gill, Ross Dalgleish and the Gohel brothers, Bharat and Kanu. Kanu was a lynchpin of the Vags attack for many years, while Bharat, after leaving Vags, represented Hong Kong. Recent Hong Kong players Ravi Sujanani and David Cross continue to wave the Vags flag, while many anonymous cricketers have contributed in their own way to the Vags cause.

Every season since its beginning in 1977, a question mark has hung over the future continuance of the team. There is a constant struggle for players, and the Vags can offer only a game of cricket – there is no comfortable clubhouse to relax in after the matches.

Despite these difficult struggles, the friendly cameraderie that has persisted over the years, still led by such stalwarts as Steve Weatherley, brought the side another coveted trophy, the Rothman's Cup, which they won at the end of the 1993–94 season.

Fortunately, this hidden strength remains amongst the stalwarts who have guided the Vags over the years. Veteran team captain Phil Glenwright is still there with consistent batting performances, ably supported by Alex Price, Stephen Whitton, David Steer and 15-year-old Allister Williams, who marked the 1998 New Year with his maiden century. This independent team, spawned by an enthusiast, spurred on with spirit, and recently sponsored by Ansett Australia, now has the players and the backing to become a potent force in the Sunday league.

Sunday League – Batting Performances 1977–78 to 1993–94

Season	Player	500 runs plus	Centuries
1977–78	D Clinton	577 at 52.45 (2)	115* v Scorpions
1978–79	D Race		105 v Army
1979–80	D Greenwood	599 at 54.45 (1)	147* v Wanderers
	D Race	553 at 36.86 (10)	
	D A Reeve		117* v Police φ
1980–81	D A Reeve	917 at 70.54 (1)	119 v Infidels, 113 &
			108 v Brit. Forces,
			107 v Optimists & 104 v LSW
	D Greenwood		100* v Infidels
1981–82	D Greenwood	725 at 72.50 (1)	102* v Wanderers & 102 v Infidels
	D Race	560 at 46.67 (7)	161 v Brit. Forces, 134 v Infidels
			& 101 v Wanderers
	D A Reeve		156* v Brit. Forces
	B Ellis		102 v IRC
1982–83	D Greenwood		123 v LSW
1983–84	D Greenwood	613 at 38.31	106 v Police
	D Sharwood	595 at 35.00	106 v Wanderers
1984–85	D Greenwood	587 at 45.20 (10)	
	D A Reeve		117 v Police & 105* v Optimists
1986–87	C Dean	504 at 50.40 (7)	135* v Infidels
	J Ellis	594 at 42.43 (10)	119* v Scorpions & 102 v Templars
	D Clinton		102 v LSW
1987–88	C Dean	525 at 52.50 (4) (only batsman 500 plus)	103 v Comb. Services #

243

Sunday League – Batting Performances (cont'd)

Season	Player	500 runs plus	Centuries
	D Greenwood		126* v Brit. Forces
1988–89	D Greenwood	558 at 39.86	
	J Shaw		114* v Templars
1990–91	S Marsden		107 v IRC
1991–92	P Glenwright		100 v Optimists
1992–93	A Williams		117 v Scorpions
	C Dean		115 v Wanderers
	M Hallam		100* v IRC
1993–94	J Garden		129 v LSW
	J Penrose		121* v IRC & 115 v LSW
	D Clifton-James		117* v Optimists
	A Williams		103 v Pak. Assn.

- ϕ Rothman's Cup
- #   Super League
- (1)   Position in averages
  - HKCC – Optimists/Scorpions/Wanderers
  - KCC – Infidels/Templars

Sunday League – Bowling Performances 1977–78 to 1993–94

Season	Player	7 plus (for 50 runs or less)
1977–78	C Forse	8–51 v Police
1978–79	C Forse	8–49 v Police & 7–21 v IRC
1980–81	E Ismail	7–33 v HKCC Scorpions
1981–82	D A Reeve	7–24 v IRC
1984–85	S Weatherley	9–53 v HKCC Scorpions
	D A Reeve	8–67 v HKCC Optimists
1986–87	D Uttamchandani	8–70 v KCC Infidels

THE SERVICES

In 1841, the Commander in Chief, Lord Hill, gave orders that a cricket ground should be built at every Army barracks in England. When the Colony of Hong Kong was ceded to Great Britain in January 1841, the Services were there, and wherever soldiers were quartered and the Fleet represented, the game of cricket would have been played, no doubt following Lord Hill's orders.

In F S Ashley-Cooper's book, *Highways and Byways*, he stated: 'we find matches taking place in Hong Kong in 1840, although the Hong Kong Cricket Club was not actually formed until 1851.' A supposition, and as no details were given, 1840 was probably a little too early.

In the HKCC Centenary Booklet 1851-1951, under the section on Royal Navy cricket in Hong Kong, it was stated: 'Although there are no records available it is probably safe to say that the Navy has played cricket in Hong Kong as long as anybody.'

E W Hamilton, who wrote cricket articles under the name of R. ABBIT, also stated in the HKCC Centenary Booklet that from memory, as his own records had been lost in the POW camp at Stanley during the war: 'Cricket in Hong Kong was undoubtedly first played by the Services shortly after 1841, in all probability and certainly only at Happy Valley.'

The author has probably discovered the earliest written reference to cricket being played in Hong Kong from the *Cree Journals*. These record the voyages of Edward H Cree, Surgeon RN 1837–1856. Tuesday, 27 April 1841: 'Dine with the 18th and after went over to Kowloon to see a cricket match between the officers of the Navy and the Army. The Chinese looking on appeared to be greatly interested.' The Chinese looking on were more likely to have been intrigued and mystified rather than interested, as the Chinese as a race, have never taken to cricket.

At the time of the first Opium War (1840–1842), the following British regiments were stationed in Hong Kong: 18th, 26th, 49th, 55th and 98th Foot. Various Indian regiments also took part in this war, as well as a multitude of HM ships, some of them being: Blenheim, Cornwallis, Hyacinth, Melville [with Rear Admiral the Hon. George Elliot, Commander in Chief aboard], Modeste, Nimrod, Sulphur and Wellesley all providing a nucleus of service personnel for local cricket matches.

Inter-Unit and Inter-Service cricket matches probably followed this early game in 1841, becoming more frequent after the swamps in Happy Valley were drained in 1846 and sports fields prepared, and then more regularly after the founding of the HKCC in 1851, when part of the former parade ground was also used for cricket by the Services.

Early records on Services cricket are scarce. However, on special occasions, like the visit of the Duke of Edinburgh to Hong Kong in November 1869, when the local press commented on the match between the HKCC and the United Services, the United Services being represented by the 25th Foot (1st Cameronians), the 59th Foot (2nd East Lancashire) and the Royal Navy, the researcher is a little luckier.

The weather was all that could be desired, a bright sun tempered by a cool breeze, afforded promise of a day on which everything would look its best; and certainly the cricket ground showed to an advantage. The green sward, the line of white tents gaily ornamented with flags of all the nationalities and colours, and the blue line of the harbour beyond. The northern boundary of the ground was washed by the harbour and a hit for six would land in the sea. A Chinese coolie, referred to as 'Catchee ball' was posted on that edge with a long-handled net to retrieve such. Mr H E Wodehouse, father of the humourist novelist, P G Wodehouse, played for the HKCC. Tiffin was served under the tents and during the afternoon, in the presence of the Duke, a military band performed during the tea interval.

Other early records were provided by Miss Rait Kerr, the then Curator of the MCC Library, to the President of the HKCC in 1951 on the occasion of their centenary. These match extracts were taken from *Cricket* dating from 1885 up to WWI.

By local rules, every match was decided on the first innings, if not played out in two afternoons.

1885	The Buffs:	106 and 135	(E J Coxon 8–72)
Nov 7	HKCC:	116 and 108–8	(D'Aeth 6–73)
& 8			

HKCC won by ten runs on the first innings.

| Nov 21 | HKCC: | 133 (Coxon 78) and 97 |
| & 22 | Garrison: | 99 and 134–7 (D'Aeth 70) |

In the match Coxon took 7–89, Druit 9–108 and Rice 10–41 for the Garrison

| Nov 29 | HKCC: | 135 and 51–3 |
| | XIV Garr. NCOs: | 121 |

HKCC won by 14 runs on the first innings.

| 1887 | Hong Kong: | 131 and 101 |
| Mar 4 | United Services: | 120 and 85–8 |

Hong Kong won by 11 runs on the first innings.

The following was a closely fought First Division match won by the RGA. The details were recorded by the SCMP and are not from *Cricket*.

| 1909 | HKCC 'A': | 68 (E C Oliver 22, Capt Garnett 6–35) |
| Mar 20 | RGA: | 73 (Capt Garnett 42*) |

1909   HKCC: 242–7 (T E Pearce 88)
May 15 Garrison: 213–8

The Hong Kong Garrison then embarked on a tour of Shanghai and Japan. The team was: D C K Greenway (Capt), Capt H H C Baird, H W Green, J Crookenden, I C Innes, D K Anderson, (The Buffs); Capt G T Brierley, H Bagnall, Capt H J M Beasley, Capt G E Garnett, T Whyte, (RGA); E G J Byrne & E J H Houghton, (105th Mahratta LI), and C R Satterthwaite, (RE).

Dec 12 Hong Kong: 222–2 (Dick Hancock 103*)
        The Navy: 100

1910   Army: 370 for 4 (Staff Sgt Power 144*, Capt Baird 125)
Dec 16 Navy: 275 for 5 (Com Lewis 149)

    It makes you wonder what the bowling was like, with 645 runs scored in a day!

Details of the following three matches were also extracted from the microfilmed SCMP at the British Library, Colindale, North London.

1912   KOYLI: 157   (Lt Collis Browne 34*, P Currie 4–51, H H
Mar 12   Taylor 4–52)
        CCC: 158–9 (R Pestonji 28*, W H Viveash 27, Pte Kilkayne
                       2–14)

1914   RE: 164 (Cpl Morrish 110, E Kelly 5–41)
Mar 7   Police: 58 (Cpl Morrish 7–34)

        Garrison: 144 (Maj Bowen 42, Lt Bagnall 32, R N Anderson
                      3–40)
        HKCC: 110 (A G Stokes 38, Lt Bagnall 6–23)

After WWI, a triangular tournament involving the HKCC, the Army and the Navy took place annually during the Christmas week and over the New Year. This annual tournament was maintained fairly regularly between the two world wars, with the RAF joining in later to make it a quadrangular tournament.

1919   Army: 282 (Lt Sutherland 60)
              128 (Donelly 5–64, Day 5–60)

247

HKCC: 166 (A A Claxton 51)
        280 (A A Claxton 125)

The HKCC won by 36 runs after following on!

Army: 157 and 308–5 (Col Coles 100, Capt P Havelock-Davies
                        105*)
Navy: 210 and 208–8

Match drawn.

Navy: 257 (Surg Com Hall 55, Lt Franks 58) and 113
HKCC: 382 (Dick Hancock 156, E J R Mitchell 68, A A
             Claxton 62)

The HKCC won by an innings and 12 runs.

Mar 8   Navy: 99   (Mr Cary 26, C P James 5–22)
          Kowloon: 106   (J P Robinson 40, Sig Hack 7–42)

KCC won this close league encounter with the Navy

1920   Army: 200
                   220 (Capt C O Oliver 59, Capt P Havelock-Davies 54)
        HKCC: 213 (Dick Hancock 86, E J R Mitchell 69, Capt
                 Havelock-Davies 6–62)
                 195 (T E Pearce 80, Capt Havelock-Davies 5–44).

Army won by 12 runs. It must have been quite a match.

Army: 271   (Capt Havelock-Davies 59, Capt Spinks 57)
       202–9 dec (Capt C O Oliver 71, E B Reed 5–78).
Navy: 193–9 dec (Lt Com Jotham 75) and 124 (Capt Havelock-
             Davies 10–38)

The Army won by 156 runs, thanks to Havelock-Davies's fine performances.

Navy: 180 (Lt Stewart 54, G R Sayer 6–66)
        192 (Lt I B Franks 69, E B Reed 5–77).
HKCC: 184 (Hayter 6–74)
      167 (Hayter 6–69)

The Navy won by 21 runs.

When the league cricket competition commenced in the 1903–04 season, the Services provided four of the eight sides in the then First Division: Army Ordnance Corps CC, RAMC, Royal Engineers and HMS Tamar. Army Ordnance became the first league champions. HMS Tamar dropped out in the second season when the fleet had to sail up to North China to protect British interests during the Russo-Japanese War of 1904–05. The RGA and Army Staff sides joined in to fill the gap. 'The weather was beautifully fine for these friendly matches played in 1903.'

1903	Garrison:	178	(Capt Ratcliffe RE 74, Lt Smith RA 29, T Sercombe Smith 3–45)
Nov 14	HKCC:	196	(E Mast 43*, W C D Turner 34, J T Dixon 27, F Maitland 22, A R Lowe 22, Lt Heath 4–81, Maj Chichester 3–33)
	RAMC:	98	(Lt Harvey 45, Cook 22, E R Herton 8–30)
	CCC:	94–7	(L Lammert 48, Cook 4 wickets)
	CSCC:	55	(Hon J M Atkinson 30, E Crabtree 7–26)
	Tamar:	43	(E Crabtree 16, P T Lamble 5–7)

Between the seasons 1903–04 and 1940–41, Service teams won the First and Second Division four times. After the Army Ordnance, it was the RGA in 1918–19 and 1919–20 and the Royal Navy in 1925–26. In the Second Division, the RE's won in 1923–24 and 1925–26, the RASC in 1934–35, and the Royal Navy in 1937–38.

1920	HKU:	153	(J H R Freeborn 56, I T Pun 31, Capt Davis 5–48)
Mar 27	RGA:	159	(Capt Oliver 100, F A Redmond 7–71)

RGA won a close contest on the military ground at Happy Valley.

1926	Army:	250–7 dec	(Capt Morris 121, Lt Warters 86, J C Lyall 5–92)
Feb 28	Vols:	153	(A W Ramsay 67, H C Burgess 28, Pte Moore 6–42)
Nov 18	United	134	(Capt A G Dobbie 28, Dr W E O'Hara 6–46)
& 19	Services:	210	(Capt C A Bridgeland 90, J A Isaacs 5–52)
	Shanghai:	268	(Capt E I M Barrett 133, Capt Dobbie 6–83)
		44–7	

An upset win for the Services was thwarted by the time factor.

1926   CRC: 76   (J L Youngsaye 24, Capt A Dobbie 7–31)
Dec 11 KOSB: 191–2 (Lt Hankey 104*)

        CSCC: 98 (E C Fincher 32, Spr Goodyear 5–36)
        RE & Signals: 31 (F J Ling 5–14, G R Sayer 5–17)

These two friendly matches were followed by Garrison knock-out competition matches in November played at CRC, KCC, HKU and IRC.

1927   Queen's ('D' Co): 126   (L/Cpl Miles 32)
        RASC: 182–6 (QMS Moss 43*, Capt Morris 37)

        Scots Guards: 155   (Capt Graham 39, Capt Dobbie 4–26)
        KOSB: 107–4 (Lt Hankey 45*)

        Scots Guards: 94   (L/Cpl Burger 6–15)
        RAOC: 102–7 (Dvr Stiven 6–26)

        Queen's Regt: 122 (Taylor 62, S/Maj Hale 4–40)
        RAOC: 67 (Elbourne 5–17)

That same month Malaya and Shanghai were in town for the triangular Interport matches.

        United Services: 182   (Capt I Erskine 56, D W Leach 4–33,
                                T L Rawsthorne 4–34)
        Shanghai: 186–5 (J Quayle 58)

        Malaya: 136–8 dec (R L L Braddell 42 retd)
        United Services: 114–5   (Capt Graham 30)

1928   HKCC: 143 (G P Lammert 50*, A W Hayward 31, Lt Col
Oct 27   Christian 5–22)
        Army: 132 (L/Cpl Miles 38, J Bonnar 5–24)

1929   HKCC: 173 (A W Hayward 34, Lt Musson 4–71, BSM Leach
Mar 30   4–74)
        RA: 77 (BSM Leach 45, H Owen Hughes 4–11, H V Parker
                     4–32)

Nov   Army: 80 (F Oliver 3–16, U M Omar 3–24, R E Lee 3–36)
CCC   CCC: 90 (U M Omar 32, Reynolds 5–20, Lt Col F J Wyatt
                     4–25)

250

1930   Navy: 136 (Lt F M R Stephenson 50, Lt Col F J Wyatt 4–23)
Jan 16 Army: 140 (Lt W A H Maxwell 71, Comdr F C Baker 5–36)

The Navy/Army First Division match was played from 11.00 a.m. till 4.00 p.m. in breach of league rules! C-in-C Vice Admiral Sir A K Waistell scored 16 for the Navy, who batted for 51.4 to the Army's 28.1 overs. The previous three matches were also First Division. The annual club and Services match at the HKCC that followed began in 'dull and cold weather'.

Jan 30 HKCC: 140 (T E Pearce 79, Comdr F C Baker 4–30)
& 31   133 (E J Mitchell 24, Capt J R Reynolds 3–16, Comdr
                     Baker 3–17)
        United 170 (J G Wolfe-Barry RA 50*, Comdr Baker 38,
        Services: Lt A H Musson RA 34, A C Beck 3–27)
                96 (Lt Col F J Wyatt RE 34, A Reid 5 & A C Beck
                     4 wkts)

HKCC squeezed a win by seven runs on this wicket which was 'soft on top but hard underneath.'

1933   Navy: 20   (A T Nomanbhoy 6–10, E L Gosano 4–8)
Feb 4   University: 63–1   (D J N Anderson 26*)
                               at King's Park.
Mar 4   Army: 143   (Capt Williams 70, A T Lee 4–40)
        University: 145–8   (E L Gosano 31, Lt Garthwaite 5–48)
                               at Pokfulam.

Nov 19 Navy: 186–7 dec (Lt A R Cheyne 56,
                                   Sub/Lt A Sinclair 51 retd)
        Lincoln's: 138   (A B Large 3–33)

Nov 21 United Services: 182 (Lt/Com F M R Stephenson 39) at HKCC.
        Shanghai: 181 (D W Leach 58, Lt Garthwaite 5–73)

  'T W R Wilson skied the ball, Capt Williams dropped the catch, but ran out T A Madar going for the second winning run.'

Except where stated, the following were all First Division matches.

Nov 25 Navy: 191–7 dec (Lt Eaden 43, Lt Garthwaite 3–56)
        Army: 131–7   (Maj Bonavia 44, Lt Eaden 3–31)
                          at King's Park.

251

1934   University: 68   (CSM Elwin 7–44) at Pokfulam.
Mar 3   Army: 97–8 (Capt P Williams 17)

Mar 10 CSCC: 66   (CSM Elwin 5–28, Lt Garthwaite 4–30)
        Army: 156–5 (Capt Mitchell 51 retd)
                          at Happy Valley.

'The openers passed the Civil Service score without being parted.'

Mar 24 IRC: 141   (A H Madar 50, Lt Garthwaite 5–45) at Sookunpoo.
        Army: 143–4 (Capt Mitchell 36, Capt Walsh 34)

Oct 27 University: 41   (Capt D B Mitchell 7–16) friendly at Pokfulam.
        Army: 125–6 (Lt Garthwaite 49, Pte Dewey 47, H L Ozorio
                          4–33)

1935   Navy: 69   (E L Gosano 8–23) at Pokfulam.
Jan 5   University: 54   (E L Gosano 14, Lt Crunden 7–18)

1936   RASC: 232–5 (Capt Walsh 132, Pte Willey 34)
Mar 23 RAMC: 89   (Pte Thompson 29, L/Cpl Muir 5–6, Cpl Ballard
                    4–46) Second Division at Sookunpoo.

1939   Navy: 156–7 dec (G P Longfield 4–37) at King's Park.
Jan 28 HKCC: 159–1   (H Owen Hughes 64*, L T Ride 41, T A
                      Pearce 37*)

The following matches were friendlies before the resumption of league
cricket in 1948–49:

1947   HKCC: 220 (J E Richardson 113, L D Kilbee 50, A Stepto
                  6–43)
Dec 26 Army: 127 (Maj Hope 47, F Howarth 7–21) & 91 (F Howarth
                  6–36)

1948   KCC: 181   (N Hart-Baker 59, Sterns 6–40)
Jan 1   Navy: 125–8 (R E Lee 6–40)

Just prior to the resumption of league cricket in Hong Kong in 1948–49, a
few enterprising prewar HKCC members, who had fought in the battle for
Hong Kong and survived the hardships and deprivations of their POW
camps, planned a 'Services' tour to Singapore and Malaya. Captained by
Lt Col H Owen Hughes, the team comprised the following members:

252

G N Gosano, J Hope, F Howarth, L D Kilbee, R E Lee, M Little, W Murray Brown, A Panton, T A Pearce, A Steptoe, and F R Zimmern.

There was no Cathay Pacific sponsorship in those days, so ingenuity had to be used to get the team down to the warmer climes of the Malayan peninsula. Laurie Kilbee informed the author that the transportation problem was resolved by Panton, a Squadron-Leader in the RAF, who said he could arrange for flights if all the players were service personnel. Most were or had been in the Hong Kong Volunteers, except for Frank Howarth, a key bowler. So for the purposes of the tour, Howarth was made an honorary corporal. The 'Services' team then embarked for Singapore by Sunderland flying boat, courtesy of AOC-in-C, Far East, Air Marshal Sir Hugh Pugh Lloyd, also of Surrey CCC.

Major Rowland Bowen reported in the *Cricketer Quarterly* 1966: 'The match in 1948 betwen Malaya and Hong Kong was a Combined Services match and in no sense part of the Interport Series.'

The Army were particularly strong in the 1950s and 1960s, especially so during the period of national service, when county and minor county players were recruited. Army won the First Division 12 times (once jointly) from 1950–51 to 1969–70. They were so strong the squad was split into Army 'North' and Army 'South' and still took turns to win the league title during the seasons 1955–56 to 1958–59. In the Second Division, the Services, in such guises as Army, Army 'B', Army 'North', Garrison and RAF, won the title 11 times from 1950–51 to 1970–71.

Army 'B' set a Second Division record in 1953–54 by winning all 20 matches played. Their highest scores were 262 for 4 dec v IRC and 256 for 4 dec v HKU, each innings taking 112 minutes. 2nd/Lt Cochrane scored 108 not out in the HKU match. Capt Petty smashed exactly 100, when Army blasted past Recreio's 176 in only 21 overs to win by seven wickets. Army's strength lay in their bowling, with seven bowlers taking 12 or more wickets in the season at less than nine runs per wicket. Major Evans led with 41 wickets at an average of 5.70 runs per wicket.

In 1955, a Hong Kong Combined Services (HKCS) side toured Singapore and Malaya. The tour party included Lt Pritchard and acting Sergeants Carnell and Dhabher. The three names are very familiar former Hong Kong Interporters. They qualified for the HKCS as volunteer members of the Hong Kong Regiment. The author, like Carnell and Dhabher, was a private in the same 'Home Guard' during 1953 and 1954.

Jul 12 & 13	HKCS:	123 & 212–5	(Lt Pritchard 110*, Maj Howard-Dobson 73)
	S'pore CS:	172	(Sgt Carnell 7–33)
		100–6	(Lt Spooner 4–36)

'The 19-year-old fast bowler Carnell sent back five Singapore batsmen for a paltry seven runs.'

15   HKCS: 152 (Howard-Dobson 65*, Pritchard 33, K T
                     Ratnam 4–23)
     Univ of Malaya: 106 (A Delilkan 42, Pritchard 4–14, Lt Spooner
                     4–28)

'Major Howard-Dobson won the toss on an easy paced matting wicket.'

Jul 16   HKCS: 123   (2nd/Lt Ford 41, Farmer 5–31)
         SCC: 129–5 (B C N Carnell 3–32)

'Major Chubb won the toss on a perfect grass wicket on a bright hot day.'

The next morning, a very weary team climbed into a Valetta aircraft at Singapore's Changi airfield at 6:30 a.m. for the flight to Butterworth.

Jul 17   HKCS: 103   (P Howard-Dobson 50*)
         Penang Sports Club: 104–6 (Urquhart 50, Lt Spooner 4–24)

'Major Chubb won the toss, pitch lively at times.'

19   HKCS: 124 (G H P Pritchard 69*, Barron 5–39)
     Army Singapore: 81 (J/T Birley RAF 8–18)

The side was always a happy one, due largely to Major Chubb's cheerful leadership, without whose enthusiasm indeed the tour would never have taken place. This was to become the forerunner of many such tours between Hong Kong and the Singapore Services teams, organised by similarly dedicated and enthusiastic Service cricketers from both regions.

As already stated, the 'purple' years were in the 1950s, when Army North, captained by Major Pat Howard-Dobson, and Army South, captained by Major Peter Chubb – all 6 foot 7 inches of him – took on the rest of Hong Kong and won, Army South in 1955–56, (jointly with KCC in 1956–57) and in 1958–59, while Army North won in 1957–58. Reported the *SCMP*: ARMY SOUTH WIN LEAGUE TITLE

Army South's easy victory over the Police by nine wickets at Sookunpoo gave them a well deserved title under the captaincy of Major Peter Chubb, league champions for the season 1955–56. In this match, Bill Withall reached a milestone, scoring his 700th run of the season, only the third player postwar after George Souza (CCC) and Pat Dodge (KCC) to accomplish this feat. The Police who batted first found the home team's attack almost unplayable, Yates messing up the front four batsmen while Withall dealt with the latter half of the order.

Police: 49   (Yates 4–12, Withall 4–4)
Army South: 53–1 (Withall 33*)

Although the Police opening bowlers Danny Renton and Tony Whitehead were swinging the ball considerably, Bedson, who joined Withall after Chubb had been dismissed, had no trouble scoring the 50 runs required for victory and the title.

The author visited Peter and Mary Chubb on a fine and sunny early July day in 1993 at their lovely home, The Rectory, near Northampton, to chat about Hong Kong in the 1950s and to seek out some of Peter's pertinent cricket records. He was obviously very proud of his Army South side of 1955–56.

In November 1955, the Malayan team visited Hong Kong and won the Interport by 10 wickets. The Hong Kong selectors chose six players from the Services for the Interport, four such players being Cpl M Birley, Major P J Howard-Dobson, Lt J H Lipscombe and Capt W N Withall, who had all performed well for the Combined Services against the Malayans. But a three-day Interport was quite a different proposition, as they soon found out.

Majors Peter Chubb and Pat Howard-Dobson were the inspirational force behind the creation of an Army social side which they named the 'Chopsticks'. Major Chubb led the Chopsticks to victory in their first match against a strong KCC XI at KCC in 1955.

Chopsticks: 198–6 (Major D Ball 75*, Lt G Crook 51*, B C N Carnell 2–37)
KCC XI: 128   (D G Coffey 41, C M Guilford 36, Lt P Dew 4–20)

The author also spoke with Sir Patrick Howard-Dobson, now a retired General, but failed to borrow his 'too bulky' scrapbook. However, he was full of enthusiasm for the cricket history. Hopefully, Peter Chubb's records, plus a contribution from Bill Withall, a retired Major General, whom the author knew in Hong Kong as a mere captain in 1953–54 and only located again in January 1994, will suffice for Services cricket in the 1950s.

255

In early April 1964, E W Swanton brought a very talented Commonwealth side to Hong Kong.

Apr 3   Comm. XI: 243 (R Benaud 64, M Griffith 48, N Pretzlik 41, T
                        Machin 4–54, I Lacy-Smith 3–63)
         CBF's XI: 166 (W Skelland 49, S Ramadhin 4–39, G Sobers
                        3–48)

Some highlights in the 10-year period from 1965–66 to 1974–75 were: the league double in 1969–70, when Capt Tony Vivian led the senior side to the title, well-backed by Rocky Daniel (top batsman with 457 runs) and Peter Mitchell (top bowler with 79 wickets at 8.54). Capt A L Bridger led by example to capture the Second Division title (top bowler with 31 wickets at 8.70, including two 'hat-tricks'). Carl Myatt, *SCMP*, said:

> Tony always played the game of cricket above the end result itself. He threw down the rank barriers on the field and fostered comradeship. This had the effect of bringing Army teams closer into contact with civilian clubs, thereby enhancing the atmosphere in which cricket is played here.

Ian Vaughan-Arbuckle, an influential member of that championship side, also played a very important role as Army cricket secretary during a great part of this period – apart from his stylish batting for the Army and Hong Kong.

R G Daniel, 'Rocky', headed the senior division batting three times. On the third occasion in 1970–71, he also topped the league bowling averages, the only player to complete this particular double in the First Division. Carl Myatt, *SCMP*, said:

> One of the most colourful personalities to grace the cricket fields of Hong Kong. Hails from Barbados, but played mainly in Jamaican cricket before joining the Army and going to England. Played for the Army in England. An aggressive batsman who goes for his shots; useful right arm spin bowler and good fielder.

His only apparent weakness came to light during the Hong Kong tour of Malaysia and Singapore in May 1965, when he 'succumbed' to the one-arm bandits at the Singapore Cricket Club. Rocky commented: 'They've got me!'

Sir Edwin Bramall, on 15 March 1975, scored the last league hundred on the HKCC Chater Road ground, playing for the Army against the

HKCC Witherers. In a letter to the author, Lord Bramall in his own words recorded:

The Commander British Forces, General Edwin Bramall opened the batting and, after 'an inordinately long time', completed a half century, which matched his age at the time. At this stage, as he felt he had earned his keep, he promptly aimed 'an almighty blow over extra cover', only to see the ball go straight up, gather ice, swirl around and come down next to a hapless fielder. As his luck seemed to be in, he took a new guard and when the Army declared had an undefeated 112 runs.

A memorable contribution from Field Marshal The Lord Bramall (Commander British Forces in Hong Kong 1973-76), made on an historic ground.

| 1966 | Army: | 146 | (J Holman 37, A Vivian 36, M de Witt 4–31) |
| | Singapore Police: | 149–1 | (G Krishnan 67*, N Sivamayam 60) |

1967	S'pore CS:	196	(D Oakley 56)
Oct 13	HKCS:	130	(R Pellew 7–32)
	Army:	112	(G Broomes 42)
	CCC:	67	(G Broomes 6–20)

| Nov 25 | Army | 146 | (I Vaughan-Arbuckle 64, J K Fawcett 6–38) |
| | Scorpions: | 134 | (J K Fawcett 53, J Murphy 33, G Broomes 8–43) |

'Broomes, broad-shouldered, his face streaked with sweat, set the match alight with a sensational four wickets in a one-over burst which included a hat-trick.'

The HKCC Scorpions were 134-6 with John Fawcett on 53, seemingly heading for victory. Broomes took out Fawcett, then Patton and Cannon to complete his 'hat-trick' and Army won by 12 runs!

1969	S'pore CS:	187–7 dec	
Oct		53	(P Mitchell 7–11)
	HKCS:	120	
		109	

'Mitchell tore in like some angry typhoon to scatter the visitors like chaff.'

Nov 5   Singapore CA: 215–4 dec (R A da Silva 86, R Tessensohn 67)
        HKCS: 117–5   (D Gregory 41, A Lewis 3–14)

1970   Army: 245–7 dec (I Whittaker 112*)
Feb   Sabah CA: 148   (A Dews 37, A Murugesu 33, Bilner 4-13)

'Whittaker batting at No.8 mauls Sabah attack.'

        Army: 248–6 (R Daniel 97*, I Vaughan-Arbuckle 65)
        LSW: 154   (D Gregory 56, R Daniel 3–20, I Whittaker 3–35)

'Army won off the penultimate ball of the match.'

1970   RAF: 96   (P Mitchell 6–40)
Apr   Army: 97–6   (R Daniel 43*)

'The Army certainly had some anxious moments before clinching
their match at Kai Tak to wrap up the title.'

1971   Inaugural Rothman's Cup Final

Apr 18 Scorpions: 185–6 (N Hooper 67, R Shearburn 3–37)
        Army: 186–3 (R Shearburn 91*, R Daniel 41, M Alexander
                            39)

'Shearburn with the Gods on his side, kept striking the ball firmly.'

Denys Roberts (HKCA President) in thanking Ian Gow and Rothman's,
expressed the hope that this tournament would become a regular feature in
the cricket calendar. Both Denys (now Sir Denys) and Ian would be glad
to know that the Rothman's Cup has been played annually since that
auspicious start in 1971.

1971   LSW: 273–7 dec
Oct 24 Army: 276–1   (R Daniel 129*, M Alexander 121*)

'The two West Indians, the compact Rocky Daniel and the lanky
Martin Alexander, decimated Saiwan's attack in a manner which
would have made Attila the Hun proud.'

Nov 10 HKCS: 177   (R Daniel 41, Jagdev Singh 6–30)
        Malaysian CA: 183–9   (G Singh 96*, R Graham 6–71)

On a cool dull evening after the shadows had lengthened into almost dusk, the tall imperious sikh, Gurucharan Singh, from Kuala Lumpur strode to the wicket as acting captain, with seven wickets down for 66 and his side facing certain defeat. Gurucharan's innings, the most clinical piece of destructive attacking cricket seen in years, contained eight sixes and seven fours, his unbeaten 96 coming off only 58 balls.

Carl Myatt, *SCMP*

The Saturday and Sunday League Cups were won in 1975–76 and 1976–77 respectively.

| 1975 | Army: 188–9 (D Budge 106, R Minns 3–43) |
| Nov 22 | KGV: 145–3 (D Clinton 74) |

Two more league trophies followed – the first in 1984–85, when British Forces, led by Peter Wood, 'Player of the Year' and a Hong Kong representative cricketer, captured the Sunday league title, and their last time in 1985–86 when the Army, led by their physio 'Ginge' McAllister, defeated the Police Sentinels for the Gillette Cup.

| 1978 | Singapore CA: | 95 | (J Jackson 6–48) |
| Nov 8 | HKCS: | 99–2 | (B Elworthy 38*) |

1979	Brit. Forces:	220–5	(J Bell 55, A Swift 52*, D Hurren 41, K
Nov 21			McLean 35)
	Malaysia CA:	213–9	(R Ratnalingam 109, P Banerji 48, I White 5–57)

1980	Papua NG:	273–8	(D Moody 75*, A Leka 54, G Guma 42, V
Apr 9			Amini 38)
	Brit. Forces:	179	(J Desmond 74, V Amini 5–18, A Leka 3–7)

Oct 26	Brit. Forces:	247–7 dec	(T Gregson 74, J Bell 47, I White 47, J
			Desmond 38*)
	Vagabonds:	169–9	(D A Reeve 108, J Aldridge 6–64)

John 'Sid' Aldridge and Ian White were a formidable pair of opening bowlers. Sid, using his height, would get extra bounce from the wicket, whilst Ian, with his prodigious inswinger would literally turn the batsman around as he tried to negotiate the rapidly moving ball. Coupled with Martin Walker, that great 'hitter', this trio were a force to be reckoned with in local cricket.

```
1982      UKCS U-25:  168
Nov 1     Brit. Forces:  65  (J Kneale 7–24)


1983      Brit. Forces: 254–6 dec  (G Jones 78, S Collett 56, P Wood 43,
Oct 30                               R Pritchard 35*)
          IRC:          120         (T Weerakoon 54, N Perera 43, S
                                     Collett 6–7)


1984      Scorpions:    282–7  (B Kwong 68*, P Varty 30)
Dec 9     Brit. Forces: 268    (P Wood 128)
```

The 1988–89 'Player of the Year', blond left-arm opening bowler Ian Collier, who headed the bowling in both leagues (62 wickets at 17.03, including two 'hat-tricks') and (45 wickets at 9.60, including an amazing 10 for 13 against the Centaurs), ended the season on a real high playing for a Hong Kong Selection against Worcestershire on 11 April 1989. He removed Ian Botham's middle stump! With the 'belligerent' Botham staring back down the wicket at him, Collier wasn't sure he should smile! What a memorable end to a remarkable season.

Hong Kong cricket has been very fortunate. Most of the CBFs and some others in charge of local Services cricket in Hong Kong throughout the years have been firm cricket supporters, thus Service players have been readily released for Hong Kong representative matches ever since the first Interport against Shanghai in 1866. General Bramall (now Field Marshal The Lord Bramall) has been mentioned elsewhere; John Desmond was another who 'melded' very well with the civilian sides, and one of the 'others', Colonel (now Major General) David Burden, during his tour in the mid-1980s was not only involved with British Forces cricket, but also had a lot to do with the HKCA on cricket matters. It was particularly nice to see a senior Services person, together with his wife Sue, also involved in the local social scene. David left his own mark on cricket in Hong Kong, and in his own words:

> Firstly, when backing to take a catch at deep mid-wicket while playing for Commander British Forces' XI against the Chief Justices' XI at the HKCC, I tumbled over the boundary boards and ended up prostrate in front of the Pimms' drinking spectators! Secondly, I led a tour to Bangkok, the first British Forces cricket tour to Thailand, a country noted in the past for other forms of entertainment.

From the HKCA's point of view, the other precious commodity has been the number of grounds the Services have made available in Hong Kong for this great game. Sadly, the British Forces withdrew from Hong Kong when

Hong Kong became a Special Administrative Region of China on 30th June 1997, bringing to an end an association of over 150 years. Their withdrawal has resulted in the loss of the Sookunpoo ground with the Mission Road venue presently on hold, with a good chance of its retention for sport.

First Division/Sunday League – Batting Performances 1965–66 to 1993–94

Season	Player	500 runs plus	Centuries
1965–66	R Daniel	829 at 55.27 (1)	100 v Optimists
	J F Ryder		111 v Scorpions
1966–67	A C Vivian		112 v Optimists
1967–68	I Vaughan-Arbuckle	516 at 23.45	
	G Hartley		115 v Valley #
1970–71	R Daniel	536 at 53.60 (1) (only batsman 500 plus)	
1971–72	M Alexander	826 at 55.07 (1)	151 v Templars, 121* v LSW & 117* v Optimists
	R Daniel		129* v LSW

R Daniel & M Alexander (2nd) 225* v LSW (1)

Season	Player	500 runs plus	Centuries
1972–73	R S A Shearburn	499 at 24.95	
1973–74	R H Coleman		100* v Optimists
1975–76	D L Budge	692 at 43.25 (7)	121* v Templars
	R Litherland		105* v IRC
1976–77	R G Smith	502 at 35.86 (2)	103 v Wanderers
	R Litherland	503 at 33.53 (3)	102* v Templars
1979–80	K McLean	563 at 43.31 (4)	
	D Hurren		100* v IRC
1981–82	P Dean	604 at 46.46	155 v Vags & 149 v Optimists
	R Litherland		110 v Wanderers
	P Wood		115 v Wanderers

P Wood & S Collett 200 (1st) v Wanderers (2)

Season	Player	500 runs plus	Centuries
1984–85	P Wood	646 at 43.06	128 v Scorpions φ
1985–86	T Lerwill	696 at 49.71	110 v Optimists & 109 v Scorpions
1986–87	T Lerwill	676 at 56.33 (4)	131* v Scorpions & 116 v Vags
	J Howard		102 v Optimists & 101* v Wanderers

T Lerwill & A Inions 208 (3rd) v Scorpions (1)

First Division/Sunday League – Batting Performances (cont'd)

Season	Player	500 runs plus	Centuries
1988–89	R Plowman	534 at 53.40 (8)	108* v Infidels & 101 v IRC
	A Kennedy		118* v Templars
1990–91	A Kennedy		148* v LSW & 125 v Infidels
1991–92	B Carter		124 v IRC ϕ
1992–93	C Dahl		125 v Infidels
	B Carter		118* v IRC
1993–94	C Dahl		110* v IRC

- \#   Includes 'Super' League
- ϕ Rothman's Cup
- (1)   Position in averages
- (1st) Wicket partnership over 200 runs
  - HKCC – Optimists/Scorpions/Wanderers
  - KCC – Infidels/Templars

First Division/Sunday League – Bowling Performances 1965–66 to 1993–94

Season	Player	50 wickets plus	7 plus (for 50 runs or less)
1965–66	J H Bennett	55 at 8.51 (3)	
	W Davison	50 at 9.40 (5)	8–13 v IRC
1966–67	G Paul		7–22 v Police
	G Broomes		7–46 v LSW
1967–68	G Broomes		8–43 v HKCC Scorpions incl. 'hat-trick'
1969–70	P A Mitchell	79 at 8.54 (1)	7–38 v Police
1971–72	J Whitehill		7–33 v LSW
1973–74	J M Jones		7–47 v Police
1974–75	A P Greig		7–35 v IRC
	P R Holcroft		'hat-trick' v HKCC Optimists
1978–79	T Richardson		8–68 v HKCC Wanderers
1979–80	I White	51 at 13.41 (2)	8–30 v IRC
1984–85	K Hardman	52 at 20.15 (8) (only bowler 50 plus)	
	P Wood		7–13 v IRC
1985–86	J Sutherland		9–85 v Vagabonds
1986–87	E Maunsell		7–19 v Vagabonds

First Division/Sunday League Bowling (cont'd)

Season	Player	50 wickets plus	7 plus (for 50 runs or less)
1988–89	I Collier	62 at 17.03 (1) (only bowler 50 plus)	8–74 v HKCC Scorpions incl. 'hat-trick' v HKCC Optimists

(1) Position in averages

Second Division/Saturday League – Batting Performances 1965–66 to 1990–91

Season	Player	500 runs plus	Centuries
1970–71	J Bird		100* v IRC
1971–72	F J Preston		105* v HKCC Nomads
	A C S Gordon		103* v Police I
1973–74	R H Stopford	724 at 90.50(1)	132* v DBS & 129* v Centaurs
	R A Lewis		100* v DBS
1974–75	Sir Edwin Bramall		112* v HKCC Witherers
	H D H Keating		101 v Islanders
1975–76	D L Budge	725 at 45.31(9)	106 v KGV & 102 v Islanders
	F W Cadman		178* v DBS
	R Litherland		103* v CCC
1976–77	R Smith (1LI)	791 at 32.96	106 v Islanders
	E Mountstevens (1LI)	617 at 29.38	130* v Kai Tak
	P Richards (1LI)	505 at 26.58	
1977–78	P Richards (1LI)	503 at 35.93	
1979–80	I White		126* v Police Strollers
	R Wright		107 v Islanders
1980–81	J Dean	660 at 44.00	115* v DBS
	J Desmond	530 at 26.50	
1983–84	P Wood	786 at 49.13 (10)	113* v HKU
1984–85	P Wood	792 at 46.50	
	A Kennedy		102 v KCC Crusaders
1985–86	R Harrison	605 at 35.10	
	P Willey	771 at 59.30(7)	128 v CCC & 100 v Police Strollers
1986–87	T Lerwill		119* v IRC

Also included:

1953–54	2/Lt Cochrane		108* v HKU
	Capt Petty		100 v Recreio

(1) Position in averages
(1LI) 1st Light Infantry

Second Division/Saturday League – Bowling Performances 1965–66 to 1990–91

Season	Player	50 wickets plus	7 plus (for 50 runs or less)
1966–67	G Paul		8–15 v St George's
	S Dyal		7–40 v IRC
1968–69	A Jones		7–37 v KGV (incl 'hat-trick')
	J Goodridge		7–38 v IRC
1969–70	A L Bridger		'hat-tricks' v KGV & PRC
	N Thompson	59 at 11.40 (10)	
	R Carrington		7–11 v IRC
1970–71	M Green	63 at 9.60 (2)	
1972–73	J Burke		8–15 v CCC
1974–75	H D H Keating		7–14 v Islanders
1975–76	A W Harling		8–30 v LSW
1976–77	D Knapton (1LI)	53 at 15.60	
	R Smith (1LI)	56 at 17.21	
1977–78	R Smith (1LI)		7–32 v Centaurs
1979–80	I White		7–31 v Police Strollers
1983–84	P Wood		'hat-trick' v DBS
1988–89	I Collier	45 at 9.60 (1) (only bowler 40 plus)	10–13 v Centaurs (incl. 'hat-trick') & 8–22 v Islanders
1990–91	J Axhorn		7–45 v St George's

(1) Position in averages

Royal Navy

Saturday League – Batting Performances 1973–74 to 1982–83

Season	Player	500 runs plus	Centuries
1973–74	L Williams		112* v DBS
1975–76	P W Anderson	828 at 51.75 (4)	
1976–77	P W Anderson	1225 at 72.06 (1)	113* v Centaurs, 107* v KGV & 113* v HKCC Witherers
	K Robinson	516 at 21.50	
1977–78	P W Anderson	832 at 92.44 (1)	
1978–79	M Walker	819 at 39.00 (8)	
	E Ismail	802 at 34.87	106 v Police 'A'

First Division/Sunday League – Batting Performances (cont'd)

Season	Player	500 runs plus	Centuries
	G Bacon	565 at 25.68	
	D Coulson	630 at 25.20	
1979–80	M Walker	948 at 47.40 (8)	155* v Police Strollers & 123* v Police Sentinels
	E Ismail	741 at 30.87	121* v Police Sentinels
	I Laidlaw		101* v Islanders

E Ismail & M Walker 203* (2nd) v Police Sentinels (4)

Season	Player	500 runs plus	Centuries
1980–81	P W Anderson	835 at 83.50 (1)	103* v KCC Tartars & 100 v Islanders
	T Burns	727 at 40.38	136 v Police Strollers & 104 v DBS
	E Ismail	751 at 39.52	
1981–82	P W Anderson	784 at 49.00 (7)	
	G Bacon	520 at 37.14	

(1)   Position in averages
(2nd)   Wicket partnerships over 200 runs

NB. Although these statistics come under the heading Royal Navy, as the team was called, the players were not in the Navy. Most of the players were employed by the Government's Independent Commission against Corruption.

Gillette Plate Final at HKCC

1982   Royal Navy: 199–7 (E Ismail 67)
Apr 12 Nomads: 186   (A Lorimer 71, K McConnell 50)

A very rare trophy for the pseudo-Navy side.

Saturday League – Bowling Performances 1973–74 to 1982–83

Season	Player	50 wickets plus	7 plus (for 50 runs or less)
1975–76	P W Anderson		7–40 v CCC
1976–77	R Grisenthwaite	78 at 10.90 (4)	9–11 v DBS & 7–42 v LSW
	D Whiting		7–29 v Islanders
1977–78	R Grisenthwaite		8–35 v DBS & 7–38 v KCC Saracens

Saturday League – Bowling Performances (cont'd)

Season	Player	50 wickets plus	7 plus (for 50 runs or less)
	G Bacon		'hat-trick' v HKCC Witherers
1978–79	E Ismail	53 at 13.47 (3)	
	G Bacon	54 at 17.72	
1979–80	G Bacon	53 at 15.74 (7)	
	E Ismail	54 at 17.83	
1980–81	E Ismail		7–21 v Police Strollers

Wicket-keeping Performances

Season	Player	30 plus Dismissals
1976–77	K Robinson	40 (1)
1979–80	M Walker	49 (1)

(1) Position in averages

Volunteer Cricket in Hong Kong

The first call for a Corps of Volunteers was made by the Hong Kong Government and listed in *Gazette* No. 37, of June 3, 1854. No doubt some Volunteers played cricket during the latter part of the 19th century, one being Surgeon Lieutenant J A Lowson, who was to captain Hong Kong in Interports, and who was one of the two survivors of the *SS Bokhara* disaster in 1892.

The *SCMP* on 26 October 1903 reported that the members of the Corps amused themselves in a variety of ways during the Volunteer Camp on Stonecutter's Island. In a cricket match, the First Right beat the Left Right by five wickets. A S Watson's representatives played a particularly good game, Uphill and Austen distinguishing themselves. However, organised Volunteer cricket probably did not start until after the compulsory enrolment in the defence corps came with the enactment of the Military Service Ordinance of 1917. The then named The Hong Kong Volunteer Corps became The Hong Kong Defence Corps, to be changed again in 1920 to The Hong Kong Volunteer Defence Corps (HKVDC).

At that time a Volunteer cricket week was started during the Hong Kong Race week, when the HKCC ground was given up solely to the Volunteer matches against the Army, Navy and Combined Services. Matches were also played against the KCC on their own ground in Kowloon. These Volunteer cricket weeks became so popular that after a few years, the

Volunteers were able to run a regular Sunday team to play other clubs on their grounds. This continued right up to the outbreak of the Pacific war.

The following Interport cricketers made the supreme sacrifice during the Battle for Hong Kong in December 1941: Lieut Donald J N Anderson, Bombardier Ernie F Fincher, Pte Tam E Pearce. There were many others who had played cricket in prewar Hong Kong who also gave up their lives in the cause of freedom.

The Volunteers who played cricket before the Pacific war came from all walks of life and played league and friendly cricket for the various recreation clubs in the Colony. Summarised results of some of these matches, mostly organised by Harry Owen Hughes, are recorded hereunder:

1924   Vols v Army at HKCC, tiffin at noon with stumps drawn at 4.30 p.m. The Vols team comprised: E J R Mitchell (capt), H Owen Hughes, A C I Bowker, G R More, A W Ramsay, E F Stewart, J Finnie, W W Mackenzie, I D McNicoll, H E Hollands and J C Fletcher.

1926   Vols XI: 164   (A Ramsay 62, Lightfoot 5–16)
A A Rumjahn's XI: 205–9   (E F Fincher 63)

Other Vols were: E J R Mitchell, J C Lyall, E C Fincher, H V Parker, S Jex, Capt N C D Brownjohn, F G L Wheeler, E G Renton, C D Wales, J M M Andrews and J A Summers.

CRC: 127   (C Choa 47, H V Parker 5–10)
Vols XI: 262–4   (H V Parker 100*, F E Lawrence 66)

1929   University: 228   (A A Rumjahn 58, D J N Anderson 41, S R Kermani 34, H Owen Hughes 5–68)
Vols XI: 264   (H Owen Hughes 82, G E R Divett 61, K H Batger 32, D J N Anderson 3–26)

The match was played on Sunday, 17 February, at Pokfulam, where the University batted for 50 overs and the Vols for 64 overs.

Vols XI: 170   (F I Zimmern 51, A W Hayward 36, Capt Weir, RM 3–23)
Comb. League: 89   (D J N Anderson 30, C D Wales 6 31, J Bonnar 4–20)
             109–3   (Capt Weir 53, J R Hinton 34)

The match was played at KCC on Sunday, 10 March. 'It was a perfect Cricketers day with a bright sun and a cool breeze.' W Hunt played for the Volunteers, this being the nom-de-guerre of the well known player, W C Hung.

| 1930 | Vols XI: | 163–8 dec | (A C Beck 50) |
| | Royal Navy: | 167–8 | (Lt Eaden 47*) |

1931	Vols XI:	272	(R M Wood 87*, R H Griffiths 44, E J
Feb 28			R Mitchell 33, F Goodwin 3–35)
Mar 1		72–9	(R H Griffiths 38, G C Burnett 8–25)
	KCC:	300	(E F Fincher 84, W C Hung 75, F I
		48–1	Zimmern 39)

1932	Vols XI:	40	(E L Gosano 4–4)
Jan 10	University:	242–8	(A Rodrigues 52 retd., E L Gosano 50,
			P M N da Silva 37*, G C Moutrie 3–48)

1934	KCC :	209	(W C Hung 89, A C Beck 4–52)
	Vols XI:	153	(L D Kilbee 53, Hung 3–35)
	Vols XI:	171–5 dec	(E C Fincher 50 retd.)
	DBS:	124	(A J Hulse 32, J L Youngsaye 21)

While the author was scrutinising some of the late Teddy Fincher's wartime records a few years ago, he came across a 'gem', the full scoresheet of a cricket match played in the Shamshuipo POW Camp in April 1942. How did the prisoners get the equipment to play cricket? Sir Albert Rodrigues, then one of the internees, supplied the answer:

In Shamshuipo, when officers and men were together, the Camp Commandant was asked to obtain the necessary paraphernalia for cricket, hockey and volley-ball, and some local boys went with the Japanese in trucks to various clubs where they obtained the bats, balls, stumps etc for cricket as well as for hockey. We had a fairly good cross section of cricketers from the Army, HKCC, KCC, Recreio and made up sides as we felt like it. The time we played when there was an air-raid, we ran for shelter more from the ack-ack shells that fell from the Japanese defenders, and the sentry guards were shooting at the planes with their rifles. When the officers were sent to the Argyle Street camp and then some POW's were sent to Japan, the numbers as well as the inclination to play dwindled. I recall some names when we were sort of at full strength – Officers: Capt Chris

Mann, Lieut Alec & John Pearce, Lieut P M N da Silva, and others ... the Zimmerns (Francis, Archie), Ted Fincher, Tinker Lee, the Gosanos (Gerry, Luigi and Zinho, now father Zinho), Toto Prata and brother and self.

We played wearing only the *fanduchy*. Imagine my playing at first slip with Archie Zimmern squatting in front of me as wicket-keeper, with his large backside in *fanduchy* only, but fully padded. Would have been an ideal subject for a cartoon.

Nick Jaffer, camp cartoonist, where were you to miss this once in a life-time opportunity?

```
1938      Vols XI:  99  (F A Dunnett 40, C Pope 5–16)
Mar 26 PRC:     98  (J L Stephens 30, A E Carey 22, W S Stoker 5–24,
                     N D Lloyd 4–25)
```

The Volunteers scraped home by one run at Happy Valley.

After the Pacific war, the Corps was reconstituted on 1 March 1949 as The Hong Kong Defence Force, and two years later awarded the prefix Royal, in recognition of the heroic part and sacrifices made by the HKVDC in the defence of Hong Kong.

Admiral Sir Robert Burnett, Captain of Destroyers in Hong Kong in the 1920s, recalled an occasion when the Volunteers were playing one of their Sunday matches with the Navy at King's Park, Kowloon. Bob Burnett, captain of the Navy side, asked the captain of the Volunteers whether he bowled, and on receiving the reply in the negative said: 'Neither do I, so what about my bowling to you and you bowling to me so that we can make some runs!'

In 1951, compulsory service for all English-speaking males over the age of 18 years and resident in Hong Kong, was introduced. This compulsory service netted many good cricketers from the various clubs. Apart from these special games, Volunteer cricket never again attained its prewar popularity. These matches only continued until the late 1950s, when compulsory service ceased.

During the Volunteer Centenary celebrations in 1954, the RHKDF easily defeated the Combined Services in a match at Chater Road, even though Service teams were at their strongest at this time. The Combined Services batted first, and due to a fine 5th wicket partnership between Lieut Bill Withall and Major Bailey, were able to declare their innings at 150 runs. The main wicket takers for the RHKDF were: Lieut 'Spotty' Pereira (Recreio) 3–14, Pte Peter Hall (KCC) 2–19 and Sgt Gerry Gosano (Recreio) 2–47. After tea, Lt Cdr Laurie Kilbee (HKCC) 82 not out and

L G Gosano (Recreio) 50 not out, in a brilliant unbroken partnership, took the RHKDF to a memorable victory by 10 wickets. The RHKDF team was selected from:

*Cpl David Coffey (KCC), *Pte Buji Dhabher (CCC), *Major E L Gosano (Recs), *Gerry Gosano (Recs), L G Gosano (Recs), Pte 'Spikey' Guterres (Recs), *Pte Peter Hall (KCC), Lt Cdr Laurie Kilbee (HKCC), Pte Kenneth Lo (KCC), *Lt Alec Pearce (HKCC), Lt 'Spotty' Pereira (Recs), Lt Micky Remedios (Recs), and others.

* Hong Kong Interport Cricketers

Hong Kong was handed back to China on 30 June 1997, and as part of this handover, the Royal Hong Kong Regiment (Volunteers) was disbanded on 3 September 1995. The end of another long and proud connection with Hong Kong, when 'so few gave so much' for peace in our time. May the Hong Kong Volunteers remain forever in our memories.

Cricket Match – HKVDC v Army

12 April 1942 (the match was actually played on Saturday 11 April)

Volunteer XI

D Crary	111211112141	st Logan b Tropp	17
J M Gosano	1141111421	c Webb b Tropp	17
N A E Mackay	12212	c & b Tropp	8
E C Fincher	4111141112	c J Pearce b T A Pearce	17
E J R Mitchell	41211112111211131121122422411	not out	47
N D Lloyd	22122	c & b Denyer	9
F R Zimmern	11114	st Logan b T A Pearce	8
A Zimmern		c J Pearce b T A Pearce	0
G Aikenhead	1111	c Ratcliffe b Denyer	4
R T Broadbridge	2	not out	2
G S Winch		did not bat	
		Byes	1
			130

Fall of wickets: Gosano 34 Crary 34 Mackay 47 Fincher 71 Lloyd 88
F Zimmern 105 A Zimmern 105 Aikenhead 107

Army XI

J L C Pearce		c Broadbridge b Aikenhead	0
C Logan	112122411212121211111211112	c Broadbridge b Zimmern	38
T A Pearce	22	lbw Lloyd	4
Swaine	112121	lbw Crary	8
Skipworth	2112122111211	b Winch	18
Webb	14	c Mitchell b Zimmern	5
Ratcliffe	4422144122112	st Zimmern b Lloyd	30
Denyer	1	run out	1
Blount	1	b Aikenhead	1
Tropp	21112	not out	7
Goss	1	run out	1
		Byes	16
			129

Fall of wickets: J Pearce 1 T A Pearce 6 Swaine 34 Logan 78 Skipworth 80
Denyer 85 Webb 117 Ratcliffe 120 Blount 125 Goss 129

Bowling	Army				Bowling	Volunteers			
	O	M	R	W		O	M	R	W
Tropp	7	2	26	3	Aikenhead	6	1	20	2
Ratcliffe	6	–	38	–	Lloyd	4.1	–	21	2
Denyer	6	–	32	2	Crary	4	–	23	1
Pearce	6	–	33	3	Zimmern	6	–	24	2
					Winch	3	–	25	1

THE SCHOOLS

The first schools to play cricket in Hong Kong were all located on Hong Kong Island, and in the early days, the students walked to Happy Valley to play their games. These schools were the Diocesan Boys' School (DBS), Queen's College (QC), St Joseph's College (SJC) and the Victoria English School (VES). In the 1920s, the Central British and the Ellis Kadoorie Schools also started playing cricket, joined by La Salle College in the 1930s.

Prewar Hong Kong saw a Combined Schools XI involved in friendly matches.

1932 University: 115 (J T Ride 26, M el Arculli 5–28)
Oct 26 Comb. Schools: 95 (A A Rumjahn 42*, E L Gosano 7–5)

'Remarkable bowling by E L Gosano was the cause of the dismissal of the Combined Schools for 95 runs. A A Rumjahn, however, alone withstood the attack and carried his bat for a splendidly compiled 42 runs.'

1934	CCC:	185–9	(R Lee 56 retd, A T Lee 43,
Mar 3			E Zimmern 35)
	Comb. Schools: 150–8		(G T Lee 38, A H Baker 36)

| 24 | Recreio: | 90 | (W Reed 28, A J Hulse 6–17) |
| | Comb. Schools: 106 | | (A J Hulse 22) |

J L Youngsaye (Capt), A Zimmern, A J Hulse, W Rapley, G T Lee (DBS); R Holden (CBS); A Baker, A Kitchell (St Joseph's); M Usuf (Ellis Kadoorie), Afzal (Queen's) and Alvis (La Salle).

1935	Comb. Schools: 116	(R Trowt 20, E L Gosano 2–5, E B Reed
Jan 13		2–24, A R Minu 2–27)
	G R Sayer's XI: 95	(H Owen Hughes 32, R Holden 6–21)

'Bowling a deadly length and breaking both ways, R Holden ran through Sayer's illustrious eleven.'

After the Pacific war, the Ellis Kadoorie School, La Salle, Queen's and St Joseph's Colleges all ceased to play cricket. Only DBS and the Central British School, later KGV School, continued after the 1950s. St George's School joined them in 1962, followed by Island School in 1968, and later still South Island School.

By 1971–72, a quartet of schools collaborated in organising schools' cricket on a formal basis. In order to give strength to the new system, schoolmaster Graham Wills (the first convenor of the Hong Kong Schools' Sports Association Cricket League) withdrew KGV from the Second Division to join with DBS, Island School and St George's in Saturday morning inter-school cricket matches. The Juniors – Forms 1, 2 and 3 – played for the Peter Kuruneru Trophy, whilst the Seniors – Forms 4, 5 and 6 – for the Graham Wills Shield. Additionally, Centaurs donated a Cup for a splendid Six-a-Side Competition at the end of the inaugural Schools' season.

Although KGV had some initial doubts about leaving the Second Division, this proved to be the making of organised schools cricket in Hong Kong. Many of the nationalities within the schools became involved in the game, but gaining the interest of Chinese boys has proved difficult. KGV won both divisions and the knock-out competition, whilst schoolboys such as Yarman Vachha, Noshir Shroff, Paul Varty (KCC) and Bharat Gohel (IRC) also played for club sides.

From the 1976–77 season, four schools in Hong Kong, DBS, Island School, KGV and South Island School, competed for the Ted Wilson Trophy, with the final being played at the HKCC each April. The St George's senior school side had become the St George's Cricket Club.

Keen pupils would find opportunities to play cricket. Junior school competitions were introduced in the earliest years at each of the secondary schools mentioned. The HKCA made annual grants to these schools, with additional amounts to those participating in the Saturday league. The best chance to improve one's game depended upon getting a regular place in either one of the school sides, i.e., DBS, KGV or Island School, or in playing for one of the club sides in the Saturday league. Although Saturday league matches are played to rules unsuitable for schoolboys (limited overs), many clubs bear this in mind when playing against school teams. It is in this league that the students obtain vital experience by playing with and against adults, gaining a maturity far faster than their contemporaries in other cricketing countries.

Dermot Reeve, who stepped up from the KGV 1st XI to the England team, said that being thrown in at 'the deep end' as a youngster gave him an early advantage over English boys, who until recently, normally played within their own age groups during their formative cricket years.

A major problem facing a school team was when to let students play an important role in the game. Often a more competent adult would grab the key position, thus denying students the chance and experience of performing under difficult conditions. The more enlightened, such as David Clinton, knew when to give the students the reins and when to get on the horse himself. A balance had to be struck: involving more talented boys whenever possible to enable them to improve, whilst at the same time monitoring the game to avoid too many losses which could destroy a player's and a team's confidence.

In 1983, a schoolboy team from the Haberdashers' Aske's School in England made their first visit to Hong Kong to play two matches against Hong Kong Schools. The first at KCC and the second at HKCC.

1983   Haberdashers: 202–6 (R Bate 51, R Harris 33, A Griffiths 31)
Dec 30 HK Schools: 197   (D Sharwood 68, J Thadani 42, S Myles 32)

Haberdashers won a closely fought match by five runs.

1984   HK Schools: 160   (D Sharwood 38, D Wigley 31)
Jan 3   Haberdashers: 164–9 (A Miles 40, R Bate 33, J Thadani 3–16)

Haberdashers squeezed out another victory by one wicket.

Haberdashers returned in late 1985 with either a stronger team or met a weaker Hong Kong Schools selection for two 50-over matches.

1985   Haberdashers: 219–7 (A Evans 57, A Griffiths 36, J Crawford
                                33, J Ellis 3–29)
Dec 30 HK Schools: 185   (J Ellis 55, J Marsden 46, D Preest 3–31, R
                                Downes 3–42)

Haberdashers won by 34 runs at KCC.

1986   Haberdashers: 265–8 (J Burrows 136)
Jan 2   HK Schools: 155   (A Morgan 36, Gunasekera 4–44, D Preest
                                3–15)

Haberdashers overwhelmed Hong Kong by 110 runs at HKCC.

HK Schools bowling and fielding lacked bite and was very ragged towards the close. It was a useful experience for the local boys who lack variety of opposition at schools level.

Scoreboard March 1986

Later that year, the first official overseas schoolboy cricket tour took place in December 1986 with a visit to India. At the suggestion of Mr Chatripal Sinh, Regional Manager of Air India in Hong Kong, a keen cricketer himself, a party of 16 schoolboys, captained by Steve Marsden, with Peter Anderson as Manager (the then recently retired captain of the Hong Kong side and now Chief Executive of Somerset CCC) and Geoff Lever as Assistant Manager (then Chairman of the HKACU), undertook a two-week tour, after a formal farewell cocktail party at the KCC, to play six matches around Bombay and Delhi in India.

The Hong Kong schoolboys played against some very good and competent cricketers, and as a result, had to raise their own game to compete. They responded extraordinarily well, the whole venture being very worthwhile. After the poor display against the Haberdashers earlier in the year in Hong Kong, the team's excellent fielding was a feature of their play in India. The Hong Kong schoolboys won one, drew two and lost three matches. Members of the team were: S Marsden (Capt), A Bailey, R Broadbridge, I Chakrabarti, A Chiba, C Dean, J Ellis, N Gulzar, C Jones, M Lever, J Marsden, R Seed, D Sinh, C Starling, D Uttamchandani and M Wake.

Results of the six matches played:

HK Schools: 152–6 (J Ellis 38, S Marsden 31)
Raj Kumar College OB: 155–9 (N Gulzar 3–38)

At one stage the Old Boys were 135–9, but it was the two run-outs that cost the Hong Kong team dearly. If only ...

HK Schools: 131–4 (C Dean 88*)
Raj Kumar College: 130   (A Bailey 3–29)

Craig Dean's superb innings and two excellent run-outs by Michael Wake and Martin Lever were special features of this match.

Bombay CC U19: 251–9 (Broadbridge 3–32)
HK Schools: 166–4 (S Marsden 77, J Ellis 55)

The match was played in intense heat and the Hong Kong captain, Steve Marsden, after keeping wicket for four hours, opened the batting!

Air India Boys: 179   (N Gulzar 3–22, D Uttamchandani 3–60)
HK Schools: 140–6 (S Marsden 60)

What an experience playing in Bombay's Brabourne Stadium.

HK Schools: 118
Delhi Colts: 119–6

On a damp wicket, HK batted disappointingly, and had Delhi 28–6 at one stage!

Delhi Schools: 219 (A Bailey 4–49, M Wake 3–29)
HK Schools: 210 (J Ellis 63, J Marsden 50, M Lever 38)

HK Schools dearly wanted to win this last match against the champion school. The Delhi School was equally eager – 'their quick bowler was held back to the end and promptly operated at full pace in the fast receding light.'

On the first day of the second Cathay Pacific/Wharf International Sixes, held in October 1993, a number of local primary school teams went onto the field at lunchtime to show their skills in a junior sixes competition. The teams were selected from Bradbury Junior School, Clearwater Bay Junior School, Glenealy Junior School, Kennedy School, Kowloon Junior School and Quarry Bay School.

As part of a new four-year development programme, the HKCA's initiative in this particular area is beginning to show results which should be encouraged, in order to provide the impetus for local schools to play more cricket in Hong Kong.

In the meantime, DBS, Island School and KGV School continue to participate in the Saturday league, sometimes strengthened by past students, or persons with a paternal affinity, or some with no connection at all.

The future health of schools' cricket in Hong Kong will depend largely upon the continued strength of the HKCA. At this point of time, the HKCA strongly supports the participation of students in schools' cricket, by assisting with coaching and funds. The HKCC and KCC hold junior cricket 'clinics' on Saturday mornings during the cricket season. From October 1996, these coaching sessions were expanded to CCC (Mondays and Fridays), Mission Road (Saturdays), Sandy Bay, HKU (Fridays), and Discovery Bay, Lantau Island (Wednesdays).

Ted Wilson Schools Trophy

Season	Winners	Runners-up
1976–77	DBS	KGV
1977–78	KGV	DBS
1978–79	KGV	DBS
1979–80	KGV	DBS
1980–81	KGV	DBS
1981–82	KGV	Island
1982–83	KGV	South Island
1983–84	Island	South Island
1984–85	KGV	DBS
1985–86	KGV	Island
1986–87	KGV	Island
1987–88	KGV	Island
1988–89	KGV	South Island
1989–90	South Island	KGV
1990–91	Island	DBS
1991–92	Island	KGV
1992–93	South Island	DBS
1993–94	South Island	Island
1994–95	South Island	KGV
1995–96	DBS	South Island
1996–97	South Island	DBS
1997–98	Island	DBS

A Tim Davies Trophy, as a further encouragement for schools cricket, was benefactored by Tim for matches played between Hong Kong and Kowloon Schools. Kowloon Schools 190–5 (N. Foue*) defeated Hong

Kong Schools 126 (N. Fung 4–16) to become the first winners of the trophy in 1994–95.

Diocesan Boys' School

In 1860, on Bonham Road, Hong Kong Island, a school called the Diocesan Native Female Training School was opened. In September 1869, under a new constitution, the name was changed to the Diocesan Home & Orphanage. The boys were given a wide and liberal education, fitting them well for professional, commercial and clerical careers. A particular feature was made of all kinds of sport, particularly those which created and inspired teamwork, such as cricket and soccer.

In the School Annual Report of 1888, cricket was mentioned, but no details were given. There were only 125 pupils, including day girls. All the girls had left by 1892.

The Government had provided some land near Robinson Road, West Point, Hong Kong Island, for the use of schools in that area. These included St Joseph's College, the Victoria English School, as well as the Diocesan Home & Orphanage. In 1897, the HKCC presented three cricket bats to the school. With the advent of Mr A O Brawn in 1901, the school held its own with, and usually led, the other schools of the Colony in cricket and soccer.

In 1902, the school became the Diocesan Boys' School & Orphanage. In 1905, being a Church of England school, the Anglican Bishop offered prizes for cricket and tennis matches between the School and St Joseph's College. Later that year these matches became a feature of life between these two schools.

'Pleasant and sometimes successful games were played with the second elevens of the Civil Service, Police and CCC in 1906; and in 1908 also matches with the masters, the Sailing Ships' Apprentices, CCC, and the 'A' teams of the Civil Service and the Kowloon Clubs.'

From 1915 to 1918 there were no proper practice grounds for cricket and soccer. Around 1920, 70 per cent of the pupils were Chinese, with the remainder made up of twelve other nationalities. The 1922 School Annual Report stated:

In games we have decided to join no Leagues or Associations, we are willing to play any school in friendly matches. The League system is

277

not a good system for schools, nor are the systems for holding sports for prizes or for International contests for school boys.

In 1923, two nets for cricket practice were put up on the lower tennis court at the school and matting and general cricket equipment supplied. Mr J L Youngsaye organised the cricket. In 1926, the school moved from Hong Kong Island to its new site off Argyle Street in Kowloon. The school buildings were taken over by the Military Authorities and used as a hospital until 1928.

In the 1927–28 season, 24 matches were played: 13 won, 6 lost, and 5 drawn. The captain, Donald Anderson, scored over 1,000 runs for the school, including two centuries. A T Lee also scored a century. Both mentioned also shared the bowling honours with Kwan and R E Lee (President of KCC 1954–62). Matches won included those against IRC 'A' & 'B', CCC and HKU 2nd XI, all league sides.

During the next season, matches were won against the second elevens of both the HKCC and the KCC, the two premier cricket clubs. At that time 34 DBS old boys were playing cricket in seven local cricket clubs. In 1929, Donald Anderson, captain of the school in 1928–29, played his first Interport for Hong Kong in the Triangular Series against Shanghai and Malaya. Other old boy Interporters at that time were Teddy Fincher and F I Zimmern (1930).

In J L Youngsaye's 1928 School Cricket Report, he said:

D J N Anderson easily remains the best batsman and all-rounder in the team, and R Lee, the best bowler. Forceful batting is now being more encouraged with those who have learnt the rudiments of straight play, and bowling has not been allowed to degenerate into a mere task, The most encouraging point, however, is that quite a number of Chinese boys are taking to the game, and we hope before long to be able to turn out really decent Chinese players.

R ABBIT, who wrote cricket articles for the *Hong Kong Daily Press*, reported in 1929:

I have received through my Editor an interesting note from the Rev W T Featherstone, the Headmaster of the Diocesan Boys' School. I know of course that D J N Anderson and Freddie Zimmern were old boys of that Alma Mater, but I did not know Teddy Fincher also learned to lisp his infant school numbers there. I was interested to learn that that ripe sportsman (I hope 'ripe' is not actionable! call it 'veteran'!), A O Brawn first seriously encountered the game there, and

278

in 1922–23 a matting wicket and nets was put on a tennis court at the old school buildings, and the great thing was to slog a ball onto Bonham Road. In 1924, came Mr J L Youngsaye to the staff, and the school is now a really fine nursery of local cricket.

JL was dedicated to DBS cricket; he was also a very keen orchid grower right up to his 90th year. In the early 1950s, he taught the author, on a private basis, general mathematics – train 'A' leaves platform 'B' travelling at 25 mph … He was a very nice, quiet, smiling gentleman. It was a great pleasure knowing you, JL.

Before the Pacific war, DBS played school cricket regularly against the Central British School (later KGV School), the Ellis Kadoorie School for Indians, La Salle, Queen's and St Joseph's Colleges. The school also played friendlies against most of the Second Division clubs and the Services. The first match of the season was usually a Past v Present match on the school ground.

1931   University: 154–7 (E L Gosano 54*, A Prata 5–40)
Nov 4   DBS: 66–8   (N Broadbridge 14, H Nomanbhoy 3–12, C E
                            Clarabutt 3–18)

1934   Volunteers: 171–5 dec (E C Fincher 50 retd)
Mar 11 DBS: 124   (A L Hulse 32, J L Youngsaye 21)

    14 DBS: 133   (G T Lee 34, Broadbridge 29, B Singh 2–18)
        Queen's: 137–3 (M el Arculli 76, Y P Tsui 43*)

1936   DBS: 143–6 dec (F J Lay 37, G Hong Choy 35, Ismail Ali
Mar 18   3–52)
        Queen's: 79–9   (N Lee 54*, R Broadbridge 5–38, Y T
                            Barma 3–16)

Drawn match at Sookunpoo.

1938   DBS: 129   (F J Lay 48, A J M Prata 34, G A V Hall 4–14,
                        D J N Anderson 4–20)
        KCC: 137–8 (K M Baxter 62, C B R Sargent 4–46)

KCC 2nd XI scraped home on a friendly Wednesday afternoon.

        Queen's: 57 (N Singh 33, D Crary 5–9, C N Matthews 4–18 incl
                      'hat-trick')
        DBS: 80 (A J M Prata 35, K M Rumjahn 7–35)

DBS passed the Queen's College total with 3 wickets down.

Like most recreational clubs and schools, the Pacific war had wrecked havoc with the buildings and grounds, and it wasn't until the 1947–48 season that cricket was played again on a limited scale. DBS joined the Hongkong Cricket League Second Division in the 1950s.

In 1960–61, when DBS won only six matches out of 22, Thomas Chadd scored 753 runs, highest 88, averaging 37.65, and captured 71 wickets, averaging 8.83 per wicket. He was probably instrumental in the wins against IRC (twice), KCC, KGV and Recreio. Jimmy Lowcock, who played cricket for the school in the immediate post-war period, then became headmaster for many years until the late 1980s, said of Chadd: 'Thomas Chadd was one of the best all-rounders since the war. Unfortunately, he was killed in an accident the year he left the school.'

In the mid 1960s, Roger Poynton was the strength behind DBS cricket. The 1st XI played in the Second Division of the Hongkong Cricket League; the 2nd XI played mainly against KGV, La Salle and St Joseph's Colleges, while the Junior XI played against Kowloon Junior School. Three teams were formed from 29 seniors and 24 juniors.

In the school magazine *Steps* it was reported: 'The nets near the railway did not empty until 5.00 p.m., except for the occasional retreat of the acolytes to seek their missing orb lost in the railway wood.'

Over $2,000 was spent on cricket equipment, 60 per cent being provided by old boys, such as H T Barma, E S Cunningham, J Fenton and J L Youngsaye. The students contributed $1.00 for each 1st XI home game. In 1963–64, Roger Poynton's 103 against IRC was the highest score in league cricket by a DBS boy, and was the highest score in the Second Division. Michael Shu, who umpired with the School 1st XI, was the first Chinese umpire to become one of the Colony's 12 qualified umpires, after attending an HKCC course and sitting for the UK umpires' examination.

Two close finishes were recorded:

DBS: 94 and KGV: 91

KGV were 83–2, then Poynton and Willis dismissed eight batsmen for eight runs. A remarkable win by three runs!

DBS: 125 and KCC 2nd XI:122

KCC were 103–9, the KCC captain hits two sixes ... the score moved to 122–9. Poynton bowled to the KCC captain: 'BANG! the ball was thumped high and far towards Shamshuipo for six runs – it was all over .... but wait!?! a DBS fielder catches something and a round

280

object strikes the bank around the field. What's going on?? The fielder is clutching the outer leather case of the ball, it's the core which has gone for six!! A rare miracle – the ball had split on the winning hit. A 'dead ball' was declared and the next over started with the formidable KCC captain facing the bowling again. Willis bowls ... a sharp snick – Barma lunges forward – OWZZAT! Win by two runs.'

Steps, 1964

Played 22, won 11, lost 11, position 6th. A good season ably led by Roger Poynton.

The usual two non-league annual matches were played, the Boxing Day fixture against the old boys and the Youngsaye Shield at KCC.

In 1964–65, the two outstanding players were:

R Poynton – an aggressive batsman who scored 326 runs, highest 59 not out, averaging 27.20. As a fast bowler, he took 73 wickets, averaging 8.96, including five wickets eight times with a best of 7–33.
R Nolasco – a medium-pace bowler, who took 63 wickets averaging 12.73, including five wickets five times, with a best of 6–56.

The school magazine *Steps* had this to say:

A far greater number of youngsters from the primary section of the school must be encouraged to partake in the game so that the spirit, as well as the technicalities of cricket can be fostered.

From the early 1990s, the HKCA has spent considerable sums of money toward the improvement of the wicket and the upkeep of the ground at DBS, in its efforts to retain as many grounds as possible for cricket in Hong Kong.
Two of Hong Kong's top cricketers 'guested' for the DBS team, Stewart Brew in 1990–91 and Jason Penrose in 1992–93, when the school came 8th out of 18 teams in each of these seasons. In the last four seasons DBS has slipped back into the lower half of the league table, but now led by Roy Lamsam, who gained valuable experience with the Hong Kong Representative squad in Malaysia in 1997, have put in some fine performances.

Diocesan School [Past & Present] v Craigengower CC

Friendly: Saturday, 3 March 1906

Diocesan School

A O Brawn, c Fairholm b Pestonji	15					
R C Witchell, c & b Pestonji	7	*Bowling*				
G Evans, c & b Lammert	38		*O*	*M*	*R*	*W*
W Wong, c Lammert b Fairholm	14					
A Arnold, c Fairholm b Irving	2	Pestonji				4
W Thom, c (sub) b Pestonji	12	Lammert				3
H Anderson, c & b Lammert	0	Fairholm				1
G Lee, b Pestonji	8	Irving				1
W Jenkins, run out	0					
Chan Wing To, b Lammert	7					
T Jex, not out	1					
Extras	12					
Total	116					

Craigengower CC

E Irving, b Wong	4					
R Pestonji, b Wong	7	*Bowling*				
J Fairholm, b Wong	0		*O*	*M*	*R*	*W*
L E Lammert, not out	64					
R Basa, b Wong	1	Wong				4
L A Rose, b Witchell	23	Witchell				1
H Ropp, b Brawn	13	Brawn				3
F Loureiro, c & b Brawn	0					
A E Asger, c Chan b Brawn	9					
F Drude, not out	4					
T Loft, did not bat						
Extras	15					
Total (8 wickets)	146					

At a reunion of ex-internees of Stanley POW Camp, Hong Kong, at Leamington Spa on 12 April 1997, I spotted a cricket photograph which belonged to Bill Macauley, a member of the 1940–41 DBS team. Bill said:

> I never meant to play cricket but turning out for the 'house' team taught me the difference between a baseball and a cricket bat. Always

282

as a boarder – appetite and stomach motivated and good with numerals, I started as a scorer, a very quiet and sedate job, sitting in the shack enjoying refreshments and the end of the match teas. But the leisurely life as a scorer came to an end when we were short and I was drafted as the 11th – 1940.

Members of the team: Jim Macauley (captain, elder brother of Bill), Edward Reed, Chernakoff, Cyril Kotewall, Rosselet, Eric Randall, David Lloyd, Ahmed Ibrahim, Charley Whitfield, and Chin Fen Jnr.

Appendix

Old boys and pupils playing for local clubs in 1928
[Date indicates year of leaving school]

Club de Recreio

L J Guterres   1926

Craigengower C C

E Mow Fung	1899	W A Youngsaye	1922
W J Howard	1919	Ernest Zimmern	1923
R C Reed	1919	E B Hamson	1924
A B Hamson	1920		

Chinese Recreation Club

Charlie Choa	1917	G Chue	1926
J L Youngsaye	1918	A Hung	1926
H C Hung	1920	H Q Hung	1926
W C Hung	1920		

Hong Kong University C C

H T M Barma	1923	F I Zimmern	1926
S V Gittins	1925	A T Lee	1927
J Hunt	1926	D J N Anderson	1928
E A Lee	1926	A J Nomanbhoy	1928

Indian Recreation Club

A H Rumjahn   1908

Kowloon Cricket Club

Starling Jex	1906	D S Green	1918
George Lee	1910	E C Fincher	1919
G A V Hall	1913	E F Fincher	1922
W M Gittins	1914	N A E Mackay	1926

Sindhi Merchants

A T M Barma	1919	A S A Kyum	1928

Second Division/Saturday League – Batting Performances 1963–64 to 1993–94

Season	Player	350 runs plus	70 plus (to 1972–73)	
1963–64	R Poynton		103 v IRC	
1968–69	A Suffiad	429 at 22.58	79 v Centaurs	70 v PRC
1969–70	A Suffiad	386 at 21.44		
1970–71	F Ah King	393 at 17.86		
	S Abbas	358 at 17.05		
1971–72	J Lamb	573 at 28.65	89 v Witherers	84 v Nomads &
			79* v Saracens	
1972–73	S Abbas	386 at 24.13	85* v Army	
	F Prata	368 at 18.40		
1973–74	E Ismail	600 at 28.57	100* v PRC	96 v Royal Navy
1974–75	E Ismail	500 at 29.41	101 v ?	
1975–76	E Ismail	690 at 31.36	103 v Witherers	
1978–79	J Lamb	431 at 30.79	96* v HKU	
	M Hung	361 at 30.08		
1983–84	E Ismail	538 at 35.86		
1984–85	N Perera[a]	627 at 39.10		
	E Ismail[a]	627 at 37.80		
1985–86	J Lamsam	562 at 40.14		
	E Ismail	582 at 36.37	111* v HKU	
1990–91	S Brew[b]	1505 at 215.00 (1)	139* v CCC	131* v Strollers,
			129* v Saracens	121 v Sentinels,
			115* v LSW	107* v Islanders,
			107 v Centaurs	105* v Witherers
1991–92	S Brew		204* v Strollers	133* v Crusaders
1992–93	J Penrose	833 at 69.42 (4)	155 v Kai Tak	112 v Islanders
	S Brew		134* v Crusaders	100 v Kai Tak

S Brew & J Penrose 207 (1st) v Kai Tak (5)

Mistake in the 1984–85 handbook, similar totals!

An Australian expatriate assisting DBS cricket

(1) Position in averages

(1st) Wicket partnership over 200 runs

HKCC – Nomads/ Witherers

KCC – Crusaders/ Saracens

Police – Sentinels/ Strollers

Second Division/Saturday League – Bowling Performances 1964–65 to 1993–94

Season	Player	40 wickets plus	7 plus (for 50 runs or less)
1964–65	R Poynton	73 at 8.96 (5 plus eight times)	7–33 v ?
	R Nolasco	63 at 12.73 (5 plus five times)	6–56 v ?
1966–67	R Nolasco	48 at 18.46	'hat-trick' v Army
1968–69	F Ah King	53 at 15.77	
1969–70	M Whitcombe	54 at 9.38 (3)	8–48 v IRC
1970–71	M Whitcombe	64 at 12.04 (10)	
	L Huang	41 at 24.20	
1971–72	M Whitcombe	62 at 17.92	7–23 v St George's
1973–74	E Ismail	45 at 13.36 (10)	
1974–75	E Ismail	44 at 16.64	8–30 v Navy
1975–76	E Ismail	46 at 19.17	
1978–79	E Tse		'hat-trick' v RGJ (Army)
1980–81	B Lin		'hat-trick' v KCC Saracens
1985–86	E Ismail	55 at 13.84 (4)	

(1) Position in averages

Ellis Kadoorie School for Indians

The author was not aware that this particular school had played a part in the history of Hong Kong cricket until he found the results of a few cricket matches played in 1933. The names Arculli and Abbas had featured in a number of these matches.

| 1933 | Queen's: | 119–6 dec | (M el Arculli 39 retd, W Abbas 4–52) |
| Nov 22 | Ellis Kadoorie: | 121–8 | (M Singh 27, W Abbas 26, M Afzal 4–20) |

285

Letters were then written to Dr N P Karanjia, a former President of CCC and to the Hong Kong Director of Education. Dr Karanjia said he had contacted the Arculli and Abbas families, but to no avail. However, he did mention two former headmasters:

Sutherland, a Scotsman, and later Fletcher, an Englishman, encouraged the boys to play the game as much as possible. After the re-opening of the school around 1947, owing to insufficient 'local Indians', there was a mixed bag of students and cricket was not a popular game.

As the Director of Education did not even acknowledge the author's letter, a copy was sent to Alec Reeve, a former headmaster of KGV School, asking for his assistance. Alec spoke to A K Suffiad (a pupil in the 1920s) and to Miss Lala Curreem, the Principal of the school in the 1950s. Miss Curreem stated:

Sir Ellis Kadoorie School for Indians (sometimes called the S K Indian School) was founded by Ellis Kadoorie, a very wealthy Parsee businessman and began operations in 1898 as a primary school in Sookunpoo in Eastern Hospital Road. It wasn't until 1959 that it began to operate a Form 1 (secondary level). It was the policy of the Government to appoint expatriates as heads before the Pacific war.

A K Suffiad said he wasn't much of a cricketer himself, but did play for IRC: he and Lala confirmed that the school produced some good cricketers, including the Madar brothers (one of whom played in the Inter-port matches against Shanghai), the Rumjahns and the Arcullis. Miss Curreem added that the school's records were either destroyed or lost during the Japanese occupation of Hong Kong during the period from 1941 to 1945.

While in Hong Kong in November 1992, the author had spoken to Sir Sidney Gordon, his former boss at Lowe, Bingham & Matthews (now Price Waterhouse), the Kadoorie's trustee and financial adviser, about this school. The above information was sent to Sir Sidney in September 1994. That letter was passed onto Jimmy Lowcock, a former headmaster of DBS, to reply. Jimmy said that although the school was now completely localised, it still had a good proportion of Indian pupils who were very active in Inter-School hockey. Jimmy added:

The E K (Sookunpoo) did not have a full secondary school until well after WWII. Their boys, those who were able, usually ended up at either Government or aided secondary schools for the final three years of their secondary education.

Jimmy had spoken to George Hong Choy, a former Hon. Secretary of the Hongkong Cricket league, who confirmed:

the Rumjahns went up to Queen's College while the Arcullis went to St Joseph's and even though these local Indian boys learnt their basic cricket at Sir E K, they didn't really flourish until they were at Queen's or St Joseph's.

On Jimmy Lowcock's suggestion, the author then wrote to Conrad Salat Rumjahn, son of Arthur Abdul Aziz Rumjahn, former Hong Kong Inter-porter, and grandson of Usuf Rumjahn, one of the first two Vice Presidents of the IRC. Conrad said:

In 1961· the 5 storey building was completed, the name SIR ELLIS KADOORIE AM/PM SCHOOL was adopted. There are classes running from 8:00 a.m. – 1:00 p.m. for the Indians or so-called local boys. The 1:30 p.m. – 6:30 p.m. was a Chinese school with different principals, teachers and curriculum.

and added that his father A A Rumjahn:

had devoted many afternoons to teach pupils of SEKS in IRC's play-ground to play cricket in the 1950s.

Without available records, no one seemed to know when cricket was first played by the Sir Ellis Kadoorie School for Indians. However, it seems they continued to play cricket after the Pacific war for a short period at schools' level in the 1950s.

Island School

Cricket at Island School was introduced in 1968 by the then Head of Geography, Keith Garner, who later became the Manager of the HKCC, now recently retired to France. Unlike their 'friendly' rival, King George V School, Island School was not blessed with a sports ground, so cricket had to struggle to secure a position as a mainstream sport.

In the early days the school was fortunate in being able to use CCC for net practice and Saturday morning matches for 13–14 year olds. The HKCC ground at Chater Road was also used for net practice during the 1968–69 season.

In 1974, the senior master, Mike Taylor, took the 'historic' step of forming the Islanders Cricket Club (the Islanders), which consisted of staff, parents and pupils to compete in the Saturday league. The Islanders won its first match against the Royal Navy in 1975. In the same year the school acquired its own cricket nets, perched precariously on top of one of the teaching blocks. Being only 20 metres in length, it barely sufficed. In those days a collection of CCC stalwarts – Keith Garner, Graham May, John Sharman and Gareth Buckland – helped with the coaching.

Successes as well as defeats have been plentiful over the years. One of the most notable 'embarrassments' was against St George's in 1976, when the school team was skittled out for 4 runs, with extras top scoring!

Early junior cricket prodigies were an Australian batsman, Paul McGrath, who opened for CCC at the age of 13, and 'Rob' Gill, who later joined KCC and went on to represent Hong Kong. The Islanders have since established themselves as a permanent member of the adult cricket scene under the respective captaincies of Mike Taylor, Bob Dewar, Chris Forse, Alan Honeyman, Peter Anderson (also a Hong Kong captain) and Bob Fotheringham.

Islanders shared the Gillette Plate in 1979–1980. They won the CCC Sixes in 1984, defeating KGV, LSW, HKCC and KCC in successive rounds. Mention should also be made of the 1983–84 and 1986–87 teams, both of which won ten or more matches in the Saturday league with only a token adult participation. The school's greatest victories were over HKCC Nomads in 1984, their only defeat in two years, and the PRC in the 1987 Gillette Plate Final. The Ebrahim Inter-School Sixes competition has been won several times, including a run of three successive victories in the late 1980s.

With the introduction of the Ted Wilson Trophy for senior boys in 1976, it was possible to play a school 1st XI for the first time. This knock-out cup is regarded as the premier Inter-School competition in Hong Kong, and the school emerged winners in 1984, 1991, 1992, and 1998 being runners-up on five occasions.

1990   Centaurs: 184–4 (S Brew 116*, M Beck 45)
Mar 3   Islanders: 186–2 (L Wark 95*, N Stearns 39*, R Seed 34)

Island School upset Centaurs in excellent win.

The school's most successful season was in 1990–91, when they finished third behind the strong HKCC Nomads and KCC Tartars. During the season they were 'aided and abetted' by Hong Kong representatives Nigel Stearns and Warren Symcox, with schoolboys Matthew

Johnson and Rohan Chandran performing well alongside their more illustrious elders.

Among the talented individuals who came to maturity as a result of Saturday league cricket were Damon Sharwood (who scored 1054 runs in 1983–84), Keith Parsons, Nadir Mirmohammadi, Garic Howles, Ayez Ebrahim, Indi Chakrabarti, Martin Lever and Rohan Chandran, who have all played a high standard of cricket in Hong Kong, UK or Australia in recent years.

Junior and Intermediate teams continue to play on Saturday mornings, made possible by staff members' altruistic support. Others who have also given their valuable time besides the CCC stalwarts were Mike Higgitt, Mike Taylor, Alan Riddy, Paul Jackson, Peter Clarke and, more recently, the first official Hong Kong coach, David Wilson. The school has also been blessed with a superb team of scorers, including Shelagh Dewar, Melanie Forse, Indrani Chakrabarti, Meera Chandran and Margaret Schofield.

The Islanders are indebted to KGV for providing a home ground, the HKCC for the use of their nets, and the HKCA for financial support.

At the end of the 1992–93 season, Island School cricket reached its first milestone, its 25th Anniversary.

The way ahead, tied in with the future of Hong Kong, is uncertain. But given a chance and continued support, the author feels sure that the spirit that has carried the school this far will see it confidently progress into the future.

Saturday League – Batting Performances 1974–75 to 1993–94

Season	Player	500 runs plus	Centuries
1978–79 a	P W Anderson	520 at 32.50	100* v KGV
1979–80	P W Anderson	604 at 43.14	
	K Parsons	752 at 31.33	133* v CCC
	N Mirmohammadi		101* v Police Strollers
1980–81	A Ebrahim	501 at 23.86	
1982–83	A Honeyman		106* v Royal Navy
1983–84	D Sharwood	1054 at 52.70 (8)	137 v CCC, 103* v Tartars & 103* v Saracens
1985–86	M Lever	507 at 28.20	
1986–87	M Lever	534 at 31.41	
1987–88	I Chakrabarti	706 at 39.22	121 v St George's
1988–89	L Wark	636 at 42.40	
1989–90	L Wark	752 at 62.67 (9)	
1991–92	M Johnson		125 v Police Strollers

Saturday League – Batting Performances (cont'd)

Season	Player	Centuries
1992–93	K Chandran	101* v Centaurs
1993–94	K Chandran	126 v HKCC Witherers
b	L Jayasinghe	117 v HKU

a Hong Kong captain from 1978 to 1986
b Sri Lankan appointed as assistant HKCA coach in 1993

(1) Position in averages
    KCC – Saracens & Tartars

Saturday League – Bowling Performances 1974–75 to 1993–94

Season	Player	50 wickets plus
1975–76	C Forse	56 at 16.57
1976–77	C Forse	61 at 14.72

King George V School

In Nathan Road, Kowloon, next to St Andrew's Church, is the permanent home of the Antiquities and Monuments Office. This building was originally the Kowloon British School, the forerunner of King George V School (KGV).

In 1900, Mr Ho Tung (later Sir Robert) donated $15,000 to the Government to erect a school in Kowloon. The foundation stone was laid on 20 July 1900 by the Governor Sir Henry Blake. The school was officially opened on 19 April 1902 as a primary school for some 60 pupils. Designed by Palmer & Turner, the building was a typical Victorian structure but adapted to local climatic conditions, with wide verandahs, high ceilings and pitched roofs.

The Kowloon British School was a co-educational primary school. It was not until after the 1914–18 war that pupil numbers rose above 100. The first headmaster was Benjamin James, a former master at Queen's College and the progenitor of their school magazine *The Dragon*.

Some secondary schooling was provided for girls till 1923, the boys having to cross the harbour to the Victoria English School on Leighton Hill. This arrangement was most unsatisfactory, so in 1923, the Kowloon British School catered for all students from 9 to 18 years. In December 1923, the name was changed to the Central British School (CBS).

By the 1930s, pupil numbers were reaching 300, so a move was made in September 1936 to new school premises in Homantin, where immediately postwar, CBS was opened to pupils of all races. The school is still on this site, being renamed King George V School in 1948.

Cricket was played in the 1930s against such schools as DBS, the Ellis Kadoorie School, La Salle, Queen's and St Joseph's Colleges, with friendlies against KCC 2nd XI and Service teams.

| 1933 | St Joseph's: | 98–7 | (G Windsor 28, Sharpham 5–19) |
| Nov 22 | CBS: | 69 | (Mr Mulcahy 27, H Asome 4–21) |

| 1934 | Royal Fleet Aux: | 114 | (Lacey 32, N B Whitley 4–20) |
| Mar 3 | C.B. Assn: | 78 | (Russell 5– 3) |

The CB Association was formed by old boys of the CBS. It was originally called the Kowloon British School Former Pupils Association.

| Mar 14 | CBS: | 36 (R Silva 4–11) |
| | La Salle: | 72 (L Gosano 18, R Holden 3–22) |

'Played at Recreio, La Salle passed the CBS score with five wickets down.'

| Mar 21 | CBS: | 18 (M Usuf 4–7, H Ali 4–2) |
| | Ellis Kadoorie: | 52 (Cassim 13) |

'... passed the CBS score with one wicket down.'

David Clinton, a senior master and cricket coach at KGV, who is writing a history of the school, mentioned that he had come across references '... balls were lost after being struck over the fence into the paddy fields below. After a game the players could stroll across the fields to Hung Hom and the beach for an evening swim.'

A tremendous impetus was given to sport after the opening of the new school at Homantin in 1936. The cricket team won 22 of 28 matches played in 1936–37; a second XI was also active, and a full programme of house matches instituted.

| 1937 | KCC: | 175–4 dec (A W Ramsay 40*, B D Lay 38, E F Fincher 34, D McLellan 3–46) |
| Mar 20 | CBS: | 80 (D E Street 18, R E Lee 2– 3, W L Mackenzie 3–19) |

Fincher, Lee and Ramsay were all Interport cricketers!

By 1938, there were three concrete practice wickets, and Messrs McLellan and Mulcahy became the first of a long line of teachers who had much to do with the promotion and success of cricket at KGV School. Such names as W Gegg, C Hosegood, N J Booker, R Holden and K Baxter were frequently mentioned.

1938   CBS: 77   (W Gegg 17, C N Matthews 4–19)
Mar 16 DBS: 90–7 (F J Lay 46*, W Gegg 5–26)

The best prewar player was F A 'Tony' Weller, who scored the first century on the school ground against an Old Boys' XI in 1939–40. Tony, a hard-hitting batsman, represented Hong Kong in the 1960s. School matches continued against DBS, La Salle and St Joseph's. David Clinton could not find any further mention of Queen's College, the school's early cricket nemesis.

After the Pacific war when the ground had been re-turfed in 1947, the indefatigable duo of McLellan and Mulcahy organised inter-form and house matches, but the school team friendly matches could not be resumed until 1948–49. M Koodiaroff and M Slater were the stars of the team, whilst B P Dhabher made his first appearance as a bowler. School matches were played against DBS, La Salle and St Joseph's.

The next season saw the school team enter the Second Division of the Hongkong Cricket League, with Buji Dhabher scoring the first KGV league 50. F Bottomley and B Dhabher were selected for the 'Rest of the League' against the champions, KCC. Near the end of the season, B Carnell and J Shroff made their first appearances for the school team. These two players, with Dhabher, until he left in 1951, dominated the school team in the early 1950s, and all three went on to gain representative honours for Hong Kong. They were ably supported by such players as Q Almao, J Basto, G Bendall, E McCosh and D Robb. From the mix of the names mentioned, it can readily be seen that cricket had also benefited from the opening of the school to all nationalities in 1947.

Jalu Shroff, described 'as an inspiring captain', scored a brilliant century against IRC 'B'. Clinton marks this, from available records, as the first league century by a KGV pupil. A magnificent four-run win against Recreio was another highlight of the 1954–55 season.

In 1959, KGV were at the receiving end of two remarkable bowling performances.

1959   KGV: 18   (O Adem 10–10)
Nov 7 IRC: 22–1

'Young IRC off spinner, Osman Adem, set an all-time Colony record by capturing 10 KGV wickets for 10 runs in 6.5 overs.'

292

Nov 14 HKU: 164–5 dec (A R Kitchell 60*, J T Hung 43)
        KGV: 9   (S M Teh 8–0)

'Six of the nine runs were extras!' Teh bowled 5.4 overs.

In the early 1960s, Frank Findlay, the headmaster and a former captain of the Hong Kong team, maintained the school's interest in cricket. Frank was tragically killed in a road accident in the UK in June 1963. Gopal Lalchandani emerged as an outstanding player, who later represented Hong Kong for many years. He had so many blazers he nearly opened a shop in Nathan Road! Tony Tebbutt, an all-round athlete of great ability, was also selected to play for Hong Kong.

1967–68 proved to be the school's most successful in the Second Division, finishing 4th after winning 11 of the 20 games played. Graham Varty spearheaded many of these victories with his record haul of 81 wickets at 6.10 each. Varty and Kanu Gohel each also scored over 390 runs.

1967   Centaurs: 100 (G Varty 6–19)
Oct 28   KGV: 70 (B Hemshall 5–15)

Nov 25   KGV: 115 (K Gohel 84*, J Beckett 2–18)
          SGS: 89 (T Self 36, A Gough 22, G Varty 8–18)

'Gohel and Varty manhandle St George's.'

The schoolboys were well supported and inspired with enthusiasm by teachers Graham Wills and Alec Reeve. Graham recalled an incident in the mid-1960s:

the school batted first and were shot out for 33 (grass wicket prior to present artificial one). Police decided to reverse their batting order – some 15 overs later they were all out for 31 to some very fast (and dangerous) 'wrong foot' bowling from Graham Varty, and a new boy from Australia, Rodney Howells.

1970–71 saw the names of the future 'spin twins', Bharat Gohel and Yarman Vachha, appear for the first time. They have both since represented Hong Kong on numerous occasions, and were both in the Dermot Reeve-coached 1994 Hong Kong squad for the ICC Trophy in Kenya.

KGV withdrew from the league after the 1970–71 season, to form with DBS, Island School and St George's schools' cricket on a formal basis. The Schools' competition settled down after three years, allowing KGV to rejoin the league in 1974–75 to a changed format. KGV would now play in the new Saturday league, which included many of the best players in Hong Kong. Under Clinton's captaincy, the team initially consisted mainly of teachers, this emphasis gradually giving way to pupils by the end of the 1970s. The school team won the Saturday League Plate in 1977–78.

1975   CCC: 136–8 (A Hale 37, I Talbot 7–53)
Nov 1 KGV: 97–7   (R Cooper 3–18)

In 1980–81, a strong school team, led by David Clinton, had many difficult hurdles to overcome during their march towards the Gillette Cup final.

1981   KGV: 165–5 (D A Reeve 71, D A Hall 32*, B Hemshall 3–32)
Apr 4 Centaurs: 157   (P Olsen 51, J Hughes 47, D A Reeve 5–14)

KGV, riding on their confidence, then defeated a strong Army side at Sookunpoo in the semi-finals. Now for the final against HKCC Nomads, always a strong side to be reckoned with.

1981   KGV: 130–5 (D A Reeve 45, J Evans 34*)
Apr 18 Nomads: 134–8 (J Hollioake 38, D O'Hara 5–34)

Paul Dunnett, not known for his batting, scored a four off the last ball to win this nail-biting Gillette Cup final.

The highest Saturday league position was achieved in 1987–88, when the school came third out of 18 participating teams.

1984   Sentinels: 142   (B Wigley 50, S Myles 5–31, R Marsden 3–30)
Feb 18 KGV: 143–3 (J Evans 75)

In addition to David Clinton, many post-1970s pupils have represented Hong Kong: Craig Dean, David Evans, Bharat Gohel, David Jones, Martin Lever, Frank MacLeod, Jason and Rob Marsden, Simon Myles, Dermot Reeve, Ravi Sujanani, Ian Talbot and Yarman Vachha.

David Clinton, Craig Dean and Dermot Reeve have also achieved the ultimate honour in local cricket, being chosen 'Player of the Year' whilst playing for the school. Dermot, Warwickshire County captain (1994–96), has played for England in Test matches and One-Day Internationals, whilst Simon Myles has played an important role in the highly successful Staffordshire Minor Counties side.

Since 1988, the School side has been less successful in terms of league position. However, with Jim Francis as Head of PE, not only joining

Clinton in the league side, but giving great impetus to the sport in the lower echelons of the school, there are now more boys playing cricket than ever before. It should be noted, however, that although between 1976–1988 the inter-school Ted Wilson Trophy almost became KGV's exclusive property, since 1989 it has not been won once. However, the tradition of cricket is still felt very strongly in a school where it remains an activity of major interest and importance. The self-sufficient identity of the Saturday side that genuinely represents the school community remains jealously guarded.

David Clinton, February 1994

David Clinton's immense contribution has done much for Schools' cricket and cricket at KGV in particular, and he deservedly should close this brief chapter on cricket at KGV.

Second Division/Saturday League – Batting Performances 1965–66 to 1993–94

Season	Player	500 runs plus	Centuries
1967–68	G Varty		102* v Crusaders
1974–75	D Clinton	810 at 62.31 (1)	110* v RAF
1975–76	D Clinton	1019 at 78.38 (1)	108* v CCC
1976–77	D Clinton	893 at 55.81 (3)	
1977–78	I Talbot	578 at 30.42	
1978–79	F McLeod	514 at 23.36	126 v Police 'B'
	I Talbot		110* v Islanders
1979–80	F McLeod	670 at 37.22	102* v Centaurs
	D A Reeve	566 at 29.79	
	D A Jones	605 at 26.30	
1980–81	D A Reeve	1029 at 64.31 (2)	145 v Tartars & 143* v CCC
	D A Jones	860 at 45.26 (5)	111* v Nomads
	D Evans	641 at 33.73	
1981–82	D A Jones	930 at 51.67 (5)	
	S Myles	519 at 25.95	
1982–83	J Evans		120* v Islanders & 113 v HKU
	S Myles		103* v HKU
1983–84	S Myles	617 at 36.29	
	J Evans	725 at 34.52	106 v Tartars
	D A Reeve		141* v Witherers
1984–85	D Clinton	613 at 51.10 (8)	
1985–86	C Dean	496 at 49.60 (9)	

295

Second Division/Saturday League – Batting Performances (cont'd)

Season	Player	500 runs plus	Centuries
	J Ellis	563 at 31.30	
1986–87	C Dean	604 at 60.40 (1)	
	J Ellis	552 at 50.18 (6)	125* v DBS
	S Marsden	525 at 40.38	
1987–88	C Dean	731 at 121.83 (1)	117* v Nomads & 110* v Witherers
	R Marsden	394 at 98.50 (2)	
	J Marsden	561 at 51.00 (9)	
1988–89	D A Jones	1032 at 79.38 (2)	133* v CCC, & 115 v Army, 104* v Centaurs, & 100* v Kai Tak
	I Ashraf		132* v DBS
1989–90	D A Jones	775 at 64.58 (7)	113 v Gap Ramblers & 105* v Strollers
	J Francis	539 at 44.92	111 v CCC & 100* v Centaurs
	C Dean		123* v LSW
1990–91	D A Jones	669 at 60.82 (5)	129* v HKU
	C Dean		158* v Strollers & 120* v Army
1991–92	J Francis	650 at 43.30	101* v Gap Ramblers
1992–93	J Francis	568 at 47.33	135* v Saracens
	R Sujanani	631 at 39.44	104* v HKU & 101 v Nomads
	D Clinton		111 v Tartars

J Francis & R Sujanani 205* (1st) v HKU (6)

Season	Player	500 runs plus	Centuries
1993–94	R Sujanani		149* v Strollers
	J Francis		115 v HKU & 105* v Kai Tak

(1)   Position in averages
(1st) Wicket partnership over 200 runs
       HKCC – Gap Ramblers/Nomads/Witherers
       KCC – Crusaders/Saracens/Tartars
       Police – Strollers

Second Division/Saturday League – Bowling Performances 1965–66 to 1993–94

Season	Player	40 wickets plus	6 plus (for 50 runs or less)
1965–66	G Varty	59 at 8.24 (3) (5 plus four times)	7–10 v HKU, 6–22 v LSW

Second Division/Saturday League – Bowling Performance (cont'd)

Season	*Player*	*40 wickets plus*	*6 plus* (for 50 runs or less)
	R Howell	59 at 9.86 (5)	6–18 v CCC, 6–19 v HKU
	K Gohel	36 at 7.97 (2) (exceptional)	8–15 v LSW, 6–31 v Centaurs & 'hat-trick' v Centaurs
1966–67	G Varty	57 at 13.60	
1967–68	G Varty	81 at 6.10 (1) (6 plus seven times)	8–18 v St George's & 6–19 v Centaurs
1975–76	I Talbot	43 at 18.26	7–53 v CCC
1976–77	I Talbot	61 at 14.87	
1977–78	I Talbot	47 at 15.28	
1978–79	D A Reeve	42 at 17.76	
	I Talbot		7–29 v HKCC Nomads
1979–80	D A Reeve	47 at 15.11 (6)	
1980–81	D A Reeve	47 at 11.59 (4)	'hat-trick' v Army
	S Myles	61 at 15.77 (only bowler 50 plus)	7–39 v LSW

(1) Position in averages

La Salle College

Brother Aimar, who was to become the first Principal of La Salle College, purchased a site at the very edge of Kowloon in 1932, and La Salle College was opened with the pupils of St Joseph's Branch School forming the nucleus of the student body.

After the outbreak of the European war in 1939, the Government used the school as an internment camp for enemy aliens: the Japanese took over the premises as a hospital during their occupation of Hong Kong, expelling the Brothers, who did not return until 1946.

In 1949, the British Army took it over as a Military Hospital, and it was another ten years before the Brothers could return to the college. Dr Albert (later Sir Albert) Rodrigues and others had helped to obtain the return of the premises to the college. In the meantime the college had to operate in cramped barrack quarters in Perth Street, Kowloon.

When La Salle was built in 1932, its architectural beauty and magnificence held people in awe. 47 years later, it was still magnificent externally, but functionally totally inadequate to cope with pupil numbers and their requirements. So in 1979, the college authority decided that in

297

its best interests, it would be more practical to knock down the old edifice and in conjunction with a local public property company, construct a new building with up-to-date facilities such as centrally air-conditioned classrooms, a spacious library, a soundproof auditorium, two lecture theatres, an indoor gymnasium and standard-sized swimming pool together with an all-weather track and artificially turfed football pitch. The downside was that it lost a substantial area of land for residential development right next to the college. It was hoped that with modern facilities, the work and progress of the college would be guaranteed for many years, making La Salle one of Hong Kong's major schools for boys.

Little information on cricket has been found. The present Principal, Bro. Francis O'Rourke, informed the author that:

La Salle was taken over as a hospital during the war years, and as a result practically all records etc. were lost. La Salle ceased to play cricket after the war, so I am sorry I cannot help you in this matter.

1934   CBS: 36 (R Silva 4–11)
Mar 14 La Salle: 72 (L Gosano 18, Holden 3–22)

'La Salle passed the CBS score with five wickets down.' This match was played on the Recreio ground in King's Park, Kowloon.

It appears that many Portuguese attended La Salle College in prewar days. Micky Remedios, who captained Recreio in the 1950s, informed the author that while still a schoolboy at La Salle he played cricket for Recreio. Arnaldo de Oliveira Sales, 'Sonny' to his many friends, President of Club de Recreio and the Club Lusitano, Hong Kong, is a distinguished old boy.

Queen's College

Queen's College, originally the Central School/Government Central School, founded in 1862, was situated in Gough Street, Hong Kong Island, until 1889. In 1892, Mr W A Machell coached his non-Chinese boys in cricket and football in the lower playground. He had hoped that healthy exercise would wear them out and make them less lively in class. In the same year, Charlie Wallace, an old boy and member of the Hong Kong Interport team, was drowned when the *SS Bokhara* sank off the Pescadores in a typhoon whilst returning to Hong Kong from Shanghai.

In 1894, new premises were built in Aberdeen Street, with space for three playgrounds. The school was renamed Victoria College at the Governor's suggestion, but due to a similarly named school in Pottinger Street, it was renamed Queen's College on 31 January 1894. Since then the school has been known to the Chinese as the 'College of Royal Benevolence.'

In 1897, two sports grounds, the Wong Nai Chung ground at Happy Valley, and the other behind Causeway Bay, where the present Queen's College is situated, were used for cricket and soccer. The first recorded school cricket match was played in 1899, when the 1st XI, captained by D Rumjahn, comprising eight Indians, two Portuguese and a Jewish boy, defeated the Diocesan School at Happy Valley.

By 1901, several Chinese boys were playing in the 1st XI, still captained by D Rumjahn. Chinese boys in Class 4 started their own cricket club, captained by Choa Po Min. Seniors coached them in the lower playground.

> Some shaped very well, but others – could not get out of the Chinese habit of standing with clasped hands hidden in their sleeves, catching the ball being furthest from their thoughts.
>
> Gwenneth Stokes, *Queen's College, 1862–1962*

In 1902, the 1st XI was captained by Hung Kwok Leung, the first time by a Chinese. In fact he was an Eurasian, his English name being Joseph Overbeck Anderson. In the same year, Mr R E O 'Dickie' Bird, a keen cricketer and nephew of the famous Yorkshire captain Lord Hawke, joined the staff.

Next year, Choa Po Min was 1st XI captain and Ko Po Sham (Francis Grose) was vice-captain. 'Dickie' Bird played for Hong Kong from 1903–20, while Mr Hugh Arthur, an old boy, played for Hong Kong from 1897–1904. Hugh Arthur was killed in WWI. In 1904, 'two and a half days break in honour of Interport matches played in Hong Kong', was added to the annual school holidays, no doubt in honour of Messrs Arthur and Bird.

In 1909, in the Interport match against Shanghai, the 6 foot 3 inches moustached 'Dickie' Bird had a match analysis of 9 for 81 runs. In the 1920 Interport against Shanghai, he captured 7 for 47 in their second innings.

The few Chinese who joined their English and Indian colleagues at cricket were 'athletic curiosities'. Chinese students were still showing very little interest in cricket, but Indian students were missing 'tiffin' in order to practice at the nets. Old boys remembered how Mr Fletcher, an indefatigable cricket coach, with his little band of enthusiastic Indian students would come puffing and panting into the afternoon classroom, not having heard the bell!

In 1921, in a match against *HMS Ambrose*, Douglas Laing took 6–16, including the 'hat-trick'. Mr F J de Rome, a master, and A A Rumjahn, an old boy, played for Hong Kong in the Interport against Shanghai.

In 1931, Archie Hung, head prefect, captained the 1st XI to their most successful season.

1932   Queen's: 86–6 dec (M el Arculli 37, Y P Tsui 24, E Esmail 3–10)

Mar 29 St Joseph's: 84–5   (H Asome 30, A Rumjahn 28*, M el Arculli 4–25)

'... Queen's College was nearly beaten by St Joseph's.'

Other Queen's players: G Lee, S Lee, O el Arculli, A R Markar, M Afzal, F R Abbas, M A Wahab, A H Suffiad, A M Abbas.
Other St Joseph's players: E Souza, H Ozorio, G Souza, S Hamet, T Jeffery, R Laurel, A Bakar, A Esmail.

In the same year, two old boys, A H Madar and A R Minu, played well in the Interport against Shanghai. Both had received their first cricket coaching from the 'indefatigable' Mr Fletcher, in the lower playground on matting over concrete.

1933   Queen's: 119–6 dec (M el Arculli 39 retd, W Abbas 4–52)
Nov 22 Ellis Kadoorie: 121–8   (M Singh 27, W Abbas 26, M Afzal 4–20)

This match was played on the IRC ground at Sookunpoo.

1934   DBS: 133   (G T Lee 34, Broadbridge 29, B Singh 2–18)
Mar 14 Queen's: 137–3 (M el Arculli 76, Y P Tsui 43*)

The Causeway Bay sportsground, which was renamed the Queen's Recreation Ground in 1913 solely for the use of Queen's College, was re-turfed in 1934.

Just prior to the Pacific war, cricket was still a mystery to most Chinese pupils. One conscientious master spent hours reading and explaining the cricket match described in *Tom Brown's Schooldays*, but to no avail. The 'Chinese' previously mentioned as members of the 1st XI were in fact all Eurasians.

When the Japanese attacked Hong Kong in December 1941, the school building known as the 'Old Lady of Aberdeen Street', constructed in 1889, was badly damaged by shell-fire and later looted. A building at No. 26 Kennedy Road was used as temporary premises for Queen's College until

22 September 1950, when Lady Victoria Lo cut the ribbon, whilst her husband Sir Man Kam Lo opened the oak door with a gold key and declared the new school building officially open. The two-storey building is situated in Causeway bay, where the Queen's Recreation ground was located.

Abbas el Arculli and A H Rumjahn, former pupils, became leading figures in the founding of IRC, Arculli as President, and Rumjahn as the first captain of the 1st XI. Although Queen's College itself no longer participates directly in Hong Kong cricket, their enthusiastic masters in days gone by certainly assisted some of their keen and talented pupils to take part in local cricket leagues and also gain representative honours playing for Hong Kong.

St Joseph's College

St Joseph's College was founded in 1875 out of a reorganised St Saviour's School. During the author's research into the history of Queen's College 1862–1962, he came across references to cricket matches with the Diocesan Boys' School and St Joseph's College.

This reference was followed up with a letter to Bro. Thomas, the present Principal of St Joseph's College, asking for some information on the years when his college played cricket in Hong Kong. A reminder letter brought the following response from Bro. Thomas: 'I deserve to be hit over the head with a cricket bat! Sorry for not replying to your letter of January 13th.'

He also enclosed a comment on cricket from their 1933 school magazine, plus a photocopy of a photograph showing nine members of the school team, which the author has since discovered was taken in front of the original IRC matshed pavilion.

The cricket comment read:

During the course of the year our cricket eleven played several clubs and a few schools. Considering that we are newcomers in this branch of sport we did very well. We won two matches against DBS and suffered defeat twice at the hands of our old rivals, the Queen's. Of eight other matches, we won three, drew three, and lost two. I take this opportunity to thank the Hongkong Cricket League for its generous financial help, the Indian Recreation Club, the Club de Recreio, the Craigengower Club, and the University Club for the use of their respective grounds.

Sir Albert Rodrigues, a distinguished St Joseph's Old Boy reminisced:

301

In my time at St Joseph's College, it was mainly baseball that was played, but I recall the occasion when we arranged a match with the Ellis Kadoorie School and obtained the use of the Civil Service Club, the ground diagonally across from the CCC. [The land is now where the Volunteer HQ lies – 1994.] The French teacher was to arrange everything including tea, which we told him as hosts we had to provide. Imagine our dismay when we found that he had taken us literally on this, and produced several large chatties of tea and some soft drinks only. We had to rush off to nearby restaurants for sandwiches and cakes – but this was not all. Our team, mostly baseballers, without knowledge of cricket rules, but with a 'good eye', and when batting promptly hit the ball, dropped their bats and ran!

Sir Albert said he did not play much cricket after those embarrassing moments at school. DBS in those days was the best school side, benefitting much from the guidance of J L Youngsaye and later from Jimmy Lowcock.

As many records were lost during the war years in Hong Kong, it has been difficult to gather any information on some of the schools, never mind on matters pertaining solely to cricket. However, while at the British Library at Colindale, North London, the author did find a few scores relating to matches played by St Joseph's.

1933　Ellis Kadoorie:　54　(W Abbas 26, C Amery 5–18)
　　　　St Joseph's:　　143　(A H Bakar 52, Y Esmail 30, W Abbas 6–48)

This match was played on the IRC ground.

Nov 22　St Joseph's: 98–7　(G Windsor 28, Sharpham 5–19)
　　　　CBS:　　　　69　(Mr Mulcahy 27, H Asome 4–21)

This match was played on the Recreio ground at King's Park.

Arthur White from Exmouth, Devon, England, grandson of Henry White who emigrated from Exmouth to Hong Kong in the 1880s, and who was probably a founder member of Craigengower, said in a recent letter to the author:

I was a pupil at St Joseph's from 1932 to 1939. In the mid 1930s cricket went into decline. However, about 1937, the maths teacher Hugh Asome formed a team. We played under the title 'Asome's Eleven'. I was wicket-keeper. Other members were: Fred (Buster)

302

Hollands, Ronald Ho, brother of Algy Ho, who was killed when the Japs landed, and Eric Ho, later of the HK Legislative Council. The Souza brothers both played for S.J.C. in the early 1930s with A Bakar, Y Esmail and W Abbas. The games were mostly played at IRC.

INTER HONG CRICKET

Inter-Hong cricket started in Shanghai between Jardines (Ewo), Butterfield & Swire (Taikoo), Dodwells, and The Hongkong and Shanghai Bank (Wayfoong). According to Stuart Barnes, these four senior 'Hongs' did not allow any other Hong 'pretenders' to join in the competition!

1924	Ewo:	188	(W W Mackenzie 52 retd, G H Piercy 45)
Nov 22	Taikoo:	47	(H E Hollands 5–18, W B Carnaby 3–16)

This match, easily won by Jardines, was played on the CRC ground.

1932	B & S:	210–4	(R H Dowler 102, H B Williamson 35)
Apr 9	HK Bank:	150	(E W Stagg 61*)

After the Communist takeover of China in 1949, the 'Hong' matches were traditionally played annually on the HKCC Chater Road ground until it closed in 1975, then continued at their new ground at Wong Nai Chung Gap Road, Hong Kong Island.

1952	Bank:	202	(P C Annesley 39*, P E Hutson 33, J M Beazley
Mar 23			25, J A Borthwick 22, J V Sellors 5–70, C
			Barclay 3–83)
	Jardines:	96	(D I Bosanquet 33, R G Craig 5–59, J K Mills
			3–30)

Michael Turner and Freddie Knightly were playing for the victorious Bank side.

1954	Swires:	170	(A E V Brown 65, J Lancashire 34, C J B Leader 22,
			F Young 5–53)
Nov 14	Bank:	170	(R E H Nelson 49, S T B Lever 43, F Young 39, A
			Brown 6–44)

This must have been a 'nail-biter'; unfortunately I only found the scores.

1956	Swires:	69	(P D Soughan 4–7, F J Purcell 4–15)
Dec 2	Bank:	70–8	(P D Soughan 24, T G C Knight 6–18)

1957   Bank: 138 (C W D Hall 60, G M Mills 4–50, H Barton 3–41)
Feb 3   Jardines: 117 (N D Booker 31, H Barton 26, R M Gault 6–47, P
                        Soughan 4–36)

In July 1968, the Inter-Hong matches were briefly reported in the *The Thistle*, Jardines' corporate magazine:

> The Barton Trophy, the subject of the traditional four-way cricket competition each year between Jardines, Butterfield & Swire, Dodwells, and The Hongkong and Shanghai Bank, went to the Bankers in the 1967–68 round of matches.
> The Jardines side was hampered by the unavailability of several leading players, and could manage only one win in the three matches played. The success came against Dodwells by 23 runs following sound batting performances by Cyril Blott (62) and Ian Pullen (52*). Dodwells started well, and looked to have the game well in hand at 135 for four, but Stuart Barnes, with five wickets for 35 runs, was instrumental in bundling out the side for 157.
> Jardines looked comfortable against the Bank with 171 runs on the board, John Heywood (35), but could not capitalise in the field. The Bank coasted to a relatively easy eight wickets win.
> A powerful Butterfield & Swire line-up declared at 271 for nine in the final match, and routed Jardines for 87 for an easy win.

1973   Jardines: 214 (R Wright 108*)
Dec 22 Dodwells: 118 (R Henley 3–9, M Costello 3 wickets)

> 'Jardines batting first, amassed a total of 214 runs – the highest total scored for eight years. The main feature was undoubtedly the performance of Russell Wright who scored 108 not out. (18 4s & 2 6s)'

1974   Swires: 124 (W Downey 4–47, T Lillywhite 3–27)
Dec 7   Jardines: 104 (H Wilken 26)

> 'After losing the toss, Jardines bowled out Swires for 124 runs. Bill Downey once again proved his worth by taking 4–47. The early dismissals of Lunn and Barnes for 14 runs was a sharp setback for Jardines.'

1980   Jardines: 154
Mar 16 Dodwells: 155–9 (I L J Stevens 81)

This was the last recorded match between Jardines and Dodwells.

1992   Jardines: 254–1 (M Wiggett 105*, J Weston 75*)
        Bank: 105

Jardines, captained by Steve Foster, won the toss and rapidly scored
their runs in the allotted 35 overs. '... saw Jardines emerge victorious
by 149 runs, one of the largest winning margins for many years.'

1993   Jardines: 293–6 (P Fitzgerald 103, R Rittson-Thomas 90, R
                          Langford 31)
Mar 21 Bank: 180   (J Hennessy 68, W Manning 59, J Tedd 4–23, S
                          Grant 3–20)

Jardines obviously intend to extend their winning streak having
recently 'recruited' the Hong Kong captain Pat Fordham, who is
employed by one of their subsidiary companies (MPFC).

1995   Bank: 180   (R Rittson-Thomas 5–22)
May   Jardines: 181–1 (N Robinson 99*, S Foster 46*, H Wilken 27)

This emphatic victory at KCC, after the earlier defeat of Swires, ensured
that Jardines retained the Barton Cup. As this match was Harry Wilken's
last for Jardines before his 'enforced' transfer to Bermuda, Tim Addison
(Bank) had organised a special farewell cheer for this stalwart of Jardines.
    Swires defeated both the Hongkong Bank and Jardines to win back the
Barton Cup in 1995–96, but the last match was not played until early
1997. It seems that a combination of fewer expatriates, fewer grounds and
Harry Wilken no longer around to get the machinery moving, may see the
end of this competition.

The Barton Cup

1952–53	Dodwells		1973–74	Swires
1953–54	Hongkong Bank		1974–75	Swires
1954–55	Jardines		1975–76	Swires
1955–56	Swires		1976–77	Hongkong Bank
1956–57	Dodwells		1977–78	Jardines
1957–58	Hongkong Bank		1978–79	Jardines & Swires (J)
1958–59	Jardines & Hongkong Bank (J)		1979–80	Swires
1959–60	Dodwells		1980–81	Jardines
1960–61	Hongkong Bank		1981–82	Jardines
1961–62	Swires		1982–83	Swires
1962–63	Swires		1983–84	Swires
1963–64	Swires		1984–85	Swires

1964–65	Jardines		1985–86	Swires
1965–66	Dodwells		1986–87	Swires
1966–67	Jardines		1987–88	Swires
1967–68	Hongkong Bank		1988–89	Swires
1968–69	Hongkong Bank		1989–90	Swires
1969–70	Hongkong Bank		1990–91	Swires
1970–71	Hongkong Bank		1991–92	Swires
1971–72	Hongkong Bank & Jardines (J)		1992–93	Jardines
1972–73	Jardines		1993–94	Jardines
			1994–95	Jardines
			1995–96	Swires

(J) Joint winners

The Barton Cup, presented by Hugh Barton, the then 'Taipan' of Jardines, was first competed for in 1952. Four 'Hongs' became three when Dodwells withdrew in the early 1980s.

CHARITY CRICKET

The Taverners' squad for the tour to Hong Kong in October 1989 was in three distinct parts:

(a) dedicated cricketers whose entire adult life had been primarily motivated by their unstinting service to the great game – Peter Skellern, Richard Stilgoe, Bill Wiggins, Christopher Blake and the President, Tim Rice;

(b) casual carefree dilettante playboys, denizens of every top showbiz haunt, to whom the twin imposters of success or failure with bat or ball were matters of little import – D I Gower, J E Emburey, N G Cowans, J D Carr, F M Engineer and M J K Smith, and

(c) Caroline Driver, who superbly handled the tour's finance, management and travel. At very short notice she managed to upgrade to club class ten members of the team, 'only the President suffered, forced to slum it in the middle of the plane for the first time since *Jesus Christ Superstar* flopped in Amritsar in '76.'

Sham and Gopa Chakrabarti met the squad at Kai Tak and bussed them to Hong Kong Island's Grand Hyatt Hotel, not yet finished – 'but as is the case with W Wiggins, the few parts that do work do so very well.'

After the customary press conference and a freshen-up, the XI reported for a happy hour with the cream of Hong Kong's Senior Service society at HMS Tamar.

306

'The view over the harbour was as breath-taking as Farokh Engineer's aftershave and it was a glowing party that went down to the
Go Down Club for dinner and later to Jo Bananas where Norman
Cowans began his determined quest to by-pass the 20 year wait for
membership by qualifying as a playing member.'

The following evening a gala ball in aid of both the Taverners' and numerous Hong Kong charities was, fortuitously for the Taverners', held at their
hotel. Richard and Peter's sensational act was received with ecstasy by the
'well-heeled mob of nobs that had flocked to the Grand Hyatt.'

The following morning, a bright-eyed and bushy-tailed team crossed
back to the mainland to do battle at the KCC, 'the pictureque park that
nestles amid a forest of both man-made and natural high-rise construction.'

'Fighting off the long-term handicap of a shot shoulder and the newer
threat of the galloping trots, Gower played as if E R Dexter was in
the well-appointed pavilion, impressing all with his gay bladesman-
ship.'

That evening the hard-worked side split into two groups – the Stilgoe/
Skellern axis repaired to the Hong Kong Football Club to rib-tickle the
capacity crowd there, while the pros entertained with cricketing yarns at
the HKCC, leaving the crowd that had turned out at KCC wondering
what they had done wrong to miss out on the Taverners' wit!

Sunday saw the Taverners' at the Army ground at Sookunpoo pitted
against Sir Denys Robert's XI. The match balls were being delivered by
helicopter for Lady Fiona to commence the proceedings. 'What do I do
with these balls!' she was heard to remark.

Various stalls had been set up on the adjoining area by an army of
hardworking helpers for public spending purposes. The match proceeded:

'Skellern pocketed the first amateur's catch of the tour and Gower
two quite sensational ones off the tempting floaters of Stilgoe. Farokh
was here there and everywhere, operating both as stumper and pur-
veyor of leg-breaks, all but simultaneously. Emburey cut a dash in the
showers. A magnificent Welsh male choir entertained in the luncheon
interval boosted by the vocal skills of the Taverners' middle order.'

That evening The Hong Kong Club proved to be the most delightful of
hosts, while later the hottest of Szechuan meals was served in honour of
the impeccable Miss Driver. If Gower had partaken, he could have 'flown
back under his own power'.

307

The Chakrabartis were charming hosts and with the Taverners' coffers being swelled by £3,000, not to mention the assistance given to several Hong Kong charities, the venture must go down as one of the most enjoyable and worthwhile. [Mostly squeezed from Tim Rice's article in the 1990–91 *HKCA Handbook*]

KCC Charity Sixes, the inaugural event won in 1991 by Thomas Spencer (captained by Dai Thomas), has also become a feature in a more light-hearted cricket programme for the benefit of the less fortunate members of the Hong Kong community.

The charity weekend of 12/13 December 1992 saw quite a few new overseas 'Stars' supporting the event, who were distributed amongst the various teams.

AUSTRALIA	ENGLAND	INDIA
Trevor Chappell	Neil Foster	Farokh Engineer
Alan Davidson	Graeme Fowler	Madan Lal
David Hookes	Wayne Larkins	Gunduppa Vishwanath
Graham Yallop	Matthew Maynard	
	Mark Nicholas	
	James Whitaker	

At the KCC sixes on the first day, Thomas Spencer, with visiting stars Neil Foster and Graeme Fowler as back-up, retained their trophy in an all-business final against BUPA, who had Matthew Maynard as support. A total of 81 was brushed aside by a breezy 'Fozzie' Foster innings of 34.

At the HKCC the next day for the double-wicket competition on a warm, sunny day, the professionals agreed the HKCC format 'presented an interesting tactical challenge'. Strines I (Trevor Chappell and David Hookes) edged out Poms II (Mark Nicholas and James Whitaker) in the final. Functions on 11 (KCC) and 13 (HKCC) December were relaxed, enjoyable and entertaining affairs, enhanced by the highly amusing anecdotes provided by the professionals.

These charitable events, run by many volunteers and backed by the generosity of financial concerns, still mainly stage managed by Sham and his wife Gopa, have continued to the present day. Familiar and new overseas faces, cricket and comic, seem to turn up each time; it must be the 'Szechuan Specials' they keep coming back for!

In order to put Hong Kong's charitable cricket onto a more official footing, the HKCA set up its own charitable trust for just this purpose.

308

INTERPORT CRICKET

In 1866, 15 years after the founding of the HKCC, a long series of Interport cricket matches was inaugurated between Hong Kong and Shanghai: at this same time W G Grace (aged 18) was enjoying one of his greatest seasons, scoring 173 not out for the Gentlemen of the South v The Players, and 224 not out for England against Surrey. The Hong Kong and Shanghai Interport series lasted until 1948, just prior to the Communist takeover of China in 1949.

With the emergence of the first Interport match in 1866, the foundation was laid for the highest grade of competitive cricket to be played amongst selected representatives of the big ports of the Far East – Hong Kong, Shanghai and Singapore. In those days, just past the middle of the Victorian era, lob or underarm bowling was the only legalised method of delivering the ball to the batsman – the MCC had as yet not permitted 'square arm' or 'shoulder high' bowling.

In January 1890, another series began between Hong Kong and the Straits Settlements (the 'Straits'). The Straits came into being in 1819 and comprised Penang, Malacca and Singapore. The Straits team has also been known as All Malaya.

After Singapore left the Federation in 1968, that series continued with separate Interports being played against Malaysia and Singapore. The standard of cricket remained generally high until more recent years when the non-promotion of cricket in their schools led to a lowering of standards. Hopefully the position will improve again under the right influential leadership.

Triangular tournaments, mostly played in Hong Kong, took place from 1897 to 1933, involving Hong Kong, Shanghai and the Straits/Malaya. In the first triangular tournament in 1897, because the Straits had an exceptionally talented side, beating both Hong Kong and Shanghai teams by an innings, an additional match was arranged between the Straits and a combined Hong Kong & Shanghai XI. The Straits thrashed the combined side by an innings and 231 runs!

The Straits: 381 (R M Mackenzie 163, Lt Woodroffe 74, T R Hubback 58)
Hong Kong 86
& Shanghai: 64 (J G MacTaggart 6–39)

Mackenzie from Perak also took 8–81 in the match.

Major Rowland Bowen, editor of the *Cricket Quarterly*, said: 'It could be argued at periods before the last war that all Malaya fielded a first class team.'

It is interesting to note that the nomenclature 'Interport Cricket' is characteristic to people resident in the Far East only. The term is easily discernable in the Far East, but it might require a second thought to understand its precise meaning when read by cricketers not acquainted with this particular part of the world.

Interport Cricket meant cricket initially played between the best representative teams selected by the ports of Shanghai, Hong Kong and Singapore, thus 'Interport'.

The standard of cricket in these competitive matches might be equated with those of the better cricket clubs in England. Some of the best Interport cricketers have played first-class cricket in the British Isles; the name Alec Pearce, of Kent and Hong Kong, comes readily to mind. Others are listed in the appendices.

Arthur Rumjahn writing on Interport cricket, mentioned other names such as R E O Bird, 'that great wizard with the ball, who could give life to a piece of red spheroidal but dead leather'; his contempory, 'Lobster' Reed, who carried on where R E O left off; A C I 'Acky' Bowker, 'a glutton of power in bowling, batting and on the field'; Captain Havelock-Davies, the Oxford Blue, 'who made many a good batsman look that colour'; A A Claxton, 'who played those beautiful off shots.' Others such as Dr J A Lowson, Frank Pereira, 'Fatty' Minu and Teddy Fincher – must not be allowed to slip into oblivion. The author remembers some others who were still playing in the early 1950s, that debonair Shanghai all-rounder Donald Leach of Interport vintage (1920), Arthur Rumjahn (1921) and Lt/Col Harry Owen Hughes (1923).

In the more recent postwar era, such Service players as Capt Bill Withall (Worcestershire 2nd XI) and Major Pat Howard-Dobson; Cpl 'Rocky' Daniel, an attacking West Indian batsman from Barbados who had played his earlier cricket in Jamaica and England; Buddy Carnell, a fast bowler who was greatly 'feared' by the Malaysians; Jalu Shroff, the Parsee with the 'trotting' run and the superb big match temperament, and Dermot Reeve, the only Hong Kong-born cricketer to play for England – the last three named learnt their cricket at KGV School in Hong Kong; Des Greenwood, a useful all-rounder who went about his job quietly and efficiently; John Fawcett (Middlesex 2nd XI) a very effective all-rounder; Carl Myatt, another great wizard with the ball; Peter Davies, a most prolific scorer in local cricket; John Bygate, the 'dour' Yorkshireman, another heavy scorer with the cultured left-handed blade; Peter Anderson, known affectionately as 'Plod', remembered as a 'no-nonsense' Hong Kong captain and an administrative trailblazer, and the 'stylist' Nigel Stearns, who holds the record for the highest score of 169 in Interport cricket. There are many other accomplished cricketers who have graced the local scene and in other country fields whom I have not mentioned; to them my apologies.

The ambition of most cricketers in the Orient was to gain selection into their respective national teams, Interport representation being the ultimate 'goal' of all cricketers in that part of the world.

The Interports were played at the HKCC and the KCC in Hong Kong; the Shanghai Cricket Club; the SCC and the Singapore Recreation Club in Singapore; the Royal Selangor Club, Kuala Lumpur, the Kilat Club and the Penang Sports Club, Penang, in Malaysia. Brief histories of the Shanghai, Singapore and Royal Selangor clubs appear elsewhere in this book.

There were many other 'interports' played in the Far East, mainly for pleasure, of a less competitive nature and generally of a lower standard. These are mentioned briefly here, so as not to give the impression that only the three main ports played cricket in the Far East.

Prior to the Pacific war, various 'foreign elements' were involved in cricket. Batavia played Singapore, Kobe played Yokohama, and on the Chinese mainland matches were played between Hankow, Tientsin and Tsingtao. In more recent times, in an excess of anti-British fury, a mob in Djakarta deliberately destroyed the wicket at the British Cricket Club – familiarly known as the 'Box Club'.

Other lesser 'interport' club cricket matches continue between the HKCC and Manila Nomads, Yokohama CC and Singapore CC; between the KCC and the Royal Bangkok Sports Club (RBSC) and Singapore CC; and between the Centaurs and the RBSC, to name a few.

Hong Kong Interports 1866–1987

Hong Kong Batsmen who have scored 70 runs plus

Runs	Year	Player	Opponent	Venue
169	1984	Nigel Stearns	Singapore	Hong Kong
156	1971	Jal S Shroff	Malaysia	Hong Kong
145*	1923	T E 'Tam' Pearce	Shanghai	Shanghai
136	1903	Lt Lumsden	Shanghai	Shanghai
127*	1936	Ernie F Fincher	Shanghai	Shanghai
126*	1981	Nigel Stearns	Singapore	Hong Kong
122	1920	T E 'Tam' Pearce	Shanghai	Hong Kong
119	1909	W N Edwards	Shanghai	Hong Kong
112	1977	John Bygate #	Singapore	Singapore

Hong Kong Batsmen who have scored 70 runs plus (cont'd.)

Runs	Year	Player	Opponent	Venue
108	1929	Harry Owen Hughes	Malaya	Hong Kong
107	1892	Capt John Dunn	Shanghai	Hong Kong
104*	1963	Jal S Shroff	Malaysia	Hong Kong
99	1866	R D Starkey	Shanghai	Hong Kong
94	1901	H R B 'Dick' Hancock	The Straits	Hong Kong
92	1980	Des Greenwood	Singapore	Singapore
88	1903	W C D Turner	Shanghai	Shanghai
85	1904	J T Dixon	Shanghai	Hong Kong
85	1912	G R Sayer	Shanghai	Hong Kong
83	1923	R H Wild	Shanghai	Shanghai
83	1933	A W 'Tom' Haywood	Shanghai	Hong Kong
82	1980	Des Greenwood	Malaysia	Kuala Lumpur
81	1933	E C 'Teddy' Fincher	Shanghai	Hong Kong
81	1955	Ivor L Stanton	Malaya	Hong Kong
80	1959	Ivor L Stanton	Malaya	Hong Kong
80	1979	Capt K McLean	Malaysia	Hong Kong
78	1979	Des Greenwood	Malaysia	Hong Kong
78	1984	Nigel Stearns	Singapore	Hong Kong
76	1909	W C D Turner	Shanghai	Hong Kong
75*	1975	P W Anderson	Singapore	Hong Kong
75	1912	A A Claxton	Shanghai	Hong Kong
74	1926	T E 'Tam' Pearce	Shanghai	Hong Kong
73	1890	Lt E M Blair	The Straits	Hong Kong
73	1974	J Manning	Malaysia	Hong Kong
72	1901	H Arthur	The Straits	Hong Kong
72	1935	E C 'Teddy' Fincher	Shanghai	Hong Kong
71*	1914	H R B 'Dick' Hancock	Shanghai	Shanghai
71	1866	T Clifford	Shanghai	Hong Kong
70	1968	I L J Stevens	Singapore	Singapore

Only Hong Kong batsman to score a century in Singapore or Malaysia.

Hong Kong Bowlers who have captured 5 wickets plus

Wkts	Year	Player	Opponent	Venue
8–60	1892	E J Coxon	Shanghai	Hong Kong
8–66	1892	Dr J A Lowson	Shanghai	Shanghai
7–)φ 1866		D H Mackenzie	Shanghai	Hong Kong
5–)				

Hong Kong Bowlers who have captured 5 wickets plus (cont'd.)

Wkts	Year	Player	Opponent	Venue
7–34)	1891	Dr J A Lowson	The Straits	Singapore
5–61)				
7–47 #	1920	R E O Bird	Shanghai	Hong Kong
7–64	1929	A C I Bowker	Shanghai	Hong Kong
7–71	1907	Cpl Sharpe	Shanghai	Hong Kong
6–24	1898	W A L Lethbridge	Shanghai	Shanghai
6–28	1890	Dr J A Lowson	The Straits	Hong Kong
6–30	1920	Capt P Havelock-Davies	The Straits	Hong Kong
6–37)	1901	R E O Bird	The Straits	Hong Kong
5–70)				
6–40)	1909	R E O Bird	The Straits	Hong Kong
5–60)				
6–46	1971	Charles Rowe	Singapore	Singapore
6–48	1969	Carl Myatt	Singapore	Hong Kong
6–49	1932	A R 'Fatty' Minu	Shanghai	Shanghai
6–52	1968	J K 'Foxy' Fawcett	Malaysia	Kuala Lumpur
6–56	1892	Dr J A Lowson	Shanghai	Hong Kong
6–65	1981	Dermot Reeve	Singapore	Hong Kong
6–68	1892	Sgt Mumford	Shanghai	Shanghai
6–70	1933	Alec Pearce	Shanghai	Hong Kong
6–74	1923	Harry Owen Hughes	Shanghai	Shanghai
6–74	1963	J K 'Foxy' Fawcett	Malaya	Hong Kong
6–76	1936	Alec Pearce	Shanghai	Shanghai
6–78)	1904	J T Dixon	The Straits	Hong Kong
5–22)				
6–97	1959	B C N 'Buddy' Carnell	Malaya	Hong Kong
5– 9)	1948	Frank Howarth	Shanghai	Shanghai
5–38)				
5–14	1947	Capt R J A Darwin	Shanghai	Hong Kong
5–15	1987	Bharat Gohel	Singapore	Singapore
5–17	1906	H E Stanger-Leathes	Shanghai	Shanghai
5–17	1965	Carl Myatt	Malaysia	Kuala Lumpur
5–19	1971	Cordell Hull	Singapore	Singapore
5–24)	1983	Jon Jenkins	Singapore	Singapore
5–28)				
5–25)	1890	E J Coxon	The Straits	Hong Kong
5–41)				
5–25	1898	Capt Langhorne	Shanghai	Shanghai
5–25	1909	R E O Bird	Shanghai	Hong Kong

Hong Kong Bowlers who have captured 5 wickets plus (cont'd.)

Wkts	Year	Player	Opponent	Venue
5–30	1972	Benny Kwong	Singapore	Hong Kong
5–32	1927	Bill Brace	Shanghai	Hong Kong
5–34	1929	A C I 'Acky' Bowker	Malaya	Hong Kong
5–35	1904	J T Dixon	Shanghai	Hong Kong
5–36	1912	Lt H F Christian (RGA)	Shanghai	Hong Kong
5–39	1926	Frank C Goodwin	Shanghai	Hong Kong
5–41	1971	Cpl Rocky Daniel	Malaysia	Hong Kong
5–44	1906	R E O Bird	Shanghai	Shanghai
5–45	1891	C S Barff	The Straits	Singapore
5–46	1968	Hatim Ebrahim	Malaysia	Kuala Lumpur
5–47	1925	A C I 'Acky' Bowker	Shanghai	Shanghai
5–50	1926	Capt A G Dobbie (KOSB)	Shanghai	Hong Kong
5–51	1903	J T Dixon	Shanghai	Shanghai
5–51	1975	Rod Starling	Singapore	Hong Kong
5–56	1924	A C I 'Acky' Bowker	Shanghai	Hong Kong
5–57	1908	Cpl Sharpe	Shanghai	Shanghai
5–63	1974	C G 'Kit' Cumings	Malaysia	Hong Kong
5–64	1897	T Sercombe Smith	Shanghai	Hong Kong
5–74	1935	A R 'Fatty' Minu	Shanghai	Hong Kong
5–87	1928	Capt I Erskine	Shanghai	Shanghai
5–94	1912	L/Cpl Dempsey	Shanghai	Shanghai

ϕ No bowling analysis. Shanghai totalled 107 & 59.
\# Includes the 'hat-trick'

Reminiscences of interport cricket Dr James Alfred Lowson, Hong Kong Interporter, 1890–1898

Mike Richardson said I must meet Dougal, who had some connection with a prewar Hong Kong Interport cricketer. Dougal lived near Mike in Park Village West, Regents Park, London. On the eve of 19 July 1994, after a hot, stifling train journey from Liverpool, Mike and I dined with Dougal Reid and his wife, Georgina. I was down for the Lord's Test, England v South Africa, the first such meeting for 29 years. Dougal produced 'the last remaining copy' of Dr James Lowson's *Reminiscences of Interport Cricket.*

I'd read about the existence of such a booklet, but never in my wildest dreams did I ever think I should lay my hands on an original, and from

314

such a source. Dougal is the maternal grandson of Dr Lowson, his mother, Catherine Jean, being the second of six children and the eldest daughter. What a lucky amazing find!

As previously mentioned, Dr Lowson survived the *SS Bokhara* tragedy in 1892, but had a lung removed and suffered healthwise as a result of his traumatic watery ordeal. He became known as 'Wun Lung' Lowson. He finally retired to England, where he died on 21 October 1935.

The following extracts have been taken from Dr Lowson's booklet. His words on the Interports should be read in conjunction with the other comments made on those matches in the relevant section of the history.

Many staunch friendships have been formed in the course of these contests. Hospitality is invariably unbounded, and only those who have experienced it can have an adequate idea of the cordiality of the reception extended to visiting teams.

These interport matches are a great experience to a rising player, and in the East have often been the making of a man. I can recommend no more enjoyable holiday to young players than one of these trips away from home, and they should strive their hardest to show up well and get chosen in the eleven.

First of all a word about two or three points in connection with these games. There are two great disadvantages no doubt which often tell heavily, and these are the change of light and ground. Now there is no better light in the world of cricket-grounds than that experienced in Hong Kong on a November forenoon, before the summer verdure has been scorched off the grass, whilst later in the day it is difficult to get a worse light for cricket anywhere. In Shanghai, on the other hand, in the middle of the day, I have usually experienced a glare, no doubt due to the flatness of the surrounding country, which effectually prevents a batsman getting his eyes opened properly – but for the same reason the evening light is much better than that of Hong Kong. In Singapore you may have any sort of light – usually a bad one from the visiting batsmen's point of view. Bright sunshine and heavy rain seem to be on tap all the time, and the variations are certainly disconcerting. The surrounding backgrounds at Hong Kong and Singapore are not favourable for cricket when the sun gets near the horizon.

The ground itself at these three centres is quite different in character, Singapore having undoubtedly the worst wickets, wet or dry; Hong Kong has the truest wicket, Shanghai the most fiery and often wearing badly. Hong Kong and Shanghai usually play their matches in weather common to both places, and neither side benefits.

Hong Kong going to Singapore however, are heavily handicapped,

315

although if Shanghai went to Singapore they would be in their element, as they also play cricket in the hottest weather. I do not think Singapore lose by going to Hong Kong, as usually the weather is not cold enough to shrivel them up, but still cool enough to act as a first-class bracing tonic.

On the choice of men – the decay of Hong Kong civilian cricket as compared to that of Shanghai and the Straits is due to several causes. In Shanghai cricket has a season of its own – summer, and little else is done in the amusement line otherwise, except some feeble opposition in the way of golf. In Hong Kong, cricket has to meet strong opposition in football, golf and racing, not to mention a little shooting, yachting and other sports, all of which have to be crammed into the winter months. The Straits have cricket all the year round, and have not the opposition of these sports that Hong Kong has – no one would dream of pushing football, for instance, in the hot tropics to the extent it is carried in the bracing winter climate of Hong Kong. In addition, Straits cricket has the enormous advantage of having the active patronage of His Excellency Sir Frank Swettenham – a most important matter – when it is remembered that the Straits Civil Service is now a fairly numerous one, and that its head is an enthusiastic cricketer.

The presence of a large garrison and a large fleet in Hong Kong in the winter has been another big nail in the coffin of Civilian cricket. This necessitates (?) a large number of matches, such as Club v Navy, Club v United Services, etc, with the result that the same civilian representatives play in nearly every match, and block out a large number of men who are almost good enough for the first eleven. Those men get tired of this state of affairs. In the old days more civilian matches of the type – Hills v Plains were played, and, consequently, more men were required more frequently. In recent years, there have been far too many return or extra matches with the Navy and the Military, and too few matches restricted to civilians alone. With grounds at Happy Valley, Army and Navy should be content with fewer matches on the Club ground. Matters may be improving again, but these are the main reasons for decay in Hong Kong cricket which was certainly visible during the latter years of the nineteenth century.

I unfortunately settled in the Colony just too late for participation in the 1889 match against our Northern opponents at Shanghai – a matter for my constant regret as it must have been a match to live for. One simply itches to have been there to lend a hand in that last innings, when Shanghai, with about 56 runs to win, had six wickets down for 25. With a big heart and plenty of luck, however, Bobby

Wickham managed to pull the match out of the fire, but if Hong Kong had had another bowler for a change it is quite on the cards that the luck and game might have gone the other way. The match will always be remarkable for the long wait for the rain to clear off, the teams lying on their oars, actually as well as figuratively, for almost three weeks before the floods cleared and a commencement could be made with the game.

Christmas Day, 1889, brought news to Hong Kong that the Straits Settlements, after a lot of trouble, had been able to arrange a visit to us at China New Year in the end of January. No doubt the exertions of the officers of the 58th Regiment had a good deal to do with getting up the team, several of them desiring to visit their old and happy hunting grounds, whilst to others the prospect of almost a month's holiday in a bracing climate was too great a temptation to be withstood. This was the first time a Straits team had ever ventured away from home, and a large company of camp followers took the opportunity for a pleasant outing and joined the merry throng which arrived in Hong Kong about the 19th of January. The team taken all round was fairly representative of the Straits at that time. Our team was certainly our best one at that period.

As usual, China New Year brought cold wet weather and rheumatism in its train for the Southerners, who were further handicapped by Fox being unable to do himself justice owing to an injury to his knee. Batting first on a wet wicket, we were able to put on 280 by steady-going play. The Straits batting was an unknown quantity, and considerable interest was aroused as to how they would fare. With the wicket in good condition on the following day, it was hoped that they would make a good fight. These hopes were early dispelled, as two of their best batsmen fell in my first over, and the procession continued right through the innings. This was a most disappointing display of batting for such a fairly strong side. There was never really a semblance of a struggle, but it must be said that the wicket, though good, gave the bowlers just enough help to make them rather dificult.

The next period to claim attention was during the new year festivities in 1891, when Ceylon, Hong Kong and the Straits met together at Singapore, a time still remembered as the 'famous fortnight.' Some of us set out on this trip with considerable trepidation, the idea of playing in such hot weather not being altogether agreeable, especially to those on whom the brunt of the work would fall. We were lucky in being able to get a fairly good team together for the campaign, as, if form went for anything, our batting, bowling and fielding appeared above the average. F M Blair was skipper. Our hopes of success were doomed to grievous disappointment.

The Straits were first tackled, and for a time fortune smiled upon us, as six of their wickets went down for 26 runs; at this period, one of those things happened which changed the whole course of the match. H L Talbot was batting and commenced to lash out at everything, when I sent four successive yorkers past him, all of which just managed to miss the wicket, whilst, misjudging the last ball of the over, he sent a fairly easy catch straight to John Dunn at mid-off, which the latter most unaccountably dropped. This was the turning point of the game. If Dunn had held the catch they probably would not have reached 40.

When we batted we were totally unprepared for the extraordinary collapse that followed, even though the wicket had had the usual douche of rain. Our procession was a most miserable affair. Fox and Mackenzie were certainly in their best form – but this was awful. On the following day most of the team arrived on the ground like boiled lobsters – so severely sunburnt by the previous days outing that in most cases it was simply agony to move about, and it was with anything but hopeful feelings that we took the field. Straits had again a dry wicket to bat upon, and Barff and I proved quite out of trim owing to the beastly discomfort of the sunburn – with the result that our opponents put up a comfortable 188, leaving us 240 to make to win. Even with 40 from John Dunn, we only reached 75, and were licked by 164 runs. We lost the toss and had to bat in the latter part of each day in uncertain light and after the usual afternoon rain, but still it was an awful walloping.

We then had to tackle the Cingalese. This match proved almost as disastrous as our first one. Several of us still suffering from sunburn. Christoffelsz was the cause of our downfall – having eight wickets for 24. I was under the impression that his action was decidedly unfair; but still that is a detail. This was another awful thrashing. Several of us felt like running away. There was some excuse for Barff and myself not batting well after our hard work with the ball, but as for the others – all sober men and true, I cannot explain it yet.

A third match was won by an innings against the Singapore Club.

Singapore Club: 156 (Birch 39, Higginbotham 32, Lowson 4–30) and 18 (Lowson 7–5)
Hong Kong: 179 (Barff 49, Campbell 24, Sercombe Smith 24, Lowson 23)

Barff bowling with half-a-gale behind, fairly frightened the batsmen, and when they got to the other end they didn't know what the ball was to do. I put in a bit of a record, getting seven scalps for a total cost of five runs. After the first days play – I think it was during the same evening that the much-talked-of artistic work on the Singapore Elephant was carried out.

The local inhabitants awoke to find that their stone elephant (the emblem of the Municipality which faced the Town Hall) was painted in many colours, green and red predominantly. Dougal confirmed that the principal artist was his grandfather.

Dr Lowson then digressed from cricket matches to discuss three Hong Kong Captains – Blair, Coxon and Dunn – during the period 1890 to 1892.

Blair was and is a splendid batsman and fielder. At Singapore, however, between having to speechify on numerous occasions and captaining the team, he seemed to be overloaded with the responsibility and certainly did not do himself justice. We certainly lost all Blair's value as a batsman by making him captain.

Dunn on the other hand, was anything but a stolid and anxious captain, and seemed to shine most when in command of a team. He had so much experience of first class cricket that he probably knew more about the game than the others, and got the most out of his team in an easy-sailing game; but first class cricket is quite another thing to Far Eastern cricket where leadership, to be successful, makes a greater demand on a man's 'savvy' and initiative than most people think. It is one thing captaining a well-disciplined county team at home where one knows the capacity of every unit; it is quite another thing in Hong Kong where every player knows – at least at that time knew – more about captaincy than all his neighbours in the field.

Neither of these men were in the same street as E J Coxon for inspiring a cheery confidence in their men, and Coxon could do this winning or losing; whilst for bringing off surprises he was almost unrivalled, though in many cases it was due to his own skill.

Our experiences in 1890 seemed to have rather choked off future teams attempting a descent upon Singapore. However, with a skipper who can fight a losing battle, and who is not afraid to change the ordinary tactics of a match, anything is possible there with a bit of luck.

Our next venture was again from home – to Shanghai in September 1891. On this occasion we also had a very good team, but alas! had to go without a wicket-keeper, and to this fact I attribute our failure to bring back the Northerner's flag.

Dumbleton opened the batting with me, but he soon fell to a magnificent catch on the longleg boundary by W H Moule. Dunn came in, and was in splendid form when the writer was bowled over by a smack on the knee. The Shanghai captain would not allow a substitute to run without a guarantee that I would not subsequently bowl; but Dunn would not have that. For a time we walked our runs, but this put Dunn (who was very fast between the wickets) out so much that he decided to retire me, when, as bad luck would have it, he was bowled. This was very hard on him and the spectators too, as I never saw him in better trim, and there is not the slightest doubt that the 'walking match' put him latterly completely off his game. Shanghai had of course their best eleven in the field and should have scored more than 180. The writer took four for 34 – merely standing at the wicket and tossing up the ball. Orman and Wallace began their second innings, I sent up a short 'Donkey Drop' with break on it. He (Orman/Wallace!) ran far out and just touched it, and Maitland, who was 'keeping' at the time, missed an easy catch and an easier stumping. After that, our weak bowling was hammered 'all over the shop.' Barff was unfortunately quite out of form, whilst I was a helpless cripple.

It is usual to talk about cricketers taking reverses 'like sportsmen', but there is a lot of bosh in this. Well, I confess to feeling very disappointed at the result, as I expected we should win. This feeling of disappointment was in no way mollified by the fact that I was successful in getting a record for Hong Kong in securing 135 wickets (1890–91) for eight runs apiece, and that too, against batsmen of the calibre of John Dunn, Dumbleton, Jeffkins, Darby, Coxon, not to mention De Robeck and Taylor of the Navy. I know that one or two more of us were disappointed, but we bottled up our wrath and patiently waited our chance at Hong Kong

The weather at China New Year 1892 proved favourable for cricket when our Northern friends paid their promised visit. Shanghai were fortunately represented by a very strong team. We had an eleven which would have given most of the second-class counties at home a good fight for victory. Shanghai won the toss and batted, the wicket was in splendid condition, although the weather broke down a bit in the Shanghai second innings.

Dr Lowson produced the scoresheets for the match without any comment on Capt John Dunn scoring the first Interport century for Hong Kong! He merely said: The following scores eloquently describe the match, and added Hong Kong's principal bowling analyses.

A pressing invitation from Shanghai led the HKCC to send up an eleven in October 1892. On this occasion, we were weakly represented. We went off with five men who had only a nodding acquaintance with Eastern first-class cricket. Shanghai batted first on a splendid wicket. Keeping up the pressure, the first eight wickets fell to me for about 30 runs, and visions passed before my eyes of making a record in these matches by getting all ten wickets – then John Dunn dropped an easy catch at mid-off. There was excuse for this missed catch and also for the failure in batting in this the last match of that great cricketer Dunn. For some time he had been suffering from astigmatism. Opening our batting, the writer was again unfortunate, as Barff lamed him with a fast ball and he was only a spectator of the game afterwards. Corporal Mumford with six wickets for 68 came to the fore with underhand grubs. The wicket was wearing badly. We were overwhelmed by a very much stronger team.

This is not the place to say much about the disaster which overtook us on our voyage home. My feelings can be imagined on reaching the shore of Sand Island at midnight and finding no one there. I began to think I was the only one who had got out of the ship alive. It is scarcely likely that I can ever forget that period, and even now when I think of my companions – some of them close personal friends – I frequently have that peculiar sinking sensation about the heart and epigastrium which no one has yet defined or described properly. To people who have experienced this it is probably best described as 'that feeling – you know!' It was a bad business from beginning to end.

Six years elapsed before we again set out for Shanghai in September 1898. The Hong Kong team was a very even one all round – except in the trifling detail of temper. Langhorne in this match was *facile princeps* in the fielding line. Our second innings was not at all a success, only producing 126, on a wearing wicket. With only 103 to make, the Shanghai men had good reason for looking forward to winning. To get the Shanghai team out for 74 was a feather in our cap. Lethbridge with six for 24, never bowled better during his stay in the East. I confess to gloating over the result with satisfaction, as it was the first time Hong Kong had won an interport away from home. I might mention that the excitement and joy at the result on the part of old Hong Kong men in Shanghai was a sight to behold.

Before completing his reminiscences, Dr Lowson discussed a few other matters.

Bowlers should practice in private and refrain from giving themselves 'away' before the opposing batsmen. Personally, I have never bowled a ball at practice when any of our opponents were looking on – no matter whether they had played against me before or not. The result has been that almost invariably my bowling analysis has been very much better in the first innings.

In the matter of fielding, Hong Kong, in my time, was always behindhand. The reason for this slackness is not far to seek. Singapore and Shanghai grounds are large, and smartness and activity are absolutely essential if a man is to retain his place in the team – a man must make some sort of a show of getting after a ball. In Hong Kong, even after a long innings, a fielder generally leaves the ground quite fresh owing to so many boundary hits being scored. The result of this is that, when any extra fielding has to be done at Shanghai or Singapore, Hong Kong men get hopelessly fagged out, and never have a chance of doing well with the bat in consequence, so that if training in a little fielding practice can be carried out it will prove a great blessing to future teams.

The author feels sure the unaccustomed heat in both Shanghai and Singapore had just as much to do with the Hong Kong team being 'fagged out' as the extra fielding. Dr Lowson would have been pleased to know that the Hong Kong team selected for the 1965 tour of Singapore and Malaya did not lose a single match whilst on tour. This team had been put through an organised, six-week vigorous training session, the first ever for a Hong Kong team about to embark on an overseas Interport. It certainly paid off, thanks to John Fawcett and Brian Wigley.

In selecting teams, particularly for a match at home, there has been, and there always will be, difficulty in deciding whether to retain in the XI a good old hand temporarily out of form or select a rising youngster who is showing decent cricket at the time. Outside circumstances may have to be taken into consideration, but, speaking generally, the man with experience of these matches is to be preferred, provided he is fairly active in the field. I am not sure that the Hong Kong practice of the Committee selecting all the team is the best. It would be better to select the captain and give him the first seven men, of whose selection there is usually no doubt, and then allow him to fill up the remaining vacancies himself.

A somewhat radical approach, which I doubt has ever been implemented. Dr Lowson added that his remarks were peculiarly apposite to Hong Kong, which is notoriously slow at learning from experience. He went on to say it would be ungracious to finish without again referring to the hospitality extended to Hong Kong teams away from home.

Dinners, dramatic entertainments, dances, smoking concerts, etcetera, not to mention the demands of private hosts, scarcely left a spare moment in the day; many most pleasant memories of these remain, more especially of Shanghai, where the local A.D.C. is particularly strong. Smoking concerts have always proved themselves popular as not requiring much rehearsal and always allowing of the introduction of topical 'stuff'. At a 'Smoker' in Shanghai in 1891, I got a reception such as the newspapers said had never been experienced in that classic city. I had sung a song with topical allusions in the costume of a Highlander of the Edward Terry type – short kilts and bathing pants sort of style – when, in response to a loud recall, what seemed a flash of genius flashed across my brain. Seizing a chair from the wings, I stuck it on the stage and stood on my head on it. The result was simple uproar – to put it mildly. Even Harry Hall, that splendid comedian who was present at the above entertainment, said: 'Well Lowson, I'm well endowed with confidence and cheek, and have often resolved to work that business of yours, but I've never yet been able to screw up my courage to the sticking point.'

I have always been lucky in being picketed – or should it be billitted? – on what seemed the choice of our hosts. What could one wish for more than live with the old 58th Officers' Mess for a fortnight? I can even now see old Bramwell peering in at the bedroom barrack door out of his deep-set eyes and roaring out, 'Doctor – brandy and soda this morning?'

As for Shanghai, if anyone can put me into better hands than those of James McKie, Brodie Clark, J L Scott or H E R Hunter, it is high time I was out in the Far East again. Living for a week even, with those who have made so much commercial history in the North of China is a liberal education itself.

One regret, however, if we ever again meet on the green sward, our fighting will have to be done in words – bad joss, though it might have been worse! Here's luck anyhow! – Chin Chin.

I hope that through a selection of his own words I have managed to convey to the reader the essence of the man – Dr James Lowson, an excellent cricketer and surely a character.

Dr Lowson was also an accomplished golfer, winning the Hong Kong championship three times.

In 1895, he beat J W Matthews, RA, by 7 and 6. In 1896 (medal play over 54 holes), he returned 255 against Capt W V Eccles's 269 and Gershom Stewart's 276. In 1899, he beat A S Anton by 8 and 7.

In E W Hamilton's T*he Royal Hong Kong Golf Club – A Short History*, which was reprinted in the *SCMP* in the 1920s, C M G Burnie, who played for Hong Kong against Shanghai in 1904, said of Dr Lowson:

> He had a most forceful personality. Pale-faced, bright-eyed and black-haired, he stood about 5' 10" and had hardly any flesh on his bones. He was a cricketer of eminence, a slashing hitter and a fastish medium bowler.

A Special Group of Cricketers

The following cricketers have played first-class cricket in the British Isles and have also played representative cricket for Hong Kong.

Name	When/Where born	Where Qualified
Atkinson, Stephen Robert	b 18 Dec 1952 Birtley, Durham	Minor Counties 1985
Blair, Everard McLeod (Lt) [later Major-General]	b 26 Jul 1866 Bangalore, India	Kent 1893–1900
Barclay, John Robert Troutbeck	b 22 Jan 1954 Bonn, W. Germany	Sussex 1970–86
Brettell, David Norman	b 10 Mar 1956 Woking	Oxford 1975–78 Blue 1977
Dale, Jack Hillen (Lt RN)	b 29 Oct 1901 Northampton	Northants 1922, RN 1928
Dumbleton, Horatio Norris (Capt)	b 23 Oct 1858 Ferozepore, India	Hants 1884
Dunn, Capt John	b 8 Jun 1862 Hobart, Aust.	Surrey 1881
Eddington, Roderick Ian	b 2 Jan 1950 Perth, Aust.	Oxford 1975–76
Findlay, Francis	b 4 Feb 1920 Aberdeen	Scotland 1948
Garthwaite, Clive Charlton	b 22 Oct 1909 Guisborough	Army 1930
Havelock-Davies, Philip (Capt)	b 30 Aug 1893 Brighton, Sussex	Oxford 1913–14, Sussex 1914 & Army 1927
Maundrell, Rev William Herbert	5 Nov 1876 Nagasaki, Japan	Hants 1900
Myles, Simon David	b 2 Jun 1966 Mansfield	Sussex 1987 & Warwicks 1988 and Minor Counties #
Orders, Jonathan Oliver Darcy	b 12 Aug 1957 Beckenham	Oxford 1978–81

Name	When/Where born	Where Qualified
Pearce, Thomas Alexander	b 18 Dec 1910 Hong Kong	Kent 1930–46
Reeve, Dermot Alexander	b 2 Apr 1963 Hong Kong	Sussex 1983–87 & Warwicks 1988–96 # World Cup 1991–91 & 1996 # Tests v NZ 1991–92
Rowe, Charles James Castell	b 27 Nov 1951 Hong Kong	Kent 1974–81 & Glamorgan 1982–84
Willson, Bernard John	b 20 Jun 1935 Strood, Kent	Combined Services 1964

Who's Who of Cricketers, 1993 and # added 1996

NB: Three other cricketers from *Who's Who* also might be the same persons who have played for Hong Kong.
1. Coxon, Ernest James De Veulle, b 10 Dec 1857, Taunton, Somerset, played for the Gentlemen of England (1890), and Coxon E J for Hong Kong v Shanghai (1889–92) and against The Straits (1890);
2. Dixon, J T, who played one match for Middlesex (1908) and once for Hong Kong v Malaya (1904).
3. Baird, Henry Hume Chisholm, b 13 Apr 1878, Haverfordwest, Pembrokeshire, played for MCC (1910) and Army (1912–13), and Capt Baird (Buffs) for Hong Kong v Shanghai and against The Straits (1909).

HONG KONG v SHANGHAI – highlights

1866 – The inaugural Hong Kong v Shanghai Interport was played in February on the HKCC Chater Road ground, where the Hong Kong civilian team selected by and comprising almost exclusively HKCC members, soundly defeated the Shanghai team by an innings and 264 runs. The Shanghai 'lob' bowlers were most inaccurate, bowling 41 wides. In Shanghai's second innings, seven of their batsmen failed to score. D H Mackenzie captured five and seven Shanghai wickets respectively, whilst R D Starkey was bowled on 99!

Hong Kong: 430
Shanghai: 107 and 59

1867 – Hong Kong travelled to Shanghai in May for the first time, but failed to repeat their home success, losing by an innings and 36 runs, J P Mollinson (Shanghai) picking up 11 wickets.

'It is of course possible that the trundlers found the Shanghai wicket not to their liking.'

Shanghai: 239
Hong Kong: 121 and 82

As there was still a day to spare, another match was played, Hong Kong losing by 81 runs. This second game, although only played over one day as a single-innings match, has been included in past Interport records. Mollinson added a further five wickets to his haul.

Shanghai: 200
Hong Kong: 119

1889 – The hardships of these long sea passages must have knocked the enthusiasm out of the respective Hong Kong and Shanghai cricketers. As a result, it was not until November 1889 that the series was resumed when a Hong Kong team visited Shanghai. On a soft wicket that had been badly affected by rain, Shanghai won a low-scoring game by three wickets. In Hong Kong's second innings, A Stewart took 5–12 off 27.3 overs. This match saw the first appearance of two future Presidents of the HKCC and the SCC – Frank Maitland and A P Wood.

Hong Kong: 67 and 80
Shanghai: 94 and 55 for 7

1891 – This visit in September saw one of the best matches played in Shanghai when, on a good batting wicket, Hong Kong scored 268 in four hours, Lowson being 'lamed' by a blow on the kneecap. He was so dreaded by Shanghai that their skipper, W Bruce Robertson, would not allow anyone to run for Lowson unless he agreed 'not to bowl against Shanghai'. J Orman was unluckily run out for 91 in Shanghai's second innings. Hong Kong were left only 80 minutes to score 213 for victory. Hong Kong had paid a severe penalty by not including a regular wicket-keeper, sundries totalling 58 in the two Shanghai innings.

Shanghai: 180 and 300 for 8
Hong Kong: 268 and 72 for 4

1892 – Two matches were played in this year, the first in Hong Kong during an 'excessively' hot February, when a very strong Hong Kong side defeated Shanghai by an innings and 132 runs. Captain John Dunn, although dropped at 45, 89 and in the 90s, batted 'brilliantly' to score the first Interport century. E W Maitland (No. 9) and G Taylor (No. 10), each with half centuries helped the side amass over 400 runs.

Shanghai were bowled out by E J Coxon and Dr J A Lowson, who had match analyses of 12 for 121 and 8 for 98 respectively.

Hong Kong: 429
Shanghai: 163 and 134

When Hong Kong visited Shanghai in October that same year, certain leading Hong Kong players were unable to make the trip. The same 'for business or other reasons' problem applied equally to Shanghai, when the Interport took place in Hong Kong.

The match result was reversed in equally dominant fashion, Shanghai winning by 157 runs. Lowson took the first eight wickets for 66 runs in Shanghai's first innings, but was 'lamed' again when batting, and couldn't bowl in Shanghai's second innings! Sgt Mumford, with his 'underhand grubbers', had the Shanghai players mesmerised and captured 6–68. But it was A G H Carruthers who devastated Hong Kong with 5–29 and 8–41 respectively.

Shanghai: 112 and 202
Hong Kong: 78 and 79

Tragedy hit the Hong Kong team as they were returning home on the *SS Bokhara*, a P&O steamship. At night near Sand Island in the Pescadores, a typhoon struck, sinking the ship and drowning 125 of the 148 persons on board. Only two Hong Kong cricketers survived the disaster, Dr Lowson and Lt Markham of the Shropshire Light Infantry. In St John's Cathedral, Hong Kong, a bronze memorial plaque with the following inscription was consecrated:

> In token of their deep regret for the loss of
> Major Turner, A.P.D.
> Captain J. Dunn, A.S.C.
> Captain Dawson, Hong Kong Regiment
> Lieutenant Burnett, 53rd Regiment
> Lieutenant C. G. Boyle, R.A.
> Sergeant Donegan, 53rd Regiment
> Sergeant Mumford, 53rd Regiment
> Quartermaster-Sergeant Jeffkins, R.E.
> G. S. Purvis, Esq.
> G. F. Taverner, Esq.
> C. Wallace, Esq.

Members of the Hong Kong Cricket team, who
Perished in the
Wreck of the P. and O. Steamer *Bokhara*
On 10th October, 1892
While on their return voyage to Hong Kong after
The Interport Cricket Match

This Window is Erected by the Members of the
Shanghai Cricket Club

No other Cathedral in the world contained a memorial to members of a cricket team. The tragic near total loss of the entire Hong Kong team dealt a severe blow to the Interport series, which did not resume again until 1897.

1897 – Hong Kong in November, provided one of the most exciting finishes in the series to date. Hong Kong, requiring 201 runs to win, succeeded with their last pair at the wicket. D M Wood and A S Anton each scored half centuries in Hong Kong's first innings, whilst Sercombe Smith picked up nine wickets in the match.

Shanghai: 173 and 189
Hong Kong: 162 and 201 for 9

1898 – After trailing on the first innings, Hong Kong, visiting Shanghai in September, won an unexpected victory by 28 runs, due to excellent bowling performances from W A L Lethbridge and Capt Langhorne, with match analyses of 9 for 75 and 8 for 48 respectively.

Hong Kong: 179 and 126
Shanghai: 203 and 74

1901 – Shanghai won their first match in Hong Kong during a fine November. After an evenly fought first innings, they gained the upper hand in the second innings and won by seven wickets. Dick Hancock, in his first appearance for Hong Kong, top scored with 68. Major Beresford-Ash scored 61 and Shanghai's J Mann took 5–70 in Hong Kong's second innings.

Hong Kong: 230 and 157
Shanghai: 239 and 153 for 3

1903 – Prior to the Hong Kong's teams departure for Shanghai, the *Daily Press* reported:

Virtually all the players were new to Interport cricket and the Hongs were threatening not to release their staff even if selected. Hong Kong still smarting from its thrashing in 1901, even managed to put its boat bookings back and leave for Shanghai two weeks late in order to get more practice in. But still, said the Press, the team had no chance.

Hong Kong proved the critics wrong and won by an innings and 23 runs in October. Lt Lumsden hit a brilliant 136 in Hong Kong's first innings. This was the debut match for Tam Pearce, father of Alec, who was to be a dominant figure in Interport cricket until his retirement in 1935. J T Dixon captured 5–51 in Shanghai's first innings.

Hong Kong: 336
Shanghai:　 122 and 191

1904 – Another triangular tournament in Hong Kong during November, when J T Dixon top scored for Hong Kong with a well struck 85 and took 5–35 in Shanghai's second innings, to lead Hong Kong to victory by four wickets. W J Turnbull answered with 82 for Shanghai.

Shanghai:　 229 and 151
Hong Kong: 274 and 109 for 6

1906 – Play was not possible on the first day. V H Lanning was practically unplayable on a rain-affected Shanghai October wicket, taking 8–10 and 5–34, to rush Hong Kong to defeat. R E O Bird had a match analyses of 9 for 104.

Shanghai:　 130 and 121
Hong Kong: 46 and 66

1907 – Winning the toss, Shanghai batted first on a pleasant November day on the Chater Road ground. Two bowlers, Cpl Sharpe for Hong Kong and T Main for Shanghai, with match analyses of 11 for 108 and 10 for 110 respectively, were the main contributors in this game, which Hong Kong won comfortably by 4 wickets.

Shanghai:　 212 and 185
Hong Kong: 261 and 137 for 6

1908 – October in Shanghai saw Hong Kong lose badly by 10 wickets, after only managing 74 runs in its first innings. Shanghai's R N Anderson

329

(74) matched the Hong Kong total. O D Rasmussen, playing in his first game for Shanghai did most of the damage, taking 7–29 and 3–41. Cpl Sharpe captured 5–57 for Hong Kong, whilst A E Lanning with 62 gave Hong Kong a semblance of respectability in their second innings.

Hong Kong: 74 and 163
Shanghai: 228 and 10 without loss

1909 – Hong Kong's emphatic win by an innings and 224 runs at Chater Road in November. T E Pearce (64) and A C E Elborough (58) gave Hong Kong a good start with a century opening partnership. W N Edwards, coming in at No. 7, rubbed it in for Shanghai, taking 119 runs off their tiring attack. Oliver 4–38 and Bird 5–25 then put Shanghai to the sword in their second innings, cutting them down for 78 runs.

Hong Kong: 455
Shanghai: 153 and 78

1912 – Two matches were scheduled, the first in Shanghai in May/June and the second in Hong Kong in November. Again, playing at home proved to be decisive. Two Interports were played to make up for the three-year absence since the previous match in 1909. A weak Hong Kong team, without Hancock, Pearce and Sayer, was beaten by an innings and 26 runs, D R McEuen taking 7–12 and 5–32. L/Cpl Dempsey captured 5–94 for Hong Kong.

Shanghai: 175
Hong Kong: 56 and 93

Later in the year, G R Sayer, making his first appearance for Hong Kong, top scored with 85, A A Claxton chipped in with 75 and Lt W F Christian (RGA) took 5–36 in Shanghai's second innings. Shanghai's Jimmy Quayle, who was to prove a thorn in many a Hong Kong side, had a debut match analysis of 5–107.

Shanghai: 200 and 181
Hong Kong: 417

1914 – When Hong Kong visited Shanghai in May, the clouds of war were gathering in the West. This was to be the last Interport until 1920. Capt Ivo Barrett, the immensely talented Shanghai batsman, made his debut and scored 100 and 43. He played county cricket for Hampshire during the war

330

years. Despite a gallant 71 not out from Dick Hancock in Hong Kong's second innings, there was no denying Shanghai's deserved win by 116 runs. R E O Bird was Hong Kong's most successful bowler with 4–59 and 3–60. 'Lobster' Reed chipped in with 4–10 to finish off the Shanghai second innings.

Shanghai: 199 and 194
Hong Kong: 153 and 124

1920 – On 11 November, Armistice Day, Hong Kong and Shanghai resumed their contests. Although there were many new faces, it was good to see a nucleus of the prewar brigade. The stars for Hong Kong in its comfortable win by six wickets were opener Tam Pearce, with a masterful 122, and R E O Bird's 7–47 in Shanghai's second innings. A young RFC and RAF officer recently demobbed, turned out for Shanghai with a match analysis of 6 for 70. Donald Leach was to become one of the better known of all the pre-Pacific war Interport cricketers, continuing after the war into the mid 1950s as a player for the HKCC Scorpions. H B Ollerdessen put together 52 and 63 for Shanghai. The *Hong Kong Daily Press* reported: 'Bird's last four wickets cost him one run. He did the "hat-trick" and was enthusiastically applauded.'

Shanghai: 166 and 189
Hong Kong: 279 and 79 for 4

1921 – May in Shanghai, after a lapse of seven years, saw Hong Kong run into the duo talents of Ivo Barrett, who had returned from England, and Dr W E O'Hara, an extremely gifted left-arm first-grade cricketer from Australia. 'One of the finest seen in this part of the world.' Barrett scored a magnificent 165, while 'Doc,' on his debut, captured 7–26 and 6–62. Hong Kong were trounced by an innings and 159 runs.

Shanghai: 391
Hong Kong: 80 and 152

1922 – Chater Road in November, the Shanghai skipper G M Billings almost single-handedly led his team to an unlikely triumph over Hong Kong. Batting at No. 10 in the first innings, he scored 38 out of 86. Needing nearly 200 for victory, by far the highest total of the match, Shanghai were in trouble after the dismissal of Donald Leach for 79. Billings coming in at a promoted No. 8, literally 'took the bull by the horns' and ended the game with a towering six. He had also taken 5–31 and 3–39, whilst newcomer T W R 'Torrie' Wilson had a match analysis of

10–117 off 50 overs. Capt Havelock-Davies was Hong Kong's most successful bowler, with 4–45 and 4–56.

Hong Kong: 140 and 141
Shanghai: 86 and 197 for 8

1923 – Hong Kong decided to send a fully representative side to Shanghai to try and reverse its many defeats there. In an evenly contested match lasting four days in May, one of the best Interports took place, when over 1,200 runs were scored. Hong Kong won by 3 wickets just before tea on the fourth day with Tam Pearce 145 not out, its first win in Shanghai since 1903. Harry Owen Hughes, another cricketer of renown and future HKCC President, on his debut took 4–92 and 6–74 with his cleverly flighted slow left-arm deliveries.

The match looked like ending on the third day with Hong Kong facing a heavy defeat, until Tam Pearce defied all the Shanghai bowlers in his memorable innings. It was even rumoured that the *Empress of Canada* had delayed its departure from Shanghai for Pearce, who was going on home leave. For Shanghai, the dependable H B Ollerdessen (96) and H E Muriel (89) were mainly responsible for their excellent first innings total. J A Quayle (84) and D W Leach (68) were the main scorers in their second innings. Quayle also captured 6–77 and 5–97 to round off a splendid all-round performance for Shanghai.

Shanghai: 351 and 255
Hong Kong: 332 and 276 for 7

1924 – A fairly strong Shanghai side could only manage just over 100 runs in each innings in Hong Kong, a match Hong Kong won by an innings and five runs. HKCC's 'Acky' Bowker, playing in his first game for Hong Kong, captured 3–16 and 5–56, including the prized wicket of Capt Barrett for 4 and 0, whilst 'Lobster' Reed matched this with 4–35 and 4–47. A bold innings of 59 by Lt Com Hargreaves, coming in at No. 8, together with 61 from opener R E A Webster helped Hong Kong to a respectable first innings total.

Shanghai: 109 and 106
Hong Kong: 220

The Editor of *HKCC Centenary 1851–1951* recalled the Shanghai duet by E G Barnes, a dogged No. 11 bat with no strokes, and Donald Leach:

Barney had a delightful falsetto voice and many will recall with

332

pleasure the duet, an adaption of the 'Keys of Heaven', which he used to sing with Donald Leach. Donald sang a good-length baritone, coming in slightly from the off-tonsil.

1925 – Hong Kong visiting Shanghai won a closely contested interesting game by seven runs over three days in May. Both sides first innings were boosted by bowlers batting at No. 9 'Doc' O'Hara for Shanghai with 62 not out, the only player to record a fifty in the match, and 'Acky' Bowker for Hong Kong with 38. Shanghai, needing only 106 to win, were bowled out for 97, Bowker 5–47 and Reed 4–37 respectively trimming their sails.

Hong Kong: 145 and 127
Shanghai:　167 and 97

'My memories of anything interesting about Shanghai cricket are limited and vague, except for the match I was playing in on 30 May 1925. Rioters had stormed up Nanking Road and threatened the police station. The police opened fire, killing probably six rioters – though the exact figure was disputed. Summons came in succession for any police, police reserves and Shanghai Volunteer Corps members to report to their units; and with the disappearance of half their players the cricket teams decided that they would have to draw stumps.'

G S Dunkley, 23 April 1994
[Dunkley was the Hong Kong wicket-keeper in 1933, 1934 and 1935]

1926 – In another close finish during a triangular tournament in Hong Kong in November, Shanghai won by one wicket. After a poor start, a determined 74 from Tam Pearce saw Hong Kong struggle to 174. Shanghai matched Hong Kong's total with 185 runs, Ivor Barrett top scoring with 45. Bowlers dominated the batting of both sides in the second innings, with O'Hara 7–57 and Leach 3–45 for Shanghai and Goodwin 5–39 and Bowker 4–45 for Hong Kong. Len Stokes and Lolly Goldman for Shanghai, and Frank Goodwin for Hong Kong, made their debuts.

Hong Kong: 174 and 121
Shanghai:　185 and 113 for 9.

1927 – A very fine innings of 146 by Ivo Barrett could not prevent Hong Kong winning by three wickets at Chater Road in November. Bill Brace and Teddy Fincher, both KCC players, had excellent debuts. Brace scored 58 and 41 and captured 4–47 and 5–32, whilst Teddy Fincher scored 62 in Hong Kong's second innings.

After five wickets had fallen cheaply, Tam Pearce, batting at a very unaccustomed No. 9, eventually won the match for Hong Kong with 41 not out. Later at the Interport dinner, the flags of the defeated teams, the occasion being another triangular tournament, were handed over to the Hong Kong captain 'amid a scene of great enthusiasm.'

Shanghai: 260 and 97
Hong Kong: 156 and 202 for 7

1928 – Service players were prominent during this match in Shanghai in May. Shanghai won by 120 runs. Some discussion over the eligibility of Service players had taken place in Hong Kong during the previous Interport. A tacit understanding was reached, whereby it was decided that Service members were eligible to play provided they had resided in the Ports for more than three months, and that not more than four Service players should be included in an Interport XI. This matter had arisen mainly because of the stationing of a large defence force in Shanghai in 1927 due to the considerable anti-foreign feeling connected with the Nationalist movement in China.

In Shanghai's second innings, Donald Leach (80) and 'Doc' O'Hara (96) had put their team on the way to victory. Then their Service bowlers, Army fast bowler Sgt Freshwater 4–30 and Lt Melsome 5–28, who later played for the Army at Lord's, scythed through the Hong Kong batting. Capt I Erskine bowled well for Hong Kong with 4–36 and 5–87. Starling Jex, Hong Kong's wicket-keeper, took four catches in Shanghai's first innings.

Shanghai: 129 and 279
Hong Kong: 186 and 102

1929 – Hong Kong began a successful Triangular contest by defeating Shanghai at Chater Road in November. There was no Ivo Barrett for Shanghai and Dick Hancock, after winning the toss, would play his last game for Hong Kong, although he would remain President of the HKCC until his death in 1948. Donald Anderson, just 17 years old, was the youngest player to represent Hong Kong. R. ABBIT, *Hong Kong Daily Press* reported:

The day was rather dull and overcast. Shanghai had the best of the opening day, the Home side being dismissed for 114 'on a slow

334

turning wicket' (Leach 5–17), of which E C Fincher made 53, being last out. The visitors by careful play put on 131 for 5 wickets. Hong Kong made a fine recovery, thanks in the main to some very fine bowling by Bowker (7–64). Going in 69 in arrears the Home side have now made 210 for 7 wickets. Fincher, Owen Hughes (61), Pearce and Anderson did particularly well. Bowker and Colonel Wyatt put up a capital last wicket stand setting the visitors 204 to win (Leach 5–72). Hong Kong had the situation well in hand, all through steady bowling backed by some brilliant catches. Shanghai were all out for 121 early in the afternoon.

Hong Kong: 114 and 272
Shanghai: 183 and 121

1930 – The match started on 19 May in Shanghai, was then rained off for the next three days and completed on 23 May! Shanghai started well with a splendid third wicket partnership between Len Stokes (66) and Donald Leach (81), which put them in a strong position. Hong Kong, bowled out for 141 in the first innings, struggled to 55 for 4 wickets in their second innings, when 'Rain rescues Hong Kong,' reported a Shanghai newspaper. Ernie Fincher joined his brother Teddy in his first Interport for Hong Kong.

Shanghai: 291
Hong Kong: 141 and 55 for 4

1931 – Shanghai thrashed Hong Kong at Chater Road in November. Donald Leach was the main architect of Hong Kong's defeat, top scoring with 59 and taking 5–30 and 3–37. R Booth 5–27 and Pat Madar 5–24, helped Leach clean up Hong Kong. Sam Kermani's debut for Shanghai.

Hong Kong: 138 and 125
Shanghai: 237 and 27 for 3

1932 – A H Madar, with 59, was the only batsman on either side to score more than 30 runs, whilst A R 'Fatty' Minu, an IRC player, mesmerised the Shanghai batsmen with his slow left-arm spinners, capturing 4–52 and 6–49. These two new faces played a large part in Hong Kong's win over Shanghai by 42 runs on their home ground in May.

Hong Kong: 108 and 180
Shanghai: 131 and 115

335

1933 – Alec Pearce made his first appearance for Hong Kong in this triangular tournament. Although primarily a classical batsman, he made his mark as an 'inspirational' third change bowler, taking 6–70 in Shanghai's second innings. Teddy Fincher (81) in Hong Kong's first innings and Tom Hayward (83) in the second, complete with broken finger, helped Hong Kong win this match by 117 runs, despite 50s from Donald Leach and Len Stokes. J A Isaacs was Shanghai's best bowler with 4–45 and 3–42.

    Hong Kong: 240 and 212
    Shanghai: 103 and 232

1934 – Hong Kong's powerful team arrived in Shanghai one day late, badly shaken en route by a November typhoon. Their second battering came from Shanghai, who won the match by a resounding 270 runs. An excellent second wicket partnership of 194 between Len Stokes and Sam Kermani in Shanghai's first innings laid the foundation for their win; Stokes finished with a brilliant 161 and Kermani an attractive 72. Pat Madar restricted Hong Kong's first innings with 5–22, whilst G R M Ricketts, a 6 foot 6 inches former Oxford goalkeeper, took 4–58 and 4–38 for Hong Kong. Len Stokes (50) and 'Peanut' Marshall (56) held the Shanghai second innings together.

    Shanghai: 335 and 188
    Hong Kong: 151 and 102

1935 – The first and only game in this Interport series in which the two Pearces, Tam and Alec, played together. Hong Kong won the toss and compiled a respectable 213, mainly due to a fine 72 from Teddy Fincher. With Donald Leach closing up one end, bowling 28 overs for 43 runs, the slow bowling of Pat Madar 7–76, reaped results at the other. In Shanghai's first innings, Sam Kermani stroked a fine 86. Leach bowled another 28 overs in Hong Kong's second innings, this time taking 5–41. 'Fatty' Minu was Hong Kong's most successful bowler, capturing 4–48 and 5–74. A fluctuating game, with Hong Kong eventual winners by 31 runs at Chater Road.

    Hong Kong: 213 and 145
    Shanghai: 180 and 147

1936 – A strong Hong Kong team travelled to Shanghai for what was to be the last Interport before the Pacific war. The cricket was of a high

336

standard and went into a fourth day, before Shanghai emerged as worthy winners by the large margin of 217 runs.

A stout-hearted 100 not out from H V Parker at No. 9 and 84 from John Leckie at No. 8, paved the way for Shanghai's massive total. Shanghai batted for 175 overs! Ernie Fincher answered with a masterful 127 not out, but without support, Hong Kong fell short of Shanghai's total by 202 runs. Len Stokes, after being dismissed for 0, turned bowler and bounced back with 5–52. Another feature of the match was the marathon bowling performance by 'Fatty' Minu, who bowled a total of 94 overs. Alec Pearce with 3–117 and 6–76 from a total 59 overs, plus a splendid knock of 61 in Hong Kong's second innings, was Hong Kong's most successful all-round player. Eddie Gosano, on his 'delayed' debut, scored 33 not out in Hong Kong's second innings.

Shanghai: 479 and 190
Hong Kong: 277 and 175

1947 – The first postwar Interport was held in November at Chater Road and resulted in an easy win for Hong Kong. Lt Broadley's 59 for Hong Kong was the only score over 50, whilst Donald Leach took 5–45 in Hong Kong's second innings. The real star of the match was Capt Darwin for Hong Kong with 5–14 and 4–22. 'A feature of the Shanghai innings was the magnificent fielding of the Hong Kong team – not a single chance was missed, and Howarth in particular, made three brilliant catches.' Most of the Shanghai team were prewar players, whilst for Hong Kong Alec Pearce, J E Richardson, Harry Owen Hughes, and 'Fatty' Minu had also represented the Colony in prewar days.

Hong Kong: 202 and 155
Shanghai: 45 and 147

1948 – A doubly historic match when Hong Kong visited Shanghai in October. It was the first time a team had travelled by air between the two ports, and it was to be the last Interport in this great Series before the Communist takeover of China in 1949.

Harry Owen Hughes and Alec Pearce each scored 50s. Sam's brother, Shanghai's Farley Kermani, with 4–64 and 6–43, and Hong Kong's Frank Howarth, with 5–38 and 5–9, both collected 10 wickets. It was Howarth's medium-paced off-cutters which destroyed Shanghai for 35 in their second innings, the lowest score in the Series.

Hong Kong: 165 and 146
Shanghai: 145 and 35.

337

A total of 38 matches were played over a period of 82 years. Summary of results:

	In *Hong Kong*	In *Shanghai*	*Total*
Won by Hong Kong	14	6	20
Won by Shanghai	4	12	16
Drawn		2	2
	18	20	38

The last words from Harry Owen Hughes: 'Let the future continue in the tradition of the past.'

Results – Hong Kong v Shanghai 1866 – 1948

Year	*Venue*	*Result*
1866 (Feb)	Hong Kong	Hong Kong won by innings and 264 runs
1867 (May)	Shanghai	Shanghai won by innings and 36 runs
(May)	Shanghai	Shanghai won by 81 runs (one-day match)
1889 (Nov)	Shanghai	Shanghai won by three wickets
1891 (Sep)	Shanghai	Match drawn
1892 (Feb)	Hong Kong	Hong Kong won by innings and 32 runs
(Oct)	Shanghai	Shanghai won by 157 runs
1897 (Nov)	Hong Kong	Hong Kong won by one wicket
1898 (Sep)	Shanghai	Hong Kong won by 28 runs
1901 (Nov)	Hong Kong	Shanghai won by seven wickets
1903 (Oct)	Shanghai	Hong Kong won by innings and 23 runs
1904 (Nov)	Hong Kong	Hong Kong won by four wickets
1906 (Oct)	Shanghai	Shanghai won by 139 runs
1907 (Nov)	Hong Kong	Hong Kong won by four wickets
1908 (Oct)	Shanghai	Shanghai won by 10 wickets
1909 (Nov)	Hong Kong	Hong Kong won by innings and 224 runs
1912 (May)	Shanghai	Shanghai won by innings and 26 runs
(Nov)	Hong Kong	Hong Kong won by innings and 36 runs
1914 (May)	Shanghai	Shanghai won by 116 runs
1920 (Nov)	Hong Kong	Hong Kong won by six wickets
1921 (May)	Shanghai	Shanghai won by innings and 159 runs
1922 (Nov)	Hong Kong	Shanghai won by two wickets
1923 (May)	Shanghai	Hong Kong won by three wickets
1924 (Nov)	Hong Kong	Hong Kong won by innings and five runs

Results – Hong Kong v Shanghai (cont'd.)

Year	Venue	Result
1925 (May)	Shanghai	Hong Kong won by eight runs
1926 (Nov)	Hong Kong	Shanghai won by one wicket
1927 (Nov)	Hong Kong	Hong Kong won by three wickets
1928 (May)	Shanghai	Shanghai won by 120 runs
1929 (Nov)	Hong Kong	Hong Kong won by 82 runs
1930 (May)	Shanghai	Match drawn (no play on 20, 21 and 22)
1931 (Nov)	Hong Kong	Shanghai won by seven wickets
1932 (May)	Shanghai	Hong Kong won by 42 runs
1933 (Nov)	Hong Kong	Hong Kong won by 117 runs
1934 (Oct)	Shanghai	Shanghai won by 270 runs
1935 (Nov)	Hong Kong	Hong Kong won by 31 runs
1936 (Oct)	Shanghai	Shanghai won by 217 runs
1947 (Nov)	Hong Kong	Hong Kong won by 165 runs
1948 (Oct)	Shanghai	Hong Kong won by 131 runs

Batting and Bowling Averages 1866–1948

	Period	Matches	Innings	Highest	Runs	Average	100s	50s	Wickets	Average	Best	Wickets 5 plus	Catches	Stumpings
Airy, J O	1904	1	1	47	47	47.00							1	
Anderson, D J N	1929–30	2	3	35	63	21.00			ϕ					
L D K	1909	1	1	4	4	4.00								
R N	1914	1	2	8	12	6.00			1	25.00	1–25		2	
Anton, A S	1897–98	2	4	64	163	40.75	1						1	
Arthur, H	1897–1904	5	9	33	115	16.43							4	2
Bagnall, H G Lt	1909–21	5	7	50	126	21.00	1		3	17.66	2–29		4	
Baines, Rev H G	1934	1	2	18	28	14.00							1	
1. Baird, Capt	1909	1	1	22	22	22.00			3	14.33	3–31		3	
Balhatchet, H N	1925	1	2	18	21	10.50							1	
Barff, C S	1891	1	2	42	44	22.00			1	57.00	1–28			
L	1891	1	1	2*	2	∞			1	27.00	1–18			
Barton (bdsman)	1908	1	2	16	20	10.00			ϕ					
Beasley, Capt	1907	1	2	1*	2	1.00			ϕ					
Beck, A C	1930–33	3	5	16*	34	8.50			6	23.16	2–45		2	
Beresford-Ash	1901	1	2	61	97	48.50	1							
Bird, G S	1866–67	3	4	28	72	18.00							2	
Lt	1901	1	2	20	24	12.00			2	65.00	1–55		1	
R E O	1903–20	7	10	5*	17	2.43			44	12.54	7–47	3	7	
Boddam, J W	1867	2	3	13	31	10.33							3	
Bramwell, G A	1889	1	2	8	8	4.00								

339

	Period	Matches	Innings	Highest	Runs	Average	100s	50s	Wickets	Average	Best	Wickets 5 plus	Catches	Stumpings
Broadley, J M Lt	1947	1	2	59	76	38.00	1							
Bowker, A C I	1924–31	5	9	38	99	14.14			35	10.86	7–64	3	4	
Boyle, Lt	1891–92	2	4	63	80	20.00	1	1	1	53.00	1–5			
Brace, W	1927–29	2	4	58	109	27.25	1		13	9.00	5–32	1	2	
Bratrix, (gunner)	1901	1	1	0	0	0.00								
Brinkley, F	1867	2	3	27*	32	16.00			4				1	1
Burnett, G C	1932	1	2	29	35	35.00			2	14.50	2–15		1	
J	1892	1	2	0	0	0.00							1	
Burnie, C M G	1904	1	2	16	16	8.00								
Butcher, Capt	1889	1	2	9	9	4.50								
Campbell, A J	1889	1	2	2	3	1.50			φ				1	
G D	1897–98	2	4	43	92	23.00			1	17.00	1–17		4	
Case, A M	1866	1	1	4	4	4.00			3				1	
Christian, Lt	1912	1	1	14	14	14.00			9	9.11	5–36	1		
Claxton, A A	1908–14	4	7	75	164	23.43		1					1	3
Clegg-Hill, G R	1936	1	2	4	8	4.00								
Clifford, T	1866	1	1	71	71	71.00	1						1	
Clifton-Browne, Lt	1901	1	2	32	47	23.50								
Colledge, W H	1936	1	2	8	16	8.00							1	
Cooke, G A	1912	1	2	5	9	4.50								
Cooper, C R S	1903	1	1	0	0	0.00			6	9.83	3–6		1	
Cox, P A	1897–1901	2	4	38*	75	25.00			1	8.00	1–0		2	
2. Coxon, E J	1889–92	2	3	20	38	12.67			19	8.95	8–60	1	1	
G S	1892	1	1	28	28	28.00								3
Crawford, Capt	1912	1	1	4	4	4.00							1	
3. Dale, Lt	1927	1	2	2	3	1.50							5	
Darby, S L	1892	1	1	16	16	16.00			φ					
Darwin, R J Capt	1947	1	2	29	35	17.50			9	4.00	5–14	1	1	
Dashwood, A P	1912	1	2	4	4	2.00							1	
Davidson, D	1866–67	3	4	45	96	32.00							2	
Davies, L J	1922–23	2	3	16	21	10.50							1	2
P G	1898	1	2	6	10	5.00			1	30.00	1–30			
Dawson, Capt	1892	1	2	7	9	4.50							2	
Deane, W M	1867	2	3	1	2	0.67			4					
4. de Robeck, J M	1892	1	1	18	18	18.00							1	
de Rome, F J	1912–21	2	4	13	15	3.75			φ				1	
Dempsey, L/Cpl	1912	2	3	22	36	12.00			10	23.40	5–94	1	2	
5. Dixon, J T	1903–04	2	3	85	91	30.33	1		12	14.25	5–35	2	4	
W	1906	1	2	11	21	10.50			φ					
Dobbie, A G	1926–27	2	4	14	39	9.75			8	14.50	5–50	1	2	
Dodds, Capt	1923	1	2	43	43	21.50							1	
Donegan, Sgt	1892	1	2	2	2	1.00			3	19.66	2–34		1	
Dorehill, Maj	1901	1	2	25	27	13.50			1	22.00	1–22			
Duckitt, E R	1930	1	2	20	34	34.00			φ					
6. Dumbleton, Capt	1891–92	2	3	16	30	10.00			φ					
Dunkley, G S	1933–35	3	6	16	26	5.20							7	6
7. Dunn, J Capt	1891–92	3	5	107	198	49.50	1		8	18.62	4–58		3	
Dyson, Capt	1898–1901	2	4	16	47	15.67			φ					
Edwards, Maj	1920	1	2	58	78	39.00		1	3	27.33	2–51		1	
W/WN	1907–09	3	5	119	211	42.20	1	1					2	

340

	Period	Matches	Innings	Highest	Runs	Average	100s	50s	Wickets	Average	Best	Wickets 5 plus	Catches	Stumpings
Elborough, A C E	1909–12	3	4	58	133	33.25		2					1	
Erskine, I Capt	1928	1	2	46	46	23.00			9	13.66	5–87	1	1	
Evans, B D	1922	1	2	11	17	8.50			2	9.00	2–18			
Farthing, F H	1920–21	2	3	9	10	5.00			2	36.50	2–14			
Fincher, E C	1927–35	7	14	81	402	28.71		4					3	
E F	1930–36	4	8	127*	221	44.20	1		φ				1	
Franklin, C S P	1901	1	2	23	23	11.50			φ					
Franks, I B	1921	1	2	25	40	20.00								
L R	1920	1	1	29	29	29.00							2	3
Garnett, Capt	1909	1	1	16	16	16.00			1	28.00	1–28		1	
8. Garthwaite, C C Lt	1933–36	4	8	59	134	16.75		1	4	30.50	2–14		3	
Gibb	1867	2	3	7	7	2.33							1	
Goodwin, F C	1926–27	2	3	10	16	5.33			6	16.33	5–39	1	1	
Gambrill	1948	1	2	13	14	7.00			3	21.66	3–62			
Gosano, E L	1936	1	2	33*	41	41.00			φ					
G N	1947–48	2	4	23	44	11.00			φ				5	
Green, L H W	1909	1	1	16	16	16.00							1	2
Hamilton, A C	1931–32	2	4	26	60	15.00			7	5.86	3–21		1	
Hancock, H	1903–07	3	5	27	83	20.75			φ				1	2
H R B	1901–29	12	21	71*	512	26.95		2	11	27.64	4–36		19	
Hankey, Lt	1927	1	2	17*	17	17.00			7	13.86	4–85		2	
Hargreaves, Lt Com	1924–25	2	3	59	109	36.33		1	1	31.00	1–24		2	
Hastings, J F A	1897	1	2	2	3	1.50			1	39.00	1–17			
Haughton, E J Lt	1908	1	2	30	30	15.00							1	
9. Havelock-Davies P Capt	1920–22	3	5	30	56	11.20			15	22.86	4–45		3	
Hayward, A W	1926–35	5	10	83	277	27.70		1					6	
Heath, P M	1904	1	2	33	36	18.00							1	
Hart-Baker, N	1948	1	2	6	11	5.50								
Home, G R Lt	1908	1	2	11	12	6.00								
Hope, J M Maj	1947	1	2	26	34	17.00								
Howard, T N	1897	1	2	31	35	17.50			4	18.25	2–32		2	
Howarth, F	1947–48	2	4	22	51	12.75			15	7.00	5–9	2	3	
Hutchison, R O	1908–12	2	3	39	39	13.00								
Hannay, Maj	1891	1	2	7	8	4.00							1	
Irvine, J R	1907	1	1	3	3	3.00			1	66.00	1–56		1	
Jeffkins, QMS	1892	2	3	45	70	23.33			φ				2	
Jex, S	1928	1	2	2*	2	∞								4
Lane, T A	1866	1	1	16	16	16.00							1	
Langhorne, Capt	1898	1	2	8	8	4.00			8	6.00	5–25	1	2	
Lanning, A E	1907–08	2	4	62	131	43.67		2						
Leach, A J	1892	1	1	23	23	23.00								
10. Lee, A H	1889	1	2	3	3	1.50								
R E	1936	1	2	10	12	6.00			3	40.00	3–103			
Lethbridge, W A	1898	1	2	15	15	7.50			9	8.33	6–24	1	2	
Lightfoot, Maj	1926	1	2	29	29	14.50			2	10.00	2–20			
Lowson, J A Dr	1891–98	4	6	37	104	17.33			20	15.05	8–66	2	2	
Lucy, Lt	1906	1	2	1	1	0.50								
Lumsden, W F	1903–04	2	3	136	138	46.00	1		5	29.40	2–37			

	Period	Matches	Innings	Highest	Runs	Average	100s	50s	Wickets	Average	Best	Wickets 5 plus	Catches	Stumpings
Macaskill, K R	1914	1	2	16	17	8.50			1	45.00	1–33		2	
Macfarlane, J K	1931	1	2	14	18	9.00							1	
Mackay, C H	1906	1	2	3	3	1.50			φ				2	
Mackenzie, D H	1866–67	3	4	15	37	9.25			16				1	
MacLean, G F	1866	1	1	12	12	12.00								
Madar, A H	1932–36	4	8	59*	134	19.14	1		1	54.00	1–7		2	
P	1932	1	2	14	14	7.00			2	11.50	2–23			
Martin-Little	1948	1	2	44	53	26.50								
Maitland, E W	1889–92	3	5	59	97	32.33		1	2	51.50	1–22			
F	1889–97	3	5	38	63	12.60			1	27.00	1–16		1	
Makin, H R	1907	1	2	14	18	9.00			1	55.00	1–35		1	
Markham, Lt	1892	1	2	19	25	12.50								
Matthews, E Capt	1914	1	2	8	13	6.50								
McInnes, I	1934	1	2	12	12	6.00			φ				2	
Mercer,T	1866	1	1	45	45	45.00							1	
Minu, A R	1932–47	6	12	22	111	9.25			33	18.51	6–49	2	5	
Mitchell, E J R	1930–34	3	6	18	50	10.00			1		1–0		1	
Moberley, H S	1898	1	2	32	33	16.50							2	
Moore, G R	1930	1	1	23	23	23.00			φ					
Morrell, G E	1906	1	2	9*	9	9.00			1	13.00	1–12			
Morris, E W Capt	1925–26	2	4	41	75	18.75							1	
Mumford, Sgt	1892	1	2	2	2	2.00			7	12.29	6–68	1		
Musson, A H Lt	1928–31	3	6	19	57	9.50			6	21.66	4–42		2	
Nazarin, K	1936	1	2	24	38	19.00								
Oliver, C O Capt	1921–22	2	4	8	21	5.25								
R E H	1909	1	1	9	9	9.00			6	9.33	4–38			
Omar, U	1923	1	2	14*	27	∞			2	40.50	2–74			
Owen Hughes, H	1923–48	10	19	61	324	17.05		2	11	23.09	6–74	1	13	
Parker, H V	1926	1	2	8	10	5.00			φ					
Patterson, W T	1932	1	2	7	7	3.50								
Payne, Rev S W	1912	1	2	18	23	11.50			1	20.00	1–20		1	
Peake, A W J	1908	1	2	21	21	21.00			φ					
11. Pearce, T A	1933–48	6	12	61	266	22.17		2	23	18.43	6–70	2	6	
T E	1903–35	15	27	145*	796	33.17	2	2	8	19.87	3–35		17	2
Pereira, F	1931–35	4	8	23	88	14.67			8	31.25	3–21		3	
Persse, D W	1935–36	2	4	37	56	14.00			1	42.00	1–42		2	
Phelips, H R	1906	1	2	0*	0	∞							1	
Platt, C	1889	1	2	10	12	12.00								
Pollard, E H	1866	1	1	4	4	4.00			1	? ?				
Powell, Rev T B	1924	1	1	17	17	17.00			2	16.50	2–33			
Prata, A M	1948	1	2	1	1	0.50								
Preedy, Pte	1901	1	2	2*	2	∞			4	14.75	4–26	3		
Quick, Rev E K	1922–28	5	9	21	65	7.22			6	40.16	2–23	2		
Ram, E A	1889–91	2	3	18	27	9.00							1	
Ramsay, A W	1924–28	5	9	39	96	10.67							4	
Reed, E B	1914–26	6	11	5*	15	2.50			27	14.81	4–10	2		
Reid, A	1929–31	3	5	10*	26	8.67			9	21.44	4–40	1		

	Period	Matches	Innings	Highest	Runs	Average	100s	50s	Wickets	Average	Best	Wickets 5 plus	Catches	Stumpings
Reynolds, J R Capt	1928–30	2	3	9	15	5.00			3	38.33	2–35	1		
Richardson, J E	1929–47	4	8	22	46	5.75			3	16.00	3–48			
Ricketts, G R M	1934–35	2	4	42	74	18.50			13	11.77	4–38		4	
Rumjahn, A A	1921–23	2	4	38	99	33.00							1	
12. Sayer, G R	1912–32	9	17	85	275	16.18	2		5	34.60	2–23		3	
13. Sercombe-Smith, T	1889–1904	3	5	16	34	6.80			15	11.20	5–64	1	3	
Sharpe, Cpl	1907–08	2	3	1*	1	1.00			16	10.44	7–71	2		
Simpson, O G	1931	1	2	27	52	26.00							1	
Smith, W H Capt	1906	1	2	21	21	10.50								1
R A Lt	1903	1	1	27	27	27.00							1	
Stanger-Leathes, H E	1906	1	2	3	4	2.00			5	9.00	5–17	1		
Stapleton, C I	1921–22	2	4	14	19	4.75								1
Starkey, R D	1866–67	3	4	99	125	31.25	1	2						
Stepto, A	1948	1	2	2	2	2.00			6	7.16	4–15			
Stewart, E F	1925	1	2	14	27	13.50								
R A	1914	1	2	9	10	5.00			4	14.75	3–37			
Stripp, A J	1924–25	2	3	18	29	9.67						1	2	
Sutton, F	1912	1	2	1	1	0.50								
Taylor, G (C G)	1892	1	1	51	51	51.00	1	φ						
Lt	1907	1	1	2	2	2.00								
Taverner, Cpl	1912	1	2	2*	2	∞			3	11.00	3–33			
G E	1892	1	2	16	23	11.50		φ						
Thompson, G W	1867	2	3	7	16	5.33								
Throp, C R T	1912	1	2	14	15	7.50		φ						
Toller, J F	1867	1	2	14	24	12.00			1				1	
Turner, J T	1867	2	3	2	3	1.50			3					
W C D	1903–20	7	11	88	272	27.20	1						3	
Vallings, Rev G	1897–98	2	4	8	16	5.33			5	16.40	3–19		1	
Wales, C D	1927	1	1	4*	4	∞			1	51.00	1–31		1	
Walker, R E Capt	1925	1	2	2*	2	2.00			3	10.66	3–21			
Wallace, C	1892	1	2	9	11	5.50		φ						
E	1866	1	1	43*	43	∞								
Ward, A G	1897–1903	3	5	17	21	4.20							1	
Waterhouse, W	1912	1	2	9	10	5.00								
Watherston, A E	1889	1	2	0*	0	0.00								
Webster, R E A	1921–24	3	5	61	132	26.40	1		4	23.75	2–4			
West, R H P Capt	1925	1	2	4	4	2.00								
White, Lt	1912	1	1	12*	12	∞			4	12.50	2–18			
Wild, R H	1923	1	2	83	117	58.50	1							
Williams, P V	1933	1	2	14	25	12.50								
Wood, A E	1923	1	2	28	28	14.00							1	
D M	1897	1	2	53	95	47.50	1	φ					2	
Woodhouse, R L	1920	1	2	21	25	25.00			3	18.33	2–39		3	
Woodward, H W	1906	1	2	2	2	1.00								
Wyatt, Lt Col	1929	1	2	24*	33	33.00			1	83.00	1–17		1	

343

	Period	Matches	Innings	Highest	Runs	Average	100s	50s	Wickets	Average	Best	Wickets 5 plus	Catches	Stumpings
Young, F N	1923	1	1	2	2	2.00			2	72.00	2–83		1	
Lt	1891	1	1	18	18	18.00								
Zimmern, A	1947	1	2	30	30	15.00							1	
F I	1930	1	2	1	1	0.50								
F R	1947–48	2	4	10	18	18.00			3	7.33	3–16		4	

φ   Also bowled without success
∞   Infinity – no average

1. MCC 1910, Army 1912–13
2. Gentlemen of England 1890
3. Northants 1922, Royal Navy 1928
4. Later Admiral of the Fleet Sir John. President of MCC in 1925
5. Middlesex 1908
6. Hants 1884. Designed the Royal HK Golf Course
7. Surrey 1881
8. Army 1930
9. Oxford 1913–14, Sussex 1914, Army 1927
10. Later Lord Lee of Fareham
11. Kent CCC 1930 to 1946
12. Director of Education, Hong Kong & author
13. Magistrate & first President of the HK Cricket League

Shanghai Cricket Club

Arnold Graham, the 'Wisden' of the Far East and founder of the Old Hands' Association, recalled cricket in Shanghai.

'Shanghai', which became a Treaty Port in 1842, had three successive sites for its first racecourses which housed the Settlement's cricket clubs. These areas, which were converted from marsh land and reed beds, were purchased outright at the then exorbitant price of £40 an acre from a Recreation Fund established by four generous, public-spirited and far-seeing British merchants.

The first of the racecourses was established in 1850 and sold in 1854. A second course was bought in 1854 and sold in 1861, when the third and largest area was purchased and developed. The latter remained the principal racecourse and recreation ground until 1949.

Apart from the impressive Race Club buildings and racecourse, the area embraced a nine-hole golf course and clubhouse, three cricket clubs and grounds, several bowling greens, two rugby pitches, a swimming bath club, and a baseball ground. During the summer months there was still ample room for various tennis clubs with temporary matshed clubhouses. In the winter hockey and rugby were also played on the cricket grounds.

Some idea of the extent of this magnificent recreational enclosure is conveyed by the size of the Shanghai Cricket Club ground, which had a playing area as large as Kennington Oval! Shanghai is sited in a vast alluvial plain, and the cricket grounds were blessed with first-class turf and wonderful light.

The Shanghai Cricket Club was formed about the same time as The Hong Kong Cricket Club – circa 1851, with mainly the Services playing games of cricket under primitive conditions during the earlier years.

The first cricket ever played here found its pitch in Hongkew, exactly where we have not been able to discover. But on Tuesday the 22nd April 1858, on the ground at Honque, there was played the first recorded cricket match in Shanghai. The sides were composed of officers from *HMS Highflyer* and a picked eleven of Shanghai residents. The naval men were no match for the residents, who scored 129 against the Highflyer's 23 and 19. Amongst the Shanghai team were a Bell, a Gibb, and a Tate.

G Lanning & S Couling, *The History of Shanghai*, 1921

(The first Interport against Hong Kong took place in 1866, and against the Straits/Malaya in 1890, highlights of which appear in the chapters on Interport Cricket.)

Shanghai cricketers first visited Japan in 1893 and initiated a series of interport matches against Kobe and Yokohama. Hankow was added to the list of Shanghai opponents early in the 20th century.

Over the years many distinguished cricketers have worn the Shanghai colours, amongst them: Capt E I M Barrett, Dr W E O'Hara, L Walker, F W Potter, W H Moule, D W Leach, C G W Robson, H B Ollerdessen, and J F Mayhew – all first-class actuals or potentials. Of these, Capt Ivo Barrett (Indian Army, Straits and Shanghai Police) is probably the best known. Dr O'Hara described Barrett as 'a beautiful left-hander of real class.'

We played our cricket during the hot weather in Shanghai; often during July and August, in temperatures of 100 in the shade and heavily humid to boot. Many people when I first came out in 1928 wore *topees* and *double-terais* on the field. But despite the heat and all the other alarums and excursions inseparable from Settlement life, we

345

enjoyed our games and the cricket clubs were cheerful and friendly institutions.

League and friendly games made a full programme from early May to early October, with three two-day matches between the Shanghai Cricket Club and a combined Recreation Club/Police XI, the domestic highlights of each season.

Alas, with the advent of political changes in 1949, the sunlit joy that is cricket was extinguished on China's fields, and the lovely expanses of green turf on the Shanghai and Recreation Clubs' grounds are now buried under the harsh concrete of a vast Peoples' Square.

Arnold Graham was born on 5 September 1905 in Carlisle, Cumberland. After leaving school he joined Thomas Cook & Sons, as he had always had the yen to travel. He played rugby for Waterloo, one of Lancashire's famous club sides. After arriving in Shanghai in 1928, as befits a young bachelor expatriate, he indulged in all the outdoor and indoor sports, and was even persuaded to join the Shanghai Volunteers, rising after eleven years to the rank of Lance Corporal! He worked for the Shanghai Gas Company for ten years until 1941. In between times he managed to get to Hong Kong in 1933 to watch an Interport and to get married in St John's Cathedral.

After WWII broke out, he sent his wife and two children to New Zealand, where he followed soon after and joined the New Zealand Engineers. He soon found life as a Sapper too mundane for an 'old Shanghailander' and got seconded to the Intelligence Corps, when he learnt Japanese and became an interrogator. When the Pacific war ended, Arnold had hoped to return to his old stamping grounds in Shanghai, but politically this was not to be. He then joined the Hong Kong & China Gas Company, becoming administration manager, a post he held until he retired in 1961. Not being the retiring kind, he then joined Binnie & Partners, Civil Engineers, as office manager.

When the Shanghai Cricket Club played its last Interport in Hong Kong in 1947, Arnold played for Shanghai against a combined KCC/Recreio side at KCC. He became a vociferous – in a nice way – member of the HKCC and edited the 1951 HKCC Centenary Celebration Report.

He used to write to the Editor of the *SCMP* on any topic he felt needed airing, chiding anyone who needed chiding. For this purpose he used a variety of noms de plume, some of which are better not repeated, but others such as 'Ancient Gweilo', 'Acidulous Grape' and, more recently, 'Agitato Gaucho', are all different interpretations of his initials. Once he even sent the full scores and summary of an imaginary cricket match between 'Old Hong Kong' and 'Old Shanghai', played at the HKCC, which was published in full in the *SCMP*. The Sports Editor nearly lost his job!

The author knew Arnold for many years – he had never lost his appetite for a leg-pull or a joke. On visiting Arnold at his home in Hong Lok Yuen in November 1992, he said: 'Peter, it's all very well living to my age, but it's the quality of life that counts,' and as he shuffled away from his front gate, added 'and there's not much of it here!'

Bless you Arnold, for the laughter and enjoyment you and your writing has brought to so many people, cricketers, colleagues, and friends. Very sorry you have left Hong Kong, but I wish you good health and every happiness in New Zealand.

[Arnold contacted the HKCC in early January 1995, said he was leaving Hong Kong to join his daughter in New Zealand, and handed over his vast and valuable collection of sporting books to Mike Walsh, HKCC Captain of Cricket. His *Wisdens* from the 1880s up to the Pacific war, included the rare 1916 edition. 'Ancient Gweilo', a real character, died peacefully in the Bay of Islands, New Zealand on 24 August 1996.]

HONG KONG v THE STRAITS/ MALAYA/ MALAYSIA & SINGAPORE – Highlights

1890 – When The Straits Settlements (the Straits) cricket team visited Hong Kong for the first time, the match was played on HKCC's Chater Road ground. 'Cold wet weather. The visitors were handicapped by the weather, which gave some of them rheumatism.'

Hong Kong won the toss, batted first and scored 280, useful knocks coming from Lt E M Blair (73) and Dr J A Lowson (59). Dr S G Fox bowled steadily taking 6–83 off 36 overs. The Hong Kong bowlers, spearheaded by E J Coxon (5–25) and Dr Lowson (6–28), quickly disposed of the Straits for 54. The visitors 'even looked cold and miserable'. When the Straits batted a second time, Coxon (5–41) and E W Maitland (4–14) soon put the visitors out of their misery, Hong Kong easily winning by an innings and 147 runs.

'J J Bell-Irving was added at the last moment as the visitors desired to play twelve men.'

Dr J A Lowson

Hong Kong: 280
The Straits/Malaya: 54 and 79

As there was a spare day, another 12-a-side match was played, Hong Kong

347

again winning, this time by 7 wickets. This second match was not included in the Interport records.

1891 – On Hong Kong's first visit to Singapore for a Triangular tournament in which Ceylon also participated, a reorganised Straits team gained their revenge, thrashing Hong Kong by the wide margin of 182 runs. Hong Kong also lost to Ceylon (see Touring Teams). The Straits batted first, and were soon in trouble with their first five batsmen back in the pavilion, none having reached double figures. H L Talbot then steadied the innings with a fine 40, but Hong Kong were well satisfied, having dismissed them for 93, Lowson (7–34) being the main destroyer. Hong Kong's innings started even more disastrously: 'Six wickets were down with only nine showing on the board.'

The innings folded for 40, only C G Boyle reaching double figures. The Straits scored a respectable 188 runs in their second innings, with Talbot (56) again being the highest scorer. C S Barff (5–45) and Dr Lowson (5–61) both bowled well. In Hong Kong's second innings, Capt Dunn scored 40 out of a total 59! Dr Fox and R Mackenzie did the damage in both innings, having match analyses of 11–36 and 7–26 respectively.

'The great heat which prevailed had prostrated almost the entire team; all suffered badly from sunburn. Fox and Mackenzie again proved irresistible.'

The Straits: 93 and 188
Hong Kong: 40 and   59

1897 – In the first Triangular tournament in Hong Kong, the Straits won comprehensively by an innings and 79 runs on a good November wicket at Chater Road. Hong Kong made early inroads into the Straits batting, with Sercombe Smith getting three wickets. Then partnerships between Glassford and Capt Talbot, and later Talbot and Stevens, took the game beyond Hong Kong's reach. Glassford (110) and Stevens (101) compiling fine centuries, with Capt Talbot (81).

When Hong Kong batted, Mackenzie was again the scourge of the local batsmen, taking 7–68 and 5–44. Only Wood, with 42 and 58, together with a first innings rearguard action by Sercombe Smith, 54 not out at No. 7 and Howard 51 at No. 9 respectively, saved Hong Kong from a more embarrassing defeat.

The Straits: 413
Hong Kong: 216 and 118

348

This powerful Straits side then played a combined Hong Kong & Shanghai XI, defeating the combined team by an innings and 231 runs! It was Perak's Mackenzie again, who scored 163 and took 4–48 and 4–33. Shanghai's J Mann (43) had hit Mackenzie for 22 in his third over, then Mackenzie struck back and took 4 for 4 off his last nine overs!

1901 – In the second Triangular, again in Hong Kong, Hong Kong gained their revenge by beating the Straits by 129 runs. In Hong Kong's second innings, Dick Hancock (94) and Hugh Arthur (72) were the main contributors to the home side's total of 296. 'Hancock had batted with freedom and skill, and richly deserved to have gained the coveted century.'

Voules and Sharp, batting at Nos. 1 and 3, were the only Straits batsmen to score over 50 runs, each scoring 71 runs in their first innings. For Hong Kong, Lt Bird bowled excellently to capture 5–70 and 6–37. 'Six trundlers were tried by the Straits and five by Hong Kong.'

Hong Kong: 192 and 296
The Straits: 253 and 106

1904 – In another Triangular in Hong Kong, the Straits managed to beat both Hong Kong by 95 runs and Shanghai by 52 runs. The bowling of Rees for the Straits, 5–42 and 6–62, and J T Dixon for Hong Kong 5–22 and 6–78, kept the game on a fairly even keel. The difference between the two sides being the only three scores of over 50 made by the Straits players: R B Rees (50), Capt E I M Barrett (53) and E W N Wyatt (74) in the Straits second innings.

The Straits: 128 and 232
Hong Kong: 155 and 110

1909 – In the last Triangular match played at Chater Road before WWI, Hong Kong defeated the Straits by 9 wickets, R E O Bird being mainly responsible, taking 5–60 and 6–40. Only Zehander, with 53 not out in Malaya's first innings, showed any real resistance. Capt Baird scored 66 in Hong Kong's first innings.

A grandstand had been erected at the lower corner in front of the Law Courts and another was situated on the Queen's Road side of the ground, while a small marquee in Royal purple was placed in front of the Club for the accommodation of H E The Governor. In the pavilion itself matting covered the entrance, and arrangements

349

were made inside for catering to the players and supplying their creature comforts.

SCMP

Malaya: 179 and 100
Hong Kong: 211 and 70 for 1.

In late November early December Hong Kong defeated a combined Shanghai/Straits team by 21 runs, Rev. Maundrell (95) just missing a deserved century for Hong Kong, whilst N Grenier top scored for the combined XI with 79. R E O Bird (6–80) and R E H Oliver (5–49) were Hong Kong's most successful bowlers.

1920 – In the first resumed match and Triangular after the war, Malaya returned to Hong Kong and won a closely contested game by 35 runs. E J Riches (62), who top scored in Malaya's first innings and took 5–55 in Hong Kong's second innings, was named 'Man of the Match'. Tam Pearce (56) in the first innings, was the only Hong Kong batsman to reach 50, whilst Capt P Havelock-Davies with 6–30, was responsible for Malaya only scoring 99 in their second innings.

Malaya: 256 and 99
Hong Kong: 161 and 159

1924 – The *Hong Kong Daily Press* on 15 March 1924 reported:

No team for Singapore – the Committee sent out invitations to about 30 cricketers to represent Hong Kong in Singapore, but as only seven were able to go, the Committee abandoned the idea for this season.

So Shanghai and Malaya came to Hong Kong again in November to continue the Triangular series. Hong Kong defeated Malaya by two wickets in a closely contested match. Top scorers for Hong Kong were Tam Pearce (62) in the first innings and the Rev E K Quick (67) in the second innings. For Malaya, Lt F H Thompson captured 5–47 in Hong Kong's first innings.

... then a drive for four by the Hong Kong captain brought the match to a conclusion. Hancock received a thoroughly well merited ovation as he returned to the Pavilion after an innings (32 not out) that had been played with admirable patience and judgement.

Hong Kong Daily Press

Malaya: 147 and 157
Hong Kong: 159 and 149 for 8

1926 – Hong Kong visited Singapore for only the second time and lost to Malaya by an innings and 112 runs. 'They should have continued playing in the cooler Hong Kong climate where they had been so successful.'

Prior to the commencement of this match, in order to give the Hong Kong team some encouragement on their first overseas venture since 1890, a local poet, Savee, from the *Hong Kong Daily Press*, who preferred to remain anonymous, cabled them the following lines:

Bar-wall have got nasty scratch
Must have bunting makee patch
Get one flag, must makee match
Can do hit ball, hold 'um catch.

Malaya batted on an easy paced wicket, with V E H Rhodes (102), R N Hamilton (96) and E L Armitage (64) going on a run rampage. Rain fell overnight and on Saturday morning the sun came out and 'Hill was unplayable'. A J Bostock Hill, the Negri Sembilan bowler, had the remarkable figures of 9–10 as Hong Kong scraped to a miserable 35 runs. G R Sayer, with a fine 54, gave Hong Kong some respectability in their second innings, whilst Bostock Hill finished with a match analyses of 12 for 49.

Malaya: 383
Hong Kong: 35 and 236

In another match against the Federated Malay States in Kuala Lumpur, Hong Kong collapsed again, being all out for 41 and 76, after the Malay States had scored 224 (V E H Rhodes 58). Bostock Hill, with a match analysis of 10 for 69, just edged out the medicine prescribed by Dr Hennessy, who captured a total 9 for 28 runs.

1927 – Back in Hong Kong, Malaya lost both to Hong Kong and Shanghai. Hong Kong defeated Malaya by an innings and 25 runs. Lt J H Dale of the Royal Navy (62) and A W Hayward (59), after W. Brace and Hayward had put on 102 for the first wicket, were responsible for Hong Kong's total. For Malaya, H G L Richards captured 5–83.

The result was very largely due to excellent batting and splendid teamwork. The fielding was excellent and nothing reasonable was put

351

down. Our bowlers kept a steady length and took full advantage of the help given them by the pitch.

Hong Kong Daily Press

Hong Kong: 264
Malaya: 98 and 141

1929 – Malaya continued their losing streak in Hong Kong, this time by four wickets. The weather was perfect. Unfortunately Dick Hancock was not fit and stood down on medical advice. Tam Pearce lost the toss to Bobby Braddell. R. ABBIT, *Hong Kong Daily Press,* reported:

Malaya made a bad start and six wickets went down for 68 runs, but they recovered to reach 148. Bowker's 5–34 was a very fine performance. He sends down a lot of loose ones but these rather accentuate the good ones. But one wishes he could cut out the full toss. Hong Kong at the end of the day are in a very favourable position leading by 30 runs with four wickets in hand.

The weather had turned colder and was quite overcast when Owen Hughes put together a fine maiden Interport century (108). He was presented with two full tosses in his first over and never looked back. The earlier Malayan batsmen made a great effort to pull things around, but after Owen Hughes had got a valuable brace of wickets in a single over, play went all in favour of Hong Kong. The day ended with Malaya 19 runs on with only 3 wickets remaining.

Next day, on an easy wicket, Braddell (56) an Oxford Blue, and Jansen (48) raised Malaya's total to a very creditable 294. E C Fincher and Richardson gave Hong Kong a splendid start (76), and though there were some anxious moments, Brace, Pearce and Owen Hughes put the issue beyond doubt.

Malaya: 148 and 294
Hong Kong: 303 and 142 for 6

The Interport dinner was held at The Hong Kong Hotel roof garden.

The outstanding cricketer of the series was undoubtedly Mr Donald Leach (applause) and he thought that his was the best cricket he had seen in that class of cricket for the last 28 years.

Tam Pearce

352

Mr Leach handed over Shanghai's flag. Mr Braddell pointed out that Malaya had no flag to give, but if Hong Kong wanted to collect one, then let them go to Singapore and try to get one.

Hong Kong Daily Press

1933 – In the last series of matches before the Pacific war, Malaya gained its revenge and beat both Hong Kong and Shanghai in two closely fought matches by 14 and 50 runs respectively. Frank Goodwin strained a muscle and was unable to bowl in Malaya's second innings. R W Hamilton, the Malayan captain with 51 in their second innings, was the only player to reach 50 in the match. Hong Kong's captain, Harry Owen Hughes, with 40 not out, produced the best Hong Kong score. His Excellency the Governor, Sir William Peel, was a guest of the HKCC at tiffin and was an interested spectator throughout the afternoon.

Malaya: 92 and 171
Hong Kong: 125 and 124

In the other Interport between Shanghai and Malaya, Shanghai was heading for victory with Donald Leach and Len Stokes at the wicket, but after they were dismissed after adding 94 for the fourth wicket, the side collapsed for 121, with G L F Willis capturing 6–64.

Malaya: 186 and 198
Shanghai: 213 and 121

1955 – After a break of 22 years, the Malayan team flew into Hong Kong to resume the series at Chater Road. Alec Pearce, who had first played for Hong Kong in 1933 against Shanghai, was to captain Hong Kong in his last Interport. Malaya compiled a formidable total of 391, due to excellent contributions from Mike Shepherdson (83), H F Sheppard (72) and Gurucharan Singh (62). Malaya won comfortably by 10 wickets. Only Ivor Stanton (81) and N Welch (49), who put on 76 for the ninth wicket in the first innings, and Stanton (62) and Bill Withall (46) in the second innings, could cope with the bowling of John Kirkham, whose 45 overs with a match total of 6 for 65 was an indication of his accuracy and effectiveness.

Malaya: 391 and 18 for 0
Hong Kong: 218 and 187

1957 – Rain interrupted play on the first two days.

353

'Three dropped catches by Hong Kong captain F Findlay after Hong Kong had dismissed 7 Malayan batsmen for 45, enabled All-Malaya to reach 127 for 8 on the first day.'

Alex Delilkan, coming in at No. 8, scored 50 after Malaya's disastrous start, and gave the home team on their Selangor Club ground a respectable total. Buji Dhabher, with an aggressive 53 runs out of 118 in Hong Kong's first innings, also had the Malayans worried in the second innings with some mighty sixes off left-arm spinner Khoo. One six landed on the club-house roof.

'The aggressive Dhabher helped himself to 30 runs off Khoo Bin Kheng's two overs.'

Malaya's bowlers, Kailasapathy and Kirkham, proved to be the match winners with hauls of 9 and 8 wickets respectively. A very sporting declaration by the home team captain left Hong Kong 146 runs to win in 119 minutes. Hong Kong accepted the offer but failed by 27 runs.

'Frank Findlay never contemplated playing for a draw which would have been easily attainable.'

Humphrey Brooke, Malayan Programme 1965

Frank Findlay, a fine batsman, excellent leader and a gentleman, died tragically in a motor accident whilst on home leave in Scotland in the summer of 1963.

Malaya: 145 and 118
Hong Kong: 118 and 118

1959 – One of the most exciting matches in the post-war period was played in Hong Kong and has since been called the 'Stan Nagaiah' Interport of 1959. When Stan came to the wicket to join Carl Schubert (Schubert had taken 5–35 in Hong Kong's first innings), Malaya were 91 runs behind with one wicket and 90 minutes of the game remaining, a seemingly hopeless task for the visitors. Hong Kong, captained by Guy Pritchard, were well on their way to an historic win, not achieved against Malaya since 1929! Ivor Stanton (80) and Buji Dhabher (54) had been the main contributors to Hong Kong's useful second innings of 291, whilst Buddy Carnell had bowled his heart out and taken 6–97 to add to his 4–39 in the first innings. However, after being 38 for 5, then 163 for 9, Stan and Carl saw Malaya through to a most memorable win, Stan ended with 81 not out.

354

'Malayan pace bowler writes name indelibly in cricket records'.

Carnell and Bell had dismissed both Nagaiah and Schubert for 'ducks' in the first innings! Jalu Shroff, who was making his first Interport appearance, takes up the story:

The champagne was on ice, and quite a large crowd turned up as the afternoon wore on, expecting to celebrate a home victory. Buddy had been bowling so well, but then Stan started to hit out, and Carl batted sensibly, and 90 minutes later we'd lost the Interport.

Buji Dhabher was another of the 'shattered' Hong Kong players. He added:

At first Stan was just having fun, giving the ball a thump. But after they'd put on 30 or 40, Carl had a word with him and obviously told him they had a chance. From then on they both batted very sensibly. We all thought it was just a matter of time before they got out. Skipper Guy Pritchard tried everything, but nothing worked. Buddy bowled a full toss to Stan, and as he went to pull, George Rowe at silly mid-on dived flat on the ground – but Stan misshit it and it lobbed gently over George's head.

The Hong Kong team were devastated. Much 'spiritual medicine' was dispensed to calm the spectators' shattered nerves. The *Singapore Press* proudly printed:

'NAGAIAH & SCHUBERT IN GREAT STAND – 92 runs for the last wicket – Stan Nagaiah, Malaya's quiet, unassuming pace bowler ...'

The author met Stan Nagaiah in Singapore in the mid-1970s during a visit from Hong Kong, and on behalf of Buddy presented him with special T-shirt (from an old friend) for his fantastic effect on that memorable occasion back in 1959.

Hong Kong: 132 and 291
Malaya: 170 and 256 for 9

Just before Guy Pritchard retired and left Hong Kong, a well-known sports editor said:

Guy Pritchard will be remembered in Hong Kong cricket not so

355

much for the many matches he won both through his captaincy and his own skills as an all-rounder, but for the one match he lost – that incredible 1959 Interport against a powerful Malayan side.

Guy bowled right-arm seamers off a short run and captured as many wickets with as much guile as he did with the incredible movement he often got in the air. He wasn't a typical left-hander in that he didn't probably hook and pull as naturally as do most left-handers, but he drove handsomely.

He was always a tough competitor, and if anything was at stake he played it harder than most – though never unfairly. He leaves Hong Kong shortly on retirement and will be remembered for many things, including the encouragement he gave to young cricketers – this writer included – and the example he always set both on and off the field.

> The one that got away, *Off the Seam*, Carl Myatt, *SCMP*

1961 – In Kuala Lumpur, Hong Kong lost to Malaya by seven wickets. Malaya won the toss and batted first. After the loss of three early wickets, Mike Shepherdson (132) and R Milner (107) put on a soul destroying partnership of 236 runs for the fourth wicket, with Gurucharan Singh chipping in with 48. Skipper Kailasapathy declared at 330 for 6.

Hong Kong started steadily, but once the openers were out, the batting all but disintegrated. Felix Pereira, a right-arm medium pace bowler, captured 6–48 off 23 overs. Following on, Hong Kong started well with a century partnership between J G Allen (53) and D G Barlow (30). Others who added useful scores to Hong Kong's total were Jalu Shroff (32), K Sillett (29), C Myatt (28 not out) and D G Beckett (24), which left Malaya requiring only 51 runs for victory. Unfortunately for Hong Kong, Buddy Carnell was unable to play, having twisted his ankle bowling in the nets in Singapore. The Malayans' relief at the absence of Buddy was audible.

Malaya: 330 for 6 and 52 for 3
Hong Kong: 117 and 263

1963 – Hong Kong, captained by David Coffey, beat Malaya by seven wickets at Chater Road, a memorable victory being the first in 34 years. Malaya had departed from their previous selection policy and had not included any expatriates. It had been rumoured the Malayans were looking for stronger competition elsewhere, as Hong Kong had not provided the necessary opposition for their cricket to progress. Batting first after

356

winning the toss, Malaya were dismissed for 135, due to Hong Kong's excellent catching and fine bowling from John Fawcett (4–52), well supported by Peter Hall (2–20) and Carl Myatt (2–26). Hong Kong then compiled a very respectable 255, with solid contributions from John Hall (69), John Fawcett (50), plus a whirlwind 64 from Tony Weller. Malaya's second innings folded at 285, after being 251 for 5, due mainly to a partnership of 128 in 102 minutes between Mike Shepherdson and John Martens (51). Shepherdson scored a polished 107 after being dropped before he had reached double figures. A Hong Kong supporter, John Leader, remarked at the time: 'I'm glad he was dropped, otherwise we would not have witnessed such a marvellous innings.'

Fawcett completed a splendid match by claiming another six wickets. Jalu Shroff, after failing in Hong Kong's first innings, changed his glasses and scored a very fine maiden Interport century, 104 not out, to lead Hong Kong to an historic victory.

Malaya: 135 and 285
Hong Kong: 255 and 166 for 3

1965 – David Coffey won the toss and put Malaya in to bat on a brown Selangor wicket. Mike Shepherdson's 70 took 153 minutes. Rain during the luncheon interval on the first day prevented any further play and turned the ground into a mirrored lake which reflected the charming railway station architecture across from the clubhouse. Malaya eventually totalled 182, scored in 4 hours 17 minutes, Mike Richardson captured 4–38. Hong Kong struggled against accurate bowling on a difficult wicket: Shroff 23 in 67 minutes, Fawcett 5 in 56 minutes, Dhabher 9 in 29 minutes, Hall 10 in 50 minutes, and Richardson 25 in 64 minutes, gave some idea of the problem in an innings of 141, which lasted 3 hours 35 minutes. Rain stopped play at 3:11 p.m. Hong Kong had Malaya in deep trouble in their second innings at 45 for 9, then a frustrating last wicket partnership between Bynoe (28 not out) and Doss doubled the score to save the situation for Malaya, allowing skipper Shepherdson to declare, which left Hong Kong 37 minutes to score 131 for victory. Carl Myatt had scythed through the Malayan batting after a 'sleepless' night to take 5 for 17.

Malaya: 182 and 90 for 9 dec
Hong Kong: 141 and 57 for 1

The Hong Kong cricket tour to Malaysia and Singapore in mid-1968 broke 78 years of tradition. The respective cricket association presidents at the time were:

357

Hong Kong	Denys T E Roberts, OBE
Malaysia	Hamzah bin Dato Abu Samah
Singapore	Punch Coomaraswamy

For the first time, Hong Kong was due to play separate Interports against Malaysia (composed of players from the Federation of Malay States) and Singapore, now a country in its own right. Thus the long-established series which began in 1890 between Hong Kong and the Straits/Malaya was terminated, with honours to the Southern Peninsula. The Straits/Malaya won ten matches, Hong Kong eight and one was drawn, the drawn match being the last Interport against Malaya in Kuala Lumpur in 1965.

Hong Kong now faced two series of equal intensity, both new national sides – Malaysia and Singapore, each wanted to outdo the other in performance – Hong Kong was certain to feel the effects of their national efforts. Looking at the other side of the coin, Hong Kong's long standing opponent had been 'watered' down into two sides.

This team is one of the strongest to come here. We left Hong Kong as individuals but have moulded into a team after a two-day stay in Bangkok.

Jalu S Shroff

1968 – Malaysia won the toss and batted 'on a perfect batting wicket in the blazing tropical sun and against the added disadvantage of inconsistent umpiring.'

'Durairatnam is a batsman of fine technique and immense patience and an extremely hard man to dislodge.'

Hector Durairatnam top scored with 55 out of a total 250, scored in just over six hours. John Fawcett bowled well to take 6–52. Hong Kong then struggled to 142, bemused by Alex Delilkan who took 5–46. Hatim Ebrahim matched Delilkan by also capturing 5–46 to restrict Malaysia to 120. The match didn't start on the third day until 12:55 p.m. due to rain. Hong Kong struggled and batted the whole afternoon to save the game against the all-spin attack of Delilkan, Jagdev Singh and Gurucharan Singh. Ghulam Abbas 14 in 79 minutes, Fawcett 27 in 116 minutes, whilst the two Ians, Vaughan-Arbuckle and Lacy-Smith, faced the final 58 balls without scoring.

Hong Kong, as a result of an inept performance with the bat, collapsed against the spin attack of Delilkan and Jagdev Singh.

358

Hong Kong salvaged the Interport against Malaysia with all the odds stacked against them, when bad light, poor umpiring and a pitch made treacherous by a sudden downpoor, played out the last 20 minutes of this dourly fought, controversial match.

Carl Myatt, *SCMP*

Malaysia cut 'International' Hong Kong down to Interport size.

Norman Siebel, Malayan Correspondent

Malaysia: 250 and 120
Hong Kong: 142 and 88 for 9.

1968 – Hong Kong won the toss and batted. '... on a hot, sticky day, the wicket quickly eased off after showing more spark than fire. Fortunately for the Colony side, both Shroff and Stevens refused to be unnerved by the situation and playing with great temperament steered Hong Kong out of this jam.' Having lost Ghulam Abbas, John Fawcett and Hatim Ebrahim for a total 8 runs, Ian Stevens (70) and Jalu Shroff (57) assisted by Ian Vaughan-Arbuckle and Julian Murphy, helped Hong Kong reach 220. John Martens, Singapore's veteran all-rounder, commanded particular respect, taking 3–47 off 25.3 overs. Rain delayed the commencement of play on the second day until 3:52 p.m. Singapore, with useful innings from Martens (56) and Reggie da Silva (49), compiled 187 runs, with Ian Lacy-Smith, Carl Myatt and Jangu Vachha each capturing three wickets. Another half century from Stevens (54) allowed Hong Kong to reach 166 for 7 when rain put an end to the match.

It was a disappointing finish to a match which promised after the first day to be an intense struggle, but the weather took a decisive hand and the game never regained the initial tempo.

Carl Myatt, *SCMP*

Hong Kong: 220 and 166 for 7
Singapore: 187

1969 – Singapore won the toss at Chater Road and decided to bat first. An excellent aggressive innings from Max Lloyd saw the visitors total 196. Carl Myatt, ably helped with three catches in Benny Kwong's safe hands, again proved to be a difficult proposition and deserved his well-earned

6–48, whilst Peter Mitchell (3–57) tied up the other end. Hong Kong's batting, with solid half centuries from Peter Davies (54), Douglas Dalrymple (60), who had replaced the injured Vaughan-Arbuckle, and Gerry Jarman (57), gave Hong Kong a useful lead. The veteran Martens took 4–85 off 32 overs. Singapore's second innings matched their first; this time K Moorthy (66) provided the backbone, with Myatt (3–18) being the most successful of the Hong Kong bowlers.

Kwong-wo stepped down the pitch and slammed Reggie da Silva for a soaring six to give Hong Kong victory against Singapore. He threw his arms in the air, a gesture both of triumph and relief.

Carl Myatt, *SCMP*

Hong Kong lost five wickets in reaching the 109 runs required for victory. Reggie and his team came off the field to a rousing ovation. It was perhaps indicative of the spirit in which the whole game had been played.

Singapore: 196 and 202
Hong Kong: 290 and 114 for 5.

1971 – Singapore won the toss and batted on a hot, humid April day at the SCC. Mike Scrutton, a very useful all-rounder, topped scored in both Singapore innings with 56 and 68 runs respectively. Cordell Hull bowled magnificently to finish with 5–19 in Singapore's first innings. Jalu Shroff (55) and Charles Rowe (34) were the only Hong Kong batsmen to reach double figures in a poor batting display. In Singapore's second innings, leg-spinner Charles Rowe bowled splendidly capturing 6–46 off 23 overs to restrict their overall total, but Hong Kong's batting failed again, with Hull's 48 being the only worthwhile score. Singapore's first innings lead dictated the game which they won by 96 runs.

Singapore were always struggling and only the fine technique of Scrutton enabled them to keep their heads above water.

Hong Kong failed because the batting never came up to expectations. The men who needed to make runs – the accredited batsmen – didn't. It was left to the bowlers and a lone all-rounder – Cordell Hull – to perform the heroics.

Carl Myatt, *SCMP*

Singapore: 209 and 144
Hong Kong: 117 and 140

1971 – Malaysia won the toss and batted on a good Chater Road wicket. After losing early wickets, the Malaysians settled down with strong batting from the middle order – Toh Choo Beng (44), skipper Alex Delilkan (85), Hector Durairatnam (50), Gurucharan Singh (71) Marimuthi (50 not out) totalling 343 in under five hours. Best of the Hong Kong bowlers were Peter Hall (3–57) and Gopal Lalchandani (3–63). Hong Kong also enjoyed the good track, surpassing the Malaysian score, with Jalu Shroff's 156 setting a new Interport record. He was ably supported by Ram Lalchandani (69), Rocky Daniel (43) and Benny Kwong (31). The batting continued to dominate the Interport, and when Malaysia declared their second innings at 253 for 8, Zahman (67) and Toh (59) being the main contributors, a tame draw was the likely and inevitable result. Daniel's off-breaks rewarded him with 5–41.

There was some fine batting, topped by Jalu Shroff's polished and well contructed 156 – the highest individual score by a Hong Kong Interporter – courageous bowling, and if the catching was a little indifferent, one took comfort in the thought that it allowed the batsmen to flourish on a good wicket.

Gerald Delilkan, *SCMP*

Malaysia: 343 and 253 for 8 dec
Hong Kong: 368 and 72 for 3

1972 – November at Chater Road, with Singapore batting first after winning the toss. Col Metcalf and Carl Myatt soon had the batsmen in trouble, each capturing three wickets, with Benny Kwong breaking up the tail. Although seven Singapore batsmen reached double figures, the highest score was Mike Scrutton's 20. Hong Kong were also soon in trouble, but a patient half century from Young England captain John Barclay (55) and a last wicket partnership of 40 between Metcalf (42 not out) and Myatt took Hong Kong to a respectable total. Kwong (5–30) and Myatt (3–9) swept Singapore away in their second innings, leaving Hong Kong 29 runs for victory. This was achieved for the loss of Barclay, Roger Booth, Ian Stevens and Martin Alexander, Scrutton claiming all four for 15 to add to his 4–36 in Hong Kong's first innings.

Not a memorable game, there was really no batting on either side. But the real villain was the Chater Road wicket, by the second day the pitch was pocked with holes. Scrutton bowled superbly for Singapore with solid and sensible batting from Hong Kong's young Barclay. The selectors must be congratulated for bringing

361

Kwong Wo into the side at the last minute. His temperament is for the big game and he has too much talent to be left out of the Colony side.

Gerald Delilkan, *SCMP*

Another view: 'Due to bad weather, there had been inadequate time in which to prepare the wicket on the already suspect square at Chater Road, and runs were very hard to come by throughout the match. Hong Kong, ably led by Carl Myatt, were more experienced and applied themselves better, and the Colony bowling hero, the Chinese boy Kwong Wo, who had a match analyses of 8–32, following his seven wickets in the President's XI match.'

Singapore: 133 and 70
Hong Kong: 175 and 31 for 4

1974 – April at the SCC saw Singapore win the toss once again and bat first. Good middle order batting from R Tessensohn (29), A de Silva (25), B Balakrishnan (49) and R da Silva (38) took them to just over 200. Mike Duggan (3–29) was the most successful of the Hong Kong bowlers. A sound 30 from John Bygate, then a mini-collapse until Martin Bulfield (39 not out) and O L Robinson (42) put together a 9th wicket partnership of 66 to save Hong Kong from disaster. The Hong Kong bowlers then had Singapore in all sorts of trouble at 51 for 6, until the experienced hand of Reggie da Silva (43) arrived at the crease to steer Singapore out of immediate danger. Hong Kong then batted the remaining 2 hours 20 minutes, struggling to 70 for 5 at stumps for a draw. Johnny Martens 'floated' four batsmen out for 16 runs off 16 overs.

In three days of bitterly contested cricket, three players really stood out – Robinson for Hong Kong with his left-arm spin bowling and bold batting in the first innings; Balakrishnan, not only for his fine work in the field, but also for two really polished innings which stamped him as a player of genuine class, and Reggie da Silva, whose batting in both innings proved that if anything the years have matured his technique and sharpened his stroke play.

Carl Myatt, *SCMP*

Singapore: 202 and 129–9 dec
Hong Kong: 168 and 70 for 5

Police - Champions Rothman's Cup - 1972-73

Courtesy: Police C.C.

St. George's Cricket Club, The British Embassy, Beijing, China - 1983

Courtesy: Alan Swift

Central British School - 1st XI 1937-38

Courtesy: Terry Lockhart

Aerial view of the British Forces and I.R.C. Grounds-Sookunpoo, late 1960's

Courtesy: Sgt. A. Kitson. R.A.S.C.

Hong Kong v Federation of Malayan States, Kuala Lumpur, June 1948   Courtesy: Laurie Kilbee

Army South, Champions First Division 1955-56   Courtesy: Peter Chubb

Inter-Hong between Ewo and Wayfoong - 21st March 1993   Courtesy: Harry Wilken

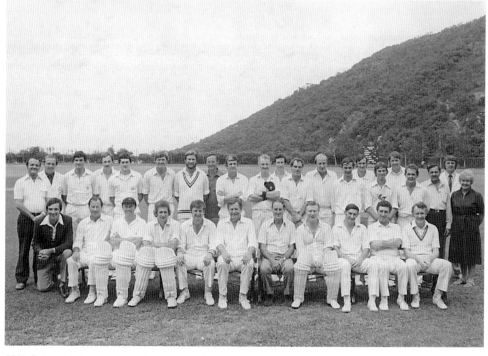

H.K.C.A. v M.C.C. at HKCC., 17th October 1981   Courtesy: Ted Wilson

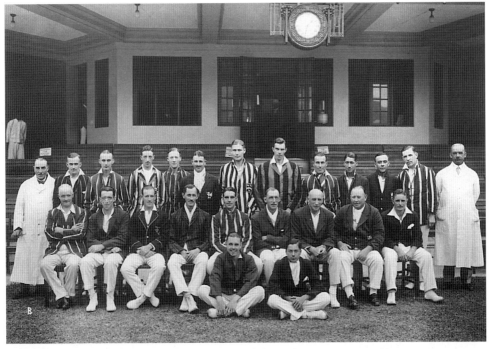

Hong Kong v Shanghai - November 9th to 12th, 1929   Courtesy: Mrs Marybud Chignell (née Hancock)

Hong Kong v Malaya - HKCC, 23rd to 25th November 1963

Hong Kong v Holland - 2nd April 1997 - Cantrell bowling to Fordham   Courtesy: Ray Brewster

Drying the Wicket, 1st Asian Cricket Council Tournament, Bangladesh 1984   Courtesy: Geoff Lever

First Hong Kong International Sixes - KCC October 1992   Courtesy: H.K.C.A.

Jack Chegwyn's Australian Team and Hong Kong - HKCC 16/17 Oct 1952   Courtesy: Laurie Kilbee

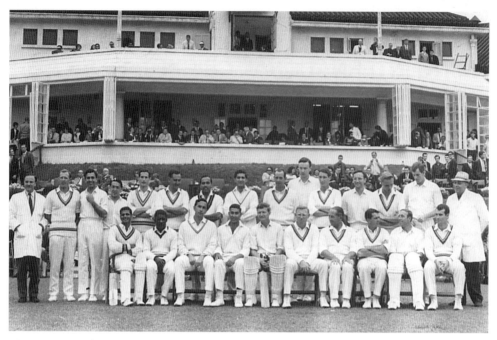

Hong Kong v M.C.C. at KCC March 1966

Hong Kong Squad at Lord's - 1976

Courtesy: Marlene Willson

1974 – Malaysia won the toss and batted at the Selangor Club, Kuala Lumpur. After a solid start from openers A Zahman (51) and L Singh Chall (49), Mike Shepherdson moved into top gear with a polished 88 not out and, aided by skipper Dennis de Silva's 39, Malaysia declared at a formidable 271 for 5 after just over five hours batting. Hong Kong were heading for a disaster when the eighth wicket fell for 75; only John Bygate (42) had showed any mettle. Carl Myatt at No. 10 then joined Gopal Lalchandani for a partnership of 85 very valuable runs before Gopal was out for 39. Carl then continued his magnificent captain's innings with last man Mike Duggan, eventually ending on 60 not out. Malaysia declared their second innings when 231 runs ahead, with Zahman, 52 not out getting his second half century. In the remaining 105 minutes, Hong Kong scored at a run a minute to end on 103 for 2. John Bygate (40) and Col Metcalf (45) were both unbeaten, putting on 83 for the second wicket. Myatt, reporting for the *SCMP*, said: 'Both sides played positive cricket and this was much appreciated by the large crowd of spectators who thronged the clubhouse on all three days.'

Malaysia: 271–5 dec and 141–4 dec
Hong Kong: 181 and 103 for 2

Summing up in the *SCMP* after the team's return to Hong Kong, Carl Myatt added:

Superior teamwork compensated for any lack of batting skills and carried Hong Kong's cricket team through a tough tour of Singapore and Malaysia unscathed. Six matches were played – and all were drawn. That doesn't look terribly exciting on paper, but in view of the fact that this was probably one of the weakest sides to leave these shores, that in itself was a considerable achievement.
All except John Bygate suffered from a famine of runs. The Yorkshireman's phlegmatic application, his courage and his dedication saw him scoring runs with astonishing consistency when most around him were floundering. In conditions as alien to him as the Sahara would be to an Eskimo, Bygate got his head down and batted with verve and nerve. In seven innings he compiled 284 runs for an average of 56.80. Players who were prepared to fight and concede nothing emerged with reputations intact, whereas players of greater skill failed because of their inability or unwillingness to apply themselves to the task.

1974 – Backed by some splendid bowling and fielding, Hong Kong swept to a nine-wicket victory over Malaysia during the last Interport played on the HKCC's historic ground at Chater Road. The Colony side, led by Carl Myatt, had the best of the weather as Dennis de Silva's Malaysian side had to field throughout the second day in damp and cold weather, conditions quite foreign to them.

Manning pulling and cutting and Shroff collecting most of his runs with delightful square cuts.

Hong Kong always had a grip on the game, even in the extras department, where one bye was the sole 'giveaway', and all in all were much the better side. There were two outstanding fielding moments in the game, both provided by Hong Kong players. The first was Benny Kwong's run-out of Mahinder Singh:

The ball, punched hard into the covers off the back foot, looked destined for the boundary, but the Chinese player, flashing across from cover point, picked up cleanly while in a flat-out sprint and whipped the return to the wicket-keeper Bulfield with the batsman comprehensively stranded halfway down the wicket, unable even to turn. It was Test-class stuff.

The second occurred on Sunday morning as Zahman attempted to hook Cumings:

As the ball flew off the top edge of the bat, Bygate backward of the two short legs, pivoted and darted after the ball. Ball and player arrived simultaneously in a welter of thrashing arms and legs. As the ball descended in front of him, Bygate flung himself forward, the ball slapping into his hand and staying there. The momentum of his effort carried the fielder skidding along his stomach for another two yards. It was an unbelievable catch.

'Off the Seam', Carl Myatt, *SCMP*

Malaysia:	163	(H Durairatnam 54, Lakbir Singh 30, O Robinson 4–46, G Butler 3–23)
	136	(Navaratnam 46*, K Cumings 5–63, O Robinson 3–19)
Hong Kong:	278–8 dec	(J Manning 73, J Shroff 63, M Bulfield 57*, Navaratnam 4–57, Jayakugan 3–49)
	22–1	

Hong Kong won by 9 wickets.

This was Hong Kong's first win against Malaysia and was celebrated accordingly in the bar after the match. This win was particularly poignant, as Malaysia was always a difficult opponent and the win marked a fitting finale for this historic ground.

1975 – Hong Kong failed by 50 runs to reach the target of 282 to win at a run a minute. In Singapore's second innings, their last three batsmen saved the match for them, taking the score from 77 for 7 to 167 all out. A fine unbroken sixth-wicket partnership of 110 in Hong Kong's second innings between Peter Anderson and Martin Bulfield, after Rod Starling had broken the back of the Singapore batting, nearly saw Hong Kong home.

The Hong Kong team, led by Carl Myatt, had three new 'caps' in Peter Anderson, David Budge and Martin Lewis. Hong Kong's disappointing first innings was the direct result of too many loose shots. As the spectators left the KCC after the first day's play, General Bramall remarked to the author, who was Chairman of Selectors: 'You were a selector, weren't you?' 'There's two days yet to play!' answered the author.

Singapore: 258 (A Patel 93, L Young 48, C Myatt 4–45, K Cumings 3–58)

167 (L Young 70, I Hamid 32, R Starling 5–51, C Myatt 3–28)

Hong Kong: 144 (B Willson 40, J Shroff 30, L Young 4–26, S Sathivail 3–35)

232–5 (P Anderson 75*, B Willson 56, M Bulfield 41*, S Muruthi 3–34)

'Interport ends in a drab draw.'

1977 – Carl Myatt led Hong Kong to a resounding win over Malaysia in Penang. 'Magnificent Hong Kong axe Malaysia'

'Hong Kong hammered Malaysia into the dust of the Penang Sports Club ground this evening to win this traditional Interport by 155 runs – Hong Kong's first postwar victory in this country.

It was a magnificent team effort by 11 players who did all that was asked of them in the field, and batted and bowled and ran as though their lives depended on it.

Hong Kong kept the pressure on Malaysia from the very first day and never relinquished their hold on the game after scoring 260 in their first innings, the highest score by a Hong Kong team in Malaysia since the war.'

Hong Kong: 260   (P Anderson 59, J Bygate 53, C Roberts 41, G
                     Lalchandani 33, D Greenwood 30, R Ratnalingam
                     3–10, P Bannerjee 3–78)
         149–8   (P Anderson 37, D Greenwood 30, P Bannerjee 3–48)
Malaysia: 117   (K Krishnasami 30, P Smith 3–16)
         137   (R Ratnalingam 28, R Litherland 3–16)

Hong Kong won by 155 runs.

1977 – Hong Kong's total of 303 runs was the highest total by a Hong Kong team in either Singapore or Malaysia since WWII, and the first time either side has surpassed the 300 mark in the series. The Singapore side, according to the experts, was one of the strongest ever selected for an Interport. Great things had been expected of their batting.

'Historic hundred by Bygate'

'Templars' left-handed opening batsman John Bygate, on his birthday, wrote his name into the history of Interport cricket with a magnificent fighting century. Bygate's 112 was the first hundred by a Hong Kong player in either Malaysia or Singapore and was an abject lesson in the art of sustained concentration under the most difficult conditions. Bygate on 93 at the tea break went to his hundred with a shot which slid off the top edge of his bat and flew over the keeper's head for four. Bygate, by now looking very tired, was finally stumped after batting for 275 minutes, hitting 10 fours. The pavilion rose to applaud a truly wonderful innings.

'It were bloddy 'ot,' said the sweat-sodden weary Yorkshireman.

Hong Kong: 303   (J Bygate 112, P Anderson 67, D Greenwood 46,
                     A Naughten 7–89)
Singapore: 243   (P Ishwarlal 83, P Singh 43, C Roberts 4–15)

Rain stopped play, match drawn.

1978 – The first Interport on HKCC's new ground 'Up the Hill' was ruined by the weather, the second day's play being delayed until 4:15 p.m. Except for Peter Olsen's two mighty sixes at the end of the Hong Kong innings, there was little to colour this drab rain-affected draw. 'One six smashed up about 15 glasses of beer on the top bar balcony, and for a few moments the hecklers dived for cover.'

Peter Olsen, Dec. 1996

'Stunning performance by lower order batsman Chris da Silva.'

Singapore: 272–9 dec (C da Silva 94, M Asher 44, M Ahmed 37, P Singh 29, C Swann 4–59, S Willis 4–73)
129–4 (S Houghton 30)
Hong Kong: 191 (J Bygate 33, N Stearns 29, S Muruthi 6–55, M Mehta 3–56)

1979 – Batting dominated this Interport at KCC. Taking first lease of the wicket, Malaysia with a third-wicket partnership of 150 beween P Banerji and Y C Chan, totalled 256. Hong Kong, after a good start from Bygate and Greenwood, saw five batsmen exceed 30 runs apiece to lead Malaysia by 97 on the first innings. Banerji continued his good form with the bat in Malaysia's second innings and was very unlucky not to reach his century:

'Harris, trying to give Banerji his century, was run out when sent back after turning for the second run. Last man D Singh was then caught for nought, leaving Banerji on 99 not out.'

Hong Kong, set 203 runs to win in 155 minutes, only managed 148 for 6, including 43 in the last 20 overs! – skipper Peter Anderson and Des Greenwood being completely 'bogged down'. Malaysia, handled intelligently by Ratnalingam, fielded like demons and bowled well. In the end, Hong Kong could only contemplate the one that got away.

Malaysia: 256 (P Banerji 82, H Durairatnam 65, Y C Chan 50, G Bacon 4–33, S Willis 3–85)
299 (P Banerji 99*, K K Koo 45, R Ratnalingam 36, S Willis 4–86)
Hong Kong: 353 (K McLean 80, D Greenwood 78, C Langford 38, G Bacon 35, J Bygate 30, H Durairatnam 5–144)
148–6 (D Greenwood 52, P Anderson 37*, P Banerji 4–51)

Match drawn.

1980 – The HKCA, MCA and SCA all agreed that it would provide a strong incentive to umpires in the three countries if they were allowed to travel with their national teams and officiate on these tours. They would gain experience in the different climatic and other cricketing conditions, and also help develop further goodwill amongst the respective umpires' panels. Thus Hong Kong Panel umpire Bernard Moore – 'was permitted to stand in Interports and one day fixtures'. In the Interport against Malaysia at the Kilat Club, Kuala Lumpur, Hong Kong erratically compiled a useful 290 for 9 declared with the seventh, eighth and ninth wickets putting on nearly 100 runs. Ian White had the Malaysians in all sorts of trouble until the 'old guard' of Banerji and Durairatnam steadied the middle order, then Des Greenwood entered the arena to demolish the tail. After a good start from Bygate and Stearns in Hong Kong's second innings, reversing the order nearly had disastrous consequences, as Hong Kong, dependent on its first innings lead of 120 runs, only managed 109 for 6 when skipper Anderson declared, leaving the Malaysians to score 230 in 240 minutes for victory. This bold initiative, rarely seen in Interports, was widely acclaimed. However, the game ended in a draw when Hong Kong failed to capture the last two wickets. Again, Greenwood and White proved to be Hong Kong's most successful bowlers.

Hong Kong: 290–9 dec (D Greenwood 82, N Stearns 59, M Walker 43, G Bacon 31, P Banerji 4–44, K Selvaratnam 3–67)

109–6 dec (N Stearns 54, J Bygate 32, H Durairatnam 3–12)

Malaysia: 170 (H Durairatnam 57, P Banerji 33, I White 4–34, D Greenwood 3–20)

173–8 (P Banerji 47, K Selvaratnam 44*, D Greenwood 4–37, I White 3–40)

Match drawn.

1980 – This match at the SCC was the first in an Interport series to be abandoned before the scheduled close of play on the third day. Muruthi had compiled a fine century in Singapore's first innings and Hong Kong's Des Greenwood had responded by reaching into the 90s, so nearly emulating John Bygate's historic century in 1977 on the same ground. However, at 5:00 p.m., since the match could not produce a result, the two captains agreed to abandon the Interport.

As a captain, I have to respect Muruthi's decision. But I also felt that Hong Kong should have been given some sort of target.

Peter Anderson, Hong Kong Captain

Singapore: 233–9 dec (S Muruthi 115*, F Martens 32, J Aldridge 3–49)
             212–7   (C Kilbee 56, R Deering 42, F Martens 36,
                        D Reeve 2–32)
Hong Kong: 267–7 dec (D Greenwood 92, P Anderson 60, A Turner 47*,
                        R Deering 4–56)

Match abandoned

As a direct result of the Singapore match, allied to the historically high incidence of drawn Interport matches, administrators in the three countries discussed the possibility of imposing a first innings limitation (of say 75 overs) for each side, which would go some way to achieving more outright results.

The Hong Kong team returned home undefeated after six matches, and came within a hairsbreadth of an excellent win against Malaysia in Kuala Lumpur.

1981 – Hong Kong won the toss at the HKCC on a sunny November morning and decided to bat. Nigel Stearns, after a slow start, then accelerated to score an excellent 126 not out, to provide exactly half the Hong Kong total of 252 when skipper Anderson declared. Dermot Reeve then ripped open the early Singaporean batting to leave then trailing Hong Kong by 45 runs when their last wicket fell. Steady batting from Hong Kong in their second innings, with five batsmen scoring 35 or more, allowed Anderson to declare, leaving Singapore the 'impossible' target of 339 to win. They, not unnaturally, put up the shutters and more or less said – you get us out if you want to win. Hong Kong bowled 105 overs (Reeve 24 overs for 28 runs) while Singapore crawled to 206 for 7.

Overall, I thought the Hong Kong team performed creditably, with Stearns and Reeve as the stars. Greenwood was as reliable as ever, and Olsen pulled off a first-class stumping in the Singapore second innings. Bacon and Eddington both bowled well on an unresponsive wicket, and Starling did the job of 'workhorse bowler' for which he was selected. I thought we maintained a good standard of fielding throughout.

Peter Anderson, Hong Kong Captain

Another view from Malcolm Grubb, cricketer and sports correspondent:

Both sets of selectors played it safe by choosing teams stacked with batting and short of penetrating bowling. Then the HKCC track played passively throughout. And finally, neither captain was willing

to risk defeat in order to snatch victory. We had the better individuals, the better team, and the better scores, but on the final afternoon never really looked like winning.

Hong Kong: 252–5 dec (N Stearns 126*, D Reeve 40)
293–8 dec (N Stearns 47, D Greenwood 44, P Olsen 38*,
J Hollioake 37, D Reeve 35, S Muruthi 4–45)
Singapore: 207 (R Stiller 57, S Muruthi 40, D Reeve 6–65)
206–7 (M Ahmed 55, L Young 33, R Stiller 32, D
Reeve 2–28)

Match drawn.

1983 – Malaysia won the toss and put Hong Kong in to bat at the Selangor
Club, Kuala Lumpur. Hong Kong struggled from the start to reach 143 for
9, after four and a half hours, rain-interrupted batting. On the second day,
with only a little over an hour's play possible, the match was abandoned.
Shades of Singapore in 1980, only this time the match was abandoned with
a whole day's play still possible. Brian Wigley, Hong Kong team manager,
said: 'The decision was thought logical as it was impossible to complete the
two innings.' Mr P Selvanayagam, a former MCA Secretary for 13 years
and connected with Malayan cricket for more than 40 years, said: 'It is not
cricket if a match is declared abandoned when there was still a day to go,
as the original arrangement was a three-day match.'

Hong Kong: 143–9 dec (C Swann 32, Amarjit Singh 4–35)
Malaysia: 32–1

Match abandoned as a draw.

1983 – The decision to play the Interport on the Singapore Recreation
Club ground instead of the traditional SCC was puzzling. The author
recalled John Fawcett causing havoc on the same ground in 1965 in a one-
day game – the pitch giving every assistance to the medium/fast seam
bowler. This time Hong Kong had 'rugby star' cricketer Jon Jenkins.

Peter Anderson maintained his perfect record by losing the toss once more,
and Hong Kong were put in. The wicket lived up to everyone's predictions
– it was quite simply awful and certainly not fit for a three-day game, but
at least it produced a result. A fighting partnership of 74 between
Anderson and Andy Lorimer and a late 'restrained' half century from
Gordon Bacon, ably supported by Rob Gill in a partnership of 44, proved
to be the key to the match. Jon Jenkins bowled magnificently on a wicket
ideally suited to his type of medium/fast off-cutters. He was the main

370

architect for Singapore failing to reach 100 runs in either innings. Hong Kong's fielding was outstanding, with Nigel Stearns picking up a total of six catches at short leg, whilst Benny Kwong's brilliant diving catch dismissed Balakrishnan in the first innings. This win by 90 runs was a splendid team effort and a grande finale to the tour.

The author, then Chairman of Selectors, was there on the Saturday and Sunday. He had asked the captain to finish the game by noon as he had to catch the flight back to Hong Kong at 2:00 p.m. The always obliging Anderson carried out this request to the tee.

The hero of the morning was the quiet man of the party, the guitar-playing seam bowler Jon Jenkins. 'I had great support from the fieldsmen and I'm still flying a little high at the moment,' the modest Jenkins said. Meanwhile the victorious captain Anderson said: 'We have had our critics at home, and I hope this silences them.

from Our Special Correspondent, *SCMP*

Hong Kong: 193–9 dec (G Bacon 53, A Lorimer 45, P Anderson 30,
                        T Seal 3–36, S Sathivail 3–39)
                91   (T Seal 4–17, M Mehta 3–22)
Singapore: 97   (G Asoka 28, J Jenkins 5–24)
                97   (J Jenkins 5–28, B Kwong 3–8)

Hong Kong won by 90 runs.

John Hansen, tour manager, reported in *Scoreboard* after the team returned to Hong Kong:

Peter Anderson approached every game with a positive attitude and this approach in captaincy contributed much to the success of the team. This was very much a team effort, and the more notable personal performances were only made possible by the dedication of the whole party to the common goal. Generous hospitality followed the team wherever it went, this was of course greatly appreciated.
The team spirit was excellent throughout – despite the efforts of the weather. There were lots of memories to be cherished over the years – Colin 'James Bond' Swann, and Chris 'BQ' Collins and their antics; Glyn 'What you doing now' Davies; Manager Brian Wigley disappearing into the hotel pool after the Singapore triumph; 'JJ' Jenkins taking over the band at the Malaysian Interport dinner; the ever-changing team song from – 'Down Under' to 'Raindrops keep

falling on my head' to 'Sexual Healing' to 'Jessie Girl'. A wonderfully enjoyable and successful two weeks.

Peter Anderson's tribute to John Bygate who had played continuously for Hong Kong since April 1974:

The omission of John Bygate should not go unnoticed. For several years he sweated blood for Hong Kong in the opening slot for Interports without any visible sign of panic. I shall never forget his all day 'ton' in the Singapore heat of 1977. His counsel and advice to me has always been wise and his general demeanor conducive to good morale within the team. Thanks John for your contribution.

1984 – Nigel Stearns' assault on a mediocre Singapore attack warmed the cockles of local cricket followers, as his 169 took him past Jalu Shroff's personal and Colony best of 156 against Malaysia in 1971. It was a great knock, but he didn't have to face the talented spin trio of Alex Delilkan, Gurucharan Singh and Jagdev Singh, as had Shroff.

Nigel Stearns' cracked an immaculate record-breaking 169 as Hong Kong assume total command of the three-day Benson & Hedges Interport cricket match against Singapore.

Cricket Correspondent, *SCMP*

The only real talking point seemed to be Skipper Anderson's decision to declare on the first day, after Hong Kong had notched up 301 for 3, instead of going for a larger total in the hope of forcing Singapore to follow on in their second innings. However, with his experience against Singapore, he knew he had to keep the game open to encourage Singapore to play to win. Singapore responded positively; gone were the old delaying tactics, as they attempted to score the formidable 351 runs to win at three runs an over on a plumb track. What a tempting target ... an interesting match for spectators and players alike, which Hong Kong won by 98 runs.

Hong Kong: 301–3 dec (N Stearns 169, M Sabine 33*, P Anderson 31*, J Barrington 30)
261–5 dec (N Stearns 78, J Barrington 55, C Collins 35*, P Wood 31, M Patel 3–89)
Singapore: 212–9 dec (S Muruthi 45, R Crapper 44, N Perera 4–54)
252 (B Piperdi 81, C Thorns 60, Y Vachha 4–42)

1987 – Very sadly, what looked like the last of the three day Interports was played against Singapore at the SCC from 15 to 17 May 1987.

The pitch was brown, damp, slow and like a jelly in places after overnight rain. Hong Kong lost the toss and were put in to bat on this non-productive batting strip. Accurate bowling by Singapore and the slowness of the pitch made scoring extremely difficult. Hong Kong struggled to a total of 128 runs after over four hours batting.

What had proved difficult for the Hong Kong batsmen became nigh impossible for the Singaporeans. Except for a solid and competent 42 from Chris Kilbee, son of the former Hong Kong player, Laurie Kilbee, the rest of the home side failed to cope with the strong and varied Hong Kong attack of medium-pacers – Alan Telford, Nanda Perera, Chris Collins, Doug Beckett, Bob Fotheringham and 'spin twins' Bharat Gohel and Yarman Vachha. Telford and Beckett were the most successful of the Hong Kong bowlers, Chris Collins didn't even get on, and Gohel and Vachha together only bowled three overs.

The pitch had dried out quite a bit by the time Hong Kong batted again. An opening partnership of 98 between Doug Beckitt and David Evans, with good support from Tim Lerwill, enabled skipper Vachha to declare at 223 for 9, after just over four hours at the crease. M. Patni, who didn't bowl in Hong Kong's first innings, captured five wickets. Hong Kong's opening bowlers, Telford and Perera, immediately had the Singapore batsmen in trouble, and once Gohel had removed Kilbee for 34 the rest of their batsmen faded away, mesmerised by his prodigious spin, as he took five wickets in 4.4 overs. Collins bowled eight overs without success, whilst Beckett was given one as a token. It was Fotheringham's turn not to get a bowl, such was Hong Kong's superiority. Jean Lever, Hong Kong's scorer, was there to record this comprehensive victory.

Hong Kong controlled the game after Singapore's first innings, completely outclassing them in every department.

Hong Kong: 128   (D Beckett 25, M de Kretser 3–21, T Seal 3–37)
           223–9 dec (D Beckett 60, T Lerwill 33, M Patni 5–45, T Seal 3–59)
Singapore: 109   (C Kilbee 42, A Telford 4–37, D Beckett 3–29)
            93   (C Kilbee 34, B Gohel 5–15, N Perera 2–4, A Telford 2–26)

Hong Kong won by 149 runs.

After the match, Vachha's men retired to the world-famous Raffles Hotel to celebrate their victory with rounds of the renowned 'Singapore Sling'.

The author, as Company Secretary of Hongkong Land, managed to arrange for the Hong Kong team to stay in the company's recently opened five star hotel, The Mandarin Oriental, built on reclaimed land just south of and only a stone's throw from the Padang, and was also fortuitously present to watch most of this match, possibly the last of the 'Test Match' Interports.

Summary of Results 1890 – 1987

A total of 39 matches were played over a perod of 97 years

		Hong Kong			
Opponents	*Venues*	*Won*	*Lost*	*Drawn*	*Total*
Straits/Malaya	Hong Kong	7	6		13
	Malaya		2	1	3
	Singapore		2		2
Malaysia	Hong Kong	1		2	3
	Malaysia	1		4	5
Singapore	Hong Kong	3		3	6
	Singapore	2	1	4	7
		14	11	14	39

Results – Hong Kong and the Malayan Peninsula 1890 – 1987

Year	*Opponents*	*Venue*	*Result*
1890	Straits / Malaya	Chater Road	Hong Kong won by innings & 147 runs
1891	– do –	SCC	Straits / Malaya won by 182 runs
1897	– do –	Chater Road	Straits / Malaya won by innings & 79 runs
1901	– do –	– do –	Hong Kong won by 129 runs
1904	– do –	– do –	Straits / Malaya won by 95 runs
1909	– do –	– do –	Hong Kong won by nine wickets
1920	Malaya	– do –	Malaya won by 35 runs
1924	– do –	– do –	Hong Kong won by two wickets
1926	– do –	SCC	Malaya won by innings & 112 runs

374

Results – Hong Kong and the Malayan Peninsula (cont'd.)

Year	Opponents	Venue	Result
1927	Malaya	Chater Road	Hong Kong won by innings & 25 runs
1929	– do –	– do –	Hong Kong won by four wickets
1933	– do –	– do –	Malaya won by 14 runs
1955	– do –	– do –	Malaya won by 10 wickets
1957	– do –	Selangor Club, KL	Malaya won by 27 runs
1959	– do –	Chater Road	Malaya won by one wicket
1961	– do –	Selangor Club, KL	Malaya won by seven wickets
1963	– do –	Chater Road	Hong Kong won by seven wickets
1965	– do –	Selangor Club, KL	Drawn (rain)
1968	Malaysia	– do –	Drawn
	Singapore	SCC	Drawn
1969	– do –	Chater Road	Hong Kong won by five wickets
1971	– do –	SCC	Singapore won by 96 runs
	Malaysia	Chater Road	Drawn
1972	Singapore	– do –	Hong Kong won by six wickets
1974	– do –	SCC	Drawn
	Malaysia	Selangor Club, KL	Drawn
	– do –	Chater Road	Hong Kong won by nine wickets
1975	Singapore	KCC	Drawn
1977	Malaysia	Penang Sports Club	Hong Kong won by 155 runs
	Singapore	SCC	Drawn (rain)
1978	– do –	HKCC	Drawn
1979	Malaysia	KCC	Drawn
1980	– do –	Kilat Club, KL	Drawn
	Singapore	SCC	Drawn (rain/abandoned)
1981	– do –	HKCC	Drawn
1983	Malaysia	Selangor Club, KL	Drawn (rain/abandoned)
	Singapore	SRC	Hong Kong won by 90 runs
1984	– do –	HKCC	Hong Kong won by 98 runs
1987	– do –	SCC	Hong Kong won by 149 runs

Chater Road	Hong Kong
HKCC	Hong Kong
KCC	Kowloon, Hong Kong
KL	Kuala Lumpur, Malaysia
SCC	Singapore Cricket Club
SRC	Singapore Recreation Club

Of Banana Leaves and Hat-tricks – Carl Myatt, 1983

My all-encompassing memories of playing cricket in Singapore and Malaysia is of the intense heat and the strange places I laid myself down to rest at night.

I often think that the cricket must somehow have been of secondary importance because it seems to have been slotted into the deeper recesses of my mind. Not that the cricket wasn't eventful and exciting. It was, but there is often a tendency to remember pain before pleasure.

I don't think I have ever felt as hot as I did the morning I walked out onto the Singapore Padang for my first net practice as a member of a Hong Kong team. The year was 1961 – the day miserable. It had just stopped raining. I don't mean the soft, gentle kind of rain you sometimes get in the spring in Hong Kong, but a leaf-rattling, tree-bending, ground-awash-with-rivers kind of rain that slopped down in bucketfuls. Five minutes after the storm had passed, the sun came out and you could almost feel the moisture being sucked out of the ground by a sun that had all the intensity of a white-hot poker. The effect was akin to turning on a vacuum cleaner. By the time we were on the ground, steam was rising off the grass like a Turkish bath. Our shirts were soon black and clinging to our bodies.

This particular Hong Kong team included two stalwarts of the Kowloon Cricket Club – Buddy Carnell and Buji Dhabher. Buddy had flown in from England at the end of his vacation to join the team, and with his friend Buji formed the new ball attack for Hong Kong. Buji bowled medium-pace stuff off the wrong foot; Buddy bowled fast stuff off the right one.

We gasped our way through the first 45 minutes of the session, the heat searing our lungs with every breath. Just as we were ending this initial stint, Buddy roared in off his long run to bowl the last ball of the day – and twisted his ankle so badly, he ended up being a passenger for the remainder of the tour. So before a ball had been bowled in anger, we were already handicapped. The gloom that afflicted the Hong Kong camp stayed with us throughout a tough tour.

But there is always light relief, and the Good Samaritan from the Singapore camp who produced a sheaf of banana leaves for the team to wear under their white floppies will long be remembered for his kindness. The banana leaves, he assured us, was a perfect 'heat shield', and it kept the head moist. We were soon to understand what he meant. Within 30 minutes of the opening day's play in the first game of the tour, the banana leaves had turned a tobacco brown – and were just as brittle. They had to be changed.

Some of the stranger places I have 'bunked down' on tour were the Station Hotel in Kuala Lumpur, the pavilion at the club in Malacca, and the Ruby Hotel, a somewhat quaint hostelry in Ipoh, that quiet, pretty little tin-mining town in Malaysia. I have also had the good fortune to stay in rather more salubrious surroundings – with the late Carl Schubert at his mansion in KL; with the former Argentinian Ambassador to Singapore, Mario Pepe, an old friend from Hong Kong days, and with the Commissioner for Prisons in Sabah in a 'cottage' in Kota Kinabalu, where orchids grew in wild profusion on the verandah, and Borneo ponies trotted about on the lawn.

Ipoh too will be remembered for a trishaw 'derby' at the dead of night that made the chariot race in *Ben Hur* look like a trot for surreys. Four trishaws went thundering down the street with the bemused, sometimes terrified owners clinging grimly to the seat of the vehicle, while a couple of sturdy middle-order batsmen and an assortment of medium-pace bowlers pedalled the hell out of the thing.

Scared, astounded faces peeped from behind barred windows and lights flickered on in several houses as we sped past to our destination – the Ruby. The climax came in a jangle of bells and grating of metal as the brakes were applied. Exhausted cricketers tumbled into the 'hotel', while two well-known 'international' tourists, fatigued by the ride – they didn't pedal for fear of creasing their silk shirts and British textile trousers – left by the back door in the direction of their favourite massage establishment.

The Ruby, despite its cockroaches and strange bathing facilities, was luxury compared to the Busman's Union in Penang, where four of our party were due to be accommodated on another memorable tour. The Union is a wayside station for tired drivers and has what could be described as basic accommodation – two sleeping 'pallets' in a room about four feet square, and a squatting toilet. We never found the shower. The gentleman accompanying us was somewhat taken aback when we informed him we were moving into a hotel. He couldn't understand what was wrong with the accommodation. Luxury isn't what a cricketer looks for on tour. He does seek comfort, however, and that includes a clean bed and a shower – essential to one's sense of well-being.

The other prerequisite to a 'good' tour – apart from the stimulant of making runs – is the choice of room mate. If you are lucky, you have a choice. If that choice falls ill in a place like the

377

Station Hotel which locks its doors at night and seems to turn off the electricity at the same time, then you have a problem. I've had that problem. It hasn't been fun. On the plus side – and in this respect, touring Malaysia and Singapore always had more pluses than minuses – was the joy of being with old friends and making new ones.

There was an occasion in 1965, on the second day of the three-day Interport against Malaya, when it rained so hard we never thought we would catch sight of the wicket for a week. So my old pal Buji and I decided to accept an invitation to dinner, something we never did during an Interport. We did take the game seriously, immaterial of what anyone thinks. That was the first mistake. The meal was one of those 'eatathons' where every effort was made by our hosts to stuff us to the brim with satays, murtabhaps, mangosteins and sticky desserts and then topped off with lashings of whiskeys and Irish coffees. True confessions – we returned to our respective digs just as the sun was creeping up into a cloudless sky. My room mate turned over just as I came out of the toilet and asked me why I had dressed so early. I didn't want to disillusion him, so I lied. I felt sick.

At the ground I sat on the steps with Buji, my mouth felt as though someone had poured sawdust into it and then used a razor-strap to clean it out. Buji's eyes looked like suitcases packed by a returning Filipino Balikaian. A friend I hadn't seen in 20 years tapped me on the shoulder, casually remarked that I looked like death and offered me a pill. Would it have an after effect; was it a drug, I asked? No, she replied, just a pick-me-up. I took it, thinking I could not feel any worse.

I stood at leg slip, took the first catch, came on first change and took five wickets for 17 runs. Perhaps there was something in that pill after all. Or could it have been the satays and the Irish coffees. I may never know the answer, but Nero always believed there was something to be said for debauchery – and I guess I must agree.

We (his teammates) now know why Carl bowled so well that day in Kuala Lumpur. He even told us he had bowled off-breaks instead of his usual 'rolling leg cutters'. If he didn't know what he was doing, no wonder the Malayans were bemused!

378

Batting and Bowling Averages 1890–1987

	Period	Matches	Innings	Highest	Runs	Average	100s	50s	Wickets	Average	Best	Wickets 5 plus	Catches	Stumpings
Abbas, G	1963–68	3	6	25	106	17.66			1	40.00	1–6		2	
Airey, J O	1904	1	2	14	24	12.00								
Aldridge, J 'Sid'	1980	1							4	17.00	3–49			
Alexander, M	1972	1	2	36	44	22.00								
Allen, G J	1961	1	2	53	63	31.50	1							
Anderson, D J N	1929	1	2	12	12	6.00								
P W	1975–84	11	18	75*	499	38.38		4	3	14.33	1–7		5	
Anton, A S	1897	1	2	4	4	2.00							2	
Arthur, H	1901–04	2	4	72	120	30.00	1						4	1
Ashworth, J	1971	2	4	31*	39	39.00			1	97.00	1–58		1	
Bacon, G	1979–83	6	9	53	166	20.75		1	16	26.25	4–33		4	
Bagnall, Lt/ H G	1909–20	2	3	18	34	11.33			φ					
1. Baird, Capt	1909	1	1	66	66	66.00	1		5	13.00	3–47		3	
Balhatchet, H N	1926	1	2	5	7	3.50								
2. Barclay, J R T	1972	1	2	55	55	27.50	1	φ					2	
Barff, C S	1891	1	2	0	0	0.00			8	10.50	5–45	1		
Barlow, D G	1961	1	2	30	48	24.00								
Barrington, J	1984	1	2	55	85	42.50	1						3	
Beckett, D G	1961	1	2	35	59	29.50			4	31.00	2–28			
3. D K	1987	1	2	60	85	42.50	1		3	10.00	3–29			
Bedson, H Lt	1955–57	2	4	9	29	7.25							1	
Bell R W	1955–59	2	4	13*	14	7.00			5	32.20	2–39			
Bell–Irving, J J	1890	1	1	0	0	0.00								
Bird, Lt/ R E O	1901–20	4	7	27*	43	14.33			27	13.22	6–37	4	4	
Birley, M Cpl	1955	1	2	4	4	2.00			1	70.00	1–59			
4. Blair, E M Lt	1890–91	2	3	73	85	28.33	1	φ					4	
Booth, R	1972–74	3	5	10	31	6.20			4	32.00	2–32		4	
Bowker, A C I	1924–29	3	5	45	65	16.25			16	17.56	5–34	1		
Boyle, C G	1891	1	2	17*	21	21.00		φ						
Brace, W	1927–29	2	3	43	96	32.00			8	14.75	3–18			
Brewster, R	1987	1	2	13	21	10.50							1	2
Budge, D Capt	1975	1	2	23	37	18.50		φ					2	
Bulfield, M	1974–75	4	6	57*	142	71.00	1						8	1
Burnie, C M G	1904	1	2	32	34	17.00							2	
Butler, G	1974	1	1	4	4	4.00			3	18.66	3–23			
Bygate, J	1974–81	11	19	112	558	31.00	1	1	φ				5	
Campbell, A J Lt	1890–97	3	5	25	44	8.80		φ					3	
Carden, Capt	1891	1	2	1	1	0.50							1	
Carnell, B C N	1957–59	2	4	10	17	4.25			14	12.50	6–97	1	2	
Catton, B	1983	2	3	3	4	1.33								
Clifton-Browne Lt	1901	1	2	27	48	24.00							1	
Clinton, D	1974	1	2	11*	16	16.00								
Coffey, D G	1957–65	3	4	17	41	10.25							2	
Collins, C	1984–87	2	3	35*	46	23.00			2	42.50	1–28		1	
Cox, P A	1901	1	2	8	0	0.00								
5. Coxon, E J	1890	1	1	19	19	19.00			10	6.60	5–25	2	3	
O S	1890	1	1	12	12	12.00								1
Cumings, C G	1968–75	4	6	18	51	8.50			11	26.91	5–63	1	2	

379

	Period	Matches	Innings	Highest	Runs	Average	100s	50s	Wickets	Average	Best	Wickets 5 plus	Catches	Stumpings
6. Dale, J H Lt	1927	1	1	62	62	62.00		1					4	
Dalrymple, D	1969	1	2	60	82	41.00		1	φ					
Daniel, R G Cpl	1965–71	3	6	43	94	15.66			6	21.00	5–41	1	1	
W	1904	1	2	4	5	2.50								
Darby, S L	1891	1	2	2	2	1.00			φ				2	
Davies, G	1983	2	3	21	40	13.33			1	27.00	1–0		1	
P H	1968–74	5	10	54	112	11.20		1					4	
Dhabher, B P	1957–65	5	9	54	166	20.75		2	6	37.00	3–26		5	
7. Dixon, J T	1904	1	2	25	30	15.00			11	9.09	6–78	2	1	
Dobbie, A G	1927	1	1	1	1	1.00			4	12.50	2–23			
Dodge, P V	1957	1	2	0	0	0.00							1	
Dorehill, Maj	1901	1	2	42	42	21.00							2	
dos Remedios, E	1963	1	1	0	0	0.00			2	24.50	1–11		1	
Duckett, E R	1933	1	2	2	2	1.00			5	7.00	3–11		2	
Duggan, M	1969–74	5	6	7	11	1.83			9	31.77	3–29		2	
Dunkley, G S	1933	1	2	17	23	11.50							1	
8. Dunn, J Capt	1891	1	2	40	40	20.00			φ				2	
Dyson, Maj	1901	1	2	13	19	9.50							1	
Eddington, R	1981	1	1	8*	8	∞			3	26.00	2–31		1	
Ebrahim, H	1968–69	3	6	24	59	11.80			6	15.33	5–46	1	2	
Edwards, Maj	1920	1	2	25	38	19.00			φ				3	
W N	1909	1	1	17	17	17.00							1	
Elborough, A C	1909	1	2	30*	31	31.00								
Evans, D	1987	1	2	23	23	11.50							1	
Farthing, F H	1920	1	2	10	11	5.50			1	36.00	1–31			
Fawcett, J K	1963–68	4	8	50	161	26.83		1	16	12.06	6–52	2	7	
Fincher, E C	1926–33	4	7	38	100	14.29							2	
Findlay, F	1957–61	2	4	13	35	8.75							1	
Fotheringham, R	1984–87	2	1	6*	6	∞			3	38.33	2–47		1	
Franklin, C S P	1901	1	2	40	49	24.50			6	18.83	4–81		1	
Franks, I B	1920	1	2	26*	33	33.00							2	3
Garnett, Capt	1909	1	1	10	10	10.00			φ				4	
9. Garthwaite, CC Lt	1933	1	2	13	18	9.00			1	19.00	1–8			
Gill, R	1983–87	3	3	19*	27	27.00							5	
Gohel, B	1987	1	2	12	19	9.50			5	3.20	5–15	1	1	
Goodwin, F C	1927–33	2	3	13	17	8.50			3	8.33	3–16			
Gordon, Col	1897	1	2	4	5	2.50								
Gosano, J	1965	1	1	3	3	3.00							1	
Gratrix, Gunner	1901	1	2	20	23	11.50			1	54.00	1–32			
Green, Lt	1909	1	1	8	8	8.00							2	
P	1974	1	2	2	2	1.00								4
Greenhalgh, W	1957	1	2	29	30	15.00			5	14.00	3–42			
Greenwood, D	1977–83	8	13	92	485	40.42		4	14	13.43	4–37		1	
Hall, J B	1963	1	2	69	70	35.00		1						
P A	1963–71	3	3	10	21	7.00			8	23.37	3–57		5	
Hamilton, A C	1933	1	2	11	11	5.50			2	11.50	1–0			
Hancock, H	1904	1	2	8	9	4.50							1	
H R B	1901–26	5	10	94	239	26.55		1	3	34.66	3–35		7	
Hankey, J A Lt	1927	1	1	1	1	1.00			4	8.00	2–13			
Hargreaves, G E Lt Com	1924	1	2	12	16	8.00			φ					

	Period	Matches	Innings	Highest	Runs	Average	100s	50s	Wickets	Average	Best	Wickets 5 plus	Catches	Stumpings
Hastings, J F A	1897	1	2	0	0	0.00			φ					
10. Havelock-Davies, P	1920	1	2	28	34	17.00			9	10.22	6–30	1	1	
Hayward, A W	1927	1	1	59	59	59.00	1						1	
Heath, P M	1904	1	2	43	44	22.00							2	
Hislop, M	1979	1	1	18	18	18.00			3	36.66	2–69			
Hollioake, J	1981	1	2	37	38	19.00			φ				2	
Howard, T N	1897	1	2	51	58	29.00		1	2	29.50	2–59			
Howard-Dobson P Maj	1955	1	2	11	18	9.00							1	
Hull, C	1971	1	2	48	49	24.50			5	7.00	5–19	1	2	
Humphreys, J D	1926	1	2	10	15	7.50								
Jarman, G	1969	1	2	57	59	29.50		1					2	
Jenkins, J	1983	2	2	2*	4	∞			11	5.36	5–24	2		
Johnstone, Surg	1897	1	2	1	1	0.50								
Kwong, B	1969–84	11	15	31	200	16.66			20	24.00	5–30	1	10	
Lacy-Smith, I	1965–69	4	5	9*	12	4.00			11	21.00	3–50		4	
Lalchandani, G	1971–83	9	13	39	177	13.62			17	31.18	3–56		1	
R	1959–72	10	16	69	220	16.92		1					17	4
Lammert, F	1891	1	2	0	0	0.00			φ				1	
Langford, C	1979	1	2	38	40	40.00			φ				3	
Leach, A J	1890	1	1	31	31	31.00							1	
Leader, C J B	1959	1	2	19	20	10.00							3	
Lerwill, T Capt	1987	1	2	33	49	24.50							2	
Lewis, M	1975	1	1	9*	9	∞			φ					
Lipscombe, J Lt	1955	1	2	5	6	3.00			3	37.33	3–105			
Litherland, R Capt	1977	2	3	6	7	2.33			4	10.75	3–16		1	
Lorimer, A	1979–83	4	6	45	121	20.16			1	1.00	1– 1		5	
Lowson, J A Dr	1890–91	2	3	59	60	20.00		1	19	7.37	7–34	3	1	
Lumsden, W F	1904	1	2	17	17	8.50			3	27.33	3–66			
Maitland, E W	1890	1	1	2	2	2.00			4	3.50	4–14		1	
F	1890–97	2	3	5	6	2.00							1	
Manning, J	1974	1	1	73	73	73.00		1					1	
Marshall, I	1972	1	2	11	17	17.00								
11. Maundrell, Rev W H	1909	1	1	4	4	4.00							1	
Maxwell, W A H	1929	1	2	21	25	25.00							1	
McLean, K Capt	1979–80	2	4	80	108	27.00		1	φ				3	
Metcalf, C	1972–74	3	5	45*	112	56.00			6	21.16	3–25		2	
Miles, Maj (RA)	1890	1	1	23	23	23.00							2	
Minu, A R	1933	1	2	21	22	11.00			1	52.00	1–33		2	
Mitchell, P Capt	1969	1	1	17	17	17.00			5	20.20	3–57			
Morgan, J	1971	1	2	27	27	13.50								
Murphy, J C G	1968	1	2	24	31	15.50			1	29.00	1–29			
Myatt, C	1961–77	15	19	60*	257	21.42		1	54	13.22	6–48	2	14	
Myles, S	1983													1 (sub)
Oliver, R E H	1909	1	1	2*	2	∞			2	31.00	2–26		1	
Olsen, P	1978–81	3	4	38*	70	35.00							4	1
Owen Hughes, H	1924–33	3	6	108	177	44.25	1		6	9.50	4–36		4	
12. Pearce, T A	1933–55	2	4	27	46	11.50			4	14.25	2–22			
T E	1904–29	6	11	62	282	25.64		2	1	41.00	1–15		4	

381

	Period	Matches	Innings	Highest	Runs	Average	100s	50s	Wickets	Average	Best	Wickets 5 plus	Catches	Stumpings
Perera, N	1984–87	2	2	19	27	13.50			8	12.00	4–54			
Pettit, T W	1957	1	2	0*	0	∞			1	57.00	1–33			
Powell, Rev T B	1924–26	2	4	10*	14	7.00			9	17.66	4–34		1	
Preedy, Pte	1901	1	2	16	16	8.00			1	37.00	1–37			
Pritchard, G H P	1955–59	2	4	35	78	19.50			4	30.00	3–29		1	
Quick, Rev E K	1924	1	2	67	72	36.00		1	3	12.33	2–10			
Ram, E A	1890	1	1	6*	6	∞								
Ramsay, A W	1924–27	3	5	42	76	15.20							1	
Redmond, T M L	1933	1	2	3	3	1.50			1	21.00	1–17			
Reed, E B	1924–26	2	3	4	5	2.50			5	32.80	2–27			
13. Reeve, D A	1980–81	2	3	40	78	26.00			11	12.45	6–65	1	4	
Reid, A	1929	1	1	6	6	6.00			3	27.33	2–46			
Reynolds, J R C	1929	1	2	52	55	27.50		1	1	44.00	1–44			
Rice, Cpl	1891	1	2	0*	0	0.00			φ				1	
Richardson, G	1974	1	2	0	0	0.00								
J E	1929	1	2	33	35	17.50								
M J B	1965	1	1	25	25	25.00			6	13.50	4–38			
T Capt	1977–78	3	4	14	25	6.25			4	28.00	2–28		3	
Roberts, C	1977	2	3	41	50	25.00			5	8.00	4–15		3	
Robinson, O L	1974	3	2	42	52	26.00			14	15.43	4–46		2	
14. Rowe, C J C	1971	1	2	34	48	24.00			6	11.83	6–46	1	1	
G T	1959	1	2	7	14	7.00								
Sabine, M	1978–84	3	5	33*	98	24.50							2	
Sayer, G R	1920–27	3	5	54	96	19.20		1	5	4.40	3–17		1	
Sercombe-Smith T	1890–1901	4	7	54*	133	22.16		1	4	43.00	4–162		3	
Shroff, J S	1959–75	12	22	156	687	38.16	2	3					7	
Sillett, K	1961	1	2	29	29	14.50							1	
Smith, P	1977	2	2	2	2	2.00			4	14.00	3–16		3	
Souza, G A Snr	1955–61	4	8	30	111	13.87			1	44.00	1–34		1	
Stanton, I L	1955–59	2	4	81	235	58.75		3	2	22.00	2–44		1	
Starling, R	1975–81	3	2	1	1	0.50			7	31.86	5–51	1		
Stearns, N	1978–87	7	12	169	605	50.42	2	3					10	
Stevens, I L J	1968–72	2	4	70	129	32.25	2	φ					2	
Stripp, QMS	1924–26	2	4	16	32	10.66								1
Swann, C	1978–83	2	2	32	36	18.00			6	15.66	4–59		1	
Taylor, A	1957	1	2	2	2	1.00			φ					
Telford, A	1987	1	2	6	8	8.00			6	10.50	4–37		1	
Toes, R	1978–80	4	2	28	28	14.00			5	57.60	2–35		2	
Tress, M	1974	1	2	1*	1	1.00							2	
Turner, A	1980	2	2	47*	74	74.00			φ					
W C D	1909–20	2	4	38	77	25.66								
Vachha, J N	1968	1	1	1*	1	∞			3	12.33	3–37			
Y	1984–87	2	2	15	23	11.50			6	16.16	4–42		2	
Vallings, Rev G R	1897	1	2	14	24	12.00			φ				1	
Vaughan-Arbuckle, I M Capt	1968	2	4	27	41	13.66								
Vergelius, R	1977	2	3	8	13	4.33							4	1
Wales, C D	1927	1	1	7*	7	∞			5	17.00	3–33		3	
Walker, M	1980	2	3	43	52	17.33							7	1
Ward, A G	1897	1	2	14	16	8.00								
Warters, Capt	1926	1	2	11	12	6.00								

382

	Period	Matches	Innings	Highest	Runs	Average	100s	50s	Wickets	Average	Best	Wickets 5 plus	Catches	Stumpings
Watts, J S Capt	1959	1	2	13	16	8.00							1	
Webster, R E A	1924	1	2	23	24	12.00			1		1– 0		1	
Wellard, D	1974	1	1	0	0	0.00			3	16.33	3–32			
Welch, N G F/Sgt	1955–57	2	4	49	73	24.33								2
Weller, F A	1963	1	1	64	64	64.00	1		φ					
White, I	1980	1	1	16*	16	∞			7	10.57	4–34		5	
Wigley, B T	1968	1	2	3	5	2.50			4	9.25	3–16		2	
Williams, P V	1933	1	2	26	35	17.50								
W E G	1961	1	2	0	0	0.00			φ					
Willis, S	1978–79	2	2	11*	13	13.00			11	24.55	4–73			
15. Willson, B J	1975	1	2	56	96	48.00	1		3	12.33	2–24		1	
Wilson, E H	1968	1	2	9	17	8.50								
Withall, W N Capt	1955	1	2	46	60	30.00			2	15.50	2–31		1	
Wodehouse, R L	1920	1	2	21	22	11.00			2	22.50	2–45		2	
Wood, M D	1897	1	2	58	100	50.00	1		3	23.00	3–69		1	
P Capt	1984	1	2	31	56	28.00								2
Wright, R	1974	2	3	26	33	11.00								
Wyatt, F J Lt Col	1929	1	1	6	6	6.00			1	92.00	1–33			

φ   Also bowled without success
∞   Infinity – no average

1. MCC 1910, Army 1912–13
2. Sussex CCC 1970–1986
3. Lancs CCC, played one one-day match
4. Kent CCC 1893–1900 (later Major-General)
5. Gentlemen of England 1890
6. Northants 1922, Royal Navy 1928
7. Middlesex CCC 1908
8. Surrey CCC 1881
9. Army 1930
10. Oxford Univ. 1913–14, Sussex 1914, Army 1927
11. Hants CCC 1900
12. Kent CCC 1930 to 1946
13. Sussex CCC 1983–87 & Warwicks CCC 1988–96
14. Kent CCC 1974–81 & Glamorgan CCC 1982–84
15. Combined Services 1964

A Brief History of the Singapore Cricket Club

In the early days of Singapore, the typical European settler could count few diversions to while away his leisure hours. The most popular was sport. Social sports in Singapore were usually contested on the Padang, the grassy expanse in the centre of town. Cricket soon emerged as the most popular of these events. Cricket may well have come to Singapore with the

British, the club being situated within two minutes' walking distance from the point where Sir Stamford Raffles first set foot on the island in 1819. The first mention of the game was a complaint against Sunday cricket lodged with the local press in 1837 by a puritanical and pseudonymous 'Z'.

Yet 'the manly game of cricket' thrived, but often with odd six or nine-men teams. In October 1852, a meeting to found the Singapore Cricket Club was convened, making it Singapore's second oldest surviving club after the Turf Club founded in 1842. Thus the Singapore Cricket Club came into being just over a year after The Hong Kong Cricket Club in June 1851, and six years before The Shanghai Cricket Club.

From a handful of 28 members in 1861, all Europeans and mostly young merchants, membership had grown to 100 by the 1870s, and to 400 by the 1890s. Women were first admitted as club members in 1938.

The clubhouse has gone through several phases. A hut replaced a simple tent in the 1860s on the south-west corner of the Padang. In 1877, a single-storey pavilion was erected and was expanded to become a splendid two-storey building in 1884. Traces of this structure, including the wrought-iron pillars and verandahs, can be seen to this day. In 1907, the gracious building we now see was completed – the two wings were added in 1922.

In pre-WWII years, the club dominated and influenced all local sport, sponsoring lively events such as 'Europeans v The Rest'. Lawn bowls and tennis were pioneered in the 1870s, soccer and rugby football in the 1880s, and hockey in the 1890s. Squash became an important club sport from the more recent 1970s.

The club has proved to be one of Singapore's most successful survivors. Although refurbished and modernised in the early 1970s, it has not lost its colonial character. Today, it is truly a multi-racial club, with membership extended to Singaporeans and expatriates alike. Programmes to teach and encourage Singaporean youngsters with sporting ability, the generous lending of the Padang for non-club events, and substantial donations to charity, have all made a lasting contribution to the quality of modern Singaporean life.

To use Singapore Prime Minister Lee Kuan Yew's words in 1970, when he accepted the title of 'Visitor' (Patron) to the club: 'There is an indefinable quality about this Club which no other club can match – it bridges the transformation from what was to what is, and represents our capacity to meet what will be.'

Tom Hughes, Singapore Cricket Club President from 1973 to 1975, said: 'This is a Club for sportsmen and sportswomen – present, past and potential.' [Source: Christopher K C Phua, General Manager, Singapore Cricket Club, September 1993]

The author first played cricket on the Padang for Hong Kong in a two-day game against the Malayan Cricket Association in May 1965, during the Hong Kong tour of Singapore and Malaya under the captaincy of David Coffey, with Denys (later Sir Denys) Roberts as the team manager. The wicket wasn't much to talk about on that occasion, but the historic clubhouse, the lasting friendships made over the years (three further visits were made in the 1980s to the Singapore Stock Exchange as Company Secretary of Hongkong Land, which slotted in neatly with the dates of the Interports), and the atmosphere of the occasions, have remained lasting and treasured memories – thanks to the likes of the late Stan Nagaiah, and fellow cricketing opponents, Cecil Cooke, Johnny Martens and Reggie da Silva.

In early 1995, the author met up with Cecil and Reggie in Perth during his trip to watch England play Australia in the Adelaide and Perth 'Ashes' Test matches. At Lord's in June 1996, during the England v India Test match, the author was surprised to see Johnny Martens strolling with friends behind the pavilion. These are the 'gems' the great game produces.

A Brief History of the Royal Selangor Club, Kuala Lumpur, Malaysia

With the arrival of the British and other races, it was not long before an International Sports and Social Club was mooted with the Acting Resident, J P Rodger, as President. A site was selected and acquired at the Gombak Bridge corner of the Parade Ground (the Padang), with stables where St Mary's Church is today. Originally cleared for fruit and vegetable cultivation, the central section was used by the Police as a Parade Ground. Captain Syers, Superintendent of Police, used to shoot snipe in the swampy land which sloped away at either end of the Padang. Thus The Selangor Club came into being in 1884.

Although the actual date when the first cricket match was played on the Padang is not known, 'we may assume that it was played between 1884 and 1886 ... Selangor's first State match appears to have been against Malacca in 1887 at Kuala Lumpur. The Selangor v Perak series was inaugurated in 1889, followed by Selangor v Singapore in 1891.'

In 1885, the Government lent the Club M$900 to improve their buildings. By 1892, the membership had risen to 140. Cricket received an immense filip with the arrival of the enthusiastic E W (later Sir Ernest) Birch as Acting Resident. During his time the raising and turfing of a portion of the Padang was completed, the cricket pitch formed and the swamp area filled in.

By 1907, The Selangor Club, complete with newly installed electric lighting and fans, had a membership of 650. The clubhouse was also the headquarters of the Turf Club, the Choral Society and the Automobile Club. By 1910, The Selangor Club had undergone further structural

385

changes when the existing long Tudor-type building was evolved. The ballroom was added to accommodate the reception for the Prince of Wales in 1922, the same year in which the Federated Malay States Board of Cricket Control (BCC) was formed.

Before the Klang River was straightened, Kuala Lumpur was subject to frequent floods, the worst being in 1902 and 1926, when the Padang was a veritable sea!

In June 1927, a visiting Australian 'Test' team, led by C G Macartney which included W H Woodfull and W A Oldfield, was defeated by an All-Malayan cricket team captained by N J A Foster, a planter and member of a distinguished English cricketing family. Dr P H Hennessy, 'a slow bowler who combined leg-breaks and off-breaks', captured 7–42 to help bowl Australia out for 85 in their first innings.

In 1964, the great Gary Sobers, a member of E W Swanton's Commonwealth team, perhaps in revenge for being bowled first ball by Malaysia's Dr Alex Delilkan 'caused a sensation by taking the first five wickets in five consecutive balls.'

Most of the club records were lost during the Japanese occupation. In 1948, the Malayan Cricket Association (MCA) was formed and took over from the BCC. The MCA continues to control all cricket in Malaysia to this day.

By the early 1960s, following extensive redecoration, air-conditioning was installed in the club dining room and ballroom, an amenity never dreamed of by those early members in their attap and plank clubhouse of 1884.

[Sources: The Selangor Club looks back, January 1962
        Selangor Club Centenary Year Sports Souvenir Programme, 1984]

Hong Kong played its first Interport at the Selangor Club, the 'Dog', against Malaya in May 1957. The author clearly recalled the 'mirrored lake' when he played there in the drawn game against Malaya in 1965. The most recent against Malaysia, and hopefully not the last, was in May 1983.

Earlier matches between Hong Kong and The Straits/Malaya were played in Hong Kong from 1890, during triangular tournaments with Shanghai, the exceptions being in 1891 and 1926, when the matches were played at the Singapore Cricket Club.

The Selangor Club, known as the 'Dog', launched its Centenary Celebrations on 15th January 1984, and on the same day was declared a Royal Club by His Royal Highness, the Sultan of Selangor.

ONE-DAY CRICKET

INTERNATIONAL CRICKET COUNCIL

The International Cricket Council was originally called the Imperial Cricket Conference when it was founded in 1909, with Australia, England and South Africa as its first members. In 1962, Pakistan proposed a 'junior section' to include any country where cricket was 'firmly established and organised.'

In 1965, it became known as the International Cricket Conference, and included teams from outside the British Commonwealth. During the year, Ceylon, Fiji and the USA joined as the first Associate Members. In 1989, it became known under its present title, the International Cricket Council (ICC).

Hong Kong became an Associate Member of the ICC in 1969, but did not participate in the first competition for associate members in 1979, because the strict qualification rules precluded nearly half the Hong Kong national side from taking part. All participants, unless born in Hong Kong, must have been resident there for at least eight out of each twelve-month period for each of the four years prior to the commencement of the tournament. This rule hit Hong Kong particularly hard, due to the transient nature of its non-local business population. Very few local Chinese played cricket.

Despite this disappointment, even after strenuous efforts by the President of the HKCA (Ted Wilson) and the Chairman (Bryan Hemshall) at ICC meetings at Lord's to gain some relaxation of this four-year rule, the HKCA Executive Committee decided Hong Kong must enter the next competition in 1982. It was considered necessary for Hong Kong to take its rightful place in international cricket; to make and strengthen its ties with the other then 15 Associate members, and to fly its flag in the English midlands. Hong Kong has since also participated in the 1986 (England), 1990 (Netherlands), 1994 (Kenya) and 1997 (Malaysia) competitions. Prior to the commencement of the 1994 tournament in Kenya, certain countries wanted the qualification rule extended to seven years! At the next ICC tournament in 2001, Hong Kong will play as Hong Kong Special Administrative Region, People's Republic of China, and the Hong Kong team must include nine players qualified by birth and citizenship.

The author, as Chairman of Selectors, also endeavoured to obtain some relaxation of the four-year rule prior to the 1986 and 1990 competitions, but likewise to no avail. In the recent tournament in Kenya, some doubt about the United Arab Emirates team strictly following the qualification rule seemed to have been ignored by the ICC at the time. However, at the annual conference of the International Cricket Council at Lord's in July 1995, a revised ICC Selection Policy was agreed which stated that: Provided a cricketer has not played for another Associate for 5 years or a Test country for 10 years, a cricketer qualifies:

1. for the country of birth;
2. as a citizen, or entitled to hold the passport of a country, provided he is in residence for a minimum of 240 days in each of the 5 years preceding an ICC Trophy;
3. by residence for a minimum of 240 days in each of the 5 years – but no more than four players in this category for 1997, (2 players in 2001).

John Cribbin, Hon. Secretary, HKCA, said:

The policy is rather more stringent than Hong Kong expected, particulary given that we have now committed ourselves to development. There are many anomalies, nevertheless, insofar as it will encourage our development plans, we should accept the new policy in a spirit of enthusiasm.

2nd ICC Trophy in England – 1982

16 June – Papua New Guinea won the toss at the Bourneville CC ground and put Hong Kong in to bat on a wet wicket, in Hong Kong's first match of this 60-over competition. Wickets fell steadily in what was an unsatisfactory performance. Tight bowling and tenacious, 'give nothing away' fielding by Hong Kong made the Papuans work hard, but the small total was never enough to stop the Papuans from their deserved win.

Hong Kong: 100   (D A Reeve 38, K Ila 3–14, V Pala 3–25)
Papua NG: 101–6   (T Vai 33, D A Reeve 2–26)

Papua New Guinea won by four wickets.

18 June – Rain delayed the start until 1.33 p.m., reducing this match to 45 overs each. Israel won the toss and put Hong Kong in to bat. After the early loss of skipper Peter Anderson, Hong Kong rattled up a respectable 200-plus

runs. Israel never came to terms with the varied Hong Kong attack, and were all out for 84. A last-wicket partnership of 20 runs boosted their total.

Hong Kong: 207–7 (A Lorimer 53, D Reeve 43, P Olsen 37*, N Reuben 3–7)
Israel: 84 (S Waller 3–18, G Bacon 2–9, D Greenwood 2–13)

Hong Kong won by 123 runs.

21 June – Hong Kong v Canada at Burton CC. Without a ball being bowled, the match was abandoned due to rain.

25 June – Hong Kong v USA at Aldridge CC. Hong Kong won the toss and put USA in to bat. Rain then prevented any play. Match abandoned.

28 June – The match at the Walmley CC ground was reduced to 45 overs due to the rain-affected conditions. Hong Kong won the toss and put Gibraltar in to bat.

'Gibraltar were acknowledged as one of the weaker teams from the start, and Hong Kong were lucky to get a 40-over match in, and a comfortable eight wicket win.'

Gibraltar: 129–8 (J Jacks 35, G Bacon 4–37, G Lalchandani 2–22)
Hong Kong: 130–2 (D Greenwood 56*, D Reeve 56*)

Hong Kong won by eight wickets.

30 June – Kenya won the toss and fielded first at Streetley CC.

'Although suffering the worst of the wicket Hong Kong did not bat well, and it was only through some late defiant batting from Gopal Lalchandani and Rob Gill, who put on 34 for the last wicket, that the side even reached three figures. Again the opposition were made to fight, but the low score was always within their reach.'

Hong Kong: 105–9 (G Lalchandani 27*, Z Sheikh 3–22, R Patel 2–6, S Joshi 2–9)
Kenya: 108–7 (H Mehta 39*, N Verjee 29, G Bacon 2–15, D Reeve 2–22)

Kenya won by three wickets.

389

5 July – Hong Kong won the toss at Bewdley CC and decided to bat against Zimbabwe, the favourites and eventual winners of the competition.

'Hong Kong's best performance. The batting was consistent and full of application. The stand between Andy Lorimer and Martin Sabine was an absorbing piece of cricket, as they together, went through three phases, defence (as three quick wickets had fallen), stabilisation and attack.

'Lorimer's overall score was really the best innings I have seen from a Hong Kong player. Bacon with his accurate bowling, and with the fielding reaching new heights that day, the Zimbabwean players were left scratching their heads in wonderment as to how Hong Kong ever lost to Papua and Kenya.'

Hong Kong: 192–4 (A Lorimer 72*, P Anderson 41*, M Sabine 36, V Hogg 3–34)
Zimbabwe: 196–3 (A Pyecroft 83*, J Heron 51, D Fletcher 33*)

Zimbabwe won by seven wickets.

After the competition, a first for Hong Kong, skipper Peter Anderson said:

Hong Kong has nothing to fear from other Associate Members. Quite obviously, the overall standard of cricket played here is equal to anything that may be served up from Fiji to Canada. Naturally, one or two outstanding individuals who consistently perform well in any team would raise that standard.

He added that Dermot Reeve was easily Hong Kong's best player, but did not make the impact in the competition games he had expected. However, without him, Hong Kong would have looked very naked.

A total of ten friendly matches were also scheduled on this tour. Hong Kong won eight, lost one, and one was abandoned due to the ground at Hereford CC being waterlogged.

3rd ICC Trophy in England – 1986

11 June – This first match, played at the lovely Bridgnorth ground, was dominated by Simon Myles's superb batting performance – 172 runs, the highest individual score of the competition.

Hong Kong: 324–5 (S Myles 172, N Stearns 62, White 3–46)
Gibraltar: 180–5 (G De'Arth 63, S Perez 36*, N Perera 2–32)

Hong Kong won by 144 runs.

13 June – The aggressive Bermudan side scored a record 407–8 at the County Ground, Nuneaton, Gibbons hitting 125 not out in 114 minutes (15 4's). A resolute 55 from Martin Sabine helped a 'shell-shocked' Hong Kong to 180 for 6 in reply.

I have never felt so humiliated on a cricket field as on that occasion.

Peter Anderson, Hong Kong Captain

Bermuda: 407–8 (N Gibbons 125*, R Hill 84, S Lightbourne 50, W Reid 42, R Fotheringham 4–51)
Hong Kong: 180–6 (M Sabine 55, P Anderson 31, T Burgess 3–16)

Bermuda won by 227 runs.

18 June – With Nigel Stearns (85) and Simon Myles (82) leading the way, Hong Kong scored 261–7 after winning the toss and batting against the fancied Canadians at Halesowen. Peter Anderson said: 'the best equipped, organized and dedicated amateur cricket ground I have ever seen.'

Much to Hong Kong's disappointment, Canada won with four wickets and an over to spare.

Hong Kong: 261–7 (N Stearns 85, S Myles 82, M Sabine 44*)
Canada: 265–6 (O Dipchard 76, P Prashad 40, F Kirmani 34)

Canada won by four wickets.

20 June – Holland's innings of 327 for 7 on the Wroxeter ground was dominated by a 200-run partnership for the 2nd wicket between S Atkinson (107) and R Gomes (101). Against a fast, lively and accurate attack, Nigel Stearns (47) and Martin Sabine (45) achieved some respectability for Hong Kong, who reached 157–9.

Holland: 327–7 (S Atkinson 107, R Gomes 101, R Elferink 35, G Davies 3–61)
Hong Kong: 157–9 (N Stearns 47, M Sabine 45, R Lefebvre 3–12, P Bakker 2–20)

Holland won by 170 runs.

23 June – Hong Kong, put in on a 'green wicket' at Leamington, collapsed to 58 for 6 before a determined partnership of 52 between Chris Collins and Yarman Vachha stretched the total to 144. The USA won comfortably as the wicket 'eased'.

Hong Kong: 144   (C Collins 53, Y Vachha 28, Mody 2–12, K Lorick 2–16)

USA: 148–5 (S Shivnaraine 36, T Foster 34, H Blackman 31, N Smith 2–31)

USA won by five wickets.

Four successive defeats, albeit all against strong sides, was no disgrace, but it did dent the confidence and severely affect the morale of the side.

25 June – After reaching 101 for 2 at Barnet Green, Israel collapsed and were dismissed for 158, Simon Myles picking up three wickets. Then Myles, with a fine 87 not out, dominated the Hong Kong reply of 159 for 2.

Israel: 158   (S Perlman 41, N Jhirad 32, S Myles 3–30)

Hong Kong: 159–2 (S Myles 87*, B Catton 31)

Hong Kong won by eight wickets.

27 June – Fiji, batting first at the very pleasant and affluent Knowle and Derridge Club, were completely mesmerised and demoralised by the left-arm spin of Bharat Gohel as soon as he was introduced into the attack.

'Gohel slays Fiji with magic spell.'

Gohel's figures (6–11) was the second best ever recorded in the competition. [Bangladesh's Ashraful Haque had taken 7–23 against Fiji in 1979]. a performance which 'poor old Yarman Vachha will have to hear about from his spin-twin for at least a decade.' Hong Kong had no difficulty in scoring the required runs for its third win.

Fiji: 87   (S Koto 38, B Gohel 6–11, R Fotheringham 2–10)

Hong Kong: 88–3 (R Brewster 36, B Catton 25, S Campbell 2–16)

Hong Kong won by seven wickets.

30 June – Hong Kong, after an excellent start from Brian Catton and Ray Brewster, should have passed the 300 mark, but over confidence and the tiredness of a very demanding tour, removed this wasted opportunity, to the disappointment of their followers. In the end, only a fighting unbroken ninth-wicket partnership between the 'spin-twins', Vachha (22) and Gohel (32), enabled Hong Kong to pass the 250 mark. After a confident start, Papua always looked in contention, as Hong Kong's bowling and fielding was indifferent, winning with an over to spare.

Hong Kong: 257–8 (B Catton 63, R Brewster 55, B Gohel 32*, Myles 32, Maha 3–44)
Papua NG: 259–8 (T Vai 55, W Maha 50, A Leka 37, D Lohia 31, C Collins 3–48)

Papua New Guinea won by two wickets.

Nine other matches were played – four were won and five lost – making a total of 17 matches in 21 days. A very full and hectic schedule, but as the skipper, Peter Anderson said: 'Who would have thought there would be no rain in June!'

Peter Anderson's comments after his last representative appearance for Hong Kong:

Have Hong Kong anything to fear, and should they go again? I hope so, because it is a chance for players to perform in a very competitive, international event. I think we will always be able to provide players of sufficient ability to uphold the credibility of Hong Kong cricket, but from what I have seen, to come in the first three, young quick bowlers are essential; I doubt this will ever happen in Hong Kong.

Peter's final comments as his tenure as Hong Kong's captain came to an end:

It was a very enjoyable period in my life and I am grateful to have had the chance. Throughout the period, Peter Hall as the Chairman of Selectors and Brian Wigley were pillars of strength to whom I could always refer various problems and receive back sensible, reliable advice.

Whatever I achieved would not have been possible without the unswerving loyalty of most of the players who at varying times played under me. To my successor, whoever he is, good luck. To the players, a captain can only operate with confidence if you accept his authority and judgement. Some of the decisions he has to make both on and off the field are unpleasant and difficult. Those are made as he sees it from a match, tour or team point of view. If the representative side is to function properly, he needs your support which really means loyalty. Thank you for yours, and the memories.

4th ICC Trophy in the Netherlands – 1990

6 June – The Netherlands won the toss and put Hong Kong in to bat. A courageous opening partnership of 79 between Krish Kumar and David Evans in 1 hour 50 minutes against an attack spearheaded by 6 foot 8 inches Andre van Troost and Somerset's Roland Lefebvre, laid the foundations for a respectable total. All Hong Kong's good work was then brutally blasted away by Barbadian Nolan Clarke, whose whirlwind 116 not out (eight 6s and eleven 4s) took the Netherlands to victory in only 25.5 overs!

Hong Kong: 178–7 (K Kumar 43, M Sabine 40, D Evans 26, R Lefebvre 3–24)
Nederlands: 184–3 (N Clarke 116*, R Gomes 40)

Netherlands won by seven wickets.

8 June – Papua NG won the toss and batted. When Hong Kong's turn came, David Jones, brought in to replace the injured Kumar (knee), played one of the best innings of the tour in scoring 71. He and Nanda Perera took the score from 87 for 4 to 167 ... 'pushing Hong Kong close to victory after a spluttering start'. Hong Kong's defeat meant its main interest in the tournament was over.

Papua NG: 220–7 (R Ila 56, V C Amini 50, G Davies 3–28)
Hong Kong: 184 (D A Jones 71, N Perera 43, J Marsden 31, K Loi 5–34)

Papua New Guinea won by 36 runs.

What kind of tournament is 'all over' after two matches, when there are seven matches to be played? Surely such a ludicrous system must be changed before the next competition takes place in Kenya in 1994.

10 June – Hong Kong tossed correctly and elected to bat first. Sound knocks from Nigel Stearns and David Jones enabled Hong Kong to reach 230 for 9. Excellent spells of spin bowling from David Paull and Salauddin Tariq dismissed the South Americans for Hong Kong's first win.

Hong Kong: 230–9 (N Stearns 57, D Jones 30, Extras 41, A Morris 4–38)
Argentina: 167 (T Ferguson 57, D Paull 5–27, S Tariq 4–34)

Hong Kong won by 63 runs.

12 June – The skipper called correctly again and launched Jason Marsden in to smash the Israeli attack for 150 in 3 hours, which paved the way for Hong Kong's 'swashbuckling' 323 for 4. Hong Kong bowlers then took turns to dismiss the opposition batsmen.

Hong Kong: 323–4 (J Marsden 150, M Sabine 60*, K Kumar 58)
Israel: 179 (S Erulkar 46, C Callender 37, A Moss 31, D Brettell 4–53)

Hong Kong won by 144 runs.

15 June – Malaysia, put into bat, managed a modest 168 on a treacherous wicket. Hong Kong found run-getting just as difficult, and after being in trouble at 135 for 7, Riswan Farouq and skipper Glyn Davies steered Hong Kong to victory with 10 deliveries remaining.

Malaysia: 168 (S Bell 61, G Davies 3–27, N Perera 2–22, D Jones 2–32, S Tariq 2–35)
Hong Kong: 169–7 (N Stearns 34, J Marsden 26, A Stephens 3–28, S Muniandy 2–23)

Hong Kong won by three wickets.

16 June – Hong Kong's luck departed with the loss of the toss. After a sound if cautious start, Hong Kong's batsmen failed to gain any momentum. A final total of 182 never being enough. Fiji romped home with some 'explosive, uninhibited hitting'.

Hong Kong: 182 (K Kumar 46, N Stearns 32, J Marsden 30, N Maxwell 4–30)
Fiji: 185–4 (C Browne 65, J Sorovakatini 57, N Maxwell 41*, D Paull 2–51)

Fiji won by six wickets.

18 June – Put in to bat, the East Africans were restricted to 203 by Hong Kong's spinners, Salauddin Tariq and Dave Brettell. Hong Kong, after another unspectacular start, many anxious moments and never mastering

the bowling, eventually came out winners. Luckily for Hong Kong, extras top scored with 41.

E & C Africa: 203   (G R Shariff 42, H Patadia 34, H Tejani 33, S Tariq
                    4–46, D Brettell 3–33)
Hong Kong: 204–7 (J Marsden 38, D Brettell 32*, N Stearns 32, S Naik
                    2–23)

Hong Kong won by three wickets.

A magnificent team spirit and business-like efficiency, combined with some solid rather than spectacular batting and accurate and resourceful bowling, carried Hong Kong to their best finish in the tournament with four wins.

                                                    Jeremy Walker, *SCMP*

Player of the Tour: Salauddin Tariq. Friendly matches were played, but the results were not available. In fact, the author had to write to the Koninklijke Nederlandse Cricket Bond, who very kindly provided copies of the scoresheets for all the Hong Kong ICC matches.

5th ICC Trophy in Kenya – 1994

The tournament format was changed from the previous debacle, with the 20 participating teams grouped in four pools of five for an initial round robin series. The two leading teams in each group then proceeded to the quarter-finals and beyond. The third and fourth teams in each group entered a Plate competition, and the fifth placed teams played in a Bowl competition. All were 50-over matches played on grass wickets in the Nairobi area.

An old Kenyan cricket hand, Jasmer Singh, said: 'Time is nothing. The African has plenty of spare time and they don't mind spending it playing cricket.'

The Hong Kong squad, coached by Hong Kong-born Warwickshire captain Dermot Reeve, who played for Hong Kong in the 1982 ICC competition, started their quest for honours with two easy wins in friendly matches against Israel and Malaysia.

Israel: 110   (N Ward 41, J Strachan 2–10, B Gohel 2–23, T
                    Davies 2–27)
Hong Kong: 113–2 (M Eames 39, S Brew 30, both retired)

Hong Kong won by eight wickets.

Hong Kong: 277 (M Eames 73, R Farcy 44, P Fordham 36, J Garden
                 34)
Malaysia: 116 (R Menon 26, Y Vachha 4–28, R Farcy 2–9)

Hong Kong won by 161 runs.

At the Carnivores Restaurant the night before the first trophy match, skipper Fordham showed his leadership qualities when telling the head waiter to 'bring the boys everything', which led to the inevitable quip: 'Waiter! bring me a crocodile sandwich – and make it snappy.'

13 Feb – Stewart Brew in one memorable over took four wickets including the 'hat-trick', a first in the competition. Denmark, prior to this devastation, had reached 189 for 5 in their 38th over, then added only a further three runs. When a thunderstorm stopped play, Hong Kong were 80 for 4. The next day Jonathan Orders, playing sensibly, carried on the good work with various partners to see Hong Kong nervously edge home by tying the score in the last over. Ole Mortensen, the Derbyshire opening bowler, had grabbed the first four Hong Kong wickets in a hostile spell. Stewart Brew was named 'Man of the Match'.

Denmark: 192   (A Ahmed 61, A Butt 38, S Brew 4–43, D Cross 3–19)
Hong Kong: 192–8   (J Orders 63*, S Brew 42, J Garden 32, O Mortensen
                    4–21)

Hong Kong in dramatic win over Denmark in a tied match by virtue of losing less wickets at the Nairobi Gymkhana Club.

15 Feb – Hong Kong started badly after being put in to bat, losing Brew, Mark Eames, Steve Atkinson and Farcy for a meagre 35 runs to a fiery Bermudan pace attack at the Nairobi Jaffery Club ground. Only Pat Fordham, Orders and Garden reached double figures, Fordham's well-struck 79 saving the day for Hong Kong. Rain stopped play again, but not before Hong Kong had removed four of the Bermudan top order for 66 runs.

With Bermuda struggling at 106 for eight in the 41st over, Hong Kong were in sight of another great win.

Alvin Sallay in Kenya

But dropped catches let Bermuda off the hook, allowing D Minors at No. 9 to take his score to 46 not out and tie with Hong Kong off the last ball of the last over. If only . . . .

397

Hong Kong: 154   (P Fordham 79, A Edwards 5–27)
Bermuda: 154–8 (D Minors 46*, D Smith 44, Y Vachha 3–9)

Bermuda won this tied match in the same way that Hong Kong had beaten Denmark in the previous match.

17 Feb – On a good batting wicket at the Nairobi Aga Khan Club, Fiji were reduced to 77 for nine by the guile of Brew and Vachha, but as the run rate was vitally important to Hong Kong in Group 'D', skipper Fordham called on vice captain Steve Atkinson to bowl. In what became 'the Kenya historic over', Atkinson delivered four 'wides', one 'no-ball' and was hit for seven boundaries, in all a total of 37 runs!

He was heard before bowling his 11th delivery, saying: 'Sorry skip, I seem to have lost my loop.'

Dermot Reeve, *Out of Africa*

Fordham and Farcy then knocked off the required runs in 17 overs. Pat Fordham was named 'Man of the Match'.

Fiji: 126   (A Tawatatau 31*, S Brew 4–16, Y Vachha 2–15)
Hong Kong: 127–3 (P Fordham 50*, R Farcy 48)

Hong Kong won by seven wickets.

19 Feb – A second-wicket partnership of 161 between Stewart Brew and Steve Atkinson, followed by a third of 82 between Brew and Pat Fordham, saw Hong Kong to a massive 355 runs in their 50 overs. Stewart Brew was named 'Man of the Match'.

Brew with a superb 124 thumps Hong Kong to record victory. Hong Kong's cricketers smash a wayward West African bowling attack apart to score their highest total ever in the ICC Trophy competition at the Sir Ali Club, Nairobi.

Alvin Sallay in Kenya

Hong Kong: 355–8 (S Brew 124, S Atkinson 68, P Fordham 58, R
                  Farcy 47, S Kpunden 4–65)
West Africa: 110   (S Elliott 29, R Farcy 2–14, Y Vachha 2–16, S Brew
                  2–23)

Hong Kong won by 245 runs.

Discussions continued on the required run rate after Hong Kong's third win out of four matches. If Bermuda beat Denmark, Hong Kong would come second in Group 'D'. But if Denmark beat Bermuda, then all three teams would have the same number of points. As Bermuda won, Hong Kong went through to the quarter-finals for the first time, a very satisfactory achievement. No doubt inspired by their coach, Reeve.

'Plucky Hong Kong to face top guns Holland and Kenya' rang the headline as Hong Kong were grouped with the tournament's two top seeds.

23 Feb – The home team, Kenya, burst Hong Kong's bubble with an awesome performance of bowling and batting as they sped to victory before lunch at the Nairobi Gymkhana Club. Replacement Njuguna, a right-arm off-cutter, made full use of the variable bounce to record a career best 5–24. Kenyan opener Kennedy Otieno then blasted his way to a masterly half century to wrap up the match.

Kenyans show no mercy to hapless Hong Kong.

Alvin Sallay in Kenya

Hong Kong: 86   (A Njuguna 5–24, M Suji 3–17)
Kenya: 90–2 (K Otieno 52*)

Kenya won by eight wickets in 16 overs.

25 Feb – Hong Kong's dreams of World Cup glory slipped into oblivion under a hot Kenyan sun as Holland inflicted a crushing 134 run defeat at the Nairobi Club.

Alvin Sallay in Kenya

If only ... Steve Atkinson had caught Nolan Clarke off Riaz Farcy's first ball of the match – Clarke went on to score 113! Stewart Brew was again Hong Kong's key player, taking three wickets and looking like the 'only batsman capable of holding his own.' Once he went for a sound 61, the rest offered little resistance.

Holland: 288–8 (N Clarke 113, S Lubbers 63, B Kuijlman 34*, S
                     Brew 3–43, T Davies 2–50)
Hong Kong: 154   (S Brew 61, F Aponso 3–43, S Lubbers 2–15, F
                     Jansen 2–18, R Lefebvre 2–30)

Holland won by 134 runs.

399

27 Feb – Hong Kong go down in a spin.

Alvin Sallay in Kenya

Hong Kong failed to find an answer to the Bangladeshi spinners and were bowled out in the 48th over, after being 140 for 3. Bangladeshi skipper, Minazul Abedin, top scored with 66, then captured four wickets, including the prized scalp of Stewart Brew.

The wicket was extremely dry and the ball turned alarmingly.

Dermot Reeve, Out of Africa

Bangladesh: 238–8 (M Abedin 66, F Ahmed 43, S Shaheed 42*, S Brew 3–58, D Cross 2–43)
Hong Kong: 181 (J Orders 58, P Fordham 39, M Abedin 4–40, E Haque 3–27)

Bangladesh won by 57 runs.

One-day specialist and Hong Kong coach Dermot Reeve, in summing up, said:

I'm certain the players have learnt much from the three weeks here. Stewart Brew has been Hong Kong's most outstanding player. Without him we would not have made the last eight. Fordham has led from the front and has been our most dangerous batsman, but unfortunately the experienced pair of Riaz Farcy and Steve Atkinson did not perform against the top three seeds. Hong Kong has however done extremely well with their resources. An average age of 35 has shown in the field and our catching let us down. We were not consistent enough with the bat against good bowling and on the whole, techniques were limited for one-day cricket.

The umpiring during the tournament was inconsistent, to say the least. The Canadian umpire for the Hong Kong/Kenya match was replaced for the remainder of the competition. Hong Kong's own umpire, Geoff Lever, had the honour of being invited to officiate in the final, but unfortunately, had to decline due to his work commitment in Hong Kong.

6th ICC Trophy in Kuala Lumpur, Malaysia – 1997

22 teams representing their respective countries participated in the 6th ICC Associate Members' competition in the heat, humidity and later dampness of Kuala Lumpur. The teams were split into four groups, with six each in

400

Groups 'A' and 'B' and five each in Groups 'C' and 'D'. The two top teams in each group would progress to the quarter-finals. All matches were played on artificial pitches.

Hong Kong, coached by David Trist and managed by Glyn Davies, were drawn in Group 'D', along with Bermuda, Italy, Papua New Guinea and Scotland.

25 March – Bermuda, put into bat on the Victoria Institute ground, reached a respectable 227 for nine off their 50 overs, due mainly to a fifth-wicket partnership of 96 from A Steede and A Manders. Hong Kong used eight bowlers. When Hong Kong batted, a second-wicket partnership of 67 between Riaz Farcy and Rahul Sharma laid the foundation for Hong Kong's unexpected exciting win over the favoured Bermuda side, with just two balls remaining.

Bermuda: 227–9 (A Steede 65, A Manders 65, M Zubair 3–31, M
                         Hussain 3–37)
Hong Kong: 228–7 (R Sharma 69, R Farcy 65, R Blades 3–42)

Hong Kong won by three wickets.

'Revenge is sweet, but what matters is that we have got off to a good start', said Fordham.

Alvin Sallay, SCMP

26 March – Scotland batted first at Kelab Aman and reached 221 for 6 after their allotted 50 overs, with solid contributions from M Smith, skipper G Salmond, G Williamson and M Allingham. Hong Kong again tried eight bowlers without any causing real trouble. Hong Kong were blown away by the 10th over, tottering at 46 for 5, the damage being caused by John Blain and G Williamson. A brief recovery of 61 between Mark Eames and skipper Pat Fordham, plus 25 extras, made up most of Hong Kong's total.

Scotland: 221–6 (M Smith 67, M Allingham 35*, G Salmond 34, S
                         Brew 2–46)
Hong Kong: 134   (P Fordham 32, Kennedy 3–15, J Blain 3–23, G
                         Williamson 3–26)

Scotland won by 87 runs.

Brittle Hong Kong melt away in Malaysian heat.

Alvin Sallay, SCMP

28 March – A brilliant century from Riaz Farcy on the new Selangor Club ground, Farcy's first 50 came in 46 balls and his second in 44. Other useful contributions came from Stewart Brew, Pat Fordham and M Hussain, Hong Kong being dismissed with two balls remaining. Farcy then removed Italy's first two batsmen without a run on the board; it was downhill thereafter for ICC's newcomers, with only S de Mel and B Giordano making any headway against Hong Kong's seven bowlers.

Hong Kong: 282 (R Farcy 102, S Brew 39, M Hussain 39, P Fordham 36, B Giordano 3–35, S de Mel 3–40, A Akhlaq 3–67)
Italy: 137 (B Giordano 32, S de Mel 25, D Jones 3–14, R Farcy 2–9, M Zubair 2–19, R Sharma 2–27)

Hong Kong won by 145 runs.

Beating Italy was never in question.

Alvin Sallay, *SCMP*

29 March – Hong Kong won the toss and batted at the Kilat Kelab. Solid batting from the middle order of R Sharma, M Eames and P Fordham saw Hong Kong to 232 for 8 in their 50 overs. R Farcy made the early breakthrough and with the help of S Brew had the Papuans 7 for 3. J Oria with 62 and a late contribution of 29 from R Ipi allowed Papua to reach 151. Hong Kong again utilised their eight bowlers with no one bowling 10 overs.

Hong Kong: 232–8 (P Fordham 71, R Sharma 57, M Eames 33, F Arua 2–43, T Raka 2–45)
Papua New Guinea: 151 (J Oria 62, S Brew 3–22, R Farcy 2–15, M Zubair 2–31)

Hong Kong won by 81 runs

Fordham smote four sixes and five fours in an innings which had all the ingredients – courage, determination and fighting spirit.

Alvin Sallay, *SCMP*

After the completion of the four Group 'D' matches, Hong Kong and Scotland, with three and four wins respectively, went through to the quarter-finals, Hong Kong being drawn to play Bangladesh, Holland and Ireland. Bangladesh would be tough opponents as Hong Kong had never beaten them. Coached by Gordon Greenidge, the Bangladeshis were determined to qualify for the World Cup.

402

1 April – Bangladesh put Hong Kong in to bat at the Royal Military College ground. After an opening partnership of 44, Hong Kong 'ran out' of steam and were dismissed in 45.2 overs, R Farcy being the only batsman able to cope with their varied attack. After being 71 for 3, A Islam and Skipper Akram Khan saw Bangladesh comfortably home in 38.2 overs.

Hong Kong: 145 (R Farcy 38, M Rafique 3–20, M Abedin 2–27)
Bangladesh: 148–3 (A Islam 53*, A Ali 29, A Khan 25*)

Bangladesh won by seven wickets.

Poor running between the wickets and superb ground fielding by Bangladesh contributed to Hong Kong's loss.

Alvin Sallay, SCMP

2 April – Hong Kong wickets fell steadily throughout their innings, which closed after 47.5 overs. The heavens opened during the sixth over of Holland's reply, handing Hong Kong a very welcome one point.

Hong Kong: 170 (P Fordham 34, R Farcy 28, Khan 4–18, R Lefebvre 2–27)
Holland: 16–0

A tropical thunderstorm handed Hong Kong an unlikely lifeline. The organisers should have made allowance for reserve days from the quarter-finals onwards, said a disgusted Holland captain Tim de Leede.

Alvin Sallay, SCMP

History beckons for Hong Kong. A win over Ireland would almost certainly see Hong Kong into the semi-finals of the ICC Trophy. The top three then qualify for the 1999 World Cup in England. A farfetched dream!

4 April – Hong Kong won the toss and put Ireland in to bat at Kelab Aman. At 175 for 6 with only five overs remaining, Hong Kong seemed to be on target. A superb 54 in 61 balls from Angus Dunlop and 48 runs from those last five overs resulted in Ireland totalling 223 for 7. Both Hong Kong's openers were in the pavilion with the total on 22. S Brew, showing much improved form, added 55 for the fourth wicket with R Sharma, but Ireland's spinners had made run scoring very difficult and Hong Kong were dismissed a disappointing 51 runs astray.

Ireland: 223–7   (A Dunlop 54, J Benson 33, R Sharma 3–29, D Jones
                       2–30)
Hong Kong: 172   (S Brew 50, McCrum 3–30, P Gillespie 3–42)

Ireland won by 51 runs

Ireland trounced Hong Kong by 51 runs and ended the territory's
dream of playing in the semi-finals of the ICC Trophy. The inexperi-
ence showed under real pressure, when all that mattered was line and
length, the Hong Kong bowling got ragged.

Alvin Sallay, *SCMP*

5 April – Ray Brewster, Mike Swift and Roy Lamsam all get their
chance. Fordham stepped down as captain, when Hong Kong played-
off for seventh place against Canada at Perbadanan Kemajuan Negari
Selangor. Shuffling the batting order, even if Hong Kong felt the match
was 'meaningless' after being dismissed from the main trophy games,
nearly always proves fatal from a match-winning point of view. When
Stewart Brew, the skipper, was sixth out at 97, the writing was on the
wall. Despite the low score, Canada were made to fight for their victory.
'Man of the Match' M Diwan steadied Canada and took them to seventh
place.

Hong Kong: 125   (S Brew 46, L Bhansingh 3–13, D Joseph 3–25)
Canada: 126–6   (M Diwan 35, R Sujanani 2–16, M Hussain 2–22)

Canada won by 4 wickets

Pat Fordham, outgoing Hong Kong captain, remembered with pride the
last two ICC tournaments when Hong Kong surpassed all expectations
by entering the quarter-finals. In Kenya, Hong Kong scored an upset
over Denmark; this time it was Bermuda. 'What Hong Kong must
achieve next time around is to get into the quarter-finals and then win
some matches at that stage.'
    Youngster Roy Lamsam, the grandson of John Fenton, who had
played his cricket at the Diocesan Boys' School and KCC, was brought
into the Hong Kong squad when Justin Strachan had been unable to join
the team because of work commitments. Although Lamsam played only
in the last match against Canada, the tour would have been a wonderful
learning experience for him.

ICC Trophy Competition Results – 1982 to 1997

2nd Competition – England 1982 (Won 2, Lost 3, Drawn 2)

Hong Kong v	Papua New Guinea	Lost by 4 wickets
	Israel	Won by 123 runs
	Canada	Abandoned – rain
	USA	Abandoned – rain
	Gibraltar	Won by 8 wickets
	Kenya	Lost by 3 wickets
	Zimbabwe	Lost by 7 wickets

3rd Competition – England 1986 (Won 3, Lost 5)

Hong Kong v	Gibraltar	Won by 144 runs
	Bermuda	Lost by 227 runs
	Canada	Lost by 4 wickets
	Holland	Lost by 170 runs
	USA	Lost by 5 wickets
	Israel	Won by 8 wickets
	Fiji	Won by 7 wickets
	Papua New Guinea	Lost by 2 wickets

4th Competition – Netherlands 1990 (Won 4, Lost 3)

Hong Kong v	Netherlands	Lost by 7 wickets
	Papua New Guinea	Lost by 36 runs
	Argentina	Won by 63 runs
	Israel	Won by 144 runs
	Malaysia	Won by 3 wickets
	Fiji	Lost by 6 wickets
	East & Central Africa	Won by 3 wickets

5th Competition – Kenya 1994 (Won 3, Lost 4)

Hong Kong v	Denmark	Won on tied score
	Bermuda	Lost on tied score
	Fiji	Won by 7 wickets
	West Africa	Won by 245 runs

Hong Kong came second in Group 'D' to reach the quarter-finals

Hong Kong v	Kenya	Lost by 8 wickets

| | | Holland | Lost by 134 runs |
| | | Bangladesh | Lost by 57 runs |

6th Competition – Kuala Lumpur, Malaysia 1997 (Won 3, Lost 4, Drawn 1)

Hong Kong	v	Bermuda	Won by 3 wickets
		Scotland	Lost by 87 runs
		Italy	Won by 145 runs
		Papua New Guinea	Won by 81 runs

Hong Kong came second in Group 'D' to reach the quarter-finals

Hong Kong	v	Bangladesh	Lost by 7 wickets
		Holland	Abandoned – rain
		Ireland	Lost by 51 runs
		Canada	Lost by 4 wickets

Batting and Bowling Averages – 1982 to 1997

	Period	Matches	Innings	Highest	Runs	Average	100s	50s	Wickets	Average	Best	Wickets 5 plus	Catches	Stumpings
Anderson, P W	1982–86	13	11	41*	139	15.44			1	53.00	1–11		4	
Atkinson, S	1994	6	6	68	110	18.33	1	ϕ					3	
Bacon, G	1982	5	3	2	3	1.00			10	10.00	4–37			
Beaman, L	1994	4	4	14	16	4.00			2	48.00	1–16		2	
Brettell, D	1990	3	1	32*	32	∞			8	16.87	4–53			
Brew, S	1994–97	15	14	124	420	30.00	1	2	25	17.00	4–16		9	
Brewster, R	1986–97	10	10	55	184	20.44		1					4	4
Catton, B	1982–86	5	5	63	157	31.40		1						
Collins, C	1986	8	5	53	78	39.00		1	10	35.00	3–48		2	
Cresswell, P	1994	3	2	2*	4	4.00			2	22.50	1– 3		1	
Cross, D	1994	7	4	4*	8	4.00			8	23.38	3–19		4	
Davies, G	1986–90	11	11	23	86	9.55			12	25.58	3–27		5	
T	1994	5	5	3*	7	2.33			4	30.50	2–50		3	
Eames, M	1994–97	15	14	33	212	16.31							7	
Evans, D	1990	5	5	26	51	10.20							4	
Farcy, R	1994–97	14	14	102	387	27.64	1	1	12	20.42	2– 9			
Farouq, R	1990	1	1	20*	20	∞								
Fordham, P	1994–97	14	14	79	453	34.85		3					14	2
Foster, S	1997	2	2	5	9	4.50								
Fotheringham, R	1986–90	13	5	8*	17	8.50			19	22.95	4–51		1	
French, A	1997	4	4	13	22	5.50								
Garden, J	1994	7	7	32	65	9.29			ϕ				2	
Gill, R	1982–86	5	2	15*	16	16.00							3	1
Gohel, B	1986–94	2	1	32*	32	∞			7	10.71	6–11	1		

406

	Period	Matches	Innings	Highest	Runs	Average	100s	50s	Wickets	Average	Best	Wickets 5 plus	Catches	Stumpings
Greenwood, D	1982–86	7	6	56*	103	20.60		1	2	27.50	2–13			
Hussain, M	1997	8	8	39	114	14.25			7	23.29	3–37			
Jones, D A	1990–97	12	11	71	157	17.44		1	8	20.62	2–32		5	
Kumar, K	1990	5	5	58	162	32.40		1					4	
Lalchandani, G	1982	3	2	27*	39	39.00			3	18.33	2–22			
Lamsam, R	1997	1	1	8	8	8.00			φ					
Lever, M	1997	6	5	15	37	9.25			φ					
Lorimer, A	1982	5	5	72*	149	37.25		2	φ				1	
Marsden, J	1990	7	7	150	315	45.00	1						3	
1. Myles, S	1986	8	8	172	410	58.57	1	2	6	29.67	3–30		3	
Olsen, P	1982	2	2	37*	40	40.00							3	
Orders, J	1994	7	6	63*	159	31.80		2					2	
Paull, D	1990	7	4	3	5	1.66			11	24.09	5–27	1	1	
Perera, N	1986–90	13	11	43	118	13.11			6	71.83	2–22		3	
Raza, K	1997	8	7	15	42	8.40			6	32.50	2–41			
2. Reeve, D A	1982	5	5	56*	138	34.50		1	7	15.71	2–22			
Sabine, M	1982–90	19	17	60*	413	31.77		2	φ				7	
Sawney, T	1990	1	1	22	22	22.00							1	
Sharma, R	1997	8	8	69	190	23.75		2	6	25.67	3–29		4	
Smith, N	1986	2	1	1*	1	∞			3	17.33	2–31			
Starling, R	1982	5	2	1	1	0.50			1	85.00	1–9			
Stearns, N	1982–90	20	18	85	425	25.00		3					12	
Strachan, J	1994	2	2	3	3	1.50			1	49.00	1–28		1	
Sujanani, R	1994–97	6	6	23	45	11.25			3	26.33	2–16			
Swift, M	1997	1	1	11	11	11.00							1	
Tariq, S	1990	7	4	5	9	4.50			16	18.25	4–34		2	
Toes, R	1982	2	1	2*	2	∞			1	60.00	1–12		1	
Vachha, Y	1982–94	19	11	28	73	9.13			12	45.75	3–9		4	
Waller, S	1982	1	1	1*	1	∞			3	6.00	3–18			
Walsh, M	1986	2	2	9	11	5.50								
Zubair, M	1997	8	7	6	9	2.25			10	21.10	3–31		1	

∞ Infinity   no average
φ Also bowled without success

1. Staffordshire & Berkshire CCC
2. Sussex & Warwickshire CCC

ASIAN CRICKET COUNCIL (ACC)

The Asian Cricket Council was established in 1983 and includes India, Pakistan and Sri Lanka as Full Members. There are a number of Associate Members, but their membership and status remained to be clarified.

1st S-E Asian Tournament – January 1984

The first South-East Asian Tournament took place in Bangladesh between Hong Kong, Singapore and two Bangladeshi teams, Bangladesh and Bangladesh U-25s (Tigers), as Malaysia had withdrawn just prior to the start of the tournament. The teams played each other twice (45 overs) on a league basis, and the top two teams then contested the final.

Hong Kong practised on the afternoon of arrival in the huge Dacca Stadium. Straight away interest centred on the mud wicket, which had a mirror-like sheen. Barbed wire protected terraces overlooked the ground. The first two matches against Bangladeshi sides were lost, mainly because the Hong Kong batting never came to grips with the tight bowling, variable bounce and the efficient fielding of their opponents.

The team then embarked on a six-hour road journey to Mymemsingh, a mere 67 miles due north of Dacca, for the third match and a comfortable win against Singapore. Young Simon Myles scored a chanceless 106 not out. The start of the next match was delayed due to overnight rain and reduced to 40 overs. Before the start, the clay pitch was 'fired' by using sawdust soaked in petrol. This dried out the surface upon which a mat was placed. No one in the Hong Kong side had ever seen such a drying technique!

Although Hong Kong reached the final played in the Dacca Stadium, and had improved on their previous two outings against Bangladesh, the batting never gathered momentum and the total of 151 runs was too low a score to be successfully defended.

Sir Denys Roberts, President of the HKCA, remarked in the 1983–84 Handbook:

> The Hong Kong side played with skill and determination and was only defeated in the final by Bangladesh by three wickets. The President attended the match; it is thought that, without his constant advice to the Captain, Hong Kong might have won.

The Hong Kong Captain, Peter Anderson, in summing up, said: 'It was an extremely competitive tournament in which good, tight cricket was played. It is only by participating in such tournaments that our own standards will rise.'

Chris Collins, a member of that Hong Kong team and former *SCMP* Racing Correspondent, recalled some 'Memorable Moments':

> Hong Kong fought back after a sluggish start to make the final against the home side before a crowd estimated at 15,000 in the Dacca National Stadium.

408

The crowds in Bangladesh, as in India and Pakistan, are very knowledgeable on the finer points of the game and were very fair towards the visiting teams, Hong Kong and Singapore. If anything, they were harder on the home side.

As soon as the large and noisy crowd would start their chanting and slow hand clapping, the Bangladeshi batsmen would immediately want to hit out and please the spectators. Skipper Peter Anderson would then slow things down to frustrate the batsmen, and most times would be rewarded with a wicket.

Apart from the pipe-smoking Geoff Lever, who travelled with the party, the umpires seemed to lack a full understanding of the rules and their interpretations often differed greatly from what Hong Kong players were used to.

The tour was something of an ego trip for most of the team, as the entire party were treated like Test players, rather than part-time performers from Hong Kong.

There are always the people who say 'we could have done better.' However, to my mind the selected squad more than did their share to promote a good image for Hong Kong cricket. Their attitude both on and off the field, endeared them to the locals, and the fact that several players have already hinted they would love to return to Bangladesh for another tournament speaks for itself.

Playing before a crowd of 15,000 will stay in my memory forever. The Bangladesh experience may be over, but it is certainly not forgotten.

Results of all Hong Kong matches:

Chittagong, 13 January 1984

| Bangladesh Tigers: | 172 | (Nannu 44, Rafique 43, C Swann 4–39, C Collins 3–30) |
| Hong Kong: | 108 for 9 | (P Wood 42, Gani 3–16) |

Hong Kong lost by 64 runs

Dacca, 14 January 1984

| Hong Kong: | 115 | (Dipuroy 3–24) |
| Bangladesh: | 118 for 3 | (Lipu 48*) |

Hong Kong lost by 7 wickets

Mymemsingh, 16 January 1984

Hong Kong: 221 for 4   (S Myles 106*)
Singapore: 68   (J Jenkins 4–4, C Swann 4–22)

Hong Kong won by 153 runs

Mymemsingh, 17 January 1984

Bangladesh Tigers: 141 for 8
Hong Kong: 142 for 4   (P Wood 47)

Hong Kong won by 6 wickets

Dacca Stadium, 19 January 1984

Hong Kong: 121
Bangladesh: 125–4   (Rahman 69*)

Bangladesh won by 6 wickets

Dacca Stadium, 20 January 1984

Hong Kong: 240–6   (P Anderson 52, P Wood 50, N Stearns 50, Mehta
                      3–33)
Singapore: 123–8   (C Collins 3–26)

Hong Kong won by 117 runs

Dacca Stadium, 21 January 1984 – Final

Hong Kong: 151   (Dipu 3–17, Badsha 3–29)
Bangladesh: 152–7   (Ashraf 40)

Bangladesh won by 3 wickets

Hong Kong had shown gradual improvement in each match against Bangladesh but are still not in the same class as this team of semi-professionals.

At one of the pre-tour team meetings a list of Health & Hygiene 'Do's and Don'ts' were given to each player to learn and digest. The 'Don'ts' were:

1. Don't take chances with drinks; don't take ice in drinks; don't be put off by chlorine taste; don't use untreated water for teeth cleaning.
2. Don't eat seafood, salads, fast fried food, fresh cream, fruit except oranges.

410

3. Don't walk around in bear [sic] feet anywhere.
4. Don't approach any animals from horses to cats (rabies), and avoid snakes, spiders and insects.

These instructions were obviously well 'digested' as the whole party returned intact with no one suffering from 'Delhi Belly'.

2nd S-E Asian Tournament – January 1988

Hong Kong, as promised by Sir Denys Roberts, hosted the 2nd S-E Asian Tournament in cool, dreary January weather. The matches were played on grass as well as artificial wickets on a 45-over basis. Malaysia, due to financial difficulties, again declined to participate, so a second Hong Kong team, an HKCA President's XI, joined in to complete the quadrangular tournament.

With a weak Singaporean team taking part, it looked odds on that there would only be two teams in the competition, but an efficient President's XI, ably led by David Jones, nearly caused an upset when they played against the Hong Kong side. Krish Kumar, their opening batsman, after scoring 103 not out against Singapore, the only century in the tournament, was heading for another big score against Hong Kong when 'Perera accounted for the dangerous Kumar on 64.'

'Beckett destroys Singapore. Doug Beckett hammered four sixes and six fours on his way to 86 off just 59 balls.'

Beckett and schoolboy Craig Dean commenced with an opening stand of 117 runs. Beckett also captured the first three wickets and took two catches in Hong Kong's easy win over Singapore at KCC in the first match of the tournament.

Jan 18   Hong Kong: 320–5   (D Beckett 86, C Dean 70, M Eames 51, D Evans 43*, N Stearns 36)

        Singapore: 101   (Y Vachha 4–17, D Beckett 3–10)

        Hong Kong won by 219 runs

Bangladesh warmed up with an easy seven wicket win on the artificial pitch at Mission Road. Put in to bat, the HK President's XI made slow progress, and despite a second wicket stand of 96 between Krish Kumar and John Ford, were all out in the 43rd over. No batsman from No. 4 reached double figures. The Bangladeshi openers, Misha and M Rashid, put on 133 to set up their victory.

411

Jan 18   HK Pres. XI: 161   (K Kumar 58, J Ford 48, A A Khan 3–22,
                                  G Nausher 3–23)
         Bangladesh: 164–3   (M Rashid 74, Misha 52, D Uttamchandani
                                  2–16)

Bangladesh won by 7 wickets

'Champs crush sad Hong Kong.' A 7th wicket partnership of 82 between
Nigel Stearns and Nanda Perera helped Hong Kong to total 184. 'A score
which never looked to be enough.' After being dropped early on, Ather Ali
combined with M Abedin to take the Bangladesh team to victory, putting
on an unbroken 87 for the 4th wicket.

Jan 20   Hong Kong: 184   (N Stearns 53, C Dean 39, N Perera 36, G
                                 Nausher 3–39)
         Bangladesh: 186–3   (A Ali 92*)

Bangladesh won by 7 wickets

'Angry tourists storm out. The touring Bangladesh party stormed out
of the Kowloon Cricket Club following a controversial 'Man of the
Match' award yesterday, writes Chris Collins.
Match adjudicator, former outstanding batsman 'Tug' Willson, surprisingly declared Hong Kong spinner Bharat Gohel the award
winner. Gohel only took one wicket but picked up the $500 cash
prize. Bangladesh star batsman Ather Ali struck a match-winning
92 not out as well as dismissing Hong Kong danger man Mark
Eames.
'Bowlers win matches and Bharat bowled well,' Willson told the after-
match function. Hong Kong did not win yesterday's match, and there
were plenty of red faces after the award presentation.
'An amazing decision,' a Bangladesh spokesman said.

Chris Collins, *SCMP*

'Kumar, Collier combine to cut down Singapore.' Left-handed opening
batsman Krish Kumar batted throughout the innings, hitting 103 not out
off 138 balls. He was well supported by Brian Catton and the consistent
John Ford. Singapore were immediately in trouble when Ian Collier dismissed their first four batsmen: Chris Kilbee (0), A Dass (14), Bob Stiller (8)
and B Balakrishnan (0), which left them stranded, to be all out in the 42nd
over.

Jan 20 HK Pres. XI: 214–6 (K Kumar 103*, J Ford 41, B Catton 34)
Singapore: 145 (K Martens 30, I Collier 4–31, J Ford 3–16)

HK President's XI won by 69 runs.

Put in to bat by David Jones, skipper of the President's XI, Hong Kong reached a respectable total after some early scares, due mainly to two good partnerships. Craig Dean 'played an innings of immense maturity,' and put on 86 for the 4th wicket with Mark Eames. Then Eames and Nanda Perera added 83 for the 6th wicket; Perera's 47 came off only 32 balls and included four sixes. At 123 for 2 and then 173 for 5, the President's XI kept the pressure on Hong Kong, but could not quite get on top of the bowling, eventually being all out in the 44th over, still 38 runs short.

Jan 22 Hong Kong: 232–6 (C Dean 72, M Eames 66*, N Perera 47,
I Collier 2–30)
HK Pres. XI: 194 (K Kumar 64, G Davies 34, B Gohel 4–57)

Hong Kong won by 38 runs.

'A lethargic Bangladesh ambled to a comfortable five-wicket win over Singapore at KCC to confirm their place in the final.' The Bangladesh skipper, Ghazi Ashraf said: 'Singapore are not a strong side, and it is not easy gearing up for the whole match when you know you are going to win.'

Jan 22 Singapore: 179–6 (C Kilbee 88, G Nausher 3–32)
Bangladesh: 180–5 (A Ali 69*, T Cooke 2–30)

Bangladesh won by 5 wickets.

The President's XI completed a miserable week for Singapore to take third place in the S-E Asian competition. Glyn Davies and John Ford punched a huge hole through the middle of the Singapore batting – Stiller, Cooke and Kilbee failed to score. A late spirited innings from Rajalingam took them to a more respectable total after being 82 for 8. After losing Kumar, steady batting then saw the President's XI through to a comfortable win.

Jan 23 Singapore: 133 (M Rajalingam 32, J Ford 3–16, G Davies
3–19)
HK Pres. XI: 134–3 (T Sawney 37, R Farouq 35*, D Catton 31)

HK President's XI won by 7 wickets.

In the final at the mist-shrouded HKCC, the Bangladeshi team, after a fascinating see-saw contest, gained what they had come to achieve, a somewhat flattering win over Hong Kong. Ather Ali was again the batsman who made the difference with a fine 64 runs.

'Once again, Hong Kong had fallen at the final hurdle in an international, but the fact that the home team had more than managed to hold their own against a well-drilled, highly professional outfit offers at least some consolation.'

Jan 24   Bangladesh: 194–7   (A Ali 64, M Abedin 36, B Gohel 3–44)
        Hong Kong: 143   (D Beckett 34, Y Vachha 28*, M Badsha 3–13)

Bangladesh won by 51 runs.

For Bangladesh, Ather Ali, a tall, elegant right-handed batsman, was nominated 'Player of the Tournament'.

Some of the Bangladeshi cricketers were quite surprised to learn that none of the Hong Kong cricketers were paid for their services, and that the Hong Kong lady scorers also provided their services free!

3rd S-E Asian Tournament – June 1992

In the 3rd S-E Asian Tournament hosted by Singapore on a hot and sultry Padang, Malaysia and Thailand joined the previous participants, Bangladesh, Hong Kong and Singapore. Now, when these five countries participate in the S-E Asian Tournament, another competition for the Tuanku Ja'afar Cup also takes place without any additional matches being played. The overall winner is the S-E Asian champion, whilst the winner of the Tuanku Ja'afar Cup is the best of the other sides, excluding Bangladesh.

In Hong Kong's first match they easily accounted for Malaysia, bowling them out for 76. Put in to bat on a 'slow, lifeless' wicket, Martin Sabine top scored with 43 not out, after retiring earlier from dizziness brought on by the heat. Other useful scores came from Nigel Stearns and Glyn Davies. During Malaysia's short innings, Yarman Vachha was hit for 16 in one over. Bharat Gohel broke the back of the Malaysian batting with a match winning 4–13 from his 10 overs. 'He was pitching it in the dust and turning it two feet!' said Hong Kong team manager, Jim Middleton, who added: 'The track was abominable, it looks like the Gobi Desert with no grass whatsoever.'

In the second match, Hong Kong faced its nemesis Bangladesh once again. Unfortunately the different surroundings of the Singapore Padang didn't change the result.

'After losing the toss, Hong Kong were sent in to bat on another slow wicket but their openers, Steve Atkinson and Pat Fordham, laid the foundations for a solid total with a partnership of 95.'

At lunch Hong Kong were 115 for 1 with 11 overs remaining. Hong Kong's batting then collapsed dramatically, adding only 26 runs for the loss of seven wickets when the allotted 50 overs had expired. A Islam, 4–5 after lunch, finished with a fine 5–19 off his ten overs. Fordham tried seven bowlers in his endeavour to capture wickets, but their batting proved too solid and they reached their target in 41.3 overs. After bowling three overs, Nanda Perera had to retire with a recurrent back injury.

Skipper Fordham won the toss in the third match and put the opposition in to bat. Mendis and Ansari gave Thailand an excellent start, then 'David Crowe gave a 'Man of the Match' performance, the accurate left-arm paceman took 5 for 21 in 9.4 overs to help dismiss Thailand for 169.'

Steve Atkinson and Mark Eames gave Hong Kong a good start, and with solid quick fire knocks from Steve Foster, Fordham and Leigh Beaman, Hong Kong reached their target in 44.5 overs.

The fourth match saw Hong Kong play Singapore, the host country. 'Singapore began their innings briskly, openers Crossley and Goh taking 40 off the first seven overs.' However, Hong Kong soon took control with steady accurate bowling from Glyn Davies and Leigh Beaman, with Ravi Sujanani coming on fifth change to wrap up the Singapore innings. After the dismissal of Steve Atkinson, Steve Foster joined skipper Pat Fordham and their partnership took Hong Kong close to their target, achieved later in the 47th over.

Having beaten Malaysia, Singapore and Thailand, Hong Kong for the third time in as many tournaments, had another chance to avenge the defeats by Bangladesh. Jeremy Walker, reporting for the *SCMP*, said:

Hong Kong humbled in Cup Final – Hong Kong crumbled to a six wicket defeat at the hands of holders Bangladesh after being dismissed for a paltry 79 in the South-East Asian Cup Final at the Singapore Cricket Club yesterday.

Pat Fordham, the Hong Kong captain, blamed the pitch for his team's dismal performance. He said after the match: 'This pitch is not fit to play cricket on. You just can't do anything on it. No one can play a decent game on such a track.'

His Bangladeshi counterpart, Minazul Abedin, agreed that the pitch played havoc when Hong Kong batted. 'It was a crucial toss for us to win,' Abedin said. 'If we had to bat first, it would have been terrible for us.'

The 3rd S-E Asian Tournament had come and gone with Hong Kong still failing to find a way to defeat the strong Bangladesh XI.

Results of all Hong Kong matches:

15 June Hong Kong: 149–8 (M Sabine 43*, N Stearns 37, G Davies 23,
(SCC)   A Stephens 3–9)
         Malaysia: 76   (B Gohel 4–13)

Hong Kong won by 73 runs

16 June Hong Kong: 141–8 (S Atkinson 65, P Fordham 34, A Islam
(SCC)   5–19)
         Bangladesh: 142–3 (A Islam 45, F Ahmed 31, S Foster 2–19)

Bangladesh won by 7 wickets

17 June Thailand: 169   (K Ansari 70, C Mendis 30, D Crowe 5–21,
(SRC)   L Beaman 2–14)
         Hong Kong: 170–5 (S Atkinson 45, M Eames 31, P Fordham
                                 25, S Foster 23)

Hong Kong won by 5 wickets

20 June Singapore: 144   (M Thaiyar 33, K Imran 28*, J Crossley 28,
(SCC)   R Sujanani 3–10, L Beaman 3–17, G Davies
                                 2–20)
         Hong Kong: 147–4 (S Foster 51, P Fordham 45)

Hong Kong won by 6 wickets

21 June Hong Kong: 79   (S Atkinson 23, S Islam 4–14, J Alam 4–32)
(SCC)   Bangladesh: 81–4 (F Ahmed 42, L Beaman 2–12)

Bangladesh won the Final by 6 wickets

4th S-E Asian Tournament – 1996

The 4th S-E Asian Tournament, played in Malaysia from September 10 to 15, was renamed the Asian Cricket Council Trophy. [details not available.]

Under 19 Tour of Sri Lanka – 1997

In July 1997, the Hong Kong Under 19 squad visited Sri Lanka and played at three Sri Lankan Test match venues: P Sara Stadium, Galle Esplanade and Asgiriya Stadium. The competition as expected was tough, but it gave the players an insight into the standard required in order to qualify for the Youth World Cup later in the year in South Africa.

Under 19 Youth Asia Cup – 1997

From November 30 until December 7, the following countries participated in the Under 19 Youth Asia Cup in Hong Kong: Bangladesh, Fiji, Hong Kong, Malaysia, Nepal, Papua New Guinea, Singapore and Thailand, to determine which country would represent the region in the Under 19 World Cup matches in South Africa. Hong Kong played six matches, winning five (beating Fiji, Nepal, Papua New Guinea and Singapore) and losing once to Bangladesh. Bangladesh, the strongest cricketing country in the region, defeated Papua New Guinea in the final to earn the right of representation.

This is the area, the Under 19 Squad, where I feel the HKCA should concentrate their resources and their efforts. All the members of the squad play in the local cricket leagues, and because of the new qualification rules, will have to form the basis of the Hong Kong teams of the future for all matches played under the auspices of the ICC.

Batting and Bowling Averages 1984 to 1992 (incl Tuanku Ja'afar Cup 1992)

	Period	Matches	Innings	Highest	Runs	Average	100s	50s	Wickets	Average	Best	Catches	Stumpings
Anderson, P W	1984	7	6	52	121	24.20		1	4	17.00	2–25		
Atkinson, J	1988	3	3	14*	25	12.50			φ			3	
S	1992	5	5	65	165	33.00	1					5	
Bacon, G	1984	7	6	22*	35	7.00			4	29.50	1–11	3	
Beaman, L	1992	4	4	17*	42	42.00			7	6.86	3–17	2	
Beckett, D K	1988	4	4	86	141	35.25		1	5	17.80	3–10	3	
Brewster, R	1988	3	2	2	3	1.50						1	
Broadhurst, N	1984	5	4	33	77	25.67						2	
Caley, S	1984	3	3	12	31	10.33			1	24.00	1–13	1	
Collins, C	1984	7	6	26	77	12.83			13	11.85	3–26	1	
Crowe, D	1992	4	1	1*	1	∞			6	12.00	5–21	2	
Davies, G	1984–92	8	7	23	56	9.33			2	33.50	2–20	3	
Dean, C	1988	4	4	72	188	47.00	2		φ			3	
Eames, M	1988–92	8	8	66*	194	27.71		2					

417

	Period	Matches	Innings	Highest	Runs	Average	100s	50s	Wickets	Average	Best	Catches	Stumpings
Evans, D	1988	4	4	43*	65	21.67							
Fordham, P	1992	5	5	45	118	23.60						1	2
Foster, S	1992	5	5	51	80	16.00		1	3	22.33	2-19		
Fotheringham, R	1992	2	1	15	15	15.00			φ				
Gohel, B	1988-92	9	5	8	14	4.67			16	18.63	4-13	2	
Henley, P	1984	4	4	20*	47	15.67							
Jenkins, J	1984	7	4	1*	3	∞			9	15.44	4- 4	1	
Lalchandani, G	1984	3	1	5*	5	∞			φ				
Myles, S	1984	7	7	106*	191	31.83	1		2	18.00	1- 2	3	
Perera, N	1988-92	6	6	47	100	16.67			5	28.80	2-11	1	
Sabine, M	1988-92	4	4	43*	61	20.33						1	
Scott, A	1984	1	1	0	0	0.00			1	22.00	1-22		
Stearns, N	1984-92	13	13	53	261	21.75		2	φ			4	
Sujanani, R	1992	5	3	1	2	0.67			6	9.83	3-10	1	
Swann, C	1984	7	4	35	60	15.00			12	16.08	4-22	1	
Telford, A	1988	4	2	7	8	8.00			4	32.00	1- 9	1	
Thompson, J	1992	2										2 (sub)	
Vachha, Y	1988-92	7	4	28*	28	9.33			7	28.14	4-17	1	
Wood, P	1984	7	7	51	183	26.14		1	φ			3	

HK President's XI

	Period	Matches	Innings	Highest	Runs	Average	100s	50s	Wickets	Average	Best	Catches	Stumpings
Catton, B	1988	4	4	34	93	23.25						2	
Collier, I	1988	4	2	9	9	4.50			7	18.86	4-31		
Davies, G	1988	4	3	34	55	18.33			5	19.60	3-19	1	
Farouq, R	1988	4	4	35*	44	14.66						1	
Ford, J	1988	4	3	48	100	33.33			6	13.83	3-16		
Fotheringham, R	1988	1							φ				
Gill, R	1988	4	2	1	1	0.50						6	1
Jones, D A	1988	4	4	16	31	10.33			1	66.00	1-43	3	
Kumar, K	1988	4	4	103*	230	76.67	1	2				1	
Marsden, R	1988	2	2	4	4	4.00			1	35.00	1-10		
Sawney, T	1988	2	2	37	39	19.50						1	
Tariq, S	1988	4	3	17	17	5.67			5	23.20	2-21		
Uttamchandani, D	1988	4	2	1*	2	∞			2	57.50	2-16		

∞ Infinity · no average   φ Also bowled without success

THE TUANKU JA'AFAR CUP

Tuanku Ja'afar is the son of the ruler of Negri Sembilan, one of the Malay States. In 1971 his brother, Tuanku Imran (Peter), toured Hong Kong with the Malaysian team as the reserve wicket-keeper. Peter had attended King's School, Canterbury, and Nottingham University, where he played most of his early cricket. He had represented Negri Sembilan on numerous occasions and played against touring sides. Apart from cricket, he was a fine squash player and a tennis, hockey and rugby enthusiast. In 1991, the Tuanku Ja'afar Cup was inaugurated for matches between Malaysia, Hong Kong and Singapore, with Thailand joining the competition in June 1992.

Peter's brother was crowned the 10th King of Malaysia in 1994. The two of them have been instrumental in the recent revival of cricket in Malaysia.

These one day matches are all part of the S-E Asian region's preparation for the four-yearly ICC Associate Members' competitions. They also act as a focus for the development of each country's own domestic cricket programmes.

In 1991, a splendid century from A Stephens at the Royal Selangor Club, ably supported by S Bell with a half century, put the Malaysians in a strong position. After both batsmen were run out, Hong Kong's bowlers brought the Malaysian innings to a close. Stewart Brew matched Stephens with his own fine century, and with good supporting roles from James Barrington and Steve Foster, saw Hong Kong to victory in a high-scoring match.

1991   Malaysia: 245–8   (A Stephens 118, S Bell 55, N Perera 2–42)
Sep 13   Hong Kong: 246–5   (S Brew 126, S Foster 43*, J Barrington 28)

Hong Kong won by five wickets.

In the next match against Singapore, Hong Kong lost Brew early on, but a fine partnership from Pat Fordham and Barrington paved the way to a reasonable total when Mohmed stepped in with five wickets to restrict Hong Kong to under 200 runs. Nanda Perera removed both openers, and only Ahmed and later Field showed any signs that the Hong Kong total would be threatened.

Sep 14   Hong Kong: 183–9   (J Barrington 57, P Fordham 34, T Mohmed
                                        5–34)
        Singapore: 135   (M Ahmed 36, N Perera 3–28, G Davies
                                          2–25)

Hong Kong won by 48 runs.

The matches from June 15–21, 1992 were played as part of the S-E Asian Tournament in Singapore.

Apart from the 'hiccup' in 1991 against Thailand in Hong Kong, Hong Kong has dominated these competitions. However, Hong Kong itself is brought down to earth in the S-E Asian tournament, whenever Bangladesh participate, having met the 'professional' Bangladesh team numerous times without success.

Hong Kong, Malaysia, Singapore and Thailand next met in Bangkok in February 1993 for the Tuanku Ja'afar Cup (quadrangular) and the Volvo

Cup (triangular – without Singapore) competitions. These are now firmly established matches played on the 50-overs format.

Hong Kong were drawn to play Malaysia first in the Tuanku Ja'afar series of matches in Bangkok, Thailand in 1993:

In a match played at the Sports Club ground, defending champions Hong Kong, hottest favourites to win the Quadrangular and the Volvo Cup Triangular, gobbled up Malaysia, winning by eight wickets. V Segaran and S Bell were shaping well, but once they were back in the pavilion, their batting was in tatters. Glyn Davies and David Cross wrought havoc with the ball, bundling the Malaysians out for 94. Despite spirited bowling by the Malaysians, Hong Kong's powerful batting line-up didn't waste time and achieved their target in 27 overs. Stewart Brew who compiled an unbeaten 45 was declared 'Man of the Match'. He and skipper Pat Fordham hoisted victory with an unbeaten 32 runs.

Edward Thangarajah, Bangkok

1993   Malaysia: 94   (S Bell 27, D Cross 3–24, G Davies 3–25)
Feb 26 Hong Kong: 96–2 (S Brew 45*)

Hong Kong won by eight wickets.

Starting slowly on the Sports Club ground, Hong Kong, with sound innings from Brew, Dai Thomas, and Steve Atkinson, paved the way for a whirlwind partnership of 108 in just over 10 overs between skipper Pat Fordham and John Garden, which clocked up the side's daunting total of just over 300 runs. Singapore were all but out of the picture at 83 for 4, then a swashbuckling 84 from middle-order batsman Sunder Mani, which included six sixes – Brew and Cresswell being the main sufferers – put them in sight of achieving a spectacular victory. But once Mani was out the run-chase withered, with Hong Kong eventual winners by 22 runs. Mani was deservedly nominated 'Man of the Match'.

Feb 27   Hong Kong: 303–4 (D Thomas 64, P Fordham 60*, S Brew 52, J
                              Garden 51*, S Atkinson 44, S Muruthi 2–46)
         Singapore: 281–9 (S Mani 84, G Wilson 62, D Cross 3–25, R
                              Greer 3–42)

Hong Kong won by 22 runs.

Batting first at the Polo ground after winning the toss, Hong Kong was

420

again given a solid start by openers Brew and Thomas, who put on 101 runs. Atkinson then emerged as the 'Man of the Match' with a sparkling 70 off 58 balls coupled with an outstanding fielding display. Skipper Fordham, batting at number 6, hit 46 off 29 balls and 'rushed Hong Kong to 288 for 7 off 50 overs.' Apart from a 53 run middle-order partnership between Geoff Cooper and Adam Caro, Thailand never looked in the picture, and in the words of the *Standard*'s T M T Samat:

> Hong Kong turned in a fine professional performance to retain the Tuanku Ja'afar trophy by registering a 119 run win over Thailand in Bangkok yesterday.

Feb 28 Hong Kong: 288–7 (S Atkinson 70, D Thomas 51, S Brew 49,
                                      P Fordham 46, S Mohammed 3–54)
        Thailand: 169   (G Cooper 64, A Caro 33, P Cresswell 2–36)

After the Tournament, Team Manager David Wilson said:

> This is a good Hong Kong cricket team; they work hard and play together with a great team spirit. This is the sort of application and determination that will be needed in the ICC Trophy in Kenya next year.

Other Matches:

> Singapore: 244 (C Kilbee 72, Z Hasib 3–52)
> Thailand: 223 (G Cooper 68, K Ansari 32, K Deshpande 3–18,
>   S Mani 3–41)

Singapore won by 21 runs.

> Malaysia: 219–9 (B Nair 127, Z Hasib 3–41, L Tongyai 3 wkts,
>   Altaf 2–42)
> Thailand: 174   (G Cooper 52, C Price 30, J Lopez 3 wkts)

Malaysia won by 45 runs.

> Singapore: 217–7 (G Stanley 71*, K Deshpande 60, J Lopez
>   2–58)
> Malaysia: 199   (V Segaran 54, D Ramadass 38, S Muruthi 4–39)

Singapore won by 18 runs.

The *Bangkok Post* reported:

The Deputy Governor of the Sports Authority in Thailand, Dr Nat Intrapana; Riche Monde's Joint Managing Director, Dr Tasman Smith and Caltex's Managing Director, Bryan Baldwin, took part in last night's Awards Ceremony at the Polo Club Hall. They congratulated Jack Dunford and Mohideen A Kader for organising a fine tournament.

In November 1994, it was Hong Kong's turn as hosts for the popular Tuanku Ja'afar Trophy tournament, other participating countries being Malaysia, Singapore and Thailand. As part of its development programme, Hong Kong named seven locally born players in the 16 strong squad, including three 'Chinese' players:Tony Correa, Maurice Ling and Eddie Tse.

Winning the toss in the first match, Singapore put Hong Kong in to bat at KCC. After a slow start Hong Kong accelerated, with the impetus coming from Riaz Farcy (44), skipper Pat Fordham (85) and 51 not out off 38 balls from new man, 26-year-old left-hander John Storey. At 50 overs, Hong Kong had reached a formidable 282 for 6. The same Storey, then bowling a good line with his left-arm spinners, wrecked the Singapore batting taking six wickets. Only T Graban looked like stemming the tide, Hong Kong winning by 107 runs.

Nov 16 Hong Kong: 282–6 (P Fordham 85, J Storey 51*, R Farcy 44)
      Singapore: 175 (T Graban 70, A Vijay 33, J Storey 6–36, R Farcy 2–22)

The territories three 'Chinese' cricketers shared five of the nine Malaysian wickets that fell victim to bowlers in a one-sided match at HKCC. Hong Kong, batting first, saw Rahul Sharma and Rory MacLeay put on an opening stand of 149 runs, Sharma narrowly missing his century. Big John Storey, coming in at No. 5, 'bludgeoned his way to 60 (six 6s and four 4s) off only 27 balls.' Malaysia's openers put on a slow, steady 31, but they were never going to cause Hong Kong any concern and folded for 120 runs in 40.5 overs.

Chinese connection plays key cup role.

Alvin Sallay, *SCMP*

Nov 17 Hong Kong: 271–8 (R Sharma 98, J Storey 60, R MacLeay 54, R Selvaratnam 3–26)
      Malaysia: 120 (D Ramadass 25, Y Vachha 2–7, A Correa 2–18, M Ling 2–21)

Hong Kong won by 151 runs.

In the last of the round-robin matches, Hong Kong easily defeated Thailand at the HKCC. Taking first lease of the wicket, Hong Kong's solid batting line-up had 317 runs on the board in their allotted 50 overs. Rahul Sharma again led the way, this time with a fine century. John Storey weighed in with his third consecutive half century. After an opening stand of 44, Thailand were never in the game as Hong Kong's seven bowlers tied them down to just over 100 runs.

Nov 18 Hong Kong: 317–6 (R Sharma 118, J Storey 53, M Eames 40, S
                            Brew 38, Z Hasib 3–52)
        Thailand: 109   (K Ansari 38*, Y Vachha 2–6, J Iqbal 2–18,
                            S Brew 2–23)

Hong Kong won by 208 runs.

Singapore caused a great upset in the final match against Hong Kong at HKCC. Stewart Brew (73) and Mark Eames (49) had figured in a 100 run 3rd wicket partnership to help Hong Kong reach a respectable 234 runs.

There was little sign of the hurricane to hit Hong Kong bowlers at the start. When Naushad walked in, Hong Kong were in the driving seat with Singapore struggling at 124 for 5 in the 37th over, chasing a target of 235.

Alvin Sallay, *SCMP*

In six overs, Singapore hammered 88 runs. Stewart Brew, with 2–16 off his first seven overs, ended with 2–48 off nine! The winning runs came in the 49th over. From the author's armchair position in distant England, it would appear that after taking Singapore apart in the preliminary round, Hong Kong, after some easy wins, became too complacent!

Hong Kong managed to lose from an invincible position.

Geoff Lever

Nov 19 Hong Kong: 234–8 (S Brew 73, M Eames 49, K Deshpande 3–51)
        Singapore: 236–8 (M Naushad 53, K Deshpande 50, Z Shroff
                            40, B Hall 2–39)

Singapore won by two wickets.

According to Alvin Sallay's report, Hong Kong's biggest problems would appear to be poor running between the wickets and the lack of facing good accurate bowling. Alvin mentioned the number of boundaries hit by Hong Kong batsmen and felt sure that when Bangladesh visited over Chinese New Year they wouldn't be so accommodating.

In 1995, four matches were played in Kuala Lumpur from September 20 to 25. In the first match against Singapore, Hong Kong, with the aid of a splendid century from Rahul Sharma, led the run-chase which was achieved in the 48th over.

Singapore: 243–9 (M Naushad 104, S Mani 34, R Sujanani 4–45, A Ashman 3–35)
Hong Kong: 244–4 (R Sharma 109, P. Fordham 43*, T Smart 38, M Lever 32)

Hong Kong got in some good batting practice against Thailand before the weather threatened to give Thailand an advantage as they only required 96 runs from 20 overs in a rain affected match. After five overs they were well on target, but fortunately for Hong Kong, that was to be the extent of their innings before the rain closed the proceedings.

Hong Kong: 233   (M Lever 50, P Fordham 48, R Sujanani 36*, A Caro 3–37)
Thailand: 25–0

Cheered on by the Crown Prince of Malaysia, Tuanku Imran, Malaysia recorded a first time victory over Hong Kong in this tournament. The Malaysians, all local-born players, had outplayed Hong Kong in almost every department.

Malaysia: 246–5 (D Tallala 59, S Navaratnam 54, S Jalil 45, S Singh 30)
Hong Kong: 237–8 (R McGregor 68, P Fordham 54, D Jones 32, R Menon 3–24, J Prakash 3–32)

Hong Kong, with the best run-rate, edged out Singapore for the right to meet Malaysia in the final, and a chance to avenge its earlier 'shock' defeat. After dismissing the home side for a modest 120, a 'cocky' Hong Kong soon found itself three wickets down for six runs. 'The salt was rubbed in by the gleeful Malaysians who brilliantly piled on the pressure with their fielding, superb field-placing and accurate bowling.'

Alvin Sallay, *SCMP*

Malaysia: 120 (S Jalil 32, R Menon 31, R Sharma 3–19, R McGregor 2–11 off 10 overs)
Hong Kong: 80 (S Navaratnam 3–13, A Muniandy 2–5 off 8.3 overs)

For the second year in a row, Hong Kong were beaten in the final.

Hong Kong headed for Singapore in June 1996, in an attempt to 'lay the ghosts' of the previous two Tuanku Ja'afar Cup tournaments. Hong Kong triumphed in emphatic fashion.

After a solid build-up to the tournament, the team clearly established a determined frame of mind and won all four matches, setting a world record in the process. Hong Kong's 415 against Thailand was the highest score ever recorded in an international 50-over match. Riaz Farcy's brilliant 178 was the highest ever by a Hong Kong player, beating Simon Myles's 172 against Gibraltar in the 1986 ICC Trophy tournament.

The victorious tour was a genuine team effort with all members of the squad contributing in one way or another. Glyn Davies, former Hong Kong Captain, was moved to say: 'the spirit in this side is the best of any Hong Kong team I've ever been associated with.'

Jun 27　Hong Kong: 300　(S Brew 138, R Farcy 52, R Sharma 51)
　　　　　Malaysia:　 215　(R McGregor 3–28, S Hussain 2–14)

Jun 28　Hong Kong: 415　(R Farcy 178, S Brew 94, R Sharma 54, A
　　　　　　　　　　　　　　Dartnell 51*)
　　　　　Thailand:　 221

Jun 29　Singapore:　 194　(R Sharma 4–36)
　　　　　Hong Kong: 197–3　(S Brew 72, R Sharma 47)

Jun 30　Hong Kong: 296–8　(S Brew 88, R Sharma 71, M Lever 38)
　　　　　Singapore:　 277　(M Zubair 3–38, D Jones 2–20)

In the final against Singapore at the Ceylon Sports Club, Hong Kong won the trophy in a high-scoring match. Stewart Brew was the star of the tournament, aggregating 392 runs in four innings, whilst Farcy and Sharma both exceeded 200 runs.

In 1997, this time in Thailand from January 15 to 19, Hong Kong, now subject to the revised ICC qualification rules, fielded six players making their debut at this level and failed to reach the final for the first time, after a one wicket defeat in the opening match against Malaysia. Two of the six, Alex French and Grayson Tyndale, scored their maiden half centuries against Malaysia and Thailand respectively.

> ... they will have learned the respective lessons of character, perseverance and humility.
>
> Nick Waters, *ATV*

As part of its continuing development programme, the HKCA has started sending junior sides to participate in various tournaments within the region. In June 1997, an Under 15 team went to Singapore to participate in the first Tuanku Ja'afar Under 15 tournament, which saw Hong Kong win against Thailand but lose to Malaysia and Singapore. The important lesson learned seems to have been the need for these young players to bat for longer periods of time.

Batting and Bowling Averages 1990–95 (includes Volvo Cup)

	Period	Matches	Innings	Highest	Runs	Average	100s	50s	Wickets	Average	Best	Wickets 5 plus	Catches	Stumpings
Ashman, A	1995	4	3	4	8	4.00			5	22.20	2-35		1	
Atkinson, S	1993	3	3	70	130	43.33		1					4	
Barrington, J	1991–2	5	5	57	165	33.00		1					1	
Beaman, L	1992	2	1	7	7	7.00			2	20.00	2–14			
Brew, S	1991–4	11	11	126	621	69.00	1	5	13	25.92	2–1		7	
Correa, A	1994	1	1	0	0	0.00			2	9.00	2–18			
Cox, J	1990	1							3	35.00	2–52			
Cresswell, P	1993	3	1	6*	6	∞			3	35.66	2–36			
Cross, D	1993–5	5	1	1*	1	∞			7	15.71	3–24			
Crowe, D	1991	1							φ				1	
Davies, G	1990–3	8	5	30	60	15.00			13	23.00	3–25		6	
T	1993	2							1	51.00	1–24		1	
Eames, M	1991–5	9	8	49	188	23.50							6	
Ebrahim, A	1990	1	2	16	24	12.00								
Eddington, R	1990	1							1	59.00	1–39			
Farcy, R	1994	4	4	44	74	18.50			2	31.00	2–22		2	
Farouq, R	1990	1	2	70	122	61.00		2	1	8.00	1–8			
Fordham, P	1990–5	17	17	85	514	42.83		3	2	11.00	2–22		19	11
Foster, S	1991	3	3	43*	80	40.00			6	22.50	2–29		3	
Garden, J	1991–3	6	5	51*	74	24.66		1					3	
Gelling, D	1990	1	1	3*	3	∞							4	
Gohel, B	1991–5	5	3	12	27	9.00			φ				2	
Graham, M	1990	1	1	12*	12	∞							1	
Greer, R	1993	2	2	20	27	13.50			4	13.50	3–42		2	
Hall, B	1994–5	7	6	17*	53	17.67			4	47.25	2–39		1	
Hussain, S	1994–5	4	3	22	29	9.67			2	27.50	2–36		2	
Iqbal, J	1994	3							2	34.50	2–18		2	
Johnson, M	1993	2							φ					
Jones, D A	1995	3	3	32	47	15.67			1	44.00	1–44		2	
Kumar, K	1990–1	2	3	75	115	38.33		1					4	
Lever, M	1995	3	3	50	93	31.00		1					1	
Ling, M	1994	1							2	10.50	2–21		1	
McGregor, R	1995	4	3	68	86	28.67		1	5	17.00	2–11		1	
MacLeay, R	1994	2	2	54	82	41.00		1						
Nissim, R	1990	1												
Nuttall, R	1991	1	1	2*	2	∞							1	
Penrose, J	1992	2	2	86*	111	111.00		1						

	Period	Matches	Innings	Highest	Runs	Average	100s	50s	Wickets	Average	Best	Wickets 5 plus	Catches	Stumpings
Perera, N	1991–2	4	2	20*	30	30.00			7	14.71	3–28			
Scattergood, A	1991	1	1	1*	1	∞			2	26.00	2–52			
Sharma, R	1994–5	8	8	118	381	47.62	2	1	4	18.75	3–19		2	
Smart, T	1994–5	6	6	38	120	20.00							2	
Stearns, N	1991–3	5	4	16*	36	18.00								1
Storey, J	1994	4	4	60	167	55.67		3	9	8.33	6–36	1	2	
Strachan, J	1994	1							φ					
Sujanani, R	1994–5	7	7	36*	82	20.50			7	21.71	4–45		3	
Symcox, W	1992	2	1	3	3	3.00			3	20.66	2–33		1	
Tariq, S	1991–2	3							4	14.00	2–1			
Thomas, D	1993	2	2	64	115	57.50		2						
Tse, E	1994	1							1	18.00	1–18			
Vachha, Y	1990–4	11	6	39	97	32.33			17	22.06	4–86		1	

φ Also bowled without success
∞ Infinity – no average
N.B. 1996 has been omitted as detailed scoresheets were not available.

VOLVO CUP

The Volvo Cup was inaugurated in January 1990 by Ron Endley of Bangkok. Ron was then working for Volvo and persuaded his company to donate a trophy for officially recognised Thailand v Hong Kong cricket matches. Ron had represented the Royal Bangkok Sports Club in cricket matches against the KCC for many years, and played in the inaugural Volvo match for Thailand against Hong Kong on the Polo Ground, Bangkok.

1990	Thailand Cricket League:	179–7	(Larn Tongyai 77, N White 28, G Davies 3–63)
Jan 26		239	(P Davies 90, R Endley 55, Y Vachha 4–86)
& 27	HK Cricket Association:	206–5	(K Kumar 75, R Farouq 52, N Malik 3–65)
		187–5	(R Farouq 70, Y Vachha 39, K Kumar 36)

Hong Kong won by 27 runs on the first innings, which is limited to 50 overs.

1991	Hong Kong:	236–6	(S Brew 77, J Barrington 40, P Fordham 26)
Mar 16	Thailand:	240–7	(Larn Tongyai 67, A Zakhariya 62, Luke Tongyai 34)

427

Thailand won the toss at KCC, put Hong Kong in to bat and won by three wickets in an upset result.

When Hong Kong returned to the Polo Ground, Bangkok, in February 1992, the format had been changed to that of a triangular tournament with Malaysia joining the competition.

1992   Thailand: 247 (Larn Tongyai 108)
Feb 5   Malaysia: 164

Thailand won by 83 runs.

After Malaysian skipper Banerji was brilliantly caught by Glyn Davies for 8, 'the remaining batsmen failed to master Hong Kong's variation of pace and spin.' An aggressive 2nd wicket partnership of 140 between Stewart Brew and Jason Penrose then sealed Hong Kong's victory by nine wickets.

Feb 6   Malaysia: 166–9 (Tan Kim Hing 64*, S Tariq 2–18, S Brew
                             2–23)
        Hong Kong: 167–1 (J Penrose 86*, S Brew 53*)

'In-form Brew produced a disciplined knock of 87 off 108 balls.' Glyn Davies and Nanda Perera put on 48 for the 9th wicket after a middle order collapse had seen the score slump from 174 for 3 to 218 for 8. Although Thailand started aggressively, wickets fell at regular intervals to the six bowlers employed by Hong Kong. At 53 for 5, the writing was on the wall. Skipper Fordham collected six wickets behind the stumps, Hong Kong winning by 143 runs.

Feb7   Hong Kong: 266–9 (S Brew 87, G Davies 30, A Zakhariya 4–60)
        Thailand: 123   (E Pacha 24, S Tariq 2–1, L Beaman 2–14,
                            G Davies 2–21)

The matches involving Bangladesh, Hong Kong, Malaysia, Singapore and Thailand, as stated in the ACC Section, became interwoven in recent years without any clear defining line between the original differing competitions. It seemed that the Asian Cricket Council tournament played every four years incorporated the Tuanku Ja'afar trophy, and the Tuanku Ja'afar that of the Volvo Cup. The author was told in 1995 that there are now only two tournaments, the ACC and the Tuanku Ja'afar.

428

SILK CUT SINGLE-WICKET COMPETITION

First Competition – 1986

The first 'Silk Cut' sponsored single-wicket competition was played over two fine days at the HKCC in December 1986. A good crowd, swelled by a large contingent of Pakistanis, as the charismatic Imran Khan was scheduled to play, were enthralled by the individual talents of such renowned players as Graham Gooch, Richard Hadlee, Imran Khan (the eventual winner), Madan Lal and Clive Rice. The fielders were selected from the more mobile of the HKCA's best cricketers, while the HKACU provided the umpires and the scorers. Fielding turned out to be quite an 'ordeal' for those participating, as the ball was projected much faster from hand and bat than had previously been experienced by the Hong Kong players. Good experience, they say.

During the luncheon interval, Cathay Pacific provided some 'hot air' entertainment in the shape of their much-advertised air balloon. After the competition, Imran was mobbed by autograph hunters. Whether he had won or not would have made no difference to his obvious popularity. It was a highly successful, well organised and entertaining way of promoting cricket, an occasion to be repeated.

Second Competition – 1987

The idiosyncrasies of the single-wicket game, such as points deducted for dismissals, was more or less understood by players and spectators alike when the second competition took place the following year at KCC. An even larger crowd of cricket enthusiasts, this time including the 'hospitality' element of cricket supporters, were given another excellent two days of entertaining, competitive cricket.

The timing of this second Hong Kong Silk Cut was subject to the availability of the 'big catch', Ian Botham. He was to be the main attraction, ably supported by a host of established stars such as Richard Hadlee, Malcolm Marshall, Greg Matthews, R J Ratnayeke, Clive Rice and Hong Kong's own Dermot Reeve. Up to the last minute it was rumoured that Imran Khan would come to defend his title, but it was not to be. Fortunately, Phil Edmonds was in town, so he obligingly agreed to take the eighth place. Unfortunately for the keen followers of the game, Mr Botham was apparently not aware that he had been specially brought out to Hong Kong for this grand occasion. It had been noticed the previous evening at the cocktail party for the players and cricket enthusiasts that, whilst Marshall and Rice were drinking coke, Botham appeared to be partaking of much stronger stuff.

429

On the first day of the competition, showing little interest in the proceedings, Botham was knocked out by Dermot Reeve, much to the disappointment of the crowd. Malcolm Marshall had the crowd spellbound watching him bowl, wondering how he managed to generate such speed off his short run-up to the wicket. The ever-keen and competitive Clive Rice, mathematically calculating each run and dismissal, played hard and deservedly took the title on the second day. This time the fielders were a mix of HKCA players supplemented by a number of MCC Young Professionals, flown out specially for the competition.

After the 'no show' by Ian Botham, and possibly the added difficulty of gathering the right mix of star players together at one given time, Silk Cut declined to carry on the sponsorship of the single-wicket competition, one which had proved very popular with players and spectators. A sad end to such a promising spectacle for the participants and the local cricket enthusiasts.

HONG KONG INTERNATIONAL SIXES

The first Cathay Pacific/Wharf Holdings Hong Kong International Cricket Sixes took place at the KCC on Saturday and Sunday 3/4 October 1992.

Hong Kong cricketers have been in the forefront in popularising 'Sixes' cricket in S-E Asia. Local sixes were inaugurated by CCC in 1961, and have continued in their original format up to the present day, now played at KCC. Two of the popular venues for the region's 'international' sixes have been in Bangkok and Chiangmai in Thailand, where many of the participating teams were strengthened by current and former Test players.

The idea of a truly international sixes was first germinated in October 1991, after an extremely successful six-a-side tournament in Hong Kong as part of a charity cricket weekend. The HKCA gave its full blessing to the chief organisers, Cricket World International – headed by Brian Catton (a Hong Kong representative cricketer and former Chairman of the HKCA) and Papu Butani, a Kowloon-based jeweller and cricket fanatic, backed by chief sponsors, Cathay Pacific and Wharf Holdings.

Eight of the nine Test-playing nations were represented, including the limited-overs world champions Pakistan, led by Javed Miandad, with the 'formidables' Wasim Akram and Waqar Younis at his beck and call. Zimbabwe replaced South Africa, who were unable to take part. With each innings lasting only five overs and each game taking around 40 minutes to complete, cricket lovers were entertained to 20 mini-matches spread evenly over two days. The picturesque KCC ground had never seen so many spectators – 2,800 on Saturday and 3,200 on Sunday. Ingenuity somehow fitted them into the available space.

The respective groups, teams and captains were:

Green Group	Australia	David Hookes
	Hong Kong	Pat Fordham
	Pakistan	Javed Miandad
Blue Group	England	Derek Randall
	Sri Lanka	Arjuna Ranatunga
	West Indies	Vivian Richards
Red Group	India	Ravi Shastri
	New Zealand	Martin Crowe
	Zimbabwe	David Houghton

On the first day, in the Red group, Zimbabwe surprised India and beat them by nine runs

There were no surprises in the Blue group, but the crowd had eagerly awaited the arrival of the legendary Viv Richards on his first visit to Hong Kong, and gave him a rousing welcome when he walked to the wicket. He didn't disappoint the crowd, retiring after scoring 32 runs, which included four scorching boundaries. The great man at the end of the first day said: 'I think this tournament is a good idea. We need ideas to beef up cricket and lure people into the grounds. Things like this have to continue.'

The Green group, in which Hong Kong had been drawn to play against Australia and Pakistan, provided the shock results of the first day. The crowd watched enthralled as Hong Kong beat a sluggish Australia by 28 runs, then in total disbelief, as Hong Kong sneaked pass Pakistan's 88 for 1 off the last ball in their second match.

An euphoric Pat Fordham said: 'It's fantastic, absolutely incredible. We are just a team of good club cricketers and we've just beaten the world champions!' Hong Kong's splendid achievement was the only defeat inflicted on the world and eventual champions of the first Hong Kong International Sixes.

The second day saw the respective professional teams taking the game much more seriously, as Hong Kong soon found out, being well beaten by England and India in the Grace Group. India also beat England by six runs to head that group. Pakistan, the pre-tournament favourites and fully recovered from their practice match against Hong Kong, showed why they were world champions by beating the West Indies and New Zealand in the Bradman Group, to go through to meet India in the final.

In a low-scoring, tense final, watched by Governor Chris Patten flanked by Hatım Ebrahim, HKCA President, Pakistan, reinforced by Salim Malik, saw Sohail hammer two sixes in the last over to see Pakistan safely home with one ball remaining.

Javed Miandad said: 'A lot of people were thinking it would be festival cricket, but it was not like that at all – it was real cricket.' Ravi Shastri, the losing captain, added: 'The tournament has been a big hit with the players.'

In the Plate final, Zimbabwe were well beaten by Sri Lanka, being unable to repeat their earlier easy win over that country.

A participating local umpire and KCC member exclaimed: 'A brilliant weekend of entertainment and of spectacular cricket.'

2nd Hong Kong International Sixes – 1993

Eight of the nine Test-playing countries were represented at the 2nd Hong Kong International Sixes, now a popular fixture on the world cricket calendar. After Hong Kong's success in the first sixes, they were invited as the ninth team instead of Zimbabwe. Future competitions might well see all nine Test countries vying for the trophy.

The first match of the 1993 Cathay/Wharf sixes set the tone for the entire tournament, when unfancied South Africa defeated the seeded Kiwis by six wickets. An amazing innings from Rod Latham (NZ – 36 retired from only nine balls) relegated Richie Richardson's West Indians to the Plate competition. England's well-balanced side were impressive, and Hong Kong's moment of glory came when they managed to hold off the West Indies for a two-run victory in the Plate.

In the first semi-final England reached 79 for 1, after a great start from Philip DeFreitas and Neil Fairbrother, and defeated South Africa by 15 runs. Sri Lanka in the second semi-final reached a useful 78 for 5 against Australia, and when Mark Waugh failed for the first time with the bat, Australia were left 18 runs short. In the final, Arjuna Ranatunga won the toss and batted, and although Dermot Reeve only conceded nine runs in the first over, Sri Lanka compiled a very respectable 74 for 1. The early loss of both DeFreitas and Fairbrother, who had both been such successes in the earlier rounds, brought tension to the England camp. However, local hero Reeve, with another of his 'Houdini' acts, steered and drove seven of the 11 balls he received to the boundary, then had to retire after scoring 31 with only two runs required from the last three deliveries. Next batsman Gladstone Small, after missing the first ball, scrambled the winning runs off the penultimate to give England a deserved, narrow victory.

Ranatunga said: 'Reeve's unorthodox stroke-making, particularly the reverse sweep, threw my side out of their rhythm after they had captured the wickets of in-form Neil Fairbrother for four and Phil DeFreitas for eight runs.'

Dermot Reeve was named 'Player of the Final' and Philip DeFreitas 'Player of the Tournament.' DeFreitas had scored crucial runs and only conceded 21 runs from five overs for his two wickets. Mark Waugh must have run him close for this honour having scored 186 runs for only once out.

DeFreitas said: 'It's been a wonderful two days and the seven of us have already decided we want to come back next year and defend the title.'

With the KCC playing area shrinking to accommodate the 4,200 spectators (1992 – 3,200), thoughts about a larger venue are uppermost in the minds of the organisers and sponsors to allow for the increased demand for seats coupled with spectator safety. There is no doubt Hong Kong has now cemented this international cricket fixture into the calendars of many cricketing organisations, local and overseas.

3rd Hong Kong International Sixes – 1994

Persistent heavy rain during September had threatened this special event. However, the organisers, sponsors, players and spectators were fortunate that sunny weather blessed the 3rd International Sixes on 1/2 October 1994.

After some very close matches coupled with dashes of excellence in the field, England won the 3rd Cathay/Wharf International Sixes by beating 'the old enemy' Australia to retain the trophy in an enthralling final at the pictureque KCC.

Hong Kong-born Dermot Reeve led six other English Test cricketers to a winners' cheque for HK$187,500 (£15,375). The West Indies, captained by Richie Richardson, beat South Africa to capture the Plate, whilst India, led by Mohammed Azharuddin, beat Hong Kong to win the Bowl.

'Man of the Final': Neil Fairbrother (England) – Most Sixes: Nolan Clarke (Holland) – 'Man of the Tournament': Robin Smith (England).

The playing arena continued to shrink as crowd numbers increase each year. Now nine deep in places, and interspersed with hospitality boxes, great vigilance is an absolute must, as white leather balls constantly bisect fielders and head for dodging spectators. Sadly, but surely, the venue has to be moved to the spectacular newly refurbished Hong Kong Stadium. Not only to save some future cricket spectator from possible injury, but also to give the sponsors a chance to show some return for their generous support of this great occasion. I say sadly, because the crowded atmosphere of KCC will be lost in the vast expanse of the new stadium. But like the International Rugby Sevens before, this change will be necessary for the continued financial success of this great event.

Participants and captains of this third competition were:

Australia	Damien Martyn
England	Dermot Reeve
Holland	Steven Lubbers
Hong Kong	Pat Fordham
India	Mohammed Azharuddin
New Zealand	Ken Rutherford
Pakistan	Ijaz Ahmed
South Africa	Hansie Cronje
West Indies	Richie Richardson

Richie Benaud and Tony Greig covered the action for SKY TV, whilst international umpires Tony Crafter and Merv Kitchen joined the experienced local umpires Geoff Lever, Rod Starling and Alan Swift, together with TV scorers Kay Barnett and Gordon Vince and others, to help make the two-day proceedings an enjoyable and memorable occasion.

At the completion of the two-day cricket bonanza, the ICC Chief Executive, David Richards, a guest at the Sixes, said: 'I've been impressed, the players love the event and the hospitality is excellent.'

For a whole three or four days I get the chance to be a professional cricketer, which is what I've always wanted to be, but was unfortunately not good enough.

Pat Fordham, Captain Hong Kong team

It gives spectators the chance to see the cricketers in action without any inhibitions. The time frame of a match encapsulates all the fundamentals of the game in one explosive package. Ideal for television. It hits everything else for six.

Alvin Sallay, Sports Correspondent, *SCMP*

4th Hong Kong International Sixes – 1995

England led by Dermot Reeve were hopng to take home the Butani 'diamond encrusted golden' cricket bat for three wins in succession, but it was not to be. The South Africans led by Hansie Cronje 'robbed' England of the trophy when Adrian Kuiper hit a hurricane 36 after being caught by Reeve when 20. However, the umpire declared that DeFrietas had bowled a beamer and was no-balled! India beat the West Indies in the Plate Final afer losing to Hong Kong in an early round, whilst Holland, an Associate Member, won the Bowl Final defeating New Zealand. Hong Kong had earlier beaten Holland, but lost to New Zealand in the Bowl competition.

434

Pat Fordham, the Hong Kong captain, said: 'Beating India [Azhar-uddin, Jadeja, Kambli, Manjekar, Prasad and Tendulkar] was fantastic. Every year we have played in the tournament we have beaten one of the big teams and that is one of our aims.'

The ICC gave official recognition to the Hong Kong International Sixes at their annual conference held at Lord's in July 1996.

5th Hong Kong International Sixes – 1996

With the recent proliferation of international cricket matches, the organisers ran into logistics problems in trying to re-schedule the tournament to attract the best available Test countries and players, and by bringing the date forward ran the additional risk of inclement weather.

Despite the rain and the more than 30,000 empty seats, Nick Waters, *ATV News*, said: 'the venue switch from the KCC [to the Hong Kong Stadium] was correct, but the tournament must sharpen its act for a healthier bottom line.'

The ICC chief executive, David Richards, said: 'I would like to see more people coming to watch the Sixes, at a time which suits more of the top cricketers.' A view echoed by many (including the author), as most of us had to flick through *Who's Who* to pick out many of the players – not a good sign.

A relatively unknown West Indian squad defeated India to win this waterlogged tournament in which Hong Kong had had its worst result. In fact, such an all-round miserable weekend was best forgotten for all concerned. South Africa won the Plate Final by five runs from Sri Lanka.

6th Hong Kong International Sixes – 1997

Pakistan, with Wasim Akram's 30 not out, beat Adam Hollioake's England by 3 wickets to clinch the Cup Final, Adam going for 23 runs in the last over. Sri Lanka pipped the West Indies by four runs to win the Plate in an exciting high scoring match. Hong Kong surprised itself with its most successful Sixes tournament, beating both South Africa and India to win the Bowl title. Mohammed Zubair, in his debut tournament, achieved a 'hat-trick' against South Africa, who were bowled out for 20! Stewart Brew, playing in his sixth tournament, but first as captain, said: 'It is a great feeling. Hopefully, it will encourage the development of the game here.'

The last two International Sixes were held in the Hong Kong Stadium, but due mainly to the relatively poor attendances in this modern spectacular 40,000 seat stadium, the HKCA and World Cricket International, the organisers, are now reconsidering their future options.

435

Hong Kong – Results

1st International Sixes – October 1992

Hong Kong	beat	Australia by 28 runs
		Pakistan by 4 wickets
	lost to	India by 5 wickets
		England by 5 wickets

2nd International Sixes – October 1993

Hong Kong	beat	West Indies by two runs
	lost to	Sri Lanka by 66 runs
		Pakistan by 5 wickets
		India by 4 wickets

3rd International Sixes – October 1994

Hong Kong	beat	Pakistan by 21 runs
	lost to	New Zealand by 4 wickets
		England by 3 wickets
		India 5 wickets

4th International Sixes – October 1995

Hong Kong	beat	India by 3 wickets
		Holland by 10 runs
	lost to	Sri Lanka by 5 wickets
		New Zealand by 5 wickets

5th International Sixes – September 1996

Hong Kong	lost to	Pakistan by 6 wickets
		India by 3 wickets
		New Zealand by 4 wickets
		Australia by four runs

6th International Sixes – September 1997

Hong Kong	beat	South Africa by 40 runs
		India by 17 runs
	lost to	England by 15 runs
		Pakistan by 24 runs

TOURING SIDES

TO HONG KONG

Many international teams have visited Hong Kong, the main games being played at the HKCC Chater Road ground, in the central business district of the City till 1975, and on the picturesque KCC ground in the centre of metropolitan Kowloon. After 1975, when the HKCC moved up the hill to its new ground at Wong Nai Chung Gap Road, these matches continued to be shared by HKCC and KCC.

Jack Chegwyn's Australian Team 1952

Jack Chegwyn's team of Australian Test players were invited to Hong Kong in October 1952 to participate in a series of cricket matches as part of the HKCC Centenary Celebrations. The HKCC first approached the MCC, but were turned down. The MCC were very sorry they could not participate as they were heavily committed to the Test countries for fixtures at that time, and so the HKCC Committee looked to Australia.

Laurie Kilbee, one of the stalwarts of the HKCC and Hong Kong cricket, whilst on leave in Sydney contacted Ginty Lush, who put him in touch with Jack Chegwyn, the then captain of the NSW State side. Before Laurie continued onto the United Kingdom to complete his leave (it was six months in those days), agreement had been reached for Jack to bring a team to Hong Kong, consisting of at least eight to nine Test players, subject to Hong Kong financing the trip and arranging suitable accommodation.

On Laurie's return from 'home' leave on the P&O liner, *SS Canton*, he had the good fortune to meet up with Sir Arthur Morse, Chief Manager of the Hongkong Bank and Chairman of the Jockey Club, a fellow passenger. Sir Arthur, a very keen sportsman in his younger days, took a great interest in sport in Hong Kong, and through the Jockey Club, the big 'Hongs' and other businesses, the necessary funding was achieved. The Australians were put up in private residences to alleviate the financial cost of the tour. The whole venture was a resounding success, and was the forerunner of many more such tours which greatly enhanced the quality of the cricket scene in Hong Kong.

Several matches were played, culminating in a two day game against the

Colony at the Chater Road ground. In the earlier matches, Ray Flockton scored a double century at KCC against the Hong Kong Civilians, whilst Arthur Morris scored a century against the Combined Services on the Recreio ground. In the two-day game Hong Kong batted first, and Capt Haycraft (RA) scored a magnificent 105 runs. The Colony side reached a very respectable 224 runs, with Keith Miller 'chipping in' with 7–98.

Brilliant catches by Alexander and Francis Zimmern had helped dismiss Arthur Morris and Jim de Courcy, and when Frank Howarth had both Ray Flockton and Alan Davidson back in the pavilion without scoring, Hong Kong were looking good. At the end of the first day, the Australians were 151 for 5, but Keith Miller was waiting in the wings!

The next day, Miller, in partnership with Colin McCool and Don Tallon, showed why he was called the 'best all-rounder' in the world, remaining unbeaten on 118 out of a total 402 for 9 declared. Alexander had bowled well to take 4–95.

The Australians applied more pressure in Hong Kong's second innings and had them all out for 134 runs, thus winning by an innings and 44 runs.

Sir Arthur Morse had promised £100 to any player who could hit a six and break a window in the old Bank of China building. Even the great Keith Miller couldn't manage this feat.

Bill O'Reilly, who captained the touring Australian stars, said after the two-day match:

He and the remainder of the Australian team were amazed that Hong Kong had so much cricketing talent for such a small community. They were particularly pleased with the enthusiasm shown, not only by the players, but by the spectators. O'Reilly added that he hoped to come again – but not as a player – the tour had been too good!

Hong Kong: 224 and 134
Jack Chegwyn's XI: 402–9 dec

The Bob Haycraft Story

It took a very sad occasion to uncover a 'lost' cricket memento. At the Formby Golf Club in March 1995 after the funeral of Noel Cooke, a fellow cricketer and colleague of the author, a number of former Liverpool Competition cricketers had gathered to meet in his memory. Peter Rumjahn, one such cricketer, casually mentioned to the author that he had a cricket memento which had been sent to him by his uncle, Arthur Rumjahn, many years ago from Hong Kong for a certain Bob Haycraft. He had no idea who this person might be.

Peter's father, 'Doc' Jaffir Rumjahn, Arthur's elder brother, had left Hong Kong in 1901. Arthur had played for Hong Kong against Shanghai during the 1921–23 period and was a Hong Kong selector in the early 1950s. Peter phoned a few days later to describe this memento:

An ivory cricket bat 3 1/8" by 1 5/8" with inscriptions on gold. One side read – HK v Australia 1st Innings 105, 2nd Innings 33. United Services v Aust. 43. On the reverse R E (Bob) Haycraft from Arthur Rumjahn Selector.

The name Haycraft immediately rang a bell – I looked up my score sheets, Hong Kong v Jack Chegwyn's XI, October 1952, and there he was: Capt R E Haycraft (RA), 105 and 33.

I phoned Lt Col Keith Hitchcock, Army cricket secretary at Aldershot, who put me in touch with Major John Craiger, RA cricket secretary. He suggested I call the Glasgow pension office and if unsuccessful, then to contact RA headquarters in London to place an appropriate paragraph in their *Gunner* magazine. As I didn't have Bob's Army number, the pension office couldn't help me. I then wrote to John Braisby at Artillery House with my story and 'appropriate paragraph'. This 'paragraph' would appear in the May edition.

By now I was really hoping that Bob Haycraft would still be alive to personally receive this long-lost memento. How old was he in 1952? On Friday morning 5 May 1995, the phone rang and a somewhat surprised Bob Haycraft was on the line – fantastic, was my immediate reaction. He's 75 and lives in the old charter town of Wallingford, south of Oxford. Very sadly, his wife Jo had died suddenly the previous January.

Peter brought the memento to me on Monday 5 June, and I drove down to Wallingford two days later to personally deliver it to Bob, its rightful owner, after an absence of nearly 43 years. Such an unexpected surprise and special trophy brought a little sunshine back into Bob's life. His son, Roland, who has an antique furniture restoration business in Wallingford, would make his father a wooden case for this treasure.

When the author asked Bob whether he could remember any particular incident during his innings, he recalled batting out of his crease to Keith Miller in this match, and Miller, on being told by Don Tallon of this, immediately bowled a 'beamer' at the 'upstart' to remind him who was boss!

Bob has been the only postwar cricketer to score a century for a fully representative Hong Kong XI against a first-class touring side. Many others have 'been allowed' to get close and then would be castled. Bob must have had a special talent.

Bangkok – 1959

Buddy Carnell was too fast and menacing for the Bangkok batsmen, and after he had 'softened' them, Buji Dhabher, bowling left-arm swingers off the wrong foot, bamboozled them to claim five wickets. After an early scare, Jalu Shroff hit an aggressive 86 to put Hong Kong firmly into the driver's seat for an eventual easy victory.

Dec 6	Bangkok:	167	(R Lambert 30, R B Jones 28, M Forshaw 23, B Dhabher 5–30, B C N Carnell 3–18)
& 7		100	(R W Bell 4–18, B C N Carnell 3–17, B Dhabher 3–21)
	Hong Kong:	259–7 dec	(J Shroff 86, I Stanton 39, G Souza Snr 35, G H P Pritchard 31, M Forshaw 4–91)
		10–0	

After the match, as Hong Kong had proved too strong for Bangkok, Tommy Madar (RBSC) and Robbie Lee (KCC President) agreed to play annual two-day matches between the respective clubs, which contests continue to this day (see KCC section).

Ron Robert's Commonwealth Team – 1962

Ron Robert's Commonwealth side, led by Richie Benaud, played three matches against local sides: 'The magnetic quality of Benaud's leadership, his perfect reading of the game, and his flawless judgement in making each and every match an exciting one.'

In the first game against an Hong Kong Island XI, the Commonwealth scored 230 (McLean 64), and bowled the home team out for 222. John Hall was undefeated with 101. Hall's century was just reward for cool-headed batting under most difficult circumstances. Benaud gave nothing away and Hall had to fight desperately for every run. His was an innings 'that will be long remembered in Hong Kong.' As the Island XI's score crept closer to their target of 231, Bobby Simpson, fielding in the slips, said to Benaud, 'get yourself out of this one Richie.' Benaud immediately called back Neil Adcock, the South African fast bowler and gave him strict instructions to bowl fast full tosses at the wicket. Adcock ended the Island innings, taking 6 for 6, including the 'hat-trick'!

In the second match the Commonwealth side 'moved up a gear' and trampled on the Mainland XI. They were taking no chances.

| Commonwealth XI: | 326 for 6 | (R A McLean 129, Benaud 123* 'blasted the bowlers') |
| Mainland XI: | 133 | (S Ramadhin 5–49 'mesmerised the batsmen') |

440

In the main game against Hong Kong the Commonwealth scored 217 after an early wobble, when Buddy Carnell tore into their celebrated batting line-up, bowling Everton Weekes for a duck, and ending up with the very fine analysis of 5–48. Tom Graveney top scored with 60. Hong Kong replied with 182. David Coffey returned to the pavilion 'black and blue' after hitting a brave 57 against a fiery and fast Neil Adcock. Benaud did take a certain amount of pity on the local players in only bowling his two fast men, Adcock and Ian Meckiff, for six and five overs each. A little light comic relief was provided by Carnell and Ramadhin towards the end of the Hong Kong innings, when Buddy hit Sonny for four 4s. Sonny then tightened up his 'line and length' and had Buddy flailing at thin air before bowling him.

Another memorable tour had taken place for a 'privileged few'. The attendances had been unaccountably poor throughout the visit.

Commonwealth XI: 217
Hong Kong: 182

E W Swanton's Commonwealth Team – 1964

Hong Kong has a reputation as one of the world's great international cities. People of many nationalities and religions reside and earn their living there. This cosmopolitan flavour was particularly evident in the composition of the All Hong Kong team which met the Commonwealth XI at KCC on 4/5 April 1964.

Tony Weller, the captain, was an Englishman born and educated in Hong Kong, who played his cricket in Hong Kong, Sydney and England. John Fawcett, a comparative newcomer to the Colony, had represented the Middlesex 2nd XI, and played club cricket of a high standard in England. Peter Langston, who opened the attack with Fawcett, was the only other Englishman in the side. Buji Dhabher and Jalu Shroff are Parsees, both of whom learnt their cricket in Hong Kong. Shroff, however, did go overseas and enjoyed much success when representing London Universities. Rocky Daniel hailed from Barbados, but represented Jamaica in inter-island matches. This West Indian had a refreshing approach to the game, well in keeping with the traditions of his illustrious countrymen. Carl Myatt came from Ceylon, but played most of his cricket in England and Hong Kong. Peter Hall, a Hong Kong-born Eurasian, had considerable experience of cricket both in Australia and in Liverpool. Ghulam Abbas, a stylish batsman and useful spin bowler, had played for the Pakistan Eaglets, and was at one time on the fringe of Test cricket. Ram Lalchandani, the Colony wicket-keeper, was from Bengal in India. He reached maturity whilst playing for IRC in the local league. Last, but by no means least, there was Edo dos Remedios, the only Portuguese cricketer in the side, who learnt his cricket at Folkestone in England.

Swanton's team, with Richie Benaud joining the tour in Hong Kong, also had Seymour Nurse, Nawab of Pataudi and Sonny Ramadhin in the side. But it was the presence of the great Gary Sobers who dominated the game – in a nice sort of way! When he batted, he gave his wicket away after scoring 106 runs. On reaching his century, he asked Tony Weller, the Hong Kong captain, to put 'that man over there' back on again. To Myatt's first ball Sobers danced down the wicket and 'missed' the ball. Lalchandani, the keeper, was so surprised he fumbled the stumping chance. 'Watch the ball, "sonny,"' said the great man, and then repeated the same shot, to be stumped. Myatt had bowled well and earned his excellent analysis of 5–75.

In Hong Kong's first innings total of 173, Sobers had taken 4–51 with his spinners. In Hong Kong's second innings, Benaud had denied Sobers the ball until only five wickets remained, then bet him a bottle of Johnny Walker Black Label he couldn't get the last five. Buji Dhabher was the first hapless victim, and on his way back to the pavilion said to the incoming author, 'Don't lift your bat, Peter!' The author blocked the first ball which went for four through the covers, edged a four through the slips and was then also back in the pavilion. Sobers was bowling fast 'in and away' swingers and ended the innings with 5–19 plus the bottle of whisky, which Laurie Kilbee had obtained from the KCC bar.

Hong Kong:	173	(R G Daniel 41, F A Weller 33, G Sobers 4–51)
	144	(R G Daniel 41, F A Weller 30, G Sobers 5–19)
Commonwealth:	276	(Sobers 106, I MacLachlan 91*, K Taylor 31, C Myatt 5–75)
	44–4	(C Myatt 2–11, P Langston 2–32)

In an earlier match on April Fool's Day at HKCC, the Commonwealth XI, 292 for 5 declared, had Seymour Nurse (88), Ken Taylor (69) and Richie Benaud (53) piling on the runs, whilst their 'second string' bowlers Piachaud and Coghlan sorted out the President's XI for 88.

In June 1966 at Old Trafford in the first Test against England, the author watched Sobers score a scintillating 161 runs, 'as though he was facing the Hong Kong bowling'. England's attack included Jeff Jones, David Brown, Ken Higgs, David Allen and Fred Titmus!

What an unassuming, great cricketer, Garfield St Aubrun Sobers, later to be knighted in Barbados for services to cricket.

Worcestershire CCC – 1965

The English champion County side made a pre-season visit to Hong Kong in March 1965, playing against the Colony side at KCC.

Batting first, they rattled up 359 runs, mainly from the flowing blade of Tom Graveney, who scored 132. Don Kenyon, the captain, had been bowled early on by an inswinger from left-armer Mike Barros, which had straightened after pitching. Kenyon studied the spot on the wicket, then walked off, none too happy. From then on he made Hong Kong pay for its indiscretion in removing the visiting skipper cheaply. Hong Kong players spent the rest of the day chasing leather. Rocky Daniel and Carl Myatt bowled steadily and deserved their five and four wickets respectively. When Hong Kong batted they faced a new experience, pressure for the first time from very close-in first-class fielders. When Basil D'Oliviera and Norman Gifford were bowling, Ron Headley and Dick Richardson were literally a yard from the batsman, one on each side of the wicket. No Hong Kong batsman was clean bowled, but Headley and Richardson took eight catches in the match – 'right off the bat'. John Fawcett batted well for his hard-earned 58 runs in Hong Kong's first innings.

Worcestershire: 359 (T Graveney 132, D Slade 51, D Richardson 47, M Horton 45, R Headley 40, R Daniel 5–90, C Myatt 4–86)
Hong Kong: 150 (J Fawcett 58, B D'Oliviera 5–51, N Gifford 3–38)
          108 (C Myatt 21, B D'Oliviera 5–21, N Gifford 5–48)

Mike Smith's MCC Team – 1966

The most renowned team to visit Hong Kong was Mike Smith's full MCC side in March 1966, on their way back to England after the drawn Test series in Australia. The MCC couldn't make it in 1952, but this first MCC visit coincided with the 100th Anniversary of the first Interport against Shanghai in 1866.

Such players as Geoff Boycott, Colin Cowdrey, Eric Russell, David Brown, Ken Higgs, Jeff Jones, and John Murray were in the party. Batting first on the KCC wicket, Russell gave his wicket away after scoring 59. When asked: 'How about his partner,' he replied: 'You'll have to get him out.' Geoff Boycott went on to top score with 108. Jeff Jones and Ken Higgs were then let loose on the unfortunate Hong Kong batsmen. The constant procession back to the pavilion was causing some embarrassment, so Mike Smith took the pressure off after the fifth wicket had fallen at 42. Jeff Jones was just too quick for the local batsmen and was rested, having taken 2 for 6 off six overs. The lucky incumbents, the author with the Hong Kong captain David Coffey, then took full advantage of the temporary lull in hostilities, rapidly moving the score onto 119, when the author was run out for 41. Coffey continued to hit out, but when he had reached the mid-80s, Mike Smith decided that was enough and brought back Jones, who promptly ended Coffey's and the Hong Kong innings. Jones finished with 4 for 5 off seven overs. If you want to score runs against a first-class touring side who mean business, never bat in the first five! Coming in at No. 7, Coffey scored a creditable 88 before being castled.

Mar 20 MCC: 266–6 dec (G Boycott 108, E Russell 59, M C
                                   Cowdrey 46, I Lacy-Smith 2–34, P A
                                   Hall 2–47)
        Hong Kong: 192   (D G Coffey 88, P A Hall 41, J Jones
                                   4–5, D Allen 4–28)

Prior to the main game the powerful MCC side were struggling at 149–7 when rain stopped play against the President's XI at Chater Road. Magnificent bowling by Aussie Col Metcalf (not Colonel), whose 5–41 (Eric Russell, Geoff Boycott, Mike Smith, Colin Cowdrey and John Murray), read like a *Who's Who* of MCC's illustrious batsmen. I'm sure Metcalf must regard this haul as his most memorable cricketing achievement in Hong Kong. His tenacious approach, coupled with his all-round ability, made him a 'feared' opponent. You were very glad when he had been dismissed and lucky if you didn't have to face his medium-pace cutters on a helpful bowler's wicket when batting.

Cricket Club of India – 1967

The Cricket Club of India, on their first visit to Hong Kong, coasted to an easy win over the Hong Kong President's XI at Chater Road. Only Ram Lalchandani (28) showed any technique against the left-arm spin of A Mulani (5–47). Hong Kong had an excellent chance of winning the main match at KCC, but appeared overawed by the stature of their opponents and sadly fell away to lose by 16 runs. Hong Kong's reading of the game had their visitors baffled (see section HK Parsee CC).

Jan 8   CCI XI: 179–7 (A Chaturvedi 62, S Dharsi 30, P Umrigar 25,
                              B Carnell 4–68)
        Hong Kong: 163–8 (J Shroff 51, B Dhabher 21, A Mulani 7–70)

444

Singapore Services – 1967

Oct 15   HK League XI: 206–8 dec (J Fawcett 65, P Davies 62, R
                                   Pellew 7–59)
 & 16   Singapore Services: 52   (J Murphy 4–9)
                        120   (J Fawcett 4–11)

Whilst R Pellew bowled extremely well for Singapore and captured seven
wickets, it was the Scorpion's 'twins' who wrecked the Services batting.
Julian Murphy included a 'hat-trick' in his four-wicket burst at the
HKCC.

Melbourne University CC – 1967

In a rain-affected match against the Melbourne University CC in
December 1967 at the HKCC, the Hong Kong President XI's openers,
Jalu Shroff (144) and Ghulam Abbas (77), put on 214 runs out of a total
of 301 for 6.

J Lister's International Team – 1968

In the first match against the President's XI led by the author, most of
the Hong Kong batsmen were not particularly interested in facing
Geoff Arnold and Harold Rhodes on a 'dicey' HKCC wicket, never mind
Derek Underwood as well. The author remembered batting two feet
outside the crease when facing Harold Rhodes. 'Sonny,' said Mike
Denness from the slips, 'where are you going?' 'I want to be able to reach
the pitch of the ball before it takes my head off!' was the reply. Buji
Dhabher also struck out and hit Derek Underwood for consecutive
boundaries.

Apr 5   Lister's XI: 233–8 dec (K Suttle 61, M Stewart 57, B Ibadulla
                                  56, B Wigley 4–57, P A Hall 2–30)
        President's XI: 74   (P A Hall 23, B P Dhabher 19, H
                              Rhodes 5–16)

At KCC over the next two days, only John Fawcett in Hong Kong's
second innings showed he had the necessary class and technique for the
occasion. Micky Stewart, captaining Lister's star-studded side, was determined to show Hong Kong the difference in playing standards between a
strong representative English county team and a local side. We were not
impressed with his approach to what is always a learning curve for local
cricketers.

445

Apr 6   Lister's XI: 353   (B Ibadulla 70, M Denness 52, D Amiss 46, H
& 7   Latchman 42, G Arnold 41, M Stewart 40, R
                               Tolchard 33*, J Murphy 5–65, J K Fawcett
                               3–67)
         Hong Kong: 66   (E H Wilson 20, H Latchman 3–29)
                        73   (J K Fawcett 31, D Underwood 4–13, H
                               Rhodes 4–28)

Hong Kong lost by an innings and 214 runs. A game to savour.

I was impressed by some of your players, but they will only improve
if you improve your wickets.

Micky Stewart

Singapore – 1969

The President's XI drew with Singapore in a 'topsy-turvy' match.
'What was on paper a strong Hong Kong batting side staggered
almost drunkenly to the abyss of a total collapse.' Da Silva, 3–21
off 18 overs, bowled his leg-breaks to a nagging length in Hong
Kong's first innings. In the second innings, Peter Davies 'often took
his life in his hands, being dropped once at deep backward square
leg (where else!) and then missed on 99!' Gerry Jarman 'made his
runs with an assurance which must have been aggravating to the opposition.' Hatim Ebrahim 'batted more solidly than he had done for a long
time.'

Nov 1   HK Pres. XI: 110 & 294–3 dec (P Davies 110, G Jarman 97*, H
                                        Ebrahim 53*)
& 2   Singapore: 203 & 26–1   (M Lloyd 45, G Jarman 4–35)

Melbourne 29ers – 1970

The President's XI failed to hold onto their chances and drew with
Melbourne 29ers at the HKCC. 'Ian Vaughan-Arbuckle played an
innings of courage and technique on a fiery wicket.' 'Jarman's elegant
batting soon took the initiative away from the Australians.'

Jan   HK Pres. XI: 205–9 dec (G Jarman 65, I Vaughan-Arbuckle
                                       62)
         Melbourne 29'ers: 131–8   (K Cumings 4–13)

MCC – 1970

Throughout the Far East we took the field in colourful and unusual surroundings, but I suppose the conditions for our match against the Hong Kong President's XI were as bizarre as any I have encountered. The ground was so wet that mats were laid each side of the main matting wicket. They certainly aided the running between the wickets and the bowlers' follow-through. It was a very dark, cold drizzling day. The ground of course is famous, because it is couched in the city centre of Hong Kong, dwarfed by skyscrapers, probably the most expensive piece of cricket ground in the world. So there we batted, on soaking mats, peering through the gloom, with the trams and the traffic of the city in full view – the ground is open on three sides. The lights went on in the trams towards the end, and this murky ritual was enacted at the feet of the Malayan Bank, the Hong Kong Club, the Supreme Court, the Bank of China and the Hong Kong Hilton Hotel. These giant buildings I am sure nodded their approval. It was everything they must have heard about the cricket game – a spot of English madness! And in case the Supreme Court was having second thoughts, Don Wilson smacked a massive blow right between the upstairs windows, just to prove we meant business.

Mar 14   MCC: 204   (D Wilson 57, B Kwong 4–79)
         President's XI: 140   (B Kwong 36, D Wilson 6–58)

In a 50-over match, the MCC easily defeated the President's XI in this two-man game.

The many good cricketers who represented the Hong Kong Colony side the next day would have given us a good contest over two days. As it was, only five wickets fell in the nearly six hours of play on a placid matting wicket, and the contest had to continue in the KCC bar.' The MCC dominated the day's proceedings during the main tour match at the KCC (also see Ted Wilson's reminiscences)

Mar 15   MCC: 190–0   (A Jones 104*, G Boycott 79*)
         Hong Kong: 134–5   (I Vaughan-Arbuckle 35, P Davies 28, G
                             Abbas 23, R Daniel 22*)

After a tour of such incredible variation and colour, of such humour and such friendship, how could one possibly say enough 'thank you's' to one's hosts. It is impossible.

All quotes: A R Lewis, Captain MCC, 1970

Lancaster Park CC – 1971

The author led a KCC Invitation XI against a talented New Zealand Lancaster Park side on a hot, humid August afternoon at KCC. Only the three named batsmen made any progress against a young seam bowler called Richard Hadlee, while P Burney proved to be their match-winner.

'HADLEE GIVES OUR MEN A VERY HOT TIME
Hadlee, a tall, wiry 20-year-old, turned an idyllic morning into a scorcher for the KCC batsmen, most of whom were Colony caps.'

KCC XI: 125 (R Daniel 39, P Hall 33, C Myatt 21*, R J Hadlee 4–34)

Lancaster XI: 126–7 (P Burney 65)

Malaysia – 1971

Nov 6 Malaysia: 161 (A Christie 41, A Delilkan 35, R Graham 3–30, C Hull 3–42)

& 7 206–6 dec (R Singh 57, A Zahman 51, G Singh 33, J Ashworth 4–56)

HK Pres. XI: 103 (I Marshall 26, A Delilkan 9–36)

187–7 (J Shroff 59, C Hull 43, M Alexander 29, A Delilkan 3–68)

Assured in control, consistent in length and direction, and with as many tricks in his repertoire as Merlin the Magician. Delilkan didn't simply outwit the opposition – he mesmerised them.

SCMP

Hyderabad Blues – 1972

Carl Myatt declared at tea on New Year's Eve, leaving the 'Blues' to score 182 to win in the final two-hour session. They achieved this mainly due to a fine innings from Ali Baig. Jaisimha, with many years of Test experience, was an excellent 'Blues' captain and ambassador for the game.

Dec 30 Hong Kong: 176 (C Myatt 32*, J Ashworth 30, V V Kumar 7–66)

& 31 167–8 dec (I Stevens 45, P Davies 36, V V Kumar 3–78)

'Blues' XI: 162–4 dec (P K Belliappa 97, B Kwong 2–49)

184–6 (A A Baig 70, N Mehta 31*, B Kwong 3–51, J Barclay 2–29)

Midlands Club Cricket Conference – 1973

The Midlands CCC, on their first Far East overseas tour and in their Silver Jubilee Year, arrived in Hong Kong from Australia on the first day of the Chinese New Year holidays and helped to bring in the Year of the Ox. On the following two days, in superb weather, not a good Chinese omen for Hong Kong, they scored the winning runs in the last over. Three declarations, the last by Carl Myatt, although somewhat generous, produced excellent cricket and provided first-rate entertainment for the holiday crowd at the HKCC.

Feb 4   Hong Kong: 202–7 dec   (M Alexander 73, P H Davies 36,
                                         D Barber 3–72)
  & 5   125–4 dec   (M Alexander 34, P H Davies 32, D R
                                          Cook 3–13)
          Midlands CCC: 180–9 dec   (D Lowe 74, C Myatt 5–29,
                                          M Duggan 3–53)
                      148–5   (A S Everitt 44*, C Myatt 3–32)

RAF (UK) – 1974

RAF (UK), led by 'Tug' Willson, who was later to work in Hong Kong for Cathay Pacific, comfortably won this match by eight wickets at KCC. The *SCMP* reported: 'Bearded West Indian, Oswald Richie, thrived under these dangerous conditions but not the local batsmen, and soon Hong Kong's decision to take first lease of the wicket was beginning to prove disastrous.'

Sep 27   Hong Kong: 90   (B Kwong 28, O Richie 5–16)
  & 28   159   (B Kwong 39, J Manning 34, C Bynoe
                                          4–28, O Richie 3–42)
           RAF (UK):   200–9 dec   (J Willows 40, F Boucham 38, B Willson
                                          36, O Robinson 4–42, C Myatt 4–44)
                      52–2

MCC – 1975

'AMISS AND WOOD BATTER HONG KONG XI'

'After chasing leather for just under three hours, Hong Kong's openers John Bygate and 'Tug' Willson saw off the MCC opening attack of Chris Old and Barry Wood to put on a well-deserved 50 partnership. From then on it was a procession of "comings" and "goings" to the wiles of Derek

Underwood and Fred Titmus at the HKCC.'

Mar 13 MCC: 234–3 dec (D Amiss 101*, B Wood 68, A Greig
                                     38*, C Myatt 2–62)
        Hong Kong: 132   (J Bygate 46, D Underwood 4–13,
                                     F Titmus 4–43)

Queensland Colts – 1976

        Qld. Colts: 292–6 (D Regeling 68, P Shackleford 64, R
                             Lawrence 48, A Parker 43, C Myatt 5–96)
        Hong Kong: 224–9 (D Clinton 57, J Bygate 56, D Budge 54, A
                             Parker 6–17)
    Match drawn

D H Robin's Team – 1977

Due to the damp conditions, this match was reduced to 40-overs played on
the artificial wicket at KCC. John Lever didn't risk bowling. Other visitors
included Mike Denness (capt), Colin Cowdrey, David Gower and Mike
Smith. The previous day's scheduled match at the HKCC had been rained
off.

Oct 2   D H Robin's XI: 167   (P Willey 48, A Intikhab 46)
        HKCA XI: 94–9   (A Intikhab 3–16, J Emburey 3–21, P
                              Willey 3–21)

Capercailzies – 1978

A couple of memories from this drawn match at KCC. Frank Robertson
blasting out Hong Kong's openers John Bygate and Nigel Stearns – Peter
Olsen keeping to Steve Willis, using KCC practice gloves, his hands were
'black and blue'. The Colony keeper without his own gloves!

The Capercailzies played four matches, winning one and drawing three.
D Stewart scored their only century (106*) against the HKCC, and E
McIntyre took 6–47 against KCC.

Oct 8   Capercailzies: 191–4 dec (H More 78, R Swan 58, S Willis
                                    4–69)
        HKCA Pres. XI: 188–5   (P Anderson 53*, M Sabine 47, G
                                 Lalchandani 36, F Robertson 2–28)

The cricket was enjoyable and of a very good standard, but depend-
ant on who is 'passing through' Hong Kong at the time. The Hong

450

Kong XI, however, ran the Capers quite close, the latter being virtually a Scottish XI.

Euan McIntyre

Club Cricket Conference – 1979

Feb 8   CCC: 225–5 dec (A Scott 60*, J Kilbee 41, M Hislop 2–46)
        HKCA XI: 202   (N Stearns 53, A Lorimer 48, P Anderson
                              29, R Cruttenden 6–42)

CCC won by 23 runs.

Surrey CC – 1979

        Surrey CC: 219–4 dec
        HKCA XI: 109

Surrey CC won by 110 runs.

Malaysia – 1979
Nov 21 Brit. Forces: 220–5 (J Bell 55, A Swift 52, D Hurren 41, K
                              McLean 35)
        MCA: 213–9   (R Ratnalingam 109, P Banerji 48, I White
                              5–57)

An excellent drawn match at Sookunpoo.

RAF (UK) – 1980

On 23 March in a match against the RAF (UK), Hong Kong batted first and declared at 179 for 4. RAF (UK) replied with 141 for 3.

Papua New Guinea – 1980

During their inaugural four-match tour, Papua New Guinea won two and lost two matches.

Apr 7   HKCA XI: 192   (F McLeod 54, A Turner 34, N Stearns 32, K
                         Loi 4–31)
        Papua NG: 195–5 (D Fox 85, A Leka 51*, A Turner 4–30)

HKCA XI lost by five wickets at HKCC.

   10   The President's XI (244–4) defeated the powerful PNG tourists
        (241–6) at KCC where 'Tug' Willson scored a 'scintillating' 124.

MCC – 1981

The MCC side included Mike Denness, Fred Titmus, Nick Cook and Harold Rhodes, but was not as strong as previous sides. The Hong Kong selectors picked 44 different players for the four matches against the MCC, and didn't lose any of the matches. It was said at the time that the visitors tended to bat too long! In the Island v MCC match, Brian Wigley took the first five wickets and had the MCC reeling at 59 for 6 wickets, ending with a very fine 5–30 off 18 overs.

Oct 17 MCC: 190–8 dec (P Kippax 52, C Ingleby-Mackenzie 41, N Briers 30, R Eddington 4–38, R Starling 4–48)

           HKCA: 163–9   (P W Anderson 39, S Waller 33*, P Kippax 4–34)

  Match drawn

Worcestershire Wanderers – 1982

In early October, Worcestershire Wanderers played three matches in Hong Kong, winning one and losing two. Due to the late withdrawal of a sponsor which limited their party, the tourists, led by E Helmsley, with Alan Ormrod, Glen Turner, Mike Denness, Jack Simmons and Jim Cumbes, were supplemented by local players, so the results were not important.

Combined Services U25 – 1982

UK Combined Services U25 won four of the five limited-overs matches, only losing to a KCC Invitation XI in their last match.

Oct 27 Comb. Services U25: 162–9 (C Clark 41, J Kneale 30, G Davies 3–29)

           HKCA: 100–9 (J Bygate 27, Flynn 3–6)

Combined Services won by 62 runs at Mission Road.

Club Cricket Conference – 1983

'CCC's approach to the game was thoroughly professional and David Smith's and Mike Gear's centuries were first-class. There was little that Peter Anderson and his bowlers could do later in the CCC innings to stem a merciless onslaught. Glyn Davies played a fine innings, and his confident 70 included some sparkling boundaries. Des Greenwood batted courageously against a physical assault and collected a well-deserved 50. Hong Kong were certainly outplayed but far from disgraced.'

Jan 18   CCC: 252–2 (M Gear 108*, D Smith 102*)
KCC   HKCA: 192–4(G Davies 70, D Greenwood 51*)

In early January 1984, the HKCA defeated the touring Trinidad and Tobago Customs & Excise XI in two limited-overs matches.

HKCA: 213–5 (D Sharwood 50 retd)
T & T: 83   (D A Jones 3–19)

T & T: 225–7 (R Glasgow 89)
HKCA: 228–7 (P W Anderson 82)

Singapore – 1984

Nov 28 HKCA Pres XI: 255–5 (P H Davies 103*, K Kumar 87, M Patel 3–31)
        SCA XI: 95   (B Piperdi 29, E Ismail 5–38, K Hardman 3–14)

A demoralising heavy defeat for the Singaporeans just before the Interport.

Oxbridge – 1985

An entertaining evening at Sir Denys Roberts's superb Peak residence, prior to the match, failed to give the Hong Kong team any advantage. They lost the 50-over game at KCC by 86 runs after Steve Henderson paved the Oxbridge way to victory with a well-struck century.

Dec 12 Oxbridge: 248–6 (S Henderson 135*, C Collins 2–34)
        HKCA: 162–8 (G Davies 43, G Toogood 2–19, J Carr 2–38)

In the next match the HKCA threatened Oxbridge for awhile, but eventually lost by 17 runs at HKCC.

Dec 13 Oxbridge: 224 6 (P Rocbuck 86, J Carr 42, N Smith 3–28)
        HKCA: 207–7 (K Kumar 70, P Willey 40, S Henderson 2–3, A Scott 2–33)

Berkshire – 1985/86

Despite the early success of dismissing Graham Roope cheaply, Berkshire cruised home by 93 runs at the Police Training School ground, Aberdeen.

Dec 29   Berkshire: 193–6   (K Murray 68, M Simmons 45, G Davies 2–28,
                            C Collins 2–30)
         HKCA: 100   (B Catton 33, J Woollhead 3–9, T James 3–20)

Hong Kong's scoring ground to a halt against the accuracy of Berkshire's spinners, losing a match they were never in by 102 runs at HKCC. Hong Kong has to learn to work the ball for ones and twos when the bowling is tight and accurate. Unfortunately, the quality of the bowling in the local leagues does not apply this sort of pressure.

Jan 4   Berkshire: 245–5   (G Roope 115, M Simmons 59, N Smith 3–32)
         HKCA: 143–7   (S Myles 44, R Brewster 43, P Lewington 2–16)

On 21 February the HKCA: (M Walsh 58, N Stearns 56) defeated the British Forces – Germany: (D Alexander 77, N Scott 56), by two wickets in a high-scoring match.

New Zealand – 1986

New Zealand won by 92 runs in a match at HKCC reduced from 50 to 40 overs.

Apr 23   New Zealand: 223–6   (E Gray 63*, M Sneddon 36, T Blain 33, D
                              Beckett 3–34)
         HKCA: 131–7   (P W Anderson 34*, J Barrington 24, E
                              Gray 3–34)

New Zealand won the next match at KCC by 201 runs, as 'Hong Kong, fielding their ICC squad, were put to the sword, Crowe scoring 71 off 39 balls. Myles played some excellent shots all round the wicket.'

Apr 24   New Zealand: 329   (M Crowe 71, K Rutherford 67, C Collins
                            3–59)
         HKCA XI: 128   (S Myles 58, R Brewster 21, E Gray 3–34)

The New Zealanders were so impressed with Simon Myles's batting they gave him some of their cricket equipment.

454

Sri Lanka – 1986

Sri Lanka 'smashed Hong Kong' at HKCC to win by 186 runs. The Sri Lankans had heard about Doug Beckett having played for Lancashire – he never saw the first two fast deliveries from Labrooy, whilst the third uprooted his stumps. Poor Doug didn't know why he had been singled out for special treatment. He had only played in one one-day game!

Oct 29   Sri Lanka U23: 248–6 dec (A Gurusinghe 100, G Wickrama-
                                        singhe 36, Y Vachha 2–47)

         HKCA: 62   (G Labrooy 4–14, C Ramanayake
                                          3–12)

Gurusinghe had hit 171 in an earlier 50-over match against the HKCA Chairman's XI, which the Sri Lankans won by 213 runs. Spectators present at these matches were shown in no uncertain manner the wide gap in cricketing ability between the two countries. Mind you, there were a few very doubtful under-23s in their party!

Club Cricket Conference – 1987

Mar 5   CCC: 284–5 (J Fry 87, P Garner 73*, D Gorman 38, S
                             Edwards 37, N Hames 30, D Greenwood 2–36)
        HKCA: 180–6 (C Dean 54, N Stearns 31, S Edwards 2–48)

  CCC won this 50-overs match at KCC by 104 runs.

Mar 6   HKCA: 111 (D A Jones 23, C Collins 21, J Jones 3–10)
        CCC: 109 (M Roberts 47, P Garner 22, C Collins 3–18)

  CCC were surprisingly (for them) beaten in a close encounter at HKCC.

Capercailzies – 1987

The Capercailzies made their second tour to Hong Kong playing six matches, only losing to the Combined Services.

Oct 10   Capercailzies: 215 (W D G Loudon 76, P G Duthie 34, J D
                              Sutton 31, A Telford 3–36, Y Vachha 3–42,
                              N Perera 3–43)
        HKCA: 182 (M Sabine 49, T Lerwill 47, D C Bell 3–30)

Euan McIntyre, Capercailzies tourist and archivist, when asked by the author in July 1994 whether he had any succinct comments, said: 'I seem to recall the veterans of 1978 informing the young brigade of 1987 – Oh, we usually win this fixture ...!'

Euan had been found via Hamish More. The author, whilst waiting for Dermot Reeve outside the Warwickshire changing room at Lord's on Saturday, 9 July 1994, after the Benson & Hedges final, met up with Hamish after an absence of 16 years. Our eyes were the same but our hair colour had changed – no wonder we didn't recognise each other.

Australia – 1988

Oct 18   Australia: 398   (D Jones 131, M Valetta 88, A Border 47*, J Siddons 38*, C McDermott 32, D Paull 6–124)

         Hong Kong: 219–8   (M Sabine 60, G Davies 34*, B Gohel 33*, D Beckett 30, D Jones 3–51)

Australia crushed Hong Kong in this 50-over match at KCC. Dean Jones was awesome (eight 6's and thirteen 4's), scoring 131 runs off 72 balls!! David Paull, although mauled at times, finished with a very creditable and well-earned six wickets.

> With the rigours of a three Test series in humid Pakistan behind them, Alan Border's men went on a picnic as they romped home winners by a huge 179 runs. The Australian attack tried hard to be as hospitable as our own.
>
> T M K Samat, *Hong Kong Standard*

Worcestershire CCC – 1989

Worcestershire CCC last played in Hong Kong in 1965, also as reigning champions, then captained by Don Kenyon. This time Phil Neale brought his championship side to Hong Kong after a wet pre-season tour of Australia.

The Hong Kong selectors decided to include three guest players who were visiting Hong Kong at the time – to make it more of a contest and to give local cricket fans a chance to see the 'legendary' Graeme Pollock. The other two guests were Mike Proctor and Clive Rice.

Apr 11   Worcs CCC: 274–4   (G Lord 120*, D D'Oliveira 61, T Curtis 45, C Rice 2–28, I Collier 2–65)

         HK Pres XI: 249–6   (G Pollock 79, M Proctor 47, N Stearns 36, M Sabine 27*, M Eames 23, I Botham 2–70)

The author, as Chairman of Selectors, had asked Pat Fordham, the President's XI captain, not to bowl Clive Rice at Graeme Hick until Hick was 'off the mark', as local cricket followers had come to see Botham, Hick and Pollock. But Pat, a Yorkshireman down to his left bootlace, took not the slightest notice, and Hick was yorked without scoring by the ever-competitive Clive Rice.

Watching Pollock facing Botham (the first time for either) was enthralling; the next best thing to seeing Botham's middle stump being despatched by Hong Kong's Ian Collier. Collier wasn't sure whether he should smile or apologise for such affrontery!

Gavaskar's Indians – 1990

Mar 9 Gavaskar's XI: 251–9 (A Sippy 61, R Shastri 58, S Kirmani 30)
   HKCA: 234–9 (S Atkinson 88, R Punjabi 4–45)

The 'Little Master' was out for 12 at HKCC, falling victim to S Tariq, one of four Hong Kong bowlers to capture two wickets each.

Mar 11 Madan Lal's XI: 247 (R Shastri 84, A Sippy 82)
    HKCA Pres. XI: 234–9 (D Evans 66, T Sawney 61, A Kennedy
             35)

The President's XI nearly made it at KCC in the second of these Indian matches.

Club Cricket Conference – 1991

An excellent opening partnership of 91 between Krish Kumar and Steve Atkinson on a pleasant, sunny January day at KCC gave Hong Kong the impetus for this very fine win over the Club Cricket Conference.

Jan 17 CCC: 205–5
   HKCA: 206–5 (K Kumar 67, S Atkinson 38, P Fordham 36*)

Royal Navy – 1991

Nov 18 Royal Navy: 139 (J Baker 48, W Symcox 3–16)
   HKCA: 140–1 (S Brew 96*, M Eames 25)

'Hong Kong's big guns sink Navy side.'

The Navy, brimming with confidence after a highly successful tour, were brought down to earth by a thoroughly professional performance by Hong

Kong. This was the Royal Navy's first official cricket tour of Hong Kong. Unfortunately for them, they came up against Brew and Symcox in fine form. 'These two were a class act in a solid team performance.'

Zimbabwe U19 – 1992

'Zimbabwe U19 humble shoddy Hong Kong.'

T M K Samat, *Hong Kong Standard*

Jan 28 Zimbabwe U19: 227–4 (S Carlisle 84*, S Davies 47*)
HKCA: 188–9 (P Fordham 62, J Garden 30, H Streak 3–21)

After being 109 for 4 in 30 overs, Steuart Carlisle and Sean Davies rallied bravely, helped by Hong Kong's shoddy fielding, to add 118 runs off the last 20 overs. Fordham batted with 'admirable determination' and after the match at KCC said: 'It's very disappointing, but when we bowled, fielded and batted so badly, the result isn't surprising.'

Air India – 1993

Jan 2   Air India: 243 (S Samant 77, K Patel 50, S Koli 44, R Sujanani 3–24)
HKCA: 111 (S Brew 26, S Joshi 5–29, P Soneji 3–22)

A strong Air India side spun Hong Kong to defeat by 132 runs at KCC.

Two other matches against a Connaught League XI and a President's XI ended the same way for Hong Kong, as the local batsmen 'struggled to compile competitive scores in all three games, largely due to the consistency of Air India's bowlers.'

Bangladesh – 1993

As part of Hong Kong's preparation for the 1994 Mini World Cup in Kenya, the HKCA invited Bangladesh to Hong Kong in December 1993. A three-match series for the sponsored Dragonair Cup was comfortably claimed by the visitors.

Dec 17 Batting first, Bangladesh knocked up a formidable 260 for 9. Apart from Mark Eames (56) and Pat Fordham (34) Hong Kong disappointed, being all out for 149 at KCC.

Dec 18 Put in to bat by Bangladesh, Hong Kong reached a respectable 198 for 7 in 50 overs, Rahul Sharma (50), Stewart Brew (42) and Riaz Farcy (36) building that total. Rain cut the overs to 45, and Bangladesh passed the new target of 179 in their 43rd over.

Dec 19 After the first two matches at KCC with the series captured by Bangladesh, Hong Kong were put in again by Bangladesh at HKCC. The top order batted steadily, with Farcy (65) being the most productive in Hong Kong's total of 198 for 9. Bangladesh 'cruised to the target in 48.2 overs for the loss of five wickets,' to take home the inaugural Dragonair Cup.

The Bangladeshi flavour was still in the air when the HKCA's next invitees, the talented Air India side, returned for the Butani Cup double match to complete Hong Kong's main overseas preparations for the ICC Kenya competition.

Air India – 1994

In the first leg, Air India had little trouble passing the HKCA's total and won by five wickets at HKCC.

Jan 1 HKCA: 235–7 (S Brew 86, S Atkinson 62, R Farcy 23)
      Air India: 237–5 (N Phadnis 73, P Soneji 47*, R Sanil 38, Y Vachha 3–47)

In the second leg of the Cup at KCC, Air India emerged even easier winners.

Jan 2 Hong Kong: 181   (S Atkinson 58, J Strachan 27*, P Soneji 2–11)
      Air India: 182–3 (R Sanil 83, S Koli 61*, N Phadnis 30)

Air India had also won an earlier match against a Butani XI at Mission Road, and culminated their four match tour with an easy victory against an Invitation XI at KCC, which included Hong Kong coach Dermot Reeve. Even he couldn't dent their impressive all-round match play.

India U19 – 1995

In September, 'on a sultry day at the HKCC, the Hong Kong President's XI came very close to upsetting arguably the best national youth side in the world. It showed the competitive level Hong Kong has attained in recent years,' said Stewart Brew.

HKCA Pres. XI: 201   (T Smart 43, S Foster 28)
India U19:   203–8

Army CA – 1995

The Army CA visited Hong Kong during the second half of October for a number of matches. In the main game at KCC, the HKCA lost to the Army.

Army CA: 195 (R Greatorex 98)
HKCA: 169 (R McLeay 68, D Clifton-James 36)

In an earlier match, the HKCA President's XI defeated the Army by one run at the HKCC.

MCC – 1997

The MCC played two 50-over games, and with the arrival of the MCC President, Colin Ingleby-Mackenzie, who had visited Hong Kong with an MCC team in 1981, were determined to remain unbeaten on the last leg of their three weeks Fiji/Hong Kong tour.

Mar 8 HKCA: 174   (P Fordham 45, R Flack 3–31)
       MCC: 180–2 (T J G O'Gorman 86*, M P W Jeh 47*
                      P D Carroll 45)

MCC won by 8 wickets.

The next day, MCC won a high-scoring friendly match by 6 wickets.

The Hong Kong philosophy of 'work hard, play hard' is certainly true and the last few days of the tour had profound effects on our health.

MCC Cricket Yearbook 1997–98

World XI v Australian XI – 1997

A special pre handover 40-over match took place at KCC on 11 May between an Australian XI and a World XI. The Australian XI scored the winning runs in only 28.4 overs.

World XI: 245–8 (S Manjrekar 80, R Gavaskar 50*, A Malik
                     36, L Klusener 30, B Julian 3–44, A Bichel
                     3–56)

460

Australian XI: 248–6 (M Waugh 116, S Waugh 45, R Ponting 35*, R Gavaskar 2–43, L Klusener 2–52)

[World XI: S Brew, R Chauhan, P Fordham, R Gavaskar, A Gurusinghe, M Kamal, L Klusener, B McMillan, A Malik, S Manjrekar (C), S Pollock.
Australian XI: A Bichel, G Blewett, I Healy, B Julian, K Kasprowicz, J Langer, R Ponting, M Taylor (C), S Warne, M Waugh, S Waugh.]

Many teams from Australia to Zimbabwe have toured Hong Kong postwar and would continue to do so, for their own enjoyment and for the betterment of Hong Kong cricket.

FROM HONG KONG

Many Hong Kong cricket teams have ventured to other lands to play cricket. The HKCC prewar played 'Coast Port Matches' against Swatow, in China, whilst postwar sides from various clubs have visited Australia, China & Taiwan, England, Japan, Indonesia, Malaysia, Philippines, Singapore and Thailand. This section is mainly concerned with Hong Kong representative teams (excluding Interport sides) touring overseas.

An 1891 cricket fortnight in Singapore. 'With commendable enthusiasm, the cricketers of Singapore arranged for a series of matches to occupy a fortnight. Their efforts were so well supported that the three colonies of Ceylon, Hong Kong and the Straits Settlements were ready to place elevens in the field.' Despite Ceylon and Hong Kong having to undergo all the inconvenience and expense of such long journeys, 'with the one object of participating in the friendly rivalry of the cricket field. No effort was spared to make the visit of the Ceylon and Hong Kong teams in every way enjoyable, and those who came from afar to take part in the high revels at Singapore are not likely to forget the generous hospitality extended to them on all hands during their stay there.'

Hong Kong lost their first match on 3/4 January 1891 against a very strong Straits Settlements side by 166 runs. Dr S C Fox (Straits) had a match analysis of 11 for 36.

Straits: 95 and 188
Hong Kong: 40 and 75

Hong Kong's second match, the first Hong Kong – Ceylon encounter, was played at the SCC on 5/6 January. Ceylon was designated 'A Colombo Team'.

Colombo defeated Hong Kong by 10 wickets – although Colombo's batting failed, the accuracy of Christoffelsz and Kelaart, who bowled unchanged in both innings was too much for the Hong Kong team. Nine batsmen were clean bowled in the second innings and eight of Christoffelsz's 13 victims were bowled. Lt Blair, described as the 'best all-round cricketer in the Far East', bagged a pair.

S S Pereira, Sri Lanka, March 1971

Hong Kong: 49 (Capt Dunn 15, E Christoffelsz 8–24)
47 (Capt Dunn 17, E Christoffelsz 5–22, T Kelaart 4–25)
Colombo: 92 (W Courtenay 26, C S Barff 4–33, Dr Lowson 4–43)
5 for no wicket.

Hong Kong then beat Singapore on 9/10 January by an innings and four runs.

Hong Kong: 179
Singapore: 156
18 (C S Barff 7–5, Dr Lowson 3–11).

As the fifth match had finished early, the last match in the fortnight took place between Hong Kong/Colombo and the Straits which ended in a draw. Capt Dunn, Lt Blair, Dr Lowson, A J Campbell and C S Barff represented Hong Kong in the combined side.

Hong Kong/Colombo: 98 (Dr S C Fox 4 wkts)
99–3 (Capt Dunn 55*)
Straits Settlements: 130 (T Kelaart 3–39, E Christoffelsz 2–45)

1909 Hong Kong XI: 89 (F C Wright 23, H M Morris 6–21, Capt Somerville 3–22)
Feb 21 Manila XI: 117 (J W Cairns 53, R Thursfield 5–45, J R Bedfern 3–24)

Manila won by 28 runs in Manila.

The first representative Hong Kong team to venture abroad after the Pacific war took place in June 1948 to Singapore and Malaya. As this team went 'disguised' as a Services side, how they organised the trip and the names of the participants is recorded under the Services section of this

462

book. Matches were played against Singapore, Singapore Combined Services and Federated Malay States.

1948	Hong Kong XI:	88	(L D Kilbee 18*, M Kailasapathy & C
Jun 19			Colling 4 wkts each)
& 20		91	(G N Gosano 35, C Colling 3–22, A C Growder 3–25)
	Singapore XI:	135	(Khoo Ong–lee 29, A Stepto & F Howarth 4 wkts each)
		46–2	(Cheong Thiam-siew 20*)

Singapore won by eight wickets at the SCC after Hong Kong won the toss and batted.

'Hong Kong's batsmen obviously lacked practice and failed badly against the accurate bowling of left-arm spinner Colling and the bite of Kailasapathy.'

A feature of the play when Singapore batted was the brilliant spell of bowling by A Stepto, who performed the 'hat-trick' in obtaining the last three Singapore wickets to cut short what promised to be a commanding lead. In his earlier spell Stepto was erratic and caused little trouble, but those three balls of his were lovely to watch, even against Singapore's 'rabbits'.

SCMP

I wonder what the late Stan Nagaiah, the first of Stepto's victims, would have thought of being called a rabbit (see Hong Kong v Malaya, 1959). In the second match, Hong Kong lost to the Singapore Combined Services by 10 wickets.

Hong Kong XI:	79	(M M Little 21, Kenyon 5–22)
	168	(H Owen Hughes 28, A Panton 23, F Zimmern 22*, Syrett 5–63, Kenyon 4–35)
S'pore CS:	190	(Leggett 58, Senior 45)
	64–0	(Harding 38*)

The Hong Kong team then flew to Kuala Lumpur for the game against the Federated States of Malaya on the Padang at the Selangor Club. The High Commissioner, Sir Edward Gent, in welcoming the Hong Kong and Federation teams, said:

there is no game which has the same flavour as a cricket match – vigilant rivalry on the field and no less vigilant concern of the spectators. Whether in the rigours of an English May or the steady warmth of the Malayan June, a cricket match is a peerless form of rivalry and comradeship at all times. I hope this Hong Kong match at Kuala Lumpur will set the standard for a future series.

Official Souvenir Programme, 1948

Jun 23	Hong Kong:	161	(Panton 38, Kilbee 36, Chue Eng Cheng 4–31, J Andres 3–44)
& 24			
		176–8	(Kilbee 74*, Howarth 48, Andres 4–47, Khoon 3–66)
	Fed. States:	139	(Eu Cheow Teik 44, Stepto 5–37, Howarth 3–32)
		68–4	(G S Walker 31, R E Lee 2–9, Howarth 2–24)

Owen Hughes won the toss, and after a late start elected to bat in bright sunshine on a good wicket. The Malayan bowlers were 'evidently worrying the batsmen' for runs were slow, the hundred coming up after two hours and ten minutes. In the Hong Kong second innings, 'Kilbee and Howarth opened their shoulders, putting on 76 in 55 minutes.' After Hong Kong's declaration, rain eventually caused the abandonment of the game.

Michael John Barr Richardson was in the Army in Hong Kong in 1965 when the Colony cricket trials were taking place prior to the Hong Kong team being selected to tour Malaya and Singapore. The author and other prospective tourists had seen the cricketing potential in 'Big Mike', but he just couldn't perform in the trials, even when playing for both sides in the same match! He was eventually selected, his selection being vindicated in the important two-day match against the Malayan Cricket Association at the SCC in May 1965.

1965	Malayan CA:	66	(R Singh 37*, M Richardson 4–13, I Lacy-Smith 3–21) ·
May 15			
& 16		93	(J Martens 30, R Singh 27, M Richardson 6–19)
	Hong Kong:	222	(M Richardson 83, J Shroff 41, C Myatt 31*, Marimuthi 4–35)

Hong Kong won by an innings and 63 runs after the MCA won the toss and batted first on a hot and sunny day. Coming in at No. 9 and No. 10,

Richardson and Myatt put on 104 runs for the ninth wicket, the hundred coming up in only 59 minutes! This was a very important moral victory for Hong Kong as the MCA had fielded a very strong side, which included established stars such as Mike Shepherdson and Reggie da Silva.

'Big Mike' had scored 107 in 1952 at the Oval in a Young Amateurs match – Surrey v Middlesex, and also 126* for the MCC. However, the selectors were not aware of these statistics in 1965.

Hong Kong's second encounter against Ceylon (now Sri Lanka) came in 1971, 80 years after the first, as part of an ambitious tour of Ceylon, Singapore and Sabah.

1971   HKCA XI: 174–8 dec (J Shroff 41, Jayaweera 4–41)
Mar 21 S. Provinces: 125–6   (Sathasivam 32, Paranathala 32)

Match drawn at Galle.

Mar 22 HKCA XI: 76   (Illingaratnam 6–12)
Nat. Services: 80–3 (Pathirana 44, Jayaweera 31)

'Hong Kong's batsmen contributed to their own downfall with some rank bad shots' at Colombo.

In the main two-day game against the Ceylon Board of Control President's XI, Hong Kong lost by 10 wickets. Rocky Daniel cracked a glorious 56 in Hong Kong's first innings, but dropped catches cost Hong Kong dearly.

Mar 24 Hong Kong: 155   (R Daniel 56, R Lalchandani 35, N
  & 25   Seneviratne 2–14)
                 101   (M Tissera 3–16, M Pieris 3–17)
  CBC Pres. XI: 249–6 dec (J Fernando 108, R Sathasivam 26, C
                 10–0   Myatt 3–41)

The two highest scorers for the CBC President's XI were both school-boys!

Those carefree sporting cricketers from Hong Kong ran into a cricket cyclone in the form of the Board of Control President's XI, who demolished the visitors by 10 wickets, like their 'Colombo' counter-parts 80 years before in Singapore, in their two-day game on the Colombo Cricket Club ground.

Daily Mirror, Ceylon

465

Ted Wilson, the Hong Kong team manager, invited Ceylon to send a side to Hong Kong. A Sri Lankan Under 23 team subsequently toured Hong Kong in 1986 [see Tours to Hong Kong].

The Hong Kong team then travelled to Singapore for the Interport [recorded elsewhere], and matches against the Combined Services: 197–9 (J Morgan 71, G Lalchandani 5–39) – HKCA: 145–5 (C Rowe 61), and Singapore President's XI: 142 (R Daniel 4–34) – HKCA: 146–4 (R Daniel 84*). 'Glorious 84 by Daniel sparks Hong Kong win.'

An inaugural visit to Sabah then followed, where the main match against Sabah State Cricket Association took place at the Kepayan Police Padang, Kota Kinabalu.

1971

Apr 6	Sabah SCA:	190	(A Zahman 74, K Vijiratnam 47, Duggan 4–45, Middleton 3–50)
& 7		81	(C J C Rowe 5–25)
	Hong Kong:	189	(P H Davies 67, R Lalchandani 42, J Osmund 3–44)
		83–4	(C J C Rowe 23, M Richardson 3–33)

Hong Kong won by six wickets.

Malaysian State player, Alwi Zahman, put together a solid 74 for Sabah in the first innings, but no one had an answer to Charles Rowe's leg-breaks in their second where, on an easy-paced wicket, Rowe finished with an analysis of 11–3–25–5.

'At last – a vintage Davies innings. Given freedom to play his pull shot, Peter grew in confidence as his innings progressed and never looked in any kind of trouble.'

Despite the presence of ex-Hong Kong Interporter Mike Richardson in their side, Sabah, unlike Singapore, did not bait Peter at backward square leg or short third man!

The Sabah SCA had gone to a tremendous amount of trouble to ensure that Hong Kong players lacked nothing in comfort. Ground facilities and other arrangements have been excellent.

Carl Myatt, *SCMP*

1973 – Hong Kong's first official tour to Australia took place in March

466

1973, when an HKCA team visited Western Australia, captained by Carl Myatt and managed by Ted Wilson.

HKCA XI: 185–5 dec. (P H Davies 75, M Alexander 58, Penter 3–32)
Taverners: 134–7   (McLean 35, B T Wigley 3–27)
            Match drawn.

HKCA XI: 147–7 (R Booth 60, Grove 4–36)
Incogniti: 149–5 (Baker 38, Dry 37*)
            Incogniti won by five wickets.

In the next match the HKCA: 93, lost to W Perth CC: 96–2, by eight wickets, but then beat Combined Services by 18 runs.

HKCA XI: 198–7 dec (G Turner 73, P H Davies 44)
Comb.Services: 180   (Aunger 75, B T Wigley 4–26)

Hong Kong's last outing was against the University of Western Australia in a two-day match, which ended in a hard fought and equitable draw. Hong Kong required two wickets and the University 25 runs respectively for victory. A fitting finish to a memorable tour.

HKCA XI: 176–7 dec (M Alexander 54, R Booth 39)
          190–9 dec (I Marshall 71, R Booth 70, Nicholls 3–38)
Univ. WA: 178–5 dec (Scarff 81, Penter 50, M Duggan 4–24)
          163–8   (Penter 53, Abbott 44, Kwong Wo 5–52)

Hong Kong found that they were up against many players of a standard well above their own, including Tony Lock and several who had helped Western Australia to win the Sheffield Shield during the current season.

Ted Wilson, 'Chinaman', *The Cricketer*, May 1973

1976 – Hong Kong's most ambitious overseas tour was to England in July 1976 [see Ted Wilson's reminiscences], when eleven matches were played, including a most memorable one against an MCC side at Lord's. For those cricketers fortunate enough to be selected for that match, to have played on the 'hallowed' ground would remain forever in their memories.

Eight matches were drawn. Old Hong Kong: 223–6 – HKCA: 139–8; RAF: 259–4 – HKCA: 137–5; Coventry & N Warks CC: 208–8 dec – HKCA: 150–8; Wolverhampton CC: 220–6 dec – HKCA: 140–7; Club Cricket Conference: 109–3 (rain); Free Foresters: 190–5 dec – HKCA: 103–7 and the British Army and MCC. Three matches were lost. HKCA: 216 – Lloyds: 217–5; Warwick Pilgrims: 177–9 dec – HKCA: 170, and HKCA: 121–9 dec – Stratford CC: 122–4. Details of the Army and MCC matches follow.

Jul 6 & 7	British Army:	229–9 dec	(V E Nurse 42, L M Sanderson 36, C Myatt 4–61)
		151–4	(R G Daniel 85*, V E Nurse 35*)
	Hong Kong:	254	(J Bygate 56, B J Willson 49, P Anderson 33, N Scott 5–89)

The author obtained the Army match results from Lt Col Keith Hitchcock, Secretary of the Army Cricket Association, who said: 'I enclose photocopies of the 1976 match but have no idea what happened to HK's second innings – perhaps a typhoon?!' The Army records were detailed enough for the author to add up the total time for the match – 11 hours and 46 minutes. Hong Kong batted 5 hours and 24 minutes for their 254 runs. There wasn't any time left for a Hong Kong second innings! Later back in Hong Kong that year it was reported:

> After the match the Army entertained the Hong Kong team at an old French style chateau of such old-world charm it evoked memories of Dumas and the Three Musketeers. This was the Royal Engineers Officers' Mess, one of whose senior men was an ex-Hong Kong type, name of Bill Withall. Bill, of course, is now a Brigadier and that evening we were graced by the presence of three of the top Generals in the British Army. Lt General Sir Patrick Howard-Dobson and Lt General Sir Edwin Bramall are old friends of Hong Kong. The third was General James Wilson, known in sporting circles as James Wilson, soccer writer for the *Sunday Times*. Amid the pomp and splendour of an elegant room, a lengthy banqueting table, silent waitresses and gleaming silver, an evening of memorable speeches and comradeship.

Carl Myatt, 'Off the Seam', SCMP

Thus to the highlight of the England tour – a visit to Lord's for a match against an MCC XI containing such renowned players as Colin Cowdrey, Ted Dexter and Mike Smith. The actual full scoresheet printed by the MCC is shown here to highlight an historic occasion.

Carl Myatt and Peter Anderson, two former Hong Kong captains, were asked by the author for their most memorable moments whilst representing Hong Kong at cricket. Without hesitation, they plumped for the match against the MCC. Incidentally, both performed well, Carl with the ball and Peter with the bat.

Match Drawn

(5p) LORD'S GROUND (5p)

M.C.C. v. HONG KONG

Monday, July 12th, 1976   (1-day Match)

M.C.C.	First Innings		Second Innings
1 W. E. Russell	b Myatt	47	
2 A. Stewart	b Lalchandani	4	
3 M. J. K. Smith	c and b Myatt	66	
†4 M. C. Cowdrey	not out	66	
5 E. R. Dexter	c and b Myatt	0	
*6 B. Taylor	c Hughes b Myatt	19	
7 J. K. Fawcett	not out	21	
8 A. C. Smith			
9 N. J. Evans		Innings closed	
10 D. W. Henry			
11 L. J. Champniss	B 3, l-b 2, w 2, n-b	7	B , l-b , w , n-b
	Total	220	Total

FALL OF THE WICKETS

1—5   2—107   3—118   4—118   5—156   6—   7—   8—   9—   10—
1—   2—   3—   4—   5—   6—   7—   8—   9—   10—

ANALYSIS OF BOWLING	1st Innings					2nd Innings					
Name	O.	M.	R.	W.	Wd. N-b		O.	M.	R.	W.	Wd. N-b
Starling	11	6	32	0	2 ...		...	...	...	...	... ...
Lalchandani	4	0	31	1	... ...		...	...	...	...	... ...
Willson	17	2	56	0	... ...		...	...	...	...	... ...
Myatt	16	0	73	4	... ...		...	...	...	...	... ...
Mulready	5	0	21	0	... ...		...	...	...	...	... ...

HONG KONG	First Innings		Second Innings
1 J. A. Bygate	l b w b A. Smith	31	
2 B. J. Willson	c M. Smith b Champniss	30	
3 D. L. Budge	l b w b Champniss	1	
4 R. W. Mulready	b Champniss	0	
5 D. Clinton	l b w b Champniss	17	
6 P. Anderson	b Cowdrey	39	
7 G. Lalchandani	c Evans b Champniss	13	
8 R. Starling	c and b Dexter	8	
9 J. Hughes	not out	26	
*10 M. R. Bulfield	not out	18	
†11 C. M. Myatt	B 7, l-b 8, w , n-b 1,	16	B , l-b , w , n-b ,
	Total	199	Total

FALL OF THE WICKETS

1—49   2—53   3—53   4—89   5—89   6—124   7—135   8—165   9—   10—
1—   2—   3—   4—   5—   6—   7—   8—   9—   10—

ANALYSIS OF BOWLING	1st Innings					2nd Innings					
Name	O.	M.	R.	W.	Wd. N-b		O.	M.	R.	W.	Wd. N-b
Henry	9	1	32	0	... ...		...	...	...	...	... ...
Evans	4	0	22	0	... ...		...	...	...	...	... ...
Champniss	21	5	72	5	... ...		...	...	...	...	... ...
A. Smith	11	6	18	1	... ...		...	...	...	...	... ...
Dexter	6	2	24	1	... ..		...	...	...	...	... ...
Cowdrey	3	1	15	1	... 1		...	...	...	...	... ...

Umpires—C. Mitchell & H. E. Robinson   Scorers—E. Solomon & J. Danks

† Captain   * Wicket-keeper

Play begins at 11.30 a.m.   Stumps drawn at 6.30 p.m.

Luncheon Interval 1.30—2.10

Tea Interval 4.15—4.35 (may be varied according to state of game)

Hong Kong won the toss and elected to field

1979 – The second HKCA tour to Australia took place in April 1979, this time to Eastern Australia (NSW and Victoria), captained by Peter Anderson and once again managed by Ted Wilson. Ted was not only an experienced cricketer (Kenya and Hong Kong), but he was also one of the few persons who could 'somehow' manage to get the time off for such tours!

Apr 14 Melbourne CC: 143 (C Coutts 32, D Greenwood 2–7, P Anderson 2–17)
        HKCA XI: 144–0 (N Stearns 70*, D Greenwood 66*)
        HKCA won by 10 wickets.

Apr 15 A.C.Soc: 204–6 (B Green 83, O Wright 46, C Swann 4–52)
        HKCA XI: 152 (M Walker 35, A Turner 32, P Anderson 31, S Luddwyk 3–12)
        Australia Cricket Society won by 52 runs.

Apr 19 HKCA XI: 203   (N Stearns 66, C Langford 64)
        Griffith CA: 144   (L Jebsen 33, G Bacon 6–29, S Willis 3–40)
        HKCA won by 59 runs.

Apr 21 NSW SDCC: 119   (W Dooley 45, S Willis 4–26, C Swann 4–30)
        HKCA XI: 121–5 (M Walker 42*, P Olsen 29*, N Murphy 3–30)
        HKCA beat NSW Southern District CC by 5 wickets.

Apr 22 HKCA XI: 211–5 (M Walker 78*, A Lorimer 70, J Hawkesley 34, T O'Brien 3–60)
        NSW SD: 148   (J Poedevin 37, J Croker 31, M Hislop 3–45)
        HKCA beat NSW Southern District by 63 runs.

Apr 25 HKCA XI: 142–7 (C Langford 45, M Walker 36, D Jamieson 3–8, R Tregeale 3–27)
        Briars CC: 121   (D Jamieson 49, K Holley 33, S Willis 5–30)
        HKCA beat Briars CC, Sydney, by 21 runs.

Apr 26 HKCA XI: 145–6 (P Anderson 40, A Turner 32)
        I Zingari: 107   (C Swann 5–44)
        HKCA won by 38 runs.

Unfortunately, the last fixture in Sydney, against the Old Aloysians, was washed out. Bryan Hemshall, assistant manager, reported fully on the tour in the HKCA Handbook 1979–80. Apart from the privilege and the experience to be gained from such a tour, this particular one was planned as part compensation for Hong Kong cricketers following the decision of the HKCA not to participate in the ICC Associate Members World Cup Competition in England in May 1979.

Bryan Hemshall commented on various highlights of the tour:

Just over 1,000 miles were covered from Melbourne to Griffith, Goulburn, Canberra, and then onto Sydney in an Ansett Pioneer coach. The driver, Arthur Austin's sessions on the mike were a source of entertainment.

Whilst at the MCG, their famous cricket museum was visited and later Ian Johnson, former Australian captain and secretary of the MCG, joined the party for drinks.

In Sydney, WD & HO Wills, who market Benson & Hedges in Australia, hosted a magnificent cocktail party which included such notables as: Ian Craig, Alan Davidson, Neil Harvey, Harold Larwood, Keith Miller, Arthur Morris and Bill O'Reilly.

These were some of the 'Australian All Stars' who had previously been invited to Hong Kong to commemorate the closing of the HKCC's Chater Road ground in 1975.

'The phenomenal hitting of Martin Walker was memorable and completely turned several matches in Hong Kong's favour. But, above all, the clinch of the success was the high quality of ground fielding, throwing and close catching.

'The wickets varied from true hard fast strips at Melbourne and Goulburn to soft green difficult wickets in Sydney.

'The hospitality afforded by our hosts was at all times warm and friendly.'

All in all, a successful and enjoyable tour, ably led and managed by Messrs Anderson, Hemshall, Wigley and Wilson.

Specific HKCA overseas tours to particular countries after 1979, except for Interports against Malaysia and Singapore, were replaced by ICC Associate Members Competitions, the first for Hong Kong in 1982; South-East Asian Tournaments, and the more recently introduced Volvo and Tuanku Ja'afar Trophy competitions.

1987 – Hong Kong's last Interport tour to the Malayan peninsula took place in May 1987, led by Yarman Vachha. The HKCA crushed a SCA President's XI in the run-up to the three-day Interport.

HKCA:	266–5	(N Stearns 119, D Evans 39, T Lerwill 39,
		C Collins 39, S Sivalingam 2–23)
SCA Pres XI:	122	(A Ramaswami 24, B Gohel 3–30,
		R Fotheringham 2–15, A Telford 2–20)

1994 – In November 1994, the second oldest cricket club in Hong Kong, the Craigengower Cricket Club, mentioned in the CCC section, skippered by Kevin Styles, visited Shanghai as part of the club's Centenary celebrations. [This was the first cricket tour of any kind to Shanghai since the last Interport between Hong Kong and Shanghai in 1948.] Kevin said:

Craigengower's long-standing contacts with the Shanghai Sports Federation led to a ground being made available, the first discussions were about 18 months ago. Richard Graham provided the focus for the Shanghai group. About 70–80 from the re-born Shanghai Cricket Club (SCC) attended the Saturday evening dinner near the old Jin Jiang Hotel. The Hon. President of the SCC, the Indian Consul General, Mr P N G Subramaniam, spoke, as did I, Richard Graham and Terry Smith. *Reuters* covered the weekend, and at 9:30 p.m. on Saturday night cricket made the news on Shanghai Channel 8 (all over China). Must have thought we were mad!

Reuters' Andrew Browne's message was reported in the UK *Times*:

The first ball of the first over of the first innings in Shanghai since 1948 was bowled by Terry 'Smudge' Smith, president of the Hong Kong Cricket Club. 'I've always played cricket everywhere I've been,' explained Mr Graham. 'This has been absolutely marvellous fun.' For Craigengower Cricket Club, the tour had a serious intention: Kevin Styles and his squad are trying to make the game more popular in China.

1995 – The HKCA toured Bangladesh early that year for a series of 50-over matches as part of its development plan for improving its own players. Stewart Brew, one of Hong Kong's leading cricketers, was injured during the first international against Bangladesh, and as a 'penance' for not completing the tour as an active player wrote it up for *Scoreboard*. This summary has been extracted from Brew's article.

The team, with manager Bharat Gohel and coach David Trist, were based in Dhaka. For the first match against Bangladesh Under 19 they flew off to Sylhet to play on a wicket of rolled mud, slightly lighter in colour than the almost black mud wicket at the Dhaka stadium. Hong Kong scored 139 for 9, thanks to an educated 66 not out from Rahul

Sharma. After the match-winning shot by Bangladesh, helped by some dropped catches, an excited crowd of over 10,000 invaded the pitch with the team being escorted off by a cordon of armed riot police! Rahul gave the team some pointers on how to play on these low bounce wickets.

In complete contrast to the previous day, only a few thousand people watched this international match in Dhaka's 80,000 seat stadium. Bangladesh knocked up 230 in their allotted overs. Hong Kong started well but from 150 for 5 collapsed to 159 all out. Bangladesh used their world class spinners to bowl the final 20 overs on the black, low and turning wicket, making it nearly impossible for Hong Kong to find the boundary. Brew with a 'hobbling' 54 and Steve Foster with 33 runs were Hong Kong's only successful batsmen.

In back-to-back matches, Hong Kong batting first reached 160 for 8 with Sharma again showing the way with 42. After teetering at 80 for 5, the strength of Bangladesh's middle order saw them home in the 42nd over, giving the impression of a contest much less competitive than it was.

The next match entailed a two hour bus ride to Comilla to meet the Bangladesh Under 19 side again. Batting first Bangladesh totalled 182 for 8, Sharma capturing 3 for 19 off his ten overs. At 44 for 0 after 11 overs, Hong Kong looked on course; however, a slow scoring period, then the all too familiar predicament of needing to drastically up the run-rate, followed by a couple of silly run-outs and errant shots, found Hong Kong wanting at 105 for 9, and eventually well short of the target. 'We then embarked on the most terrifying ride back to the hotel. Until one is faced with an oncoming bus at speed with seeming nowhere to go on either side, one cannot say he has come close to death.'

The last match took place at the National Sports Institute, where, on a wicket of more usual bounce, Hong Kong notched up 214 for 8, with R Bannister 44 and Dave Mallinson 33 not out sharing the honours. The Bangladesh Colts were restricted to 172 for 9, giving Hong Kong its first and only victory. John Storey captured 3 for 30 off his ten overs.

Pat Fordham had a great tour behind the stumps. David Trist, who moonlights as coach for Holland, said privately that Pat would walk into the Holland side, a fitting accolade to his contribution to Hong Kong cricket. As during the first tour of Bangladesh in 1984, reported by Chris Collins, the experience and camaraderie would not be easily forgotten. The team will have gained experience from playing international cricket and also learnt something about low and slow wickets. The Bangladesh Cricket Association had been wonderful hosts.

Prior to the handover of Hong Kong in June 1997, the HKCA had started to adopt a more positive and optimistic attitude towards the future of cricket by developing interest in the game at junior level to encompass a

473

wider spectrum of the local population. The SAR authorities are more likely to look favourably on an association that promotes vocation in such a commercial place. Some might say, why didn't the HKCA look toward the Chinese a few years ago and encourage them to take up the game. Chinese cricketers have played the sport in Hong Kong over many years, usually as members of non-Chinese teams [but see – Chinese Recreation Club]. In answer to the question as to why tours to China have not been promoted before now – they have, prewar and one to Beijing in 1983. The real reason is that the facilities for the game in China are just not available, and the Chinese to date are not particularly interested in the game.

REMINISCENCES

Major E I M Barrett's Memories of Cricket in the Far East

[From the Winter Annual of *The Cricketer* 1921–22, and reprinted in the Hong Kong Cricket Club Centenary Booklet 1851–1951]

The Editor of *The Cricketer* remarked that wherever Englishmen are gathered together, even in the most remote corners of the globe, there they will be found playing cricket, defying all disadvantages of conditions and climate. In the Far East, comprising for purposes of this article, the Federated Malay States, China and Japan, cricket is played with considerable keenness, and the grand old game helps to keep Englishmen in touch with their home so many thousands of miles away.

During my eighteen years in the Far East, four years in Federated Malay States and fourteen in Shanghai, I have had the opportunity of meeting all the best-known cricketers in these parts, and have played on most of the cricket grounds, some of which are excellent. I have also had the opportunity of comparing cricket in the Far East with that at home, having taken part in first-class cricket for Hampshire during the seasons of 1903, 1906, 1912 and 1918. Cricketers out East are drawn mainly from the business community, and the number of Public School and Varsity boys available has, up to date, been few. Nevertheless several self-made cricketers have made their mark, and would, given the opportunity and experience, do well in English cricket.

In the Federated Malay States and Straits Settlements all cricket is played on grass. The wickets are slow and easy.

As the rain it raineth every day in this country, a good fast wicket is a rarity. I remember on one occasion, in the little town of Taiping, Perak, it started to rain as we left the field for lunch. By the time we sat down to lunch the ground was a lake, with the stumps alone visible. On the middle stump at one end sat a kingfisher! Notwithstanding, we resumed cricket at 4.30 p.m., which speaks well for the drainage.

Straits cricket owes a great deal to those keen cricketers and able administrators, Sir Frank Swettenham, Sir Ernest Birch and Colonel Frowd Walker, these were the pioneers of cricket in the Straits, and qualifications for Government appointments were considerably enhanced under this regime if the applicant was a cricketer.

Perhaps I owe my own billet to this fact. I remember taking a team to Singapore to represent Perak when the Resident-General of the Federated Malay States put his steam yacht at our disposal for the journey to and from Penang to Singapore. I don't think the Government could stand for that in those days! The more important matches were between Perak, Selangor, Penang and Singapore. I had the honour of taking part in the first match between the Federated Malay States against Penang and Singapore combined in Kuala Lumpur in 1905. Incidentally, I collected 150 odd for the Federated Malay States, who won comfortably. The teams included S C G Fox (Incogniti), A B Hubback (now commanding a London District), R T Reid, and the two Muglistons, 'Sonnie' and Gerald.

My first visit to Hong Kong was in 1904, when the Straits had a good side, which defeated both Hong Kong and Shanghai. Captain H L Talbot was captain, and a very good one too. He will be remembered by many old Incogs., for whom he made a heap of runs when on leave from his job as Commissioner of Police, Federated Malay States. Our side included T R Hubback, who kept wicket occasionally for Lancashire, and a leg-break bowler, R B Rees, who I believe, formerly represented one of the Australian States. He was quite first-class, and I remember his indignation when his skipper, who had no opinion of Rees as a batsman, put him in last. Rees, quite undismayed, tackled the huge Henry Talbot with, 'Surely to goodness I am better than Perkins?' – Perkins being a 'rabbit'! Talbot insisted on his going in last, but put him in first in the next innings, whereupon Rees gathered in an excellent and invaluable 50!

The Malays do not take kindly to cricket. Beyond occupying positions as groundsmen and practice bowlers, they have not taken to the game. I recall a tall Malay groundsman at Singapore who had that delightful flail-like action with a natural leg-break. He was distinctly fast, and would have delighted the heart of many a county committee today. He was the exception to the rule. [He was known as Panjang, meaning 'lanky'.]

As a class, I should put the representative cricket of the Straits Settlements at a higher level than that of China; but probably considerably lower than Colombo, from all accounts. During the rubber boom the estates were full of good cricketers; but it is not easy to get eleven representative players to travel 2000 miles to Hong Kong for six days cricket. In spite of the difficulties of distance and expense, our representative matches take place fairly regularly.

Apart from these Interport matches, cricket in the Far East is restricted to Saturday afternoons. Frequently the heat is overpowering, particularly so during July and August in Shanghai, where the cricket season coincides with that at home. In the Straits cricket is played all the year round, as the climate hardly varies; but in Hong Kong the season is from November to

476

April. It will be seen that it is not easy to fit in matches convenient to both Hong Kong and Shanghai, as one side or the other is beginning or ending its season.

Hong Kong cricket is usually in a flourishing condition, owing to the presence of a Naval and Military Garrison. In addition to an annual match v Shanghai, Hong Kong is the scene of a triangular tournament every three or four years, with Shanghai and the Straits as their guests. Unfortunately the ground is not a good one, being very small and the light indifferent. The wicket is fair, usually faster than Shanghai, but will not last more than two or three innings. Surrounded by trees and buildings, in the heart of the town, the light is very difficult for the visitors. Hong Kong has had a number of excellent cricketers during recent years, notably H R B Hancock, who at Charterhouse, played inside to the famous G O Smith, and T E Pearce. Both of these players would have gone far in English cricket, given practice in the best company. Of service members, H H C Baird (Cheltenham and 'The Buffs') did an immense amount of good for cricket in Hong Kong about 1908, as also the Rev W H Maundrell (Cambridge hurdler and Hants XI) a year or so later. Mention must also be made of that wily old left-hander, R E O Bird, who has probably more wickets to his credit than any bowler who ever came East.

The ground bowlers, both at Hong Kong and Shanghai, are Chinese; but as a nation the Chinese are not likely to take up cricket. The majority regard us as so many fools, in that we do not pay someone else to play for us! At my first visit to the nets in Hong Kong in 1904, I was shocked at being clean bowled by a Chinese coolie who bowled very respectable leg-breaks. My chagrin increased when, hitting a mighty drive to the far end of the ground, I was caught one-handed by another ragged-looking coolie, after climbing up on the bandstand among the chairs and music stands! The Chinese students in Hong Kong are, I believe, showing some ability and keenness for cricket, and, at the moment, the best exponents of tennis in that island are Chinese. Nevertheless, I fear that it is hopeless to expect China to produce any sort of a team before the Judgement Day.

Shanghai boasts of a very fine ground, in area as big as the Oval, with excellent turf and good light. The wicket is usually on the slow side, never very difficult, although I imagine Barnes would be pretty beastly on it at any time! At the moment of writing the game is in a flourishing condition. A league (five teams) has been started, and with the hoped-for revival of trade and expansion of the city, cricket should continue to flourish. A good Shanghai side would not do much more than compete on level terms with a strong London club, such as Hampstead; but has contained some cricketers of note, who have made big club reputations at home.

477

L Walker (Surrey), F W Potter (Bedford), and W A H Moule (Black-heath) are three of the mainstays of the game in the past, and a pillar of strength lately has been Dr W E O'Hara*, who played for Scotland v Australians in the 'nineties. A beautiful left-hand bowler of real class who has unfortunately had no opportunity to show his merit in first-class cricket. [*In the Shanghai v Hong Kong Interports, Dr O'Hara is referred to as an Australian.]

It must not be forgotten that a match between Hong Kong and Shanghai entails a sea journey of 1600 miles and at least a fortnight's holiday. To play Hong Kong, Singapore must travel some 2000 miles and take three weeks' holiday. Such is the lure of cricket.

Cricket in Japan is confined to the British residents in the two ports of Kobe and Yokohama. Owing to Government restrictions, they have great difficulty concerning their grounds, and the number of players is very limited. An annual match between the two ports is practically all the serious cricket which occurs, but I shall know more about this on my return in October. The wickets are matting over grass, though why this should be so when we have good grass wickets in China I cannot quite understand.

The interest in home cricket out in the Far East is enormous. As at home, when we pick up the newspaper, we turn first to the cricket cable of the Test match or county cricket. We, too, select the English Test teams, and marvel at the exclusion of this or that player, with no sort of sympathy for the poor Selection Committee! 'Tis ever thus. Nevertheless, we try to play cricket in the proper spirit, never fearing that those 'ashes' will come back from Australia so long as cricket is played as our fore-fathers intended it should be played.

Capt E I M Barrett played once for the Straits against Hong Kong in 1904 and scored 36 and 53. In seven matches for Shanghai against Hong Kong from 1914 to 1928, he scored 651 runs, including three centuries (highest 165 in 1921) averaging 50.08.

After the triangular tournament in Hong Kong in 1927, T E Pearce, the acting Hong Kong captain, said at the Interport dinner: 'Captain Barrett's was a remarkably fine innings, when he scored 146 out of a total 240 runs.'

The Straits captain, N J A Foster, added his tribute by saying: 'The innings of Capt Barrett was a masterpiece, and it would be difficult to find anything in the Far East to defy it.'

[Edward Ivo Medhurst Barrett was born in Churt, Frensham, Surrey, on 22 June 1879, and died on 10 July 1950, following an accident. He was a fine hard-hitting middle order right-hand batsman, and played 80 matches for Hampshire from 1896 to 1925. He had a highest score of 215 against Gloucestershire in 1920. He also represented England at rugby in 1903.

Who's Who of Cricketers, 1993]

Reminiscences – Sir Denys Roberts and Ted Wilson

For all his success as a batsman and as an administrator, I believe that his greatest contribution to the game was his impeccable behaviour on the field, where he remained courteous and good-humoured in all circumstances. Indeed, I recall that he was still able to smile when, hopelessly deceived by my flighted chinaman, he tripped over his abdominal protector and was stumped as he lay on his face several feet up the wicket.

Sir Denys Roberts

I do not, however, intend to retaliate, but anyone familiar with the writings of Sir Denys will realise that, apart from attempts at humour in one or two paragraphs, the facts stated will be far from accurate, particularly where they are derogatory. Most people are aware, Sir Denys made a reputation as the slowest bowler in S-E Asia which led to his being invited to play in various parts of the world – even in Hong Kong.

Ted Wilson

Ted (HKCC Scorpions – capt.) receives the Gillette Cup (Super League 1967–68) from Denys. Buji Dhabber eyeing the scene, seems to be thinking: 'Looks like the Old Boy network!'

Sir Denys Roberts, KBE, QC

[President of The Hongkong Cricket League/Hong Kong Cricket Association 1966–71 and 1982–88]

I first arrived in Hong Kong in 1962. I was delighted to be there, as an uncle of mine, severely injured in a brawl there in a brothel before the war, could not speak too highly of the place.

I had travelled in a ship with a guitar. Consequently I was written off by the more serious-minded, who were always fortunately in a small minority in Hong Kong, as an intellectual lightweight. Their views would have been reinforced if they had known that, concealed in my baggage, were two cricket bats. One was yellow in colour and had not been used for its proper purpose for several years. I kept it for sentimental reasons because I had struck a jackal which had found its way onto the verandah of my house in Africa. I had, of course, hit the animal with the inside edge, which is how I made many of my runs. The other bat, however, was carefully bound with white tape, which covered most of its lower half. It had seen many of my triumphs in Gibraltar, from where I was transferred in a hurry when they needed my post there for the nephew of one of the legal advisers in the Colonial Office. I had used this bat in many matches, in several of which I had reached double figures. I was eager to repeat my success in Hong Kong.

After I had been there a few days, I asked Maurice Heenan, the agreeable New Zealander who was then the Attorney General (before the office fell into disrepute with my appointment to it), if anyone played cricket in Hong Kong.

'You must join the Hong Kong Cricket Club.'

'Do I have to find a seconder?'

'Not necessarily, Denys. I'll find someone who has not met you to do that. To be on the safe side,' he added with a smile.

I was taken around the Committee a few days later.

'Are you African?' enquired one of the members. I discovered later that he was deaf and that my answers were irrelevant.

'My putative father is not,' I replied. 'Though he isn't sure where he came from as he was left in a rubbish bin in Kew. With the cuttings,' I added to give respectability to my origins.

'I see that you have ticked the box which asks if you play any games?'

'Yes, sir. I've also said I play squash. Will that help?'

'Of course it will. We have no squash courts. I'm not so sure about cricket. Do you really want to play, or have you ticked the box to impress us?'

'I'd quite like to play, if you can give me a game or two, sir.' I was at my most humble, which is not an attractive sight.

'We have about five hundred members. We provide the best uneatable cheap lunch in town and the beer drinkers keep the subs down. Welcome to the club.'

The following day, I suffered severe indigestion at lunch from the club bubble and squeak. I can only suppose the caterer, Mr Chow, had contracts with several hotels, to purchase the vegetables which they threw out as unsuitable for human consumption.

Fighting back the pains in my chest, I examined the notice board. There was an advertisement for a North Point nightclub. 'Open all night. Men five dollars, girls free.' In the middle of it was the notice of a production of *The Tempest*. Under the advertisement for the play, was a notice asking members to indicate which team they would like to play for and their previous experience.

I decided to appear to be modest, a dishonesty which has served me well. I asked to be considered for the Nomads, a second division team. To my surprise, it was apparent that somebody read the notice, I was telephoned on the following Friday evening.

'You won't know me,' he began.

'If you are an anonymous heavy breather,' I answered, 'you should try another number, because I am too.'

'No, no, my name is Hall. I'm the captain of the Nomads.'

'Well done, Hall. Was that expensive?'

'I was appointed on merit,' he replied indignantly. 'The Nomads are a cricket club team. You said you wanted to play. We've just had someone drop out at the last moment. Otherwise I would not have phoned you at all.'

'Of course not,' I agreed. 'What happened to the other chap?'

'He's been refused bail. It's a disgrace, as it's quite a trivial matter. It's called embezzlement, I think. We had been counting on him. He was one of our opening bats. Do you open?'

'No.'

'Fine. That's settled then. Please be at Craigengower Cricket Club tomorrow. We start at one thirty, Do you keep wicket?'

'No.'

'That's solved another problem.'

He rang off before I could ask him what that was. I found out next day. I arrived half an hour early, which was not difficult for me as I was working for the Government. Nobody came until after half past one, when Hall arrived. I recognised him at once, he was wearing a silk scarf.

'You must be Roberts,' he said plying me with handshakes as if I was attached to a rusted pump. 'I've lost the toss. We did it on the phone, to save time. What a good thing you've come. Did you bring your wicket-keeper's things?'

'I don't have any. I haven't kept since I was expelled from school twenty years ago.'

'Onanism, I expect,' he replied, using rather a sophisticated term which I did not follow until I looked it up, after which I was resentful. How did he know? I would have lost my hair anyway. 'Well,' he added cheerfully. 'We must make do with what we can get.'

I hobbled onto the field a few minutes later, followed by Hall and six others, two of them in shorts. Four of the eight belonged to CCC, which owned the ground in Happy Valley. Next door was the Police Sports Club, full of cheerful coppers playing cricket in huge boots. CCC, as everybody called it, including my taxi driver who had driven me twice to his favourite brothel, was a small ground, which had once been a large one. A piece had been excised by the lawn bowls players, who remained bent double, so that you could only see their backsides, until they imagined that a cricket ball was about to reach their grass, when they straightened up and made varied use of improper language and signs.

An even larger area was devoted to several lawn tennis courts, mainly occupied by girls in short skirts, who shouted 'Jolly good show' continuously. This distracted long on and long off so badly that our outfielding was virtually useless.

I thought, considering that I had not kept wicket since 1940, when I took over from Small Minor, who stunned himself on the square leg umpire when trying to poach someone else's catch, that I had done rather well. There were 34 extras, but that could happen to anyone. It would have been rather more if I had not stood well back to the slow bowlers.

I wish I had been as successful with the bat. Before I had scored, however, I was given out by one of our own batsman, who was sulking because he had been run out by his colleague who had shouted 'Yes,' 'No,' 'Wait,' 'Yes,' 'Back, you fool'. I struck the ball firmly to mid-wicket and had already run two when I was given out lbw.

I was phoned the next day by Tony Weller, a delightful man who was, for that week, captain of the Scorpions, a first division side. There seemed to be a different one each Saturday, except on the field when there were never less than four, giving contradictory instructions which were usually ignored.

'I say,' he began, 'it's Weller here.' I had not heard the name since I was forced to read Dickens at school. 'I'm captain of the Scorpions for next week. I hear you were the top scorer at CCC yesterday, with 34?'

'That is one way of looking at it,' I agreed.

'We are going to be very short next weekend, or I would not ask you.'

'Of course not,' I agreed.

'We need a wicket-keeper. I hear you keep.'

482

'No,' I replied.

'Good, good. That's settled. And you open the batting too?'

'No, Mr Weller, I do not.'

'Fine, fine. See you on Saturday next at the Army ground in Soo Kun Poo.' Weller had not taught me how to pronounce it, so I saw quite a lot of the area before I arrived at the ground. I tried the direct language method with the taxi driver, but it is not easy to act a cricket match, without becoming certifiable.

When I arrived, at two-ten for one-thirty, we had already lost four wickets. This was not on merit, as Weller explained to me later, because the last four in our order happened to reach the ground first. As I arrived eighth, I joined Weller, temporarily, on the fall of the sixth wicket.

'Jolly good of you to come,' he said shaking my hand and making me feel needed, even though I knew this was not so at all. I remained long enough for Tony Weller to reach 50 before I was dismissed for four, my highest score of the season. My dismissal was due to the unhappy combination of bad light, a mole in the pitch and poor umpiring. Tony Weller remained in a good mood. I thought this was because his was the highest score and he had taken a couple of cheap wickets before his tendon went, loudly like an old piano wire. Only later did I realize that he was always in a good mood.

'Please play again next week,' he said, as he limped off the field. 'We are bound to be short again.'

It was the sort of warm invitation which cannot be resisted.

I then played regularly for the Scorpions in 1963–64. Towards the end of that season, a member of the team told me that I was second in the batting averages, and I remained so until the last match, against a KCC side known as the Templars.

I can only assume that the Templars were as short of bowling as they were of fielding practice. I had always been a batsman with limited strokes, though difficult to dislodge. On this occasion I remained limited but the edges, which were responsible for most of my runs, worked well. I only remember being dropped six times in the field, so that my innings of 126 not out, was as nearly flawless as I was likely to get. This put me above Thompson, who passed to me a message from Weller that I should hit out before Weller declared. Naturally, I ignored this, as I had decided that it was more important that I should remain not out than that the Scorpions should win.

[The author remembers this episode very well. Buddy Carnell and I had tried our damndest to get Denys out, but the ball always found the edge of his bat, which he manoeuvered with only the slightest of movements. It was like bowling at a brick wall with certain embellishments which directed the ball away in different directions.]

Some years later, my attitude was amply confirmed by an act for which I shall never forgive the perpetrator.

I played, at the urgent request of Peter Davies, a solicitor who has since retired to Australia in spite of my prayers for his early and painful demise, for the Optimists, the other HKCC first division side. He first appealed to my sense of loyalty to HKCC. When this was unsuccessful, he promised me that I could both open the innings and bowl. I had not bowled all season, this being a skill which I had perfected but was little appreciated.

Our opponents were the Police, though the red mist which covers my recollection of the occasion has obscured the ground on which this atrocity took place. [HKCC – 22.11.70.]

I batted, with care and rare skill, from one-thirty to four-ten, I was then, thanks to lapses in the field by police officers who wanted to ensure their early promotion, 99 not out. I find it as difficult to believe as the reader, but Davies declared, without any warning that he intended to do so. I assumed that it was an act of personal malice, activated by some imagined slight, even though I could think of nothing which could possibly have justified such barbarity.

Davies attempted, as I hurled my bat through the changing room window, in what I thought to be a restrained manner, to justify his behaviour by arguing that he had to declare in order to be sure of dismissing the Police in time. The Police were all out 40 minutes before the close of play. I was not asked to bowl. I have my pride, battered though it may be. I have never played for the Optimists again.

It was before this tragic episode that John Leckie, who had been President of the Hongkong Cricket league for some years, telephoned me. 'Denys, old chap,' he began. This ought to have alerted me. Nobody calls me 'old chap' unless they want something from me. 'I am being posted by the Trade Development Council to Brussels next year.'

'That is disgraceful,' I replied, deciding that I ought to offer him some sympathy.

'Is it, really? he replied. 'Oh dear, well it is what I asked for, and I didn't ring you about that. It was about the Hongkong Cricket League. As you know, I am President of it.'

'What a splendid job you've done too.'

'Nice of you to say so. I have to find a successor.'

'Do you want me to give you some names? I can think of several men who would do the job admirably.'

'I want you to do it, if you are willing.'

'Why me? I've only been here about four years.'

'The Committee thought it was time we had a President who had some standing. You have just been appointed as Attorney-General.'

'That was an accident,' I yelped. 'I only got the job because I happened to be here and they didn't want to pass me over.'

'That may be, but you've got it.' Leckie showed a distressing reluctance to argue with me. 'So we'd be greatly honoured if you would become President. There's a meeting next week, at 5.30 in HKCC.'

'Yes, but ...'

'I expect you are full of ideas,' he concluded. I was. I was trying hard to think of reasons why I was an unsuitable appointment. I failed. Indeed, by the time of the first Cricket League meeting which I attended, I had persuaded myself that I was an inspired choice.

I occupied the position of President of the Hongkong Cricket league, from the mid-sixties when I succeeded George Rowe, on his retirement, at the HKCC. It was, in many ways, a desirable post, bringing with it a measure of prestige in the cricketing world, but little demand that anything should be done. During this somewhat barren period in the history of Hong Kong cricket, the leagues were re-organized, so that they took place on Saturday and Sunday. The high rate of divorce among cricketers from 1970 onwards shows that this was successful, as many husbands no longer went home at weekends.

Umpiring for the league was revised, so that, in all first division matches at least, independent qualified umpires would be available. It was thought that this would stifle criticism that the umpires were biased because they were provided by the batting side. Although the change was successful in this respect, it did not prevent the umpires from being told they were, if neutral, still blind, deaf, insensitive and impotent and ought to perform improper functions upon themselves.

It is greatly to the credit of the umpires' panel that, in spite of constant threats, they continued to stand. For this I should claim the major credit.

The Cricket League (later the Hong Kong Cricket Association – HKCA), also arranged for overseas tours to Singapore and Malaysia. They were a success, if judged by the percentage of players who disgraced themselves in various ways.

It was only later when Ted Wilson, secretary to the HK Telephone Company, with even less to do than me, took over as President, that other tours were arranged, to Sri Lanka, Australia and the UK.

In 1972, I handed the office of the President of the HKCA to Ted Wilson, as I thought that this would conflict with my assumption of a similar one in HKCC. In 1981, when Ted Wilson left, I resumed the HKCA presidency, as by then, after a couple of years on the bench, I was no longer pretending that a conflict of interest mattered.

The HKCA, however, before it invited me to succeed Ted Wilson, had ensured that I would not be able to do anything. The real work of the association was done by a Chairman who, with his committee, carried out its functions admirably. He consulted the President only when a problem was insoluble or when a course of action was so likely to arouse controversy that it would be useful to have someone else to blame. Under this system, I was re-elected to the post each year until shortly before I left Hong Kong in 1988.

I first became a member of the HKCC committees about 1965, when George Rowe had just become President. It was, at that time, extremely difficult to find anyone unwise enough to join it. There was seldom a contested election for the HKCC committee, as this was thought to be poor manners for a club of that kind. About 1970 there were three candidates for one vacancy. All withdrew, rather than lose face by being defeated, so that the committee was obliged to co-opt someone else to make up the numbers.

At my first meeting, I was asked to deal with the suggestions book, which was covered in badly scarred blue leather. I retrieved this from behind the bar. It had been thrown, by a disgruntled member, at the barman who had refused to serve him at two in the morning, shouting 'Bar close, no dlink,' at the protestor. The latter replied 'Bar open, plenty beer,' in a regional accent which the barman did not understand.

I looked carefully at the entries for the last year. More than half of them suggested that the committee should either resign, or that it should remain in office and carry out a range of perversions which I found disturbing. It was some months before I was able to relax with other committee men. I reported to George Rowe that nothing had been put in the book for some months. 'They put something in the book if they're angry. Usually they've forgotten about it the next day. If anyone follows it up, I say that we will appoint a sub-committee. So far that has shut them up.'

'Don't they ask how the sub-committee is getting on?'

'If they do, I say it's a very difficult and important matter. I've been a civil servant for nearly thirty years, and it always works there.'

A couple of years later, I discovered that there had been another reason for my appointment to the committee. It was wrongly thought that I might have some influence when sporting leases were granted.

HKCC did not own its own ground, although it had occupied most of the same area since 1851. It held the ground only on a 10-year lease, which was due to expire in 1971. A recent report had recommended that the lease should not be renewed, but that HKCC should be given an alternative area at Wong Nai Chung Gap, about three miles away from the centre of the city. This recommendation was due to come before the Executive Council, to which I had been appointed ex-officio in 1966. HKCC members assumed that I would ensure that the club's lease was renewed. When I received the Council papers, I saw that the adoption of the Report was recommended.

Before the paper was to be discussed, the Governor called me to his office. 'Have you read this sports lease report?' he asked me. 'Yes, I have, sir, and ...'

'I believe you are a member of the Hong Kong Cricket Club committee?'

'Well, yes, but ...'

'There's a lot in the Report about HKCC. Don't you think that you had better declare an interest and withdraw from the Council.'

'If you say so, sir.'

'I don't, you do. It's your decision. Just because some unofficial members remain and argue about things they're interested in is no reason why the official members should do the same. Don't you agree?' I did.

When the item was called upon for discussion, I declared my interest and left the chamber. When I returned, nobody would look at me, which I thought must mean that the Report had been approved. Some weeks later, HKCC was told that no new lease would be given to it of the ground in the centre of town, as this would be needed in future for a public purpose. In time, it was said, a park would be built there, open to all, whereas the present occupiers were a private club, composed mainly of expatriates.

I explained to the members, when an extraordinary meeting was called to discuss the Report, that I had not argued against it in Executive Council because I had been obliged to withdraw. Few believed me. It was generally thought that I had opposed the Report inadequately and that it was my fault that it had been accepted.

'As Roberts has let us all down,' commented one of the members, 'what are we going to do next? Do what the Report suggests and take up a new ground out of town, or just close down this club and go home?'

Largely due to George Rowe, who was firmly in favour of making the move, the decision was made to go to the new ground on the way to Repulse Bay. It was then a rough valley alongside a main road and would have to be levelled and turfed before it could be used.

A few months before he left in 1973, George Rowe, who had been President of HKCC for several years, spoke to me in the dressing room at the club. I was in an unusually happy mood, as I had achieved double figures for the second time that season, in only a dozen or so innings. 'I shall be retiring in a few months,' he began.

'I know that, George. I shall be happy to organize a collection for you, though I can't imagine who will contribute. Except perhaps Henderson, if you give him a long bowl.'

'It's not that,' George replied, rubbing another tranche of linament onto his thigh. 'I want to be sure that the club is in good hands, now that we have decided to move.'

'A good idea,' I agreed. 'Were you thinking of Armitage or Bliss? They've both been on the committee for years.' 'Armitage has just been posted to the Gulf, and Bliss shouted 'Over my dead body' and ran from the room when I asked him. So that leaves you as the next most senior member of the committee.' 'These posts should not go on seniority alone,' I protested, ignoring my years in the public service, in which this seemed to be the main principle at work.

'I knew you would see it my way,' George went on. 'You are the obvious choice for the job, apart from Armitage and Bliss, of course.'

It is difficult, in the face of such fierce enthusiasm, to refuse. I therefore found myself the successor to George Rowe as President of the HKCC, a post which I occupied until shortly before I left in 1988.

I was thus able, for about 15 years, to smile cheerfully at matters which I did not understand and leave the difficult problems to Bill Conway, the secretary/manager. It was his firmness and good humour which transformed the club.

As expected, the move from the old ground at Chater Road would not take place without difficulty. Halfway through the construction of the new clubhouse, it was suggested that an extra floor should be added, on what was supposed to be a flat and empty roof. Instead of walking out, as architects, quantity surveyors and builders might be expected to do anywhere else, if the time for completion was not extended, the building as redesigned was completed on time.

The playing area presented its own problems. An English consultant had been engaged, at a substantial fee, to advise on the best type of grass for the new ground. This had been firmed by filling in a ravine with soil taken from a nearby hill. It was admirable earth for the growing of weeds, thistles and wild flowers. The consultant had been chosen by someone else. I therefore felt that I could criticize him freely. This I did, on a visit to the Gap, early in 1975. The surface of the new ground, in one corner, was covered with green. At first I was delighted, until I discovered that the green was a patch of weeds, which would have to be removed. The rest of the ground was black, having been covered with Irish peat, excellent for growing potatoes, of which I found several. Here and there were a few struggling shoots of grass.

No doubt the advice of the consultant would have produced an admirable lawn of the English type at Blenheim Palace in 50 years or so. It was not of much help at the Gap, where we had to try to produce a playing surface in a few months. The grounds convenor, Alan Bailey, a man of resource, discovered a Chinese contractor who had been responsible for

488

putting down grass at the Fanling Golf Course. He was employed to dig up the turf at Chater Road and take it to the Gap. It was a rough kind of grass, which grew sideways rather than upwards, but it was durable and well adapted to local conditions.

For the first season, the drainage at the Gap was poor. Parts of the ground would dry fast, other parts, however, were waterlogged. This was dealt with by Alan Bailey, who prowled the ground during matches and knocked spikes into it whenever a damp patch was discovered. This crude method, which should have failed lamentably, was most successful. The Gap drains admirably, though Bailey, for many years, had to be restrained from running onto it with a handful of spikes whenever it rained.

After being President of the HKCC for about eight years, the members of the committee suggested that it would be sensible if, in future, the committee was presided over by a Chairman, who would run the club, so that I could become no more than a figurehead.

This was shortly after I had found myself in a minority of the committee in advocating the election of women as full members.

'He only wants them to be full members for immoral purposes,' whispered one member, who did not realize that even four years in the Royal Artillery had not ruined my hearing.

'Have you seen him watching the swimming pool with those binoculars?' replied another.

'Quite revolting when you think of his age too. He ought to be past that sort of thing.'

I was therefore suspicious of the real motive of the committee, in wanting to ensure that I was absent when something important was discussed.

I resorted to a device which I have found, after 40 years in the public service, to be invariably successful. I agreed with what was said, which, I added, was the result of careful thought and wise decision. I then continued to attend all meetings, as if the suggestion had not been made that I should do so. As usual, matters of importance were dealt with by Bill Conway, who reported them to the committee when he thought it would be useful to have its approval recorded. It also gave him someone else to blame in case things went wrong.

HKCC organized a series of tours to Manila. These were supposed to be justified by matches played against the Manila Nomads, a team which appeared to be composed mainly of expatriate non cricketers.

The matches were played on a ground borrowed for the day from the footballers. The pitch was 'sporting', which meant that it was unsafe, unreliable and unpredictable. Only abominable bowling and lax fielding could have ensured that the batting side reached 50, as it always did.

A few of the younger members, unfortunately, joined the Hong Kong visitors for other reasons. Some of them, shocking though this may be, were more interested in the local girls than in the cricket.

On the afternoon of my first, and I am glad to say only, visit to Manila, the visitors were asked to a tea party. Naturally, I put on the rather soiled suit which I had brought with me; I have never managed my food very well.

Soon after we arrived, and were sipping tea in the large salon where we had been met by some of our opponents, a dozen girls arrived, escorted by an older lady, who seemed to be in charge of them in some way.

I assumed that these were the wives, or perhaps the fiancees, of our opponents and chatted with one of them about the price of copper futures and the conduct of the Manila stock exchange. It was a rather one-sided conversation, but I did not mind that. She had a pleasant smile and nodded her head from time to time, which was all I required.

After a few minutes, the older lady, whom I later discovered was known as 'Big Annie', a tribute to her generous size rather than to her generosity, clapped her hands loudly. The girls excused themselves and disappeared. I asked a senior team member, who had been to Manila before, if they were likely to come back. He replied, with what in retrospect must have been a lascivious smile, that I had not seen the back of them yet.

As I was talking to him, the girls returned, wearing the sort of underclothing which is sometimes worn by women of ill virtue in the pornographic videos that, alas, I have been obliged in the past to watch as part of my duties as a prosecutor. I turned to express my horror to another member of the touring party. He was doing his best to pretend that he was not outraged by what he saw.

'I say,' I began. At this point, I noticed that a scantily dressed girl was standing at my elbow, wearing a garter belt and black undergarments.

I thrust my hands firmly into my pockets (those in the jacket of course) and talked about the best kind of flowers to plant in tropical climates in the spring, and the prospects for an economic revival in the Philippines. She did not seem to be well informed about either.

Big Annie again clapped her hands. I noticed that it took rather longer to remove the girls from the room, as some of the younger visitors seem to have taken advantage of the lack of clothing of the girls. Within minutes, the girls were back, this time wearing nothing but their high heeled shoes. It then dawned on me, for the first time, that this was not a respectable tea party, as I had imagined, but an entertainment arranged for us by our hosts. I did not, of course, want any of them to be upset and I did not wish to cross Big Annie, who was likely to be dangerous if roused. I was, however, much heartened by the conduct of some of the tourists, who left early with some of the girls, who had dressed before they left. I assume they were appalled at what they had seen and intended to escort the girls home to their families.

In 1964, I was asked by the Hongkong Cricket League if I would manage the team it intended to send to Singapore and Malaysia. This was still called the 'Interport' series, although Shanghai was no longer part of it, having been replaced by Kuala Lumpur. Although KL was around 30 miles from the sea, the name remained.

I suggested that it might be helpful, since the members of the touring party came from different clubs and probably did not know one another very well, to play a match in Bangkok, before proceeding on to Singapore and Malaysia. The proposal was greeted with reservation by the committee, but with much enthusiasm by the team themselves. When we boarded the plane to leave Bangkok, I realized why.

I had taken into Thailand 16 relatively fit young men. Some of them had performed well enough in our match at the Royal Bangkok Sports Club, the day after our arrival, others had difficulty in keeping awake in the field. When I enquired as to the reason for this lack of energy, I was told it was due to the bathhouses, although some of the team insisted that they had only visited them in order to get to know other members better, as I had instructed.

I decided to visit one of these bathhouses myself, only so that I would know what the others were talking about. There was a bath in my hotel room, but I was determined, for the sake of solidarity, to visit a communal place. I had last been to one in Wales, where there were few bathrooms at the time. It was full of miners singing bawdy songs. The Bangkok one was different.

When I arrived at the place recommended by the hotel, called the 'Most Excellent Bath Room', I was dismayed to find that I could only take my bath in company with a woman. I was obliged to select what was described as my 'bath hostess' from a line of women, dressed in black bikinis, sitting behind a glass panel. Each carried a soiled cardboard notice with a number. I selected number nine who appeared, from the welcoming way in which she looked at me, to be desperate for custom. I followed her to a bath cubicle, in which I took off my clothes, in some embarrassment, not only because she was present, but because of the condition of my underpants, and entered the bath.

I did not realize, until then, that I must have been dirty, as she scrubbed me vigorously with her soap and flannel back and front, including pieces of me that I did not often bother about. My bath hostess then offered me, for another 100 baht, what she described as a 'special massage.' It was only when she tried to cover me with oil that I realized what she meant. I replied, 'Unhand me, woman,' which was appropriate even if she didn't understand me, and walked from the cubicle.

[Many of the team were actually in the same bathhouse at the time, without realizing the manager was also present, until they heard his shout of – 'Unhand me, woman'!]

The team left Bangkok in poor shape. Most of them had been bathed a number of times. I had never seen them so clean, so friendly or in such poor physical shape. For the rest of the tour, they got on admirably together, so that my visit to Bangkok was more than vindicated, even if they were too exhausted to do anything effective for the first week.

Ted Wilson left Hong Kong in 1982, having stirred the HKCA from the torpor into which it had descended during my years as President. Before he left, he asked if I would succeed him as President. 'Why?' I asked. I had not done much the first time. I assumed that they wanted a period of inactivity after Wilson's energetic leadership. 'Because we want a name,' he replied. 'And you occupy a prestigious post.' 'It was my turn to be CJ,' I answered defensively.

'It's not as if you know anything about the game,' he went on. I thought this quite unmerited coming from the man who had made more runs with the cow shot, which he insisted on describing as the pull drive, than anyone else in the 1960s. 'So,' he went on, 'we have re-arranged the HKCA so that there is a working chairman, who will do all the work and send you copies of the minutes of the meetings. There is a President, who will do nothing much except attend the AGM's, congratulate everybody else on how well they have done, whether they have or not, and take the blame for things he never knew about. We thought you would be ideal for that.'

It is difficult to resist flattery, even when it is obvious what it is. I became President of the HKCA for the second time, though I was not allowed near anything important.

I tried, however, on one occasion, to show an independence of mind by insisting on attending a competition, in which Hong Kong took part, in Dacca, for a South-East Asia Cup. The other teams were supplied by Bangladesh, Malaysia and Singapore.

[Malaysia subsequently dropped out before the competition commenced, with Bangladesh then adding their under 25 team, the Bangladesh Tigers.]

I arrived in time to see the Hong Kong team beaten in the final by Bangladesh, in a crumbling stadium, which was full of spectators who were apparently more interested in cricket than in their own survival.

In addition, I was called upon to speak on numerous occasions, among which was the presentation of the cup at the ground; the dinner given to celebrate the victory of Bangladesh, which was planned some weeks before; the meeting of the competitors to arrange the next competition, and the reception given for the visiting teams by General Ershad. By the end of the tour, my slim stock of jokes was exhausted and members of the Hong Kong team only listened to see if I would say anything new.

Part of my leave in 1986 coincided with the World Cup for Associate Members, in which Hong Kong took part. I was able to arrange to see three matches, in each of which Hong Kong sustained heavy defeats. I was thanked for my presence, but it was suggested that Hong Kong might be more successful if I did something else.

I spent the remainder of my leave in 1986, sulking among my rhododendron bushes in Dorset. They did not bloom. Hong Kong did not lose again.

Shortly before I left Hong Kong in 1988, a young man who had just arrived asked me if I had had anything to do with cricket during my 25 years in the place. He had joined HKCC in order to play squash.

'I suppose I have,' I replied. 'I've been run out by Stuart Barnes several times; I caught typhoid from the bubble and squeak at the old club; I doubted the wisdom of moving here; I opposed the opening of the library at HKCC because I did not think there were many members who could read, and I voted for the admission of women as members.'

'You don't seem to have done much, then?'

'Maybe not,' I replied, 'but I have enjoyed playing and administering the game. I would not have missed it for anything.'

[The author had known Denys during the whole period of time he spent in Hong Kong, and apart from his wise counsel, his doggedness with the bat, recalled his extraordinary ability to render you helpless with side-splitting laughter whenever he made his after-dinner speeches, whether to cricketers at clubs or to the Institute of Engineers at the Peninsula Hotel. An era to savour and to be remembered.]

HKCC President's Reports [selected extracts]

'1983–84 contained an anniversary of some importance to the Club, being the centenary of the death of the only President of the MCC to die in office. It will be recalled that he expired in the Long Room after being told that the prices of both a new ball and a woman with her shine gone had been raised to eleven pence.'

'Like the wives of so many of our members, the ground has again responded cheerfully to the unreasonable demands made upon it. And as usual, having been worn out in one position, it performed just as well when turned sideways, in traditional oriental fashion.'

493

'A project to provide floodlighting for lawn bowls is under what public servants call "active consideration," which is the phrase used when you do not wish to do something but cannot think of any rational objections to it.'

'A hundred sun-loungers have been purchased for use at the poolside, where there is room for thirty. Your Committee hopes that this will encourage the atmosphere of personal hostility and sexual tension which members so value.'

'The old ground, convenient though its location was, had become little more than a traffic island, noisy, dirty and surrounded by tall buildings into which the ball merged when hit high. The facilities were simple and limited; the standard of food was similar to that provided for prisoners of war. The Club was regarded by many members as a convenient place for a simple, if inedible beer and good company. Children were locked into a primitive playground where a selection of rusty and lethal equipment ensured that they were unlikely to leave unscarred.'

'The members of our staff, of whom there are over a hundred, have continued to serve members with loyalty, courtesy and patience, often under pressure from those of us who always imagine that we are in a hurry for something, even if we have not discovered what.'

'The Club has continued to be a cheerful, friendly, active place, even if not providing the sort of environment which any decent member would care to introduce an unmarried daughter over the age of eleven.'

'It has been a pleasure to serve as President of the Club since November 1972. Now that my palsied hands are to be removed from the helm, it can be assured of a bright and successful future.'

Denys Roberts

E H Wilson, MBE

[Ted Wilson's contribution to Hong Kong Cricket in the wider sense]

When I landed at Kai Tak for the first time in early 1965, cricket was not uppermost in my mind. As things turned out, I couldn't have become more involved with cricket for the next 18 years, and it all started on the Saturday afternoon following my arrival.

After moving into the Mandarin Hotel, my family having been left temporarily in the UK, I wandered down the road to the old HKCC ground at Chater Road. The first thing I noticed was that the wicket-keeper was wearing the cap of the Kenya Kongonis, a club of which I was a member. This turned out to be John Townsend, the Scorpions captain. A few minutes later, one of the fielders recognised me on the boundary and came across with a warm greeting – this was Noel Hooper, with whom I had played a good deal of cricket in Uganda. Inevitably, I ended up in the HKCC bar drinking with the Scorpions and their opponents, and not long afterwards found myself a regular member of the team. Alec Pearce was President of HKCC and George Rowe, a senior figure who spurned league cricket, ran the 'Real Wanderers'. It was a club with a happy atmosphere and, being in the middle of town, was always busy.

My first away game at KCC was something of a disaster. We were knocking up on the outfield before the match, when Noel Hooper hit a screamer of a drive which hit me on the head with a most frightful crack. Collapse of Wilson, with shirt and flannels covered in blood and only just conscious. I sat in the casualty ward for hours waiting for the X-ray results, whilst a constant stream of unfortunates, who had been run over by a bus or jumped off a high-rise building, paraded before my bleary eyes. Eventually, it was decided there was no crack; a copious amount of bandage was wrapped around my head, and I returned to the KCC. Noel must have apologised, as I played tennis with him regularly for the next 18 years! I missed a game or two but recovered to enjoy my cricket that season and for many subsequent years. That first game in Kowloon did not allow me to get to know the many fine sportsmen who wore the KCC colours, but over the years I played with and against them, and always looked forward to participating in the friendly rivalry which existed between the two clubs.

The Scorpions did not win the league that season, and in fact had not done so for 13 years. I must have expressed the opinion, in too loud a voice, that I thought we had a good enough team to be champions; that we hadn't tried hard enough, etc. The eventual outcome was rather unexpected, in that I was appointed captain for the next season, and was told to get on with it and prove my point. We had an excellent opening attack, two useful spin bowlers, several capable batsmen and good fielders, and with great enthusiasm we finished on top of the league. The celebration party was quite memorable. I then decided, for business reasons, to resign the captaincy and handed over to John Fawcett, under whom the Scorps won again the next season and narrowly missed making it a hat-

495

trick. As it happened, the Scorpions did not win the league again for another 14 years!

I can relate one story which illustrates the excellent team spirit which existed within the Scorpions at that time and the tough captaincy of J Fawcett, known to all as 'Foxy'. We were playing the Police at Chater Road, batted first, and I was going rather well, having collected about 80, when I was joined by our tall opening bowler wearing his FF sweater. He seemed to be in good nick right from the start and was soon 30-odd, whereas I faced little of the bowling and hadn't reached 90. At the end of an over during which he had faced six balls and had taken a single off the last, I walked up the pitch and said: 'Julian, old boy, d'you think I could have some of the bowling – I'm on a ton here.' 'B***** you, Jack,' he replied, 'I'm on a 50.' He didn't get his 50, and Foxy declared when I was in the mid-90s.

A member of the team whose style I greatly admired was Tony Weller, whose speciality was driving the ball on the up, and while he was at the crease the scoreboard rattled merrily along. Tony played soccer as well as cricket for Hong Kong, and my admiration for him increased when I learned that his war, as a guest of the Japanese, was a good deal more unpleasant than for most of us.

In Hong Kong, it was the admirable practice for the home team to run a drinks chit on which teams, their wives and girlfriends, and a few other fortunate individuals, drank until the chit was closed by the captain, if he was still there and conscious. In theory, if each team contained players of equal capacity and habits, everything would even out financially over a season. In practice, of course, some teams contained several heavy drinkers, whereas others – although I cannot remember playing against them – had in their ranks three or four abstainers, or people who had to dash off home for domestic reasons. It would be quite uncharitable of me to name the 'early closers', but I can relate an almost libellous tale against the team for which I played for many years. Geoff Foster, of Optimists' fame, was heard to express the opinion that at Scorpions home matches, if you weren't out of the shower and into the bar 15 minutes after the end of the game, you were very likely to find the chit closed. Geoff was, however, prone to exaggeration, as I can distinctly remember on more than one occasion the Scorps' chit being open for almost half an hour.

[The author clearly recalled a match at Chater Road, when on reaching the bar the chit had already been closed. We (Templars) all ordered drinks and signed the chit 'John Fawcett'.]

Whilst on the subject of liquid refreshment, I must mention the splendid practice which existed in the league whereby bottles of whisky could be won by a batsman scoring 69 or more (VAT 69), and bowlers taking 5 wickets or more. On one occasion I enjoyed a partnership with Ivor Stanton, another stalwart of the league-winning side of 1966–67. We were playing the RAF at Kai Tak, and for some reason or other our regular scorer was absent. We did not expect applause from our team-mates for a half-century as this was of no importance, the magic number being 70, resulting in a bottle which would be shared by the team. After one shot of mine, there was enthusiastic applause from the dressing room, and I realised that I had been credited with reaching 70. Ivor was convinced that several of his runs had been credited to me by the RAF scorer and that the bottle of whisky should have been his. He may have been right, but this was of no consequence, as the bottle went 'behind the bar' for general consumption, it being severely frowned upon in most teams for a player to take his prize home.

One of the better batsmen who played for the Scorpions and the Colony in the late 1960s was Gerry Jarman. He was a stylish player, but unfortunately a person who upset a few people from time to time. Gerry played for Kenya during the time I played for Uganda, and I remember one occasion in Kampala when he came to the wicket wearing a bright red turban which he had borrowed from one of his Sikh team-mates.

On another occasion (March 1970), Gerry was playing at KCC for the Colony against prestigious visitors who included Geoffrey Boycott. Conditions were very wet, but the visitors agreed to play so long as they could bat first. The outfield was slow, and no quick singles were taken as the square was quite slippery and the scoring rate was far from exciting. Crossing between overs, Gerry remarked in a voice sufficiently loud for the England openers to hear, that this was a pretty poor performance by Test batsmen against the Colony bowling. This comment, needless to say, led to a large not out score from Mr Boycott.

I never scored a century in Hong Kong, unlike Lord Bramall – then Sir Edwin, Commander of British Forces in the Colony – who went into the history books as the last batsman to score a hundred in a league match at the old Chater Road ground. Sir Edwin was a very keen and good cricketer (full Army cap) and played whenever he could and supported the Cricket Association in many ways. In later years, both he and Sir Denys Roberts became Presidents of MCC.

Sir Denys built up a reputation as the slowest bowler in S-E Asia, and his batting was greatly admired by the purists. Many is the time I have enjoyed his company and humour on and off the field. One of his bowling performances, however, requires to be recorded for posterity. We were on tour in North America with the Mandarins and were playing NCCA Presi-

497

dent's XI at Saratoga. I was captaining the side that day, and as I have the scorebook in my possession, can quote accurate bowling analyses figures. Smith, Ebrahim, Fletcher and Barnett had each had a few quiet overs when I brought on D Roberts to bowl to a new batsman. His first over cost 22 runs. I have always thought it harsh of a skipper to take a bowler off after one over. Denys's second over was slightly more expensive – 24 runs. He did, however, take a wicket, so continued with a third over, which cost a further 20 runs. At this stage I suggested to him that he might like a rest, but he said he thought he had the batsmen worried, so I left him on. The fourth over cost another 22 runs, and he packed it in with the analysis – 4 overs, no maidens, 88 runs and one wicket. We later discovered that the batsman doing the damage was a Ceylon international, who had been recruited at the last minute. He retired with 109, including 15 sixes. Mel Pulford had to bring in extra supplies of liquid refreshment to revive both bowler and captain.

In the late 1960s, it was considered by the HKCA that the Saturday league, with its short playing hours, afforded inadequate preparation for the bigger games – in particular the Interports. Hong Kong was an exceptionally busy place, and the five-day week was unheard of. To leave work at 1.00 p.m. on Saturday meant an inevitable rush, and the light was inadequate for play after 6.30 p.m. A long innings, except for a few people at the top of the order, was seldom possible.

The experimental solution was the Gillette Cup or Super League, to be played on Sundays and involving the following four teams:

Hong Kong Cricket Club
Kowloon (KCC & Recreio)
Valley (CCC, IRC, LSW, & PRC)
Combined Services (Army, Navy & RAF)

I much enjoyed captaining HKCC when winning the Super League in its first year 1967–68. This was an exceptional year for HKCC cricket, as Optimists were runners-up to Scorpions and Nomads joint champions of the second division.

The experimental Super League did not last long. It was then decided to replace the first and second division leagues with separate Saturday and Sunday leagues, which format has continued until the present day. As to whether or not these changes led to better performances by the Colony team may be judged by results which are recorded elsewhere in this book. What was rather surprising for me personally, was to be selected to play for Hong Kong in 1968 (with no relatives on the Selection Committee) against Joe Lister's International Touring XI. This team included such stars as Dennis Amiss, Geoff Arnold, Mike Denness, Keith Fletcher, Harold Rhodes, Micky Stewart, Derek Underwood and other well-known players. To play against Test bowlers such as this team possessed was, to say the least, interesting, and of course we were heavily defeated.

It was in this game that I had what air traffic controllers call a near miss. The bowler concerned was Geoff Arnold, of Surrey and England, who had a reputation for being not only fast, but also very aggressive. After rapping me on the pads and getting his animated appeal turned down, Geoff snarled and I prepared myself for the worst. With my mind in turmoil, up rushed the angry Mr Arnold, bowled the inevitable bouncer, and I instinctively tried to hook! What I remember to this day is a bright red flash about an inch from my eyes as the ball flew past to the keeper standing somewhere near the boundary. A near miss indeed! Geoff was also displeased when Jalu Shroff smiled down the wicket after scoring a top-edged four off another bouncer.

Then came along the next Interport matches, with Hong Kong due to travel to Malaysia and Singapore. I was appointed as Player/Manager, and was heavily involved in preparations for the tour, administratively and otherwise. This involved strenuous physical training under the eagle eye of Brian Wigley, a well-known Police cricketer and fitness expert. Running round the KCC ground several times and finishing with 20 or 30 press-ups was, at my age, rather a strain but, I was pleased to note, not more so than for several of the younger players. Bearing in mind the climatic conditions in which we would play, I have no doubt that such training pays dividends, but I can't say I enjoyed it.

We visited several pleasant places in Malaysia, and in Malacca, Ian Vaughan-Arbuckle and I were fortunate to be billetted with the Manager of the Hongkong Bank. Needless to say, this was a magnificent house right on the beach, but I found great interest in the hobby of the lady of the house, who was an expert in growing orchids. Seldom have I seen such a superb show of flowers, and the house was full of them.

I played in the Interport at Kuala Lumpur, but contributed very little. The heat and humidity were quite exhausting, even though I had played in Uganda on the equator for many years. One memory I have of this match concerns Julian Murphy, the tall Scorpions fast bowler. Julian was unfortunate to have developed a boil in an awkward place and was unfit to play, but sufficiently well to participate in the social rounds. He had somehow made the acquaintance of the daughter of the British High Commissioner, and while we were sweating it out in the nets the evening before the Interport, Julian rode past with his lady friend in her father's Rolls, waving in the Royal manner and smiling broadly at the troops working their fingers to the bone. The match was drawn due to rain.

I clearly remember Carl Myatt bowling his heart out in Singapore and requiring treatment for dehydration. The humidity seemed to come out of the ground and hit you – some said it was worse when the tide came in.

The touring side included the Lalchandani brothers, Ram and Gopal. They were both fine cricketers, but of very different temperaments – Ram the quiet and steady fellow, and Gopal the extrovert with the low sports car and other trimmings. One evening in Singapore we visited the famous Raffles Hotel where, sitting in the garden sipping our fruit juice, we watched an artistic shadow show with the dancing girls behind a large screen. During one of the between-show periods, the lights came on behind the screen and the outline of a slim male figure started gyrating and removing items of his clothing. After his shirt had been divested, authority stepped in and the impromptu show came to an end. This was Gopal's way of relaxing after a strenuous day's cricket.

Having attended ICC meetings at Lord's and befriended representatives from various cricketing countries, I felt that Hong Kong should widen its experience and visit parts of the globe other than Malaysia and Singapore. The HKCA Committee agreed, and during the next tour, for which I was Manager, we visited Sabah after matches in Singapore and Sri Lanka.

A special memory of the Sri Lankan tour was to find that one of our games in Colombo clashed with an annual fixture between the two top schools. We were invited to attend on the first day and found a huge crowd and a Test-match atmosphere. This was a real training ground for young cricketers. We played in Colombo the next day, but our match was relatively unimportant and only a handful of spectators came to watch.

The Sri Lankans were wonderful hosts. I had been told that they found it extremely difficult to obtain cricket gear, so we took along extra bats and pads and left them there. We presented a bat to a 17-year-old who scored a century against us, and one would have thought that we had given him a sackful of gold. At one stage of the tour, Jalu Shroff and I were housed with a tea estate manager in a really beautiful part of the country.

Not all tours by cricketers from Hong Kong are as serious as those undertaken by Colony teams. Others, properly categorised as social, took place from time to time. One year, I went on the first HKCC tour to Japan. After Geoff Foster and I had helped to land the jumbo jet at Tokyo in a severe storm, I found myself billetted, along with Mike Duggan and Jim Hughes, at the British Embassy, a smaller version of Buckingham Palace. Her Majesty's Ambassador lent us a Rolls to go to Yokohama for one game.

I understand KCC had no difficulty in finding suitable teams to visit Bangkok; and Graham Fletcher and his civil service colleagues much enjoyed visiting up-country Thailand.

Tourist statistics show that 65% of visitors to Thailand are male, and this figure rises to 80% in respect of the Philippines. I have heard that Tunisia is a popular venue for German lady hockey teams. I have no idea if all this has much to do with sex which, to quote from the famous Forty Club dinner speech, is now for me merely a Latin numeral, but it occurred to me in my early Hong Kong days that my education would be enhanced by joining in a social cricket tour to one of the exotic neighbouring countries.

I was therefore delighted when Guy Pritchard, an experienced Colony and Optimists player and well-travelled businessman, organised an HKCC visit to the Philippines to play the Manila Nomads, and kindly invited me to participate. I had never been to the Philippines and didn't quite know what to expect, particularly as I was told that the Nomads' field was the only cricket ground in the country. The weekend was a delightful experience, involving canoeing down some rapids with Chris Shaw, evening musical gatherings with Laurie Roberts ensuring that we only listened to the right composers, and various other 'cultural' activities. The captain was generous with his advice, based on many business visits to Manila, and we even played some cricket. I made subsequent tours to Manila after that first pioneering trip and played against the Nomads on their reciprocal visits to the HKCC, but eventually retired on the grounds that I could no longer keep up with the pace required. My bowling, you understand.

The closing ceremony of the Chater Road ground in 1975 was one of the saddest cricket occasions I can remember, but it was inevitable, and the new club at Wong Nai Chung Gap, with all its facilities and family atmosphere, was a big improvement in so many ways. The appearance of the Australian All-Stars for the closure of the old HKCC ground was quite memorable for all who were there. Never in my wildest dreams had I imagined that I would captain a side containing half a dozen famous Aussie Test players, but it happened, thanks to Cathay Pacific and in particular Keith Sillett. The master-stroke by Cathay was to include in the party three old cricketing greats – Bert Oldfield, Clarrie Grimmett and Harold Larwood. How marvellous it was to hear these three chatting about the old days.

As the light faded after the final match, the Army beat the retreat and the Union Jack was slowly lowered in the far corner of the ground. Thus had almost 150 years of cricket on that particular piece of turf ended. There was scarcely a dry eye amongst those present.

In the late 1970s, the ICC approved the idea of a competition for Associate Members – i.e. about 16 non-Test playing countries. The prime mover was John Gardiner who, although not American, represented the USA at that time. John, with whom I had been on Forty Club tours in Europe, presented a handsome trophy and took on most of the administration himself. Unfortunately for Hong Kong, when the regulations were published, we found that the residential rule meant that about half the current Colony team would not be eligible. This posed a difficult problem for the HKCA Committee which decided, rightly or wrongly, that they should not enter the competition unless they could take their best side. ICC, understandably, said the rules could not be bent to accommodate Hong Kong, so we did not participate in the competition which was held in the English Midlands in 1979.

The Colony players and others, including myself, were very disappointed and, as funds had been promised, an alternative tour was then planned to a country where, although the cricket would be tough, it would further broaden our overall experience. As a result, we went to Western Australia and had some excellent cricket, with Carl Myatt as usual doing a great job as skipper.

Also in the 1970s, I had an ambition as HKCA President for Hong Kong to play at the headquarters of cricket. I had played at Lord's myself and had never forgotten the experience, and to see the Colony team walk through the Long Room and down those famous steps on to the hallowed turf seemed a worthwhile aim. I had a few friends at court in the UK and wrote many letters. The usual splendid team worked hard in Hong Kong to raise the necessary funds, and the cricket-loving Taipans were generous, as usual.

The result was a tour itinerary to England in 1976 which included games against the Army, RAF, and other excellent fixtures, but the big occasion was to play MCC at Lord's. The day dawned bright and sunny, and there was a special buzz of excitement as our coach neared the most famous cricket ground in the world. The MCC did Hong Kong proud with such renowned players as Colin Cowdrey (Captain), Ted Dexter, M J K Smith, Alan Smith and Eric Russell turning out. They also included our own John Fawcett, a member of MCC who had retired from Hong Kong some years earlier. Carl Myatt won the toss and elected to field. The full scorecard of this historic match is included elsewhere in this book, but I must refer to Carl's noteworthy feat of having Dexter caught and bowled for 0, and finishing up with 4 wickets for 73 runs. MCC kindly put on a cocktail party at Lord's afterwards, which was a very pleasant occasion attended by many friends and supporters of Hong Kong cricket, a fitting end to a memorable day for Colony cricket.

502

Later in the decade, we toured South-Eastern Australia, playing in Melbourne, Sydney, Canberra and up-country towns. This party included two real workers for Hong Kong cricket – Bryan Hemshall (Manager Administration) and Brian Wigley (Manager Cricket) – and both did a superb job. Peter Anderson was captain, and he served the Colony very well, both on and off the field. As I write, Peter is the Chief Executive of Somerset CCC.

It has been said that we in Hong Kong did not do enough to encourage schools cricket and coaching in general, and it is a fact that in my time there were very few professional coaches engaged to lift the general standard of play. Although we had several enquiries over the years, it was always difficult to find enough keenness, and therefore money, for the engagement of professional coaches from overseas. There were exceptions, of course, and I recall no less a person than Geoffrey Boycott coaching a bunch of schoolboys at HKCC and KCC in ever-worsening weather conditions, ending the sessions in his raincoat, so determined was he, and his pupils, to finish these courses.

Hong Kong has, over the years, had a few very keen schoolmaster-cricketers who have done a splendid job, but cricket was not a game which really appealed to the Chinese. In an effort to encourage the boys, I presented a cup for competition between the schools, and I am pleased to say that the Ted Wilson Trophy matches were always played with great keenness and continue to this day. Whilst we cannot claim a stream of prospective first-class players emanating from the schools, we can be proud of what Dermot Reeve has achieved.

During my time as HKCA President, we had tremendous support from several people who held top positions in business and showed their enthu-siasm for cricket in the most practical way. A reasoned request for funds to support tours or visits invariably resulted in a favourable response. Mike Sandberg and Peter Williams were two examples of supportive Taipans. They were not only initiators of cheques, but were real cricket fans, attending matches and the Association dinners and prize-presenta-tions. Ruttonjee's Shroff brothers were also great supporters, as were senior executives of Cathay Pacific, where Keith Sillett was a tower of strength on numerous occasions – and no mean player on the field himself. Hatim Ebrahim and Ian Stevens were fine cricketers and brought support from their respective companies, Essabhoy Ebrahim (HK) Ltd and Caldbeck Macgregor. I always regarded Hongkong Land as a rugby company, but Peter Hall was their company secretary and they contributed regularly to cricket. Rothman's and Gillette were, of course, very much involved, as in other parts of the world, and Ian Gow for Rothman's and

Leslie Stokes for Gillette were keen supporters and regular presenters of our knock-out trophies. Many other firms and individuals have contributed to the well-being of Hong Kong cricket and the HKCA's grateful appreciation is recorded in the annual handbook.

Umpiring is, as we all know, a vital part of our great game. Poor umpiring can spoil a match, but in all the cricket I have played in various parts of the world (over 30 countries!), I can remember very few instances of a deliberately bad or prejudiced decision. Umpires are only human and like players make mistakes, but on the whole they do a fine job, and seldom receive adequate thanks.

We were fortunate in Hong Kong to have a well-run Umpires Panel and a number of keen and competent officials. During my early playing days in the Colony I remember having full confidence in Bert Mellowes and Wally Hampton, to name but two. Jangu Vachha's name is commemorated by his memorial trophy awarded to the 'Umpire of the Year', and the list of winners contains the names of some splendid umpires who not only stood, week in week out, but also contributed by organising the work of the Panel.

I have a story from my own – very limited – umpiring experiences. This involved a Mandarin match on the Test ground at Port Elizabeth, South Africa. The home team were fielding and an off-spinner who was bowling from my end, something of a master of his craft, bowled one which turned and kept very low, hitting the batsman just above the boot playing back. There was a strong appeal by bowler and keeper, but I gave 'not out', being of the opinion that the ball would have missed the leg stump. As I handed the bowler his cap at the end of the over he asked: 'Was that one too low?' I was stumped for an immediate reply, as it was rather like being asked, 'Have you stopped beating your wife?' After the game we had a beer together and, having had time to meditate, told him that it had been too low, but only just. I hope he was satisfied.

As I said earlier, cricket so far has not appealed to many Chinese, but there are exceptions to the rule, and it was very encouraging to see several with potential. During my time in Hong Kong we saw the development of one very useful Chinese all-rounder, who eventually became a regular in the Colony team. Benny Kwong was the son of the groundsman at Chater Road; as a youngster he was always on the field, involved with the nets and preparation of the wickets etc., and soon got a feel for a cricket ball. He became a very useful leg-break and googly bowler at the nets, was a splendid fielder with a strong throw, and batted pretty well. He graduated to the Scorpions and made a useful contribution over many years. As a fielder he was in the mould of Derek Randall or Colin Bland at cover point, but it was his bowling which really impressed.

At Chater Road in March 1975 Benny clean-bowled an England Test player, who shall be nameless, but he is presently Chief Executive of the TCCB. MCC were batting, and our distinguished visitor played two leg-breaks then shouldered arms to what he thought was a third, only too late to see the googly knock off his leg bail. Drinks all round!

Benny himself became head groundsman at the new HKCC ground and continued to play. After I left Hong Kong I learned that he was suffering from a serious illness. However, the Club had a worldwide whip-around, and members past and present contributed handsomely. Benny was able to have a major operation and made an excellent recovery, and is now helping to coach the first Hong Kong All-Chinese cricket squad.

In the late 1970s, I decided to form a cricket side of friends who, whilst having a fair idea of how to handle a bat and/or ball, had contributed to Hong Kong cricket in one way or another, and would be primarily selected for this reason. This team would tour to parts of the world whose people were not specifically known for their cricketing skills, but which I knew to be hospitable and would welcome such a side. Too many people met my requirements, but eventually I ended up with 14 players and a tour itinerary which started in Honolulu and ended in Hollywood, taking in Vancouver, San Francisco and various other places in California.

Carl Myatt and Peter Davies agreed to be joint captains; Bill Conway, the hard-working Secretary-Manager of HKCC and Graham Fletcher who, apart from his ferocious bowling, did such a fine job as HKCA statistician, agreed jointly to handle the managerial duties. The rest of the party included Hatim Ebrahim, Arthur Barnett, Noel Hooper, Terry Smith, Jim Hughes, Martin Lewis, Buji Dhabher, Fahmy Jowharsha and Denys Roberts. I went along as Officer I/C Discipline, but took my kit. [The author was invited but couldn't get leave.]

Thus the Hong Kong Mandarins was born. We had a most enjoyable tour in 1980, so much so that it was decided to repeat the exercise every three or four years.

Peter Davies, that scorer of a vast number of runs, took over as chief organiser after I left Hong Kong, and set about arranging a most interesting tour to South America in 1983, which included games in Peru, Brazil, Argentina and Chile. Several wives, including my wife Edith, were included in the party which, apart from the cricket, visited many fascinating places such as the Inca ruins at Macchu Picchu and the Iguacu Falls.

In 1987, the Mandarins went to South Africa, a country which at that time was re-emerging from the sporting wilderness. We played in Jo'burg, Cape Town, Port Elizabeth and Durban, travelled on the Blue Train (on which our captain and his wife Lesley entertained us at a cocktail party in his luxurious accommodation), visited a game park, did the Garden Route and met with tremendous hospitality everywhere.

In 1990, Peter organised a tour to New Zealand, starting with a game in Sydney against ex-Hong Kong cricketers living there. Edith and I had visited New Zealand a quarter of a century earlier, and we found it to be the same friendly and beautiful country. The cricket in both Islands was most enjoyable, and the Mandarins managed to hold their own on and off the field. One pleasurable event during this tour was to meet up in Auckland with Buddy Carnell, the stalwart ex-Colony and KCC fast bowler. Buddy and Peta had settled in New Zealand, and we had a most enjoyable chat about old times whilst watching the Mandarins play on the second ground at Eden Park, after which we were shown round its magnificent new facilities.

A fifth tour was organised for 1993 with games scheduled in England, Denmark, Belgium and Holland, but did not materialise. It is unlikely that further tours will take place, so the history of the Mandarins covered one decade only, but included four memorable tours, thanks largely to the administrative and organisational skills of Peter Davies.

In the late 1960s, I started to contribute regular articles to *The Cricketer*, the UK publication which claims to be the most widely read cricket magazine in the world. Hong Kong was, of course, already well known as a place for cricketers to visit, and touring teams were always welcome. I felt that publicity in such a magazine could do no harm.

I wrote monthly articles during the Hong Kong season under the nom-de-plume 'Chinaman'. I am not sure why, but after several years the articles appeared under my own name, and were included in the 'Round the World' section, which then featured cricket in many interesting and out-of-the-way places. My contributions were far from being literary masterpieces, but I trust they helped to keep Hong Kong cricket on the world map, and I have met at least two people who said they found them interesting.

On the subject of the written word, may I here pay a tribute to Carl Myatt who, for many years as a sports journalist as well as a Colony player, made a considerable contribution to Hong Kong cricket. His comments were invariably interesting and fair, and I always felt that we were fortunate to have such a knowledgeable person writing about the local game.

An innovation during my HKCA presidency was live broadcasting of cricket matches. After relinquishing the captaincy of Uganda, I had regularly broadcast a commentary on the big matches there, and in the early 1970s, persuaded the relevant authorities in Hong Kong to 'give it a go' on Radio Hong Kong. The first occasion was for the visit of an MCC side playing at Chater Road. Later radio commentaries were made from time

506

to time by Kit Cumings, another ex-Colony player, but it appears that the small listening audience did not warrant the expense involved, and the broadcasts ceased.

Anyone who has had experience of the office of team selector knows full well that it is impossible to please everyone. To be Chairman of Selectors is not a job which one would normally wish to hold on to for very long as, for example, Ted Dexter found in England in recent years. However, the author of this book held that post for 14 years until his retirement from Hong Kong in early 1990 and did a fine job without, so far as I know, ever receiving life-threatening letters.

I served on the HKCA Selection Committee for several years and did not experience a great deal of acrimony. We always tried to pick a balanced side and on the whole the results were not too disastrous. As with most team selections, it is relatively easy to select the first eight or nine players, but often difficult to agree on the last two or three. May I wish selectors, of whatever sport and wherever they may serve, the very best of luck. Normally they need it.

For many years Hong Kong has been a very popular venue for visiting cricket teams. Although the grounds are very small and the pitches not what the professionals in particular are used to, the off-the-field facilities must be as good and as interesting as most places, for the Association was never without a list of requests from prospective tourists from various parts of the world.

This book will include the details of many visits, but during my time in the Colony we enjoyed hosting a huge variety of sides, including the full England Test team, the Australian All-Stars, MCC, Derrick Robin's XI, Hyderabad Blues, Club Cricket Conference, Midlands Club Cricket Conference and many others, not forgetting a team of enthusiasts from a pub in Somerset. I met this last-named bunch at the HKCC and found them sufficiently keen to be having a net. I spoke to one fine fellow, who had brought the party from Taunton to Heathrow. He said he was not really a cricketer, but having arrived at London Airport decided that he would like to do the rest of the trip, and there he was padding up in the fading light thoroughly enjoying himself.

The England team visited Hong Kong in 1966 on their way back from Australasia. I like to think, but can't be sure, that I had something to do with influencing MCC to allow the Test team to call in at Hong Kong on their way home. In any event they duly arrived, with two people I knew well as Captain and Manager. Both Mike (M J K) Smith and Billy Griffith had been members of the MCC side which visited East Africa in 1957–58, and I had played against them, both in Kenya and Uganda.

During this MCC visit to Hong Kong, a golf day at Shek-O was organised, and I played in a four-ball with Mike, Colin Cowdrey and Michael Melford of the *Daily Telegraph*. I have always found a round of golf to be particularly enjoyable when playing with cricketers or ex-cricketers, and this game was no exception.

The cricket was rain-affected, but I remember an inevitable century in Kowloon by Geoff Boycott, splendid knocks by David Coffey and Peter Hall for Hong Kong, and a top-class short fast-bowling spell from Jeff Jones to win the game for the visitors.

I left Hong Kong in February 1982, and in 1985 somewhat unexpectedly became involved in the organising and fund-raising for an Oxbridge tour to Australia. Rather naturally I suggested that the boys would benefit enormously if they took in Hong Kong on their way to Oz. This was agreed and I was delighted to accompany the team to Hong Kong, along with Mike Smith, who was then the OUCC President. Matches were played at HKCC and KCC, and a good time was had by all.

In 1980, it was announced from Lord's that the HKCA President, Ted Wilson, had been elected an Honorary Life Member of MCC. Ted said:

I am of course delighted to have joined a list of people who have made a tremendous contribution to our great game in many parts of the world, but apart from the personal angle I regard this as an honour for the Association and cricket generally in Hong Kong.

[The author has known Ted and Edith for many years and asked Ted, with his wide experience, if he would kindly put some of his past Hong Kong-related cricketing thoughts down on paper for posterity, and also for cricket lovers everywhere to read about and also reminisce – many thanks, Ted.]

RECORDS AND STATISTICS

Unfortunately for Hong Kong cricket there was only one George Lemay, the designer of the all-enveloping scorebook used by all clubs and by the HKCA for representative matches, which has recently been updated. The original was designed in August 1966 by the late G A Lemay and drawn by W H Tung for the HKCC.

George scored for the HKCC and for Hong Kong, but his life's work was his monumental special edition: HKCC 1st Division League Records 1948–1968, listing all persons who played for the HKCC 'Scorpions' and 'Optimists' during this period, with their complete statistical analyses. I managed to borrow a copy from Charles Rowe, son of the late George Rowe. Both father and son played for Hong Kong.

The Pacific war destroyed most clubs' cricket records, and Hong Kong's postwar lifestyle has not helped, as there was no continuity in HKCA personnel, a vital ingredient for the creation and safe-keeping of archives.

The statistics for the Hong Kong v Shanghai Interports from 1866 up to and including 1936 were extracted from Arnold Graham's typed Record book. The information for the two postwar matches in 1947 and 1948 were obtained from the Hong Kong Public Records Office and Nina Pearce (widow of Alec Pearce) respectively. Most of the Hong Kong v The Straits & Malaya pre the Pacific war from 1890, were obtained by the author personally researching the microfilmed old Hong Kong newspapers lodged at the British Library in North London. The postwar Interport scores up to the final match at the Singapore Cricket Club in May 1987 were obtained by various other means.

The Hongkong Cricket League committee started including the previous season's statistics in their handbooks from the 1966–67 season. The amount of information contained therein varied from time to time. Prior to this, postwar, the slim handbooks recorded only the names of the committee, the fixtures for the season, and the laws of cricket. Before the Pacific war, such sophistication, according to a reliable source, did not exist.

Statistics for the ICC, S-E Asian Tournament, the Volvo and Tuanku Ja'afar Trophy competitions have been obtained from the Association's scorebooks and newspaper articles, except Hong Kong's record at the 1990 ICC Competition in Holland, which the author obtained from the Nederlandse Cricket Bond.

509

Certain inaccuracies were discovered in the newspaper articles and handbooks. The figures have been incorporated as printed, for without the original team scoresheets it has not been possible to verify them. Very frustrating at times, as the author tried to marry up the batting totals with the bowling analyses, now not possible without the detailed breakdown of extras, as wides and no-balls are added to penalise the bowler. In a venture of this magnitude attempted by one person, there are bound to be some other inaccuracies and omissions, the author's responsibility entirely.

By calling up old friends and others connected with Hong Kong cricket and badgering them, by delving wherever there might be some information, but mainly by perseverance, I have collated the records, made my comments and compiled the statistics. I hope the reader will find them interesting and informative, which might be sipped when rain or bad light have stopped play or whenever cricketers past and present gather together for whatever reason.

Finally, rather than include a mass of statistical data at the end of the book, the usual format, the author considered it more appropriate to include statistics at the end of each relevant section – as the head is attached to the body.

CONCLUSION – THE FUTURE

By June 1997, after an association of over 150 years, the hugely important element of Services cricket will be no more, while its ancillary benefits to Hong Kong cricket in the form of grounds will be a negotiable commodity.

The HKCA, led by hard working and dedicated officials, continues to progress its rolling four-year development programme begun in 1991. The Saturday and Sunday cricket leagues are still flourishing numerically; touring teams are still jamming the calendar, and the local 'Dragons' team, which started participating in league cricket from the 1994–95 season, is now affiliated to the KCC.

The two premier clubs, the HKCC and the KCC, have both had their private recreational leases extended to 2008 and 2011 respectively.

Hong Kong, together with Bangladesh, Malaysia and Singapore (all Associate Members of the ICC) and, hopefully, Thailand in the near future, play an important role in the East Asian region in the promotion of cricket (S-E Asian and Tuanku Ja'afar tournaments), and collectively the present four form a crucial segment of the ICC Associate World Cup matches every four years.

Cricket has been played in China since the 1860s, albeit mainly by the foreign residents carrying on business at the time. More recently, successful tours to Beijing and Shanghai have been undertaken by St George's CC and Craigengower CC. So China is not unaware of this 'strange' game which has been played on its doorstep for many years, even though its own people are rarely seen to participate.

The appointment of John Hung, an Eurasian born in Hong Kong, as President of the HKCA, brought a former Hong Kong representative cricketer and the first Chinese-speaking person to this important post. With his many business (as a director of Wharf Holdings and Wheelocks) and sporting connections and his good standing in the community, it was hoped that John could help the HKCA successfully through its forthcoming difficult years during Hong Kong's transition from being a British governed territory to that of a Special Administrative Region of China after June 1997.

In a 1994 interview, John pinpointed two basic factors on which the future of the game in Hong Kong depended:

511

(a) Only through mass popular support will we convince the Hong Kong Administration to back cricket with the preservation of cricket grounds we need.
(b) Cricket must, therefore, be taken into local schools if we are to get the necessary groundswell of support needed.

John's suggestion was firstly to introduce cricket sixes into schools, sponsored by the HKCA, as a full day's cricket would not initially attract the locals. Later, when interest and enthusiasm had developed, the proper game could be advanced. John also stressed that the HKCA must not lose sight of the fact that the active participation of expatriate players, who had kept the game alive over the years, was likewise very important.

My belief is that the development of cricket must involve nurturing home-grown players and expatriates at the same time. This can be done. After all, wouldn't it just be 'One Country, Two Systems' under a new guise?

July 1997 is barely three years away. However, with the will and dedication of those who understand the intricacies of this complex issue, and the right support, I am confident that the game of cricket can continue through 1997 to 2047, and beyond.

John T Hung, President, Hong Kong Cricket Association, June 1994

On 30 June 1997, the British Colony of Hong Kong, part of which [Hong Kong Island] was ceded to the United Kingdom in perpetuity on 26 January 1841, was officially handed back to China amid much ceremony and pouring rain. Since that auspicious date, cricket has continued to flourish and expand in Hong Kong, now a Special Administrative Region of China.

In the short time since the Development Programme was implemented [1994], it has produced significant changes in the direction and quality of Hong Kong cricket, with a range of locally funded and sponsored initiatives serving to broaden and enhance local cricket, particularly at 'grass roots' level, the level from which the sport's future will grow.
The number of locally-based cricket coaches seeking internationally recognised coaching accreditation more than doubled in 1996 (up to 70, from 33 in 1995); while at the helm of youth development, the Brierley International Ltd's sponsored Hong Kong under-18's won

the coveted Tuanka Ja'afar Under-18 Cup (this side included six Under-18 'Dragons').

Concurrent with the strengthening of the infrastructure and future of our local cricket, there has been a push to increase the overall cricket strength of the greater Asian region, thereby increasing our access to affordable international competition; and to particularly develop cricket awareness and participation in China. To this end, The Hong Kong Cricket Association has initiated appropriate relationships with Chinese sporting organisations and in 1996 assisted Chinese cricket with pitch technology and general development.

MCC Tour to Hong Kong Brochure, March 1997

Hong Kong was recently represented at the Beijing Sixes tournament [September 1997]. Entries had also been received from Australia, England, Japan, Korea, Spain and South Africa.

The big problem is the lack of cricket grounds. The HKCA has approached Government in order to retain or replace open areas lost, principally due to the evacuation of the British Forces from Hong Kong.

The procedure requires a number of steps and is time consuming. Firstly, the policy has to be agreed and then the right sites have to be properly zoned in land use terms by the Planning Department and then the site, once zoned, has to be allocated by the Lands Department, in the urban area to the Urban Services Department or in the New Territories to the Regional Services Department. Only then will any serious money be committed for development.

Roger Nissim said that the HKCA's needs have been officially recognised in a recent review of Government's Planning Standards and Guidelines on Recreation and Open Space which read:

it is proposed to provide a multi-purpose grass pitch of 1.2 hectares per district for rugby/baseball/cricket uses as a standard provision of core activitites.

He added that, so far the dialogue with the USD has been on a very co-operative basis and they will be looking to the HKCA in future for guidance on standards for grass, pitch maintenance etc.

Roger Nissim, Chairman HKCA Grounds Committee, March 1998

The HKCA's attention had been focussed on saving the Mission Road ground which was a very likely candidate for housing development. The

Planning Department was now in the process of zoning it 'Open Space'. Once zoned, it could be allocated to the USD.

The HKCA are also in contact with the Peoples Liberation Army (PLA) regarding two other former Army grounds at Sek Kong and Stanley Fort. It is hoped that cricket can continue to be played at these grounds, and that the PLA can get involved in the cricket scene.

BIBLIOGRAPHY

The Cree Journals – Michael Levien, Webb & Bower, 1981
Cricket – Neville Cardus, Longman's, 1949
The Cricketer Quarterly – Major Rowland Bowen, Vol. 4 1966
The Cricketer International – 1973
The Diocesan Boys' School & Orphanage, History & Records 1869–1929
Rev. W T Featherstone, Hong Kong 1930
Double Century. The Story of MCC and Cricket – A R Lewis, London
1987
Highways and Byways – F S Ashley-Cooper, Allen & Unwin
A History of Hong Kong – G B Endacott, Oxford University Press, 2nd
Ed. 1979
A History of the Hong Kong Cricket Club 1851–1989 Spencer Robinson,
Centurion Books, London 1989
HKCA 'Scoreboard' & Annual Handbooks and Brochures
The Hong Kong Cricket Club Centenary 1851–1951
Kowloon Cricket Club: Annual Report 1960–61
　　　　　　　　　　A History – Peter Hall, SCMP, Hong Kong 1979
Mapping Hong Kong, A Historical Atlas – Hal Empson, Hong Kong 1993
Queen's College 1862–1962 – Gwenneth Stokes, Hong Kong 1962
Reminiscences of Interport Cricket – Dr J A Lowson
St George's Cricket Club 25th Anniversary – John Dykes, Hong Kong 1987
75 Not Out – Tony Clark and Graham Fletcher, Hong Kong 1978
Who's Who of Cricketers – Philip Bailey, Philip Thorn and Peter Wynne-
Thomas, Hamlyn, 1993

Newspapers – The Friend of China & Hong Kong Gazette
　　　　　　　The Hong Kong Daily Press
　　　　　　　The Hong Kong Standard
　　　　　　　The South China Morning Post
　　　　　　　The Straits Echo
　　　　　　　The Straits Times
　　　　　　　The Times

LIST OF CONTRIBUTORS

The following is a list of cricketers, ex-cricketers and friends who have very kindly provided photographs, reminiscences, newspaper cuttings, notes, interviews, or contributed in some other way. To them all, my sincere thanks.

Anderson, Peter
Andreassend, Gordon
Bailey, Alan
Barnes, Stuart
Bell, Bob
Bramall, Edwin (Lord)
Brewster, Ray
Burden, David (Maj Gen)
Bygate, John
Campion, Bob
Chamberlain, Joe
Chandran, Krish
Chignell, Marybud
Clark, Tony
Clinton, David
Conway, Bill
Chubb, Peter
Cooke, Cecil
D'Almada Remedios, Micky
Davies, Peter
de La Mar, A
Dhabher, Buji
Dunford, Jack
Dunkley, George
Ebrahim, Hatim
Evans, Dafydd
Fairhall, Vic
Fawcett, Geoff
Fawcett, John
Fincher, Mussie
Forse, Chris
Garner, Keith
Goldman, Lolly
Gosano, Eddie (Dr)
Graham, Arnold
Green, Stephen
Greenwood, Des
Hall, Louis
Hamilton, Sandy
Haycraft, Bob
Hitchcock, Keith (Lt Col)
Johnson, Julie
Karanjia, Navel (Dr)
Kilbee, Laurie
Kinsey, Sara
Kong, Shiu Chung
Lacy-Smith, Ian
Lalchandani, Gopal
Lay, Bertram
Lee, Margaret
Leopard, Mark
Lever, Geoff
Lever, Jean
Lewis, Joe
Liu, M C William
Lockhart, Terry
Lowcock, Jimmy
Macauley, Bill
Mackay, Doug
Mackie, Jock
McIntyre, Euan
Mak, Anthony
Middleton, Jim
Munusamy, Gopal
Myatt, Carl
Nissim, Roger
Ogden, Brian
O'Rourke, Francis (Bro)
Parsons, David
Pearce, Nina
Phua, Christopher
Prata, Alfred
Pritchard, Guy
Powell, Ian
Reeve, Alec
Reeve, Dermot
Reid, Dougal
Richards, Stewart
Richardson, Mike
Rigg, Nigel
Roberts, Denys (Sir)
Rodrigues, Albert (Sir)
Rowe, Charles
Rumjahn, Peter
Rumjahn, Salat
Shepherd, Snr. Jim
Shroff, Jalu
Slack, Peter
Smith, Sue
Souza, Irene
Stephenson, J L (Lt Col)
Styles, Kevin
Swift, Alan

517

Thomas, Bro
Walker, Kathy
Williamson, Tim
Willson, 'Tug'
Wolfe, Harold

Turner, Tony
White, Arthur
Wills, Graham
Wilson, Ted

Vaughan-Arbuckle, Ian
Wilken, Harry
Willson, Marlene
Withall, Bill (Maj Gen)

A special thank you to the author's son, David, for designing the first cover for the book.

If I have missed anyone, as some information has reached me via the HKCA and other second-hand sources, my humblest apologies and no less my grateful thanks.

INDEX

This is specifically a personal name Index, but includes the names of cricket associations, clubs, teams and sponsors. It excludes the names in full scoresheets and statistical schedules. The same person might inadvertently appear more than once in a different guise, e.g. Lt Bagnall and later as a civilian, Bagnall, H.G. Was this the same person? Kitchell, A. (St Joseph's), and later Kitchell, A.R. playing for HKU: are these two different persons? The author has where possible, checked out some of these anomalies with ex-Hong Kong cricketers worldwide.

528

529

537

Melbourne University CC 445
Melford, Michael 508
Mellor, F/O 173
Mellowes, H.F. (Bert) 69–71, 73–4, 205, 504
Melsome, Lt 334
Mendis, C.(Thai) 415–16
Mendonca, M. 20, 94
Menon, R. (Malaysia) 397, 424
Menzies, Sir Robert xxi
Merchants CC 39, **214–15**
Merry, Malcolm 157
Metcalf, 'Col' 26, 31, 205, 207, 361, 363, 444
Miandad, Javed 430–2
25th Middlesex 116
Middlesex CCC 11, 465
Middleton, Jim 37–8, 71, 74, 184, 187, 189, 220–1, 236, 414, 466
  Jim Middleton Trophy 238
Midlands CCC 449
Miles, A. (Haberdashers) 273
Miles, Lt/Cpl (Queen's) 250
Miles, Margaret 70
Miles, Mike 131, 180
Miller, K.R. (Keith) xiii, 438–9, 471
Millett, A. (Tony) 70, 74
Mills, George 108
Mills, G.M. (Jardines) 304
Mills, J.K. (Hongs) 305
Mills, L.W.R. (Laurie) 80
Mills, Tim 189
Mills-Owen, Richard 126, 206, 226
Milner, R. 356
Minors, D. (Bermuda) 259, 397–8
Minu, A.R. 'Fatty' 19–20, 107, 120, 122, 154, 164–6, 272, 300, 310, 335–7
Mirmohammadi, Nadir·289
Misha (Bangladesh) 411–12
Mistry, K.M. 147
Mitchell, Capt D.B. 252
Mitchell, E.J.R. (Eric) 106, 117, 122, 173–4, 248, 251, 267–8
Mitchell, Peter 256–8, 360
Modi, Rusi 163, 170
Mody, J.H.N. 95
Mody, (USA) 392
Mohammed, S. (Thai) 421
Mohmed, T. (Singapore) 419
Mollinson, J.P. 325–6
Monteiro, Sonny 90

Moody, D. (PNG) 259
Moody, Tom 185
Moor, O. 120
Moore, Bernard 69, 72, 368
Moore, Pte 249
Moore, S.S. 78, 116
Moorthy, K. 360
More, B. 74
More, G.R. 267
More, Hamish 450, 456
Morgan, A. (Haberdashers) 274
Morgan, A. (Tony) 35, 38, 129
Morgan, D. 228
Morgan, J. (Singapore Services) 466
Morgan, John 69, 73–4
Morgan, T. 230
Morris, A. (Argentina) 395
Morris, A.R. (Arthur) 438, 471
Morris, Capt 249–50
Morris, Eric 82
Morris, H.M. 462
Morris, Noel 71, 73
Morrish, Cpl (RE) 247
Morse, Sir Arthur 97, 437–8
Mortensen, Ole 397
Moss, A. (Israel) 395
Moss, QMS (RASC) 250
Moule, W.H. 319, 345, 478
Moutrie, G.C. 268
Mugliston, Gerald 476
Mugliston, 'Sonnie' 476
Muir, D. (BF) 242
Muir, L/Cpl (RASC) 252
Muirhead, Hamish 125
Muirhead, Robert 34, 207–8
Mulani, A. 444
Mulcahy, (CBS) 20, 291–2, 302
Mumford, Sgt 321, 327
Muniandy, A. 424
Muniandy, S. 395
Muriel, H.E. 17, 116, 332
Murphy, J. (Centaurs) 228
Murphy, J.C.G. (Julian) 23, 125–6, 257, 359, 445–6, 496, 499
Murphy, N. (NSW-SDCC) 470
Murphy, P. 227
Murray, John 443–4
Murray, K. (Berkshire) 454
Murray Brown, W. 253
Murugesu, A. 258
Muruthi, S. 365, 367–70, 372, 420–1

Army Champions First Division 1969–70

Courtesy : Ian Vaughan-Arbuckle